History
of Psychology

History of Psychology

SECOND EDITION

David Hothersall
The Ohio State University

McGraw-Hill, Inc.
New York St. Louis San Francisco Auckland Bogotá
Caracas Lisbon London Madrid Mexico City Milan
Montreal New Delhi San Juan Singapore
Sydney Tokyo Toronto

This book is printed on acid-free paper.

History of Psychology

Copyright © 1990, 1984 by McGraw-Hill, Inc. All rights reserved. Printed in the United States of America. Except as permitted under the United States Copyright Act of 1976, no part of this publication may be reproduced or distributed in any form or by any means, or stored in a data base or retrieval system, without the prior written permission of the publisher.

67890 DOC DOC 943

ISBN 0-07-030509-9

This book was set in Palatino by the College Composition Unit
in cooperation with Monotype Composition Company.
The editors were Susan Badger, James D. Anker, and Jennifer Sutherland;
the production supervisor was Stacey B. Alexander.
The cover was designed by Karen Quigley.
R. R. Donnelley & Sons Company was printer and binder.

Cover illustration adapted from photograph by Leonard Lessin/Peter Arnold.

Library of Congress Cataloging-in-Publication Data

Hothersall, David.
    History of psychology/David Hothersall.—2nd ed.
        p.   cm.
    Includes bibliographical references.
    ISBN 0-07-030509-9
        1. Psychology—history.   I. Title.
BF95.H67   1990
150'.9—dc20   89-13167

About
the Author

David Hothersall is a Professor of Psychology at the Ohio State University. Born and raised in England, he came to the United States in 1965 and received his Ph.D. from the University of Tennessee in 1968. Since then he has been at Ohio State. The recipient of a number of teaching awards, including Ohio State's Alumni Award for Distinguished Teaching, he has taught courses on the history of psychology to both undergraduate and graduate students. In addition to the history of psychology, his research and teaching interests include comparative, experimental, and physiological psychology. He has written numerous papers on these topics and an introductory psychology text published in 1984.

As before:
To Lesley, Carol, Mark, and Hilary

Contents

Preface

In this second edition of *History of Psychology* I have continued to use a biographical approach, emphasizing both the contributions of the great psychologists of the past and the circumstances of their lives that influenced their contributions. As in the first edition, psychologists of the past are presented as men and women who made important contributions to the development of psychology but who also had successes and failures, triumphs and tragedies, hopes fulfilled and hopes dashed. I believe such a biographical approach to be effective in countering the unfortunate assumption held by so many students that the history of psychology is dull, tedious, and largely irrelevant to contemporary psychology. Many of the lives and careers of psychologists described in this book were far from dull, and their contributions continue to be important influences on contemporary psychology. Wherever possible, I have shown the connections between the past and present.

Changes in the New Edition

In the second edition I have responded to the comments and suggestions of faculty members who have used this text and shared their perceptions of its strengths and weaknesses. In addition, I was pleasantly surprised by the students who wrote to me concerning this book. In one case a whole class provided their comments and questions on tape. Students' interest in the book and their developing fascination with the history of psychology were especially encouraging. Once again I would like to thank the students, both undergraduate and graduate, in my own classes on the history of psychology. Some of the changes in this second edition were suggested by those students in their evaluation of the text. An early draft of this second edition was reviewed by several psychologists who had used the text in its first edition. Their reviews were most comprehensive and their many suggestions were both detailed and constructive.

Psychology is fortunate in that there is a lively and active area of scholarship and research on its history. Many works on the history of psychology are published each year, and the years since the publication of the first edition in 1983 have been a particularly active period. That activity is reflected in the fact that some 90 percent of the new citations in this edition are to works published since 1983. The second edition is as up-to-date as I can make it and reflects contemporary scholarship on the history of psychology and the history of science. I am pleased to acknowledge my indebtedness to the many scholars whose work I have included.

Major changes in this second edition include a discussion in the Introduction of current developments in American psychology and their implications for psychology as a whole. History is proposed as a possible unifying force within contemporary psychology. The chapters on the scientific and philosophical antecedents of psychology (Chapters 1 and 2) have been expanded to include Galen's views on more specifically psychological topics and a discussion of Aristotle's analysis of causation. The origins of the scientific method in psychology are presented with reference to the experiments of Galileo and Newton. Locke's intriguing answer to Molyneux's question is discussed in more detail, using contemporary clinical reports of the sensory experience of patients whose sight is restored.

In Chapters 4 and 5 the research contributions of Wundt and Titchener are again emphasized, together with a more detailed description of the laboratories they established and the experimental procedures they used. Additional details on the life and career of Hugo Münsterberg are presented. Münsterberg is increasingly recognized as having been a major figure in the history of psychology and so his career and contributions are again a major focus. In Chapter 6 the historical development of psychophysical procedures is outlined and their use in contemporary psychological research described. Recent assessments of the lasting value and importance of the research contributions of Ebbinghaus are also included. Finally, in Chapter 6 the relationship between the cognitive psychologies of the 19th century and contemporary research on cognition is made clear.

In Chapter 8 the section on early institutions for the insane has been expanded and includes an assessment of recent controversial claims that such institutions were in fact not as barbaric as they have often been described. A major new section in Chapter 8 on radical treatments of insanity describes the development of lobotomies, shock therapy, and the use of psychoactive drugs. Recent biographies on Freud and my own visit to the Freud Museum in London led to revisions in the section on Freud.

In Chapter 9 the sections on both Galton and Darwin have been expanded, with the latter being influenced by my visit to the wonderful Darwin Museum near London. Some changes have been made in the descriptions of Hall and James. Chapter 11 on the uses and abuses of intelligence testing was the most controversial chapter in the first edition. The discussion of Broca's craniometry now introduces the chapter and provides a good illustration of the dangers in using physical measures to assess intelligence. New material on Goddard and eugenic thinking within psychology and the nature/nurture question has been added. On a more positive note Terman's study of genius is again presented as an example of psychological research at its best—but this edition also addresses criticisms of Terman's research. In Chapter 12 more detail is provided on the contributions of both Watson and Pavlov. Watson's career after leaving psychology is described in some detail. Chapter 13 discusses some of the continuing contributions of Skinner, especially his provocative views on aging.

The second edition also includes new charts, diagrams, and photographs. The use of illustrations, especially photographs, was once considered inappropriate for a textbook. But in my experience students find such photographs appealing and they seem an especially fitting complement to a biographical approach to the history of psychology.

This edition, as was the first, is intended for advanced undergraduate students majoring in psychology and for beginning graduate students. It is my hope that they will find this book of interest and that in some small way it will reinforce their commitment to psychology.

Acknowledgments

I would like to express my sincere appreciation to a number of people who helped make this second edition a reality. I am extremely grateful for the helpful comments of the following reviewers: Mark Garrison, Kentucky State University; Terry Knapp, University of Nevada, Las Vegas; Sandy Lopater, Christopher Newport College; Douglas Mook, University of Virginia; Robert Presbie, State University of New York, New Paltz; William Sanderson, Calvin College; Kurt Wallen, Neumann College; and Deborah Warnath, Western Oregon State University. At Random House Barry Fetterolf first encouraged me to work on a second edition. Susan Badger, my editor at Random House, commissioned the reviews of the first edition and of drafts of the revised chapters for this edition; her editorial assistance was very helpful. At the time of the transfer of my book from Random House to McGraw-Hill the support of Executive Editor James D. Anker was greatly appreciated. At McGraw-Hill I was fortunate to have the assistance of two superb professionals, Eric Lewenkron, the copyeditor, and Jennifer E. Sutherland, my project editor. Eric Lewenkron's copyediting showed not only his impressive professional skills but also a knowledgeable and enquiring mind. Jennifer Sutherland was uncompromising in her insistence on clear writing, excellence in presentation, and the importance of deadlines. Her encouragement, enthusiasm, and interest in the book were very much appreciated. My association with the editorial staff at McGraw-Hill has been a source of great pleasure.

Much of the writing of this second edition was done during a faculty leave of absence. I would like to express my appreciation to the Ohio State University for providing this leave. Finally, I would like to thank my colleagues, especially Donald R. Meyer for his interest and support during some very difficult times and David S. Tuber for his continuing delight in the history of psychology.

David Hothersall

Introduction

RECURRENT QUESTIONS OF PSYCHOLOGY

In 1910, just thirty years after Wilhelm Wundt founded the first psychological research laboratory in 1879, Hermann Ebbinghaus described psychology as having "a long past but only a short history" (Ebbinghaus, 1910, p. 9). Compared with the established sciences of astronomy, anatomy, physics, chemistry, and physiology, psychology indeed had a "short history." But as Ebbinghaus noted, that "short history" was complemented by a "long past" in that many of the questions and concerns of psychology can be traced back to the ancient worlds of Egypt, Greece, and Rome (Chapter 1).

Perhaps the most pressing question throughout psychology's "long past" has been whether a science of the mind, a psychology, is possible. If it is, how is it to be defined and what should its methods be? In the nineteenth century Auguste Comte denied the possibility of a science of the mind. The mind, Comte asserted, can study all phenomena but its own. His contemporary, John Stuart Mill, refuted Comte's assertion and proposed a science of the mind, a model of the mind's operations, and a method for studying its contents (Chapter 2). Mill's position was adopted and extended by Wilhelm Wundt (Chapter 4) when Wundt established a science of psychology and developed methods that allowed the classic question of the epistemologists—"How do we see and perceive the world?"—to be addressed scientifically. One of the triumphs of the first generation of psychologists was Ebbinghaus's research on human memory (Chapter 6). He was able to show that memory can be studied scientifically and that the methods of psychology can be as rigorous and its results as reliable as those of older, established sciences. Ebbinghaus's results remain unchallenged today.

In the twentieth century J. B. Watson (Chapter 12) asserted that psychology abandon all concern with the mind and study only behavior. His radical proposal and methods gave birth to behaviorism, which, through the influence of his successor B. F. Skinner, became the dominant approach to psychology in America. Today, study of the "mind" in the form of cognitive psychology is experiencing a renaissance within psychology, and much of the research being done by cognitive psychologists bears a striking similarity to research and theories developed by Franz Brentano and Oswald Külpe (Chapter 6) and Edward Tolman (Chapter 13). Psychologists have struggled to define both the subject matter and the methods of psychology throughout its history. Their struggles are described in this book.

A second recurrent question in the history of philosophy and psychology concerns the nature and locus of the mind. As we will see, the ancient philosophers had curious ideas about the seat of the mind. Aristotle located it in the heart. Today we confidently locate the mind in the brain and describe mental functions as products of the brain's operations. The brain is seen as central. Since the nineteenth century (Chapter 3), great progress has been made in understanding the brain, and today's neurosciences, of which physiological psychology, or psychobiology, is but one, represent a large collection of investigators from many disciplines. Perhaps because of its complexity, the brain—with its 100 billion nerve cells and estimated 1 quadrillion potential connections between them—is often described as the most complex structure ever studied; a complete description of the relationships between the brain and behavior as well as between the brain and consciousness eludes us.

A related problem for philosophy and psychology has been to find a way of describing the relationship between mind (brain) and body—to find a model of their relationship. Are they separate and distinct, parallel, interacting, or inseparably linked? Each of these positions has had advocates, and their views continue to influence models of mind-body interactions. Today's holistic models, for example, in which mind and body are seen as one, are sometimes presented as being new and revolutionary. In fact, such models are ancient and can be traced back through *A Guide to the Perplexed,* a medical book written in the twelfth century by Maimonides, to the ideas of the Greek physician Hippocrates in the fifth century B.C. (Chapter 1).

The relative contributions and importance of nature (the genetic constitution) and nurture (the environment) to development and individual differences have been debated endlessly. Aristotle favored an environmentalist position, stressing the importance of nurture. Indeed, it was Aristotle who first used the lasting metaphor of the mind at birth as a *tabula rasa,* or blank tablet, to be filled by experience. Plato recognized the importance of individual differences in temperament, character, and ability, but he believed that such dispositions are largely inborn and therefore adopted the position of a nativist (Chapter 1). Throughout the history of psychology these empiricist and nativist positions recur: empiricism in the philosophies of John Locke, James and John Stuart Mill, and the later psychologies of J. B. Watson and B. F. Skinner; nativism in the philosophies of René Descartes and Immanuel Kant and the psychologies of Francis Galton, G. Stanley Hall, and Lewis Terman. Nature versus nurture is still one of the most actively debated and divisive concerns of contemporary psychologists. Indeed, the divisions are so deep that it has been argued that rational discourse between proponents of environmental accounts and proponents of genetic accounts of the development of intelligence has become out of the question (Crawford, 1979). This conflict is best understood within its historical context (Chapter 11).

LESSONS FROM PSYCHOLOGY'S PAST

Psychology textbooks describe psychologists' successes. This history of psychology describes both their successes and their failures. At times the most eminent psychologists have advocated with great confidence and conviction answers to the questions of psychology that later proved to be wrong. To describe past errors is not to discredit, debunk, or diminish past psychologists, for often they answered other questions correctly; rather, it is to make the history of psychology complete and, most importantly, to alert us to our own fallibility. We must also avoid the tendency to interpret and evaluate past contributions according to the standards of the present and to evaluate the contributions of earlier psychologists on the basis of what we know today. Raymond Fancher (1987) labeled such tendencies "Whig history." This book will not be a Whig history of psychology.

In many instances our errors may not be readily apparent to us because they are supported by the shared beliefs and assumptions of a particular era. The leading historian of psychology, Edwin G. Boring (1957), described such influences as coming from the *Zeitgeist*, or spirit of the times. An illustration of the effects of the *Zeitgeist* is seen in the research of Pierre-Paul Broca. His studies of the localization of speech in the human brain (Chapter 3) are still considered distinguished, but Broca was also convinced that women are an inferior product of evolution, that their brains are significantly less developed than those of men, and that this difference in brain size increases with each generation. We now know that his conclusions not only were in error, but were based on inadequate and poorly conducted research. However, since they were in harmony with the prevailing assumptions and beliefs of the time, they went unchallenged.

A similar example can be found at the beginning of the twentieth century. At that time the consensus among leading psychologists such as Henry Goddard and Lewis Terman (Chapter 11) was that existing psychological tests measured basic intelligence in diverse groups of people, even those from different racial, ethnic, and cultural backgrounds. Today we are aware of the inherent cultural bias in many psychological measures and strive to develop "culture-fair" tests. Unfortunately, in Terman and Goddard's times the cross-cultural validity of existing tests was not questioned, and results from their application to different ethnic, cultural, national, and racial groups were accepted, largely because such results agreed with prevailing assumptions and beliefs about those groups. The consequences of this misapplication of psychological tests were both unfair and tragic (Chapter 11), yet both Goddard and Terman made other contributions to psychology that are still recognized as important. In the 1920s Goddard established one of the first enrichment school programs for gifted children, while Terman planned, initiated, supported, and for many years conducted one the most respected psychological studies ever done, his long-term study of children of genius.

Failure to question research findings that agree with prevailing political and philosophical ideology represents one of the effects of the *Zeitgeist*. Having seen how the *Zeitgeist* operated in the past, we may be more aware of its influence on contemporary psychology.

Of course, the influences of prevailing political, philosophical, and scientific ideology are not always negative. In many instances the spirit of the times as reflected by the interaction of all the sciences and technology can stimulate new ideas and creative solutions to problems. One such positive influence can be seen in the models and metaphors chosen to describe behavior and consciousness. Descartes (Chapter 2) described the body as a machine like the machines he saw in the gardens of seventeenth-century France. William Harvey, living during England's industrial revolution, saw the heart as a pump whose task is to drive blood through the body. Wilhelm Wundt and Edward Titchener (Chapters 4 and 5) set out to emulate Newtonian physics and modeled their psychology on that science not only in what they hoped would be the rigor and elegance of the methods of psychology but also in what they saw as the goals of the new science. Early in the twentieth century the behaviorists and neobehaviorists (Chapters 12 and 13) adopted a switchboard model of behavior and saw the task of psychology as accounting for connections between stimuli and behavioral responses. Today computer models of behavior and consciousness are in vogue, and psychologists refer to cognitive processes in terms of information processing, storage, input and/or output, and storage capacity—all terms and concepts drawn from computer science. Twenty years from now this computer model may appear as outmoded as switchboard models of stimulus and response do today. But throughout history we see that the value of such models does not reside in their accuracy or verisimilitude as descriptions of psychological phenomena but in their capacity to direct psychological research and theorizing.

Another aspect of psychology's past that will be stressed in this history is that earlier psychologists conducted research and speculated about psychological phenomena in ways that have turned out to be remarkably prescient. At times such research and speculation have been forgotten by generations of psychologists, only to be rediscovered later. In the seventeenth century John Locke described a clinical procedure for overcoming excessive fears (Chapter 2) that bears a remarkable resemblance to the systematic desensitization procedures developed by Joseph Wolpe and other contemporary behavior therapists for the treatment of phobias. Hugo Münsterberg (Chapter 5), in the first decade of the twentieth century, wrote extensively on the reliability of human memory and particularly of eyewitness testimony. During the 1970s research similar to that of Münsterberg was again conducted (Loftus, 1980). In the 1920s Sidney Pressey invented teaching machines and conducted research on their effectiveness compared with more traditional teaching methods. But his machines were a commercial failure, and his work has been largely forgotten. In the 1950s B. F. Skinner developed his own teaching machines, and that application achieved considerable fame. The contrast between the obscurity of

Pressey's pioneering teaching machines and the fame achieved by Skinner is best understood in a historical context (Benjamin, 1988).

Gustav Fechner, the father of psychophysics (Chapter 2), knew in the nineteenth century that the human brain has two cerebral hemispheres linked by a band of fibers, the corpus callosum. He speculated that if it were transected or cut, two separate streams of consciousness would result. The mind would be, in effect, split in two. In recent decades the corpus callosum has been transected in human patients to prevent the spread of epileptic seizures from one side of the brain to the other (Sperry, 1961). Reports describing these "split-brain" subjects have changed dramatically our understanding of the brain and in many ways have confirmed Fechner's speculations. In 1981, nearly 100 years after Fechner's publication, Roger Sperry shared the Nobel Prize for medicine for his pioneering research on the consequences of sectioning the corpus callosum. Such contributions and anticipations of later psychological findings are indeed impressive, but we must be careful not to read more into the work of earlier psychologists than was actually there. We must understand historical contributions as they actually were rather than stressing how well they anticipate later findings.

HISTORY AS A UNIFYING OR CENTRIPETAL FORCE WITHIN PSYCHOLOGY

The first organizational meeting of the American Psychological Association was held in 1892 and was attended by twelve charter members (Chapter 9). The APA's first annual meeting was held in December of that year with eighteen members in attendance. In 1893 the association had forty-three members and a budget of $63. In 1988 the APA's ninety-sixth convention had some 12,000 registrants. The association now has 65,000 members, 20,000 affiliates, forty-seven divisions, and a 1988 budget of over $40 million. Psychology is now well established as a science and a profession, and psychologists are prominent in many areas of contemporary life. Yet all is not well, for powerful centrifugal forces within contemporary psychology threaten its unity and the continued existence of the APA (I. Altman, 1987): science versus humanism, research versus practice, tough- versus tender-minded approaches, and the ever-increasing specialization of psychologists and the division of psychology. Given such forces, a former president of the APA, Janet Spence, raised the question "Will the center hold?" and outlined a "doomsday scenario" in which institutional psychology is decimated (Spence, 1987, p. 1053). Leonard Goodstein, in a valedictory column as the APA's chief executive officer, described the association as having an overly large and slow-to-move governance structure; a plethora of divisions; an abundance of boards, committees, subcommittees, and task forces; and some strongly alienated constituencies. He also reported less and less reasoned discourse and creative problem solving within the APA and a virtual disappearance of comity within the organization (Goodstein, 1988). In 1988 a proposed reorganization of the APA that would have established several semiautonomous societies was defeated. That defeat increased the likelihood of further strengthening disaffected splinter groups and alternative organizations such as the American Psychological Society, which was founded in 1988. That organization has as its mission "advancing the scientific discipline and the giving away of psychology in the public interest." Significant numbers of psychologists have elected to join the APS, including some former presidents of the APA. Some psychologists have selected membership in both organizations as the best option, while others have chosen to be members of the APA or the APS.

Centripetal forces unifying contemporary psychology seem to be much weaker, but one source of unity is the common history all psychologists share. That history distinguishes and identifies psychology. William James, Alfred Binet, Dorothea Dix, Ivan Pavlov, Kurt Lewin, and Lewis Terman belong to all psychologists. Their contributions and those of the many other men and women discussed in this book established and defined psychology. From them we can learn what psychologists have in common, what unity there is within the diversity of contemporary psychology.

THIS BOOK'S APPROACH TO THE HISTORY OF PSYCHOLOGY

Many books on the history of psychology focus on the major theoretical systems of philosophy and psychology and the ways in which they are linked conceptually from one generation of psychologists to the next. Such an approach allows the reader to understand how systems of thought evolve within a broad historical context. However, there is a danger in such an approach, especially if it is used exclusively, of neglecting the lives of the individuals who create those systems and the sometimes unlikely situations and personal experiences that have prompted new ideas and stimulated new directions of research and study.

During World War I Wolfgang Köhler was marooned on Tenerife, a lonely island in the Atlantic (Chapter 7). Tenerife had a colony of primates for research studies, so Köhler studied problem solving and insight learning by these animals. His results are still a feature of psychology textbooks, and his research did much to establish the Gestalt approach to psychology. Whereas Köhler's situation during World War I ultimately had a positive outcome, for other German psychologists the war had lasting unfavorable effects. Before World War I Franz Brentano, Carl Stumpf, and Oswald Külpe (Chapter 6) established an active tradition of cognitive research in Germany. Because of the war, this research was abandoned and their approach and findings were neglected. Only in recent years have psychologists returned to the cognitive topics pioneered by these psychologists. Knowledge of earlier cognitive research allows both an assessment and an appreciation of contemporary work.

In the case of other psychologists it was personal circumstances rather than geopolitical events that altered their careers. J. B. Watson, the founder of behaviorism and a former president of the APA, was forced to resign his university position and exile himself from psychology because of a scandal in his private life

(Chapter 12). His successor within American psychology was B. F. Skinner. Skinner's acknowledged influence on psychology is based on his experimental research and innovative applications of psychological knowledge (Chapter 13), but he also has a broader reputation and influence. Indeed, a 1970 poll numbered Skinner among the 100 most important people in the world (Robinson, 1970). For this broader audience Skinner is the archbehaviorist and master controller of behavior. These were the roles Watson played during his brief career. What, then, would Skinner's role have been had Watson remained active in psychology throughout his life? Any answer would be speculative, but surely Skinner's career and perhaps even his contributions to psychology would have been different.

These examples illustrate this book's approach to the history of psychology. We will trace the development of psychological systems within their social and political context, but we will also examine the effects of events in individual psychologists' lives. In this way we will be able to examine not only the historical context in which these individuals worked but also how their personal motivations, private tragedies, and chance good fortune affected their work. By focusing on these individual aspects we will get a more complete picture of *why* certain historical figures made the contributions they did. For instance, Sigmund Freud (Chapter 8) maintained his position of leadership of the emerging psychoanalytic movement as much from an imperative to dominate and lead as from a commitment to the development of his theoretical system or methods of treatment. Alfred Binet was strongly motivated to contribute to psychology and did codevelop the first successful intelligence test (Chapter 11). His work was clearly a form of self-rehabilitation and an attempt to compensate for the flawed research he did early in his career. Clark Hull (Chapter 13) dedicated his life to showing that though he was a man "who walked with a limp," he was as good as any man and could make contributions to psychology that would "stand the test of time." In both his research on hypnosis and his development of a behavioral system, Hull achieved this goal.

At times strong, dogmatic personality characteristics have worked against individual psychologists. Titchener (Chapter 5) did much to establish psychology as an independent science in the United States, but his rigid insistence that his was the only true psychology and his aggressive criticisms of all attempts to apply psychological knowledge actually impeded the development of psychology. Toward the end of his career Titchener withdrew completely from the field as it became apparent that his hopes for a "pure psychology" would never be fulfilled.

Titchener's disappointment is not unique among the historical figures of psychology. Freud was ridiculed when he returned to Vienna and described his views on hypnosis and hysteria (Chapter 8). Ivan Pavlov was urged by one of the leading physiologists of his day, Sir Charles Sherrington, to abandon his experiments on classical conditioning and return to "real physiology" (Chapter 12). Edwin Twitmyer (Chapter 12) described classical conditioning experiments contemporaneously with Pavlov (Chapter 12) but saw his reports completely ignored. Kurt Lewin (Chapter 7) and Hugo Münsterberg (Chapter 5) never received the recognition from their contemporaries or the place in psychology's history they clearly deserve, possibly because they were Europeans who never quite became a part of American psychology or society. How different the history of psychology might have been if the lives of these psychologists had been different.

In this personalistic account of the history of psychology we will also see the effects of good fortune—the good fortune to have an inspiring teacher or to read the right book at a crucial stage in a career. William James's *Principles of Psychology* (Chapter 10) inspired a whole generation of psychologists. For others, it was the happy accident of being in the right place at the right time. Max Wertheimer interrupted his summer vacation plans, got off a train in Frankfurt, and there met Wolfgang Köhler and Kurt Koffka (Chapter 7). Together they formed the great triumvirate of Gestalt psychology. Robert Yerkes, a student of animal behavior, was president of the APA in 1917, when the United States entered World War I, so he was chosen to organize psychologists' contributions to the war effort. As a result Yerkes directed the most ambitious psychological testing program ever conducted, the Army Testing Program (Chapter 11).

Despite such seemingly chance events, history is not chaotic, random, or entirely serendipitous. All these psychologists, and many of the others whose careers and contributions we will consider, were prepared by intellect, motivation, and ability to take advantage of their fortunate circumstances. The ways in which they did so alert us to the importance of similar opportunities in our own lives.

Aristotle. (Culver Pictures)

1

Psychology and
the Ancients

The roots of Western civilization can be traced to the ancient worlds of Greece and Rome. In particular, two major areas of human inquiry—philosophy and natural science—had their origin in the work of ancient Greek and Roman thinkers. Since psychology emerged as an independent discipline from philosophy and gradually adopted the methods of the sciences, it is appropriate to examine the ancient foundations of its two parent disciplines.

Though the theories of the ancients did not include a theory of psychology per se, we will see that many psychological issues and topics were addressed by the ancients. Among the earliest accounts of phenomena we would call psychological are a series of Assyrian "dream books" composed on clay tablets in the fifth and sixth millennia B.C. (Restak, 1988, p. 3). Assyria was one of the great empires of the ancient world, stretching at its peak from the Mediterranean Sea in the west to the Caspian Sea in the east, between modern-day Armenia and Arabia. These "books" describe dreams of death and of the loss of teeth or hair and, most interesting of all since they show self-knowledge, dreams about the shame of finding oneself naked in public. But our most complete knowledge comes from the ancient worlds of Egypt, Greece, and Rome. There ancient physicians and philosophers speculated about the nature and locus of the mind, sensation and perception, memory and learning. More generally, the ancients provided us with a number of different ways to view human nature and to approach the problems of psychology. These different approaches, or intellectual orientations and paradigms, arose from advances that the ancients made in mathematics and philosophy as well as from their conceptions of the nature of the universe.

ADVANCES IN MEDICINE: A BIOLOGICAL APPROACH

At various times during its history, psychology has had a close alliance with medicine, physiology, and neurology. Psychological processes and behavior were seen as having a biological basis. In fact, much of "psychology" during those periods would now be considered within the field of medicine. For this reason we begin with a brief consideration of early Greek medicine. In doing so we will discover that the Greek physicians had theories concerning the locus of mind as well as how physiology may affect temperament.

Early Greek Medicine

Before 500 B.C. Greek medicine was in the hands of priests who resided in temples and were believed to know the secrets of Asclepius, the Greek god of medicine. These Asclepiadae were reputed to be able to cure various illnesses and restore health, especially in cases of blindness, deafness, and various forms of paralysis. Their techniques were closely guarded secrets. A patient who desired treatment was socially isolated in the temple and subjected to a variety of rituals. The priests recounted the powers of Asclepius, read case histories written on the temple walls, and made powerful suggestions that a cure would occur. Finally, the patient would pay a substantial fee to the priests for their services.

Around 500 B.C. a Greek physician named Alcmaeon began to dissect the bodies of animals to study their skeletons, muscles, and brains. Earlier descriptions of the body had been made, but those of Alcmaeon were probably the first to be based on objective observations. He taught his methods to students at a medical school he established in his hometown of Croton, hoping to counter the influence of the priests and replace templar medicine with a rational, nonmystical, observational approach to illness. This approach was holistic in nature, as Alcmaeon believed that health and disease are the product of a balance or imbalance of the body's systems.

Hippocrates

Alcmaeon's successor, Hippocrates, was the most important figure in Greek medicine during this period. He was born around 460 B.C. and received his early education at Cos, one of the great centers of templar medicine. Like Alcmaeon, he came to reject the mystery and superstition of the priests and founded a medical school to teach others an uncompromisingly objective approach to medicine. Hippocrates taught his students that all disease results from natural causes and must be treated using natural methods. He insisted that the healing power of nature allows the body to heal itself and rid itself of disease. Consequently, Hippocrates believed that the physician's first responsibility is not to interfere with this healing power; the physician must first do no harm. Hippocrates, like Alcmaeon, adopted a holistic approach to medicine. The body must function in a harmonious state, so Hippocrates often prescribed rest, exercise, improved diet, music, and the association of friends to restore the body's natural harmony. It is striking to see Hippocrates advocating an approach that has been described in the twentieth century as being without historical precedent.

Hippocrates, an acute observer, was able to draw some remarkably accurate conclusions from his observations. He concluded correctly that the right side of the body is controlled by the left side of the brain, and the left side of the body by the brain's right side. This insight, which is counterintuitive, resulted from Hippocrates' observation that injury to one side of the head often produces paralysis of the opposite side of the body.

More evidence of Hippocrates' observational skills can be found in the case notes and clinical procedures that he detailed in a work entitled *The Art of Healing*. In this treatise he presented clear descriptions of melancholia, mania, postpartum depression, phobias, paranoia, and hysteria. Hippocrates was mistaken about hysteria, however, as he restricted the disease to women, thinking it was due to wanderings of the uterus. The misconception of hysteria as a sex-linked illness persisted until it was challenged by Freud early in the twentieth century.

In his treatise *The Nature of Man*, Hippocrates presented a theory of humors. Empedocles had described the universe as composed of four unchangeable but intermingling elements: air, earth, fire, and water. According to Hippocrates, these elements form four basic humors in the body: black and yellow bile, blood, and phlegm. An imbalance or excess of any of these humors produces disease or illness. Phlegm collects in the nose and throat when one has a cold; when the skin is broken, blood is seen; bile is excreted from the body following a serious wound. Hippocrates' theory of humors influenced the diagnosis and treatment of disease for many centuries. Bloodletting to vent excessive blood was practiced well into the nineteenth century. The red and white striped barber's pole still seen today was originally the sign of a bloodletter.

Hippocrates' basic humors also were thought to affect temperament and personality. Individuals with too much black bile would be ill-tempered, peevish, and possibly melancholic; individuals with too much yellow bile would be irascible, choleric, easily angered, and perhaps manic; individuals with too much phlegm would be apathetic, dull, and sluggish; individuals with too much blood would be overly cheerful, happy, and optimistic. The staying power of this theory is seen in the contemporary usage of words such as bileous, phlegmatic, and sanguine in the way Hippocrates employed them. We also ask: "What sort of humor is Mr. X in today?"

Hippocrates' most important work, *De Morbu Sacro* (Concerning the Sacred Disease), described the dread disease of epilepsy. At the time, epileptic seizures were seen as being a result of direct, divine intervention. Men and women who became mentally ill and who were buffeted by powerful, uncontrollable forces during grand mal seizures suffered because the gods had taken away their minds. Belief in divine retribution posed an ominous problem: How could a person appease a pantheon of gods and goddesses any one of whom at any time could intervene to strike that person down? Since the Greek deities were a notably capricious group, the problem was indeed serious.

Such fatalistic attitudes were countered by Hippocrates' natural view of epilepsy. The opening sentence of *Sacred Disease* shows his clear intention to break from such mysticism:

> It [epilepsy] appears to me to be in no way more divine, nor more sacred
> than other diseases, but has a natural cause from which it originates like

other affections. Men think it is divine merely because they don't understand it. But if they called everything divine which they do not understand,
why there would be no end of divine things. (Hippocrates cited by Zilboorg
& Henry, 1941, pp. 43–44)

Hippocrates rejected earlier views of epilepsy, calling people who held them nothing more than "conjurors, putrefactors, mountebanks and charlatans." He considered epilepsy a disease caused by the brain's disharmony and predicted that examination of the brain of an epileptic would reveal the cause of that person's illness.
He held an optimistic view that epilepsy might be cured by natural methods of
treatment.

The theory of thirst formulated by Hippocrates is still considered partially
correct by contemporary theorists of motivation. According to this theory, as we
breathe air over the buccal mucosae of the mouth and throat, they become dry and
parched. These dry mucosae give rise to certain sensations that we interpret as the
feeling of being thirsty, and so we drink to relieve these sensations. The dry-mouth
theory came to be widely accepted after being reformulated in the eighteenth century by Albrecht von Haller (1747) and Pieter Jessen (1751). It was not until 1855
that the great French physiologist Claude Bernard presented evidence which caused
physiologists to question the sufficiency of Hippocrates' dry-mouth theory. Bernard
found that if he implanted cannulae in the esophagi of horses so that the water they
drank never reached their stomachs, they would continue to drink large quantities
of water long after the buccal mucosae of their throats had been bathed with water.
Even though Bernard demonstrated that Hippocrates' dry-mouth theory did not
provide a complete explanation of our motive for drinking, the theory still accords
well with everyday experience, and its persistence is found in such statements as "I
need a drink, my throat is parched" and "I need to slake my thirst."

Hippocrates, "the father of medicine," has become almost a mythical figure,
perhaps even a composite of the ideal physician's qualities. For centuries he was
regarded as an authority on medical matters, and today medical students qualifying
as physicians take the Hippocratic oath. But Hippocrates might also be regarded as
an ancient "father of psychology." He described natural causes of psychological
conditions, recommended holistic treatments, presented the first clear descriptions
of many behavioral problems, and formulated long-lasting theories of temperament
and motivation. Our knowledge of him can be traced largely to the work of a Greek
physician, Galen, who lived some 600 years after the time of Hippocrates. As Daniel
Robinson (1981, p. 130) comments, not only did Galen keep the Hippocratic system alive for subsequent historians, he also kept the idea of the critical importance
of observation alive for subsequent scientists.

Galen: A Link with the Past

Galen lived from A.D. 130 to 200. He left a great system of physiological ideas
derived both from the works of his predecessors and from his own experiments and
observations. His system influenced biological thought until the sixteenth century
and the beginning of the modern scientific era. Galen was trained as a physician and

anatomist at the Museum and Institute of Alexandria. That great institution of learning and research, with its 700,000-volume library, had been established in 323 B.C. after the death of Alexander and the division of his empire. The museum's staff included the mathematicians Euclid (330–275 B.C.) and Archimedes (287–212 B.C.) and many skilled anatomists whose knowledge of the human body derived from their dissections of human cadavers. These were the anatomists whom Galen studied. In A.D. 169 Galen moved to Rome and took an appointment as the court physician of the Roman Emperor Marcus Aurelius Antonius. As such, he had access to the Imperial Library's vast collection of texts sent to Rome from all corners of the empire. Believing that all knowledge derives from ancient wisdom, Galen made good use of these texts. However, he was also committed to personal observation and experiment, and so his works report both the wisdom of his predecessors and his own empirical findings.

Between A.D. 165 and 175 Galen wrote a seventeen-book treatise, *De Usu Partium* (On the Usefulness of the Parts), describing the structure and functions of the body. In addition to the ancient anatomic literature, Galen drew upon three lines of evidence: what he had learned from the museatic anatomists, his own clinical experience as surgeon to the gladiators of his hometown of Pergamon, and finally, his dissections of small apes, goats, cattle, and possibly some human cadavers, though the latter would have been done surreptitiously since dissection of the human body was illegal in Imperial Rome.

Although he was not a Christian, Galen was a vigorous opponent of the atheistic materialism of the ancient atomists and mechanists. He found their belief that all matter is the result of purely chance encounters between hypothetical atoms totally unacceptable since it ignored what seemed a fundamental fact revealed from his anatomic studies: evidence of divine design in the structure of the body. Galen stressed that the intricacy, harmony, and beauty of the body could not have been an accident. He claimed to have shown that no part of the human body is superfluous. For instance, he noted that it is no accident that we have two hands. If we had but one, we would be unable to do many of the things we can easily do with two; if we had three, one would be superfluous. If we did not have a thumb, we would be unable to oppose the thumb and forefinger and thus would be incapable of the exquisite manipulation our hands allow. Galen cited the impossibility of conceiving of a substitute for any part of the body that would perform all the normal functions of that part as further evidence of divine design. What substitute, for instance, could be as versatile as the human hand?

Galen's notion of the improbability of creation without divine design has been elaborated throughout the ages. In the eighteenth century the archbishop of Canterbury, John Tillotson, applied Galen's idea to the creation of poetry, prose, books, and portraits (Bennett, 1977). How often, Tillotson asked, might a person take a bag of letters, shake it vigorously, and cast the letters on the ground before creating a poem or a prose passage? How often before the letters formed a book? How often might colors be sprinkled on a canvas before they made a portrait? Poems, prose, books, and portraits are assembled only when human intelligence is applied; so too, Tillotson argued, divine intelligence must have been applied in the creation of human beings and the world. Such views have perpetuated through the ages Galen's notion of our spiritual nature.

Galen's descriptions of the functions of the heart also reflect his spiritual approach to an understanding of humankind as well as what he had learned in Alexandria. The museum's anatomists noticed that a person's breath is warm and that warmth in general characterizes a living body, whereas chill characterizes a dead one. They thought that this warmth was created by a fire in the heart; breath seen on a frosty morning was considered the fire's smoke. To test their theory, the museum's anatomists sacrificed slaves, rending open their chests in search of the biological flame. When they did not find it, they concluded that the chests had not been opened fast enough so that there had been time for the fire to go out. Galen believed that the heart's biological flame distilled from the blood the spiritual substance responsible for movement and sensation: the vital spirit. He failed to recognize the heart's role as a pump, a recognition that was in fact delayed some 1,500 years until the work of an Englishman, William Harvey (Chapter 2).

Galen also described a method for "recognizing and curing all diseases of the soul" in his treatise *On the Passions and Errors of the Soul* (Hajal, 1983). Galen believed that diseases of the soul arise from passions such as anger, fear, grief, envy, and violent lust. Such passions, according to Galen, are governed by an irrational power within us that refuses to obey reason. To free oneself from such passions, a person must strive for understanding and self-knowledge. But that task is difficult because self-love blinds us to our own faults and causes us to see only the faults of others. Galen asserted that a good and noble mentor-therapist is essential. He wrote:

> If [a person] wishes to become good and noble, let him seek out someone who
> will help him by disclosing his every action which is wrong.... For we must
> not leave the diagnosis of these passions to ourselves but we must entrust it to
> others.... This mature person who can see these vices must reveal with
> frankness all our errors. Next, when he tells us some fault, let us first be
> immediately grateful to him; then let us go aside and consider the matter by
> ourselves; let us censure ourselves and try to cut away the the disease not only
> to the point where it is not apparent to others, but so completely as to remove
> its roots from our soul. (Galen quoted by Hajal, 1983, pp. 321–322)

This passage stands today as a description of an ideal relationship between therapist and patient or counselor and client.

Galen's works were not superseded in antiquity, and Galenism dominated medicine until the time of the Renaissance. Even during the great scientific revolutions of the decades following the Renaissance, most medical texts, especially those on anatomy, began with an acknowledgment of Galen. Most important, it is largely through Galen that we know of ancient scientific and medical theory.

ADVANCES IN MATHEMATICS: THE SEARCH FOR ORDER

The ancient Egyptians were indefatigable measurers and counters, but theirs was a practical approach. To levy taxes on land fairly, they needed accurate measures of the increases and decreases in the area of land surrounding the Nile caused by periodic floods. Geometry, the measurement of the earth, was developed to meet that need. In addition, the Egyptians were concerned with matters such as determining the north-south and east-west axes for the correct alignment of a temple and the measurements and calculations involved in the construction of such colossal structures as the pyramids. These were major achievements, but it was the Greeks who used the mensurative techniques perfected by legions of Egyptian geometricians and surveyors as the basis for mathematical theory.

For the Greeks, numbers were something more than a useful tool to summarize and describe measurements. Mathematical theory could also allow prediction of future events. Thales of Miletus played an important role in this development. In 585 B.C., using mathematical theory, he predicted a solar eclipse. This awe-inspiring feat won him great popular acclaim but also fixed in the mind of the public the still popular idea of absentminded scientists with their heads in the clouds unable to see things on the ground. Thales, it was said, fell into a ditch while contemplating the stars. An old woman asked: "How can thou know what is doing in the heavens, when thou seest not what is at thy feet?" (Turnbull, 1956, p. 81).

One of Thales' pupils was Pythagoras (584–495 B.C.), the Greek mathematician who gave us the Pythagorean theorem. It is not surprising that Pythagoras understood the power of prediction and sought to extend it to the psychological world. He was able to describe elegantly a mathematical relationship between the physical world and the psychological experience of harmony. Pythagoras demonstrated that when a single, stretched string of a musical instrument such as a harp or lute is plucked, it produces a ground note; when divided into two parts, four parts, or any other exact division and plucked again, it produces notes which are harmonious with the ground note. When string divisions are made at points other than exact divisions, the notes are not harmonious with the ground note. Pythagoras had shown that notes pleasing to the human ear correspond to exact divisions of the instrument's strings.

Having defined the relationship between the length of a lute's string and the experience of musical harmony, Pythagoras was able to predict the quality of musical experience for any combination of strings. Successes such as these led Pythagoras to conclude that all is number, that the principles of mathematics are the principles of all things.

Pythagoras' conclusion had wide appeal. His lectures and demonstrations attracted large, enthusiastic audiences, including many women who ignored a ban on their attendance at public meetings. His followers went so far as to organize themselves into a secret society, the Order of Pythagoreans, dedicated to using their knowledge of mathematics to understand their world and eventually influence it.

The academic tradition surrounding Pythagoras and the early Greeks also spawned Western science and influenced Western philosophy and, much later, psychology as it struggled to define itself as a science. Psychologists still attempt to "measure" complex psychological processes such as motivation, creativity, and intelligence. If precise relationships could be found between such phenomena and numbers, might it be possible to write psychological laws in the same way we have established the physical laws of the universe? Might it be possible to predict human behavior and thinking processes with the same accuracy with which the ancient Greeks predicted the movements of the heavens? Psychologists still debate this possibility.

ATOMISM: THE MIND AS MATTER

During the period between the seventh and fifth centuries B.C. the Greeks were concerned with theories of the cosmos, or *cosmology*. This area of inquiry resulted in *materialism*, or the position that the universe can be understood in terms of the basic units of the material world. It was from this intellectual tradition that Democritus (460–370 B.C.), the great philosopher of Thrace, developed *atomism*.

Democritus and an Ancient Theory of Perception

Democritus thought that tiny atomic particles in ceaseless motion are the basis of all matter. He saw the world as a mass of such atoms that ran itself without need of outside forces. The human mind was not excluded from this physical world. It too was seen as a collection of atoms which could influence and be influenced by events in the external world. Consequently, the mind's contents as shown by its arrangement of atoms were considered by Democritus to be the result of experience. It is important to note that this theory was very different from later conceptions of the mind, such as that of Descartes, who felt the mind was separate from the body and was governed by laws different from those governing the physical world.

Democritus believed that objects in the external world emit beams of atoms that impinge upon the mind of the perceiver to produce perceptions. The atomic beam is a representation of the object: a rectangular object emits a rectangular beam; a circular object, a circular beam; a sour-tasting object, a beam of angular, small, thin atoms, and so on. Icons in the brain represent perceived objects. Not until relatively recent discoveries of the functional anatomy of the brain and the central nervous system was this notion of iconic representation completely abandoned.

Zeno's Paradoxes

According to M. Cary and T. J. Haarhoff (1959), the general problem of the relationship between mind and matter became important as the Greeks began to question the reliability of the sensory systems. The strongest support for this position was offered by Zeno of Elea, a Greek philosopher who lived in the fifth century B.C. Zeno used paradoxes and logical argument to demonstrate the inadequacy of the senses. The most famous of Zeno's paradoxes centers on an imaginary race between Achilles and a tortoise. Zeno always gives the tortoise a head start, so as soon as Achilles reaches the place where the tortoise began, the tortoise has moved to a new point; as soon as Achilles reaches that point, the tortoise has moved a little farther, and so on. Even though Achilles is the "fleetest of all men," he will never win the race. According to Douglas Hofstadter (1979), Zeno hoped to use his paradox to show that "motion" is impossible and that it is only in the mind that it seems possible. Motion is a perceptual illusion.

Zeno's paradoxes challenged the notion perpetuated by atomism and materialism that human thought processes and the soul can be understood in terms of the laws of the physical world. As Cary and Haarhoff (1959) stated, under these new influences the Greek thinkers came to decide that "man is the measure of all things" and that therefore "the proper study of mankind is Man." This "humanistic tendency" set the stage for advances in philosophy.

ADVANCES IN PHILOSOPHY

The three major philosophers who grew out of the humanist tradition were Socrates, his pupil Plato, and Aristotle. These great thinkers established *epistemology*, the branch of philosophy that investigates the origin, nature, methods, and limits of human knowledge. They were also concerned with several psychological issues, including learning, memory, and conscious awareness.

Socrates (469–399 B.C.)

Socrates has been portrayed through history as a great observer and skeptic. For Socrates the unexamined life is not worth living. He sought knowledge everywhere—in the streets, the marketplace, the gymnasium, and the countryside—intensively questioning people. He asked: what is truth? or what is justice? or what is courage? and rigorously examined the answers, pointing out logical flaws and poor or inadequate reasoning. Socrates questioned every assumption, doubted the obvious, and ridiculed cant and pretension. He expected that his logical, rigorous approach would produce true answers to these and similar questions. His approach was that of a rationalist.

Fundamental to Socrates' philosophy of education was his belief that truth cannot be defined by an absolute authority but rather lies hidden in every mind. A teacher's role is to uncover this dormant truth and might be compared to that of a midwife, who has no part in the implantation of semen that fertilizes the ovum but is responsible for assisting in the baby's delivery. So too, according to Socrates, the teacher's role is not to implant truths in the pupil's mind but rather to assist in their emergence. To facilitate learning by discovery, Socrates devised a teaching method analogous to his street dialogues. The teacher asks a series of questions designed to lead the pupil to truth by illustrating flaws in the pupil's reasoning. In this Socratic method, teaching is a partnership between pupil and teacher rather than a superior-subordinate relationship. Socrates rejected fees for his instruction and lived a life of simplicity and moderation.

To demonstrate the power of this method Socrates led an untaught boy who had no knowledge of geometry to discover for himself the theorem of Pythagoras (Lamb, 1967, pp. 303–311). Socrates claimed that he had not taught this theorem to the slave but had facilitated its emergence from a dormant state in the slave's mind.

As a result of the power and force of his arguments, Socrates was often able to discredit whatever answers were given to his questions concerning definitions of truth, justice, and courage. It is not surprising that he made many enemies. After all, we believe that we know what truth, justice, and courage are. It is embarrassing and annoying to be shown that perhaps we do not. Eventually his fellow citizens tired of his behavior, and so at the age of seventy Socrates was charged with undermining the religion of the state and corrupting youth. He was tried in front of 501 jurors and, by a margin of 60 votes, was found guilty and sentenced to death. Socrates accepted the verdict as legitimate though unjust, spent his last minutes comforting friends, then drank the hemlock poison.

Plato (427–347 B.C.)

Plato was Socrates' pupil and successor. In fact, much of what we know of Socrates comes from Plato's record of their dialogues. Plato founded an academy in Athens, a society of scholars and students that lasted for 916 years. His aim, like that of Socrates, was not to give his students a collection of facts but rather to train them to see below the surface of things, to seek the eternal reality underlying all. However, this task was a difficult one, for like Zeno and Socrates, Plato acknowledged the unreliability of sensory information. Knowledge does not derive from sensations, which are sometimes misleading, but from the processes of reasoning about sensations.

Plato stressed the difference between sensations deriving from our senses and what he called "forms," the eternal structures that order the world and are revealed to us through rational thought. Plato considered forms to be suprasensory, with an existence independent of the sensations that constitute them. Sensations corrupt, decay, and die. They are unstable. Plato's "forms" are more real and permanent. To illustrate this distinction Plato used an allegory of being in a cave, chained in such a way that all one can see of objects outside the cave are shadows cast by the flickering flames of a fire. The shadows are the analogue of sensations; the things outside the cave are the "forms." Our world of sensations is for Plato a world of dancing, flickering shadows of which we can never be sure.

For Plato the only way to increase the accuracy of our knowledge of the world is through the use of measurement and deductive reasoning. He was well aware of the contributions of Pythagoras and, like him, sought to describe the world using mathematical principles. Over the entrance to his lecture hall at the Academy he inscribed the words "Let no one destitute of geometry enter my doors." When one of his students asked, "What does God do?" Plato replied, "God always geometrizes." Human geometricians could measure the earth, but what of the human psyche? Could it too be measured? Pythagoras had shown that at least some aspects of human psychological experience could be measured. Plato suggested others. He recognized that people differ in their skills, abilities, talents, and aptitudes, categorizing them as individuals of gold, silver, brass, or iron. Society must recognize these individual differences and what Plato saw as their inevitable consequence: some must rule while others serve. In *The Republic*, Plato described a utopian society with an oligarchical system of government in which a small number of people endowed with superior reason, the Guardians, ruled under a philosopher-king. Those with superior courage would be warriors; those with a superior sense of beauty and harmony would be artists and poets; those with little talent or ability would be servants and slaves. Plato believed that such differences came from the gods, but having recognized them, society must select and preserve needed qualities through prearranged marriages and controlled breeding. His position was avowedly nativistic in that it assumed a hereditary basis for human characteristics and intelligence. But how could such qualities be measured? Plato believed that these qualities are localized in different parts of the body: reason in the head, courage in the chest, and appetite in the abdomen. His was a bodily phrenology without the exaggeration of later phrenologies (Chapter 3). By proposing to assess individual differences by measuring different parts of the body and then assigning people to various tasks based on their psychological strengths, Plato anticipated the modern field of psychometrics.

Aristotle (385–322 B.C.)

Aristotle, the last of the three major Greek philosophers, is accurately described as more of a natural scientist than either of his two predecessors. As a young man he lived in Athens and was a devoted student of Plato for some twenty years. In his middle years he was forced, because of his politics, to leave Athens, and he spent years traveling, working for a time as a tutor to the boy who later was to become Alexander the Great. He returned to Athens at the age of forty and founded a school of philosophy and science at Lyceum. It was during his years there that he wrote most of his important works on biological and psychological topics.

Aristotle is of interest to us because he was one of the first Greek philosophers to take an inductive, observational approach to his work. As mentioned earlier, Zeno pointed out the unreliability of our perceptions. Zeno's contemporary, Thales, stressed to his pupil Pythagoras the importance of deductive methods in uncovering the truth. Socrates also relied on logical proof to uncover truth in the minds of his students. Finally, Plato contended that our sensations are but imperfect representations of reality, not to be trusted. Reality can be known only through reason and logic.

If we cannot trust our sensations and perceptions, an inductive approach will not suffice. Yet it is just such an approach that Aristotle advocated. He emphasized careful observation and distrusted purely rational methods. After all, the world may not run as logically as Socrates and Plato assumed. If it does not, their conclusions, based on deductive methods, might not have been entirely true. Aristotle came to some remarkably accurate conclusions using an inductive, observational approach, but as we will see, his methods of inquiry also led him to some interesting but false conclusions.

From his observations of his own cognitive processes as well as those of others, Aristotle developed basic principles of human memory that have been restated many times in the history of psychology and are still fundamental to many contemporary accounts of memory. In his treatise *De Memoria et Reminiscentia* (Concerning Memory and Reminiscence), Aristotle outlined his theory that memory results from three associative processes. Objects, events, and people are linked through their relative similarity to one another or their relative difference—how much they contrast with one another. Things are associated if they occur together in time and space. These three basic principles of association—similarity, contrast, and contiguity—were supplemented by two other important influences on the strength of a particular association:

1. *Frequency*. Aristotle held that the more often a particular experience is repeated, the better it will be remembered. In many twentieth-century theories of learning, the relationship between the number of times a habit is reinforced and its strength and retention is a central concern.
2. *Ease*. Aristotle also recognized that some associations are more easily formed than others. Some events are more easily remembered than others. Modern studies of learning and memory have clearly demonstrated that certain associations are more easily formed and remembered than others.

Memories are particularly important because they reflect our experiences of the world. Experiences in turn are responsible for the contents of the mind; without experience our minds would be blank. The mind at birth has the potential for thought, but for this potential to be realized it must be acted upon by the world. The mind, for Aristotle, is furnished by experience, just as a writing tablet is filled with letters. Aristotle adopted the position of an empiricist: all the ideas we have, including those sometimes considered to be innate or inborn, are the result of experience. His position anticipated that of John Locke and other empiricist philosophers (Chapter 2) and through them influenced the materialistic behaviorist psychology of John Watson (Chapter 12).

Aristotle also developed a sophisticated and influential analysis of causation, his theory of causes. To illustrate his views Aristotle described examining a statue; let us follow his example by considering different causes of Michelangelo's *David*.

1. Upon examining the statue we find that it was sculpted from a huge block of white unflawed Carrara marble. It is a marble statue. That is a description of what Aristotle termed a *material* cause.
2. We also know that the statue is not just a block of marble but has an essence or form. That is the *formal* cause.
3. How did the statue come to have that form? One answer might be through the strokes and blows of the sculptor's hammer and chisel. That answer describes what Aristotle called the *efficient* cause.
4. Finally, in describing the statue, we attribute it to the sculptor. It is Michelangelo's *David*. The statue is the product of Michelangelo's genius and supreme talent. That is what Aristotle called a *final* cause.

The concept of a *final* cause represents a teleological aspect of Aristotle's analysis which gives an appearance of certainty but in effect has explained nothing. Such explanations have often been proposed in psychology but usually with little profit. Rather, psychologists seek *efficient* causes and explanations of behavior and consciousness.

Aristotle also held remarkably perceptive views on psychological catharsis. In his *Art of Poetry* he described drama as sometimes arousing emotions that have a purgative effect on the audience. In the twentieth century, Sigmund Freud was to make catharsis a central concept in his psychoanalytic theory. Today the Aristotelian view of catharsis is often heard in the debate about the effects of media violence on the tendency of people to behave aggressively. Some authorities, together with media executives, argue that exposure to movie or television violence can be beneficial as it allows viewers to purge themselves of hostile or aggressive impulses—a cathartic response. On the other side of the debate, equally prominent authorities argue that some individuals are led by such portrayals to behave aggressively, that filmed violence is a preparatory school for violence in our society, and that such consequences are especially likely in immature or emotionally unstable individuals.

Aristotle saw all life as forming a "ladder of creation," a continuous series of gradations from the lowest to the highest forms of complexity. He outlined three levels of life: nutritive (plants), sensitive (animals), and rational (humans). Thus linked, the whole of nature was to be studied. This conception of a scale of nature (*scala naturae*) has been a major influence on biological thought throughout the centuries. Charles Darwin, for example, in formulating his theory of evolution, acknowledged Aristotle's influence. Aristotle's conception of a scale of nature has not been entirely beneficial for psychology, since at times it has led to the belief that all animals, including humans, can be ranked on a scale of unitary, continuous, graded dimensions. Lovejoy (1936) pointed out that the notion of a scale of nature eventually led to more theological than scientific conceptions in which God was at the top of the scale and all other creatures were seen as increasingly imperfect copies of His perfection. Thus the angels were somewhat imperfect, humans more imperfect, apes still more imperfect, and so on "down" the scale.

One of Aristotle's most interesting misconceptions concerns what he thought to be the locus of the mind. As mentioned earlier, Hippocrates felt the brain was the seat of sensation, perception, and thought. Colin Blakemore points out how whatever scientific evidence is prominent at the time influences "intuitions" concerning the seat of consciousness:

> It seems inconceivable today that anyone could ever doubt that one's mind is
> in the brain. For me, the "me-ness" of me is undoubtedly situated in the
> middle of my head. But I am sure that I feel this with such confidence
> because I accept the currently fashionable scientific evidence that this is so.
> (Blakemore, 1977, p. 9)

For Aristotle, the "currently fashionable evidence" led him, understandably, to a radically different conclusion: the heart is the seat of thought. For instance, Aristotle studied the development of the chick embryo and noted that the heart is one of the first organs to move. He also observed that while an injury to the head may produce a period of unconsciousness, the person often recovers, whereas a wound to the heart is invariably fatal.

Aristotle's contention that the heart and not the brain is the most important part of the body might also have been influenced by his knowledge of ancient Egyptian burial practices. The Ba spirit of an ancient Egyptian was not in the head but in the bowels and chest. To preserve the body for its journey to Osiris, body parts such as the liver, stomach, lungs, and heart were extracted and embalmed in miniature coffins. However, there was no container for the brain, which was probably retracted through the nose with a spoon during embalming and destroyed.

Careful observations and knowledge of Egyptian history were not the only things that prompted Aristotle to choose the heart as the locus of the mind. He might have been influenced by a model readily available to him from his everyday experience: the agora, the central public meeting place of Greek towns. At the agora the town's citizens would meet to discuss and debate current events, politics, sports, religion, and local gossip. From these discussions common themes would sometimes emerge. To Aristotle such themes were analogous to the thoughts that emerged from the mingling of sensations, images, and memories in the *sensorum commune* of the heart. The brain's function was to cool the blood. This example is one of the many we will find throughout the history of science and psychology that demonstrate how a shared world view, characteristic of a particular historical period, influences the choice of models which philosophers and scientists use to illustrate their theories.

Some other interesting misconceptions that resulted from Aristotle's inductive methodology concerned his beliefs about animals. In his books *Historia animalium* (A History of Animals) and *De partibus animalium* (About the Parts of Animals), Aristotle attempted to classify animals on the basis of such characteristics as number of legs and presence of blood. He also described animal locomotion and parental and sexual behavior. Aristotle gave a correct account of the behavior of foraging bees, but since he relied on observations by others, he concluded that bees do not make honey but rather collect it on their wings as it falls from the sky. He also noted that caged birds' beaks often grow long, which indeed they do, but concluded that the growth is a punishment because they had been inhospitable to a guest in a previous world.

Aristotle's theories about the locus of the mind and animal behavior are examples of conclusions resulting from a preference for inductive methods that would have benefited from qualification through a rational critique. Even so, as we have seen, several contributions derived from Aristotle's inductive approach are echoed in contemporary theories of memory, catharsis, and evolution.

Post-Aristotelian Philosophy

A number of different schools of philosophy flourished for short periods in post-Aristotelian Greece, the most interesting of which from a psychological point of view were the Stoic school and the Epicurean school. They gave radically different answers to such questions as How are we to find happiness? and What should we do with our lives? Both groups of philosophers aimed to develop all-inclusive philosophical systems applicable to physical phenomena as well as to political, social, and moral conduct and concerns. The leading Epicurean philosophers were the Greek Epicurus (341 B.C.–270 B.C.) and the Roman poet Lucretius (99 B.C.–55 B.C.). They asserted that all knowledge originates in sensations that are retained in memory. A very similar view was to be proposed in the seventeenth century by John Locke (Chapter 2). For the Epicureans human life is a brief episode in the eternal history of atomic collisions. Theirs was a stochastic or statistical view of creation; they asserted that to consider the earth the only populated world is as absurd as to conclude that in an entire field sown with millet only one grain will grow. For Epicureans the goal of life was to enjoy whatever pleasures are possible consistent with minimizing the pain and suffering of others. Major Stoic philosophers were the Greek Zeno of Citium (336 B.C.–265 B.C.) and the Roman dramatist Seneca (4 B.C.–A.D. 65). Stoics believed that a rational principle (*logos*) guides the universe and that each person has a duty to follow and promote reason in both personal conduct and affairs of state. Passions and emotions were to be subdued. The Stoics influenced Immanuel Kant (Chapter 2). In a memorable metaphor, the American philosopher and psychologist William James (Chapter 9) described these philosophical schools as "tender-" and "tough-minded," respectively.

THE IMPORTANCE OF THE ANCIENTS

Now that we have reviewed briefly some of the issues and questions that concerned the ancients, it should be evident that those questions are still being addressed by contemporary psychologists. Like Democritus we still ponder the nature of the mind, and like Aristotle, its location. We attempt to describe behavior and information processing in terms of mathematical laws, just as Pythagoras attempted to define mathematical laws of perception. Like Galen we still ponder the nature of humanity.

But the importance of the ancients lies deeper than these similarities. Why do we still ask the same questions as did the Greeks and Romans? Is it only because we have not yet arrived at satisfactory answers? Not completely. Rather, it is because we share with the ancients a similar world view—a view of the world which they defined. The European languages we speak are derived from Greek and Latin. Our systems of ethics emerged from ancient philosophy. Aristotle's inductive method and Plato's deductive approach are basic to modern science. In fact, the importance of having scientific theories at all—so as to be able to predict and control events in our world—was first recognized by the ancients.

René Descartes. (The Bettmann Archive)

chapter

2

Philosophical and Scientific Antecedents of Psychology

Nearly 1,000 years passed between the final collapse of the Roman Empire in the fifth century A.D. and the beginning of the Renaissance. For several centuries successive waves of barbarian tribes—the Ostrogoths, Visigoths, and Vandals—rampaged across Europe, occupying various sections of the shrinking empire and leaving death, destruction, and devastation in their wake. Roman law could no longer be upheld, and the universal Roman monetary system was replaced by crude barter. It is not possible to give a date for the "fall" of the Roman Empire, but by A.D. 476 the governance had fallen to Odoacer, the German "King" who deposed the last Roman emperor, Augustulus. *Sic transit gloria mundi* (Thus passes the glory of the world).

The early Middle Ages, from the beginning of the ninth century to around the year A.D. 1000, have often been considered the Dark Age of Western civilization. However, there were technical and scholarly achievements before, during, and immediately after this era. In the seventh century, stirrups were used for the first time to support a rider's foot; they allowed a rider to mount and maneuver a horse more easily and wield a weapon with greater force. The ninth century saw the publication of a major biography of the Emperor Charlemagne. In 1180 the windmill was invented, an invention so successful that within ten years the Vatican levied a papal tax on all new windmill installations.

Psychological questions were often the province of religion. Saint Augustine, the Bishop of Hippo, lived in the fourth century. For Augustine, God is the ultimate truth and knowing God is the ultimate goal of the human mind. But what of people? How are we to understand human actions and conduct? Augustine recommended turning inward, for the truth dwells inside every person. In his *Confessions* Augustine disclosed his own emotions, thoughts, motives, and memories.

At times his disclosures are startling, as when he candidly describes his passions and the temptations of a mistress. For this work of public disclosure Augustine has sometimes been called "the first modern psychologist" (Misiak & Sexton, 1966, p. 8). The label seems premature, but Augustine's *Confessions* is still of great interest for its analysis and description of one man's psyche. In the seventh century the prophet Mohammed firmly established Islamic civilization, and Muslim scholars and intellectuals preserved many of the works of antiquity. In the thirteenth century Saint Thomas Aquinas reinterpreted Aristotle and firmly established scholasticism, the discipline that readmitted human reason as a complement to religious faith in the search for truth. However, with its emphasis on faith and acceptance of papal authority, scholasticism was not conducive to the development of formal science, though it did set the stage for a reawakening of intellectual activity.

The thirteenth century saw the establishment of fourteen universities, including those at Bologna, Paris, and Oxford. Eventually these institutions became vital to the development of science, but the century that followed was a time of terrible turmoil and strife. Barbara Tuchman (1979) described the "calamitous fourteenth century" as a time of civil war in England and France; nearly continual war between France, England, and Italy; mad popes and kings; lawless knights; debilitating taxation; and finally, the horrors of the black death (1348–1350), the plague that killed perhaps one-third of the population of Europe. This terrible century was followed by a rebirth of science, learning, art, and literature during the fifteenth and sixteenth centuries—the Renaissance. It is in the Renaissance world that we find the first formal philosophical and scientific antecedents of psychology.

THE RENAISSANCE WORLD

The Renaissance began in Florence, a beautiful walled city of 70,000 people on the banks of the Arno in northern Italy. Perhaps the most spectacular achievement of the Italian Renaissance was the work of artists such as Fra Angelico, Andrea Mantegna, Michelangelo Buonarotti, and Leonardo da Vinci. Leonardo was the quintessential Renaissance man: a brilliant artist and sculptor, an inventor, a skilled anatomist who made the first cast of brain ventricles, and a medical illustrator whose anatomic drawings were the first to give the observer more than one perspective of the subject depicted. Leonardo's most celebrated anatomic drawing, a human embryo in the womb, was so expert that it appeared in anatomy texts for hundreds of years.

The greatest technical achievement of the Renaissance was the invention of printing. The first printed manuscripts had appeared in China as early as the eighth century A.D. However, those books were block-printed; that is, characters and figures were carved by hand on the face of wooden blocks, ink was applied, and a print was made. Such printing was time-consuming, laborious, and inflexible. Shortly before 1450, after much labor and many financial and technical difficulties, Johannes Gutenberg developed a method of casting movable type that could be used to print numbers of books relatively cheaply. By 1450 Gutenberg had sufficient confidence in his method that he signed a contract for the "making of books," one of which was the Bible. Between 1450 and 1459 Gutenberg printed 185 Gutenberg Bibles, 48 of which exist today. By the end of the century printing presses had been established in at least thirteen European cities. For the first time knowledge was available to a relatively large number of people. Scholars were able to publish their own works and read the works of others.

The Renaissance was the era of Niccolò Machiavelli and William Shakespeare, but in addition to literary volumes, the first books in many areas of knowledge, including psychology, were printed. The first author to use the word *psychology* in a book title appears to have been Rudolf Goeckel (Lapointe, 1970). In 1590 he published a collection of works by different authors on the nature of humanity, particularly the human soul. The title of his book was *Psychologia hoc est, de hominis perfectione*, which might be translated literally as "Psychology This Is, about the Perfectability of Man" or, more freely, as "Psychology on the Improvement of Man." This first psychology book was a success and went through three printings before the end of the century.

During the Renaissance, knowledge of the geography of the earth expanded as never before. Portugese navigators sailed 1,500 miles down the African coast and established a lucrative trade in gold, ivory, pepper, and slaves. The most lucrative trade routes were those through Constantinople to the East. When that city was sacked by Sultan Mohammed II in 1453, a sea route to the East became imperative. The first sea trip to India was made in 1497 when Vasco da Gama successfully rounded the Cape of Good Hope. Christopher Columbus sought a shorter route to the East by sailing west from Europe but found the New World instead, and Ferdinand Magellan rounded Cape Horn, proving once and for all that the earth is round and that the continents of Asia and America are separate.

It would seem that such an enlightened age might have given birth to the formal study of human beings, psychology. After all, the Renaissance was an era of exploration, discovery, and artistic achievement. Leonardo had made beautiful drawings of the human anatomy, but equally detailed studies of the mind were not produced during this era. The reasons why may be revealed by examining the reactions of the Renaissance theological community to the development of a very different science—astronomy.

RENAISSANCE SCIENCE

The Place of Human Beings in the Universe

During the Renaissance, conceptions of the cosmos and of the place of humans within it underwent drastic change. The change began in 1543, when Nicolaus Copernicus (1473–1543) published his heliocentric view of the universe. Copernicus was a distinguished Polish cleric, humanist, and astronomer. After many years of astronomical observations, he concluded that the earth-centered (geocentric) view of the universe originally formulated by Ptolemy in the second century A.D. was incorrect. According to Copernicus, it is the sun, not the earth, that sits enthroned at the center of the universe and around which the planets orbit. The daily rising and setting of the sun, he said, is due to the earth's rotation on its axis, and the annual progression of the seasons is due to the earth's revolution around the sun.

This sun-centered (heliocentric) view of the universe was not entirely original to Copernicus. As early as the third century B.C. Aristarchus of Samos had argued that the earth revolves around the sun. In the second half of the fourteenth century Nicholas Oresme, a follower of the English Franciscan William of Ockham (after whom Occam's razor—the principle that the simplest explanation is best—is named), had proposed the same idea. But such views had been rejected, for certainly they were contrary to common sense. Surely, it was thought, this solid earth is not spinning through the heavens; anyone with eyes can see that the sun moves through the sky each day while the earth remains fixed. More important, such views were contrary to the teaching of the church. As God's special creation, humans should occupy a privileged position at the center of the universe. After all, the Bible states that God labored for five days to create the earth, but spent only one day on the remainder of the universe, and rested on the seventh. Having made men and women in his image and having lavished such care and time on the earth's creation, surely God would not have then placed the earth in a peripheral position, spinning giddily around the sun. The earth must be at the very center of the universe.

Such arguments were difficult to counter. When backed by the tradition and authority of the church, they had the force of dogma. To oppose them was heresy. Anticipating an unfavorable reaction to his theory, Copernicus delayed the publication of *De revolutionibus coelestium orbium* (On the Revolution of the Heavenly Spheres) for thirty-six years and, according to tradition, saw it for the first time in 1543 as he lay on his deathbed. Fearing an unfavorable reaction, his assistant, Andres Osiander, inserted a preface asserting that the rotating and revolving earth was to be considered a hypothesis, a mathematical convenience to simplify the description of planetary motion.

Copernicus was called by some the reformer of astronomy, a second Ptolemy, a man who had changed forever conceptions of the universe. But his theory was also unacceptable to many, especially to the church. His system was labeled absurd and antireligious. One cardinal riposted: "The Holy Spirit intended to teach us how to go to heaven, not how the heavens go" (Kesten, 1945, p. 316). Most important, Copernicus had demoted humans from a central to a peripheral position in the universe. Were human beings no longer the sacred creation of God? An even more shattering view was proposed later by a Dominican monk, Giordano Bruno (1548–1600), who lectured in Rome, Geneva, London, Oxford, and Paris, defending Copernicus and extending his system. Bruno proposed the existence of not just one sun but innumerable suns, not just one earth but innumerable earths, each revolving around its own sun and potentially inhabited by sentient beings. He described a limitless universe. Such views cost Bruno his life. Among the market stalls of Rome's Campo dei Fiori a statue marks the spot where Bruno was burned at the stake in 1600.

The telescope used by the Italian astronomer Galileo in 1609 to observe the solar system. (Courtesy, Department of Library Services, American Museum of Natural History)

Galileo Galilei

Italian Renaissance astronomy was advanced further by Galileo Galilei (1564–1642), who took advantage of the development of telescopes. In 1606 Hans Lippershey, a Dutch lens maker, noticed while walking between racks of lenses that when he looked through two that happened to be aligned, the distant spire of a church appeared nearer. He mounted two lenses a certain distance apart in a tube so that light would be collected by a lens at the far end of the tube and the image would be magnified by a smaller lens, the eyepiece. He had constructed the first refracting telescope. In 1609 Galileo increased the magnification factor of his telescope from 3 to about 30 and pointed it toward the stars. He saw "wondrous sights": four new planets, the satellites of Jupiter, and mountains and valleys on the moon's surface, which he captured in a series of wash paintings. Galileo also concluded that Copernicus had been correct and that the sun was indeed the center of the universe.

He described his observations and presented his conclusions in *Sidereus nuncius* (Message from the Stars), published in Venice in 1610.

The year 1610 was less than 100 years after Martin Luther's denunciation of the papacy in 1517 and the Reformation that split Western Christendom into Roman Catholic and Protestant churches. It was no time to challenge the church's authority. On February 24, 1616, the Congregation of the Index, the censorship body of the church, condemned the teaching of Copernicanism. The earth, not the sun, was the center of the universe, and Galileo was firmly instructed to stop advocating the new theory by the powerful Robert Cardinal Bellarmine, who was in charge of the Inquisition (Redondi, 1987). On August 6, 1623, Maffeo Cardinal Barberini, a friend of Galileo, became Pope Urban VIII. With his anticipated support and that of the powerful Medici family, Galileo felt free to resume his advocacy of Copernicanism. In 1632 Galileo published a *Dialogue on the Two Chief World Systems,* in which he created a hypothetical debate on the heliocentric system. With clarity and wit the debaters argued that the sun, not the earth, is the center of the cosmos and that the earth is not at rest but rotates on its axis and revolves around the sun. At the debate's end the participants conclude that Copernicus had been correct. Pope Urban had supported Galileo, insisting only that the *Dialogue* carry a disclaimer that Copernicanism was a hypothesis. When Galileo placed that disclaimer in the mouth of one of the debaters, Simplicius, a simpleminded fellow of shallow thoughts and limited ability, his fate was sealed.

The *Dialogue* was placed on the Vatican's Index of Prohibited Books. Galileo was summoned to Rome, tried by ten cardinals, and on June 22, 1633, found guilty of teaching doctrine judged to "be absurd, false in philosophy and formally heretical...that can in no way be probable, which had been already declared and finally determined contrary to the Divine Scripture" (Galileo's sentence, in Fahie, 1903, p. 315). For unknown reasons, three of the ten cardinals did not sign Galileo's sentence. In this confrontation between observation and authority, authority had triumphed. It seems likely that Galileo was at least shown the instruments of torture before being made to kneel before the cardinals and sign the following abjuration:

> I abjure, curse and detest the said errors and heresies, and generally every
> other error and sect contrary to the said Holy Church; and I swear that I
> will never more in the future say, or assert anything, verbally or in writing,
> which may give rise to a similar suspicion of me. (Galileo's abjuration, in
> Fahie, 1903, p. 320)

Legend has it that even as he signed the abjuration, Galileo muttered *"Eppur si muove"* (But it does move). Galileo was forbidden to publish, all copies of his books that could be found were burned, and he was confined to his villa for the rest of his life. In his final years, the man whose observations had enlarged the vision of the Renaissance world a thousandfold became almost totally blind.

In 1979 Pope John Paul II, speaking before a special session of the Vatican's Pontifical Academy of Sciences, acknowledged Galileo's outstanding contribution to science, and recognized the bitter conflict between church and science his case had caused. John Paul expressed the hope for "a fruitful concord between...church and world" (Pope John Paul II, 1980, p. 11).

Galileo was also a pioneer experimentalist. In his experiments he studied the relationship between the distance an object had fallen and its speed. Contrary to myth, these observations were not made by dropping objects from the Leaning Tower of Pisa but by rolling balls down inclined planes. He carefully manipulated such factors as the weight of the ball and the incline of the plane; he measured the time the ball took to cover a fixed distance and its speed. Galileo formulated the law of free fall: the distance an object has fallen from rest equals the square of the time since it was released. Speed is proportional to the time of the fall. So precise were Galileo's descriptions of his experimental procedures that a contemporary investigator, Stillman Drake (1975), was able to replicate them exactly. One puzzle apparently solved by Drake is how Galileo made such precise time measurements, since there were at the time no reliable clocks or watches to measure intervals shorter than a second. Drake suggested that Galileo used musical beats and half beats to time his intervals. Singing "Onward, Christian Soldiers" at a crisp tempo of about two notes per second, Drake recorded time intervals very close to those reported by Galileo (Drake, 1975, p. 101). The careful control and measurement of variables Galileo achieved in what he termed his "novelties" provided a model for the physical and biological sciences and eventually for psychology.

In his *Dialogue*, Galileo predicted that Italian science and trade would be overtaken by northern rivals unless scientists were guaranteed freedom of inquiry. In the margin of his own copy of the *Dialogue* Galileo wrote:

> In the matter of introducing novelties. And who can doubt that it will lead to the worst disorders when minds created free by God are compelled slavishly to an outside will? When we are told to deny our senses and subject them to the whim of others? When people devoid of whatsoever competence are made judges over experts and are granted authority to treat them as they please? These are the novelties which are apt to bring about the ruin of commonwealths and the subversion of the state. (Galileo in Newman, 1956, p. 733)

Galileo's passionate plea for untrammeled freedom of inquiry resounds through the centuries. He believed absolutely in the power of reason, for

> in questions of science the authority of a thousand is not worth the humble reasoning of a single individual. (Galileo in Newman, 1956, p. 734)

Conditions in Italy were manifestly inhospitable to the rationalist approach to the acquisition of knowledge Galileo advocated. Just as he predicted, the next great scientific advances were to be made in Germany and England, Protestant countries of northern Europe.

Two Contributions from England

Sir Isaac Newton (1642–1727) was born on Christmas Day of the year Galileo died. He was trained as a clockmaker. While visiting Trinity College at Cambridge University in 1955, the American psychologist Ernest Hilgard (Chapter 13) was shown a clock made by Newton that was still ticking (Hilgard, 1987, p. 8). Like his contemporaries, Newton was fascinated with light. It was everywhere; so too were colors. But in white light where did the colors come from? In 1662, Newton de-

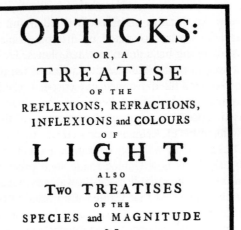

The title page of the 1704 edition of Sir Isaac
Newton's "Opticks." (From the cover of *Science*,
January 16, 1976, vol. 191, no. 4223.)

scribed to the Royal Society how he had "procured me a Triangular glass-Prisme
and conducted experiments on the 'phenomena of colors.'" White light passing
through the prism was refracted into its component colors: brilliant red, orange,
yellow, green, blue, indigo, and violet fell on the wall of Newton's study. When the
refracted rays were made to converge by passing through a second prism, the result
was whiteness, a phenomenon Newton found even more wonderful than the color
spectrum itself. Newton's demonstration that white light can be refracted into its
component colors and then individual rays can be recombined to produce whiteness
was a definitive scientific demonstration of the seventeenth century.

Newton's analysis of light was a triumph of physics. A later generation of
philosophers, the British empiricists, tried to do for human consciousness what
Newton had done for light, that is, to refract consciousness into its elements. This
was the model of the mind adopted by some members of the first generation of
psychologists in the late nineteenth century.

Voltaire said of Newton that he had been more fortunate than any other scientist could ever be, since it could fall to only one man to discover the laws that
govern the universe. Newton's great discovery was that the same force that pulls an
apple to the ground also holds the moon in its orbit around the earth and the earth
in its orbit around the sun. That force is gravity. In his majestic *Principia*, published in 1687 when he was twenty-five years of age, Newton described a lawful,
clockwork universe designed by God the "Great Watchmaker" and understandable

through mathematics and the application of the calculus Newton had invented. The Newtonian universe was lawful and predictable. In the eighteenth century the British astronomer Sir Edmund Halley reasoned that three spectacular comets recorded in 1531, 1607, and 1682 were the same one. Using Newton's law of universal gravitation to plot its orbit through space, Halley predicted that the comet would return seventy-six years later in 1758 and every seventy-six years thereafter. Halley died in 1742 and did not see the comet's reappearance on Christmas Day of 1758, just as he had predicted. Halley's demonstration of the predictability of a physical phenomenon showed the power of the human mind to understand the universe through the application of scientific laws. It was a triumph of what came to be known as the Age of Enlightenment.

William Harvey (1578–1657) demonstrated that such observational methods can be applied to a biological phenomenon. He found blood in animals as varied as frogs, chickens, pigeons, goats, sheep, oxen, and mice and even in such seemingly less promising specimens as eels, crabs, slugs, snakes, snails, wasps, and flies. The pervasiveness of blood in the biological world fascinated Harvey in the same way that light had fascinated Newton. Before that time the heart had been thought to "concoct" blood. Harvey weighed the amount of blood in a human corpse and in a sheep. The amounts were comparable, about four pounds. Next he bled a sheep and measured the amount of blood that was ejected with each beat of the heart. By noting the number of beats per minute, Harvey calculated that in thirty minutes more blood would have been forced from the heart than he had measured in the whole body. If the heart continued to "concoct" blood, in an average day some 4,000 gallons of blood would be ejected from the heart. Where did this blood come from? How could the heart make so much? Harvey's conclusion was that the heart does not make blood but rather pumps it. The heart ejects blood, which flows around the body and then returns to the heart to be ejected again. Blood circulates.

Harvey's work was important for a number of reasons. He had demonstrated that a biological system can be studied with the same experimental rigor with which physicists studied physical systems. Consequently, the success of his demonstration pointed the way to experimental biology. Harvey also speculated that "blood is the cause not only of life in general but also of longer life, of sleep and of waking, of genius, aptitude and strength" (Harvey, 1628, in Miller, 1982, p. 228). In the twentieth century blood-borne circulating hormones were shown to be important factors in temperament, cognition, emotion, and sleep. Finally, Harvey's research began the demystification of the heart that was to lead in the twentieth century to public acceptance of heart transplants.

RENAISSANCE PHILOSOPHY

René Descartes (1596–1650)

In addition to advances within science, developments within Renaissance philosophy provided an important foundation for psychology. As the Renaissance philosophers pursued knowledge of things and their causes, they developed insights and theories that greatly influenced later psychologists. René Descartes was a leading French mathematician and philosopher during the years preceding and immediately following Galileo's trial. He was born in 1596, the son of a councilor at the provincial parliament of Brittany. His family inheritance allowed him to pursue a life of study and travel unencumbered by the need to earn a living. From 1604 to 1612 Descartes was schooled by Jesuits, the intellectual foot soldiers of the Catholic church. From them he received a rigorous classical education with a strong emphasis on the humanities, mathematics, religion, and philosophy. By claiming frail health, Descartes was able to convince the school's rector that he should be excused from early morning religious exercises and allowed to stay in bed. All his life Descartes believed that he did his best thinking in the morning, in bed. Bertrand Russell said of Descartes that his mind worked best when he was warm (Russell, 1945, p. 558). Descartes' biographer reports that staying in bed became for him "a habit which he maintained all his life and which he regarded as above all conducive to intellectual profit and comfort" (Mahaffy, 1880, p. 12).

In 1617 the previously contemplative and reclusive Descartes volunteered for service in a mercenary army. One November evening during a military campaign in 1619, he had been alone thinking about mathematical ideas, when he fell asleep, and in a dream the "Spirit of Truth" entered his mind. This dream changed his life. The next day he renounced what he saw as his past idleness and resolved to devote himself to the search for truth and the unification of science through the power of reason. At the age of twenty-three Descartes resolved to write a rationalist manifesto. His first great success was the invention of analytic geometry. He developed methods that allow geometric propositions to be translated into algebraic terms, geometric curves to be described by equations, and the position of a point to be defined by coordinates with reference to two perpendicular lines. Descartes carried the ideas of analytic geometry with him through a number of battles and misadventures before publishing them eighteen years later in *La Géométrie* (Geometry). The work was an immediate success and secured Descartes' reputation as a mathematician. *La Géométrie*, he said, was written in a "contemptuous vein" and was intended to show what Descartes knew, more than to instruct the novice. He concluded his exposition with this ironic comment: "I hope that posterity will judge me kindly, not only as to the things I have explained, but also as to those which I have intentionally omitted so as to leave to others the pleasure of discovery" (Descartes, in Newman, 1956a, p. 237). On both counts his hopes have been fulfilled.

Descartes left France for Holland in 1629 to seek a life of scholarly solitude. So great was his need for peace and quiet that during the twenty years he was in Holland, Descartes lived in twenty-four different houses in thirteen different towns, allowing only a small number of trusted friends to know his whereabouts. Despite these precautions, his fame came to the attention of Queen Christina of Sweden. She wanted to know how to live happily and still not annoy God. Who was better qualified to answer her question than Europe's foremost thinker? In 1649 Queen Christina summoned Descartes to Stockholm to adorn her court and act as her private tutor in philosophy and mathematics. Upon receiving her summons, Descartes is said to have had a presentiment of death, but he had no option but to comply, especially when Christina sent a warship to transport him to Sweden. The young queen proved to be an inept student and, even worse for a man of Descartes' habits and temperament, insisted on having her lessons at 5 A.M. Descartes withstood the queen and the Swedish winter for only four months before dying of pneumonia in February 1650. In a grisly irony of history, the only available coffin was undersized, and so Descartes' head was severed from his body before burial and the two were never reunited (Boakes, 1984).

In addition to his contributions to mathematics, Descartes was also a founder of modern Western philosophy. He hoped to build a radical new system of philosophy from the ground up—a logical, scientific system of thought. He presented it in *Discours de la méthode* (Discourse on Method), published in 1637. Above all else Descartes sought truth: that which could not be doubted, knowledge that was certain. He adopted a rigorously scientific attitude, resolving

> First never to accept anything for true which I did not clearly know to be
> such; that is to say, carefully to avoid precipitancy and prejudice, and to
> comprise nothing more in my judgment than what is presented to my mind
> so clearly and so distinctly as to exclude all grounds of doubt. (Descartes,
> 1637, in Rand, 1908, p. 113)

The Jesuits who had educated Descartes made the proud claim "Give us the boy and we've got the man." Indeed, Descartes considered himself devout and always insisted that his many different homes be within walking distance of a Catholic church. However, at times he doubted the existence of God and believed that even the most passionate theist must occasionally have similar doubts. From an empirical standpoint we cannot be absolutely certain of God's existence. Such views were heretical to Catholic theologians. Descartes' works were placed on the Index of Prohibited Books, and booksellers were not allowed to print them. The theologians of Utrecht in Holland, at that time under the control of Catholic Spain, even brought Descartes before a court to answer charges that he was "an atheist, vagabond and profligate" (Newman, 1956a, p. 236). Fortunately, the charges were dismissed.

Along with his doubts about the existence of God, Descartes also concluded that it is possible to doubt and question such apparent givens as the very existence of the world and even of ourselves. He found himself in an acute existential dilemma— a dilemma he resolved by concluding that at any instant the only thing he could be certain of was that he was thinking about something. Thus for Descartes, the final proof of his existence was his act of thinking: *Cogito ergo sum* (I think therefore I am) (Descartes, 1637, p. 52).

If thinking is the final proof of our existence, it is important to know how and where we think. For Descartes, we think with our *res cogitans* (thinking thing), the mind. But the mind is different from the body. It is unextended, free, and lacking in substance. In contrast, the body is extended and limited and has substance. There is, Descartes claimed, a dualism of mind and body. Not only do the mind and body have these different characteristics, but in their functions they follow different laws. The body's actions are governed by mechanical principles and laws, for the body is nothing more than a highly complex machine. Our bodies are largely self-regulating physical systems performing many functions without the involvement of our minds. We do not have to "will" the digestion of lunch, nor do we have to think before withdrawing a hand from a flame. Likewise, we do not have to think about each breath or each beat of the heart. The body takes care of these things automatically.

Just as Aristotle was influenced by the agora when he chose a model for the heart, Descartes' conception of the body as mechanical was influenced by his observations of clockwork statues that bowed to a passerby, clocks with cuckoos that would call the hour, fountains, and other "amusements" that were popular at the time in the homes and gardens of the aristocracy. A person strolling through such a garden might step on a hidden trigger that would cause a mechanical bear or mannikin to spring from a concealed position in a hedge, a fountain to start spraying water, a gargoyle to nod its head, or musical instruments to play. In Descartes' time such diversions were considered highly entertaining, but Descartes was more impressed with them as models of the human body. Obviously, the bear and mannikin do not think before leaping out. Like our bodies, they behave in a simple, mechanical way. In *Traité de l'homme* (Treatise on Man, 1637), Descartes included an engraving of such figures and their driving mechanisms from the royal gardens of Saint-Germain-en-Laye.

How does the body's machine work? Descartes believed that there are hollow tubes or minute threads in the body that contain subtle airs, or breaths, sometimes called animal spirits. These animal spirits are heated and pressurized by the heart and flow from the sense organs, giving rise to sensations, to the muscles, giving rise to movements. They do so in a form of reflex arc described by Descartes as follows:

> Finally, it is to be observed that the machine of our body is so constructed that all the changes which occur in the motion of the spirits may cause them to open certain pores in the brain rather than others, and, reciprocally, that when any one of these pores is opened the least degree more or less than is usual by the actions of the nerves which serve the senses, this changes somewhat the motion of the spirits and causes them to be conducted into the muscles which serve to move the body in the way in which it is commonly moved on account of such an action. (Descartes, 1649, *The Passions of the Soul,* Article XV, in Rand, 1912, pp. 172–173)

In the brain, the opening and closing of certain pores allow or block the passage of animal spirits. Descartes' model is a hydraulic, pathway conception of the nervous system. In modern terms, the pores play the part of synapses, and the animal spirits that of nerve impulses.

What is the difference between our bodies and such human-made machines as the garden bear and mannikin? Descartes' answer shows the influence of Galen. The difference, he said, is one of complexity. The human body, having been designed by God, is infinitely more complex than any machine of human invention. What is the difference between the bodies of animals and the bodies of humans? Whereas the bodies of animals are governed solely by mechanical principles,

Descartes felt that the human mind can control the opening or closing of certain pores as well as their orientation. Thus, through an exercise of the mind, certain reflex actions of the human body can be controlled. Lawrence of Arabia was able to hold his finger in a candle flame. We scratch an itch, but not when hanging by one hand from a trapeze.

Given that our minds control our bodies, where does the interaction actually take place? What is its locus? Descartes chose as the site a pea-sized structure in the brain, the conarium, or pineal gland. In this brain structure, he said, the mind exercises its functions "more particularly than in other parts" (*The Passions of the Soul*, Article XXXI). He selected the pineal gland because he believed that it is not, unlike most other cerebral structures, duplicated in both sides of the brain. To Descartes a unitary structure seemed a logical site for the interaction between mind and body. His choice was simply a hunch, for he had no idea how the interaction might occur or what the functions of the pineal actually are. Even today there is some mystery about the pineal. We know that it secretes serotonin precursors, which control activity cycles, and that it becomes increasingly radiopaque with age. Consequently, it is often used as a landmark in brain x-rays.

Descartes believed that there are two major classes of ideas in the mind: innate ideas, which are inborn and do not depend on experience, and derived ideas, which arise from experience. Examples of ideas Descartes considered to be innate include the ideas of self and God; conceptions of time, space, and motion; and geometric axioms. Other ideas come from individual experience and are based on memories of past events. Descartes believed that a particular experience produces alterations of the nervous system and that these alterations, or neural traces, have effects on the mind when it acts to recall experiences. His analogy for the way in which memories are formed is characteristically original. Descartes imagined that the passage of animal spirits through certain pores in the brain forces open those pores and produces a lasting representation of their path. He compared the pores to the holes made in a linen cloth when it is punched with a set of needles. When the needles are withdrawn, the holes stay partially or completely open. The "memory" of the needles lingers on. When the mind seeks to recall something, this act of volition causes the pineal gland to change its inclination from one side to the other, causing animal spirits to flow through the enlarged pores.

One final characteristic of humans, according to Descartes, is that we have passions. These passions arise from the body, are passively experienced by the mind, and lead without further volition to bodily actions. For him, the six primary passions are wonder, love, hate, desire, joy, and sadness. All other human passions are mixtures of the primary six.

One important consequence of Descartes' notion that animals do not possess minds, let alone a will of their own, was that dissection of their bodies is permissible. Descartes performed many such studies. He is usually given credit for the first description of the retinal image, published in 1637. He extracted the eye of an ox, cut a window in the back of it, and placed a piece of paper in the opening. Holding the eye up to the light, he saw on the paper a tiny inverted image of his room. This was the first demonstration of the inverting function of the eye.

Descartes' influence on philosophy is widely acknowledged, but he was also important in the historical development of psychology. His clear statement of a dualism of mind and body provided a model and paradigm which has adherents even today. The Cartesian position that different principles and laws govern the actions of the body and those of the mind has obvious implications for psychology, the science of the mind. Finally, his distinction between innate and derived ideas anticipated the paradigm of nature and nurture which has been a prominent feature of many psychological systems.

Julien de La Mettrie (1709–1751)

In 1748, almost 100 years after Descartes died, Julien de La Mettrie published a work entitled *L'Homme machine* (Man the Machine) in which he developed an extension of mechanistic materialism. He argued that people are solely machines and that their actions can be explained exclusively through mechanistic principles. According to La Mettrie, we differ from other animals only in the complexity of our machinery, not, as Descartes had stated, because we have minds or, as the theologians believed, because we have souls. He attacked the conception of the person as a rational animal, arguing that we, like other animals, are motivated solely by the need to seek pleasure and avoid pain—by hedonistic drives. In considering thought, La Mettrie believed that degrees of thought are present in animals as well as humans. He described cognition as falling on a continuum, with greater and lesser amounts being present in different organisms. According to his position, it is just as incorrect to say that there is no rationality in apes and other animals as it is to say that there is perfect rationality in humans.

More specifically, La Mettrie challenged the assumption that only humans are capable of acquiring and using symbolic language. He predicted that if an ape were taught sign language with as much care and diligence as is commonly used in teaching a deaf child, the ape would show clear evidence of an ability to use language. After this training, such an animal, La Mettrie predicted,

> would no longer be a wild man, nor a defective man, but he would be a perfect man, a little gentleman, with as much matter or muscle as we have, for thinking and profiting by his education. (La Mettrie, cited by Limber, 1982, p. 432)

For more than 200 years both La Mettrie's views and his suggestions were rejected. Language came to be regarded as a unique attribute of humans, a function that even our closest primate relatives are not capable of developing. Recent research by comparative psychologists has demonstrated that a number of chimpanzees can acquire symbolic language (Savage-Rumbaugh, Rumbaugh, & Boysen, 1978). A lively controversy over these findings has developed (Terrace, 1979; Epstein, Landa, & Skinner, 1980), showing that at the very least they are provocative.

POST-RENAISSANCE PHILOSOPHY: EMPIRICISM, ASSOCIATIONISM, AND NATIVISM

The Early Empiricists

During the years after the Renaissance several advances were made in philosophy that ultimately laid the conceptual foundations for psychology. The early empiricists— Thomas Hobbes, John Locke, and George Berkeley—emphasized the effects of experience on a passive mind. The later empiricists—David Hume, David Hartley, and James and John Stuart Mill—considered the role of the active mind in the formation of associations, thus setting the stage for the psychological study of learning and memory. However, philosophers from Germany—Gottfried Wilhelm von Leibniz and Immanuel Kant—perpetuated nativism, the view that the contents of the mind are not solely the product of experience but are influenced by its inborn structure.

THOMAS HOBBES (1588–1679)

Thomas Hobbes was an acquaintance of both Galileo and Descartes. Hobbes not only anticipated British empiricism and was a major influence on seventeenth-century philosophical and political thought but also studied the contents of the mind and held a view of human nature that is still quoted by twentieth-century thinkers. This view of human nature formed the basis of his social and political theories concerning the origins and organization of groups. Why did humans first assemble in groups? Having done so, how did they stay together? Since Hobbes felt that we are basically aggressive animals, he believed that in the past small groups of people came together to protect themselves from the aggression of others. However, the social proximity of individual members increased the chances of self-destructive internal aggression. According to Hobbes, the only way the group's integrity could be sustained was through a strong, centralized authority, and without such authority there would be

> no arts, no letters, no society and which is worst of all, continual fear and danger of violent death, and the life of man solitary, poor, nasty, brutish and short. (Hobbes, 1650, p. 85)

In his most important book, *Leviathan* (1651), Hobbes argued that the centralized power his analysis of human behavior had shown to be essential should be held by a hereditary monarch. Kings and queens claimed to have been chosen by God and to be subject only to God. As King Louis XIV of France proclaimed, "Homage is due to kings; they do as they please." Hobbes considered the monarchy essential to any system of government, not because of any divine right of kings but because the designation of successive leaders would be undisputed, thus avoiding the possibility of conflict. Hobbes translated these beliefs into political action, supporting King Charles I in the civil war of 1642 to 1646 against Oliver Cromwell's revolutionaries. The monarchists were defeated in 1646; Charles I was found guilty of treason and was executed in January 1649. After Cromwell established a republican government, Hobbes fled to political exile in France and became tutor to the future Charles II. After the restoration of the monarchy and the coronation of his former student in 1660, Hobbes returned to England and obtained a position in the diplomatic service.

Hobbes's view of human nature is reflected in the thinking of recent sociobiologists. David Barash (1977) pointed out that it is difficult for a naked, unarmed human being to kill another human being. We, unlike some other animals, lack the lethal equipment for such killing. Barash argued that lacking this equipment, we also lack the biological inhibitions that other species have against intraspecific killing. Today, with the availability of weapons and armaments that allow mass killing at a distance, we find ourselves in a deadly evolutionary bind.

John Locke (1632–1704)

John Locke was the first major British empiricist. He was born in the country village of Wrington on August 29, 1632. His father, a country attorney and small landowner, showed a great deal of tenderness and affection for his two sons but made certain they learned to exercise the Puritan virtues of sobriety, discipline, and endeavor. Locke was taught to love simplicity and hate excessive ornament and display. In 1647 Locke entered Westminster School adjoining Westmister Abbey in London, where he received a rigorous classical education with emphasis on Greek and Latin. In addition, Locke and his schoolmates must have been aware of the momentous political events occurring, sometimes quite literally, on the other side of their schoolyard wall. Charles I was tried in Westminster Hall, and Locke might have seen him executed. We do know that one of his contemporaries, Samuel Pepys,

John Locke. (Culver Pictures)

attended the execution, for he recorded the event in his diary. Such political events must have affected a boy of Locke's intelligence and sensitivity, but despite these distractions he was an excellent student. He was appointed a king's scholar in 1647 and was elected to a junior studentship at Christ Church, Oxford, in 1652. For the next thirty years, Locke made Oxford his home. As a student he was especially attracted to research in medicine. Though he qualified as a physician, he did not become a professional doctor in that his occasional practice was never for money.

Locke found the philosophy being taught at Oxford sterile and dull. While acknowledging that Descartes had been a liberating influence on his intellectual development, the Puritan Locke regarded the Catholic Descartes with suspicion. In particular, the Cartesian doctrine of innate ideas and the conception of animals as automatons were unacceptable to Locke. He also rejected pure speculation as a method of inquiry. Instead, Locke, no doubt influenced by having been elected a fellow of the Royal Society, advocated the experimental, observational methods that were being developed by such scientists as Harvey and Newton. Locke had read Newton's account of his triangular glass-prism demonstration discussed earlier. The elegance and precision of this demonstration served as a model for Locke's work. Even today, psychology models its standards of scientific rigor on Newtonian physics.

In 1667 Locke began his association with Lord Ashley, later the earl of Shaftesbury, an English political figure of some importance. Locke served as his adviser, secretary, and family physician and as tutor to his son. Later Shaftesbury appointed Locke his secretary of presentations, a position that placed him at the center of political events. When Shaftesbury's political influence declined, he was imprisoned in the Tower of London. Fortunate to escape, Shaftesbury found exile in Holland. Because of Locke's close association with him, Locke too feared political persecution, and in 1683 he fled to Holland. After the overthrow of King James II by William of Orange in 1688, Locke returned to England at the age of fifty-six.

Understandably, given his experience, Locke had a great interest in politics and government. One year after his return to England he published his most important political work, *Two Treatises on Government* (1689). Locke saw government as based on a social contract between the governors and the governed. The state has an obligation to its citizens to protect and preserve certain inalienable rights: personal liberty, equality before the law, and religious equality—although Locke was not sure that equality should be extended to Catholics. To prevent the loss of these rights, Locke believed that the state's power must be limited through a system of checks and balances, with the most important being division of government into executive, legislative, and judicial arms. If a government persistently abused its powers, Locke believed that it would have broken its contract and debased its trust and so could be overthrown. His contention that certain revolutions are justified and his conception of the way a government should be organized had an acknowledged influence on the American revolutionaries and the framers of the American Constitution. Locke's clear statement of the dignity and worth of the individual and his advocacy of respect for fundamental human rights are reflected in twentieth-century codes of professional ethics, including the Ethical Principles of Psychologists (American Psychological Association, 1981).

Locke's Philosophy of Education   In contrast to the Hobbesian belief that human beings are aggressive animals, Locke held a much more optimistic and liberal view of humanity. He believed that the original state of nature of humans was good and that all people are born equal in their potential, so that their education is critical. Locke held that access to a good education should be available to all children. Locke's views on education were published in 1693 as *Some Thoughts Concerning Education*, a book written for a specific and limited purpose. During his exile in Holland, Locke had corresponded with Edward Clarke, an English gentleman who had written to him for advice on the upbringing of his eight-year-old son. Locke's letters formed the first draft of his book. According to Locke, children are what they are because of the experiences they have had. When they are young, children are "travelers newly arrived in a strange country of which they know nothing" (Locke, 1693, p. 173).

As an empiricist, Locke denied the existence of innate tendencies, dispositions, or fears in children. Why, then, are so many children afraid of the dark? According to Locke:

> If children were left alone, they would be no more afraid in the dark than in
> broad sunshine; they would in turn as much welcome the one for sleep as
> the other to play in. (Locke, 1693, p. 149)

But often this is not the case. If, for example, a foolish nursemaid tells a child that witches, ghosts, and goblins are abroad in the night looking for bad children, the child will probably fear darkness. Similarly, Locke said that children are accustomed to receive their "food and kind usage" from only one or two people. If they were to be exposed to more than a few people, they would go into the arms of a stranger as readily as into the arms of a parent. According to Locke, the only things we innately fear are pain and loss of pleasure. Through experience we learn to avoid objects associated with either of these consequences:

> The pleasant brightness and lustre of flame and fire so delights children,
> that at first they always desire to be handling of it. But when constant
> Experience has convinced them by the exquisite Pain it has put them to,
> how cruel and unmerciful it is, they are afraid to touch it and carefully avoid
> it. (Locke, 1693, p. 151)

Why do so many children dislike school and avoid reading books? Because, Locke said, school and books are associated with canings and beatings—practices that were routine in some British classrooms until the middle of the twentieth century. Thus are fears acquired.

Locke also gave explicit instructions as to how "vain terrors may be removed." He used the example of a child afraid of frogs and instructed the parents to treat this fear as follows:

> Your child shrieks, and runs away at the sight of a frog; let another catch it
> and lay it down a good distance from him; at first accustom him to look

upon it, and see it leap without emotion; then to touch it lightly when it is
held fast in another's hand; and so on till he can come to handle it as
confidently as a butterfly, or a sparrow. By the same way any other vain
terror may be removed if care be taken, that you go not too fast, and push
not the child on to a new degree of assurance, till he be thoroughly confirm'd in the former. And thus the young soldier is to be trained on to
the warfare of life. (Locke, 1693, p. 151)

Locke's view on the acquisition and treatment of fears is remarkably similar to that
of John Watson (Chapter 13), and the procedure Locke advocated is almost identical to the one used by Watson and his colleague Mary Cover Jones in overcoming
a fear of animals in a young boy (Watson, 1928a).

Locke's *Essay Concerning Human Understanding* Throughout the years of political turmoil, Locke continued to work on his *Essay Concerning Human Understanding*. This work, which marks the formal beginning of British empiricism, has
proved to be of great importance in the history of psychology. The story of how it
came to be written is instructive. Throughout his years of political involvement,
Locke attended seminars in which matters of philosophy, science, and politics were
debated. Often these sessions ended in conflicting opinions that seemed impossible
to resolve. Locke realized that before an attempt was made to resolve these differences, the characteristics of human knowledge and understanding should be un-
covered and criteria should be established that would allow certain and uncertain
knowledge to be separated. This examination proved more difficult than expected.
The enormous scope of the task, coupled with disruptions caused by Locke's political involvement, delayed a conclusion until 1690, when, at the age of fifty-seven,
he published the first edition of *An Essay Concerning Human Understanding*.

Locke's work was published just three years after Newton's *Principia* (1687).
Newton had described a majestic clockwork universe that follows a single set of
rules. Locke's aim was to find a similar set of rules for the human mind. He aimed
to "refract" consciousness into its basic elements, just as Newton had refracted
light. Once the basic elements of consciousness had been found, Locke hoped to
account for their interactions and combinations. Locke's system, like Newton's, is
atomistic and reductionistic. For him, the basic elements of the mind are ideas, all
of which come from a single source—experience. Contrary to Descartes, he rejected
the notion of innate ideas. In a frequently quoted passage Locke stated:

Let us suppose the Mind to be, as we say, white Paper, void of all Characters, without any Ideas; How comes it to be furnished? Whence comes
it by that vast store, which the busy and boundless Fancy of Man has
painted on it, with an almost endless variety? Whence has it all the materials
of Reason and Knowledge? To this I answer, in one word, From *Experience*.
In that, all our Knowledge is founded; and from that it ultimately derives
itself. (Locke, 1690 p. 104)

The analogy of the characterless white paper was not original with Locke. As mentioned in Chapter 1, Aristotle had conceptualized the mind at birth as a blank tablet

and had emphasized the role of experience. Nevertheless, Locke's statement is a classic exposition of the empiricist position.

Within our experience there are, according to Locke, two sources of ideas: sensations from contact with external "sensible" objects and reflection, an internal operation of the mind. These two are "Fountains of Knowledge, from whence all the *Ideas* we have or can naturally have, do spring" (Locke, 1690, p. 104). In the presence of a flower, we see its color, smell its fragrance, and feel its touch. These sensations provide us with ideas of the flower. But we can also reflect on the flower. We can think about it when it is not physically present, and thus we have ideas that are independent of sensations. For Locke, sensation and reflection are the mind's only source of ideas. Every idea in the mind was once either a sensation or a reflection. Like the ancient Greeks, Locke realized that our sensations are not always reliable. He cited the example of a person suffering from yellow jaundice to whom the world appears yellow; that person has false ideas based on diseased sensations. Similarly, looking at the world through colored glasses will produce false impressions. To prove his point, Locke described the following demonstration. Take three bowls of water, one cold, one lukewarm, and one hot. Arrange them in a row on a table. Place one hand in the cold water and one in hot. One hand, of course, feels cold and one feels hot; your ideas of the temperatures of the two bowls of water are correct. After they have been in the water for about thirty seconds, take both hands out and place them together in a bowl of lukewarm water. The sensations are discomfiting and confusing. To one hand the water feels cold, and to the other warm, yet they are in the same bowl of water. Conflicting sensations give false ideas of the water's temperature.

According to Locke, ideas are either simple or complex. The same object may give a number of different simple ideas—we see at once both motion and color, or the hand feels both softness and warmth—and these simple ideas are associated to form a complex idea. Ideas come to be associated as a result of experience. Complex ideas are made by the mind out of simple ideas in a number of different ways:

1. Combining a number of simple ideas into one complex idea
2. Bringing two simple ideas together and seeing the relation between them
3. Separating simple ideas from other ideas that accompany them—the process of abstraction

Locke's model of the human mind was that of a chemical compound, and it seems likely that he was influenced by the Oxford chemist Robert Boyle's demonstration thirty years earlier of chemical elements and chemical compounds.

But what would be the contents of the mind if our experience had been restricted in some way and such processes had not occurred? In one of the most fascinating passages of the *Essay*, Locke presented the speculations of his friend, the "Learned and Worthy Mr. Molyneux of Dublin," concerning the reactions of a formerly blind man, suddenly made to see, when he first encountered familiar objects visually. Wiliam Molyneux (1656–1698) had written to Locke:

> Suppose a Man born blind, and now adult, and taught by his touch to
> distinguish between a Cube and a Sphere of the same metal, and nighly of

the same bigness, so as to tell, when he felt one and t'other, which is the
Cube, which is the Sphere. Suppose then the Cube and Sphere placed on a
Table, and the Blind Man to be made to see. Quaere, whether by his sight,
before he touched them, he could now distinguish and tell which is the
globe, which the Cube? To which the acute and judicious Proposer answers:
Not. For though he has obtain'd the experience of how a Globe, how a Cube
affects his touch; yet he has not yet attained the Experience, that what
affects his touch so or so, must affect his sight so or so. Or that a protuberant angle in the Cube, that pressed his hand unequally, shall appear to his
eye, as it does in the Cube. (letter from Molyneux, cited by Locke, 1690, p.
146)

Locke agreed with Molyneux's intriguing proposition that a person born blind and
made to see would not be able to name the cube and sphere for some time. That
person would need to experience the visual world before having ideas based on
visual sensations. Locke wrote:

I agree with this thinking Gent., whom I am proud to call my Friend, in his
answer to this his Problem and am of the opinion, that the Blind Man, at
first sight, would not be able with certainty to say, which was the Globe,
which the Cube, whilst he only saw them. Though he could unerringly name
them by his touch, and certainly distinguish them by the difference of their
Figures felt. (Locke, 1690, p. 146)

As early as the eighteenth century, surgeons who learned to remove congenital cataracts provided dramatic tests of Molyneux's proposition. In 1728 an English
surgeon, William Cheselden (1688–1752), reported to the Royal Society his observations of a young gentleman, born blind, who was operated on between thirteen
and fourteen years of age. At first the boy was unable to name anything he saw, but
apparently he could distinguish shapes and was able to learn their names. After
handling a cat, he looked at it attentively and then said, "So puss! I shall know you
another time" (Chesselden, quoted by Morgan, 1977, p. 17). A number of such
eighteenth-century cases were discussed by Denis Diderot (1713–1784) in his "Letter
on the Blind" (1749). Diderot's letter ends with a poetic affirmation of our igno-
rance of ultimate reality for which he was thrown into a dungeon in Vincennes on
orders of the king of France.

In 1910 a surgeon named Moreau summarized his experiences with an eight-
year-old boy "born blind and made to see":

It would be an error to suppose that a patient whose sight has been restored
to him by surgical intervention can thereafter see the external world. The
eyes have certainly obtained the power to see, but the employment of this
power, which as a whole constitutes the act of seeing, still has to be acquired
from the very beginning. The operation itself has not more value than that
of preparing the eyes to see; education is the most important thing.
(Moreau, 1910, in Senden, 1960, p. 160)

Contemporary support for Locke's answer to Molyneux's question can be
found in Maurice von Senden's (1960) summary of the visual experiences of sixty-
five congenital cataract patients whose vision was restored. In general such people

do not experience the orderly, visual world of the sighted person. At first, they are confused by unfamiliar visual stimuli and can identify familiar objects only by touching them. Associations between visual sensations and the names of objects must be formed through experience. In many cases they are formed only with great difficulty. Richard Gregory (1974) described the case of S. B., a fifty-two-year-old man who recovered his vision through corneal grafts to both eyes. Before the surgery this intelligent, active, and curious man worked as a skilled machinist. Afterward he became confused, depressed, and unable to work. He was never able to adjust to a visual world and committed suicide two years after the operation.

Locke's immediate successor within British empiricism was George Berkeley. In our consideration of the history of psychology, we will encounter a number of pupils or successors who adopted positions more radical than those of their teachers or predecessors. That was certainly true of Berkeley, who might be said to have out-Locked Locke.

George Berkeley (1685–1753)

George Berkeley was a brilliant and precocious child who entered Trinity College, Dublin, in 1700 at the age of fifteen and wrote a treatise on Euclidean mathematics before he was twenty. Though he was deeply influenced by Locke, Berkeley's intellectual development followed a different course. Locke wrote his most important work, *An Essay Concerning Human Understanding*, when he was in his late fifties; Berkeley made his most important and creative contributions while he was in his twenties. He was well aware of this difference and rather arrogantly speculated about how it had been possible for Locke to write such an important work at the advanced age of fifty-seven.

Berkeley was a formidable and forceful writer. He published his three most important works within four years: *An Essay Towards a New Theory of Vision* in 1709, *A Treatise Concerning the Principles of Human Knowledge* in 1710, and *Three Dialogues Between Hylas and Philonous* in 1713. In the *Treatise*, Berkeley presented a radical extension of Locke's philosophy that has come to be called *subjective idealism* or *immaterialism*. In agreement with Locke, he argued that all knowledge of the external world comes from a single source: experience. But then Berkeley took an additional step and stated that the very existence of the external world depends on perception. Matter, according to Berkeley, does not exist in and of itself; it exists because it is perceived. His assertion is summarized in the Latin formula *Esse est percipi* (To be is to be perceived). To understand Berkeley's position one can retrace his arguments using a familiar object, an apple. Both Locke and Berkeley argued that all we know of the apple originally comes from our sensations: what we see, smell, taste, feel, and experience in the presence of the apple. But then Berkeley went on to assert that the very existence of the apple depends on its being sensed or perceived and further that the existence of the whole world has the same requirement. He wrote:

> Some truths there are so near and obvious to the mind, that a man need only open his eyes to see them. Such I take this important one to be, to wit,

> that all the choir of heaven and furniture of the earth, in a word all these bodies which compose the mighty frame of the world, have not any subsistence without a mind, that their being is to be perceived or known. (Berkeley, 1709, in Berkeley, 1820, vol. 1, p. 27)

The assertion that matter does not exist without a mind is a bold one and is obviously important for psychology, a discipline that was defined initially as the science of the mind. However, Berkeley's assertions invite ridicule and misinterpretation because they appear to be contrary to "common sense." Berkeley was aware that his work might elicit such a reaction, and so he deliberately omitted all mention of the nonexistence of matter from the title page, dedication, preface, and introduction of the *Treatise*. He begged his reader to "suspend his judgment" until the book had been read as a whole. His hope was that the notion might "steal unawares on the reader," who possibly never would have read the book had he or she known it contained such paradoxes (Berkeley, 1710, in Luce & Jessop, 1949, p. 23). Alas, such was not the case. When the *Treatise* was published in Dublin (1709) and in London (1711), Berkeley was accused of wildness, of solipsism (the philosophical idea that only the self can be proved to exist), and of having perpetrated a reductio ad absurdum. Gottfried Wilhelm von Leibniz accused him of seeking notoriety with his paradoxes, while the American philosopher Samuel Johnson refuted Berkeley's assertion that matter does not exist by kicking a stone and implied that a similar experience would clear Berkeley's head of such fuzzy thinking.

In a number of letters (philosophical correspondence, Luce & Jessop, 1949, pp. 271–294), Johnson further questioned Berkeley's assertion that things exist only when perceived, citing the example of a fire. When we light a fire and then leave the room, no created mind perceives it for some time; yet when we return, a great deal of fuel has been consumed. Surely we must conclude that the fire continued to burn, that is, to exist during our absence. Or consider the tree in the garden; does the tree not continue its existence when the garden is deserted? The birds that nest in the tree would certainly be surprised by an assertion that it does not. Berkeley replied to such ingenious criticism by stating that the fire continues to burn and the tree to exist when there is nobody to perceive them because they continue to be perceived in the infinite mind of God. Berkeley regarded the very permanence of the material world as definitive proof of God's existence, a proof he hoped would counter the skepticism he believed to be an inevitable consequence of the Newtonian view of the universe as nothing more than a giant automatic machine. In the twentieth century this phase of his thinking was neatly captured in the following limerick by the theologian Ronald Knox concerning a tree in one of the quads of Balliol College, Oxford:

> There was a young man who said, God
> Now doesn't it seem to you odd
> That this great chestnut tree
> Simply ceases to be
> When there's no one about in the quad?

To which the reply takes the form of a letter:

> Dear Sir,
> It really is not at all odd
> I'm always about in the quad
> And the great chestnut tree
> Never ceases to be
> In the mind of Yours Faithfully,
> God.
>   (Landa, 1981, p. 22)

Most of Berkeley's contemporaries were neither as witty nor as understanding. His views were regarded as absurd, an exercise in philosophical futility.

While the *Treatise* is open to criticism, it is generally agreed that the theory Berkeley outlined in *An Essay Towards a New Theory of Vision* is an outstanding argument in the classical debate between nativism and empiricism. The book may also be regarded as the first work in physiological optics, a discipline defined by Hermann von Helmholtz (Chapter 3) a century and a half later. Berkeley's concern in the *Essay* was visual perception, especially the problem of accounting for depth perception. In the *Dialogues* Berkeley had posed the problem:

> It is, I think, agreed by all that Distance of itself and immediately, cannot
> be seen. For distance being a line directed endwise to the eye, it projects
> only one point in the fund [retina] of the eye—which point remains invari-
> ably the same, whether the distance be longer or shorter. (Berkeley, 1709,
> in Berkeley, 1820, vol. 1, p. 237)

But perception of distance is a skill we are able to use, often in a remarkable way. Think of applying the brakes on a car to make a smooth stop at a traffic light or to come to a halt behind a slower vehicle. Given that we obviously perceive depth, how do we do it? Berkeley's answer was that through experience we learn to use certain depth cues. He described a number of these cues: interposition—objects that par- tially or completely hide other objects are judged to be nearer; relative size—larger objects are judged to be nearer; chiaroscuro—gradations of light and shade often used by artists to suggest depth in their paintings; and finally, movement of the eyes as objects move toward or away from us. Berkeley's description of this last cue is especially explicit. He writes:

> It is certain by experience, that when we look at an object with both eyes,
> according as it approaches or recedes from us, we alter the disposition of our
> eyes, by lessening or widening the interval between the pupils. This disposi-
> tion or turn of the eyes is attended with a sensation, which seems to me to
> be that which, in this case brings the idea of greater or lesser distance into
> the mind. (Berkeley, 1709, in Berkeley, 1820, vol. 1, p. 241)

Had Berkeley made experimental tests of his theory of vision, as contempo- rary psychologists have, he would have found empirical support for his theory and would also have been the first experimental psychologist. Instead, discouraged by the often hostile reactions to his work, Berkeley turned to other concerns. In 1720 he became involved in founding a university in the New World away from what he considered the degeneracy of the Old. His aim was "converting the savage Americans to Christianity by a College to be erected in the Summer Islands, otherwise known as the Isles of Bermuda" (Berkeley, 1820, vol. 1, p. VII). He used his charm and influence to secure a royal charter for the university, a contribution from the prime minister of England, and a promise of a parliamentary grant of several thousand pounds. Berkeley left England with high hopes, settling for what he hoped would be a brief, interim period in Newport, Rhode Island. Alas, in his case, out of sight was out of mind, and his support slipped away. Parliament reneged on its promise, as did many of his supporters. His visionary project failed, another acute disappointment for Berkeley.

Ironically, Berkeley's most successful work was a book published in 1744 about tar water and several philosophical topics including proofs of the existence of God. *Siris*, as the book was called, described how the resinous exudation of pine and fir trees could cure a wide variety of bodily complaints. Having used it to treat his own ailments, Berkeley became convinced that it was beneficial. Unlike many of his other publications, this book was widely read and went into six editions.

Berkeley lived in America for just two and a half years but always retained his admiration for the New World. In his will he bequeathed his library to Yale University and made a generous bequest to Harvard College. The California city of Berkeley is named after him. He died in Oxford in 1753 and even in death caused many people to shake their heads and dismiss him as an eccentric, if not worse. Berkeley believed that putrefaction is the only infallible sign of death, and so he left specific instructions in his will that after death his body was to lie before burial, unwashed, undisturbed, and covered by the same bedclothes, until it became offensive. Such instructions struck many people as bizarre, but today, beset as we are by the acute difficulty of defining death in many cases in which life-support systems make it possible to prolong biological life for extended periods, Berkeley's position appears more reasonable. Above all, Berkeley was himself a paradox. Clearly he had a powerful and original mind, but all too often he was dismissed as an unreliable eccentric.

A SEVENTEENTH-CENTURY NATIVIST COUNTERVOICE

Locke and Berkeley were influential voices in seventeenth- and eighteenth-century philosophy, but they were not the only voices; they had critics and opponents. The most important countervoices were those of a number of European philosophers who considered themselves nativist successors to Descartes. One such man was Gottfried Wilhelm von Leibniz.

Gottfried Wilhelm von Leibniz (1646–1716)

Leibniz was Locke's contemporary; the two men knew each other and often corresponded. Leibniz, known for his political writings, was also Germany's leading mathematician, renowned for his coinvention with Newton of the calculus, though Newton was never able to accept the fact that Leibniz had conceived of the calculus independently of his own work.

Leibniz considered Locke's *Essay Concerning Human Understanding* one of the most beautiful and estimable works of the period, but he also believed that Locke's account of the human mind was quite wrong. After reading a prepublication draft of Locke's *Essay* in 1688, Leibniz immediately began a rebuttal, his *New Essays on Understanding*. These essays were completed in 1704, the year of Locke's death, but Leibniz withheld their publication as he had no wish to appear critical of a dead man he admired so much. They were published in 1765, nearly fifty years after Leibniz's death.

Leibniz could not accept Locke's empiricist account of the contents of the mind. He admitted that animals might be "empirics," that is, blank tablets at birth filled by experience, and he described a number of examples of animals that were clearly products of their experience: a dog thrashed with a cane will whine and run away at the sight of the cane. Leibniz could admit that humans might be such products or empirics in three-quarters of their acts, but not in all of them. We expect that the sun will rise tomorrow because it has always done so in the past, that the rain will fall from the sky, and that summer will follow spring. But in addition to this empirical knowledge, Leibniz believed that there are necessary and eternal inborn truths, the "nonempiric" one-quarter. This nonempiric one-quarter represents the innate intellect. Locke and Berkeley had stated that nothing is in the intellect which was not first in the senses, to which Leibniz replied, nothing except intellect itself. According to Leibniz, intellect allows reason and science; it gives us knowledge of ourselves and of God and is the essence of the human spirit.

Leibniz believed that empiricist philosophers made a fundamental error when they denied the existence of inborn ideas, truths, dispositions, habits, and potentials. Rather than a sheet of blank paper to be written upon by experience, the mind at birth is a block of veined marble. The veins represent the mind's inborn dispositions. The sculptor's hand frees a figure from this marble, but the figure was present before the chisel was ever lifted. So too, ideas are present in the mind at birth, and the role of experience is to allow them to emerge.

In his book *The Monadology*, Leibniz described a system of *monads*—an infinite number of elements composing all being and activity. Monads are indestructible, uncreatable, and immutable. They have no parts and cannot be formed or decomposed. Both the physical and mental worlds were for Leibniz vast pluralisms of independent monads. Though monads may appear to have an effect on one another, they do not interact but follow parallel courses. In describing the parallelism of monads, Leibniz used his famous metaphor of the clocks:

> Imagine two clocks or watches which agree perfectly. Now this may take place in *three ways*. The *first* consists in a mutual influence; the *second* is to have a skilled workman attached to them who regulates them and keeps them always in accord; the *third* is to construct these two clocks with so much art and accuracy as to assure their future harmony. (Leibniz, 1695, in Rand, 1912, p. 219)

Leibniz believed that God had constructed the human body and the mind like two parallel clocks, a psychological parallelism. For him, the mind was an active agent, and his view might be described as an "activity psychology." As we will see, his position came to influence later theorists of "act" psychology (Chapter 6). Leibniz's view was that of an avowed *nativist*, or one who believes in innate ideas, tendencies, and dispositions. We encountered nativism previously in the philosophies of Plato, Socrates, and Descartes, and we will meet it again in the psychologies of Francis Galton and Granville Stanley Hall (Chapter 9) and Lewis Terman (Chapter 11).

EIGHTEENTH-CENTURY ASSOCIATIONISM

The ideas of David Hume and David Hartley may be considered transitional between those of the British empiricists and those of the British associationists. Whereas the early empiricists had analyzed the mind into component parts, Hume and Hartley began the search for laws that would describe how these parts come to connect or blend together.

David Hume (1711–1776)

David Hume was born in Scotland and was educated at the University of Edinburgh. As a student he was interested in the science of mental life, called at the time *pneumatic philosophy*, that is, philosophy concerned with expressions of the vital life force the Greeks called *pneuma*. In pneumatic philosophy, humans are considered a part of the world of nature and so should be studied by the methods of natural science. Pneumatic philosophy involved a study of mental life and an attempt to establish the principles underlying mental operations. Hume's two most important works for psychology were *A Treatise of Human Nature* (1739) and *An Enquiry Concerning Human Understanding* (1748). These books were only mild successes, not nearly popular enough to satisfy the intensely self-critical Hume or to secure an academic position for him. Twice he unsuccessfully sought chairs of pneumatic philosophy. He then turned to politics and diplomacy, holding a variety of positions culminating in his appointment as undersecretary of state. In 1716 Hume published a *History of England*, a work that was a success and did make his name, though not, of course, as a philosopher.

In the *Treatise*, Hume distinguished between impressions and ideas. He considered these two mental contents to be different in the degree of force or liveliness with which they impinge upon the mind. Ideas, for Hume, are faint copies of impressions, many of which come from sensations. Sensing is almost everything. For Hume, *senso ergo sum* (I sense therefore I am). According to Hume, there is a causal connection between impressions and ideas; occurring together, they become associated, and the idea comes to resemble the impression. Hume stated that simple ideas combine in the mind to form complex ones according to three laws or principles of association: resemblance, contiguity in either time or space, and cause-and-effect relationships.

In the introduction to *An Enquiry Concerning Human Understanding*, Hume advocated a new science of human nature. Human beings are part of the world of nature and must be studied using the methods of natural science. Systems of ethics, political behavior, criticism and reason, and moral behavior must all be described and explained. They were all considered by Hume to be natural products of mental processes, and he believed that they could be studied scientifically. His essay had little impact on his peers, but his suggestion for a new science of human nature prepared the way for Wundt's establishment of a science of the mind over 100 years later.

David Hartley (1705–1757)

David Hartley's most important work for psychology was *Observations on Man* (1749). Hartley was trained as a minister of the Church of Scotland (Presbyterians) but found himself unable to accept certain theological doctrines, and so he turned to medicine. As might have been expected from a medical man, his orientation was by far the most physiological among the British associationists. Both mind and body are to be studied, Hartley said, because they are related biologically. He specifically localized mental faculties in the brain, pointing out that

> the perfection of our mental faculties depends upon the perfection of this substance (the white medullary Substance of the Brain); that all injuries done to it affect the trains of ideas proportionably; and that these cannot be restored to their natural course till such injuries be repaired. Poisons, spirituous liquors, opiates, fevers, blows upon the head, etc., all plainly affect the mind by first disordering the medullary substance. And evacuations, rest, medicines, time, etc., as plainly restore the mind to its former state, by reversing the foregoing steps. (Hartley, 1749, p. 317)

Some of Hartley's observations were remarkably accurate. He described positive afterimages for both visual and auditory stimuli: the impression of a candle that continues after the flame is out, the impression of a note that continues after the chord is no longer struck. Why do we have such afterimages? Hartley held that objects in the external world act upon our sense organs, causing infinitesimally small medullary particles to vibrate in the nerves and then in the brain. These vibrations continue for a brief time after the stimulus is no longer present; hence, the afterimage is formed.

In the brain, vibrations and ideas become associated by occurring simultaneously a sufficient number of times. In his Proposition XI he described this reverberatory process:

> Any Vibrations A, B, C, etc., by being associated with one another a sufficient Number of Times, get such a Power over a, b & c the corresponding miniature Vibrations, that any of the vibrations A, when impressed alone, shall be able to excite in the Mind, b, c, etc., the Miniatures of the rest. (Hartley, 1749, p. 325)

For Hartley, such associations, were basic to all ideas, opinions, and affections.

Hartley's brand of associationism has a biological basis not found in the theories of his predecessors or those of the associationists who followed him. He had drawn on his clinical experiences as a doctor and biological scientist; such experiences were unavailable to other philosophers of the time. His work anticipated a branch of psychology that was not to be established for more than 100 years—physiological psychology.

NINETEENTH-CENTURY ASSOCIATIONISM

There were three important associationists in the nineteenth century: James Mill, his son John Stuart Mill, and Alexander Bain. Their wide-ranging interests included many of the topics that later were to form part of the subject matter of psychology. All three men were concerned with social problems and social reform. The Mills in particular were liberal activists who influenced the domestic and colonial policy of England through their many books, journals, and periodicals.

James Mill (1773–1836) and John Stuart Mill (1806–1873)

John Stuart Mill began his autobiography with the statement "I was born in London on the 20th May, 1806, and was the eldest son of James Mill, the author of *The History of British India*" (Mill, 1873, p. 1). In this remarkable statement there is no mention of his mother, nor does she appear anywhere else in his autobiography. Mazlish (1975) pointed out that in this new version of an immaculate conception both the history and the boy appear to have been produced by James Mill alone. The relationship between father and son is of great psychological interest.

James Mill was born in 1773, the son of a Scottish village shoemaker. His proud and ambitious mother dominated his early life, insisting that he devote himself to work and study. Study was his only occupation, and so James Mill, like his son, had no childhood friends. Under the patronage of Sir John Stuart, after whom John Stuart Mill was to be named, James entered the University of Edinburgh to study for the Presbyterian ministry. Licensed as a preacher in 1799, James Mill was unable to find a parish because, as Edwin G. Boring (1957) explained, his congregations could not understand his sermons. He spent the next three years as an itinerant preacher before becoming disillusioned with a religious career and immigrating to London. Taking care to lose his Scottish accent, he quickly became a member of a group of English writers and editors. To secure a position with the British East India Company, James Mill set out to write a magnum opus, or great work, on the history of British India. He began the book in 1806, the year his first child, John Stuart, was born, and hoped to write the history in two years. Actually, it took him twelve to finish—the years of his son's boyhood. His marriage, which initially had been happy, began to founder as he came to regard his wife, Harriet, as an unintelligent "hausfrau" and to disparage her both at home and in public. Despite his apparent disdain for his wife and the fact that he was one of the earliest advocates of birth control, he fathered eight more children. Mill's *History*, published in 1817, was well received and enabled him to secure a senior position as a civil servant with the East India Company. He soon became financially secure, well known for his writing, and a friend of the rich and influential. However, the years during which the book was written and John Stuart grew up must have been a time of tension and anxiety.

Above all else, James Mill was dedicated to the ethic of hard, unremitting work. He regarded himself as a successful, self-made man. Relentlessly he impressed on his son the belief that a person who works more than others will in the end excel all others. Influenced by the educational philosophy of Locke, James Mill believed that all children are born alike, with little variation in their potential for learning. He felt that the child's mind is a tabula rasa, a blank tablet or clean slate, on which teachers can imprint anything they wish. As his son's teacher, he dedicated his life to imprinting the maximum amount of knowledge upon John Stuart's mind. Four or five hours a day were devoted to the boy's lessons. In his characteristically dry prose, John Stuart Mill recalled those years:

> A considerable part of almost every day was employed in the instruction of
> his children; in the case of one of whom, myself, whatever may be thought
> of his success, he exerted an amount of labor, care and perseverance rarely if
> ever employed for a similar purpose, in endeavouring to give according to
> his own conception the highest order of intellectual education. (J. S. Mill,
> early draft of the autobiography, in Mill's autobiography, 1873, p. 37)

Indeed he did. James Mill regarded his son as a child prodigy and expected him always to behave as such. Failure to perform at the very highest level was harshly criticized. So constant was his father's criticism that as a boy, John Stuart concluded that he was somewhat backward. Starting with Greek at the age of three and Latin at five, John Stuart worked through the classic Greek and Latin texts in the original languages. He studied literature, history, mathematics, and politics, receiving one of the most rigorous educations on record. At the age of eleven he published his first serious writing, a work on Roman government that focused on the struggle between the Roman plebeians and patricians. His sympathies were clearly with the plebeians, anticipating the themes of many of his later works devoted to advocacy of the rights of the common people and undermining the power of the English aristocracy. His childhood letters show that John Stuart Mill was incredibly precocious. At age twelve, his educational level was probably comparable to that of the best university graduates. One attempt to assess his intelligence was made by Catherine Morris Cox and her associates in 1926 as part of a series of *Genetic Studies of Genius* (Chapter 11). John Stuart Mill's intelligence quotient was estimated to have been 190, the highest score they assigned, outranking those of such luminaries as Mozart (150); Jefferson, Franklin, Darwin, and Galileo (145); Beethoven (135); Newton (130); and Washington, Lincoln, and Bach (125). While the methodology of this study can be criticized, Mill's ranking is surely impressive.

Despite these achievements, this rigorous education had negative aspects. John Stuart Mill was never allowed to act like a boy. Since he had no playmates, he never learned to play. Even his relationship with his brothers and sisters was unusual,

John Stuart Mill. (The Bettmann Archive)

since his father appointed him at the age of eight to be their tutor and held him responsible for the progress of their education. The emphasis was always on hard work and cold rationality. Feelings and emotions were considered irrelevant, and their expression was actively discouraged. James Mill set out to make his son a "reasoning machine" and appears, at least for the first twenty years of the boy's life, to have succeeded. At the age of eighteen John Stuart Mill described himself as "a dry, hard, logical machine," a description that his contemporaries felt was accurate.

In 1823, at the age of seventeen, John Stuart accepted a position as a clerk, working under his father at the East India Company. He remained with the company until 1858, when he retired as chief of the office of the examiner of Indian correspondence. Soon after he accepted the position, the cold, hard, logical machine began to fall apart. In 1826 he suffered a severe mental crisis characterized by profound depression, an inability to work, and acute feelings of worthlessness. This period of crisis lasted until he was in his middle twenties, when he slowly recovered, emerging with increased self-awareness, particularly a recognition of the importance of feelings and emotions. He saw the need to recognize the irrational as well as the rational, to see that humans are something more than unfeeling machines. However, throughout his life he was troubled by feelings of depression.

In 1830 John Stuart Mill met Harriet Taylor, a beautiful, vivacious woman with whom he fell madly in love. Thomas Carlyle said of him: "Mill, who up to that time had never so much as looked at a female creature, not even a cow, in the face, found himself opposite those great dark eyes, that were flashing unutterable things while he was discoursin' the utterable concernin' all sorts of high topics" (Carlyle, in Kamm, 1977, p. 32). Harriet Taylor was married, the mother of two children and soon to bear a third. She and Mill began an apparently platonic relationship with intense emotional overtones, which lasted until her death in 1858. Until the death of Harriet's husband, the three adults lived together in a ménage à trois that scandalized some of their Victorian acquaintances (Hayek, 1951).

During 1831 and 1832 they exchanged a series of essays on marriage, divorce, provision for the children of divorced parents, and women and their role in society. Two years after her husband's death in 1849, Harriet Taylor and John Stuart Mill were finally married; they lived together until her death in 1858. In 1869 Mill published, as a tribute to his late wife, his essay "The Subjection of Women." He presented an analysis of the position of women in society and appealed for political action to secure equality of the sexes. Along with Mary Wollstonecraft's *A Vindication of the Rights of Woman* (1792), Charlotte Perkins Gilman's *Women and Economics* (1898), and Simone de Beauvoir's *The Second Sex* (1951), Mill's essay is regarded as one of the great landmarks of the movement for equal social and political rights for women (Rossi, 1970). But Mill was not merely an ivory tower theorist. During the brief period in which he served as an independent member of Parliament in the British House of Commons, he introduced a bill for women's suffrage. This bill caused consternation among his fellow members and was promptly voted down.

During the later years of his life Mill was one of the leading intellectual figures of his period. He did not hesitate to express his opinions and take a stand on controversial issues. During the American Civil War, for example, he stated his opposition to slavery publicly. John Stuart Mill died in 1873, leaving a rich legacy of works and a secure reputation as a leading liberal thinker.

The Philosophies of James and John Stuart Mill How did James and John Stuart Mill influence the development of psychology? James Mill's most important psychological work was *Analysis of the Phenomena of the Human Mind*, published in 1829. He adopted the familiar position that the two basic elements of the mind are sensations and ideas, with ideas being weak copies of sensations. To the classic five senses originally proposed by Aristotle—vision, audition, taste, smell, and touch—Mill added muscle sense, which gives rise to muscle sensations (kinesthesis); disorganized sensations such as those resulting from tickling or itching; and sensations from the alimentary canal. Sensations from these eight senses were considered the primary elements of consciousness.

Sensations, according to James Mill, lead to ideas. In a classic chapter entitled "The Association of Ideas," Mill described the process by which sensations produce ideas, which in turn give rise to trains or streams of associated ideas:

> Thought succeeds thought; idea follows idea incessantly. If our senses are awake, we are continually receiving sensations, of the eye, the ear, the touch, and so forth; but not sensations alone. After sensations, ideas are perpetually excited of sensations formerly received; after those ideas, other ideas; and during the whole of our lives, a series of those two states of consciousness, called sensations, and ideas, is constantly going on. I see a horse; that is a sensation. Immediately I think of his master: that is an idea. The idea of his master makes me think of his office; he is a minister of state: that is an another idea. The idea of minister of state makes me think of

> public affairs; and I am led into a train of political ideas; when I am
> summoned to dinner. This is a new sensation.... (Mill, 1829, p. 463)

Mill's description is linear and sequential. It is a representation of a largely passive mind that invites analysis of its elements. External events give rise to sensations, which are followed in consciousness by streams of associated ideas. Why are some ideas associated? Why do they occur together? Why did the idea of the horse's master cause Mill to think of the master's occupation? According to Mill, these ideas were associated because many times in the past he had seen this man performing the actions of a minister of state. Mill recognized that some associations are more compelling or stronger than others. His three criteria of strength were *permanence, certainty,* and *facility.* More permanent associations are stronger than less permanent ones, correct associations are stronger than incorrect ones, and associations formed readily without effort are stronger than those which have been formed with difficulty. When later psychologists began to investigate learning and memory, the factors determining the strength of different associations were their main concern.

James Mill also distinguished between simple and complex ideas. The latter were compounds, aggregates, or what Mill called "concatenations" of simple ideas, conjoined through contiguity. Complex ideas in turn could combine with other ideas, both simple and complex, to form duplex ideas, which Mill described as follows:

> Some of the most familiar objects with which we are acquainted furnish
> instances of these unions of complex and duplex ideas. Brick is one complex
> idea, mortar is another complex idea; these ideas, with ideas of position and
> quantity, compose my idea of a wall. My idea of a plank is a complex idea,
> my idea of a rafter is a complex idea, my idea of a nail is a complex idea.
> These, united with the same ideas of positions and quantity, compose my
> duplex idea of a floor. In the same manner my complex idea of glass, wood,
> and others, compose my duplex idea of a window; and these duplex ideas,
> united together, compose my idea of a house which is made up of various
> ideas. How many complex or duplex ideas, are all united in the idea of
> furniture? How many more in the idea called Every Thing? (Mill, 1829, p.
> 482)

Indeed, how many more? In this passage some of the difficulties of this mechanical model of mental compounding are apparent. The model needed revision, which John Stuart Mill provided in his *System of Logic* (1843) and his notes for a revised edition of his father's *Analysis,* published in 1869. The younger Mill developed a chemical model of the mind in which simple ideas fuse or coalesce to form complex ideas. He wrote:

> The laws of the phenomena of the mind are sometimes analogous to
> mechanical, but sometimes also to chemical laws. When impressions have
> been so often experienced in conjunction, that each of them calls up readily
> and instantaneously the idea of the whole group, those ideas sometimes melt
> and coalesce into one another, and appear not several ideas but one. (Mill,
> 1875, vol. 2, p. 441)

Thus his father's theory of mental mechanics was supplemented by a mental chemistry. For John Stuart Mill the associative whole of a complex idea is something more than the sum of the simple ideas that compose it. The mind is active and productive. Just as water is more than the simple sum of the properties of hydrogen and oxygen, and just as hydrogen and oxygen can combine differently to produce hydrogen peroxide, which is very different from water, so too for the younger Mill the complex idea of a house is something more than the sum of simple ideas of bricks, mortar, wood, glass, and other building materials.

John Stuart Mill's most important scientific work was his *System of Logic*, published in 1843. Despite its formidable title, *A System of Logic, Ratiocinative and Deductive, Being a Connected View of the Principles of Evidence and the Method of Scientific Investigations*, the book was a commercial and academic success that secured for the younger Mill an international reputation. Mill considered it the book he was best fitted to write. He was concerned with the study of the scientific process, or metascience, and with defining the assumptions that underlie all the sciences, including the social sciences—economics and psychology. For Mill psychology was defined as "the science of the elementary laws of the mind," a definition that was adopted by Edward Titchener some sixty years later (Chapter 5). In contradiction to Auguste Comte's view that there can be no science of the mind since the mind can study all phenomena but its own (Comte, 1842), Mill argued that there can indeed be a science of the mind. He grappled with questions that still trouble many psychology students today. Are human actions deterministically caused and subject to psychological laws, or are they qualitatively different from the phenomena of such sciences as physics, biology, and chemistry? Mill admitted that the science of psychology would be an inexact science, more like meteorology and tidology (the science of tides) than like physics and chemistry. He wrote of psychology:

> It falls far short of the standard of exactness now realized in Astronomy; but
> there is no reason that it should not be as much a science as Tidology is, or
> as Astronomy was when its calculations had only mastered the main
> phenomena, but not the perturbations. (Mill, 1875, vol. 2, p. 433)

But what if psychology does master the perturbations of human actions and the human mind? What if human behavior comes to be as predictable as the speed of falling objects, the appearance of comets, and the circulation of the blood? Mill was well aware of the ethical and moral questions that would then arise. If one day human actions were as predictable as eclipses of the sun and moon, would it be possible for the course of those actions to be changed and controlled by others? Given such predictability and control, what would become of free will? Would people be responsible for their actions? These are difficult questions. While psychology today is far from the position Mill foresaw, the questions he raised are critical and controversial. Perhaps the uneasy reaction of many people to such questions accounts, at least to some extent, for the hostile response to such works as B. F. Skinner's *Beyond Freedom and Dignity* (1971b, chap. 13). We all like to think we have free will and individual responsibility. To suggest that we may not invites an angry reaction.

John Stuart Mill saw the need for a subdivision of psychology called *ethology*. He defined this field as "the theory of the influence of various external circumstances, whether individual or social, on the formation of moral and intellectual character" (Mill, 1875, vol. 2, p. 457). Today, the word *ethology* refers to "the study of animal behavior in a natural setting" and is associated with investigators such as Konrad Lorenz, Niko Tinbergen, and Karl von Frisch. The modern meaning and approach are both very different from that which Mill intended.

Perhaps Mill's interest in ethology was due to his childhood experiences. What effects might such experiences have on character formation, and how could they be studied scientifically? For Mill, experimental methods are basic to any science. The study of humans, Mill argued, must leave the realm of speculation and become a science of observation and experimentation in its own right. But experimentation on human character formation is ethically prohibited, so what can the psychologist do? Instead of actively manipulating variables to determine their relative effects, Mill proposed a *post hoc* analysis: examination of an instance of some variable that occurs naturally—such as education or the lack of it, family size, or social class— and the formulation of generalizations about its effect. Mill believed that these types of observations might lend support for his intuition that different kinds of childhood experience produce different moral characters, and at the same time the procedure would not perpetuate harm. Today, developmental psychologists employ these procedures in their longitudinal studies of children.

Like Hobbes and Locke, Mill had an interest in problems of government, and like his eighteenth-century predecessors, his writings in this area reflected a personal view of human nature. In 1861 Mill published *Utilitarians and Utilitarianism*. Earlier, his father's friend and patron, Jeremy Bentham, had argued for hedonism, a philosophy in which humans are seen as motivated solely by desires to seek pleasure and avoid pain. This view had been roundly criticized by, among others, Thomas Carlyle, who had dismissed Bentham's view as "pig philosophy" that might possibly account for the actions of pigs but would certainly not do for humans. Mill argued that hedonism neglected sympathy, caring, compassion, dignity, love of beauty, and many more of the qualities that make us human. In its place he described utilitarianism, a philosophy stating that actions are wrong in proportion to the unhappiness they cause for others. This philosophy enjoyed great popularity in the eighteenth century and has adherents today.

Alexander Bain (1818–1903)

The last of the nineteenth-century British associationists we will consider is Alexander Bain. Bain was Scottish, the son of an Aberdeen weaver. His family was poor, and so Bain left school at the age of twelve to work as a piecework cloth weaver in a mill. He continued his self-education at home, teaching himself mathematics and Latin. Eventually, after many difficulties, he was able to enter a university. He was graduated with high honors and moved to London, where he became a friend of John Stuart Mill and a member of his intellectual set. Bain worked as a free-lance journalist until 1860, when, at the age of forty-two, he finally received an appointment at the University of Aberdeen.

Bain's most important psychological works were *The Senses and the Intellect* (1855), *The Emotions and the Will* (1859), and *Mind and Body* (1872). The first two books were actually one work with a four-year delay between the publication of their parts. The publisher was reluctant to publish the second part of the book because the first part had not been a financial success. In later years the two volumes were widely read. They went through a number of revisions and for fifty years were the standard British psychological texts. Finally, in 1882 Bain published an informative biography of James Mill, whose work and philosophy he greatly admired.

In 1876 Bain founded the journal *Mind,* the first psychological journal ever published. For many years he had to support the journal financially to ensure its survival. Sir Francis Galton, William James (Chapter 9), and Bain himself all published important papers in *Mind.* The journal was also important in providing an alternative publication route to the journals that were to be founded, edited, and dominated by Wundt and Titchener during the later nineteenth century. The founding of *Mind* was a considerable contribution to the development of psychology as a discipline independent of both philosophy and physiology.

Bain was closer to being what we would consider a psychologist than were any of the philosophers and scholars we have considered thus far. Like Hartley, he was concerned with developing physiological explanations of human actions and thoughts; however, he was far from being a reductionist, as he always held that conscious data are of primary importance. He recognized the importance of inner drives and so developed an active rather than a passive conception of motivation. To Aristotle's classic five senses Bain added the "organic" sense, which provides sensations from our muscles and is closely involved in the coordination of movements.

In accounting for human actions Bain believed that habits are of central importance. According to Bain, random movements, some of which lead to pleasant consequences and some to unpleasant consequences, form the basis of learning. The former tend to be repeated, and thus a habit develops, while the latter are weakened so that a particular habit does not develop. The similarity to Edward Thorndike's later law of effect (Thorndike, 1911, chap. 10) is clear, and the historical connection from Bain to Thorndike can be traced. Bain influenced an English comparative psychologist, Conwy Lloyd Morgan (1852–1936), who performed early experiments on learning and instincts in chickens. In 1896 Morgan was invited to Harvard University to give a series of Lowell Lectures describing his research on trial-and-error learning. Sitting in the audience was a student, Thorndike, who shortly thereafter began his own important experiments on learning in chickens.

Bain distrusted speculation and "armchair psychologizing." He stressed the importance of observations of the everyday activities of both human beings and animals. Such naturalistic observations were to provide an understanding of human and animal behavior, but Bain was sympathetic to experimental methods and to developmental approaches. In *Emotions and the Will* he concerned himself with problems of applied psychology: the diagnosis of character through the compilation of case histories and the possibility of devising tests for the assessment of abilities and aptitudes. Bain, who as a boy had been forced to work under a brutal piecework system, argued for enlightened labor practices and particularly for the importance of considering people's capacities and abilities when selecting them for jobs.

AN EIGHTEENTH-CENTURY NATIVIST COUNTERVOICE

Just as Locke and Berkeley had a European opponent in Leibniz, Hume, Hartley, and the two Mills had a countervoice in Immanuel Kant. He was everything they were not: a subjectivist, nativist, rationalist successor to Descartes and Leibniz. The contrast between his philosophy and epistemology and those of the men we have just discussed could not have been greater. Kant was the empiricists' *bête noire*.

Immanuel Kant (1724–1804)

Kant was born in the university city of Königsberg in East Prussia. He attended school and university there, was appointed to the university's faculty, and spent the rest of his career and life at Königsberg. Despite his fame, it is likely that Kant never traveled more than forty miles from his birthplace. In developing his philosophy, Kant was stimulated by the "beautiful discoveries" of the British empiricists, especially those of Hume, whose books, he said, "woke him from dogmatic slumbers" (Kant, 1781, Introduction). Kant published his *Critique of Pure Reason* in 1781 and his *Critique of Practical Reason* in 1788. These works established him as the leading German epistemologist and also formed a philosophical counterweight to the British empiricists.

Kant believed that the empiricists might have been correct in saying that knowledge comes from experience but that they had been absolutely wrong in failing to ask the fundamental question: "How is experience itself possible?" For Kant that was the transcendental question that must be answered. The answer he favored was that of a nativist. Kant believed that there are certain intuitions or categories of understanding that are inborn and do not depend on experience. Rather, they frame our experiences; they allow experience to have the effect it does.

In his *Critique of Pure Reason*, Kant described learning one's native language as an example of the interaction between experience and the "categorical imperative." We learn through experience to speak a *particular* language, but the ability to learn *any* language is a fundamental attribute of the human mind. The basic error made by the British empiricists, Kant argued, was emphasizing the effects of experience while ignoring the fundamental categories of the mind. Other examples of *a priori* knowledge are the concepts of space and time. Space cannot be "thought away" or separated from our minds because it is a fundamental idea that is necessary to all other ideas. Similarly, time is the prerequisite of all perceptions and ideas. Nothing can exist without time. Perception of time going forward is, according to Kant, a completely natural human attribute. He pointed out the difficulty we have in thinking of time moving backward; it is easy to imagine someone growing older but very difficult to imagine someone growing younger. In all, Kant described twelve such intuitions, including cause and effect, reciprocity, reality, existence, and necessity.

Kant's views on the nature of science were influential within German philosophy and later in psychology for many decades. According to Kant, true sciences must begin with concepts established *a priori* on the basis of reason alone. In addition, true sciences deal with objects of observation that can be located in time and space. They permit experiments on the phenomena they study, and a true science is able to establish lawful relationships that can be described through mathematical formulations. Kant believed that psychology lacked such a rational conceptual basis and so failed at the most fundamental level as a true science. He considered human rationality limited and inadequate in dealing with itself. Kant also believed that it was impossible for psychology to conduct true experiments, because observing mental states would inevitably modify the mental states being observed. Kant's views provided a powerful force against which the first generation of German psychologists had to strive in establishing their science.

While he denied the possibility of a "true" psychology, that is, a psychology that would be both rational and experimental, Kant did accept one legitimate method for psychology, that of anthropological observations of the actual behavior of people. Wilhelm Wundt (Chapter 4) was to devote much of the later decades of his life to his cultural or anthropological psychology, while John Watson (Chapter 12) was to advocate a psychology concerned solely with behavior.

Kant's *Critique of Practical Reason* is an examination of practical affairs and a formulation of a code of conduct. Duty for Kant is sublime, mighty, and fundamental. It is the categorical imperative to be obeyed and followed without question. In our practical affairs we must not merely behave so as to bring the greatest pleasure to ourselves and others but must follow the higher obligation of duty as well. In the decades that followed the publication of Kant's *Critique of Practical Reason*, this conception was an important influence on social and political behavior in both Germany and England. A common prayer in Queen Victoria's England was

We thank thee God for this food.
We thank thee God for this prayer.
And We thank thee God above all for the categorical imperative.

Kant led a life that was the epitome of rigid self-control and duty. He never married but lived with a manservant. Kant woke at the same time every day and rose immediately, believing that it was slothful and indulgent to lie in bed. He took his lunch precisely at one o'clock and then went for the same walk along the university's Philosopher's Way. He was a major figure in German philosophy and an important influence on the first generation of German psychologists.

THE IMPORTANCE OF THE RENAISSANCE AND POST-RENAISSANCE ERAS

The Renaissance and post-Renaissance eras made two major contributions to the development of psychology. With the work of Galileo, Newton, and Harvey, the Western scientific revolution began, and the scientific tradition that grew out of that revolution emphasized a certain methodology. One must carefully observe and if possible quantify phenomena, make mathematical predictions about the effects of certain variables, and verify those predictions empirically. These procedures promised to uncover truth; they became the standards of Western science and so were adopted by early psychologists attempting to establish a science of the mind.

A scientific tradition was not the only thing psychology inherited from the Renaissance and post-Renaissance eras. Psychology also inherited its philosophical foundations. René Descartes set the stage for psychology as a discipline independent of other sciences by stating that the mind is separate from the body and is subject to its own rules and principles. These rules and principles were to be the domain of the later science of psychology. Psychology was also given two major philosophical orientations: nativism and empiricism. Not only do these orientations still color psychological theory, they have also been instrumental in defining one of the major issues in psychology: Are human characteristics the result of our nature, or are they the result of the way in which we have been raised, our nurture? From our study of philosophers who have taken a "nature" or "nurture" view of humankind, it should be evident that the side one takes on this issue may be keenly influenced by one's political experiences and theological orientation. Nativism stresses inherited characteristics; it places less emphasis on the environment and consequently takes a more conservative view of the expected outcome of educational experience. This orientation would not be consistent with social reform and political involvement. At least with the two major nativists discussed in this chapter, Descartes and Kant, this was the case.

An empiricist orientation stresses the equal potential of all human beings, the importance of environmental factors on one's development, and the educational process. It is no surprise that it emerged in England during the rise of liberalism in the eighteenth and nineteenth centuries. As we have seen, its major advocates, the Mills and Bain, were self-made men who emphasized social reform. It is also no surprise that this philosophical orientation would flower in the United States and give birth to behaviorism, a position that is only now being countered by contemporary nativist schools of thought.

Pierre-Paul Broca. (Brown Brothers)

3

Early Studies
of the Central
Nervous System

Thus far we have been considering the broad, general influences that the development of Western philosophy and science had on psychology. Now we will turn to some specific advances in knowledge of the brain and spinal cord that later formed the foundation of physiological psychology. Unlike the largely speculative contributions of the philosophers discussed in Chapter 2, much of this new knowledge resulted from observation and experiment. The development of procedures for studying the brain and spinal cord and their application in both clinical and experimental settings laid the foundation for an understanding of the structures and functions of the nervous system and of the physiological basis of sensation, perception, emotion, language, and cognition.

The influence of Descartes led inevitably to speculation about the seat of the mind and the role of the brain in controlling thought and action. The bloody seventeenth and eighteenth centuries of European war and revolution provided many opportunities to study the consequences of central nervous system trauma and injury as soldiers sustained terrible battlefield injuries to the spine and brain. The ones who survived occasionally were not only treated but studied. Momentary actions were observed even after decapitation. The revolutionary mobs surrounding the guillotine saw grins, winks, and smiles and heard grunts and groans from the heads of the executed. Were such actions intentional? Was a wink or smile perhaps a final gesture of defiance or contempt? These were compelling questions both for the church, with its doctrine of the flight of the soul from the body at the instant of death, and for French thinkers steeped in the mind-body dualism of Descartes.

Pierre Cabanis (1757–1808), a leading French anatomist, considered such questions and concluded in 1795 that consciousness ends when the head and brain are severed from the body. All thought depends on one "special organ," the brain. The observed actions, Cabanis asserted, were reflexive and automatic. They were no more indicative of continued consciousness than is a headless chicken's flight around the farmyard. A German physiologist, Theodor Bischoff (1807–1882), arranged a macabre, even ghoulish, test of Cabanis' assertion on the head of a newly executed criminal. Even intense stimuli, including the shouted word *Pardon!* elicited no reaction during the first minute after decapitation (Fearing, 1930, p. 152). The conclusion of Cabanis was correct.

EXPERIMENTAL INVESTIGATIONS OF SPINAL CORD FUNCTIONS

The spinal cord is both structurally less complex and more accessible than the brain, and so it was studied first. In 1751, a Scottish physician, Robert Whytt (1714–1766), found that a frog without both brain and spinal cord was totally unresponsive, while a decapitated frog without a brain but *with* a spinal cord would respond to a pinch by withdrawing its leg. An intact spinal cord was necessary and sufficient for that reflex response. While Whytt's demonstration was of undeniable importance, it was in France, during the early nineteenth century, that the first experimental studies of the spinal cord furthered the development of physiology. That achievement was the work of many men, but the predominant contribution was that of François Magendie (1785–1855) (Lesch, 1984).

Since writing his doctoral thesis in 1808, Magendie had thought of the tracts of fibers entering the spinal cord, the spinal cord roots, as ways in and out of the cord itself (Cranefield, 1974). His anatomic findings were initially disappointing, for in most of the species he studied the roots fused before exiting from the spine and so could be reached only by breaking open the spine. In the days before anesthesia—ether was discovered only in 1847—that procedure was excruciatingly painful and almost always damaged the spinal cord. In puppies, Magendie found a different anatomic disposition of the dorsal and ventral roots of the peripheral nerves in that they come together outside the spinal column. The spinal cord roots could be exposed with relative ease in puppies. Magendie cut either the dorsal or ventral roots of one or more nerves and observed specific effects. Following a dorsal root section, part of the body lacked sensation, while loss of movement followed the section of a ventral root. In 1822 Magendie described the results of several such experiments in a now famous three-page paper published in the *French Journal of Physiology and Experimental Pathology*. He concluded that "the dorsal and ventral roots of the nerves that arise from the spinal cord have different functions, with the dorsal more particularly related to sensation, and the ventral to movement" (Magendie, 1822, p. 279).

In its significance for physiology Magendie's demonstration of the structural and functional specificity of spinal cord roots was comparable to Harvey's research on the circulation of blood (Chapter 2). Magendie's systematic experimental investigation made clear the basis of the reflex arc. That behavioral model, with its isolation of sensation and movement, was to provide the later science of psychology with one of its enduring paradigms—that of stimulus and response.

A more immediate consequence of Magendie's publication was a bitter dispute over priority of discovery. In 1811, an English physiologist and anatomist, Charles Bell (1774–1842), had privately published a pamphlet entitled *Idea of a New Anatomy of the Brain; Submitted for the Observation of his Friends* in which he speculated about the functional significance of different parts of the brain and described experiments using rabbits in which he had opened the spine and sectioned either the dorsal or ventral roots. Bell concluded erroneously that ventral roots control voluntary behavior while dorsal roots control involuntary behavior. After Magendie's 1822 publication, Bell's son-in-law, John Shaw, challenged the priority of his result. Since Bell had circulated his pamphlet among friends, Magendie had not read it. When Shaw sent him a copy, Magendie acknowledged that Bell had come *close* to discovering the functions of spinal cord roots but refused to yield his claim to priority. Bell and his students then began what Gallistel aptly described as "a clamorous, unprincipled, but largely successful campaign to claim priority for what was properly Magendie's discovery" (Gallistel, 1981, p. 359). The success of their campaign is seen in today's textbook references to the Bell-Magendie law. Such an attribution is unfair to Magendie. His experiments were far more complete and definitive than Bell's; Magendie's conclusions were clear, whereas Bell's were diffuse and obscure. Bell unfairly criticized Magendie for the cruelty of his experiments, claiming that his own experiments with "stunned rabbits" were more humane. In truth, the animals in both sets of experiments must have suffered great pain. At times Bell claimed that Magendie's experiments were unnecessary replications of his own. Both charges were seized upon by antivivisectionists and are still cited by critics of animal research and experimentation. Finally, Bell's behavior is open to rebuke, for there is historical evidence that he made certain alterations to his earlier works to support his claim for priority (Olmsted, 1943, 1944).

SENSORY PHYSIOLOGY

Though Bell's study of the dorsal and ventral roots of the spinal cord was not definitive, he was essentially correct in his argument, presented in 1823, that since nerves intervene between events in the external world and our perception of them, they must influence the quality of our perceptions. Bell believed that each nerve imposes its own specific quality on what is perceived. This doctrine predicts that the same stimulus will produce different sensations if it operates on different nerves. Since it is the nerve that imposes sensory specificity, as long as a particular nerve is active, a particular sensation will result. A powerful stimulus such as a blow to the head produces sensations of pain, flashes of light, and noises, because these different sensory systems have all been stimulated. This doctrine also predicts that different stimuli acting on the same nerve should produce the same sensation. Since it is the nerve that imposes sensory specificity, a particular sensation will result regardless of how a nerve is stimulated. Thus visual sensations, which usually are the result of stimulation of the eye and optic nerve by light, may result from chemical and electrical stimulation of the nerve itself or from pressing on the eye when the eyelids are closed. These are different stimuli, but all produce activity in the optic nerve; thus the sensation is one of light.

This doctrine of specific nerve energies was developed further by the nineteenth-century German physiologist Johannes Peter Müller (1801–1858) in his authoritative 1840 *Handbuch der Physiologie der Menschen* (Handbook of Human Physiology). Müller pointed out quite correctly that the nerves themselves must communicate different impressions to the brain or must project to different parts of the brain which in turn impose specificity. At the time Müller regarded proof of either proposition as impossible to attain. Today we know that different sensory projection areas of the brain impose the specific quality.

Hermann Ludwig von Helmholtz (1821–1894)

Further progress in sensory physiology was led by perhaps the greatest of the nineteenth-century physiologists. Hermann Ludwig von Helmholtz. Helmholtz, the son of a German schoolteacher, was born in Potsdam. He was a precocious and brilliant student who was graduated early from his high school and enrolled as a scholarship student in a school that trained surgeons for the Prussian Army. The school's curriculum was rigorous—48 lectures a week, with the first one at 6 A.M. each day—yet the hardworking Helmholtz thrived under this regimen. He even found time to attend the theater, hear recitals of Beethoven and Mozart, read Goethe and Byron, and master the integral calculus. Helmholtz received an M.D. degree in 1842 and then had to satisfy his military obligation by serving as an army surgeon for six years. He was, however, much more interested in research than in practicing medicine, and so in 1849 he accepted an appointment as professor of physiology at the University of Königsberg. There he began a long series of brilliant contributions to physiology and physiological optics; one of his technical contributions was the invention of the ophthalmoscope, allowing for the first time examination of the retina under direct illumination.

Helmholtz's research on sensory physiology occurred against a background of experimentation and speculation about electricity and the nervous system. A seventeenth-century Dutch scientist, John Swammerdam (1637–1680), removed a muscle and attached a nerve from a frog's leg. When he pinched the nerve, it caused the muscle to contract. In 1768, after a long series of experiments using frog nerve-muscle preparations, Robert Whytt concluded that "a certain power of influence lodged in the brain, spinal marrow, and nerves, is either the immediate cause of the contraction of muscles of animals, or at least necessary to it" (Whytt, 1768, Sec. 1, p. 3). The eighteenth century was the age of electricity, and so it was inevitable that Whytt's "certain power of influence" would be considered to be electrical. In the 1760s, an Italian professor at the University of Bologna, Luigi Galvani (1737–1798), used an "electrical influence" machine to stimulate the contraction of frog muscles. He had heard of Benjamin Franklin's kite-flying experiment and so decided to investigate the effects of naturally occurring electricity on muscle contraction. Galvani strung a long wire from the roof of his laboratory to the frogs' vivarium and attached one end to their muscles. When a cloud with its electrical charge passed overhead, the muscles would contract. This demonstration so pleased Galvani that he used it as an after-dinner entertainment for his guests. Galvani sought a more powerful source of natural electricity and so tried to capture a bolt of lightning with his wire. He was never able to do so, which was just as well for both Galvani and his frogs.

Galvani also observed muscle contractions when he connected a frog muscle between different metals; silver and iron produced the most "vehement reaction." He described his results in his 1791 *De viribus electricitatis in motu muscularis commentarius* (A Commentary on the Role of Electricity in Muscular Contractions). Only twelve copies of the book were printed, as Galvani could not think of any more people who would be interested in this experiment or in his thesis that electricity is inherent to the frog and possibly to all living organisms. He believed that the electricity was generated by the brain and distributed throughout the body by the nervous system. His thesis was soon to be challenged, but his insight that neural activity has an electrical component was important, and psychologists still honor his memory when they speak of the galvanic skin response.

One challenge came from Alessandro Volta (1745–1827), one of the twelve recipients of Galvani's book. A professor of physics, Volta believed that the electricity Galvani had observed was not inherent to the organism but bimetallic, that is, caused by a potential, or "voltage," difference between the metals attached to the frog. Galvani's frogs, he said, had not generated electricity but had conducted it.

Around 1850, Emil Du Bois-Reymond (1818–1896) constructed a very sensitive galvanometer to measure the flow of electrical current. When he placed one wire on a nerve and another on the nerve's sectioned end, he observed the flow of electrical current. Even more remarkably, Du Bois-Reymond found that when a frog nerve was stimulated with a mild electric current, his galvanometer could measure the spread of an electrical change along the nerve. Until experiments such as these, the nerve impulse had been rather mysterious. Some type of disturbance was known to travel along the nerve, but the nature and speed of the disturbance were unknown. Du Bois-Reymond had shown that this disturbance was electrical in nature. His two-volume *Thierische Electricität* (Animal Electricity) summarized what was known about electrical nerve conduction and also developed a polarization theory to account for neuromuscular functions.

Helmholtz Measures the Speed of the Nerve Impulse Given that the disturbance moving along the nerve was electrical, Helmholtz set out to measure its speed. First he dissected a motor nerve and muscle from a frog's leg. Helmholtz chose frogs because so much earlier work had been done with them and also because they have long motor nerves. When the nerve of this nerve-muscle preparation was stimulated electrically, the attached muscle contracted. A nerve impulse had traveled 60 mm along the nerve from the point of stimulation to the muscle. Since Helmholtz knew the exact time of stimulation and could record precisely when the muscle contracted, he was able to compute the time it had taken the nerve impulse to travel

60 mm along the nerve. This time was actually 0.0014 second. With these time and distance measures, Helmholtz calculated the speed of the nerve impulse: 43 meters per second.

Helmholtz made many such measurements with different lengths of nerves and calculated speeds between 25 and 90 meters per second. For the first time the speed of the nerve impulse had been measured. Earlier estimates, some relatively slow (9,000 feet per minute) and some blindingly fast (57,600 million feet per second), had been replaced by precise and remarkably accurate measurements. Helmholtz's experiment was considered definitive in the nineteenth century and exemplified the scientific precision sought by the first psychologists.

Helmholtz's work also prompted nineteenth-century sensory physiologists to research a host of important questions. First, what is the nature of the nerve impulse? Is it exclusively electrical, or does it have chemical components? Second, do different nerves conduct at different speeds, and do the nerves of different people conduct at different speeds? Third, does the speed of the nerve impulse depend on the intensity of the stimulus? Fourth, are nerves equally excitable at all times? In their attempts to answer such questions, nineteenth-century sensory physiologists made great advances in understanding the nervous system. These advances paralleled revolutionary changes in conceptions of brain function. Strictly empirical procedures, definitions, and descriptions were developed in contrast to those of Descartes, which had been based on logical and aesthetic rather than physiological grounds.

PHRENOLOGY

One such remarkably detailed description of the mind received great popular acclaim in the nineteenth century. *Phrenology*, as it came to be labeled, became for a time the accepted science (*logos*) of the mind (*phrenos*). Despite its carefully built empirical foundation, it was completely false. For this reason, an examination of its development is instructive.

Franz Joseph Gall (1758–1828) and Johann Caspar Spurzheim (1776–1832)

Phrenology began with the work of Franz Joseph Gall. Born in Germany, Gall qualified as a physician in Vienna in 1795 and made a number of contributions to anatomy and neurology. However, he is best remembered for his claim that personality can be inferred from bodily appearance, especially from features of the skull. As a boy, Gall had noticed that a number of his acquaintances with good memories also had large, protuberant eyes. As an anatomist, he speculated that other characteristics might be associated with external features, and so he began a systematic evaluation of this speculation. Gall believed passionately that precise measurements would lead to understanding. He traveled to foundling homes, prisons, and lunatic asylums to measure or "read" the skulls of the individuals residing in those institutions. At the same time, he compiled a large anecdotal catalogue of specific mental characteristics associated with particular bumps on the skull. For example, he found a number of convicted pickpockets who all had bumps in the same area on the side of the skull just above the ear. Gall concluded that this was the brain locus of the acquisitiveness function or power, a function obviously too well developed in the pickpockets. Not content with studying the skulls of the living, Gall also collected the skulls of the dead. So assiduously did he develop his skull collection that many Viennese specified in their wills that "their heads be protected from the researches of Dr. Gall."

As a result of Gall's ceaseless measuring, he gradually developed a "doctrine of the skull" that summarized the enormous body of data he had collected. This doctrine stated that personality and intelligence are reducible to forty-two powers or functions, six of which are domestic, ten selfish, five moral, five self-perfective, eight intellectual, four literary faculties, and four reflective. Gall believed that each of these powers is localized in a specific surface area of the brain and that the skull encapsulates the brain closely so that skull contours reflect deviations in the surface of the brain. Well-developed powers cause small bumps to appear on the skull; less-developed powers may even lead to indentations. Consequently, measurement or palpation of the skull can reveal the strength of the underlying powers. The results of such a phrenological reading of the skull were presented in charts, with the strength of each faculty shown on a rating scale.

Gall attracted many followers and supporters, but he also made powerful enemies. The Catholic church branded his work deterministic and materialistic, which indeed it was, and as having atheistic implications. In 1802, the Austrian government, under intense pressure from the Catholic church, prohibited Gall from lecturing on the close connection between brain and personality, since it held his lectures to be "subversive of religion and morals." However, as so often happens, banning Gall served only to increase interest in his views. Gall left Vienna and, after a highly successful lecture tour of Europe, settled in France. Despite the criticism of the church and the government, Gall continued to attract supporters, the most important of whom was Johann Caspar Spurzheim.

Spurzheim had initially studied theology and then had attended medical school in Vienna. He joined Gall as his secretary and assistant in 1804 and left Vienna with Gall in 1805. Between 1810 and 1819 they published together a massive five-volume treatise on phrenology. The title of the work was *The Anatomy and Physiology of the Nervous System in General and of the Brain in Particular, with Observations on the Possibility of Discovering the Number of Intellectual and Moral Dispositions of Men and Animals Through the Configurations of Their Heads.* Their aim was to develop a perfect knowledge of human nature based on extensive studies and measurements of the skulls and brains of many species. They thought of themselves as scientists and were thoroughly contemptuous of armchair philosophers and metaphysicians. The measurement procedures of phrenologists became increasingly refined, reaching an apex with the development in 1907 of the Lavery electric phrenometer, which was said to measure bumps "electrically and with scientific precision."

Even while collaborating, Gall and Spurzheim had many bitter disagreements

A Chart of a Reading by Phrenologist O. S. Fowler, dated April 20, 1876

Conditions	Very large	Large	Full	Average	Moderate	Small
Domestic						
1. Amativeness		X				
2. Conjugality				X		
3. Parental Love			X			
4. Friendship				X		
5. Inhabitiveness			X			
6. Continuity						X
Selfish						
7. Vitiativeness	X					
8. Combativeness	X					
9. Destructiveness		X				
10. Alimentiveness		X				
11. Acquisitiveness		X				
12. Secretiveness		X				
13. Cautiousness		X				
14. Approbativeness	X					
15. Self-esteem						X
16. Firmness		X				
Moral						
17. Conscientious	X					
18. Hope			X			
19. Spirituality		X				
20. Veneration		X				
21. Benevolence	X					
Self-perfectives						
22. Constructiveness	X					
23. Ideality			X			
24. Sublimity		X				
25. Imitation	X					
26. Mirthfulness					X	
Intellectual perceptives						
27. Individuality		X				
28. Form		X				
29. Size	X					
30. Weight			X			
31. Color				X		
32. Order		X				
33. Calculation			X			
34. Locality		X				
Literary faculties						
35. Eventuality		X				
36. Time			X			
37. Tune		X				
38. Language			X			

A Chart of a Reading by Phrenologist O. S. Fowler *(Continued)*

Conditions	Very large	Large	Full	Average	Moderate	Small
Reflectives						
39. Causality			X			
40. Comparison		X				
41. Human nature		X				
42. Agreeableness					X	
Size of brain			X			

From the author's collection

that grew out of their different conceptions of basic human nature. Gall had a rather pessimistic and cynical view, even designating one power or faculty "murder." He was very much a determinist who believed that powers are inborn and cannot be changed. Spurzheim's views were more optimistic and utopian. He saw humans as perfectible and phrenology as the science that would show them the way to a happy condition. Of the two, Gall was always more the scientist, Spurzheim more the propagandist.

The two men separated in 1814. Gall remained in Paris, and Spurzheim traveled the world to popularize phrenology. After Gall's death in 1828, Spurzheim and the Scottish phrenologist George Combe (1788–1858) changed phrenology from an attempt at a science to a cult. Together, they gave frequent lectures and demonstrations throughout Europe. In one such demonstration, magnets were used to stimulate a particular power. When a magnet passed over the veneration area, the person assumed a "worshipful air"; when it passed over the acquisitiveness area, the subject attempted to pick the pocket of the phrenologist.

Knowledge of this new "science of the mind" spread, and Spurzheim and Combe were invited to lecture in the United States. Spurzheim went to Boston in 1832. His arrival created a sensation. He gave a series of highly successful lectures and demonstrations at hospitals and universities and attended commencements at Harvard and Yale as an honored guest. As one contemporary observer put it, "the professors are in love with him" (Bakan, 1967, p. 331). Six frenzied weeks after his arrival in the United States, at the time of his greatest popularity, Spurzheim died. His death and funeral were major events, and interest in phrenology increased even more when an autopsy revealed that he had a massive 57-ounce (1,616-gram) brain, some 10 ounces (284 grams) larger than average. What the significance of such a heavy brain was, people were not certain, but surely it could not have been a coincidence.

Following Spurzheim's death, Combe continued to popularize phrenology. He was instrumental in forming more than forty-five phrenological societies in both Europe and the United States, many of which lasted well into the twentieth century. Combe's phrenological text *Constitution of Man* sold over 100,000 copies, and it has been said that in the nineteenth century many homes contained only three books: the Bible, *Pilgrim's Progress*, and *Constitution of Man* (Young, 1985, p. 64). Combe was elected to the National Academy of Natural Sciences and was offered a professorship of mental and moral philosophy at the University of Michigan. He devoted his life to phrenology, education, and prison and asylum reform and appears to have been dedicated and idealistic. When Combe was asked to justify the existence of slavery on the grounds that his scientific studies had shown that the skulls of black people were "inferior," he refused and stated that an educated slave could compete as a free person. He also attacked the second-class status of women, rejecting claims that they were intellectually or emotionally inferior to men. Sarah Josepha Hale, the author of the well-known verse "Mary Had a Little Lamb" and the editor of Boston's *Ladies Magazine*, said that phrenology was second only to Christianity as a force for the elevation and improvement of the status of women. Very soon, however, as a result of the popularization of phrenology, the focus of the discipline changed. It was no longer an empirical science in the manner Gall had originally defined it.

Phrenology as Big Business

Three enterprising Americans capitalized on the fadlike qualities of phrenology. Orson and Lorenzo Fowler and a man named Samuel Wells, who married their sister, established the family firm of Fowler and Wells. They marketed every conceivable type of phrenological apparatus and equipment: busts and heads with neatly lettered and numbered areas and phrenological manuals complete with detailed instructions for phrenological self-analysis. "Know thyself" was the phrenologists' motto, and the best-selling *Phrenological Self-Instructor* (Fowler & Fowler, 1859) was profusely illustrated with "proofs" of phrenology. William Teller, described as a thief and murderer, is shown with a large bump at the top of his skull in the acquisitiveness area, while Mr. Gosse, who gave away two fortunes, actually has a small dent. Aaron Burr, who killed Alexander Hamilton in a duel, was tried for treason, and was widely known as a philanderer, is shown as having a large bump in the amativeness area. "Miss Modesty," on the other hand, is pictured as having a marked depression. Fowler and Wells made extensive lecture and publicity tours, published an amazing amount of literature, and established phrenological parlors in many cities. Their phrenological cabinet in New York City was an emporium in which thousands of human and animal skulls were displayed.

The influence that Fowler and Wells had on American culture at the time was great. American businesses began to require phrenological examinations as a condition of employment. Advertisements such as the following from the *New York Sun* appeared in newspapers:

> Apprentice wanted—a stout boy not over 15 years of age of German or
> Scotch parents, to learn a good but difficult trade. N.B.—it will be
> necessary to bring a recommendation to his abilities from Messrs. Fowler
> and Wells, Phrenologists, Nassau Street. (in Schwartz, 1986, p. 33)

Young people contemplating marriage were urged to consult a phrenologist to learn

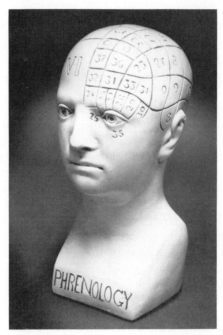

A phrenological bust with its neatly
numbered locations of different faculties.
(Leonard Lessin/Peter Arnold)

the laws of conjugal selection and to discover who ought and ought not to marry.
During the 1850 presidential campaign a phrenological analysis of each candidate
was published in the phrenologists' *Journal of Man*. Many famous figures had their
heads read. Walt Whitman was so pleased with the results of his phrenological
analysis that he had it published five times. Phrenological terms and analyses appear frequently in nineteenth-century literature: heroes have large heads, high fore-
heads, and wide-set eyes; villains have narrow heads, beetle brows, and beady eyes.
Jane Eyre was said to have an unusually large veneration area, while Sherlock Holmes
deduced from a large-sized hat that its owner was of high intellect. Today such
descriptions persist in disparaging references to "pointy-headed intellectuals" and
"thick-skulled athletes."

Given this vast enthusiasm and success, why did phrenology fail, and why do
we now regard it as at best a pseudoscience? The answers lie in its fundamental
characteristics and assumptions. First, the selection of faculties was indiscriminate.
Attempts to describe the complexities of human intelligence and personality in terms
of a limited number of faculties and powers were doomed to fail. Second, the ex-
ploitation of gullible people was unacceptable to serious students of brain function
and personality, as it probably would have been to Gall himself. Phrenology made
a great deal of money for some people but never was accepted as a valid psychometric method. Third, phrenology could not be accepted as a science, as its pre-

dictions could never be proved false. When Spurzheim learned that Descartes' skull was much smaller than average in the forehead region, in which intellect supposedly resides, he merely stated that "perhaps Descartes was not so great a thinker as many thought him to be" (Schwartz, 1986, p. 33). Finally, criticism by the nineteenth century's leading investigator of brain function, Pierre Flourens, proved devastating.

In *An Examination of Phrenology*, published in 1843, Flourens presented a logical critique of phrenology and cited his own experimental studies of the effects of the removal of brain tissue (ablation) on the behavior of animals. Thickness of the skull varies from place to place, and the contours of the skull do not correspond to the contours of the brain; thus the fundamental assumption of phrenology is wrong. The phrenologists had located amativeness in the area of the brain that corresponds to the cerebellum. In his ablation experiments Flourens had found that damage to the cerebellum interferes with motor movements but does not interfere with the strength of an animal's sex drive. Finally, Flourens opposed attempts to localize specific functions in restricted areas of the brain. Flourens was not above using *ad hominem* arguments in his campaign against phrenology. He reported with obvious delight an incident in which

> the famous physiologist, Magendie, preserved with veneration the brain of LaPlace. Spurzheim had the very natural wish to see the brain of the great man. To test the science of the phrenologist Mr. Magendie showed him, instead of the brain of LaPlace, that of an imbecile. Spurzheim, who had already worked up his enthusiasm, admired the brain of the imbecile, as he would have admired that of LaPlace. (Flourens, 1864, p. 234)

The criticisms of phrenology by Flourens were stringent, but it is important to understand any positive contributions phrenology might have made to the development of psychology. The belief that the brain is the organ of the mind was reinforced by phrenology, as was the suggestion that mental functions can be localized in the brain. Phrenologists contended that psychological characteristics can be measured, and since they used elaborate rating scales to record and score a profile of a particular individual's different powers, they reinforced the concept of individual differences, the domain that later came to be the focus of differential psychologists and personality theorists. The editor of an anthology of Gall's writings, Erna Lesky, claimed in 1979 that Gall was the father of the behavioral sciences, a great instigator of social reform, a criminal anthropologist of Cesare Lombroso's stature, and a precursor of Charles Darwin. All these claims might be challenged, but it must be admitted that phrenologists had their occasional successes. According to one report, a modern phrenologist examined Ray Kroc when he was four and predicted that he would have a successful career in food (Kroc, 1987, p. 42). Kroc later founded McDonald's and amassed a fortune of $450 million selling food.

LOCALIZATION OF FUNCTION IN THE BRAIN

Studies of the Animal Brain

Marie-Jean Pierre Flourens (1794–1867) was the most important investigator of the functions of the brain during the middle decades of the nineteenth century. He was an eminent French surgeon, the permanent secretary of the French Academy of Science, a grand officer of the Legion of Honor, a national deputy, and a professor at the College of France. A man of many honors and accomplishments, he devoted his life to investigating empirically the functions of the different structures of the brain. To Flourens the brain appeared harmonious, intricate, and beautiful. Even to an untrained eye the brain is clearly not a homogeneous mass but rather consists of many different parts, all obviously interconnected but all clearly different. Given that the brain has so many different structures, the question arises: Do they perform different functions? Flourens attempted to answer this question empirically.

Flourens was a brilliant and precise surgeon noted for the elegance of his experimental procedures and tests. One method he used was ablation, an experimental procedure in which specific areas of the brain are removed surgically. Flourens hoped to use this method to determine the functions of the different units or structures of the brain. In his experiments he followed two guiding principles. First, he believed that the parts of the brain to be studied should be anatomically separate and distinct. For Flourens, six units in the brain were appropriate for study: the cerebral hemispheres, the cerebellum, the corpora quadrigemina, the medulla oblongata, the spinal cord, and the nerves themselves. Second, his approach was to study an animal's behavior, perform a delicate surgical operation in which one of the units was removed, allow the animal time to recover from the operation, and then study its behavior again. His experimental methods allowed much greater control and precision than "nature's experiments," in which brain damage followed an accident, injury, or stroke. Flourens recognized that experimental and clinical approaches complement each other, but his approach was direct, surgical, and experimental. It still stands as a model for contemporary investigators of brain function.

Flourens summarized the results of his investigations in a paper published in 1823 entitled *Récherches physiques sur les propriétés et les fonctions du système nerveux dans les animaux vertébrés* (Experimental Research on the Properties and Functions of the Nervous System in Vertebrates). The following year he published a more extended report in a book of the same title. A second edition was published in Paris in 1842. His conclusions about the functions of the basic units of the brain were as follows: The cerebral lobes were considered the seat of all voluntary actions. Following removal of the cerebral lobes, an animal would still show reflex responses— the pupils of the eyes would dilate in the presence of a dim light and constrict in the presence of a bright one—but despite such reflexes, the animal was functionally blind. Visual stimuli were not perceived, and auditory stimuli were similarly ineffective. Following removal of the cerebral lobes, a pigeon remained motionless when a hooter sounded; before the operation, the hooter had produced immediate flight. Following surgery, the bird would eat only when food was pushed into its beak; it would not search for food. A pigeon would fly when thrown into the air; when left alone, it would not. Flourens gave the following account of the behavior of a pigeon without its cerebral lobes:

> It held itself upright very well; it flew when it was thrown into the air, it walked when it was pushed; the iris of its eye was very mobile but nevertheless it did not see; it did not hear, it never moved spontaneously, it nearly always assumed the appearance of a sleeping or drowsy animal.... When I left it to itself, it remained calm and absorbed; in no case did it give any sign of volition. In a word, it was an animal condemned to perpetual sleep and deprived even of the faculty of dreaming during this sleep; such almost precisely, had become the pigeon of which I had removed the cerebral lobes. (Flourens, 1823, p. 352, in Clarke & O'Malley, 1968, pp. 484–485)

Given such results, Flourens concluded that the cerebral lobes are the seat of perception—we see and hear in our brains—and also the province of such higher mental functions as willing, memory, and judgment. He summarized his results as follows:

> If the cerebral lobes are removed, vision is lost for the animal no longer sees; volition is lost for it no longer wishes to move; memory, for it no longer remembers; judgment, for it no longer judges; it strikes itself twenty times against the same object without learning to avoid it; it stamps on the ground when struck blows rather than fleeing. (Flourens, 1823, p. 363, in Clarke & O'Malley, 1968, p. 485)

Following removal of the cerebellum, an animal walked only with jerky, spastic, uncoordinated movements. Birds with cerebellar damage appeared to make attempts to fly, in contrast to birds with damage to their cerebral lobes, which had no such volition. But when birds with cerebellar damage were thrown in the air, they could not coordinate the movements necessary to stay aloft. Flourens found similar results when he progressively injured the cerebellum of a dog. As Flourens ablated deeper and deeper sections of its cerebellum, the dog's ability to walk disintegrated proportionately until it could no longer regulate its movements at all. Flourens correctly concluded from such systematic studies that the cerebellum controls and coordinates the motor activities involved in walking, jumping, flying, and standing.

Flourens found that animals can survive damage to the cerebral lobes and the cerebellum but not damage to the structure containing centers or areas that control the heart, respiration, and other systems that are basic for life—systems that are "vital." Consequently, he called this area—the medulla oblongata—the "vital knot."

Thus far we have considered Flourens' descriptions of the specific functions of the brain's different areas or units, what he termed their specific actions, or *action propre*. Flourens, however, also stressed that the brain is an interconnected, integrated system that functions with a common action, what he termed *action commune*. He wrote:

> The nervous system is not a homogeneous system; the cerebral lobes do not
> act in the same way as the cerebellum, nor the cerebellum like the spinal
> cord, nor the cord absolutely like the nerves. But it is a single system, all of
> its parts concur, consent, and are in accord; what distinguishes them is the
> appropriate and determined manner of acting: what unites them is a recipro-
> cal action through their common energy. (Flourens, 1824, p. 368, in Clarke
> & O'Malley, 1969, p. 485)

The unity of the brain was for Flourens the reigning "grand principle." With such views Flourens anticipated the equipotentiality and mass action concepts of a great twentieth-century student of brain function, Karl Lashley (Lashley, 1929). Flourens also studied recovery of function after brain injury. He found that small areas of the brain can be damaged without an obvious loss of function. The effects of an ablation depend on the amount of tissue removed. Some functions that were lost immediately after brain damage could, with time, recover. Flourens believed this recovery resulted from certain areas of the brain taking over the functions of the ablated areas. This sort of recovery of function may be seen in stroke victims. Immediately after the stroke the victims may be devastated behaviorally, but after some months many of them recover to some extent. These are human clinical analogues of the results Flourens reported.

Studies of the Human Brain

Above all else, Flourens believed that elegantly controlled, carefully conducted experiments are essential for an understanding of brain function. From his experiments with animals he concluded that the brain is the organ of the mind. However, the question still remained: What of humans? Do the same principles apply to the human brain? In an ironic twist of history, Flourens' conclusion was shown to be applicable to humans by the terrible consequences of an accident involving a member of a railroad construction gang. A less controlled setting for the study of brain function would be difficult to imagine, yet the conclusion was the same.

The railroad accident occurred at 4:30 in the afternoon of September 13, 1848, near the small town of Cavendish, Vermont (MacMillan, 1986). The central figure was a twenty-five-year-old railroad gang foreman, Phineas P. Gage, a man described by his fellow workers as shrewd, hardworking, pleasant, persistent, and energetic. He and his men were building a new railway line and were about to blast some rock. Gage poured powder into a hole drilled in the rock and tamped down the powder and fuse with a long iron tamping rod. Distracted by his men, Gage looked away. The tamping iron hit the rock, struck a spark, and ignited the powder. The 13-pound, 3-foot, 7-inch tamping iron was blasted from the hole, striking Gage just below the left eye. The iron exploded through his skull and rose high into the air, finally landing fifty yards away. Gage was thrown to the ground in a convulsion but within a few minutes regained consciousness and was able to speak. He was taken by ox cart to Cavendish. He got down from the cart by himself and sat on the verandah of the tavern where he lodged, awaiting the arrival of a doctor. He explained to bystanders what had happened and, when the doctor arrived, greeted him with the words "Doctor, here is business enough for you" (MacMillan, 1986, p. 74). The two local doctors who examined Gage found it difficult to believe his story, yet there could be no doubt that the terrible missile had indeed passed through his head. There were numerous eyewitnesses, the entry and exit wounds were obvious, and the tamping iron, covered with brain matter and blood, had been found. Slowly Gage recovered from his physical injuries, and by November he was out of bed and able to wander around the town. He was eager to return to work but tragically was never able to do so. John Harlow, one of the two doctors who attended him after the accident, was a follower of the phrenologist Gall, and so he was understandably fascinated by Gage. His treatment was skillful and caring, and he kept detailed case notes. Harlow described Gage's difficulties as follows:

> His physical health is good and I am inclined to say that he has recovered.... The equilibrium or balance so to speak between his intellectual faculties and animal propensities seems to have been destroyed. He is fitful, irreverent, indulging at times in the grossest profanity, which was not previously his custom, manifesting but little deference for his fellows, impatient of restraint or advice when it conflicts with his desires, at times pertinaciously obstinate, yet capricious and vacillating, devising many plans of future operation which are no sooner arranged than they are abandoned in turn for others appearing more feasible. In this regard his mind was radically changed, so decidedly that his friends and acquaintances said he was "no longer Gage." (Harlow, 1869, pp. 13–14)

The injury to Gage's brain had radically changed his mind.

Phineas Gage was unable to find a job. He was rejected by his old employer because of his erratic behavior and was forced to exhibit himself and the tamping iron at Barnum's Museum in New York City. In 1852 he left New England for employment in Valparaiso, Chile, caring for horses and driving six-horse coaches. In 1860 his health began to fail, and he returned to the United States. After a series of increasingly severe convulsions Gage died on May 21, 1860 (MacMillan, 1986, p. 76). His skull and the tamping iron are on display in the Museum of the Harvard Medical School.

The behavioral and personality changes shown by Gage after his accident are characteristic of people with frontal lobe damage; such people are often highly distractable, lacking in foresight, frivolous, and unreliable in their conduct. John Harlow's description of Gage stands as a classic outline of the consequences of frontal lobe injury. Understandably, his report of the case was often cited in the great debate over the cerebral localization of function (MacMillan, 1986, pp. 85–101). Part of Gage's brain had been destroyed, and his personality, emotions, and behavior changed beyond recognition. With such a case report and Flourens' experimental studies, the role of the brain as the organ of the mind had been established beyond dispute.

The Localization of Speech

One of the most characteristically human actions is articulate speech. The question of the role of the brain in the production and comprehension of speech was to be answered in the nineteenth century. In 1825, a French physician and follower of Gall, Jean-Baptiste Bouillaud (1796–1875), studied a fifty-one-year-old patient who was healthy and intelligent, had good hearing and vision, but had been unable to speak for two to three months (Stookey, 1963). The patient had a history of epilepsy, but his loss of speech had been sudden. In general, he spoke only in monosyllables, but one especially fascinating feature of his behavior was that when angered or aroused, he would say, "*Sacré nom de Dieu.*" This was the only time he spoke a complete sentence. Following his death, Bouillaud performed a postmortem study of the patient's brain and found extensive damage to the anterior (frontal) portion of the cerebral lobes. By 1848 Bouillaud was so convinced that disorders of speech are associated with lesions of the frontal lobes that he offered 500 francs to anyone who could show that this was not so.

Bouillaud's prize was never claimed, and his challenge lay dormant until the early months of 1861, when the question of the cerebral localization of speech was hotly debated at a series of meetings of the French Anthropological Society in Paris. At the February meeting the surgeon and neurologist Pierre-Paul Broca (1824–1880), in the tradition of Flourens, stressed the action of the brain as a whole and the relationship between brain volume and intelligence. His opponent in the debate was Ernest Auburtin (1825–1893), a thirty-six-year-old surgeon, the pupil and son-in-law of Bouillaud. He argued in favor of cerebral localization, citing his father-in-law's findings. In the climactic debate held on April 4, 1861, Auburtin challenged those who opposed his and Bouillaud's views on cerebral localization:

> For a long time during my service with M. Bouillaud I studied a patient named Bache, who had lost his speech but understood everything said to him and replied with signs in a very intelligent manner to all questions put to him. This man, who spent several years at the Bicêtre, is now at the Hospital for Incurables. I saw him again recently, and his disease has progressed; slight paralysis has appeared, but his intelligence is still unimpaired, and speech is wholly abolished. Without doubt this man will soon die. Based on the symptoms that he presents, we have diagnosed a softening of the anterior lobes. If, at autopsy, these lobes are found to be intact, I shall renounce the idea that I have expounded to you. (Bouillaud, 1861, in Clarke & O'Malley, 1968, p. 493)

Within days of this challenge a man named Leborgne was transferred from the Bicêtre Hospital to a surgical unit headed by Pierre-Paul Broca (1824–1880). Leborgne had been a patient for thirty-two years. Originally admitted at the age of twenty-one, he had lost his speech and was chronically aphasic, or what Broca termed "aphemic." The only sounds Leborgne could make when Broca met him were "Tan–Tan," so he has gone down in medical annals as Broca's patient 'Tan.' He suffered weakness in the right side of his body but apparently was of normal intelligence. Broca made a thorough examination of his larynx and speech apparatus and found

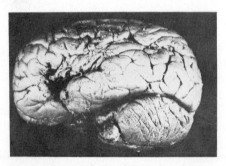

The embalmed brain of Broca's aphasic
patient Tan. The area of damage on the
lower side of the left frontal lobe is now
known as Broca's area. (Courtesy of
Musée Dupuytren)

that they were fully able to function. On April 12, 1861, Broca challenged Auburtin
to renounce his father-in-law's doctrine should the patient not have the specified
frontal lesion. Auburtin insisted on first examining Tan. Broca agreed, and after the
examination Auburtin accepted Broca's challenge.

Tan, assuring his place in history, died within a week on April 17, 1861. Broca
performed an immediate autopsy. In the posterior part of the second and third
frontal convolutions of the left frontal lobe he found a cavity the size of a small egg
filled with fluid. Auburtin had been correct. At that month's meeting of the Anthropological Society, Broca presented Tan's brain for inspection by the members,
pointing out that the lesion was restricted to the left frontal lobe. He also introduced
the term *aphemie* to describe Tan's loss of articulate speech (subsequently termed
expressive aphasia).

Next Broca saw an eighty-four-year-old man named LeLong who had suddenly lost his speech. A post-mortem examination of his brain showed a lesion in
the left frontal lobe, more circumscribed than the one in Leborgne's brain but in
the same area. The right hemisphere of his brain was perfectly normal. In 1863
Broca described over twenty-five aphemic patients, all with lesions of the left hemisphere. He considered it strange that these patients showed no signs of damage to
the right front lobe, suggesting that contrary to Bouillard's original thesis, the faculty of speech is localized specifically in the *left* frontal lobe. He had also observed
deep lesions of the third right frontal convolution in patients who were not in any
way aphemic. That the two frontal lobes, with their identical situations, size, and
symmetry, would have different functions contradicted the law of organic duality
and was for Broca a strange puzzle. It remains so today.

In 1865 Broca presented additional cases of aphemia and stated:

> I persist in thinking, until further details are available, that true aphemie, that is
> loss of speech without the paralysis of the organs of articulation and without the
> destruction of the intellect, is linked to lesions of the third left frontal
> convolution. (Broca, 1865, in Berker, Berker, & Smith, 1986, p. 1066)

The impact of Broca's finding was enormous. It radically changed the debate over the localization of function. In a review of nineteenth-century studies of aphasia, Marx (1966) reported over 3,000 papers. In 1980 the French journal *Revue neurologique* dedicated a special volume to Broca, and his memory will be forever honored in references to Broca's area.

Broca considered articulate language to be the highest achievement of human beings. Having localized that function in the, left frontal lobe, Broca went on to hypothesize that the left hemisphere develops more quickly than the right and so is more advanced. It is the superior hemisphere (Harrington, 1987). Broca's hypothesis anticipated contemporary discussions of the articulate, intellectual left brain and the intuitive, mystical right brain, the seat of the "bicameral mind," where the prophetic and visionary language of the gods can be heard (Ornstein, 1972; Jaynes, 1976).

In 1874, Carl Wernicke (1848–1905) identified another type of aphasia (Wernicke's aphasia), resulting from damage to the superior portion of the left temporal lobe; speech output can be rapid and effortless and has the rhythm and melody of normal speech, but it conveys little meaning. A Wernicke's aphasic might say: "Oh sure, go ahead, any old thing you want" or "If I could I would. Oh, I'm taking the wrong way to say, all of the barbers here whenever they stop you it's going around and around, if you know what I mean" (Restak, 1988. p. 213).

By 1874, the role of the brain in the production and comprehension of language had been described and two different language disturbances associated with damage in two distinct areas of the left temporal lobe had been identified. Progress had indeed been made.

DIRECT STIMULATION OF THE BRAIN

So far we have considered conclusions drawn from studies of the consequences of brain damage that followed accident or disease or that was produced experimentally. The nineteenth century also saw the development of a second important technique for the study of brain function: direct stimulation of the brain. The first attempts involved "agitation" of the brain surface. Around 1860, Franz von Leyden injected a solution of sodium chloride between the skull and the surface of the brain. Hans Pagenstecher conducted an extended series of studies, reported in 1871, in which a mixture of white wax and tallow heated to 50 degrees Centigrade was injected between the skull and brain of dogs. Following this injection, the animals showed derangement, loss of physical functions, stupor, somnolence, and coma together with motor disorders, convulsions, and paralysis. In 1873 Fournie made a small opening in an animal's skull through which he injected various corrosive substances. Injections into the gray matter destroyed clusters of brain cells and were associated with loss of movement of distinct groups of muscles on the opposite side of the body. However, true progress came not from these crude and often lethal procedures but from experiments in which the brain was stimulated electrically.

The first person to stimulate the brain electrically appears to have been L. N. Simonoff, who in 1860 published an account of an operation in which electrodes were implanted in the brain stem. Following the operation, he delivered electrical current directly to the brains of unanesthetized animals. However, the most important early demonstrations of the effects of direct electrical stimulation of the brain were those of the Gustav Fritsch (1839–1927), a German anatomist, and Eduard Hitzig (1838–1907), a German psychiatrist. Hitzig served as a physician in the German Army. Toward the end of the 1860s he applied a mechanical stimulus to the exposed surface of the brain of a wounded German soldier. When different brain areas were stimulated, different muscular movements would occur. After the war he collaborated with Fritsch in investigations using animals, first stimulating the brain of a rabbit and then conducting a systematic study of the effects of the electrical stimulation of a dog's brain. These famous experiments were done in Fritsch's bedroom. Wires or electrodes were placed on the surface of the brain, and current of different intensities was applied. In anterior portions of the cerebral cortex a weak current would usually elicit motor movements; a more intense current produced convulsive general movements. Using weak electrical stimulation, Fritsch and Hitzig were able to localize areas controlling five different groups of muscles involved in extension of the neck, extension and flexion of the foreleg, movement of the hindleg, and movement of the face. Electrical stimulation of one side of the brain always caused movements on the opposite side of the body.

These startling findings were quickly replicated in a number of other laboratories, including that of David Ferrier (1843–1928), first at the West Riding Lunatic Asylum in Yorkshire and later at the National Hospital for the Paralyzed and Epileptic in London. Ferrier performed a series of brilliant experiments on the localization of both sensory and motor functions. His aim was to use the technique of Fritsch and Hitzig to map the functions of the brain—to create a "scientific phrenology"—and to remove the "doubt and discrepancy" resulting from the earlier ablation studies (Ferrier, 1886, p. 222). He reported the results of his experiments in *The Functions of the Brain*, first published in 1876. Ferrier implanted brain electrodes in dogs, jackals, cats, rabbits, rats, guinea pigs, pigeons, frogs, and fish and was able to localize motor and sensory functions in their brains. In the monkey Ferrier localized fifteen different motor functions, including advance of the opposite leg, retraction of the opposite arm, opening of the mouth and protrusion of the tongue, opening of the eyes, and pricking up of the ears. So precise were Ferrier's results that he was able to transfer his monkey localization map directly to the human brain and localize the first brain tumor to be removed in a neurosurgical operation (Bennett & Godlee, 1885).

Later it was found that the amount of representation of the different body parts in the motor cortex is proportional to their function rather than to their body mass. For example, the hands are much more heavily represented than is the back. Such relationships are often shown in physiological texts by drawings of the motor homunculus, a humanlike cartoon figure drawn in proportion to the amount of cortical representation of different functions. Such figures have a rather alarming appearance with their enormous lips and tongues, large hands, and small backs. They show a cortical representation of the body, not the body we are used to seeing.

What of sensory functions? Ferrier localized vision in the occipital cortex,

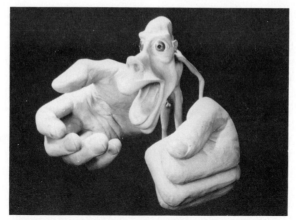

A sensory homunculus, showing the body as it is
represented in the brain's sensory projection areas.
(The British Museum of Natural History)

since stimulation of the occipital region produces movements of the eyeballs and
contraction of the pupils. Animals with one occipital lobe ablated are blind in the
eye opposite the ablation. Audition was localized in the temporal lobe; Ferrier found
that a monkey with a left temporal lobe ablation remained unconcerned when a
percussive cap was fired. The animal was undoubtedly deaf. By the end of the
nineteenth century the somesthetic senses had also been localized in the postcentral
region, posterior to the motor centers.

Further progress came from the contributions of Ferrier's compatriot and
sometime collaborator John Hughlings-Jackson (1835–1911). Hughlings-Jackson
was largely self-taught, a shy, aloof, carefully controlled man. His wife was afflicted
with a form of epilepsy now known as Jacksonian epilepsy in which the seizure
starts in one part of the body, such as a hand, and then marches through the wrist,
arm, elbow, shoulder, and neck to the face. The seizure, Hughlings-Jackson believed, spreads through the internal geography of the brain in an ordered sequence.
He also developed a conceptual model of the organization of the brain. Perhaps
influenced by the political views of Thomas Hobbes (Chapter 2), he compared the
brain to a government that can endure only by suppressing lower, less legitimate
sources of power and authority. In the human brain higher cortical centers rule by
controlling or inhibiting lower, older, and more primitive centers. Inhibition,
Hughlings-Jackson believed, is the mark of a healthy brain. What we do *not* do is
the mark of civilization. When such higher inhibitory control is removed, the result
is the behavioral, emotional, and intellectual anarchy of a man such as Phineas
Gage. Jackson's hierarchical model of cerebral organization is influential today.

Electrical Stimulation of the Human Brain

Less than five years after the first animal experiments using electrical stimulation
of the brain, a similar experiment was performed on a human patient. The time lag

seems amazingly short. Dr. Roberts Bartholow, a professor of clinical medicine at the Medical College of Ohio in Cincinnati, observed the effects of electrical stimulation of the human brain. In April 1874 he published a report of his "Experimental Investigations into the Functions of the Human Brain" in the *American Journal of the Medical Sciences*. Bartholow was aware of the earlier animal experiments of Fritsch and Hitzig and Ferrier and cited their results in the introduction to his report. However, he also stressed that similar investigations should be made of the human brain.

Taking advantage of what he termed "a clinical opportunity," Bartholow conducted just such an investigation. His patient's name was Mary Rafferty. From the case notes of the house physician, Dr. Steeley, we learn that Rafferty was a thirty-year-old domestic worker who had been born in Ireland but at the time was a resident of Cincinnati. She was admitted to Cincinnati's Good Samaritan Hospital in January 1874. Rafferty was not well nourished and appeared somewhat feebleminded. She had been in good health until thirteen months earlier, when a small ulcer had appeared on her scalp. Rafferty believed that the ulcer was produced by friction caused by a piece of whalebone in her wig. Upon admission, her skull was found to be completely eroded over a circular area two inches in diameter. Through this hole the pulsations of her brain could be seen.

Rafferty had earned her living as a domestic servant and was able to answer questions correctly and converse in a bright and cheerful manner. Bartholow inserted needles through the hole in her skull into the brain. The needles were insulated except for their tips so that electrical currents could be delivered to localized areas of her brain. The first observations Bartholow made followed stimulation of the dura mater and the brain itself. He described the results as follows:

> Needles were inserted at various points into the dura mater and into the brain. When the irritable granulations of the surface of the ulcer were touched, pain was experienced; but when the needle points were engaged in the dura mater, Mary declared, in answer to repeated questions that she felt no pain and certainly did not indicate any by her conduct. No pain whatever was experienced in the brain-substance proper. (Bartholow, 1874, p. 310)

In Bartholow's second and third sets of observations, needles were inserted deep in the dura mater and posterior lobes. When stimulated in the left posterior lobe, Rafferty reacted with muscular contractions of the right arm and leg, her neck muscles moved, and her head turned to the right. When she was stimulated in the right posterior lobe, her head deflected to the left and her left arm and leg extended. During the brain stimulation Rafferty complained of a very strong and unpleasant tingling in her arms and legs and at one point seized her hand with the opposite hand and rubbed it vigorously. Despite this, Bartholow reported that she remained cheerful throughout the observations. Rashly, Bartholow decided to increase the strength of the electrical stimulation in order to produce more intense reactions. He described the tragic result as follows:

> In order to develop more decided reactions, the strength of the current was increased....When communication was made with the needles, her

countenance exhibited great distress, then she began to cry. Very soon the
left hand was extended as if in the act of taking hold of some object in front
of her; the arm presently was agitated with clonic spasms; her eyes became
fixed, with pupils dilated, lips were blue, and she frothed at the mouth; her
breathing became stentorous; she lost consciousness and was violently
convulsed on her left side. The convulsion lasted five minutes and was
succeeded by coma. She returned to consciousness and complained of some
weakness and vertigo. (Bartholow, 1874, pp. 310–311)

While Bartholow's ingenuity and boldness in carrying out this experiment and his
honesty in reporting its results may be admired, his ethics are open to question. The
consequences were disastrous for Mary Rafferty. Three days later she was still pale
and depressed, but Bartholow planned further brain stimulation sessions. However, her condition deteriorated rapidly, and he was forced to abandon his plan. She
had difficulty walking and complained of numbness and tingling on the right side
of her body and frequent dizzy spells. Four days after the observations were made
she became incoherent, had a convulsive seizure followed by paralysis of the right
side of her body, and then lapsed into unconsciousness and died. Bartholow performed an autopsy and examined her brain. Tracks made by the electrodes were
clearly visible penetrating the brain to a depth of 1 inch in the left parietal lobe and
1½ inches in the right posterior frontal lobe. The surrounding brain tissue was
found to be unaffected. Bartholow published his findings in April 1874, ending his
account with the statement "It has seemed to be most desirable to present the facts
as I observed them, without comment" (Bartholow, 1874, p. 313).

Unfortunately for Bartholow, his report led to many "comments" by others;
in fact, it created a scandal. His procedures struck many observers as intolerable,
raising in their minds the specter of the "mad scientist" creating human robots by
direct stimulation of the brain. The public outcry forced Bartholow to resign his
academic position at the university and his staff position at the hospital. In fact, so
intense and critical was the reaction that he was forced to leave Cincinnati.

Bartholow's observations were the beginning of what David Krech has described as the era of the "surgeon-experimenter." Krech wrote:

With these discoveries the great era of the surgeon-experimenter was to
begin. From now on, every human brain exposed for medical treatment was
an open invitation to experiment. And many of these invitations were
accepted. (Krech, 1962, p. 63)

Perhaps the key phrase here is "exposed for medical treatment." Rafferty's brain
was not exposed for treatment, whereas, in modern procedures exposure of the
brain is part of the treatment. Such procedures depend on maps or atlases specifying the three-dimensional coordinates of a brain structure and thus its location
and stereotactic instruments that allow electrodes to be placed within targeted structures in the brain. The first stereotactic instrument for the human brain was designed by Aubrey Mussen around 1918 (Olivier, Bertrand, & Picard, 1983). It is
now housed at the Montreal Neurological Institute, which is appropriate, for it was
in Montreal that Wilder Penfield and his colleagues, beginning in 1928, performed

over 400 operations on patients suffering from some form of epilepsy and needing brain surgery. During the operations the brains of some of these patients were stimulated with what Penfield termed "gentle electrical currents." Motor responses following the stimulation could be observed, and since the operations were performed under local anesthesia, Penfield could ask the patients for verbal reports of their experiences. In their classic book *The Cerebral Cortex of Man*, originally published in 1950, Penfield and Rasmussen described sensory and motor areas along either side of the fissure of Rolando, an area in which speech is localized, and areas in the temporal lobe in which memories, hallucinations, illusions, and even dreams are apparently stored. Brain stimulation had indeed proved to be a powerful technique for unraveling the mysteries of the human brain.

Brain Stimulation Reinforcement

There has been a large body of research using electrical brain stimulation. One of the most intriguing findings in this body of research is that stimulation of certain brain areas is highly rewarding or reinforcing. In 1924, two French investigators, Michel Victor Pachon and Valentin Delmas-Marsalet, found a cortical area for reward. They implanted copper electrodes unilaterally in the caudate nuclei of two dogs (Kenyon, 1981). Electrical stimulation of the brain through these electrodes would rouse the sleeping dogs; they would lick their lips with "evident satisfaction" and begin to chew. With prolonged stimulation, the dogs would get up and walk. The researchers concluded that the caudate nucleus plays a role in the expression of affective states and in certain automatic movements. Thirty years later, in 1954, James Olds and Peter Milner reported that rats would lever-press at very high rates for intracranial stimulation and would continue to do so until exhausted (Olds & Milner, 1954).

PROGRESS AND CHALLENGE

Obviously, great progress has been made in the study of brain function. Looking back on the decades around the beginning of the twentieth century, it is not difficult to understand the excitement and optimism of investigators at that time. Two techniques for studying brain function—ablation and stimulation—had been developed and found to be highly productive of new knowledge. Sir Charles Sherrington (1857–1952) dedicated his great 1906 work, *The Integrative Action of the Nervous System*, to David Ferrier, expressing his admiration but also his astonishment that such imperfect procedures could produce such precise results. Even the brain mechanisms underlying the formation of associations seemed on the point of being revealed. For instance, in 1905 Baer implanted electrodes in the visual and motor cortexes of dogs. He then paired stimulation of the visual cortex with stimulation of the motor cortex and found that after a number of pairings, stimulation of the visual cortex alone would elicit the motor movements previously elicited by stimulation of the motor cortex. An association had been established within the brain, but it was a controlled association based on electrical stimulation of discrete areas. Perhaps the very cortical basis of learning and memory could be discovered.

The more optimistic investigators surely must have thought that if only a sufficient number of careful experiments using ablation and stimulation could be conducted, the mysteries of brain function might be solved. It seemed only a matter of time. Such hopes were premature. One of the most eminent twentieth-century investigators of brain function, Karl Lashley (1890–1958), concluded in 1950 that attempts to localize such psychological capacities and functions as learning, memory, and intelligence were based on oversimplified conceptions of brain function and should be abandoned. Lashley spent over thirty years searching for *engrams*, the physical or chemical changes in the brain assumed to underlie memory. He tested thousands of rats, systematically studying their behavior and brains. In 1950 Lashley reviewed this prodigious effort in a paper entitled "In Search of the Engram" and concluded:

> I sometimes feel in reviewing the evidence of the localization of the memory trace, that the necessary conclusion is that learning just is not possible. It is difficult to conceive of a mechanism which can satisfy the conditions set for it. (Lashley, 1950, p. 477)

However, an important lesson can be drawn from Lashley's conclusion. Attempts to understand learning, memory, and other psychological processes exclusively through neuropsychological techniques may not be sufficient. While great progress has been made in this field in recent years, there is still a need for behavioral assessment and evaluation—the province of psychology. While contemporary psychology is very different from the independent science first established by Wilhelm Wundt late in the nineteenth century, it is to Wundt that we turn first for a consideration of psychology as an independent branch of science with its own subject matter and, most important, its own distinct methods of investigation.

Wilhelm Wundt. (National Library of Medicine)

chapter

4

Wilhelm Wundt and the Founding of Psychology

Portraits of Wilhelm Wundt appear in many contemporary psychology books. A bearded, distinguished-looking gentleman gazes calmly at the world through wire-rimmed glasses. The reader looks back at the man often identified as the "founder of psychology" or the "world's first true psychologist." Such characterizations soon followed Wundt's founding of the first psychological research laboratory at the University of Leipzig in 1879. In 1896, at the time of the Third International Congress of Psychology, a Berlin newspaper account described Wundt as "the Psychological Pope of the Old World" (Perry, 1935, p. 145). Edwin G. Boring used as a frontispiece to his influential *History of Experimental Psychology* (1929) a reproduction of a bronze plaque of Wundt made in 1905 to mark the golden jubilee of Wundt's doctorate. Seventy-five years later, the American Psychological Association recognized the centennial of psychology with a special minting of a gold medallion bearing Wundt's profile. Clearly Wundt holds an esteemed position in the history of psychology. Who was Wundt and what did he do?

Wilhelm Maximilian Wundt was born on August 16, 1832, in the small village of Neckarau near Mannheim in the German principality of Baden. He was the youngest of four children. Wundt's father was a Lutheran pastor. His family included historians, theologians, economists, geographers, and two presidents of the University of Heidelberg. His mother's side of the family was equally prominent and included scientists, physicians, and government administrators. Some scholars have concluded that no contemporary German family had as many intellectually active and productive individuals (Bringmann, Balance, & Evans, 1975, p. 288). It seems likely that such a distinguished family background would have provided the young Wundt with a stimulating environment, yet he appears to have had a lonely and at times unhappy childhood. His brother was eight years older and away at school during Wundt's childhood, and two other siblings had died in infancy. For many years Wundt's only playmate was a slightly older retarded boy who could hardly speak. The boy was endlessly good-natured, but Wundt was always responsible for him. Wundt seems never to have had the chance to learn how to play. Throughout his life, he remained a shy, reserved person who disliked meeting strangers, hated to travel, and avoided new experiences.

Wundt's maternal grandfather took a personal interest in his education, taking him on frequent trips and tours. Together they served as sidewalk supervisors during the construction of the area's first railroad station. However, Wundt's grandfather was a stern and authoritarian taskmaster who insisted on a rigorous daily schedule and absolute precision in everything they did. Between the ages of eight and twelve Wundt's formal education was entrusted to his father's assistant, a young pastor who gave the boy the love and warmth neither of his parents could provide. When the young man moved to a church of his own, Wundt was greatly distressed. He continued his education at the local Catholic *Gymnasium* but failed his first year and later referred to this institution as his "school of suffering." Wundt then transferred to the Lutheran *Gymnasium* at Heidelberg and was graduated in 1851.

When Wundt's father died in 1845, his mother was forced to support the family on a small clerical pension. The family had never been wealthy, but now financial pressures were severe. Because of his self-admitted "unbridled daydreaming," Wundt had achieved only an average academic record and so was not eligible for a university scholarship. He also was undecided as to a career. Fortunately, his mother's brother, a professor of anatomy and physiology at the University of Tübingen, took the young man under his wing and arranged for him to enter the university as a premedical student. Wundt stayed at Tübingen just one year before transferring to the University of Heidelberg. He had little money but worked very hard and completed the medical curriculum in three years rather than four, saving a year's fees and expenses. Wundt graduated summa cum laude in 1855 and placed first in the state medical board examination. For his medical dissertation research Wundt studied the touch sensitivity of hysterical patients at the University of Heidelberg Hospital. He later described these experiments as the first steps toward his experimental work in psychology.

At Heidelberg, Wundt had done research with the chemist Robert Wilhelm von Bunsen, the man who invented the gas burner that bears his name. Among other things, Bunsen and Wundt were interested in the effects of restricted salt intake on urine composition. Since they could not find a volunteer to eliminate all dietary salt, Wundt followed a long tradition of self-experimentation in medical research (L. K. Altman, 1987) and did the experiment on himself. It turned out well. He published a paper describing his results in the *Journal of Practical Chemistry* (1853) and had the highly reinforcing experience of seeing his paper cited in the literature. Given this outcome, it is not surprising that Wundt decided to pursue a research career.

WUNDT'S EARLY ACADEMIC CAREER

In 1856 Wundt spent a semester at the University of Berlin, studying with Johannes Müller and Emil Du Bois-Reymond (Chapter 3), and in 1857 he returned to Heidelberg as a *Privatdozent* (lecturer) in the Department of Physiology. His first course offering was on experimental physiology. Only four students took the course, which he taught in his mother's apartment, but it was a beginning. Wundt worked very hard arranging demonstrations to complement and confirm his lectures. He was determined to succeed, but he overworked, became seriously ill, and was for a time close to death. Later, he recalled his experience at the time of near death as being one of "perfect calm," without fear. After his illness, he took a leave of absence to recuperate in the Swiss Alps.

In 1858 Hermann von Helmholtz (Chapter 3) was appointed the head of the new Institute of Physiology at the University of Heidelberg. He in turn appointed Wundt as his assistant. Wundt was delighted to accept the position, for he considered Helmholtz the best scientist at Heidelberg and, along with Müller and Du Bois-Reymond, one of the three great German physiologists of the time. Wundt shared a room with I. M. Sechenov (1829–1909), a young Russian physiologist who later was to influence Ivan Pavlov (Chapter 12). Unfortunately, the position was something of a disappointment as Wundt was required to be more a teaching than a research assistant. His main duty was drilling medical students in the fundamentals of sensory physiology and laboratory procedures. However, he was able to develop a new course in anthropology, or what today would be called social psychology. Wundt offered the course for the first time in 1859, and in it he addressed the relation of the individual to society. Wundt was to return to this interest in the last decades of his life and produce a ten-volume magnum opus on the topic.

During his years as Helmholtz's assistant, Wundt also wrote his first book, the *Beiträge zur Theorie der Sinneswahrnehmung* (Contributions Toward a Theory of Sense Perception), published in 1862. In this book Wundt discussed sensory functions, developed a theory of perception, and, according to Edward Titchener (Chapter 5), outlined a program for psychology that he followed for the rest of his life. Wundt saw psychology as falling between the physical sciences (*Naturwissenschaften*) and the social sciences (*Geisteswissenschaften*). Experimental and research methods comparable to those of the physical sciences were to be used to address psychological questions. Wundt saw this new science of psychology as having three main subdivisions. One of the subdivisions was psychology as an inductive, experimental science. Wundt had read and been impressed by the writings of John Stuart Mill (Chapter 2). But Mill's approach was that of a philosopher who speculates and thinks about mental life; Wundt's was that of scientist who uses experimental methods to study mental life.

Wundt believed that language, myths, aesthetics, religion, and social customs are reflections of our highest mental processes and thus should be topics of psychology. But since these processes could not be manipulated or controlled, they could not be studied experimentally. Instead, Wundt believed they could be investigated through the study of historical records and literature and by means of naturalistic observations.

Wundt conceptualized a third branch of psychology that was to integrate the empirical findings of psychology and other sciences. *Scientific metaphysics,* as he labeled this division, would develop eventually into what he saw as the ideal goal of all science: a coherent theory of the universe. As Blumenthal (1985) demonstrated, Wundt's aim was to establish psychology as a foundational or propaedeutic science that would integrate the social and physical sciences.

Just one year later, in 1863, the prolific Wundt published a major work, the two-volume, 1,000-page *Vorlesungen über die Menschen- und Thierseele* (Lectures on the Human and Animal Mind). As the title indicates, the work is both broad and inclusive, with about half the material continuing Wundt's presentation of cultural psychology.

Even though he had been able to develop his courses and was given a chance to write, Wundt became increasingly dissatisfied with his position at the institute, and in 1863 he resigned. His decision has prompted speculation that the relationship between Helmholtz and Wundt had cooled. G. Stanley Hall (Chapter 9) went so far as to report that Helmholtz found Wundt's knowledge of mathematics inadequate and so replaced him with a man of "severer and more accurate methods and greater mathematical knowledge" (Hall, 1924, p. 206). This speculation is not true, for as Wundt himself remarked, Helmholtz needed no help with his mathematics and wrote many letters of recommendation for his former assistant over a period of several years. In any event, having resigned from the institute, Wundt was left without regular income. He still held his academic rank at the university and had in fact been promoted to associate professor, but his position was without salary. Wundt established a small laboratory in his home and supported it and himself with royalties from his books.

He became intensely interested in politics and was elected president of the Heidelberg Workingmen's Educational Association, an idealistic, socialistic group dedicated to improving conditions for working people. Wundt served as a member of the Baden Parliament for two terms but became convinced that political life was not for him, and in 1871 he returned to the University of Heidelberg. There he held the rank of extraordinary professor for three years before accepting a call to the chair of inductive philosophy at Zurich. He was at Zurich for just a year before being appointed to the chair of philosophy at the University of Leipzig. This chair had been vacant for ten years because the faculty had been unable to agree on an appointment. Wundt's interest in the new psychology and his recent political activism must have caused alarm among the more conservative members of the Leipzig faculty.

THE FIRST EXPERIMENTAL PSYCHOLOGY LABORATORY

In 1876 the University of Leipzig assigned Wundt a room to store the demonstration equipment and experimental apparatus he had brought from Zurich. The room

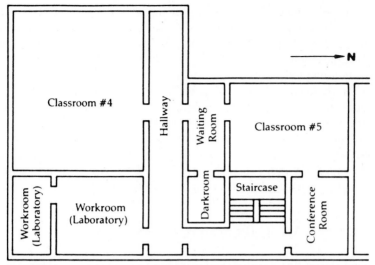

Wundt's Leipzig laboratory in 1883. (From *Wundt Studies: A Centennial Celebration* (p. 151) edited by W. G. Bringmann and R. D. Tweeney, 1980, Toronto: Hogrefe. Reprinted by permission.)

was in the *Konvikt* building constructed in 1840 to house a dining hall for poor students. At Leipzig, Wundt's first course was on physiological psychology. He presented demonstrations and experiments during his lectures, but it became cumbersome to transport equipment back and forth from the storage area to the classroom, and so a number of demonstrations were set up permanently in one room of the *Konvikt* building. Students would go there to observe the demonstrations and even to participate in simple experiments. This was the modest beginning of Wundt's Leipzig laboratory. Wundt's psychology was to become very much an experimental science of tachistoscopes, chronoscopes, electrical stimulators, pendulums, timers, and sensory mapping devices—a "brass instrument" psychology. A new student joining Wundt's laboratory was typically assigned a piece of apparatus for use in planned experiments or to develop and adapt for future research (Hilgard, 1987, p. 30). Wundt bought much of this original equipment himself, and it filled more and more rooms in the *Konvikt* building. In autumn 1879 Wundt began some psychological experiments that were not part of his course. He later suggested that these independent experiments marked the formal establishment of his laboratory of psychology, and 1879 has been generally accepted as the date of the establishment of psychology as an independent experimental science.

The Leipzig laboratory had in fact been established over a number of years, and in 1879 Wundt's laboratory was still a primitive affair. It was not officially recognized and listed in the catalogue of the University of Leipzig until 1883. Even that belated action came only when Wundt threatened to accept an offer to move to the University of Breslau. Benjamin Wolman (1960, p. 11) has suggested that establishing this laboratory was an act of courage by Wundt. He had to face opposition from colleagues who questioned the legitimacy of psychology as an experimental science and maintained that continued self-observation would drive young persons to insanity. Despite this opposition, Wundt's laboratory grew. By the mid-1880s it occupied eight to ten rooms. In 1893, the laboratory was moved to eleven rooms in a building formerly occupied by the department of gynecology; finally, in 1897, the Psychological Institute, as it was then called, moved to a new building that Wundt had designed expressly for psychological research. It is ironic that some of Wundt's most prominent students—Cattell, Kraepelin, Münsterberg, Külpe, Titchener, and Lipps—did their research in the *Konvikt* building. Wundt himself did little research in the new laboratory since by that time his interests were primarily theoretical. Wundt's last laboratory was destroyed in an Anglo-American bombing raid on Leipzig during the night of December 4, 1943.

THE WUNDTIAN THEORETICAL SYSTEM

In addition to laboratory exercises and demonstrations, Wundt needed a text for his course. In 1873 and 1874 he published the two-volume *Grundzüge der Physiologischen Psychologie* (Principles of Physiological Psychology). The book had been planned for some time. In December 1872, Wundt had described it to Wilhelm Englemann, a potential publisher, as being physiological in that it used the inductive, experimental methods of that field but also new in that those methods would be applied in areas that were not considered in contemporary physiological texts. The book's subject matter was to fall somewhere between physiology and philosophy. By physiological psychology Wundt did not mean what we mean today: the study of the physiological basis of behavior and consciousness. Rather, for Wundt it meant a psychology using experimental techniques analogous to those of physiology. The publisher accepted Wundt's book and published it in Leipzig in 1873 and 1874. In the preface Wundt clearly outlined the book's domain:

> The book which I here present to the public is an attempt to mark out a new domain of science. I am well aware that the question may be raised, whether the time is yet ripe for such an undertaking. The new discipline rests upon anatomical and physiological foundations which, in certain respects, are themselves very far from solid; while the experimental treatment of psychological problems must be pronounced from every point of view to be in its first beginnings. At the same time the best means of discovering the blanks that our ignorance has left in the subject matter of a developing science is, as we all know, to take a general survey of its present status. (Wundt, 1904, p. V)

The phrases "new domain of science," "new discipline," "experimental treatment of psychological problems," and "developing science" in this passage show that Wundt was self-consciously trying to stake out a new area of science. Thus, he is the first person we can label without reservation a psychologist. Wundt's *Principles* was a success. The book went through major revisions and expansions in

1880, 1887, and 1893. Three-volume editions were published in 1902–1903 and 1908–1911. These books are the clearest statement of Wundt's experimental psychology and so must be considered in some detail.

First Wundt described the "bodily substrate of mental life," or brain anatomy and function. Next he described the nervous system and presented his views on the forces that underlie nerve conduction. For the contemporary student of psychology, these sections are of little value as they have been superseded by more recent findings. Then Wundt discussed the characteristics of sensations; he identified quality, intensity, extent, and duration as the four fundamental characteristics and went on to develop a theory of perception. Part IV is the psychological heart of the book. There Wundt defined psychology as "the investigation of conscious processes in the modes of connexion peculiar to them" (Wundt, 1904, p. 2).

Well-established methods of the physiological sciences were to be the model for the methods of the new experimental science. However, Wundt stressed that those methods required modification to meet the specific requirements of psychological investigation. He commented that "psychology has adapted physiological, as physiology adapted physical methods to its own ends" (Wundt, 1904, p. 3). The goal of psychology was the study of "conscious processes," or what Wundt considered part of "immediate experience," as opposed to "mediate experience." To illustrate the distinction, consider two stimuli: a green sheet of paper and a tone. If we use a spectrometer to measure the wavelength of the light reflected from the paper or a sound spectrogram to measure the frequency and intensity of the tone, we are not studying the paper and the tone directly; our experience of the green paper and tone is mediated by the instruments. If we describe the conscious processes and experiences we have when the two stimuli are presented—the "greenness" of the green paper and the "toneness" of the tone—we are describing our immediate experience, our direct experience. According to Wundt, the first is the path of physics, the second that of psychology. Physicists attempt to study the external world without being a part of the situation or phenomenon being examined. Psychologists, according to Wundt, do not study the external world per se; they study the *psychological processes* by which we experience and observe the external world. They cannot remove themselves from their objects of study since they are studying their own conscious processes.

While physicists have their spectrometers, spectrographs, and many other wonderful instruments, what objective observational techniques does the psychologist have with which to study conscious processes? One technique Wundt described is *Experimentelle Selbst-beobachtung* (experimental self-observation or introspection). *Introspection* has been the word most frequently used to describe Wundt's method. The choice is unfortunate, for it may be taken to imply a type of armchair speculation, which was certainly not what Wundt meant. He dismissed such speculation as "contemplative meditation" that leads only to fruitless debate and the grossest self-deceptions (Wundt, 1904, p. 7). In 1882, Wundt in a polemical paper compared earlier introspectionists to the Baron von Munchhausen, a comic character of German folklore who rescued himself from quicksand by pulling himself up by his own hair (Blumenthal, 1985, p. 29). Wundt's introspection was a rigidly controlled, arduous experimental procedure. He believed that just as little had been learned about mechanics from casual, haphazard observations of falling bodies, little would be learned about human mental experiences from uncontrolled, contemplative meditations.

Wundt's introspection was not limited to self-reports but included objective measures, including reaction times and word associations. In fact, the majority of experiments in Wundt's laboratory included such measures. Danziger (1979) surveyed nearly 180 reports from Wundt's laboratory between 1883 and 1903. He found just four articles containing *only* introspective reports. Whenever introspection was used, highly trained observers were presented with carefully controlled sensory events and were required to describe their mental experiences. To yield valid introspections, certain rules were enforced. The observer had to be "master of the situation," that is, in a state of "strained attention," knowing when the stimulus would be presented and when the observations would be made. All observations were to be repeated many times. Finally, experimental conditions would be varied systematically to allow a general description of mental contents.

In their introspections, Wundt and his students identified two basic elements of mental life: sensations and feelings. Complex, continually changing mental processes result from connections or creative syntheses of these elements. Wundt placed this principle of creative synthesis in direct opposition to what he considered the misleading atomic elementism of some nineteenth-century associationists. Arthur Blumenthal described this situation well:

> [The associationists] had atomized mental processes into elemental ideas that became associated into compounds according to classical associationist descriptions. Wundt considered that approach to be a mere primitive analogy to systems of physical mechanics, and he argued at length that these systems teach little about the relations of psychological processes. (Blumenthal, 1975, p. 1083)

For Wundt, sensations and feelings were not simply "billiard balls" that collide and interact. Like John Stuart Mill (Chapter 2), Wundt adopted a model of the mind that emphasized chemical rather than mechanical principles. For Wundt, the mind is a creative, dynamic, volitional force. It can never be understood by simply identifying its elements or its static structure. Rather, it must be understood through an analysis of its activity—its processes. In fact, the term *structuralist*, commonly applied to Wundt, was invented later by Edward Titchener (Chapter 5) and William James (Chapter 9); it was never used by Wundt. Instead, Wundt gave the name *voluntarism* to his psychology and stressed the difference between his voluntarism and Titchener's structuralism (Blumenthal, 1979, p. 549). Blumenthal has largely been responsible for clarifying our conceptions of Wundt's true position. He wrote:

> Today I cannot help but wonder whether Wundt had any notion of what might happen the day he chose the word "Elemente" as part of a chapter title. Later generations seized upon the word with such passion that they were eventually led to transform Wundt into something nearly opposite to the original. (Blumenthal, 1979, p. 549)

Blumenthal's remarkable conclusion was that Wundt was not in fact a reductionist, not an elementist, and not a structuralist—the three characteristics most often ascribed to him. Wundt did not define psychology as the science of the mind. That definition, like the term *structuralism*, also comes from Titchener. Wundt denied that there are "minds" to be studied apart from "bodies." He vehemently opposed mind-body dualisms and believed that mental experience must be studied in terms of both the mind and the body—the so-called double aspect resolution of the mind-body problem. Finally, Wundt's introspection was not a limited method of self-report but rather a collection of objective, experimental procedures more accurately labeled experimental self-observation.

WUNDT'S RESEARCH

When we turn to Wundt's research, we find a similar situation. Rather than a restricted, tedious, largely irrelevant series of experiments bounded by introspection, Wundt and his students actually did research on a range of topics, and as we have seen, in many of their experiments classical introspection had little if any part.

Fortunately, we have an excellent historical record of the experiments Wundt and his students performed in their Leipzig laboratory. As the number of experiments increased, Wundt realized that some way of presenting their results to a wider public was needed. His *Principles* was constantly being expanded and revised, but the publication lag of the book created the need for a journal which would allow the results to be published quickly. In 1881 Wundt established the journal *Philosophische Studien* (Philosophical Studies), and he edited it until 1902. This was the first journal to be devoted exclusively to psychological research. Edwin G. Boring (1929) and Robert Watson (1978) classified about 100 of the experiments reported in this journal during a twenty-one-year period and found that about 50 percent of the studies were concerned with sensation and perception: studies of color vision and contrast, afterimages, and visual illusions. Time perception was studied by having subjects judge and estimate time intervals. Tactile sensations were studied using the psychophysical methods developed by Ernst Weber and Gustav Fechner (Chapter 6).

About 17 percent of the experiments reported in *Philosophische Studien* concerned reaction times and their measurement. Subjects had to respond after a stimulus had been detected or identified. Reaction times for identification were consistently longer than were detection reaction times; this was thought to be due to the time taken by the process of identification after the simple detection of the stimulus. These methods and assumptions appear reasonable, but around the turn of the century they were found to be inadequate. Observed reaction times varied greatly from subject to subject, in the same subject at different times, and from laboratory to laboratory. Reaction times simply did not yield the precise measurements of mental processes the Wundtians sought.

About 10 percent of the Leipzig experiments concerned *attention*. Wundt thought of attention as a mental process that creates a fixation point in consciousness. Surrounding this fixation point are regions of consciousness that became increasingly dark. Wundt defined attention as

> the state which accompanies the clear grasp of any psychical context and is characterized by a special feeling. (Wundt, 1902, p. 229)

Wundt termed the mental process that brings mental contents to clear comprehension *apperception*. Today this process would be called *selective attention*. Wundt referred to the mental contents that remain unclear and indistinct as being apprehended. He described apprehension and apperception as follows:

> We shall call the entrance into the large region of consciousness—apprehension, and the elevation into the focus of attention—apperception...
> the apprehended content is that of which we are more or less darkly aware; it is always, however, above the threshold of consciousness.
> The apperceived content is that of which we are clearly aware...that which lies above the narrower threshold of attention. (Wundt, 1912, pp. 35–36)

As you look at the words on this page, the ones at your fixation point are apperceived and those on the periphery are apprehended. Within this model of attention, James McKeen Cattell (Chapter 9), the first American student to receive a Ph.D. from Wundt at Leipzig, did many experiments to investigate span or scope of attention, that is, the number of stimulus items that can be apperceived at a single glance. To do this, he used a tachistoscope, an apparatus that allows an observer to see visual stimuli for only very brief periods. In other experiments, practiced and unpracticed observers were shown an array of sixteen randomly chosen letters for one-tenth of a second. Unpracticed observers reported three to four letters, while practiced observers reported six. Practice had widened the area of apperception. Six simple impressions could be apperceived at the same instant. In 1919 one of Wundt's most eminent former students, Emil Kraepelin, applied a model of attention to the thinking of schizophrenics (Kraepelin, 1919). Kraepelin accounted for certain forms of schizophrenic behavior as being due to reduced attention, highly erratic forms of attention, or extremely limited and poorly focused attention. Kraepelin's "impaired attention" theory of schizophrenia has seen a modern revival in information-processing approaches to the illness (Silverman, 1964).

Another 10 percent of the experiments at Leipzig concerned *feeling*. Metronome beats were played to observers, who reported that certain rhythmic patterns were more pleasurable than others: there was a dimension of feeling pleasure versus displeasure. The observers also reported a slight feeling of tension as they anticipated the next beat. Thus a second dimension of feeling involving strain and relaxation was defined. Finally, at certain metronome rates observers reported mild feelings of excitement, while at others they reported feeling calm. Thus a third dimension of feeling—excitement versus calm—had been identified. These three dimensions were combined in Wundt's three-dimensional theory of feeling, which can be diagrammed as follows:

pleasantness ←——————→ unpleasantness
strain ←——————→ relaxation
excitement ←——————→ calm

Wundt and his students devoted much effort to plotting various feelings on this three-dimensional matrix. In general, their efforts were unsuccessful, but when techniques of factor analysis became available in the twentieth century, a number of dimensional approaches to meaning and emotion were developed. For instance, Osgood, Suci, and Tannenbaum (1957) described three dimensions of meaning in their semantic differential:

good ←——————→ bad
active ←——————→ passive
strong ←——————→ weak

Harold Schlosberg (1954) described the following three dimensions of emotion:

pleasantness ←——————→ unpleasantness
high ←——————→ activation
attention ←——————→ rejection

In studying feelings, the Wundtians also used a method of "paired comparisons." Feelings were compared with each other and with a standard comparison feeling. The comparisons were made along the three dimensions that had emerged from earlier observations. In addition, measures of pulse rate, breathing, and muscle tension were taken as indices of the quality of feeling. This research anticipated the psychophysiology of today.

Finally, about 10 percent of the studies reported in *Philosophische Studien* dealt with *association*. For Wundt, association was a process of combination in a passive state of attention. Single words were presented to a subject, who was required to respond with a single word. The Wundtians recorded both the response word itself and its latency. Wundt distinguished between *inner* associations based on intrinsic connections between the words (e.g., "lion-animal," "spear-shield," "cow-milk," and "white-black") and *outer* connections based on accidental, extrinsic connections which are often the product of a person's individual history (e.g., "curve-accident" and "father-hate"). Suggestive support for the greater clinical significance of these associations was provided by Emil Kraepelin, who found that a subject under the influence of alcohol would increase the number of outer associations.

While Wundt directed research in his Leipzig laboratory, much of the day-to-day supervision was provided by his official assistants (Boring, 1957). Fifteen men held that position, including Cattell from 1885 to 1886 and Oswald Külpe (Chapter 6) from 1886 to 1893. Students usually worked on assigned experiments that were often replications of earlier work. Danziger (1985) compared the psychological experiment as a social institution at Leipzig and in contemporary research laboratories. He found striking differences in the roles of subjects and experimenters. Today there is a clear difference in power and status favoring the experimenter. Psychologists "run" their subjects, who often sign up for an experiment to meet a course requirement or receive a small payment. The experimenter is clearly in charge. The subject does what he or she is instructed to do and then receives either a participation credit or a payment. In Wundt's laboratory the subject's role was considered more important than that of the experimenter, since the subject was the data source. Subjects were highly trained, psychologically sophisticated members of the Leipzig laboratory. Sometimes they would alternate in the roles of subject and experimenter; at other times the subject and the experimenter were the same person. Especially in the laboratory's early years, Wundt himself was often the subject. "Subject" was but one term used in Leipzig reports, others being "reactor," "observer," "participant," and "individual under observation." Research in Wundt's laboratory was intensive and cooperative, conducted with a small group of people. Danziger (1985) concluded that current role patterns in psychological experiments come not from Leipzig but from studies in France on experimental hypnosis by medical investigators such as Jean Charcot (Chapter 11).

WUNDT AS ADVISER

A wide variety of experiments were done at Leipzig. Without a large number of students, such a volume of research would not have been possible. While liberal in some respects, Wundt's practice in his laboratory was to assign research problems and dissertation topics to the students, who were to use the approach he defined. Leipzig in the late nineteenth century was the center of the new science of psychology, and one of Wundt's most important contributions to the development of psychology was the students he influenced. One of the first was William James. As early as 1867 James wrote to a friend:

> It seems to me that perhaps the time has come for psychology to be a
> Science—some measurements have already been made in the region lying
> between the physical changes in the nerves and the appearance of
> consciousness....I am going to study what is already known, and perhaps
> may be able to do some work on it. Helmholtz and a man named Wundt at
> Heidelberg are working at it and I hope, if I live through this winter, to go
> to them in the summer. (James, 1867, quoted by Roback, 1961b, p. 76)

James did live through the winter and spent some time with Wundt. However, as we will see in Chapter 9, James quickly concluded that Wundt's psychology was not what he was looking for. Other students found their Leipzig experience more worthwhile. Between 1875 and 1919 Wundt directed 186 Ph.D. theses (Tinker, 1932). Of these, seventy were in philosophy and the remainder were on psychological topics (Fernberger, 1933). The majority of these students (136) were from Germany and Austria. Reading their names, Samuel Fernberger (1933) recognized only thirty-four of them. Why did many more of Wundt's students not attain psychological prominence? Possibly they would be better known to German psychologists, or perhaps, as Fernberger speculated, for most of these students a Ph.D. degree led to a career in the German *Gymnasium* system, in which research was not encouraged or required, and so they did not contibute to the psychology literature. However, Wundt did have some notable European students.

In addition to Emil Kraepelin, who has been mentioned, Hugo Münsterberg, whose career will be described in more detail in Chapter 5, made early advances in applied psychology. Wundt's students from France included Viktor Henri, who collaborated with Alfred Binet in formulating the first intelligence tests (Chapter 11), and B. Bourdon, who in 1896 founded the second French psychological laboratory at Rennes. From Russia, Vladimir M. Bekhterev, one of Pavlov's contemporaries, developed a unique theory of conditioning and a system of psychology. Wundt's students from England included the great statistician Charles Spearman as well as the individual responsible for bringing a refined version of the Wundtian system to America, Edward Titchener. These are important names in the history of psychology, but Hugo Eckener was the most famous of all Wundt's German doctoral students. He commanded the dirigible *Graf Zeppelin* on its many flights around the world, was honored with two ticker-tape parades in New York City, and was voted the best-known man in the world in a 1930s newspaper poll. The *New York Times* ranked Eckener as an explorer in a class with Robert E. Peary, Roald Amundsen, Ernest Shackleton, and Richard E. Byrd and as an aviator in a class with Charles Lindbergh (Vaeth, 1958). Doing his dissertation research on the effects of irritation and annoyance on attention, Eckener received his Ph.D. from Wundt in 1893.

Sixteen students from Canada and the United States received their degrees from Wundt. James McKeen Cattell, who later developed a prominent theory of personality, and Harry Kirke Wolfe, who established the Department of Psychology at the University of Nebraska, both received their degrees from Wundt in 1886 (Benjamin, 1987). Frank Angell, Edward Scripture, and Edward Pace, who founded psychology laboratories at Stanford, Yale, and Catholic University, respectively, all received their degrees from Wundt in 1891. The first psychological clinic in the United States was founded in 1896 by Lightner Witmer, a Wundtian student who received his degree in 1893 (McReynolds, 1987). The founder of the psychological laboratory at the University of California, George Stratten, and the founder of the Department of Educational Psychology at the University of Chicago and the psychology laboratory at New York University, Charles Judd, both received degrees from Wundt in 1896. Judd also translated Wundt's *Outline of Psychology* into English. In 1900, Walter Scott, who started the Department of Psychology at Tufts University, received his degree from Wundt. The chairman for twenty-four years of the Department of Psychology at the Ohio State University, George Arps, received his Ph.D. from Wundt in 1907 (Tinker, 1932). Finally, John MacEachran, a longtime faculty member at the University of Alberta, was granted a degree in 1910 (Arvidson,1971, p. 516). Blumenthal described Wundt's impact on students from other countries:

> In 1920, the year of Wundt's death, his Japanese students and followers were constructing a replica of the Leipzig laboratory at Tokyo University. It survived World War II, only to be burned in a student riot during the

1960s. In 1932, the centenary of Wundt's birth, the *Indian Journal of Psychology* and some followers of Wundt at Calcutta produced the largest commemorative volume on Wundt printed that year. (Blumenthal, 1975, p. 44)

By 1900 there were forty-three psychological laboratories in the United States, twelve of which had been founded by Wundt's doctoral or nondoctoral students (Garvey, 1929). Four of the first five distinguished psychologists listed by Cattell in 1903—James, Cattell, Münsterberg, and Hall—had studied at Leipzig with Wundt. Wundt so influenced the first generation of American psychologists that the majority of American students of psychology can probably trace their historical lineage back to him (Boring & Boring, 1948). Few of these psychologists remained true to Wundt's teachings and approach to psychology, but nevertheless they had received their PhDs from him. Wundt not only founded psychology but also trained a substantial cohort of the first generation of psychologists.

WUNDT AS WRITER

Throughout his career Wundt was a prolific writer. His first three books were followed in 1880 and 1883 by two volumes of his *Logic*, which went into four editions. His *Ethics* (1896) went into five editions, and his *Grundriss der Psychologie* (Foundations of Psychology) (1896), went into fifteen editions. In 1889 he published his *System der Philosophie*, and between 1900 and 1920 he published the ten-volume *Völkerpsychologie*, of which more will be said shortly. Finally, his *Einführung in die Psychologie* (Introduction to Psychology) came out in 1911, and in 1920 *Erlebtes und Erkanntes* (What I Have Experienced and Discovered) was published. His bibliography includes 491 items. Boring (1957) computed a total of 53,735 published pages, giving Wundt an average publication rate throughout his career of 2.2 pages per day, or one word for every two minutes, day and night for sixty-eight years (Boring, 1957, p. 345). Watson estimated that the average reader at the rate of sixty pages a day would need nearly two and a half years to go through Wundt's entire works (Watson, 1968, p. 272). Surely this prodigious output will never be matched. If nothing else, it shows Wundt's industry, and it is especially impressive when one learns that for the last half of his life Wundt suffered from strabismus of the right eye, which made writing and reading difficult. Cattell loaned Wundt one of the newly invented American typewriters. In 1883 Wundt bought his own typewriter and used it thereafter for all his writing. Richard Avenarius (Chapter 6) suggested that Cattell's was "an evil gift for with it Wundt wrote twice as many books as would otherwise have been possible" (Avenarius quoted by Cattell, 1921, p. 158). Though Cattell's typewriter wasn't a gift, Wundt did indeed write twice as quickly after he acquired a machine of his own (Hillix & Broyles, 1980, p. 432).

Despite this prolific output, Wundt's works are little read today. Only disconnected segments have been translated into English, and his writing style in German produces immediate discouragement. G. Stanley Hall described Wundt's writing style as being as solid as lead but just as lusterless; George Miller referred to Wundt's genius as "the kind Thomas Edison described as one percent inspiration and ninety-nine percent perspiration" (Miller, 1962, p. 24). In a letter to Stumpf, James described Wundt as aiming to be "a sort of Napoleon of the intellectual world. Unfortunately he will never meet his Waterloo for he is a Napoleon without genius and with no central idea which, if defeated, brings down the whole fabric in ruin." According to James, while critics were able "to make mincemeat of some of his views, he is meanwhile writing a book on an entirely different subject. Cut him up like a worm and each fragment crawls" (James, 1887, in Perry, 1935, vol. II, p. 68). Even Titchener admitted:

> Wundt's style has often, of later years, been termed diffuse and obscure. I should not care to call it either of these things; but I am sure that it is difficult. It has, perhaps, in a somewhat unusual degree, the typical characteristics of scientific German; the carelessness of verbal repetitions, the long and involved sentences, the lapses into colloquialism and what not. (Titchener, 1904, in Hillix & Marx, 1974, p. 118)

Wundt's Lifelong Interest

The project that concerned Wundt most during the last two decades of his life was his *Völkerpsychologie* (Cultural or Ethnic Psychology), published in ten volumes between 1900 and 1920. This major work has been largely ignored by historians of psychology. Boring (1929), in his 700-page *History of Experimental Psychology*, gave it less than a page. Recently, however, much more attention has been paid to this work, which was clearly a major undertaking (Blumenthal, 1975, 1979; Mueller, 1979). But the question remains: Why has the *Völkerpsychologie* been so neglected? Blumenthal's explanation is that rather than reading Wundt directly, psychologists have developed a number of "myths of origins," which are passed on from one generation to the next and which do not include the *Völkerpsychologie*. Another explanation is that much of our knowledge of the history of psychology comes from Boring's classic *History of Experimental Psychology* (1929). History may repeat itself, but historians repeat each other. Boring dedicated his book to his teacher, Titchener, describing him as experimental psychology's "historian par excellence," and offered his work with "great diffidence" as a "poor substitute" for the book Titchener should have written. Boring reflected Titchener's view that the *Völkerpsychologie* was of little importance. Titchener had said of it:

> I wish, however, to linger a little over the *Völkerpsychologie* in order to protest a belief, current in recent years and in some measure encouraged by Wundt himself, which I take to be grounded at best in a half truth. A legend has grown up—I cannot call it anything else—to the effect that social psychology was Wundt's first and fondest love, and that all of his life up to about 1890, was spent in clearing intruders out of the way, that he might ultimately return to it. In part the long stretch of years devoted to the *Völkerpsychologie* may be responsible; in part, as I have just said, certain statements of Wundt's own subscription; I should not accept this legend if it came with Wundt's own subscription; I should mistrust an old man's

memory. I do not think that anyone can accept it who knows intimately the course of Wundt's development as his books portray it. (Titchener, 1921b, p. 169)

Titchener dismisses the ten volumes of *Völkerpsychologie* as being due to nothing more than Wundt's lifelong weakness for "troublesome subjects of a certain sort" (Titchener, 1921b, p. 169). In a remarkable footnote, Titchener states that during his second year as a graduate student at Leipzig, he "succeeded in pigeonholing Wundt" (1921b, p. 170). The *Völkerpsychologie* did not fit into the pigeonhole Titchener had made for Wundt, and so he ignored it. As a result, our perception of Wundt's interests through the years may not be accurate. Contrary to Titchener's assertions, Wundt had long been interested in topics that he felt could not be studied experimentally. Wundt had defined "folk or ethnic psychology" in the introduction to his first book, *Beiträge zur Theorie der Sinneswahrnehmung* (Contributions Toward a Theory of Sense Perception), published in 1862, and in the *Principles of Psychology* he elaborated on his concept of ethnic psychology:

> There are other sources of psychological knowledge, which become accessible at the very point where the experimental method fails us. There are certain products of the common mental life, in which we may trace the operation of determinate psychical motives; chief among them are language, myth and custom. In part dependent upon historical conditions, they are also, in part, dependent upon universal psychological laws; and the phenomena that are referable to those laws form the subject-matter of a special psychological discipline, *ethnic* psychology. (Wundt, 1904, p. 4)

Blumenthal found other evidence of Wundt's interest in a broad range of psychological topics:

> More than any other single work, the early "Vorlesungen" reflects the breadth and direction of Wundt's interests. Already in the early 1860's, his studies of *Völkerpsychologie* (cultural psychology) were developed. And this "Vorlesungen" of 1863 contains as much on society, or on comparative psychology, aesthetics, language, or emotion, as on anything else. (Blumenthal, 1979, p. 548)

As we have seen, *Vorlesungen über die Menschen und Thierseele* (Lectures on the Human and Animal Mind) was Wundt's second book. It had grown out of a course he had offered during his early teaching career at the University of Heidelberg, "Psychology as a Natural Science." It was probably during this time that Wundt developed his philosophy that experimental and ethnic psychology must be supplemented by comparative and child psychology. Much later in his life, he wrote in the ten-volume *Völkerpsychologie* that studies of animals were important because

> the animal kingdom exhibits a series of mental developments which may be regarded as antecedents to the mental development of man, for the mental life of animals shows itself to be throughout, in its elements and in the

general laws governing the combination of the elements, the same as the
mental life of man. (Wundt, 1902, p. 308)

In a similar vein Wundt advocated psychological studies of children. Such studies
would describe the development of complex mental processes.

Two of the ten volumes of *Völkerpsychologie* concern language, two cover myth
and religion, two are on society, and one each is on art, law, culture, and history.
It is impossible to summarize a ten-volume book, but suffice it to say that at least
for Wundt's study of language, Blumenthal (1970) concluded that his work is an
important historical contribution to the development of psycholinguistics.

WUNDT THE MAN

Opinions about Wundt's personality differ. In another letter to Stumpf, James described Wundt as the very "model of a German professor" and "the finished example of how much *mere* education can do for a man" (emphasis in the original;
James, 1887, in Perry, 1935, vol. 2, p. 69). Hall (1924) gave an unflattering portrait
of the Wundt he encountered at Leipzig, describing him as "an indefatigable worker
and we rarely saw him outside his laboratory although even there he spent little time
and did little work, most of it being done in his study at home. He also impressed
me as being rather inept in the use of his hands" (Hall, 1924, p. 206). Even Titchener
described Wundt as "humorless, indefatigable and aggressive" (Titchener, 1921b,
p. 175), but more often he and other students were generous in their praise of
Wundt. Titchener gave a warm account of the first Christmas he spent in Leipzig
with Wundt and his English-speaking wife, Sophie. He remembered Wundt as
being

> unassuming, cordial, tolerant; by no means given to monologue; showing
> frequent flashes of a pleasant, wholly academic humor. There was no trace,
> as one sat with him in his own study, of the roaring lion of controversy or
> the somewhat Olympian arbiter of science and philosophy. (Titchener,
> 1921b, pp. 175–176)

Wundt showed his sense of humor in his recollection of a school examination
in psychology that he attended. The schoolmaster had brewed his own psychology,
which he required his pupils to learn by heart. In the course of the examination,
each question concerning the nature of the soul, life, mind, and body was answered
by the student with the utmost exactness. When Wundt was asked later by another
master whether the pupils were "well up" in psychology, he replied, "Yes indeed,
out of all those questions I could not have answered one" (Wundt, 1877, quoted by
Blumenthal, 1979, p. 550). Wundt must have been kind to his own students during
their examinations, for Anna Berliner, Wundt's only female Ph.D., remembered
him as "the kindest and most helpful examiner I have ever experienced" (Berliner,
1971, p. 516).

Wundt deplored the stodgy atmosphere of German universities. As a lively
and stimulating lecturer who, unlike most of his colleagues, did not read prepared

material, he attracted large audiences of Leipzig undergraduates. He was one of the first lecturers at Leipzig to use lantern slides and to bring demonstrations and experimental apparatus into his classes. Just as he had done at Heidelberg, Wundt used such demonstrations and experiments to complement and support his lectures. Titchener gave the following description of Wundt's lecture style:

> Wundt would appear at exactly the correct minute—punctuality was essential—dressed all in black and carrying a small sheaf of lecture notes. He clattered up the side aisle to the platform with an awkward shuffle and a sound as if his soles were made of wood. On the platform was a long desk where demonstrations were performed. He made a few gestures—a forefinger across his forehead, a rearrangement of his chalk—then faced his audience and placed his elbows on the bookrest. As he talked his arms and hands moved up and down pointing and waving, in some mysterious way illustrative. His head and body were rigid, and only the hands played back and forth. He seldom referred to the few jotted notes. As the clock struck the hour, he stopped, and stooping a little, clattered out as he had clattered in. (Titchener, quoted by Miller, 1962, pp. 19–20)

Wundt was to teach more than 24,000 undergraduates in this manner. Later, at Cornell University, Titchener, in the style of his teacher, was to clatter in and out of *his* lectures.

In 1889 Wundt served as the University of Leipzig's rector, and in 1902, in recognition of his achievements and contributions, the city of Leipzig made him an honorary citizen. However, during the last two decades of his life Wundt gradually withdrew from experimental psychology. Wilhelm Wirth was appointed codirector of the Leipzig institute in 1908, leaving Wundt free to concentrate on his *Völkerpsychologie* and other books. Wundt retired from the University of Leipzig in 1917.

Wundt retained an intense interest in politics throughout his life. During World War I he ardently supported the German cause with pamphlets and articles, insisting that Germany had been forced to enter the war because its existence as a great power had been threatened. In September 1914, Wundt gave a speech at the University of Leipzig in which he adamantly argued that the war was due to a conspiracy by the participants in the entente cordiale: England, France, and Russia. Wundt believed that those powers were motivated by envy and jealousy, a desire for revenge, and a dream of power, respectively. Of the three, England, and especially its late king, Edward VII, were the archvillans, responsible for the war. Wundt said:

> But the chief guilt for kindling this world conflagration lies with England. Without the instigation of the English, without English money and the English fleet, there would at least have been contact within the limits in which an honorable trial of strength had always seemed possible. England first made it into a world war. (Wundt, 1915, p. 11)

After his death, the *Times* of London stated that Wundt would have been more honored had he died earlier (Cattell, 1921, p. 158). Small wonder that Titchener referred to Wundt's wartime writings and activities as something psychologists "can only try to forget" (Titchener, 1921b, p. 163).

WUNDT IN PERSPECTIVE

Since Wundt began performing experiments independent of classroom demonstrations in his laboratory in 1879, and since he is often given credit for founding psychology as a discipline separate from both philosophy and physiology, the American Psychological Association selected 1979 as the centennial year of psychology. Yet Blumenthal characterized Wundt as the founding father of psychology that most psychologists have never known (Blumenthal, 1979). Why? Wundt is usually remembered as an advocate of a rather narrow approach to psychology—introspection—and as a strict experimentalist. But as we have seen in this chapter, his psychology was quite broad; his early *Vorlesungen* and his later *Völkerpsychologie* are testaments to his lifelong interest in a wide range of topics that could not be studied using a strict experimental approach and controlled introspection. Wundt was not merely an elementist interested only in the structure of the mind. That description would fit Wundt's student, Titchener, much better, and it is from Titchener that we have received many of our ideas about Wundt. It is no wonder that Wundt's son, Max Wundt, described the picture of his father's work in most psychology texts as nothing more than a caricature (M. Wundt, 1944).

Wundt died peacefully on August 31, 1920, two weeks after his eighty-eighth birthday. As we have seen, his many students, especially those from America, went on to found psychological laboratories and departments of psychology. Two of his students from Europe, Edward Titchener and Hugo Münsterberg, also had major roles in the early development of psychology in America. Ironically, Titchener's approach and work are remembered, but he no longer has a following, whereas the work of Münsterburg has been largely forgotten, but the concerns that he had and the approach that he took are being taken up by contemporary psychologists.

Edward Titchener. (Brown Brothers)

5

Edward Titchener and Hugo Münsterberg

Edward Titchener and Hugo Münsterberg both came to the United States in 1892, where each directed a major psychological laboratory and became an influential figure in American psychology. Though neither man became an American citizen, both lived the remainder of their lives in this country. There, however, the similarity ends.

Titchener's psychology became more restricted and inflexible than that of his teacher, Wilhelm Wundt. Anything that could not be studied using rigidly controlled introspection was excluded by Titchener from the domain of psychology. Consequently, there was no room for Wundt's cultural anthropology, comparative psychology, and child psychology within the Titchenerian system. Titchener adopted only one aspect of Wundt's psychology—the study of sensation by trained introspection—refined it, and turned it into what he termed *structuralism*, the study of the structure of the conscious mind.

Münsterberg's psychology was broader, more varied, and less amenable to the academic rigor that dominated everything Titchener did. In contrast to Titchener, Münsterberg played his life on a large stage, the friend of presidents and kaisers, a major public figure, a controversial speaker and popular writer, and a man who, when he died in 1916, was hated by more Americans than any psychologist before or since. Münsterberg's notoriety is probably the reason why his many applications of psychological knowledge to psychotherapy and to industrial and forensic psychology have often gone unrecognized.

EDWARD BRADFORD TITCHENER (1867–1927)

Titchener was born on January 11, 1867, in the old Roman town of Chichester, Sussex, some seventy miles south of London toward the English Channel coast.

113

The town is famous for its Roman ruins, which Titchener must have explored as a boy. In fact, Titchener retained an interest in history throughout his life; his family traced its ancestry to 1532, and it included schoolteachers, lawyers, and a former mayor of Chichester.

Titchener's father died in his thirties, and during Titchener's childhood the family was financially insecure. Fortunately, Titchener was a brilliant student and won a number of scholarships, including a highly competitive one to Malvern College, an English public school. Malvern was not one of "the" public schools—Eton, Harrow, Winchester, Rugby, Charter-House, Westminster, or Shrewsbury—but it provided an excellent, if expensive, education. English public schools are in fact private and charge hefty fees. In the nineteenth century less than 1 percent of all English schoolchildren attended public schools. Yet the public school graduates, or "old boys," formed a disproportionately large part of the enrollment at British universities, particularly at the two most prestigious: Oxford and Cambridge. Titchener's family wanted him to go to Cambridge, but the independent Titchener chose Brasenose College, Oxford, and entered that university in 1885.

At Oxford, Titchener was an "exhibitioner," or scholarship holder, and wore a middle-length academic gown with sleeves rather than the shorter sleeveless gown of most Oxford undergraduates. Such subtle distinctions and marks of status were important to Titchener all his life. He always knew and insisted on the socially proper way of doing things. Years later, when the president of Cornell University invited him to dinner, Titchener refused because the president had not personally delivered the invitation. When the president protested that he was too busy for such social niceties, especially with new members of the faculty, Titchener suggested that he send the invitation with his coachman. The president complied, and Titchener attended the dinner (Boring, 1927, p. 495). Titchener invariably wore his Oxford gown to his lectures at Cornell. The gown, he said, "confers the right to be dogmatic." The entrance hall to his son's Columbus, Ohio, home was dominated by a formal portrait of Titchener in full academic regalia.

At Oxford, Titchener studied classics and philosophy, and in his fifth year he worked in the laboratory of the Oxford physiologist John Scott Burdon-Sanderson (1828–1905). He also translated the third edition of Wundt's *Physiological Psychology* into English. Titchener graduated in 1890 at the age of twenty-three with a bachelor's degree and a deep interest in the new science of physiological psychology. Later that year he traveled to Leipzig to study under Wundt. Titchener was fluent in German, was an admirer of German culture and society, and had been impressed by Wundt's psychology. Titchener took his translation with him to Leipzig, hoping to publish it, but found that the prolific Wundt was about to publish a fifth edition. His time at Leipzig confirmed Titchener's commitment to the new science of psychology. He received a Ph.D. degree from Wundt in 1892 and for the rest of his life considered himself a true Wundtian. It comes as something of a surprise to find that Titchener spent just two years at Leipzig, but those years had a lasting effect.

After receiving his degree, Titchener served as an extension lecturer in biology at Oxford for a couple of months (he had published ten papers on biology and so was qualified to do so). No doubt he hoped for a regular position, but psychology was not taught at Oxford. Frank Angell, an American fellow student at Leipzig, had established a laboratory of psychology at Cornell, supported by a bequest from a person interested in phrenology. When Angell accepted a position at Stanford University, he recommended Titchener to Cornell. Titchener arrived at Cornell in 1892. After Oxford and Leipzig, he must have found Cornell a strange and alien environment. The campus had a raw, unfinished look (Boring, 1927). Margaret Floy Washburn recalled a European visitor's description of his time at Cornell as "a year in the wilderness" (Washburn, 1932, p. 341). Perhaps this alien environment caused Titchener to become even more dependent on his Oxford-Leipzig past than would have been the case at a well-established university. He was to remain at Cornell until his death thirty-five years later but was always "an Englishman who represented the German psychological tradition in America" (Boring, 1957, p. 410).

Titchener had accepted Wundt's psychology without reservation. At Cornell, he modeled not only his psychology but also his laboratory and lifestyle on Wundt's. Edwin G. Boring (1927) suggested that Titchener acquired many of his attributes and characteristics from Wundt, and that certainly seems to have been true. But it is also true that they were acquired from the Wundt Titchener remembered and might not have reflected the actual Wundt. Nevertheless, they are important in understanding Titchener and his psychology.

Titchener's Version of Wundt

A similarity that Titchener most certainly shared with Wundt was the use of demonstrations in his lectures. At Cornell, these often were elaborate, full-scale productions requiring the work of a number of assistants. Titchener insisted that he give the elementary lectures as well as the advanced ones and that the laboratory staff attend them. Titchener's student, Boring, described his professor's lecturing style as follows:

> In the first semester on Tuesday and Thursday at eleven he lectured to the undergraduates in the new lecture-room in Goldwin Smith Hall, the room with a psychological demonstration laboratory and an office built off it, and with the pitch of the seats determined by Titchener's stature. The demonstration was set out the hour before, and Titchener arrived shortly after ten to inspect it. Later the staff gradually gathered in his office. When the time of the lecture arrived, he donned his gown, the assistant brushed his coat for fear of ashes from the ever-present cigar, the staff went out the door for apparatus and took front seats, and Titchener then appeared on the platform from the office-door. The whole rite was performed pleasantly and sometimes jokingly; yet it was scrupulously observed. After the lecture the staff gathered in Titchener's office for an hour for talk and at one o'clock dispersed for lunch. (Boring, 1927, p. 500)

Often Titchener, just as Wundt had done, used these introductory lectures to present for the first time new findings from the laboratory or new developments in his system. Titchener was a powerful lecturer who attracted large numbers of under-graduate students. What must their reactions to his psychology have been?

Like his teacher, Titchener was a prolific writer. His bibliography of 216 items (Dallenbach, 1928) includes six major books, the most important of which was his *Experimental Psychology*, whose four volumes were published between 1901 and 1905. Titchener had a didactic writing style and certainly never overestimated the psychological sophistication of his readers. Since they were "beginners" in psychology who needed to follow a "primer" or "text," everything was spelled out and explained.

Titchener also trained a large number of students in his laboratory. Between 1894 and 1927, fifty-eight students received Ph.D. degrees from him. Perhaps his best known student was Edwin G. Boring (1886–1968), the author of *A History of Experimental Psychology*, published in 1929, and the president of the American Psychological Association (APA) in 1928 (Stevens, 1968).

Like Wundt, Titchener defined the problems his students should study and dictated the methodology they should use, but he was even less flexible in polemics and controversies in which the basic assumptions of his psychological system were challenged. Persistently, Titchener made certain that he and his students in the Cornell laboratory followed the "true" psychology, allowing no room for the diversity of his teacher's *Völkerpsychologie*. Consequently, for Titchener more than for Wundt, psychology was an experimental, laboratory, "brass instrument" science. He made a considerable effort to build up his laboratory and published a number of papers describing it as the model psychological laboratory.

Titchener's Psychological System: Structuralism

At Cornell Titchener taught his students the experimental psychology he had learned at Leipzig, defining it in a stream of papers and books. For Titchener, psychology was "the science of the mind" (Titchener, 1916, p. 2). Furthermore, it was the study of the normal, human, adult mind, not the study of the minds of children, animals, or the insane. Titchener's psychology was concerned with the generalized mind, not with individual minds. Titchener seemed never to tire of warning the reader that what psychologists mean by mind and what the layperson means are very different. The layperson's conception of the mind is that it is something inside the head that thinks, learns, and remembers—an internal, mental mannikin. Such a conception, Titchener said, is fruitless. In explaining thinking, for example, as being due to the activity of the mind, we have in fact explained nothing. We are still left with the problem of accounting for the actions of the mental mannikin. For Titchener (1916, p. 18), psychology as the science of the mind had a threefold task: to analyze the sum total of mental processes, identify their elements, and show how they go together; to discover the laws determining the connections between these elements; and to work out in detail the correlations of the mind and nervous system.

Titchener spent the bulk of his career on the first task: determining the elements that make up the structure of the mind. In the process, he defined his approach to psychology as *structuralism*. Titchener used this term for the first time

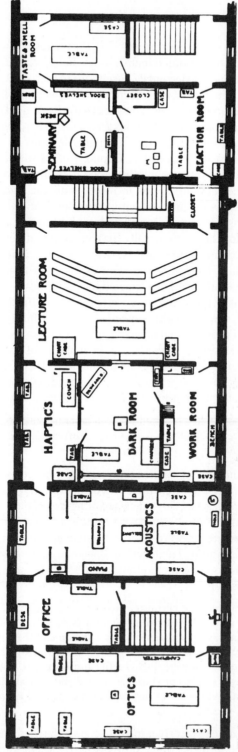

Titchener's research laboratory at Cornell, first occupied in 1895. (From "A Century of Psychology: From Subject to Object to Agent" by W. Kessen and E. D. Cahan, 1986, *American Scientist, 74*, p. 644. Reprinted by permission.)

in 1898 in a paper in which he contrasted "The Postulates of Structural Psychology" with the approach of the functionalists—psychologists such as John Dewey and Frank Angell who opposed elemental conceptions of human experience (Chapter 10). However, neither Titchener nor the functionalists were the first psychologists to use the terms *structural* and *functional*. These terms were first used in reference to the human mind by William James in 1890 in his *Principles of Psychology* (Chapter 9).

To study the structure of the mind, Titchener felt that psychology must do what all sciences do: start with careful descriptions of its subject matter. Mental processes must be observed directly and described in terms of observed facts. The observational technique, of course, was introspection—the rigorous, demanding technique of disinterested, experimental self-observation that Titchener had learned from Wundt in Leipzig. Titchener considered most ordinary, commonsense observations worthless, for they were usually inaccurate and almost always involved what he called the "stimulus error"; that is, they were descriptions of the physical event itself rather than of the mental experiences resulting from the event. They were mediate interpretations—"I saw a green light" or "I heard a pleasant tone"—rather than descriptions of the *immediate* experience per se. Furthermore, objective observation is difficult, even for highly trained observers. Children, the insane, and animals were unable to provide such objective introspections and so were excluded from Titchener's "pure" psychology, as were the majority of ordinary adults. Part of the mystique of science derives from its methods, and Titchener intended the methods of psychology to be as exclusive and demanding as those of any other science. Titchener quoted with approval Thomas Huxley's comment

> There is not one person in a hundred who can describe the commonest
> occurrence with even an approach to accuracy. (Huxley, quoted by
> Titchener, 1916, p. 20)

To ensure his students' accuracy in describing their conscious experiences, Titchener drilled them in what he called "hard introspective labor." Certain introspections were defined as correct and certain others as erroneous, with the final authority being Titchener himself. Such a procedure is never a satisfactory method for science, and its weaknesses were soon to become apparent.

Margaret Floy Washburn, Titchener's first woman graduate student, described the appeal of this introspective method and also what she and many other psychologists saw as its limitations:

> To a person with a liking for chemistry the idea of introspectively analyzing
> mental states into irreducible elements had attraction, yet one could not
> forget James' conception of consciousness as a stream and the impossibility
> that it should be at once a stream and a mosaic. I never followed Titchener
> when he developed his elaborate, highly refined introspective analysis and
> not one of the doctor's theses produced at Cornell and later at Clark [under
> John Wallace Baird] by the use of this method had any real appeal for me.
> (Washburn, 1932, p. 343)

To facilitate accurate and correct introspections, Titchener used experiments that allowed systematic introspections to be isolated, varied, and controlled. The experimental methods of psychology were described in the four volumes of his *Experimental Psychology* (1901–1905). The work's subtitle was *A Manual of Laboratory Practice,* and Titchener intended it to be used as a laboratory manual of drill exercises by both students and instructors. He considered most of the instructors of his time unqualified to teach psychology and so wrote two manuals for students and two *thicker* ones for their teachers. These manuals remained the standard laboratory manuals in psychology for more than thirty years. Oswald Külpe (Chapter 6) is said to have regarded them as "the most erudite psychological works in the English language" (Boring, 1957, p. 413). John Watson (Chapter 12) reportedly admitted that he "did not know a great deal of experimental psychology until the manuals fell into my hands" (Wickens, 1980, p. 3), and Boring described them as "encyclopedic and astonishingly accurate" (Boring, 1927, p. 497). Perhaps so, but looking through the books today, one cannot help but wonder how many students and instructors, even in Titchener's time, actually read them.

The Elements of Consciousness

According to Titchener, when immediate experiences are described correctly using introspection, we are aware only of sensations, images, and feelings. In his descriptions of the elements of consciousness, Titchener was influenced by the views of the British associationists (Chapter 2). Sensations are the "feels" of our perceptual world and come from objects that are not physically present—what the British associationists called ideas. Both sensations and images, according to Titchener, have the following characteristics:

1. A particular *quality,* which we describe as the "blueness" of a light, the "highness" of a tone, the "sweetness" of a taste, and so on. These qualities allow distinctions to be made between one sensation or image and another.
2. *Intensity,* or the strength or degree of the sensation or image.
3. *Protensity* or *duration,* or the time the sensation or image lasts.
4. *Vividness* or *attensity,* or the degree of separation between foreground and background in our mental processes.
5. *Extensity,* or the extent or "spread-outness" of a sensation or image.

The third class of mental elements, according to associationists, are the feelings—the emotional reactions that accompany certain mental experiences. Titchener (1916) agreed that feelings are elements of mental life but rejected Wundt's three-dimensional theory of feeling since it was based on psychophysiological data, which were unacceptable, and because Titchener's own introspections did not yield the three dimensions of pleasantness ↔ unpleasantness, strain ↔ relaxation, and calm ↔ excitement (Chapter 4) Wundt had described but produced only quality, intensity, and duration. Sensations, images, and feelings were to Titchener the fundamental elements from which all mental events are composed. According to Titchener, everything that occurs in consciousness is reducible to these three elements. Complex mental states are always combinations of these basic elements.

Titchener's analyses of attention and meaning provide good illustrations of his approach to psychological topics. Consider his views on attention. What is the basis of attention? The commonsense reply is that the mind attends. The mind does something that allows us to perceive certain things more clearly; it acts to focus our attention. Titchener, however, rejected such an account for two reasons. First, it is part of the mental mannikin theory, which was of no value. Second, his introspections did not yield descriptions of the act of attending. This led to a bitter controversy with Titchener's former teacher, Külpe. After leaving Leipzig, Külpe established a laboratory at Würzburg (Chapter 6). The introspections of Külpe and his students reliably yielded descriptions of such mental acts (Chapter 6). According to Titchener, careful introspections—one might add "Cornell introspections"— show that when we attend, certain sensations or ideas become more vivid and distinct while others remain dim and unfocused. Attention results from a patterning of consciousness, with certain events coming to the foreground while others remain in the dim background. However, we are never consciously aware of our actions in attending. We are aware only of the changed sensations that result from attention. Consequently, for Titchener, attention is only something that we *attribute* to our experiences—it has an "attributive status"; we never experience it directly.

Just as Titchener and his students were unable to observe the processes of attention during their introspections, they were also unable to observe meaning. What, then, is meaning? Titchener concluded that it is the result of context, the fringe of mental processes that surrounds the central sensations and images. Titchener gave the following example of the effects of context. If a particular word that initially has meaning is repeated over and over again, it eventually becomes meaningless (Titchener, 1916, p. 26). The central core of the perception is stripped of its context and so comes to lack meaning. For Titchener, meaning is what the word had before this happened. Like attention, it is something we attribute to our conscious experiences, in this case as a result of the context in which the sensation or image occurs. Meaning is an "attributional plus" factor. Titchener further pointed out that the semantic, syntactical context of a language determines and defines the meaning of particular sounds. Thus sounds have different meanings in the context of different languages and even, as with homonyms, in the same language.

Over the years Titchener's psychology grew increasingly restricted, becoming more and more a "pure psychology" limited to introspective analysis of the human mind. Titchener had no sympathy for the increasingly applied bent of many of his colleagues. He called the mental tests of James McKeen Cattell, Alfred Binet, and Lewis Terman (Chapter 11) "second rate and cheap." Ernst Meumann, his former roommate at Leipzig and Wundt's colleague at the Psychological Institute, had pioneered studies of educational psychology, but Titchener dismissed them as "educational technology." Münsterberg's work on industrial problems was an unfortunate example of "trading a science for a technology" (Titchener, 1928). The study of mental illness formed no part of Titchener's psychology, and he often quoted the complaint of H. G. Wells, who in one of his novels said that no sick soul could find help or relief in modern textbooks of psychology. Titchener regarded this complaint as a compliment. "Of course they do not," he said, "for psychology in its text books is concerned with the normal, human, adult mind, it is not the science of mental comfort and improvement" (Titchener, 1916, p. 2). Reluctantly, Titchener recognized the need for diverse areas of study, but they were not part of *his* psychology. He grouped together animal psychology, justice psychology, social and ethnic psychology, economic psychology, and even the psychology of plants as somehow impure and less important areas of psychology—impure, it is clear, because their subjects could not use introspection. Consider animals. They cannot introspect because they do not use language. Why do they not speak to us? According to Titchener, they do not speak

> because they have nothing to say...if animals thought, they could
> undoubtedly use their vocal organs for speech; and since they do not talk,
> they cannot either be thinking. (Titchener, 1916, p. 267)

It seemed to many of his contemporaries that Titchener had excluded most of the interesting and significant areas of psychology, but that did not bother Titchener. His aim was a pure psychology concerned with the study of mental processes using introspection. That others considered his approach restrictive and sterile simply showed how much they needed instruction and enlightenment. But Titchener's system could not endure. His instrospection was a rigid and limiting method and came to be regarded by more and more psychologists as what one of Wundt's former students, the British psychologist Charles Spearman, described as "a sort of inward staring" (Spearman, 1930, p. 332). Challenged by increasing criticism of introspection, one of Titchener's loyal followers, John Baird, arranged a widely publicized demonstration of correct introspections at the 1913 convention of the American Psychological Association. Seated on a stage in front of the entire convention, Baird's best introspectors were presented with a variety of carefully controlled stimuli. They proceeded to give dull, meaningless accounts of their sensations, images, and feelings that enlightened no one (Boring, 1953, cited by Blumenthal, 1985, p. 73). The demonstration was a dramatic failure.

The Controversial Titchener

The usual portrait of Titchener presented in histories of psychology is one of a powerful, dogmatic personality. It does indeed seem that beneath Titchener's brash, autocratic exterior lay a brash, autocratic interior. Who but Titchener would devote more than half a book review to listing errors made by the author (Titchener, 1922b)? Who but Titchener would refer to the flurry of interest in behaviorism (Chapter 12) and confidently state in 1914:

> The present hullabaloo will quiet down after a few critical papers have made
> their appearance; and then we shall get our perspective again. I do not
> belittle behaviorism by hoping that it may soon be set in its right place! But
> I get a trifle tired of unhistorical enthusiasms. (Titchener, 1914, in a letter to
> Robert Yerkes, quoted by Larson & Sullivan, 1965)

In his relationships with psychologists whose views he considered to be in error, and especially with former students who had gone their own way, Titchener could be harsh and unyielding. He was involved in a series of controversies, of which two will be considered here. A controversy over the reality of imageless thought began when Oswald Külpe and his students at the University of Würzburg, Alfred Binet in France, and Robert Woodworth in the United States independently presented evidence that thought is not an affair of sensations and images but at times is "imageless." Their studies were based on reports of thought processes that occurred while subjects performed complex mental activities, such as solving a difficult problem. In these situations, thinking seemed to occur without any experienced sensations or images. The subjects reported vague and unanalyzable "awareness" and "imageless thoughts" rather than Titchener's clear and discrete conscious elements. This was a direct challenge to Titchener, who argued that such reports were based on incorrect introspections. If only the introspections had been done properly, sensations and images would have been observed even in the situations these investigators had used. Subtle sensations and images had been overlooked. When more "careful and controlled observations" were made at Cornell University in such situations, these basic elements were said to have been revealed. Thus Titchener assimilated the finding of imageless thought into his system and remained convinced that sensations, images, and feelings are the sole elements of human consciousness. However, this "assimilation" failed to convince many psychologists.

Titchener also became embroiled in a controversy with James Mark Baldwin (1861–1934) over differences in sensory and motor reaction times. Baldwin had studied with Wundt at Leipzig but had received his Ph.D. degree in philosophy in the United States. At Leipzig, Wundt taught his students that sensory reaction times, which are obtained when a subject attends to the stimulus, are longer than muscular or motor reaction times, which occur when a subject attends to the reaction. The difference was on the order of one-tenth of a second and was a reliable and consistent finding in the Leipzig laboratory. Titchener accepted this finding as valid; Baldwin did not. In the United States Titchener did similar reaction time experiments using highly trained and experienced observers and found exactly the result reported by Wundt. Baldwin ran the experiment with unpracticed, untrained observers and often obtained exactly the opposite result: muscular reaction times were longer. He argued that his finding was the true, natural, and real result and that the Leipzig-Cornell results were artificial and unnatural. Further, he emphasized individual differences in reaction times and stressed their importance and significance. Psychology, said Baldwin, should adopt an evolutionary point of view and study the reality and significance of such differences rather than embarking on a futile search for the elements of the generalized human mind. Titchener dismissed Baldwin's findings and interpretations as the product of sloppy research with untrained observers. However, in Baldwin, Titchener met a formidable adversary whose rhetoric was more than a match for his own. Consider the following passage from one of Baldwin's papers on reaction times:

> The attempt to rule these results out on the ground of incompetency in the reagents [subjects] is in my opinion a flagrant *argumentum in circulo*. Their

contention is that a certain *Anlage* or aptitude is necessary in or to experimentation on reaction times. And when we ask what the *Anlage* is, we are told that the only indication of it is the ability of the reagent to turn out reactions which give the distinction between motor and sensory time, which Wundt and his followers consider the proper one. In other words, only certain cases prove their result, and these cases are selected because they prove that result. It is easy to see that this manner of procedure is subversive both of scientific method and of safely acquired results in individual psychology. (Baldwin, 1895, p. 265; for more details of this controversy, see Krantz, 1969)

In refusing to recognize individual differences in reaction times, Wundt and Titchener, said Baldwin, had made the reaction time method "simply the handmaiden to dogma." Titchener's response was to have nothing more to do with Baldwin and to avoid as far as possible any contact with the *Psychological Review*, the journal that Baldwin edited.

However, with students who remained loyal, Titchener was warm and supportive. Perhaps the most loyal of all his students was Boring, who took his Ph.D. with Titchener in 1914. Boring regarded Titchener as brilliant, outspoken, domineering, and the closest to a genius he had ever encountered (Stevens, 1968, p. 591). Such was Boring's dedication that to meet a minor subject requirement, he studied for four years the regeneration of a nerve in his own forearm, which he had cut in order to trace the return of sensitivity. Years after Titchener's death Boring wrote the following eulogy to his former teacher:

> Psychology at Cornell—at least the orthodox psychology that centered in the laboratory—revolved around and was kept in orbit by the personality of E. B. Titchener. What a man! To me he has always seemed the nearest approach to genius of anyone with whom I have been closely associated. I used to watch my conversations with him, hoping that I might gain some insight into why his thinking was so much better than mine....He was always ready with unexpected advice. If you had mushrooms he would tell you how to cook them. If you were buying oak for a new floor he would at once come forward with the advantages of ash. If you were engaged to be married, he would have his certain and insistent advice about the most unexpected aspects of your problems, and, if you were honeymooning, he would write, to remind you, as he did to me, on what day you ought to be back to work. Seldom did he distinguish between his wisdom and his convictions and he never hid them either. (Boring, 1952, p. 32)

Boring did admit that many of Titchener's able graduate students found his dominance and interference in their lives intolerable. When they rebelled, they were excommunicated and found themselves outside Titchener's circle. However, Boring and his wife, Lucy M. Boring, who earned a doctorate with Titchener, remained faithful to their teacher, for

> Quite early in our married life, we decided that we would accept "insults" and arbitrary control from Titchener in order to retain the stimulus and charm of his sometimes paternal and sometimes patronizing friendship. I

never broke with the master and I still feel that the credit remained on my side. (Boring, 1952, p. 33)

Ernest Hilgard gave an amusing account of Boring's devotion to Titchener:

> Once Boring was invited to dinner at Titchener's to celebrate Titchener's birthday. After dinner the cigars were passed and Boring could not refuse under the circumstances, though he had never smoked a cigar. The consequence was that he had to excuse himself presently because of his nausea and go outside to throw up. Still, the honor of having been invited once was so great that every year thereafter Titchener's birthday would be celebrated by dinner at the Boring home, followed by the smoking of a cigar, with the inevitable consequence. (Hilgard, 1987, p. 106)

Occasionally, Titchener could be surprisingly accommodating. Margaret Floy Washburn, after graduating from Vassar College, wanted to study the new psychology, and so in 1891 she went to Columbia University to study with Cattell (Chapter 9). At the time, Columbia had never admitted a woman graduate student, and Washburn was allowed to attend the university only as a "hearer." Cattell recommended her to Titchener, who arranged for her admission to Cornell. She became his first female Ph.D. in 1894 and went on to a distinguished career, serving as president of the APA in 1921 and being elected to the National Academy of Sciences in 1932. However, her psychology became very different from that of her teacher, and today she is best known for writing the first comprehensive text on comparative psychology, *The Animal Mind*, published in 1908 (Goodman, 1979).

To complete our picture of Titchener, it must be mentioned that he was a man of culture, varied interests, and civilized tastes who spoke several languages, was a brilliant conversationalist, and could be surprisingly warm and compassionate. Following the death of Hermann Ebbinghaus, Titchener movingly expressed his deep sense of loss (Chapter 6). He was also one of a very small number of psychologists who stood by Watson during his crisis period and supported him after his dismissal from Johns Hopkins University (Chapter 12).

Titchener's Contributions

So quickly did Titchener become an important figure in the early years of psychology that he is sometimes considered to have been one of the founders of the new science. Actually, psychology already had a "short history" by the time Titchener arrived in Leipzig. As early as 1860 Gustav Fechner (1801–1887), a pioneer sensory psychologist, had published his *Elements of Psychophysics*. Of course, Wilhelm Wundt had published his *Physiological Psychology* in 1874, and that same year Franz Brentano (1838–1917) (Chapter 6) had published *Psychology from an Empirical Standpoint*. William James (1842–1910) (Chapter 9) first offered a course on psychology at Harvard in 1874 in the Department of Physiology, and in 1875 he established a demonstration or teaching laboratory. Francis Galton (1822–1911) (Chapter 9) had opened the world's first psychometric clinic in London in 1882. The first International Congress of Psychology, attended by 120 psychologists, had been held in

1889. Finally, by 1890 the British journal *Mind* had been published for fifteen years, and Wundt's journal, *Philosophical Studies*, was in its sixth volume.

Rather than saying that Titchener was one of the founding fathers of psychology, it might be better to recognize that he was instrumental in bringing to America a strict empirical approach to psychology. Edward Bissel Holt (1873–1946) described Titchener as "the Dean of American empirical psychology" (Holt, 1911, p. 25). Titchener's writing of *Experimental Psychology* was an important contribution and

> helped speed the legitimization of the laboratory as a part of psychological instruction, and thus aided the acceleration of psychology's separation from philosophy. And that, for better or worse, helped make psychology what it is today. (Evans, 1979, p. 3)

Titchener's second major contribution was his role in the development of the *American Journal of Psychology*. This journal was founded by G. Stanley Hall in 1887 (Chapter 9) and edited by him until 1920. Titchener served as Hall's associate editor from 1895 to 1920 and as editor from 1921 to 1925. He resigned suddenly in 1925 and was succeeded by an editorial board of Madison Bentley, Edwin G. Boring, Karl M. Dallenbach, and Margaret Floy Washburn, all four of whom earned PhDs with Titchener. Titchener's contributions to this journal were voluminous, including major empirical and theoretical reports, minor studies and notes from the Cornell laboratory describing research by his students, frequent book reviews, restatements and translations of Wundt, comments, and notes and reflections on psychology. The journal was very much Titchener's, as his publication record from 1894 to 1928 demonstrates:

Years	Volumes	Pages	Pages by Titchener and His Students and Coworkers (%)
1894–1895	6– 7	1,240	83 (7)
1896–1900	8–11	2,412	109 (5)
1901–1905	12–16	3,078	60 (2)
1906–1910	17–21	2,938	91 (3)
1911–1915	22–26	3,024	196 (7)
1916–1920	27–31	2,495	153 (6)
1921–1925	32–36	3,104	202 (7)
1926–1928	37–39	1,764	0 (0)

While the number of psychologists during these years was small (the APA's membership was 53 in 1894, 162 in 1905, 295 in 1915, and 471 in 1925 [Cattell, 1929]), the percentage of contributions by Titchener and his students and coworkers is still impressive. In addition to these publications, Titchener was also writing books, translating works by Külpe and Wundt, and publishing in other journals, such as *Science* and *Nature*. However, Titchener refused to publish in certain journals because of his feuds with their editors or publishers. Titchener had dominated the *American Journal of Psychology* and had been its editor from 1921 to 1925. The journal had cost its owner, Karl Dallenbach, a considerable sum, and as expenses mounted, he suggested to Titchener that the journal might carry some dignified advertising, perhaps from book publishers or equipment companies. Titchener was so outraged by this proposal that he promptly resigned his editorship (Hilgard, 1987, p. 76). After this abrupt resignation Titchener, in characteristic fashion, tried to start a rival, "pure" journal of psychology, but his efforts came to naught.

Titchener was elected to membership in the APA by the twenty-six charter members (Chapter 9), attended the first annual meeting, but resigned shortly afterward over what he considered to be a matter of honor. He rejoined the APA in 1910 but did not attend the meetings or serve on the council and was never elected to the presidency. Even when the APA met at Cornell University in 1925, Titchener did not attend but instead held court for visitors at his house. Shortly after the turn of the century Titchener became concerned with what he considered to be the APA's increasingly applied bent. It seemed to him in danger of becoming an organization of mental testers, industrialists, and psychotechnicians. In 1904 Titchener organized a group of "pure" psychologists, the *Experimentalists*. He issued invitations to representatives of ten laboratories he considered to be doing orthodox psychological work, and the group met for the first time at Cornell in 1904. From then on they met each spring with Titchener controlling the meetings. Up to 1927 five of the twenty-three meetings were held at Cornell. After Titchener's death in 1927, the group changed its name to the *Society of Experimental Psychologists*, and it still meets every spring. Membership is by invitation and is considered a prestigious sign of recognition for an experimental psychologist.

Structuralism was the dominant approach to psychology in the United States, but it soon was challenged and then supplanted by newer, broader, and more flexible movements which grew out of dissatisfaction with Titchener's system. The psychologists who developed the newer approaches had Titchener's system to measure their own against, with the sure knowledge that Titchener would be quick to point out any weaknesses. Consequently, the new approaches were explicit and well defined. As Boring wrote in an appreciation of Titchener after his death:

> Not only was he unique among American psychologists as a personality and in his scientific attitude, but he was a cardinal point in the national systematic orientation. The clear-cut opposition between behaviorism and its allies, on the one hand, and something else on the other remains clear only when the opposition is between behaviorism and Titchener, mental tests and Titchener, or applied psychology and Titchener. His death thus, in a sense, creates a classificatory chaos in American systematic psychology. (Boring, 1927, p. 489)

Titchener in Perspective

During the last years of his life, Titchener became increasingly withdrawn and seems to have been a rather sad man. He was disappointed not to have been elected a fellow of the Royal Society of London or a member of the National Academy of the United States, and he was never offered the academic position he most desired, a chair at Oxford. He considered Harvard to be the most prestigious university in the United States, but when in 1917 he was offered a Harvard appointment, he turned it down and remained at Cornell. During the last decade of his life Titchener withdrew from both university life and psychology. He was rarely seen on the Cornell campus and became something of a legendary figure. Even after his death the Titchener legend and mystique continued, aided in no small part by the display of his brain in the Psychology Department at Cornell. In the years before his death, psychology was changing in ways he could not accept. Functionalism and behaviorism had become the dominant approaches, but they were not his approach, and Titchener was never convinced that they were even psychologies. In a 1926 Lowell Lecture at Clark University, Madison Bentley (1870–1955), one of Titchener's PhDs, said of his contributions:

> If we ask today who represents the psychology of "structure," I doubt whether we shall find anyone to acknowledge that his own brand is of that kind; though the epithet will often be accompanied by a gesture of indication toward a fellow-psychologist. We should all agree that no one in this country has done so much to expound the doctrine [of structuralism] as Professor Titchener has; but he has not for some time researched or written under its rubrics and he explicitly remarked some time ago that in his position, both functional and structural as qualifications of psychology are now obsolete terms. (Bentley, 1925, p. 383)

Bentley's use of the past tense in referring to Titchener and his contributions is noteworthy. During these years Titchener was rumored to be working on a major revision and updating of his psychological system. While occasional sections were published, the book never appeared; it is Titchener's final lost system (Evans, 1972). He devoted most of his time during these years to the study and collection of ancient coins, becoming an expert, and his retreat from psychology is clear. Even at Cornell his effect on the subsequent development of the psychology department was relatively small (Ryan, 1982). Bentley succeeded him as head of the department at Cornell and broadened course offerings in psychology to include abnormal, developmental, comparative, legal, and industrial psychology, along with aesthetics and language. Research activities were also considerably broadened under Bentley.

Titchener died from a brain tumor on August 3, 1927, at the age of sixty. His psychology had been formed and fixed during his two years with Wundt, and perhaps it also was influenced by his perception of himself as an alien in a foreign land whose task it was to instruct and teach. He was never a part of American psychology but was always a Wundtian at Cornell University. Even though Titchener lived in the United States for thirty-five years, he was always an Englishman with all the pleasures of background and accent. Still, he never returned to England, not even for a holiday. At times he appeared more German than many Germans and in fact was occasionally thought to be German, once by an English student. He was, as Keller said, always "an Englishman by birth, a German by temperament and an American by residence" (Keller, 1937, p. 23).

By the time of Titchener's death, it was clear to all, including, it seems, to Titchener himself, that his structuralism would not last. Psychology was changing, and Titchener's inflexible system and rigid approach could not accommodate such changes. Edna Heidbreder summed up the situation:

> If psychology as Titchener interpreted it could not maintain itself in the United States under the leadership of a man of his ability; if, with the prestige of priority and of an honorable academic tradition, it could not establish itself as the basis of future psychology and assimilate future developments to itself—that fact was significant. And to have revealed the fact is no small achievement. (Heidbreder, 1961, p. 148)

In contrast to Titchener, Hugo Münsterberg's approach to psychology was much more compatible with the concerns of contemporary psychologists. His research ideas and many of his findings are being investigated today, and he was a pioneer in developing important areas of applied psychology. For these reasons we will explore in detail the work of Münsterberg, the other European student of Wundt who immigrated to America.

HUGO MÜNSTERBERG (1863–1916)

Hugo Münsterberg was born in 1863 in Danzig, then part of Prussia but now the Polish city of Gdansk. Danzig was devastated by World War II bombing raids, but in the nineteenth century the city's architecture and location on the Baltic led to its being called the Venice of the North. Münsterberg's father was a prominent international lumber merchant—the city of Danzig had been founded centuries before by merchants—and his mother was an accomplished artist (Hale, 1980). He was one of four sons and led a happy, almost idyllic life until his mother's death when he was twelve. He then changed from a carefree boy to a serious-minded young man. Münsterberg became a prodigious reader, a writer of epic poetry, a

Hugo Münsterberg. (Culver Pictures)

student of archaeology, a reader of Greek and Arabic, the publisher of his school's magazine, a cello player in an amateur orchestra, and an actor in local theatricals, all while attending the local *Gymnasium* and following its rigorous curriculum. Münsterberg's father died in 1880. In 1882 Münsterberg graduated with distinction, joining the elite group qualified to wear the traditional red hat of the *Gymnasium* graduate (M. Münsterberg, 1922).

After a summer in Geneva and the Swiss Alps, Münsterberg entered the University of Leipzig, planning to study medicine in preparation for an academic career in science. In 1883 he attended a course of lectures by Wundt and was deeply impressed. He added psychology to his curriculum and worked as a research student in Wundt's laboratory. Wundt assigned him to experiments in which introspection was used to analyze voluntary activities. His introspections convinced Münsterberg that "will" is not represented in consciousness since the only conscious "will elements" his introspections revealed were sensations from the muscles, tendons, and joints involved in voluntary activities. Wundt did not agree. He rejected Münsterberg's findings as being due to his inexperience and set him to work on "simpler tasks." This was the first of a number of stresses and tensions between the two men. However, Münsterberg was able to complete his Ph.D. under Wundt. His 1885 dissertation was a nonexperimental, critical examination of the biological doctrine of natural adaptation. He then transferred to the University of Heidelberg and received an M.D. degree in 1887, writing a thesis on the visual perception of space. Münsterberg later recommended taking both degrees as the ideal preparation for an applied career in psychology.

Münsterberg's Early Academic Career

In 1887, Münsterberg was appointed *Privatdozent* (private lecturer) at the University of Freiburg under the familiar conditions of no regular salary but a small income from fees paid by students taking his courses. In 1888 Münsterberg published a small book, *Activity of the Will*, in which he returned to his earlier interest in will and voluntary activities. He restated the position he had formulated while working in Wundt's laboratory and once again was attacked and criticized by his former teacher, this time in public. Titchener joined in the criticism, describing Münsterberg's experiments as inexact and incomplete. In characteristic fashion Titchener concluded:

> Dr. Münsterberg has the fatal gift of writing easily—fatal especially in science, and most of all in a young science, where accuracy is the one thing most needful. (Titchener, 1891, p. 594)

A much more positive reaction came from William James, who regarded the book as an excellent piece of work. In his *Principles of Psychology*, James referred to the book as "a little masterpiece" (James, 1890, vol. 2, p. 505). James arranged to meet the young man at the First International Congress of Psychology in Paris in 1889 and was impressed by him.

At the University of Freiburg, Münsterberg established Germany's second psychological laboratory. Initially it was nothing more than a couple of rooms in his house fitted with apparatuses, but the laboratory was very productive. Münsterberg published a series of *Contributions to Experimental Psychology* (1889–1892), which again were criticized by Wundt and Titchener but were well received by James. In his *Principles*, James refers to Münsterberg's "beautiful examples of experiments on reaction time" (1890, vol. 1, p. 432) and "masterly experiments on time perception" (1890, vol. 1, p. 620). In 1891 Münsterberg was appointed assistant professor, and his laboratory was moved to the university. James arranged for one of his students, Edwin B. Delabarre, to work in Münsterberg's laboratory, and Delabarre's reports of the exciting research being done there confirmed James's opinion that Münsterberg was a promising young man. For James, Münsterberg's work also provided a welcome German alternative to the psychology and writings of Wundt.

As we will see in Chapter 9, by 1892 James had decided to give up his Harvard laboratory so that he could devote more time to his philosophical writings and lectures. He needed a young man to take over his duties and provide leadership for American psychology from Harvard, and Münsterberg was an obvious choice. In February 1892, James wrote to him as follows:

> Dear Dr. Münsterberg,
>
> Is it conceivable that if you should be invited, you might agree to come and take charge of the Psychological Laboratory and the higher instruction in that subject in Harvard University for three years at a salary of say, 3,000 dollars?

After this characteristic opening James forthrightly described the background to his offer:

> We are the best university in America, and we must lead in psychology. I, at the age of 50, disliking laboratory work naturally, and accustomed to teach philosophy at large altho I could *tant bien que mal*, make the laboratory run, yet am certainly not the kind of stuff to make a first rate director thereof. We could get younger men here who would be safe enough, but we need something more than a safe man, we need a man of genius if possible. (letter in M. Münsterberg, 1922, p. 33)

As additional inducements, James mentioned that after three years it might be possible to arrange a permanent Harvard appointment. There was a sum of $1,600 immediately available for the laboratory with further support promised, two research assistants would work in the laboratory, and Münsterberg's maximum teaching load would be less than six hours a week. This offer to a man still in his twenties was remarkable, but Münsterberg hesitated. He had a deep love for the German fatherland, was unsure about life in America, could read but not speak or understand English, and was confident of progressing within the German university system. However, after numerous letters of encouragement and a personal visit from James, Münsterberg accepted the position and sailed for America in August 1892. Arriving in Boston by train, he was met by the eminent Harvard philosopher Josiah Royce.

During his first three years at Harvard, Münsterberg, whose English was poor and who lacked confidence in his ability to speak and write the new language, was content to concentrate on laboratory work. However, by 1894 he was able to give his first public lecture at Radcliffe College and even to debate Hall before the Boston Schoolmasters' Club on the place of psychology in education. During his first years at Harvard he also wrote his first major book, which he published in German in 1900, the *Grundzüge der Psychologie* (Principles of Psychology). The book was very much a reflection of his German training, but already Münsterberg was being influenced by his American experiences. The work was dedicated to William James, and from that time on Münsterberg always "looked at the American world through German eyes with Harvard astigmatism" (M. Münsterberg, 1922, p. 326). In 1902 he published his first major book in English, *American Traits*, and from that time was a prolific author, writing more than twenty books in English, six in German, and literally hundreds of journal, magazine, and newspaper articles (Viney, Michaels, & Ganong, 1981). Münsterberg was a gifted writer of books that often appealed to the general public. He was also a very fast writer, able to compose a book in less than a month. However, it should be said that most of his writings were dictated, and Münsterberg cheerfully admitted that his secretary did the actual writing.

Münsterberg's Applied Psychology

Münsterberg always intended his psychology to be as broad and inclusive as possible and had no patience with restrictive approaches such as that of Titchener. In fact, Münsterberg consistently refused to give a precise definition of psychology since any definition would imply restrictions he did not intend and could not accept. He was interested in such functions or acts as understanding, memory, learning, empathy, and the search for beauty, love, and faith. His was a purpose-oriented functionalist psychology. For Münsterberg it was "more natural to drink the water than to analyze it in the laboratory into its chemical elements" (Münsterberg, 1914, p. 14). His lifetime interest was in the application of psychological knowledge in the service of humanity, and it is these applications that we will now consider. However, it is important to remember that Münsterberg always considered himself an experimental psychologist. Later he was to refer to patients coming for treatment to his "laboratory" and his "experiments" in industrial settings.

Münsterberg's Clinical Psychology

Münsterberg long had an interest in mental illness. He began to see patients in Germany and continued to do so in the United States. He was an unusual clinician. Never having a clinic, Münsterberg met his patients in his laboratory. He accepted only patients who were of scientific interest; of the many hundreds of people he treated, not one paid a fee (Münsterberg, 1909, p. ix). He believed that mental illness always has a physiological basis. First he made a diagnosis based on his observations of the patient's behavior, an interview, the patient's answers to his questions, and often the patient's responses to a word-association test. If he concluded that the case was of scientific interest and that the patient was not psychotic, treatment would be given. Münsterberg's approach was directive. He saw himself as the purposeful agent of therapy and sought to impose his will on the patient. He used direct suggestions and autosuggestions and encouraged the patient to "expect" to get better. Münsterberg thought that for patients "to lie down on a lounge on which hundreds have been cured fascinates the imagination sufficiently to give every suggestion a much better chance to overcome the counteridea" (Münsterberg, 1909, p. 222). Münsterberg also relied heavily on assurance. The therapist assures the patient that, for example, the patient will sleep that night, and the next day when they meet remarks how well rested the person appears. What Münsterberg termed "reciprocal antagonism" was used to overcome troublesome ideas or impulses. The opposite idea or impulse was "reinforced" to block expression of the undesirable one (Münsterberg, 1909, p. 218). Finally, Münsterberg used hypnosis, but in a conservative and guarded manner. He found that it was especially useful in facilitating receptivity to suggestions. His aim was direct relief of symptoms, not deep changes in the patient's personality. In an early publication, Münsterberg had sought to allay fears of hypnosis and of the belief in the evil eye. He stressed the beneficial effects of hypnosis in the hands of a skilled practitioner (Münsterberg, 1910).

Münsterberg reported success with these clinical techniques in the treatment of a wide range of problems: alcoholism, drug addiction, hallucinations, obsessions, phobias, and sexual disorders. These outcomes and procedures were described in his book *Psychotherapy*, published in 1909. He defined psychiatry as the "treatment of mental diseases" and described psychotherapy as the "practice of treating the sick by influencing the mental life" (Münsterberg, 1909, p. 1). As such, psychotherapy was but one of the approaches available to the psychiatrist and was not appropriate for certain types of mental disease, for example, psychoses and diseases due to deterioration of the nervous system. Of course the dominant voice in psychiatry at the time was that of Sigmund Freud (Chapter 8). Münsterberg, while seeing the value of Freud's emphasis on the traumatic origin of some hysterical symptoms and the sexual basis of many neurotic disorders, did not accept Freud's views on the importance of unconscious determinants. According to Münsterberg, "the story of the subconscious mind can be told in three words: there is none" (Münsterberg, 1909, p. 125). He also opposed general or schematic approaches to the treatment of illness. Münsterberg argued that no two cases are alike and that subtle differences between patients must always be taken into account.

Psychotherapy was written for a general audience and was intended to counter the half-truths and false information surrounding mental illness. Münsterberg began the book in April 1909, and it was published in May. By the end of June it had sold 3,000 copies, and in three years it went through five printings. It was successful for many years. Münsterberg's clinical work did, however, produce one unfortunate episode. One of his female patients developed a paranoid delusion centered on him and threatened him with a gun as he was leaving a lecture. Fortunately nobody was injured, but the resulting legal actions and publicity led President Eliot of

Harvard to advise him to forgo hypnotic treatment of women. Münsterberg agreed, though he did continue to do experimental research on abnormal behavior.

In one series of experiments Münsterberg sought conditions under which a second personality, often seen in hysterical patients, might emerge in normal people. He hoped that such a personality might influence certain automatic actions, and so he performed a number of automatic writing experiments. A subject would actively attend to an interesting story while holding a pencil on a blank page. Some subjects would write down some of the words they heard, but in an unconscious and involuntary manner. Münsterberg believed that these words were a reflection of the person's second personality. After some practice, a number of subjects, including Gertrude Stein, who was then a student at Radcliffe College, were able to focus their attention on a word four or five words behind the one actually being written. B. F. Skinner (1934) described these automatic writing experiments of Münsterberg and Gertrude Stein's role as a subject. Skinner also argued that evidence of automatic writing can be seen in Stein's later literary works and that this writing might have been a reflection of her second personality.

The Beginning of Forensic Psychology

Beginning in 1908 Münsterberg wrote numerous articles on the application of psychological information in legal situations—*forensic* psychology. The great interest in these articles and his own experiences observing a number of criminal trials led him to write a best-selling book, *On the Witness Stand*, published in 1908. The book went through numerous printings in both the United States and England, the most recent being in 1976. In the introduction, Münsterberg set the stage for this application of psychology:

> There are about fifty psychological laboratories in the United States alone. The average educated man has not hitherto noticed this. If he chances to hear of such places, he fancies that they serve for mental healing, or telepathic mysteries, or spiritistic performances. What else can a laboratory have to do with the mind? Has not the soul been for two hundred years the domain of the philosopher? What has psychology to do with electric batteries and intricate machines? Too often I have read such questions in the faces of visiting friends who came to the Harvard Psychological Laboratory in Emerson Hall and found with surprise twenty-seven rooms overspun with electric wires and filled with chronoscopes and kymographs and tachistoscopes and ergographs and a mechanic busy at his work. (Münsterberg, 1908, p. 3)

In this passage we see Münsterberg's characteristic delight in the mechanics and brass instruments of psychology as a laboratory science. While his own interests became increasingly applied, his first love remained the Harvard laboratory. He saw to it that the laboratory's work continued under Edwin Bissel Holt for the human research and Robert Mearns Yerkes (Chapter 11) for research with animals. As director of the laboratory, he was succeeded by one of his students, Herbert S. Langfeld.

In the first section of *On the Witness Stand* Münsterberg described eyewitness reports and the many psychological reasons for disagreements between equally trustworthy witnesses who are trying their best to give accurate and truthful testimony. Why does such testimony so often differ? Münsterberg explained the difference between subjective and objective truth. An oath to "tell the truth, the whole truth, and nothing but the truth" is in fact no guarantee of objective truth. Münsterberg described illusions to demonstrate how our senses can be deceived and showed how suggestions affect perceptions. He pointed out that memories are often unreliable, especially when we try to recall events from some time past. Münsterberg had testified at the trial of a burglar who had broken into his home that his house had been entered by a window, only to find that it had actually been entered by a cellar door. Even with the best of intentions, ideal conditions, and a short time span between an event and its recall, memories are often unreliable. To illustrate this surprising fact Münsterberg described a demonstration originally done at the University of Berlin:

> A few years ago a painful scene occurred in Berlin, in the University
> Seminary of Professor von Liszt, a famous criminologist. The Professor had
> spoken about a book. One of the older students suddenly shouts, "I wanted
> to throw light on the matter from the standpoint of Christian morality!"
> Another student throws in, "I cannot stand that!" The first starts up,
> exclaiming, "You have insulted me!" The second clenches his fist and cries,
> "If you say another word...." The first draws a revolver. The second
> rushes madly upon him. The Professor steps between them and, as he grasps
> the man's arm, the revolver goes off. General uproar. (Münsterberg, 1908,
> pp. 49–50)

The whole incident, in fact, had been staged, and once order was restored, the students were asked to write an account of what had happened. Their accounts were dramatically different. Münsterberg staged a number of these "uproarious scenes" before audiences of jurors and psychologists to demonstrate that our memories are often unreliable. When we are asked to recall events some time later, especially under the stressful conditions of courtroom testimony, inaccuracies are to be expected.

Münsterberg's description of Liszt's demonstration was the basis of a once popular demonstration in psychology classes: In the middle of a lecture the lecturer is suddenly accosted by a stranger who rushes into the room, accuses the lecturer of some heinous crime, pulls out a gun, and fires it; the lecturer falls to the floor, and the assailant dashes out. Then the lecturer "recovers," explains that the incident was staged, and asks the class to describe the assailant. Once again the descriptions vary greatly. This technique has become less popular, because according to an often repeated but possibly apocryphal account, a lecturer once staged this demonstration at an unnamed university only to have a student in the back row pull out *his real gun* and threaten to shoot the assailant.

In *On the Witness Stand*, Münsterberg also considered the prevention of crime. Münsterberg believed that criminals are made, not born; society creates the conditions that foster and produce crime. Consequently, such conditions must be changed. Münsterberg retained an interest in crime and legal affairs to the end of his life. Unfortunately, much of his work was sensationalized by the press, and Münsterberg became a controversial public figure.

The Sensational Münsterberg

Another section of *On the Witness Stand* deals with the detection of crime. Münsterberg condemned brutal, third-degree methods of interrogation. According to him, such barbaric methods should be replaced by psychological alternatives. To detect whether a person was lying, Münsterberg had used a variation of the reaction time technique in laboratory experiments. He also had an opportunity to use his techniques in the real-world setting of the sensational trial of Harry Orchard. Orchard was the self-confessed murderer of eighteen people, including a former governor of Idaho. He accused leaders of the Western Federation of Miners, including the union's president, Big Bill Haywood, of having directed and paid for the murders. (The governor had been an opponent and critic of organized labor.) Orchard was a witness for the prosecution at the trial of the union members. Orchard's credibility was crucial, and apparently it was buttressed by his claim that he had converted to the Seventh Day Adventists and thus had made his peace with God. The governor of Idaho invited Münsterberg to attend the trial in Boise and to test Orchard. In the courtroom Münsterberg's first impressions of the man were highly unfavorable. He had a "brutal, vulgar, murderous profile" and seemed far from the religious convert he claimed to be. Münsterberg resolved, however, "not to consult his antipathies but rather to rely on his experiments" (Münsterberg, 1908, p. 94).

In the initial interview with Orchard, Münsterberg sought to impress him with his scientific powers. First Münsterberg made a five-cent piece disappear by moving it through the blind spot in Orchard's visual field; then he showed him a number of perceptual illusions and distortions. When Münsterberg judged Orchard to have been sufficiently impressed, he recited a list of fifty words to him and asked him to respond to each word with the first word that came to mind. Münsterberg recorded for each stimulus word the latency of Orchard's reaction. Included in the list were a few words relating to the crimes—"revolver," "blood," and "pardon"— and to Orchard's professed religious conversion. Orchard's reaction times for the "dangerous" words were no different from his reaction times for the other words. Münsterberg stayed in Boise for four days, attending the trial, meeting with Orchard, and conducting his tests. He concluded that the man was not trying to hide anything, that his conversion was sincere, and that subjectively he was telling the truth.

On his way home the exhausted Münsterberg met a newspaper reporter and in an unguarded moment let slip his conclusion that he believed that Orchard was telling the truth. Banner newspaper headlines proclaimed Münsterberg's "verdict," and he was censured by the press for interfering in the trial, even though the jury was sequestered from the flood of sensational publicity. Absurd accounts of the techniques he had used in his interviews with Orchard appeared in the press. One California newspaper asserted that Münsterberg had performed a phrenological analysis of the thickness and dimensions of Orchard's skull. The reporter ended his account with the witticism "I'll bet a dollar to two bits that Professor Münsterberg has a head like a prize pumpkin" (M. Münsterberg, 1922, p. 147). Rumors spread that Münsterberg had used a marvelous machine, "Professor Monsterwork's lying machine." In fact no such machine existed, but in *On the Witness Stand* Münsterberg did describe ways in which various physiological indices of emotion could be measured and used: eye movements—gross movements up, down, and sideways of the eyes (though he did not recognize the significance of dilation and constriction of the pupils)—respiration, heart rate and blood pressure, hand tremor, and changes in the electrical resistance of the skin. However, Münsterberg expressed the need for great caution in using these techniques and stressed the importance of careful laboratory research. Unfortunately, such warnings have not always been heeded, and the use of physiological measures to detect deception is still controversial (Lykken, 1979).

In *On the Witness Stand,* Münsterberg also discussed untrue confessions in which people claim to have committed crimes they actually have not committed. He warned against such confessions; once again the warning was based on an unfortunate experience with the press. Richard Ivens, an apparently retarded young Chicagoan suspected of the brutal murder of a young housewife, confessed after intensive police questioning. Later he retracted the confession and established an alibi, but he still was tried and convicted. A Chicago neurologist, J. Sanderson Christison, described the case to Münsterberg and asked his opinion of the outcome. In a private letter Münsterberg replied that he felt sure that the man was innocent, that his confession was untrue, and that he had been unjustly convicted. Christison published Münsterberg's letter, which caused a sensation. Headlines referred to Münsterberg as "Harvard's Contempt of Court." Ivens's sentence was upheld, and with record crowds outside the jail he was executed. Münsterberg was convinced that a terrible injustice had been done.

In *On the Witness Stand,* Münsterberg discussed the conditions under which untrue confessions are likely to occur: intense and prolonged interrogation of people who have a need to please, people who need to comply with powerful authority figures, deeply depressed people who feel a need for punishment. Münsterberg discussed the Ivens case in detail, describing the conditions under which the man had made his confession and the suspicious fact that more and more damning details of the crime had been given under interrogation.

In 1914 Münsterberg published an article, "The Mind of the Juryman," in which he described experiments he had done at Harvard on group decision making. Students were required to make a judgment alone and then were given the opportunity to discuss the judgment with others before making a second one. When judgments were made alone, 52% were correct; when they were made in a group, 78% were correct. Münsterberg concluded that the jury system of group decision making is a psychologically sound procedure. Unfortunately, even this experiment led to controversy, for when Münsterberg repeated the experiment with female students at Radcliffe College, he found that there was no increase in the percentage of correct decisions after the discussion. He concluded that women are not capable of rational discussion and that the jury system would work well as long as women

did not serve. Newspapers all over the world reported his conclusion under headlines:

"WOMEN STUBBORN:
MEN ARE FIRM"
"WOMEN NOT FIT
FOR JURY WORK"
"A POLKA DOT PROFESSOR"

So says Professor Münsterberg
but Boston women lawyers
challenge Harvard savant's
conclusion.

(M. Münsterberg, 1922, p. 435)

ANGRY AT MÜNSTERBERG
SUFFRAGISTS
SAY WOMEN FIT FOR JURY

MÜNSTERBERG IS ALL
WRONG JURY
FOREWOMAN DECLARES

(M. Münsterberg, 1922, p. 436)

Despite this controversy, Münsterberg's experiment was a pioneer study of group
decision making and has been cited as a cornerstone of the experimental study of
group psychology (Murphy & Kovach, 1972).

While Münsterberg's work as a psychotherapist and forensic psychologist was
important in the broadening of psychology and was at times controversial, he is
most important in the history of psychology for his work as an industrial psychologist.

The Beginning of Industrial Psychology

Münsterberg is often considered to be America's first industrial psychologist, with
Psychology and Industrial Efficiency, published in 1913, being the founding work.
The book is divided into three main sections: nine chapters on "the best possible
man," which deal with selection of workers; six chapters on "the best possible
work," which discuss factors affecting worker efficiency; and six chapters on "the
best possible effect," which deal with marketing and advertising techniques.

For a company to select the best possible person for a job, Münsterberg recommended that existing self-report measures of vocational interest be supplemented
with "tasks in miniature," which assess an individual's capacity for a particular job.
Münsterberg believed that for many industrial and occupational tasks it is possible
to miniaturize the situation in which the potential employee will be working, to
develop what today would be called simulations. In these simulated work situations, the abilities of potential workers can be assessed. As an example of such an
approach, Münsterberg cited work he was asked to do in 1912 for representatives
from a number of cities that had elevated or street railways. The representatives
were concerned about the psychological factors involved in accidents on street railways. Münsterberg decided that the performance abilities of the driver or motor-
man were crucial, and so he developed a game or simulation in which the participant had to make a series of decisions and reactions in situations similar to those
encountered while driving a train through busy city streets: a pedestrian, animal,
or vehicle suddenly crosses the tracks; a brake malfunctions; and so on. He worked
with three groups of employees of the Boston Elevated Company: twenty-year vet-

eran motormen with excellent records, men who had barely escaped dismissal and
had been involved in frequent collisions and other accidents, and men with average
service records. On a simple reaction time test Münsterberg found no consistent
differences among the three groups. When tested using the game or simulation,
many of the men reported that they really had the feeling of driving a train. There
were also consistent differences in performance among the three groups. The group
with good records consistently did better than the men who had been close to dismissal. Münsterberg was convinced that the test could be used as a selection procedure and that many men who might go on to be high risks for having an accident
could be identified first. He also did some preliminary work for a number of ship-
ping companies and the United States Navy on the development of selection procedures for ships' officers. Münsterberg believed that similar selection procedures
could be used for a variety of other occupations.

As a second example of the way in which psychology might contribute in
employee selection, Münsterberg presented his work for the New England Telephone Company. The company found that among the young women successfully
trained as telephone operators, one-third were not able to perform well on the job
and either left or were dismissed within six months. In his attempt to remedy the
situation, Münsterberg began by observing the operators' work situation. They
averaged 225 calls per hour but at peak periods often handled as many as 300. He
estimated that fourteen separate "psychological processes" were involved in the
typical call, especially memory, attention to detail, exactitude, rapidity, and general
intelligence. Münsterberg developed a series of tests of these psychological functions. In the memory tests operators were asked to repeat two four-digit numbers;
then additional digits were added, to a maximum of twelve. In the attention test
they were told to cross out all the examples of a particular letter on a newspaper
page; in the test of exactitude the edges of a sheet of paper had to be divided into
two equal halves; in a test of rapidity the operators drew as many specific zigzag
movements as possible during ten seconds. Münsterberg gave these tests and one
of general intelligence to a group he was told consisted of newly hired employees.
He compared the test results with their actual work performance during their first
three months of employment. Actually, most of the people tested were newly hired
employees, but unknown to Münsterberg, the telephone company had included in
the group a number of highly experienced operators with excellent work records.
Münsterberg described the outcome of the testing as follows:

> If the psychological experiments had brought the result that these individu-
> als who stood so high in the estimation of the telephone company ranked
> low in the laboratory experiment, it would have reflected strongly on the
> reliability of the laboratory method. The results showed, on the contrary,
> that these women who had proved most able in practical service stood at the
> top of our list. Correspondingly, those who stood lowest in our psychological
> rank list had in the meantime been found unfit in practical service and had
> either left the company of their own accord or else had been eliminated.
> (Münsterberg, 1913, pp. 108–109)

The agreement of test results and work performance was not perfect, but the method
held promise.

With regard to improvement of worker efficiency, Münsterberg had much less empirical information to present. He had studied work conditions at the General Electric and International Harvester companies, the Plimpton Press, the Waltham Watch Company, and a number of other companies. Münsterberg did not agree with a common view that much modern industrial work is characterized by dreadful monotony and mental starvation. In the factories and plants he visited he made a point of chatting with the workers whose jobs appeared to be the most tedious and monotonous. Often the workers did not describe their jobs in these terms and were content with their work. In one dramatic case Münsterberg observed a woman in an electric lamp factory whose job was to wrap lamps in tissue paper—13,000 units per day. She had done the job for twelve years, and Münsterberg estimated that she had wrapped 50 million lamps. Yet she assured him that the work was "really interesting" and said that she found "constant variation" in the way she wrapped each lamp (Münsterberg, 1913, p. 196). Münsterberg concluded that the judgments of outsiders as to which tasks breed boredom and frustration were unreliable and that many of the so-called higher professions involved a great deal of tedious repetition: the work of physicians, teachers, and lawyers is far from free of monotony. Münsterberg concluded that many factors affect worker satisfaction and morale and that many more investigations were needed.

In the last section of his book on industrial psychology, Münsterberg discussed factors that stimulate consumer demand and ways in which the effectiveness of advertising can be increased. In his laboratory Münsterberg investigated the effects of the size and number of repetitions of an advertisement on its "memory value." He was convinced that advertising could be a powerful factor in stimulating product demand but also believed that it must be used responsibly. In a later article, "The Social Sins of Advertising," Münsterberg bitterly attacked as socially irresponsible the new practice of scattering advertisements throughout the text of magazines and newspapers rather than, as had formerly been done, segregating them in one section. Debate over the appropriate placement of advertisements continues today with respect to television commercials. In the United States they are scattered throughout programs; in England, on the commercial channel of the British Broadcasting Corporation (BBC) they are segregated in advertising periods at the beginning, midway through, and at the end of each program.

Even after the publication of *Psychology and Industrial Efficiency*, Münsterberg retained an interest in industrial problems. In the spring of 1913 he met with President Woodrow Wilson and the secretaries of commerce and labor to urge the establishment of a government bureau devoted to scientific research on the application of psychology to the problems of commerce and industry. His proposals were well received, although practical plans for their implementation were disrupted by World War I. In general his work in industrial psychology has proved to be of great importance, and many of his concerns and interests are current among industrial psychologists. A contemporary reviewer said of his work:

> Overall, Münsterberg's grasp of the psychology of business and industry was impressive. In two books and a handful of articles, he laid the groundwork for every major development in these fields. He specified the problems and

the goals, and indicated some of the methods to be used, for personnel psychology, vocational psychology, engineering psychology, consumer psychology, and other specializations in these areas...there should be no doubt that Hugo Münsterberg was the founder of the fields of industrial and business psychology as they exist today. (Moskowitz, 1977, p. 838)

Business Week Magazine honored Münsterberg in a series of articles on "Famous Firsts in Industrial Psychology" (Hale, 1980, p. 6).

In addition to his work in industrial psychology, Münsterberg wrote extensively on teaching, education, and several other social issues. Though he neither smoked nor took alcohol, Münsterberg opposed Prohibition and was actively involved in the debate over that burning issue. He even attempted to introduce a little levity to the controversy in an article in 1908 in the *Ladies Home Journal,* "The Temperance of Women." Münsterberg contrasted the intemperance of men for alcohol with the intemperance of women for candy and the latest fashions. A predictably outraged reaction followed the article's publication, especially when it became known that Münsterberg had solicited and received financial support from the beer magnate Adolphus Busch (Hale, 1980, p. 119). Münsterberg opposed sex education in the schools, arguing that such education would simply stimulate interest in sex. He fought a lifelong battle against what he called "naive psychology" and constantly challenged the claims of pseudo psychologists. He was also a critic of believers in the occult, mysticism, astrology, thought transference, and other psychical activities.

Münsterberg Honored and Defamed

Honors and awards came easily to Münsterberg. At the age of twenty-nine, he was a professor of philosophy at Harvard University, and in 1899, when he was thirty-six, he became chairman of the department. The year before he had declined an offer of a readership at Oxford University; in 1905, he was offered the chair of philosophy at the University of Königsberg formerly occupied by Immanuel Kant. He first accepted but then declined the position and remained at Harvard. These offers constituted an impressive recognition of his status. He played a major role in organizing a scientific congress held in conjunction with the 1904 St. Louis Exposition and traveled to Europe to extend invitations to some 150 scientists and scholars. He was president of the APA in 1899 and of the American Philosophical Association in 1907. In 1901 Harvard University awarded him an honorary master of arts degree, thus making him a "son of the house" and a "Harvard man." Münsterberg served Harvard loyally for twenty-five years. He organized the fundraising drive for Emerson Hall, the home of Harvard's Psychology Department for forty years. He was a friend of the rich, the famous, and the important. He knew Andrew Carnegie, Bertrand Russell, H. G. Wells, Presidents Theodore Roosevelt and William Howard Taft, Kaiser Wilhelm II, Hollywood movie stars and moguls, and most of the leading American and European scholars and intellectuals of the time. However, when Münsterberg died in 1916, no eulogies for him appeared in the psychological journals. Why?

Perhaps an answer to this question can be found in an examination of Münsterberg's lifelong interest in improving relations and developing greater understanding between his native and adopted countries. In one of the first books he wrote in English, *American Traits*, published in 1902, Münsterberg ridiculed the false stereotypes Germans and Americans held about each other. He described the two societies, pointing out what he considered to be the good and bad points of each. In 1903 he published *Die Amerikaner*, a book translated by his student Holt and published in English in 1904 as *The Americans*. The book provided detailed and insightful descriptions of American social, cultural, economic, political, and intellectual life intended primarily for a German audience. According to Münsterberg's daughter, this book

> made a stir among readers and, to a remarkable degree awakened interest in American life. It even inspired readers to set sail and see for themselves a land that had been painted in such appealing colors. The secret of the book's influence was not so much the clearly presented new information as the convincing power of the enthusiastic author behind its statements. (M. Münsterberg, 1922, p. 333)

Unfortunately, Münsterberg did not have as much success improving the perceptions Americans had of Germany. In 1905 Münsterberg was appointed by Harvard to serve as an exchange professor at the University of Berlin to establish a new American Institute there. The institute was dedicated to facilitating exchanges of scholars and scientists and establishing a collection of newspapers, magazines, and journals reflecting life in America. When Münsterberg returned to the United States in 1912, he constantly strove to counter the rising tide of feeling against Germany. With the outbreak of World War I in 1914, his activities became increasingly unpopular, yet he persisted in writing articles and books presenting the German position and arguing for "fair play." He received volumes of hate mail, was accused of being a German spy, and was censured, condemned, and ostracized even by some of his colleagues at Harvard. An Englishman offered $10 million to the university if the administration would dismiss Münsterberg immediately. Harvard stood firm. The canny Münsterberg offered to resign if the man would present $5 million to the university and $5 million to him. The man refused. While this episode has a touch of humor, these were terrible years for Münsterberg. Perhaps it is as well that he did not live to see American entry into World War I in 1917. The morning papers of December 16, 1916, brought news of peace offers, and Münsterberg said to his wife, "By Spring we shall have peace." He left to give his morning lecture at Radcliffe, walked to the college through bitterly cold weather, and arrived exhausted, but he insisted on meeting his class. He entered the lecture hall, began to speak, and died in midsentence from a massive cerebral hemorrhage.

TITCHENER AND MÜNSTERBERG IN RETROSPECT

Titchener and Münsterberg both earned doctoral degrees with Wundt at the University of Leipzig and shortly thereafter immigrated to the United States. As we have seen, there the similarity ends. In their definitions of psychology, approaches, and careers, they could hardly have been more different. Titchener defined psychology as the science of the mind and declared its task to be the search for the basic elements or structure of the human mind. Introspection under rigidly controlled experimental conditions was to be psychology's most important, indeed its defining, method. Münsterberg, in contrast, always refused to define his psychology, for no definition could be sufficiently inclusive. His aim was to study the workings or functions of the mind: how we learn, remember, perceive, and judge. While laboratory experiments were sometimes of value, Münsterberg favored work outside the laboratory and applications of psychological knowledge in a variety of settings: the psychological clinic, business and industry, and courts of law. Titchener adamantly opposed such applications, considering them technologies that were not part of the true science of psychology.

Contemporary psychology shows the influence of Münsterberg but little of that of Titchener. Today there are no Titchenerian structuralist psychologists; in fact, there have not been any for many years. In contrast, many of Münsterberg's interests are still being pursued by contemporary psychologists. However, histories of psychology often emphasize Titchener's role and not that of Münsterberg. Boring (1957) in his classic history of psychology devoted ten times as much space to Titchener as he did to Münsterberg; the index to Watson's *The Great Psychologists from Aristotle to Freud* (1978) has twenty-three citations to Titchener and only six to Münsterberg; Marx and Hillix in their *Systems and Theories of Psychology* (1979) devoted many pages to Titchener and none to Münsterberg. Such presentations show that Titchener continues to influence the way the history of psychology is written, but they are a misrepresentation of the relative importance of the two men.

Hermann Ebbinghaus. (The Bettmann Archive)

6

Other German Psychologists of the Eighteenth and Nineteenth Centuries

Through Edward Titchener and, less so, Hugo Münsterberg, many American psychologists trace their heritage to Wundt. As we have seen, Wundt is often given credit for the very founding of psychology and the establishment of its methods. But Wundt's laboratory at Leipzig was not without German rivals, and Wundt was not without German critics. These competing approaches to the "new psychology" of the nineteenth century were also experimental but differed from the approach of Wundt in the topics they emphasized. Unlike Wundt, many of these other German psychologists, such as Ernst Weber, Gustav Fechner, Carl Stumpf, Oswald Külpe, and Hermann Ebbinghaus, restricted their work to the study of a specific topic area: psychophysics, sensation and perception, problem solving, or memory. Others, such as Franz Brentano, did not become as widely known because they did not publish as frequently as did Wundt. But in all these cases, perhaps especially those of Stumpf and Külpe, their potential influence was diffused by World War I, the rise of competing American approaches to psychology in the 1920s and 1930s, and the political situation prior to World War II. Without loyal, dogmatic students such as Titchener to implant their approaches in America and keep them alive, much of the work of these men has been neglected. Today, with the rise of cognitive psychologies, the importance of their contributions is gaining recognition (Knapp, 1986a).

EXPERIMENTAL PSYCHOLOGY DEFINED BEFORE WUNDT

The earliest use of the term *psychology* in an English-language title was John Broughton's *Psychologia: or, An Account of the Nature of the Rational Soul,* pub-

145

lished in London in 1703 (Van de Kemp, 1983). Later that century, in 1756, Johann Gottlob Krüger, a German professor of philosophy and mathematics with a background in medicine, natural science, and mathematics, published a book entitled *Attempt at an Experimental Psychology*. According to Alexander Mintz (1954), who discovered Krüger's book, the work provided an explicit description of experimental psychology more than 100 years before Wundt. Krüger's psychology was intended to be empirical rather than metaphysical, with an emphasis on observations of consciousness using introspection and observations of external actions using the senses. Krüger's psychology was also associationistic and hedonistic; it was clearly influenced by the writings of the early British empiricist philosophers discussed in Chapter 2. Throughout the book Krüger considered what purpose each of the different psychological capacities could serve in the normal daily functioning of a human being. Krüger concluded, for instance, that the function of memory is to retain and hold knowledge for future use.

In addition to memory, the fourteen chapters of Krüger's book include topics such as sensation, cognition, imagery, waking, sleeping, dreaming, emotion, and the minds of animals. Mintz (1954) pointed out that much of this material is not what one might expect to find in such an early psychology. For example, the chapter on sensation includes a discussion of the visual experience of a blind person whose cataracts were removed by an operation—the topic addressed by Locke in response to Molyneux's query (Chapter 2)—a number of reports of phantom limbs in amputees, and descriptions of phenomena of visual contrast and mutual inhibition of sensations. These interesting and important topics were to be studied by generations of sensory psychologists. Krüger also reflected the prevailing assumptions of his time. He believed that quick learners forget more rapidly than do slower learners and that a pregnant woman's experiences mark her unborn child.

PSYCHOPHYSICS

Gustav Fechner (1801–1889)

Psychophysics, a branch of science investigating the relationship between the physical and psychological worlds, began prior to the time of Wundt's work. Gustav Fechner was thirty years older than Wundt. Wundt established his laboratory in 1879, nearly twenty years after Fechner published the book for which he is remembered today, his *Elemente der Psychophysik* (Elements of Psychophysics) (1860).

Like Wundt, Fechner was the son of a pastor, a man of independent thought and action who once shocked his congregation by placing a lightning rod on his church. "Surely," he was asked, "the Lord will protect his own?" "Perhaps," said Pastor Fechner, "but the laws of physics must also be respected" (Boring, 1957, p. 276). After the usual *Gymnasium* education, Fechner studied medicine at the University of Leipzig, where he remained for the rest of his life, some seventy years. He took a medical degree in 1822, but thereafter his interests turned toward physics and mathematics. By 1830 he had published more than forty works, including an important paper on the measurement of electrical direct current. During the next decade Fechner turned to more psychological topics and published papers on color vision and positive afterimages, or visual sensations that continue after the visual stimulus that produced them is no longer present, such as the image of a light bulb that remains for a brief period after the electricity has been switched off. For these experiments Fechner needed a bright stimulus, and so he stared at the sun. He injured his eyes and became ill and so depressed that in 1839 he had to resign his position as a professor of physics.

For three years Fechner suffered a physical and psychological crisis, but then he recovered suddenly. Fechner always regarded his recovery as the miraculous turning point in his life. He became deeply committed to Pietism, a movement prominent within the German Lutheran church of his time that stressed personal piety over religious orthodoxy. Fechner renounced what he saw as the materialism of both his earlier life and much of contemporary science. Instead of continuing to do scientific research he turned to poetry and metaphysics. When Fechner considered the perennial metaphysical question of the nature of mind and matter, he concluded that they could be related; but how could that relationship be described? The answer came to him "before getting out of bed" on the morning of October 22, 1860. He would describe the relationship between body and mind, between the physical and mental, by quantifying the relationships between physical stimuli and the mental experience of those stimuli. Such descriptions would be based on the work of his colleague at Leipzig, Ernst Weber (1795–1878).

In 1834 Weber had published in Latin a great treatise, *De tactu,* describing his experiments on touch. Weber first measured the minimum amount of tactile stimulation necessary for a sensation of touch. Very weak stimuli were not sensed; intense ones nearly always were. Between these two intensities was a *limen,* or threshold, at which tactile stimuli are first perceived—the absolute threshold. Weber also investigated the ability of people to discriminate between two weights when the weights were either resting on the hand (touch alone) or lifted (touch and muscular exertion). Smaller differences were reported in the latter case as a result, Weber believed, of sensations from the muscles.

Weber noted that two tactile stimuli are not always perceived as different. When very close together, they are often reported as one stimulation point; when far apart, as two. Between these two extremes of perception there is a threshold where one touch sensation becomes two or two become one—the two-point discrimination threshold. He found that this threshold varied on different parts of the body. On the fingertips, it was 0.22 cm; on the back, 4.06 cm. Such findings indicated that there is not a simple one-to-one relationship between the physical characteristics of stimuli and the sensations they produce.

Weber's results had shown that a physical change does not always make a psychological difference, but this insight was not original with Weber. In 1738 Daniel Bernoulli had pointed out that a franc to a poor man produces more of a gain than 10 francs to a wealthy man. Psychological gains in wealth are relative to economic status. Similarly, lighting a candle in a pitch-dark room causes a noticeable difference; a single candle added to a brightly lit room may not be noticed at all.

Weber applied Bernoulli's concept of relativity to perceptual judgments of weight. First Weber had his subjects lift a standard weight. Then they lifted a second comparison weight and made a judgment of which weight was heavier. Large differences were reported consistently, but small differences often went undetected. Weber asked how large the difference between two weights had to be before it was detected reliably. Putting the question another way, What was the just noticeable difference (j.n.d.) between two weights? Weber found that the j.n.d. was not fixed but varied depending on the specific weights being considered and was best described as a ratio of 1 to 40. If the standard was 40 units, the j.n.d. would be 1 unit, and the comparison weight would have to be at least 41 units to be detected as different. With a standard of 20 units, the j.n.d. would be one-fortieth of 20, or 0.5; a comparison weight of 20.5 units would be detected reliably as different from the standard of 20 units. The physical difference required for the same psychological difference varied with different weights.

Weber conducted similar experiments with lines of different length, lights of different brightness, thermal stimuli, tones, smells, and tastes. For each of these senses he found a constant ratio or fraction described by the formula

$$\frac{\Delta(R)}{R} = k$$

where $\Delta(R)$ is the just noticeable stimulus (in German, *Reiz*) increment, R is the standard stimulus magnitude, and k is a constant. The actual ratios Weber found were one-sixtieth for vision, one-thirtieth for pain, one-tenth for tones, one-fourth for smell, and one-third for taste. Different senses had different ratios, but in all cases there was not a linear correspondence between the physical world and one's psychological experience of it.

Weber's results provided exactly the type of precise description of the relationship between the physical and psychological worlds Fechner was seeking. Like Weber, Fechner measured the relationship between the power or magnitude of many different types of stimuli and their judged intensity. He described his results in *Elemente der Psychophysik* (Elements of Psychophysics). Fechner found, as had Weber, that as the magnitude of a stimulus increases, more and more of an increment in intensity is needed to produce a perceptible difference. Through a series of mathematical steps Fechner transformed Weber's ratio to the formula

$$S = k \log R$$

where S is the sensation, k is a constant, and log R is the logarithm of the physical intensity of the stimulus. See the graph on page 149 for what the relationship looks like. This nonlinear function shows a complex relationship between the physical and psychological worlds. Considering the difference between the linear relationship shown by the solid line and the actual relationship shown by the dotted line, one might ask: Where does the curvilinearity or bend come from? Fechner's answer was that it comes from the mind. It is the active mind that "bends" the function, and thus the bend is a measure of the mind's activity. A psychological process had been measured, with the results expressed in a mathematical equation. Fechner's

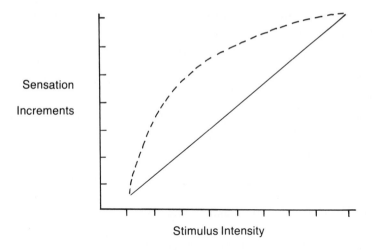

Sensation Increments — Stimulus Intensity

success contradicted Auguste Comte's (1798–1857) assertion that the human mind can measure everything but its own activity.

Psychophysics in Perspective

For most nineteenth-century psychologists, including Wundt, Weber and Fechner's experiments were a model of careful, painstaking research. They were convinced that such research was necessary for the development of the new science of psychology. However, Weber and Fechner had critics who contended that sensations are not measurable, that the j.n.d. was not a proper unit of measurement, and that Weber's law and Fechner's logarithmic transformation were invalid. For the American psychologist William James (Chapter 9):

> Fechner's book was the starting point for a new department in literature, which it would be impossible to match for the qualities of thoroughness and subtlety, but of which, in the humble opinion of the present writer, the proper psychological outcome is just *nothing*. (James, 1890, vol. I, p. 534)

A few pages later James concluded:

> But it would be terrible if even such a dear old man as this [Fechner] could saddle our Science forever with his patient whimsies, and, in a world so full of more nutritious objects of attention, compel all future students to plough through the difficulties, not only of his own works, but of the still drier ones written in refutation. Those who desire this dreadful literature can find it; it has a disciplinary value....(James, 1890, vol. I, p. 549)

Throughout his career Fechner remained confident about his approach to psychology; in 1877 he directed these defiant final words (*Nachwort*) to his many critics:

> The tower of Babel was never finished because the workers could not reach an understanding of how they should build it; my psychophysical edifice will

stand because the workers will never agree on how to tear it down. (my translation; Fechner, 1877, p. 215)

Indeed, contemporary psychological research still uses psychophysical techniques to study sensation and perception. Since the time of Fechner, catch trials (with no stimulus present) have typically been inserted into a series of stimulus presentations to keep the subject alert and attentive. Signal detection procedures today use catch trials to measure sensitivity and response bias, that is, the subject's ability to detect the signal and his or her certainty that a signal has been detected (Hochberg, 1979). Psychophysical methods have also been used to answer more complex questions of judgment: How do different cultures perceive the "absolute threshold" for criminal behavior? When are human actions considered criminal? How do different professions and careers differ in status? What are the relative intensities of different hostile acts in international conflict and friendly acts in international cooperation? (Stevens, 1966).

One of Fechner's more striking speculations concerning consciousness has found contemporary support. Fechner knew that the brain is bilaterally symmetrical, i.e., that it has two halves that are virtually mirror images of each other (Chapter 3). He also knew that there is a deep division between the two halves, which are linked by a connecting band of fibers, the corpus callosum. Fechner speculated that if the corpus callosum was transected or "split," two separate streams of consciousness would result. The mind would become two. Fechner believed that his speculation would never be tested. In that he was wrong, but it was not until the mid-twentieth century, when Roger Sperry studied discrimination learning in cats with split brains, and later, when Sperry and Michael Gazzaniga worked with epileptic patients with a sectioned corpus callosum, that Fechner's speculation was shown to be correct (Gazzaniga, 1970).

The work of Weber and Fechner was instrumental in advancing the study of sensation and perception. Other German psychologists shared an interest in these topics, but more important, they sought to extend the experimental rigor of psychophysics to the study of higher mental processes and mental actions such as learning, memory, ideation, imagination, and judgment. These psychologists challenged assertions such as that of the German philosoher Johann Friedrich Herbart (1776–1841) that experimental methods cannot be applied to psychological problems. Hermann Ebbinghaus was one of the German psychologists strongly influenced by Fechner's approach. He was to lay the foundation for contemporary psychological research on memory and to make one of the most enduring contributions to psychology.

HERMANN EBBINGHAUS (1850–1909)

Hermann Ebbinghaus was born on January 24, 1850, the son of a merchant in the town of Barmen near Bonn in the Prussian Rhineland. At the local *Gymnasium* he received a classical education preparatory to university studies. Ebbinghaus entered the University of Bonn at the age of seventeen and also studied at Berlin and Halle, two universities whose faculties he was to join later in life. The Franco-Prussian War interrupted his studies, and Ebbinghaus served in the Prussian Army from 1870 to 1871. He spent the years after his service traveling in England and France, attending university classes and seminars, and working for short stints as a teacher and private tutor. While browsing through a Parisian *bouquinerie* (used book-stall), he found a copy of Fechner's *Elemente der Psychophysik*. Ebbinghaus was captivated by Fechner's description of psychophysics and became fired with the conviction that psychology, like psychophysics, could become a natural science and that procedures similar to Fechner's objective, psychophysical procedures could be developed and applied to higher mental processes. Some time around 1877 Ebbinghaus set out to develop such procedures for studying the higher mental process of memory. Many years later, when he published his major psychological work, *Grundzüge der Psychologie* (Fundamentals of Psychology) (1902), he dedicated the book to Fechner: *"Ich hab' es nur von Euch"* (I owe everything to you).

Ebbinghaus's Early Academic Career

In 1880 Ebbinghaus was appointed a *Privatdozent* at the University of Berlin and there continued his research on memory. While there had been some speculation and reflection about memory before Ebbinghaus, his were the first systematic experimental investigations (Herrmann & Chaffin, 1988). The research of Ebbinghaus was highly original. He did not have a teacher from whom he could learn and whose materials, techniques, and procedures he could use. Fechner, who had inspired the studies, was an old man of nearly eighty, living in quiet retirement in Leipzig and more interested in aesthetics and philosophy than in experimental psychology. Furthermore, Ebbinghaus was not a member of a department of psychology and did not have a research laboratory or colleagues with similar interests and research programs. Finally, Ebbinghaus did not have access to a large pool of subjects for his experiments, and so he performed most of them on himself. Despite these limitations, he did some of the most remarkable investigations of human memory in the history of psychology (Roediger, 1985).

Ebbinghaus was a meticulous researcher who followed a rigorous set of experimental rules. His first series of experiments was completed by the end of 1880, but such was his caution that he spent the next three years replicating and extending them before describing his results in the monograph *Über das Gedächtnis* (Concerning Memory), published in Leipzig in 1885. This work was well received, and the value and originality of his contribution were widely recognized.

Ebbinghaus realized early that familiarity and meaning have powerful effects on learning and memory. To control for these effects, he set out to devise material for his memory experiments that would be unfamiliar and meaningless. The result was 300 nonsense syllables—three-letter combinations of a consonant, a vowel, and a second consonant. Devising nonsense syllables was a creative act; they had not been constructed before Ebbinghaus but have been used extensively in memory research ever since. How did Ebbinghaus come to invent the nonsense syllable? In

1871 Lewis Carroll* published *Through the Looking Glass and What Alice Found There* to popular acclaim. The first and last verses of its poem "Jabberwocky" read as follows:

> Twas brillig, and the slithy toves
> Did gyre and gimble in the wabe;
> All mimsy were the borogoves,
> And the mome raths outgrabe.
> (Carroll, 1871;
> miniature edition, 1940, p. 22)

Shakow (1930) speculated that while in London in 1876 Ebbinghaus read the famous children's story with Carroll's nonsense parody of the English language and that it gave him the idea for the nonsense syllable. Whatever their genesis, nonsense syllables with their homogeneity and lack of meaning were ideal for Ebbinghaus's experiments.

The Ebbinghaus Experiments

Ebbinghaus used nonsense syllables to investigate several broad questions. He examined the relationship between the amount of material to be memorized and the time and effort required to learn it to "complete mastery." To do this he read out loud lists of nonsense syllables and repeated them back, all in time to a metronome. Ebbinghaus recorded the number of repetitions necessary before he could repeat lists with different numbers of nonsense syllables perfectly and without hesitation.

Number of Nonsense Syllables in the List	Number of Repetitions to the First Errorless Reproduction (exclusive of it)
7	1
12	17
16	30
24	44
36	55

Ebbinghaus, 1885, p. 47.

While longer lists required more repetitions before mastery, the relationship is not a simple one.

Ebbinghaus also assessed the effects of different amounts of learning on memory. He used different lists, all of which had sixteen nonsense syllables, and varied

---

*Lewis Carroll was the pseudonym of the Reverend Charles Lutwidge Dodgson (1832–1898), a mathematics tutor at Oxford. According to one report, Queen Victoria was so delighted with *Alice* that she ordered everything else by the same author. The queen must not have been amused to receive Dodgson's *The Formulae of Plain Trigonometry, An Elementary Treatise on Determinants,* and *Symbolic Logic* (Collins, 1932).

the number of repetitions of each one. All lists were then relearned twenty-four hours later. The times required to relearn the list were recorded and are shown in the following table:

Number of Original Repetitions	Time to Memorize the List 24 Hours Later (seconds)	Result of the Preceding Study Was a Saving of (seconds)
0	1,270	—
8	1,167	103
16	1,073	192
24	975	295
32	863	407
42	697	573
53	585	685
64	454	816

Ebbinghaus, 1885, p. 56.

The relationship is clear: as the number of original repetitions increases, the time necessary to relearn the list twenty-four hours later decreases. Given such a strong negative relationship, one might wonder why Ebbinghaus did not pursue it further, using still larger numbers of repetitions. Ebbinghaus rather dryly explained:

> I have not investigated this question by further increasing the number of repetitions of unfamiliar 16 syllable series because as has been already noted, with any great extension of the tests the increasing fatigue and a certain drowsiness caused complications. (Ebbinghaus, 1885, p. 59)

Some experiments were not possible even for the dedicated Ebbinghaus. Nonetheless, this experiment suggests the importance of overlearning. Since the previous set of results showed that a list of sixteen nonsense syllables required some thirty repetitions to mastery, it is clear that a number of the lists in the second experiment were overlearned, and it is those lists which had high savings scores.

In his best-known experiment, Ebbinghaus investigated his third major research interest: the effects of the passage of time on memory. He learned eight lists of thirteen nonsense syllables until they could be reproduced perfectly twice. After varying amounts of time, the lists were relearned, and the number of repetitions required for relearning was used in the following formula to calculate a "savings score":

$$\frac{\text{Number of original repetitions} - \text{number of relearning repetitions}}{\text{Number of original repetitions}} \times 100$$

Thus the smaller the number of relearning repetitions, the higher the calculated savings score. His results are shown in the following table.

Interval between Original Learning and Relearning	% Saved	% Lost
0 minutes	100	0
20 minutes	58	42
60 minutes	44	56
9 hours	36	64
24 hours	34	66
2 days	28	72
6 days	25	75
31 days	21	79

Ebbinghaus, 1885, p. 76.

A graph of these results with the time elapsed since learning plotted on the abscissa and the percent savings plotted on the ordinate shows the course of forgetting over time. The curve that results is a classic in psychology, appearing in many contemporary textbooks. Its most startling aspect is the large initial drop in retention, especially considering the stringent learning criterion Ebbinghaus used. Over 50 percent of the material learned was lost after only sixty minutes, and 66 percent was lost after twenty-four hours. While such a curve is often identified as Ebbinghaus's curve of forgetting, Ebbinghaus did not graph the results this way. Rather, he developed a mathematical model for forgetting by writing a logarithmic equation for the function and deriving its parameters by the method of least squares (Roediger, 1985, p. 521). Such sophisticated statistical techniques were typical of Ebbinghaus. He introduced the concepts of mean and variability and developed a way of comparing performance in different conditions by seeing if the difference between means exceeded what would be expected on the basis of probable error.

Ebbinghaus also investigated the relative effects on memory of spaced versus massed, part versus whole, and active versus passive learning. He found that in general, active, spaced learning of material as a whole is most effective. He also found meaningful material, such as poetry or prose, much easier to learn and remember than material without meaning. To learn six stanzas from Byron's *Don Juan* took him only eight repetitions; a nonsense syllable list of the same length took from seventy to eighty repetitions. In addition, internal analyses of his results indicated that lists learned before he went to sleep were retained better than were lists learned at other times of the day. This finding—that sleep slows forgetting relative to waking activity—was to be confirmed some forty years later by Jenkins and Dallenbach (1924) in what has come to be a classic paper.

Ebbinghaus's *Über das Gedächtnis* was widely recognized as a highly significant contribution to the scientific development of psychology. For the first time a higher mental function had been studied experimentally. The leading American psychologist William James (Chapter 9) viewed Ebbinghaus as one of the Germans' "best men," an opinion shared by many of his American colleagues. Predictably, Titchener's reaction was initially less favorable. In 1910 he stated that

> the introduction of nonsense syllables...has nevertheless done psychology a
> certain disservice. It has tended to place the emphasis upon the organism
> rather than upon the mind. (Titchener, 1910, p. 414)

However, this was one of the rare occasions when Titchener changed his mind. In
1928 he wrote:

> It is not too much to say that the recourse to nonsense syllables, as a means
> to the study of association, marks the most considerable advance in this
> chapter of psychology, since the time of Aristotle. (Titchener, 1928, p. 125)

In a retrospective review marking the centennial of the publication of *Über das
Gedächtnis*, Henry Roediger described the book as recording "one of the most remarkable research achievements in the history of psychology" (Roediger, 1985, p.
519). In his review Roediger used words such as "remarkable," "astounding," and
"incredible" to refer to Ebbinghaus and his research on memory. Few contemporary psychologists would quarrel with such praise.

One year after the publication of his monograph Ebbinghaus was appointed
Professor extraordinarius at the University of Berlin. He was approaching the peak
of German academic life, but paradoxically, though he had promised further memory research in his book, he chose not to continue that work. Perhaps, as Roediger
(1985) suggested, Ebbinghaus was distracted by administrative duties, journal editing, and textbook writing. An additional reason might have been that the University of Berlin was the home of Hermann von Helmholtz, the world's leading
authority on sensory physiology (Chapter 3). Following his example, Ebbinghaus
became interested in sensory physiology, sensation, and perception. In 1890
Ebbinghaus and Arthur Konig established the *Zeitschrift für Psychologie und
Physiologie der Sinnesorgane* (Journal of Psychology and Physiology of Sense Organs).
Ebbinghaus edited the journal and from all accounts was fair-minded and tolerant
of views other than his own. In 1893 he published a theory of color vision, but his
contributions to sensory physiology were judged not to have been of the highest
quality, and so he was passed over for promotion to a chair at Berlin. He moved to
the University of Breslau in 1894 and stayed there until 1905, when he moved to
the University of Halle.

Ebbinghaus Tackles an Applied Problem

In July 1895, the municipal authorities of Breslau wrote a letter to the Hygiene
Section of the Silesian Society for National Culture requesting some justification for
the way in which the German school day was arranged. Children went to school in
one uninterrupted session from 8:00 A.M. to 1:00 P.M. Their fatigue and nervous
irritability seemed to increase as the day went on, and so the authorities wondered
if a different arrangement of the school day might be better—perhaps morning and
afternoon sessions with a midday break. The society appointed a committee to investigate this question and make recommendations. The committee saw the need
for an objective measure of changes in a child's mental powers during the day. H.
Griesbach, a German physiologist, proposed that two-point discrimination thresh-

olds be used to measure mental fatigue. He believed that such fatigue impairs a child's ability to distinguish between two points of stimulation on the skin and proposed to use this physical measure to assess changes in children's mental powers. Clearly he was influenced by the psychophysical research of his era.

Griesbach measured two-point discrimination thresholds when the children entered school in the morning and at the end of every class hour. As a control procedure he also tested them on free days when they were at home. Griesbach found a considerable blunting of sensitivity that reached its maximum around the third hour of the school day, and so he recommended that the day be broken into two shorter segments. The committee, most of whose members were physicians, was impressed by Griesbach's investigations, but Ebbinghaus, who was not a committee member, was less favorable in his judgment. He agreed that the testing had been done well but felt that the test procedure was not suited to the purpose. Ebbinghaus proposed psychological rather than physical measures of the mental processes of declining attention and increased fatigue. The committee accepted Ebbinghaus's criticisms and commissioned him to devise a number of tests he would consider satisfactory. He accepted the charge but quickly became concerned with the more general question of the nature of intelligence.

Ebbinghaus viewed intelligence as a general ability to combine information, see relationships and associations, and arrive at correct conclusions. This ability, he believed, is what distinguishes the outstanding person in any field, whether it be a physician who must make a diagnosis based on incomplete information; a general who must combine partial, uncertain, and at times conflicting information into a battle plan; a scholar; or a merchant. Ebbinghaus devised analogy tests and completion tests to tap this sort of reasoning ability. To do well on the analogy tests, a child had to recognize a rule to complete the analogy

> July is to May as Saturday is to _____.

The completion tests involved having a child complete a passage or sentence:

> Big things are heavier than _____ things.
> _____ are always younger than their fathers.

The appropriateness of each completion was judged, as was the speed with which it was made. Later, completion tests such as the ones Ebbinghaus introduced were used by Alfred Binet (Chapter 11) when he developed his first intelligence test. In addition to the two tests of general reasoning, Ebbinghaus used tests to measure the child's ability to do basic arithmetic.

Ebbinghaus gave his tests to schoolchildren in Breslau and compared their test scores with their scholastic records and standing. His completion tests discriminated best between children with good, average, and poor grades. Ebbinghaus believed that this test measured a combining function central to intelligence. Though Ebbinghaus made progress in understanding and measuring intelligence, the original question of how the school day should be arranged somehow got lost. Today many German schools still operate on an 8:00 A.M. to 1:00 P.M. schedule.

Ebbinghaus in Perspective

Ebbinghaus was a great innovator and pioneer but, unlike Wundt, did not have followers and did not establish a school of psychology. His influence on psychology derives from his impressive experimental research on memory, his pioneering work on the measurement of intelligence, and his writings. His *Grundzüge* (Fundamentals) and *Abriss der Psychologie* (Summary of Psychology), published in 1902 and 1905, respectively, were used as psychology texts throughout the world. When one pages through the original editions of these books, they appear formidable and intimidating, but closer inspection shows that Ebbinghaus had a clear and precise prose style. The opening sentence of the *Abriss* (Ebbinghaus, 1910, p. 9); *"Die Psychologie hat eine lange Vergangenheit doch nur eine kurze Geschichte"* (Psychology has a long past but only a short history), is a description which has perplexed and fascinated many psychologists interested in the history of their science.

Ebbinghaus died suddenly of pneumonia in 1909 at the age of fifty-nine. In an appreciation written after his death, Robert Woodworth (Chapter 10) wrote:

> The sudden death of Dr. Ebbinghaus, professor of philosophy at Halle, is felt as a severe loss throughout the world, for few psychologists were more international in their reputation and sympathies. (Woodworth, 1909, p. 253)

In a lecture at the Clark Conference (described in Chapter 9), Titchener movingly expressed his feelings:

> As I approach the topic of this lecture, what is uppermost in my mind is a sense of irreparable loss. When the cable brought the bad news, last February, that Ebbinghaus was dead, just a month after the celebration of his fifty-ninth birthday, the feeling that took precedence even of personal sorrow was the wonder of what experimental psychology would do without him. (Titchener, 1910, p. 405)

Titchener predicted that Ebbinghaus's works might prove as important as those of Wundt. From Titchener that was the ultimate accolade. Indeed, the methodology and theory of Ebbinghaus provided direction and focus for contemporary research and concerns. For instance, Sidney Pressey, the American educational psychologist, investigated retention over time of material from an introductory psychology course. As predicted by Ebbinghaus's laboratory results, Pressey found that students tested immediately after taking the course scored on average 70 percent on the final examination, but if the test was administered two years later, the average score fell to 19 percent (Pressey, 1933). As we have seen, Ebbinghaus's experiments also suggest a remedy for the rapid loss of material: overlearning, or the repetition of material beyond what is necessary to learn it initially. Interestingly, the area in which overlearning is used a great deal is athletics. Tennis professionals practice the same serve over and over again, hundreds of times, even though they already know how to execute the serve and may be serving aces. Finally, the facilitating effects of meaning on memory, as demonstrated by Ebbinghaus's work, are seen in mnemonics, or powerful devices for improving memory in which some sort of meaning is given to meaningless material; for example, the telephone numbers of radio stations are more easily remembered when the last four digits are the call letters of the station. Students of anatomy memorizing the order of the cranial nerves use the mnemonic "On Old Olympus' Towering Top a Finn and German Viewed Some Hops" (the first letters correspond to the first letters of each cranial nerve), while schoolchildren remember the color spectrum with "Roy G. Biv."

Ebbinghaus was not the only nineteenth-century German psychologist to describe an empirical approach different from that of Wundt. In the same year Wundt published the second half of his *Fundamentals of Physiological Psychology*, Franz Brentano published *Psychology from an Empirical Standpoint*.

FRANZ BRENTANO (1838–1917)

Franz Brentano was born in 1838 in the town of Marienburg on the German Rhine. His was a distinguished literary family, with his father being a published writer (Puglisi, 1924). The father died when Brentano was thirteen, and so Brentano was raised by his mother, a pious and cultivated lady whose ambition was that her son be ordained a Catholic priest. Brentano first entered the University of Berlin, where he studied philosophy, especially the writings of Aristotle, under Friedrich Adolf Trendelenburg. These studies made a lasting impression on Brentano, and all his life he looked back to the teachings of philosophers in considering psychological topics. In 1856 he transferred to the University of Munich and there was influenced by a second great teacher, Johann Joseph Ignaz von Döllinger. Döllinger was recognized as a distinguished historian and theologian of the Catholic church. He tutored Brentano in the teachings of St. Thomas Aquinas. Encouraged by his mother and inspired by Döllinger's example, Brentano decided to study for the priesthood. He was ordained a Dominican priest in the summer of 1864.

Ideological Conflicts

In 1866 Brentano accepted a position as a lecturer at the University of Würzburg while continuing to live a monastic life with his brother Dominicans. He proved to be a popular teacher, better at presenting his views orally than in books and papers. He probably was expected to follow the contemplative life of a Catholic academic, but that was not to be. The Dominicans were among the most traditional of the Catholic church's priestly orders. During the Counterreformation they had been known as the "hounds of the Lord" (*canes domini*) for their zeal in tracking down heretics. It is not surprising that they supported the controversial proposal, made in the summer of 1869, that papal infallibility be adopted as an article of faith for Catholics, that Catholics were to believe that the Pope speaking *ex cathedra* (from the pontifical chair of Saint Peter) on matters and principles of faith and dogma was incapable of error. Adoption of this proposal would mean that church members questioning papal infallibility would face excommunication, and so it aroused great opposition, with the bishops of Germany being especially active opponents.

At Döllinger's suggestion, Bishop Ketteler asked Brentano to prepare a philosophical and historical essay on papal infallibility. In his essay Brentano described a number of historical occasions on which a Pope speaking *ex cathedra* had been in error and concluded with "the firmest possible persuasion" (Puglisi, 1924, p. 415) that the proposed doctrine was impossible to accept. Given this conclusion, it came as a devastating blow to Brentano when the Vatican Council in the spring of 1870 promulgated papal infallibility as an article of faith. This promulgation led to a bitter schism in the church, but Brentano tried desperately to remain faithful and refused to follower Döllinger's lead into a rival Old Catholic church. The following three years were a terrible period for Brentano as he tried to resolve the conflict between faith and reason. He continued to teach at Würzburg, attracting many students, including Carl Stumpf, and to publish papers on Aristotle and the history of science in the Catholic church (Misiak & Staudt, 1954). In 1872 he was promoted to the rank of *Professor extraordinarius*, but shortly thereafter he decided to withdraw from the church he had been raised to serve and love. Having been appointed to the university's faculty as a priest, Brentano felt morally obliged to resign his academic position as well.

Brentano's Contribution to Psychology

Brentano was able to overcome this setback and used the time of his forced hiatus from university life to write *Psychology from an Empirical Standpoint*. The book's success secured his appointment as a layman to the faculty of the University of Vienna. Brentano spent six years (1874–1880) as a *Professor ordinarius* at Vienna before his personal life created another professional crisis. In 1880 he became engaged to a Catholic. Since marriages by former priests were forbidden in Austria, Brentano was forced to resign his university position and assume German citizenship before he could legally marry. After his marriage he was allowed to return to the faculty of the University of Vienna, but only at the lower rank of *Privatdozent*.

The psychology Brentano outlined in *Psychology from an Empirical Standpoint* was intended to be empirical in the sense that it was based on experience. Brentano hoped to use experience to construct a core of generally accepted truths. His approach appears similar to that of his rival, Wundt, but there are important distinctions. First, for Brentano, the truth and acceptability of his psychology would be determined by careful, logical examination. Experiences, which provide the empirical base of psychology, had to be analyzed according to the rules and principles of logic before they could be used to establish psychological knowledge. Wundt's inductive psychology, on the other hand, gave experimental results central importance.

A second major distinction between Wundt and Brentano concerns the modifiability of their respective systems. Since the empirical observations on which Brentano's psychology was based would not change and since the rules of logic are fixed, Brentano did not expect his psychology to change much over time. It was, relative to Wundt's psychology, fixed. Consequently, it is no surprise that Brentano chose not to write the three additional outlines of his position that he had originally planned to follow his first book. In 1874 he had said all he wanted to say, and his psychology was complete. In contrast, the prolific Wundt constantly revised and expanded his *Fundamentals* as new experimental findings became available.

Third, Brentano's psychology is an "act" psychology. Instead of studying the products of our mental actions, Brentano proposed that psychologists should study the mental *actions* and *processes* themselves. The three fundamental classes of mental acts Brentano proposed included ideating, judging, and loving versus hating. According to Brentano's analysis, mental acts may include as their objects past sensations, thus making it possible to have an idea of an object when the object is not present. The mind employs what Brentano termed *imagination*, or what Locke had termed *reflection*. Similarly, it is possible to feel an emotion when the object of that emotion is not present. In Brentano's system, one mental act may have as its object another mental act. We have ideas about ideas, judgments of judgments, and feelings about feelings. Finally, mental acts may mix; one mental act may have as its object a mental act of a different class. When we hear a harmonious sound or see a beautiful landscape, we feel pleasure. The pleasure, according to Brentano, results from the mental acts of seeing and hearing, not from the sensations themselves.

A fourth major distinction between the psychologies of Wundt and Brentano concerns methodology. Brentano's psychology did not include introspection, a method Brentano labeled "inner observation." While we are able to observe external objects, Brentano believed that it is impossible to make inner observations of our own consciousness. Brentano pointed out that in the white heat of rage or in the throes of terror, we cannot observe these emotions. If we try to do so, the very act of observing changes, diminishes, or even destroys them. As further evidence that introspection is not an appropriate method for psychology, Brentano cited the Wundtians' descriptions of the long and arduous training program needed before a psychologist could qualify to introspect, the difficulty of such self-observations, and the rigidly controlled, unnatural conditions under which they were to be made. Brentano asked why, if inner observations are as possible as external observations, such extreme precautions and procedures are necessary. He described the sorry plight of students attempting what he considered to be the impossible:

> I know of examples of young people, desiring to devote themselves to the study of psychology, who, at the thresholds of the science, began to doubt their own ability. They had been told that inner observation is the main source of psychological knowledge, and they repeatedly made strenuous attempts at it. But all these efforts were in vain; all they got for their trouble was a swarm of confused ideas and a headache. So they came to the conclusion that they had no capacity for self-observation, which is quite right. But on the basis of the notion, which had been imparted to them, they took this to mean that they had no talent for psychological investigation. (Bretano, 1874/1973, p. 30)

Having rejected introspection, what methods can psychology use to observe mental phenomena? Brentano suggested that mental acts can be observed in memory and therefore can be studied "quietly and empirically." We can look back, for example, at the last time we were angry and thus observe the mental phenomena involved in that emotion. As a second psychological method Brentano proposed imagination. It is possible to intentionally arouse various mental phenomena that can be studied. In addition to these two methods, Brentano suggested studies of the mental lives of animals and children as well as examination of the disordered mental life of idiots and the insane. These suggestions anticipated the concerns of later comparative, developmental, and clinical psychologists.

Brentano in Perspective

Nearly twenty years elapsed between Brentano's publication of his *Psychology* and that of his next psychological works. These were years in which he suffered ill health, progressive loss of vision, and personal difficulties. In 1895, following his wife's death, he resigned from the faculty of the University of Vienna and moved to Florence. That same year Brentano published three psychological papers on optical illusions, and in 1896 he attended the Third International Congress of Psychology, where he presented a paper on his doctrine of sensation. At that time his interests were becoming more philosophical, though he did attend the Fourth International Congress of Psychology in 1905, presenting a paper on the psychological qualities of tones. When Italy entered the World War I in 1917, Brentano, an avowed pacifist, felt compelled to move to neutral Switzerland. He died in Zurich in 1917.

As we have said, perhaps one reason Brentano is not as well known as Wundt or Ebbinghaus is that he was not a prolific writer. His lifetime bibliography consists of only thirty-eight works, of which perhaps eight are on psychological topics. He always considered his *Psychology* to be his major statement, and forty years after its publication he was still working on a proposed second edition, which was finally published posthumously in 1924 (Kraus, 1924). Brentano's significance for the history of psychology lies not in the volume of his published works and certainly not in his experimental research, for he did very little, but rather in his formulation of a contemporary rival approach to that of Wundt. His psychology of mental acts was an important historical predecessor of the American functional psychologies that will be presented in Chapter 10. He also trained two important students: Christian von Ehrenfels, whose conception of form quality (*Gestaltqualität*) influenced the Gestalt psychologists (Chapter 7), and Carl Stumpf, the next nineteenth-century German psychologist we will consider.

CARL STUMPF (1848–1936)

Carl Stumpf was born in Wiesentheid in Franconia, now Bavaria, southern Germany, on Good Friday 1848 and died on Christmas Day 1936. Stumpf's father was the country court physician, and his immediate family included scientists and academicians. As a boy Stumpf showed precocious musical talent, learning the violin by the age of seven and five other instruments by the age of ten and having sufficient skill to perform in public. At the age of ten he composed and published an oratorio for three male voices, and throughout his life he composed and performed musical

Carl Stumpf. (Archives of the
History of American Psychology,
University of Akron)

works (Ruckmick, 1937, p. 189). In his adult years Stumpf moved equally comfortably in the academic world of psychology and the artistic world of music and
musicians. At the University of Berlin Stumpf valued his association with the great
sensory physiologist Hermann von Helmholtz as well as his friendship with the
famous violinist Joseph Joachim, himself a friend of Mendelssohn, Brahms, and
Schumann. Later in his life, this musical background provided Stumpf with a frame
of reference for evaluating psychological research on auditory perception and especially on musical aesthetics. It also led to disputes with the experimentally oriented Wundt, whose methods Stumpf would come to label "repellent" and whose
name would become taboo in Stumpf's Berlin Psychological Institute.

As a boy Stumpf attended the local *Gymnasium* before enrolling at the age of
seventeen as a student at the University of Würzburg. He spent a semester studying
aesthetics and one studying law, the latter to prepare for a money-making career,
since he did not consider himself sufficiently talented to be a professional musician.
In his third semester at Würzburg he met the man who was to change his life, Franz
Brentano. Brentano taught the artistically inclined Stumpf to think logically and
empirically. After two semesters Brentano encouraged him to transfer to the University of Göttingen to complete his studies under Rudolph Hermann Lotze (1817–
1881), a German perceptual theorist. Even though Stumpf studied under Brentano
for just three semesters, all his life he acknowledged his indebtedness to Brentano
and regarded him as his master.

After receiving a degree from Lotze in 1868, Stumpf returned to Würzburg
to prepare for the Catholic priesthood. In 1869, he entered a seminary and studied
theology, with special attention to the writings of Saint Thomas Aquinas. Almost
immediately his career plans were shattered, for 1870, as we have seen, was a year

of crisis in the Catholic church over the doctrine of papal infallibility. For Stumpf, as for Brentano, "the whole stock of Catholic-Christian dogmatic theology crumbled to dust" (Stumpf, 1930, p. 393). Stumpf had not yet been ordained, and so his professional crisis was not as severe as Brentano's, but he went through great anguish before deciding in July 1870 to discard the black robe of the seminarian. However, unlike Brentano, he did not leave the church, and he remained a practicing Catholic until 1921.

Stumpf's Early Academic Career

Lotze welcomed Stumpf's decision to leave the seminary and arranged for him to return to Göttingen as an instructor in the Department of Philosophy. There Stumpf met Weber and Fechner and had the distinction of serving as an observer in psychological experiments for both of them. Weber demonstrated sensory mapping on Stumpf's arm and tested him as a subject in an experiment involving sensory magnitude estimation. At that time Fechner was investigating the visual appeal of rectangles with different proportions. As we saw in Chapter 1, Pythagoras and his followers believed that beauty inheres in simple ratios: a lute string divided into exact divisions of 2, 4, 8, and so on, produces harmonious notes; when it is divided at other places, the notes are discordant. Similar principles were held to govern other aesthetic experiences. Thus it was believed that rectangles having simple ratios of width to length—1:2, 2:3, 3:4, for example—would be most appealing to the eye of an observer. Fechner constructed ten rectangles with different ratios of width to length and asked a number of observers, including Stumpf, to choose the "best" and "worst" of them. The rectangles chosen as "best" by the largest number of observers had a ratio of 0.62. This modal ratio falls between 3:5 and 5:8 and is not a simple ratio. It came to be known as the "golden section," that is, the ratio of a rectangle's width to length most pleasing to the eye. This careful approach to a problem of aesthetics appealed to the young Stumpf and reinforced the lesson he had learned from Brentano that psychological acts or functions can be studied empirically.

In 1873, at the age of twenty-five, Stumpf returned to the University of Würzburg, this time as a professor in the Department of Philosophy. His homecoming, however, was not without problems. Upon arrival at Würzburg, Stumpf found that he *was* the Department of Philosophy. With Brentano's forced departure, the department at Würzburg had fallen on hard times, and so Stumpf had to teach all of philosophy and psychology. Even so, during this first year at Würzburg, Stumpf was able to complete his first major psychological work, an examination of visual perception, particularly depth perception.

Stumpf proposed a nativistic explanation of depth perception, in contrast to the accounts of such empiricist theorists as Berkeley, Helmholtz, Wundt, and Stumpf's teacher, Lotze. For these empiricists, depth perception was considered an acquired skill based on experience. Stumpf acknowledged the arguments they proposed but developed disputational counterarguments in favor of his nativist position. Stumpf accepted that muscle and other sensations associated with eye movements, what Lotze had called "local signs," contribute to our perception of depth, but in contrast to Lotze, Stumpf felt they are of secondary importance. He stressed that they were only local, after all, and that something more was involved. The "something more" was the interpretative action of a higher center in the brain. Furthermore, the cognitive act of interpretation was considered to be an inborn or native function. Stumpf compared local signs to addresses on letters. They are important, but the letters would not be delivered without the carrier's knowledge of the route. Stumpf's conception of depth perception paralleled Immanuel Kant's view of the *a priori* nature of space. Stumpf's book has been cited as a testimonial to his youthful brilliance (Langfeld, 1937, p. 319) and an outstanding early contribution to the debate between nativist and empiricist views of perception, a debate that continues in our time (Gibson, 1977).

Stumpf Gains Academic Prominence

In 1875 Stumpf began his monumental *Tonpsychologie* (Tone Psychology), a work often considered his greatest contribution to psychology. Stumpf followed Brentano's lead and distinguished between phenomena and mental functions. Stumpf suggested that phenomena such as tones, colors, and images are either sensory or imaginary. The study of such phenomena Stumpf termed *phenomenology*, and his massive *Tone Psychology* was a phenomenology of tones. The second major class of psychological experience included seeing, hearing, perceiving, and thinking—Brentano's cognitive acts. Studies of sensory and imaginal phenomena were for Stumpf "preparatory" to the study of psychological acts or functions, the real task of psychology. But here we find a paradox, for Stumpf devoted his life to studying these preparatory phenomena but always considered himself a psychologist. Accepting his own distinctions, he was, in fact, a phenomenologist. Regardless of his academic label, Stumpf did a wide range of studies of the phenomenological characteristics of the sounds of different instruments, the determinants of melody, tonal fusion, and the consonance and dissonance of tones. He also investigated auditory attention, analysis, and comparison and conducted studies of a number of extremely unmusical subjects by comparing their musical observations and perceptions with those of musical people. These were monumental investigations, and they continued to the end of his career.

In 1879, as a result of this work, Stumpf was called to the University of Prague. The first volume of his *Tone Psychology* appeared in 1883. One year later Stumpf moved to the University of Halle, staying there until 1889, when he was called to the University of Munich. Finally, in 1894 Stumpf's academic pilgrimage ended with his appointment to the most prestigious position in German philosophy, the chair of philosophy at the University of Berlin. Berlin was the capital city of Germany, the home of the kaiser and his court, and the University of Berlin was one of the finest universities in Europe.

From our perspective in the late twentieth century we may wonder why Stumpf was appointed rather than Wundt or Ebbinghaus. After all, by 1894 Wundt was well established as the leader of the new German psychology of mental content; he had published extensively and had established the world's leading psychological laboratory at Leipzig. Ebbinghaus's research on memory had been widely acclaimed, and he was also at the University of Berlin at that time. Perhaps he was considered too junior for a Berlin chair. In addition, Ebbinghaus might have harmed his chances for the chair with his criticisms of the eminent Berlin methodologist Wilhelm Dilthey. Dilthey was a skeptic regarding the new experimental psychology and believed that it would never be a true science. Ebbinghaus characterized Dilthey as having an old-fashioned understanding of science.

At Berlin, Stumpf also held an adjunct appointment as director of the Berlin Psychological Institute. The institute had been started by Ebbinghaus, but at the time of Stumpf's appointment it occupied only three dark rooms. Under his leadership, it expanded in 1900 to occupy the top floor of a Berlin apartment house, and in 1920 it was moved to twenty-five rooms in the former Imperial Palace. It was said that one of the great attractions of the University of Berlin was its proximity to the kaiser. Stumpf's psychological institute occupied part of the kaiser's former residence, a grand location that was appropriate for Stumpf's conception of psychology as a respectable experimental science.

Especially in the years prior to World War I, Stumpf held a position of great power and influence. He organized divisions within his institute devoted to medical, musical, and military purposes in addition to the basic research division. In 1896 he took charge of preparations for the Third International Congress of Psychology held in Munich. Stumpf presided over the congress and delivered the inaugural address on the relation between mind and body. He advocated an interactionist position, which he contrasted with the psychophysical parallelism held at the time by most nineteenth century physiological psychologists, including Wundt. Their position was that mental phenomena coincide with brain phenomena or are parallel with them.

The year 1900 was a productive one for Stumpf. He established an archive of phonograph records of songs, music, and native dialects from all over the world. Recordings were sent to Berlin by German missionaries, travelers, and diplomats. During World War I a commission arranged for recordings to be made of the language, songs, and music of thousands of prisoners of war held captive in Germany. In addition to this musical archive, in 1900 Stumpf and a Berlin school principal cofounded the Society for Child Psychology. Their research organization was founded just one year after Binet had organized the Free Society for the Psychological Study of the Child in Paris (Chapter 11). Both societies supported studies of children, especially their mental life. Stumpf's former teacher, Brentano, also had advocated such studies. Stumpf made observations of speech development in his own children as well as in others and studied the origins of childhood fears. Stumpf stressed the importance of direct observation of children rather than the use of questionnaires, an approach which G. Stanley Hall had pioneered in the United States and which was then in vogue (Chapter 9). Finally, Stumpf studied the musical development of a number of child prodigies as well as children with phenomenal memories.

Stumpf served as the rector of the University of Berlin from 1907 to 1908, important recognition for a psychologist. Those years were a time of political turmoil and student unrest in Germany. In his inaugural address he advocated a rigorous, observational approach to the acquisition of knowledge. As an empiricist he distrusted armchair speculations and theorizing. "Theories," Stumpf said in his autobiography (1930), "come and go." A source of satisfaction in his own life was that he had made "some good observations." Paradoxically, Stumpf never conducted large-scale experiments. He was more in the mold of his teacher, Brentano, than in that of his rival, Wundt. His reluctance to experiment might also have been due to his admitted lack of manual dexterity; as a chemistry student at Würzburg he had started a fire in a laboratory which threatened the whole building before it was brought under control.

Stumpf Studies Sensational Phenomena

In 1903 and 1904 Stumpf was involved in two well-publicized debunking episodes. The first concerned an engineer from Prague who claimed to have invented a machine that could change photographs of sound waves into sound. The entire faculty of the University of Berlin, together with many distinguished experts, attended an apparently successful demonstration. Stumpf, however, was convinced that it had been fraudulent and wrote a sarcastic article challenging the likelihood of such a machine. Not a single word of this remarkable invention was ever heard again.

The second debunking was more difficult. The late nineteenth century saw much interest in the mental abilities of animals, an interest stimulated in large part by Charles Darwin's *The Descent of Man* (1871). As Darwin presented the case for continuity in the mental life of humans and other animals, evidence of reasoning and thought in animals was eagerly sought. With the long European tradition of dressage, intelligent horses were especially popular. The horse Muhamed was part of a stable of horses in Elberfeld, Germany, trained and owned by Karl Krall. While blindfolded, Muhamed could add, subtract, multiply, divide, and calculate cube roots, tapping out the correct answer with his right foot. Scientific observers were never able to prove trickery or fraud.

The case of Clever Hans (*Der kluge Hans*), an apparently brilliant horse owned by Herr von Osten, was even more sensational. Von Osten was a former high school mathematics teacher, a dabbler in phrenology, something of a mystic, and a man who was convinced that horses are capable of "inner speech" and therefore of mathematics. To all appearances von Osten was successful in training Hans to add, subtract, multiply, divide, work with fractions, and even tell time and keep track of the calendar. For instance, von Osten might ask Hans, "If the eighth day of the month comes on a Tuesday, what is the date of the following Friday?" Hans would answer by tapping the answer with his hoof, slowing down as he approached the correct number. Hans could also count objects or people. Von Osten might ask, "Hans, how many people—or men, or umbrellas, or women—are there in this room?" Such questions could be asked orally or might be printed on cards. Von Osten exhibited him throughout Germany, never charging admission to their demonstrations but garnering great public interest wherever they went. Kaiser Wilhelm himself observed Hans, and a front-page account of the horse's mathematical abilities appeared in the *New York Times*. In his foreword to an account of the investigation of Hans the American psychologist James Angell (Chapter 10) summarized the situation:

No more remarkable tale of credulity founded on unconscious deceit was ever told, and were it offered as fiction, it would take high rank as a work of imagination. Being in reality a record of sober fact, it verges on the miraculous. After reading Mr. Pfungst's story one can quite understand how sedate and sober Germany was for months thrown into a turmoil of newspaper debate, which for intensity and range of feeling finds its only parallel in a heated political campaign. (Angell, p. v, in Pfungst, 1911).

Because of the immense public interest in Hans and his achievements, the German Board of Education appointed a commission to study him and evaluate von Osten's claims. Stumpf was asked to head the commission and select its members. He included a circus manager, a cavalry officer, an experienced veterinarian, a number of schoolteachers and administrators, the director of the Berlin Zoological Gardens, and his assistant, Oskar Heinroth, whose student Konrad Lorenz was to win the 1973 Nobel Prize for his studies of animal behavior. This commission observed von Osten's demonstrations and in September 1904 issued a report concluding that no tricks, intentional influences, or aids from the questioner were involved in Hans's performance. The question of how clever the horse actually was they recommended for further investigation. These investigations were conducted by one of Stumpf's assistants at the Berlin Institute, Oskar Pfungst (Pfungst, 1911).

Pfungst was able to befriend both von Osten and Hans, which was no small achievement since von Osten was of a tyrannical temperament and was prone to rage when the horse did not perform well. Hans too was bad-tempered and at times

Clever Hans demonstrates his "mathematical abilities." (Karl Kroll, *Denkende Tiere*, Leipzig, 1912)

difficult to control. When frustrated, Hans made the stable courtyard an unsafe place and Pfungst suffered more than one horse bite during his investigation. He tested Hans when the correct answer to the question was known by the questioner and then when the questioner did not know the answer. Pfungst chose a seemingly simple test for a horse of Hans's talents: Numbers were printed on cards, and Hans was asked to tap out the the number shown. When von Osten asked the questions "with knowledge," 98 percent of the horse's responses were correct; "without knowledge," only 8 percent were correct. Clearly the questioner's knowledge was crucial, but how did it influence Hans's behavior?

First, Pfungst investigated the role of visual cues. Hans was fitted with large blinkers and was questioned with the questioner standing either directly in front of him, where he could be seen, or to the side, where he could not be seen. When the questioner stood to the side, Hans made strenuous attempts to see him and answered the questions correctly only 6 percent of the time. When the questioner stood directly in front of Hans, 89 percent of the answers were correct. Clearly the horse required a visual cue from the questioner. With what Stumpf called his "keen eyes and iron patience" (Stumpf, 1930, p. 407), Pfungst was able to discern that when the horse was given a problem, the questioner would lean forward to watch the response being tapped out. At the correct response, Pfungst observed that the questioner would give an involuntary slight upward movement of the eyebrows and head. Nearly all the questioners made this movement, and they were all unaware of it. Once this cue had been identified, Pfungst was able to elicit any response he wanted simply by making the upward movement. Pfungst presented his evidence to Stumpf's commission, and in December 1904 a second report was issued concluding that the horse had learned to attend to slight changes in the questioner's body posture while tapping. The case of Clever Hans showed the critical influence of subtle cues and movements from an observer. It alerted psychologists to the need to control such effects and is still cited in discussions of the methodology of psychology. Von Osten forbade further studies with Hans, asserting that the investigation had failed to achieve what he considered its goal of corroborating his claims and theories. He continued to exhibit Hans, attracting large and enthusiastic crowds.

Stumpf's Later Years

The case of Clever Hans was one of Stumpf's more colorful investigations, but the bulk of Stumpf's later academic career did not consist of such sensational and interesting research. In fact, his later years were sad ones. With the outbreak of World War I, most of the young people had left the Berlin Psychological Institute to serve in the armed forces, and so it was a lonely and deserted place. The war was a wrenching experience for Stumpf since he had many British, American, and Russian psychologists as friends and had been honored by his membership in the American Academy of Sciences and the National Institute of Music in Moscow. War between his beloved Germany and the allied countries disrupted these professional relationships. Compounding his sense of loss, he was asked by the German government to organize psychologists in support of the war effort. It appears that his heart was not in such an assignment, and he admitted that his work had little success.

Stumpf retired from the University of Berlin in 1921 and was succeeded as director of the Psychological Institute by his former student, Wolfgang Köhler (Chapter 7). The last fifteen years of his life were a time of great social and political turmoil in Germany. The kaiser was in exile, and the country was wracked by inflation. In August 1922, 400 marks bought one U.S. dollar; one year later, in August 1923, the exchange rate was 1 million marks to the dollar (Rhodes, 1986, p. 16). Even so, one of Stumpf's former students, Kurt Lewin (Chapter 7), recalled that as an old man in his eighties, Stumpf would often visit the Berlin Psychological Institute to continue his observations, using the elaborate machines and instruments he had constructed (Lewin, 1937, p. 190).

Not only did the onset of World War I create a sense of personal sadness, conflict, and loss for Stumpf, it also might have been one of the reasons why much of his work was lost to the mainstream of sensory psychology. Stumpf made potentially major contributions to the field of auditory perception and to aesthetics, but his work was not elaborated by later generations of psychologists, particularly American psychologists, because their contact with Stumpf and his work had been severed. This unfortunate situation was not to affect Stumpf only. The ideas of other German psychologists, such as Külpe and his students, suffered a similar fate.

OSWALD KÜLPE (1862–1915)

Oswald Külpe was born in 1862 to a German family in the Baltic province of Latvia, which was then and is now again part of Russia. After graduating from the local *Gymnasium*, Külpe entered the University of Leipzig in 1881. He majored in history but became interested in psychology after attending Wundt's lectures. He spent two semesters at Leipzig and then, at Wundt's recommendation, transferred to the University of Göttingen to study under George Elias Müller (1850–1934). Müller had succeeded Lotze (Stumpf's teacher) at Göttingen and occupied the university's chair of psychology for over forty years.

Külpe's teacher was ardently dedicated to the new experimental psychology. The British psychologist Charles Spearman, who also studied with Müller, described him as having "a narrow outlook" and as being a man "who ran in blinkers" (Spearman, 1930, p. 305). Müller's vision might have been narrow, but his research output was broad. Initially, he followed Fechner's lead and worked on psychophysics, but like Ebbinghaus, he turned to the study of memory. Müller developed additional experimental procedures using nonsense syllables and pointed out the weakness in Ebbinghaus's experiments of having one person, most often Ebbinghaus himself, act as both experimenter and subject. Ebbinghaus had found that problem "vexing" and had taken precautions to avoid what he called "the secret influence of theories and opinions." As far as possible Ebbinghaus withheld knowledge of the outcome of his experiments until they were complete, and he always replicated his results. Müller's forceful criticisms were important in bringing such potential experimenter influences to the attention of experimental psychologists. Today much attention is paid to what are called the "demand characteristics" of experiments, that is to the subject's perceptions of the experimenter's expectations. Müller also invented an apparatus to present nonsense syllable lists, the memory drum. A horizontal drum with nonsense syllables on its surface rotates at a controlled speed and exposes one nonsense syllable at a time through a small opening. The memory drum is ideal for the study of serial learning and is still widely used today to present lists of material to be learned. Müller studied effective ways of learning and described the effects of interference—old learning interfering with new learning (Müller & Pilzecker, 1900). He also reported experiments in which memory was much better after a two-day interval, presumably as a result of the longer time available for its consolidation. With another of his students, Adolph Jost, Müller also discovered that when two associations are of equal strength, repetition strengthens the younger one more than the older one, a finding known as Jost's law. Finally, Müller studied the phenomenal ability of "lightning calculators," individuals who could do large, bulky calculations nearly instantaneously. Despite this important work, Müller was never a popular figure. He apparently had a terrible temper and was often a vicious reviewer of the work of others.

After graduating from Göttingen, Külpe returned briefly to Russia, where he considered becoming a schoolteacher. However, he quickly returned to Germany to study under Wundt. He received a Ph.D. in 1887. James McKeen Cattell, Wundt's first research assistant, had just left Leipzig for Cambridge, and so Wundt appointed Külpe in his place and secured Külpe's appointment as a *Privatdozent* at Leipzig. Külpe was promoted to the rank of *Professor extraordinarius* in 1894, but that same year he moved on to the University of Würzburg. At Würzburg, Külpe and his students performed experiments that challenged fundamental assumptions held by Wundt and especially by Titchener. Despite this apparent rivalry, Külpe maintained the warmest affection for Wundt, always regarding him as his "master teacher," and was active in the publication of Wundt's *Festschrift* (honorary anthology).

Because the faculty needed a text for the increasingly popular lectures on psychology being given in the Leipzig psychology department, Wundt encouraged Külpe to write a book that was clearer and simpler than his own *Physiologische Psychologie*. Wundt's text was in its fourth edition at the time, but it was too long, difficult, and technical for the students. In response to Wundt's request, Külpe published in 1893 one of his major works, the *Grundriss der Psychologie*. An English translation by Titchener entitled *Outline of Psychology* appeared in 1895. The book was dedicated "To my revered teacher, Wilhelm Wundt, in sincere gratitude and affection." Ironically, Wundt found the text unsatisfactory, and in 1896 he published his own book, *Grundriss der Psychologie*. It is always difficult for a pupil to present a teacher's views, but there were other reasons for Wundt's dissatisfaction. Külpe's conception of psychology was beginning to diverge from that of Wundt, and even in this first book there are clear areas of strain and difference. In Külpe's second major book, the *Einleitung in die Philosophie* (Introduction to Philosophy), published in 1895, the split was even deeper.

Külpe Defines a General Experimental Psychology

In formulating his definition of psychology Külpe was influenced by the positivist views of the physicist Ernst Mach (1838–1916) and the philosopher Richard Avenarius (1843–1896) (Danziger, 1979). As positivists, these philosophers held that all science is based on experience; when natural scientists observe and record natural events, they do so through their sensory experiences. When experiences are studied independently of a biological system, the science is physics; when they are studied in the context of a biological system, the science is psychology. Their emphasis was on observation; mentalistic conceptions and attributions of mental entities were to be abjured. Psychology was to provide objective descriptions of mental events. These men accepted the possibility of a science of psychology and respected its status as a new but nonetheless valid and important branch of natural science. Külpe aimed to develop a positivistic general psychology that would include complex phenomena such as thinking, judging, remembering, and doubting. As we have seen, Wundt believed that such complex psychological phenomena are beyond the reach of experimental methods. Such mental acts were part of what he called *social* or *ethnopsychology*, a nonexperimental complement to experimental or physiological psychology. Despite Ebbinghaus's success, it was still Külpe's responsibility to demonstrate that other higher mental functions could be studied experimentally. Külpe's research at Würzburg provided that demonstration.

Research at the University of Würzburg

Külpe was assigned one of the university's medieval buildings for his laboratory, which was supported by a private endowment. By 1896 the laboratory was full of activity. The experimental results reported from Würzburg would challenge some of the fundamental tenets of Wundt's psychology and establish a rival approach to the science of psychology.

What has come to be known as the "Würzburg school" saw its formal beginning in 1901 with a paper by two of Külpe's students, A. Mayer and J. Orth. In an investigation of the qualitative nature of associations, they questioned subjects about the associations that came freely to their minds during thinking. This method of questioning or interrogation was known in German as *Ausfrage* and came to be widely used at Würzburg. Mayer and Orth's subjects reported many different patterns and types of associations. The associations were complex and detailed, unlike those reported by Wundt and Titchener. They were more like Francis Galton's descriptions of the associations that came to his mind during his walk down Pall Mall in London (Chapter 9). Külpe was familiar with Galton's investigation and presented it in his *Outline*. Such experiments would never have been done at Leipzig or Cornell.

That same year an experiment reported by Karl Marbe (1901) was to show even more clearly the characteristics of the Würzburg approach. For many years Marbe had been a *Privatdozent* at Würzburg, succeeding Külpe as head of the laboratory. Marbe performed an experimental study of judgment, in which subjects were asked to compare weights and judge them as heavier or lighter. Of course, many weight-lifting experiments had been done before Marbe; they were, after all, a staple of the psychophysical laboratories. What was different about this experiment was an interest in the judgments themselves. Marbe's subjects were able to make correct judgments most of the time, but they were unable to describe how the judgments were made. Their introspections did not yield descriptions of the mental act of judging. Judgments just came to their minds. They did have many sensations and images, as Wundt had said they would, but the sensations and images were not the judgments themselves. In the act of judging, various other states—doubt, hesitation, searching—occurred. These states Marbe termed *Bewussteinlagen* (conscious attitudes) (Ogden, 1911, p. 9). They formed the background against which judgments were made; they attended upon judgments. Wundt's description of three basic elements of consciousness—sensations, images, and feelings—did not describe adequately the experience of Marbe's subjects.

In 1900 Külpe and one of his American students, William Lowe Bryan, conducted some abstraction experiments which show the Würzburg approach at its best. Bryan was well prepared to assist in these experiments. After attaining a master's degree in philosophy at Indiana University (1886), he went to Berlin, where he served as a subject for Ebbinghaus's memory experiments (Capshew & Hearst, 1980). He then returned to Indiana, establishing a small psychological laboratory in 1888, and took a Ph.D. degree with G. Stanley Hall at Clark University in 1892. After teaching again at Indiana University, Bryan returned to Europe in 1900 and studied with Pierre Janet (Chapter 8) and Alfred Binet (Chapter 11) before working with Külpe. In Külpe and Bryan's experiment subjects were shown cards with nonsense syllables of various colors, letters, and arrangements. The card was shown briefly, and the subject was asked to observe it and report the color, form, or number of items on it. Külpe and Bryan found that with suitable instruction their subjects would abstract a particular feature while remaining unaware of the other features. Sensations from the features alone were not sufficient to place them in the subject's mental experience (Ogden, 1951, p. 15). Külpe and Bryan believed that abstraction of the desired element was based on active mental acts they termed *apprehension*. A simple demonstration of this mental phenomenon is easily arranged. If the figure on page 173 is shown to a subject who is told to inspect it carefully as he or she will later be asked what *numbers* were displayed, the subject's recall of the numbers will usually be quite good. But if the subject is asked what the *letters* were, recall will be poor. The instructions cause the numbers but not the letters to be "apprehended."

One of the most frequently used paradigms at Leipzig was that of the simple reaction time. Külpe had done a study comparing reaction times with the favored, usually, the right, or unfavored hand. The Würzburg psychologists used the reaction time paradigm to study volitional responses. The subjects had to make a particular response to a specific stimulus through an act of will. With practice, reaction times decreased and the subjects became less and less able to report an act of will prior to the response. For one thing, the reaction occurred so quickly that there simply was not sufficient time for the introspection to be made. This created

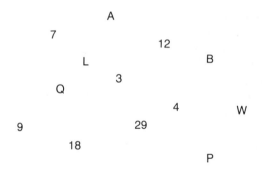

a problem, for how could a volitional act occur, as it obviously did, without being part of the subject's mental experience?

Yet another Würzburg worker, H. J. Watt, seized upon this dilemma. First he introduced the new Hipp chronoscope, which allowed reaction times to be measured with far greater precision and accuracy. It was a technical contribution that the Wundtians welcomed. What they did not accept was his conception of the reaction time response itself. Watt proposed that it be "fractionated" into four phases:

1. A preparatory period in which the subject prepares for presentation of the stimulus
2. Stimulus presentation, in which the stimulus is sensed by the subject
3. Striving by the subject for the response—the mental act prior to the response
4. The response itself

Watt believed that the volitional act occurs in the preparatory period, when subjects accept and prepare for the task. The Wundtians had failed to report it because they had been introspecting just prior to the response itself—at the wrong time. Instead, when Watt's subjects introspected during the preparatory period, they were always able to describe volitional acts or thoughts. The act of will was present for all reactions, but always in the preparatory phase.

For his dissertation research at Würzburg, Watt (1905) used a constrained association technique. Subjects were given a stimulus word and were asked to give its sub- or superordinate. For example, to the stimulus word "bird" the subordinate might be "sparrow," and the superordinate "animal." Watt's subjects were able to respond appropriately with short reaction times and without conscious mental effort. The conscious work, Watt claimed, was done when the instructions were given and accepted by the subject. These mental attitudes or preparations Watt termed *Aufgaben* (instructions). They were seen as establishing in the subject an *Einstellung* (set) to respond in a particular way. Narziss Ach, Külpe's assistant at Würzburg for fifteen years, showed the influence of a cognitive set in mental operations. When Ach's subjects were shown tachistoscopically the numbers 7 and 3, their response was almost always 10, despite the fact that they were not given specific instructions to add. Products of other arithmetical operations—4, 21, and 2.3— usually did not occur as responses. The subjects had a cognitive "set" to add rather than to perform other arithmetical operations.

In 1905, Ach reported an investigation in which he used what he termed systematic experimental introspection to analyze the mental processes by which subjects reach decisions. Ach found clear differences between his subjects which were consistent from problem to problem, leading him to classify his subjects into different "decision types." These experiments are very reminiscent of Binet's (1903) descriptions of reasoning and thinking in his two daughters: the cool, concentrated Madeleine and the impulsive, gay Alice (Chapter 11). When Ach published his results, a rather unseemly squabble resulted. Binet claimed priority and stated that the "method of Würzburg" was better named the "method of Paris." Priority was not really important; what was significant was that studies by Binet in Paris and in Külpe's laboratory were converging on the same findings (Ogden, 1911).

As the years passed, the experiments done at Würzburg became more and more cognitively oriented as they addressed increasingly complex mental activities. Some of the best known of these investigations were those of Karl Bühler. In 1907 he reported the results of an experiment in which subjects were asked questions that required a thoughtful reply rather than a simple reaction or a yes or no answer. For example, he asked: "Why is it that the smaller a woman's foot, the larger the bill for her shoes?" (Bühler, 1907, p. 298). Modern examples of Bühler-style questions might be: "Why is it that as school enrollments decrease, school budgets do not?" or "Why are utility-hole covers round?"

The thought required for such problems was the subject matter of Bühler's research. He questioned his subjects in an empathetic but detailed way to tease out the mental steps they had followed. His subjects told him that the solutions usually came to them without concrete images or sensations. Consequently, Bühler described the thought of his subjects as being "imageless." In 1906 an American investigator, Robert Woodworth, had reported imageless thought, and so the finding was not original with Bühler, but it did become a hotly debated topic between the Leipzig and Würzburg psychologists. The reality of thought without sensations and images was impossible according to Wundt, who believed that all the experiments done at Würzburg, especially those done by Bühler, were pseudo experiments or mock experiments. Bühler was not using introspection correctly, since his subjects reported what happened as they tried to solve the problem rather than reporting the mental events themselves. Their data were "highly subjective" and thus subject to bias and error (Wundt, 1908).

A final challenge to Wundt was reported from Würzburg in 1915 by another American visitor to the laboratory, Thomas Verner Moore. Moore was an ordained priest who had earned a Ph.D. at Catholic University. At Würzburg he studied the relationship of meaning to image. Moore presented words both visually and auditorily to nine subjects and asked them to press a telegraph key as soon as the word evoked meaning or to lift their hands off the key when it evoked an image. For all but one of the nine subjects, meanings came more quickly than did images. Meanings occurred within half a second on the average, while images took a second. Moore and Külpe concluded that meaning and image are distinct elements of mental experience and thus that there are at least four independent elements in human consciousness: sensation, image, feeling, and meaning (Ogden, 1951). After his work at Würzburg, Moore returned to Catholic University, where he served as chairman of the departments of psychology and psychiatry from 1939 to 1947. In 1938 Moore wrote *Cognitive Psychology*, a book that has much in common with the perspective that emerged twenty-five years later at the beginning of what has been called the cognitive revolution in psychology (Knapp, 1985). A number of procedures developed at Würzburg are used by contemporary cognitive psychologists. In an elegant series of experiments Saul Sternberg (1966, 1969, 1975) used reaction times to measure retrieval from short-term memory, and Michael Posner (1978) discovered some important facts about mental comparisons by timing people as they made mental judgments. The Würzburg procedure of direct questioning or interrogation (*Ausfrage*) has also been widely used, for example, in Roger Schank's research on semantic knowledge (Schank, 1976).

Würzburg under Attack

This Würzburg research was criticized in much detail and with great frequency by Wundt and his students. Titchener was an especially assiduous critic. Külpe had been senior to him in the Leipzig laboratory and seems to have retained a rather paternalistic attitude toward Titchener throughout his life. Ogden recalled that Külpe once told him:

> If only I could sit down with Titchener, I am sure I could make him see what we are driving at. (Ogden, 1951, p. 6)

Külpe was never able to do so, and Titchener certainly never changed his mind. More than half a century later, when Titchener's student Edwin Boring discussed Külpe in his *History of Experimental Psychology*, we see the critical forces still at work. Boring described Külpe as a psychologist who

> with the impress of G. E. Müller and Wundt upon him, began as a psychologist of content, a clear thinker of succinct thoughts and a man ready to follow whither experiment led, and who ended up, after the researches of his Würzburg school on thought, pretty well over into Brentano's camp. (Boring, 1957, p. 386)

Külpe left Würzburg for the University of Bonn in 1909. In 1913 he made his last move, to the University of Munich. Külpe was deeply committed to an experimental approach to psychology and accepted these positions only on the condition that a laboratory be established at Bonn and an existing laboratory be reequipped at Munich. He often said that "science was his bride." However, like Stumpf, Külpe was an accomplished musician and had a deep interest in music as well as literature and art. One of his American students, Robert Ogden, described him as "an esthetic personality living in a factual world" (Ogden, 1951, p. 7).

World War I had a traumatic effect on Külpe, as it had on Stumpf. He had many psychologist friends in the allied countries yet was convinced of the rightness of Germany's cause. With his death in 1915 the research program at the Würzburg school ended.

THE LOST GERMAN PSYCHOLOGISTS

With the exception of Ebbinghaus, Weber, and Fechner, many German psychologists of the late eighteenth and nineteenth centuries fell into relative obscurity. As we have seen, the major reason for that outcome was that their work and international professional contacts were disrupted by World War I and events prior to the onset of World War II. Hitler and the Nazis came to power in 1933, and the destruction of the German universities soon followed. Stumpf was the only German psychologist discussed in this chapter who was still alive. He was a very old man at the time but was keenly aware of the political situation. In one of his last letters to a former student he wrote pathetically that he "was not a good enough philosopher to maintain a complete stoicism toward the existing conditions," yet he "was endeavoring to cultivate that attitude" (Langfeld, 1937, p. 319).

The political situation prevented communication between German and American psychologists. But as we have already noted, these "other" German psychologists did not have their loyal "Titcheners" to carry their theories and approaches to America. Consequently, many of their ideas were not given appropriate consideration or were simply lost. Also, the development of other approaches to psychology in America, such as functionalism and later behaviorism, served to displace the German cognitive approach. Today cognitive psychologies with some similarities to those of Stumpf and Külpe are finally gaining a prominent position in American psychology (Knapp, 1986). If it had not been for the two world wars, however, they might have developed much earlier. The only nineteenth-century German approach that did find a footing in America was that of the Gestalt psychologists. Prior to the onset of World War II these men fled from Nazi Germany and found refuge in America. Gestalt psychology will be our concern in Chapter 7.

Kurt Lewin. (Archives of the History of American Psychology, University of Akron)

7

Gestalt Psychology in Germany and the United States

During the first decades of the twentieth century, Gestalt psychology provided a major alternative and challenge to structuralism (Chapters 4 and 5), functionalism (Chapter 10), and behaviorism (Chapter 12). Founded in Germany by successors to the psychologists discussed in Chapter 6, Gestalt psychology moved west in the 1930s and became an important influence on the development of American psychology. Gestalt means *shape* or *form,* and initially the three founders of Gestalt psychology, Max Wertheimer, Kurt Koffka, and Wolfgang Köhler, were interested in perception. Later their interests broadened to include learning, problem solving, and cognition, but within Gestalt psychology those topics were treated as wholes. Later one of their colleagues, Kurt Lewin, adopted a Gestalt approach in developing an innovative field theory, which he employed to address a wide variety of topics and concerns in child development, industrial management, and social psychology. The term *Gestalt psychology* has entered the English language and the word *Gestalt* is widely used by psychologists, sometimes without being capitalized.

THE CONCEPTUAL FOUNDATION
OF GESTALT PSYCHOLOGY

Though new and even radical, Gestalt psychology did not develop in a vacuum but rather grew out of the perceptual theories of Ernst Mach and the experiments of Christian von Ehrenfels. In Chapter 6 we encountered Mach as a positivist philosopher and saw his influence on Oswald Külpe. In his book *Analysis of Sensations* (1886), Mach described the properties of spatial and auditory forms—squares, circles, and simple melodies. As perceptual wholes these forms have qualities that

179

distinguish them from their elements; sensations are organized in consciousness to create qualities of the form (*Gestaltqualitäten*) that may be novel and to some extent independent of the sensations themselves. Mach pointed out that a table is the source of many sensations; we can see, touch, and possibly even taste it. But a table is something more than a compounding of those sensations. It has a "form quality" that persists even when the sensations change. Brightly illuminated or dimly lit, new or old, polished or stained with ink, it remains the same table. The table's form qualities give it perceptual or psychological permanence.

The second perceptual theorist who influenced the Gestalt psychologists was Christian von Ehrenfels (1859–1932). He received his training in philosophy under Alexius Meinong at the University of Graz in Austria. Meinong had been a pupil of Franz Brentano (Chapter 6). Von Ehrenfels must have been an interesting person; he wrote poems and operas and was a passionate Wagnerian, a friend of Sigmund Freud (Chapter 8), and an advocate of the legalization of polygamy (Heider, 1970). He also had a strong musical background as both a composer and a performer. Von Ehrenfels agreed with Mach that melodies have form qualities in addition to the distinct sensations from individual notes that constitute them. When a melody is played in different keys or played by different instruments, the different notes produce different sensations but the melody retains its form quality. A song sung by different voices remains the same song. Von Ehrenfels termed this characteristic *transposability*. The melody may be transposed to different keys, voices, or instruments but still retains its identity. In 1888 and 1889 von Ehrenfels lectured on form qualities at the University of Vienna, and in 1890 he published a paper describing them. One of the students who heard him lecture and read his paper was Max Wertheimer, one of the three founders of Gestalt psychology.

MAX WERTHEIMER (1880–1943) AND THE BEGINNING OF GESTALT PSYCHOLOGY

Max Wertheimer was born in Prague and attended that city's university, where he studied law. He then became interested in psychology and studied under Stumpf at the University of Berlin before taking his doctoral degree at the University of Würzburg with Külpe in 1904. In the summer of 1910, Wertheimer was on his way from Austria to the German Rhine for a vacation. Gazing out the train window, Wertheimer was struck by the apparent movement of poles, fences, buildings, and even distant hills and mountains. These stationary objects appeared to race along with the train. Millions of people before Wertheimer had ridden in trains and seen this phenomenon, but Wertheimer saw it with new eyes. He asked himself: Why do these objects appear to move? Abandoning his vacation plans, Wertheimer left the train at Frankfurt and bought a simple stroboscope in a toy store. In his hotel room he used the stroboscope to project successive images of a horse and a child.

At the right projection rate the horse appeared to trot and the child to walk. Though these movements were jerky and spastic, they were clear. Many people before Wertheimer had seen such movements—the stroboscope was after all a popular toy—but Wertheimer sought the underlying psychological origins of such movement. Again he asked himself: Where does the movement come from?

The next day Wertheimer consulted Professor Friedrich Schumann of the University of Frankfurt. Schumann (1863–1940) held a Ph.D. in physics and was an authority on space perception. Being unable to answer Wertheimer's questions, Schumann urged him to try to answer them himself and generously offered the use of his laboratory and equipment, including an improved tachistoscope that he had developed. Schumann also introduced Wertheimer to two of his Frankfurt colleagues, Kurt Koffka and Wolfgang Köhler. Koffka (1884–1941) was born in Berlin and attended the University of Berlin. He took a Ph.D. degree with Stumpf in 1909. Köhler (1887–1967) was born in Reval in the Baltic provinces (now Tallinn, Estonia) and also took a degree with Stumpf in 1909. When they met, Wertheimer was thirty years old; Koffka and Köhler were twenty-four and twenty-two, respectively. They were to become the triumvirate of Gestalt psychology.

In his first experiment at Frankfurt, Wertheimer used the Schumann tachistoscope to project successively a vertical white stripe and then a horizontal white stripe on a black background. Schumann had reported in 1907 that at certain time intervals the white stripe appeared to move from the vertical position to the horizontal position. Wertheimer's three subjects—Köhler, Koffka, and Koffka's wife—all described exactly that perceptual experience. One reported "rotation of about 90 degrees, it is impossible to think of it as a succession; it is not the white vertical that moves, but there is simply a process of transition" (Wertheimer, 1912, in Sahakian, 1968, p. 419). Another subject reported that the line appeared to "lie down" (Wertheimer, 1912, in Sahakian, 1968, p. 419). Apparent movement had been observed under controlled laboratory conditions.

Next Wertheimer shone lights successively through two narrow slits in a screen. When the lights were separated by intervals of fifty to sixty milliseconds, they appeared to move from one position to another, a phenomenon Wertheimer labeled the *phi phenomenon*. At shorter intervals, both lights were seen as being on continuously; at longer intervals, they were seen successively; but at the optimum interval, Wertheimer reported that "the motion is present compellingly and characteristically in its specific nature; it is given clearly and spontaneously and is always observable" (Wertheimer, 1912, in Sahakian, 1968, p. 422).

An experiment reported by Vittorio Benussi (1878–1927) provides another example of such apparent movement, but in a different sensory modality. Benussi was a contemporary of Wertheimer, a student of Meinong, and a professor at the University of Graz. He discovered that when two points on the skin are stimulated in rapid succession (the interval is critical), the stimulus appears to move in an arc through space, touching the skin at the two stimulation points. It is as if a flea had hopped from one spot to the other on the skin. According to Benussi, perception of the movement of the "flea" is a two-stage process. First the tactile stimulus is sensed, and then an internal mental process occurs that results in the perception of movement. Benussi labeled this internal mental process or act *Gestalt production.*

In 1972 two contemporary psychologists, Frank Geldard and Carl Sherrick, reported an effect similar to that of Benussi. They found that when electrical and mechanical stimuli were applied at certain time intervals to separate parts of the wrist and arm, the subjects reported

> a smooth progression of jumps up the arm, as if a tiny rabbit were hopping
> from wrist to elbow. If the original timing is retained and the number of
> taps (N) at each locus is reduced, the hops get longer; if N is increased (up
> to a limit), the hops become shorter. (Geldard & Sherrick, 1972, p. 178)

Clearly, in Wertheimer's and Benussi's experiments and more recently in the case of Geldard and Sherrick's "rabbit," the Gestalt, or whole perceptual experience, had a property—movement—that its components did not. The lines, lights, and tactile stimuli did not actually move but were perceived to do so. In 1912 Wertheimer published a paper, *"Experimentelle Studien über das Sehen von Bewegung"* (Experimental Studies of the Perception of Movement), reporting the results of his experiments at Frankfurt. This paper is often said to mark the formal beginning of Gestalt psychology.

Wertheimer, Koffka, and Köhler sought a newer, more dynamic psychology than that provided by Wundt's structuralism. They were dissatisfied with what they considered to be the static, sterile, and stilted state of contemporary psychology. Later Köhler recalled their views:

> His [the introspectionist's] psychology is quite unable to satisfy people for
> long. Since he ignores the experiences of everyday life, and concentrates on
> rare facts which only an artificial procedure can reveal, both his professional
> and lay audience will sooner or later lose patience. And something else will
> happen. There will be psychologists who will take him at his word when he
> says that this is the only right way of dealing with experience. If this is true,
> they will say, the study of experience can surely not interest us. We will do
> more lively things. We will study behavior. (Köhler, 1947, p. 85)

In doing "more lively things" Wertheimer, Köhler, and Koffka did indeed establish a new, more dynamic, more relevant psychology. In their outlines of Gestalt psychology, they mustered support for the new discipline wherever they could find it. Especially important was the research of the Danish phenomenologist Edgar Rubin. In 1915 Rubin described his experiments with perceptually ambiguous figures such as those on the top of page 183.

In the figure on the left, a person usually sees first a white table or urn (vase) and then, sometime later, two profiles in black. The figure therefore is described as "Rubin's vase" or "Rubin's Peter and Paul profiles." In the other figure a person sees either a white cross or a black cross. In these figures different figure-ground

 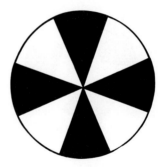

relationships lead to different perceptions. These perceptions, said Rubin, emerge as wholes, not piecemeal. Such figures demonstrate that our perceptions are active, lively, and organized. We are not simply passive receivers of sensory stimuli. Such views were adopted by the Gestalt psychologists as their own.

Gestalt Principles of Perception

According to the Gestaltists, our perceptions of the everyday world are also organized actively into coherent wholes. Consider the night sky. For eons the stars in the night sky have been perceived as belonging together in groups that are so common that they have names: the Big Dipper and the Southern Cross, for example. The principles that govern the organization of such perceptual experiences were outlined in three important works: Koffka's *Perception: An Introduction to the Gestalt Theories* (1922), Wertheimer's *An Enquiry into the Laws of the Gestalt* (1922), and Köhler's "An Aspect of Gestalt Psychology" (1925). These principles included the following.

Similarity Equal and similar elements form groups or wholes. Consider the following figures:

```
X   O   X   O   X   O        O   O   O   O   O   O
X   O   X   O   X   O        X   X   X   X   X   X
X   O   X   O   X   O        O   O   O   O   O   O
X   O   X   O   X   O        X   X   X   X   X   X
X   O   X   O   X   O        O   O   O   O   O   O
X   O   X   O   X   O        X   X   X   X   X   X
```

Typically, the Xs and Os in the array on the left are seen in columns, whereas they are seen in rows in the array on the right. Elements that are similar are grouped into perceptual units, in this case into either columns or rows.

Proximity Elements that are proximal or close together tend to be grouped. In looking at the following figure, most observers perceive two groups of three patches:

Xs and Os can easily be arranged to produce proximal grouping:

```
XX   XX   XX      OO   OO   OO
XX   XX   XX      OO   OO   OO
XX   XX   XX      OO   OO   OO
XX   XX   XX      OO   OO   OO
XX   XX   XX      OO   OO   OO
XX   XX   XX      OO   OO   OO
```

The array on the left is usually perceived as three double columns of Xs, whereas the array on the right is perceived as three double columns of Os.

Closure and Good Gestalts *Closure* refers to our tendency to "fill in" or complete the missing parts of a configuration so as to make it perceptually complete. A figure that allows us to do this easily is considered a good Gestalt. Consider these examples:

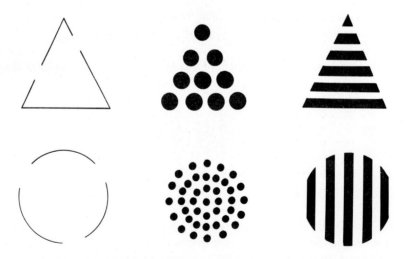

In all cases the figures are incomplete—they lack closure—yet they are all clearly seen as either triangles or circles. These geometric figures are examples of good Gestalts. Often, because of closure, just a few lines are sufficient for organized perceptions:

Most people easily see the horse on the left; the figure on the right may be less compelling. It is the movie director Alfred Hitchcock's cartoon of himself.

For those familiar with Hitchcock's profile (Spoto, 1983), it is clearly seen as the essential Hitchcock. These figures are good Gestalts in that they have closure and balance to a sufficient degree that no local change could improve them.

In these demonstrations the Gestalt psychologists showed that perceptual experiences are dynamic, not static; organized, not chaotic; and predictable, not erratic. Rudolf Arnheim considered the insight that "the world of sensory experience is made up primarily not of things but of dynamic forms" to have been the most important development in the psychology of the arts during the twentieth century (Arnheim, 1988, p. 585). To illustrate such perceptual dynamics Arnheim described the different impressions made on observers by these two simplified faces:

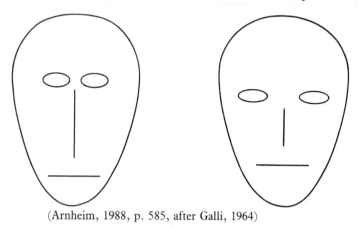

(Arnheim, 1988, p. 585, after Galli, 1964)

The face on the left is seen as aged, sad, and mean; the face on the right is seen as youthful and serene. Minor differences in the figures lead to major perceptual differences.

The Gestalt psychologists believed that principles of perceptual organization can account not only for our visual perceptions but also for our auditory and tactile perceptions and for such higher mental processes as memory. Impressive demonstrations of the generality of these Gestalt principles have been provided by Bluma Zeigarnik, Paul Schiller, and Roy F. Street.

The Generality of Gestalt Principles

Bluma Zeigarnik is a Russian psychologist best known to Western psychologists for her discovery of what has come to be called the *Zeigarnik effect* (Bieliauskas, 1977). She spent some time in Germany working with the fourth important Gestalt psychologist, Kurt Lewin. The genesis of her study was Lewin's observation that German waiters could remember for a considerable stretch of time the details of a customer's bill. However, once it had been paid, they often could not recall the amount. As long as the bill remained unpaid, the transaction lacked closure, and this tension facilitated recall; payment completed the transaction, produced closure, dissipated the tension, and erased the memory.

To test the validity of this explanation, Zeigarnik (1927) did an ingenious experiment. She gave her subjects a series of simple tasks, such as copying lines from a book and making clay figures. Some of the tasks were interrupted before completion and so lacked closure, and some of them Zeigarnik allowed the subjects to complete. One hundred sixty-four subjects were tested. A few hours later they were asked to recall the tasks. The majority of the subjects remembered more interrupted than uninterrupted tasks, and they also recalled interrupted tasks more quickly and with less effort.

Zeigarnik believed that a subject given a task feels a need to complete it. If not allowed to do so, this "quasi-need" persists, creating a state of tension, which in turn facilitates recall of that particular task. This explanation predicts that if the recall test were given twenty-four hours later, recall of interrupted tasks would be much more difficult. By that time the quasi-need would have dissipated. Zeigarnik tested some of the subjects twenty-four hours after the interrupted or completed tasks and found that by then recall of the interrupted tasks was in fact considerably reduced (Köhler, 1947, p. 304).

In our contemporary everyday world we see compelling examples of the Zeigarnik effect: the "cliff-hanger" endings of serial episodes and advertisements that pose questions without answers or set us up for closure and then fail to provide it. Such advertisements make our brains itch (Chance, 1975). Some years ago there was a particularly clever example of the latter technique in a Salem cigarette commercial played on radio and television. The commercial included a little jingle, repeated a number of times: "You can take Salem out of the country but [here a bell rang]—ting-a-ling—you can't take the country out of Salem." The jingle was repeated several times, and then the commercial ended: "You can take Salem out of the country but—ting-a-ling...." The need to complete the message was irresistible. It was a brilliant use of lack of closure to facilitate recall.

The second fascinating study of the generality of Gestalt principles was conducted at the Yerkes Regional Primate Center by Paul Schiller (1951). Schiller took advantage of the scribbling and drawing ability of a mature chimpanzee, Alpha.

When given crayons and paper, Alpha would often draw. Schiller showed Alpha the following circle with a missing pie-shaped wedge:

      Alpha filled in the open space and made few marks on the rest of the figure (Schiller, 1951, p. 106).

      When Alpha was shown the following arrays of squares, most of the scribbles were in the area of the *missing* squares (Schiller, 1951, p. 107). Alpha's drawings were remarkably consistent with Gestalt principles of perceptual organization. Like Zeigarnik's subjects and anyone who experienced the Salem commercial, Alpha expressed a need for closure.

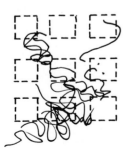 

      Closure has also proved to be of clinical significance. The Gestalt Completion Test judges a subject's ability to perceive meaningful figures in drawings such as these (Street, 1931):

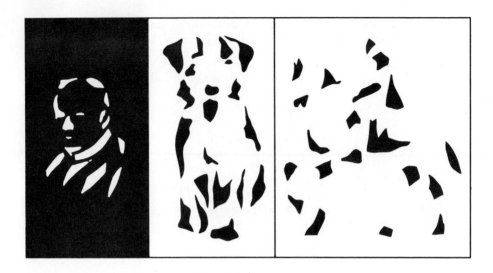

The ability to see the "man," "dog," and "horse and rider" has been used to assess the functional integrity of the right hemisphere of the brain (Gur & Reivich, 1980). Poor performance on perceptual closure tests has been associated with right hemisphere impairment (Bogen, De Zure, Tenhouton, & March, 1972). More recently, perceptual closure tests have been characterized as "noisy"—that is, influenced by many factors—but still useful measures of right hemisphere function (Wasserstein, Zappullan, Nosen, & Gerstman, 1987).

Illusions and Our Perceptual World

According to Gestalt psychologists, our tendency to organize perceptions leads to a perceptual or psychological environment that is often very different from the physical one. Consider these simple figures:

In both cases the vertical line appears longer than the horizontal line. In fact, the lines are all equal in length. Here and in general, the physical and psychological worlds often do not correspond; our tendency to organize our perceptions leads to illusions, or deceptions of the senses. Consequently, when we react to the environment, we are not necessarily reacting to physical reality; we may be reacting to a different psychological reality. In *Principles of Gestalt Psychology* (1935) Koffka used an old German legend as a dramatic illustration of the difference between what he termed "geographic and behavioral environments."

> On a winter evening amidst a driving snowstorm a man on horseback arrived at an inn, happy to have reached a shelter after hours of riding over the wind-swept plain in which the blanket of snow had covered all paths and landmarks. The landlord who came to the door viewed the stranger with surprise and asked him whence he came. The man pointed in the direction straight away from the inn, whereupon, the landlord in a tone of awe and wonder, said: "Do you know that you have ridden across the Lake of Constance?" At which the rider dropped stone dead at his feet. (Koffka, 1935, pp. 27–28)

Geographically, the man had ridden across the Lake of Constance, but behaviorally or perceptually, he had crossed a snow-covered plain. When he learned what his environment really had been, the shock killed him. Koffka also pointed out that though we may share the same geographic environment, our behavioral environments may be very different.

The Fate of Gestalt Psychology in Germany

These experiments and theoretical contributions established Gestalt psychology as a major school of German psychology in the 1920s. In that decade Germany was a nation devastated by the aftermath of World War I, and its political, economic, and social institutions were in disarray. In November 1918 riot and mutiny spread to Berlin, leading to the kaiser's flight to Holland, to the armistice, and to the founding, after more bloody riots, of the Weimar Republic. Berlin was a wide-open city of febrile rage and ferment. Starvation was common, and inflation ran at a rate difficult to comprehend. In August 1922, 400 German marks bought one United States dollar; in August 1923, the rate of exchange was 1 million marks to the dollar; and in November, it was 4.2 trillion marks to the dollar. Banks advertised for book-keepers "good with zeros" and paid out cash withdrawals by weight (Rhodes, 1986, p. 18). Yet Berlin in the 1920s was the city of the plays of Bertolt Brecht and the music of Kurt Weill, the precocious debut of Yehudi Menuhin with Albert Einstein in the audience, and Ludwig Mies van der Rohe's first glass-walled skyscraper (Rhodes, 1986, p. 17). The University of Berlin was at the center of those events, and it was there that Gestalt psychology developed and peaked.

In 1922 the ascendancy of the Gestalt approach was confirmed when Wolfgang Köhler succeeded Carl Stumpf as director of the Berlin Psychological Institute. Sadly, the institute had little more than a decade of excellence under Köhler's leadership before being wrecked by the Nazis. One of the first effects of the Nazis' seizure of the German government was the dismissal of Jewish professors from universities and research institutes. On April 7, 1933, all Jews were expelled from the civil service, which included all professorial positions in German universities.

Wertheimer was removed from his position at the University of Berlin and expelled from Germany in 1933. He immigrated to the United States, joining what came to be known as the University in Exile at the New School for Social Research in New York City. That enlightened institution rescued over 170 scholars, scientists, and their families from fascist Europe, including the historian Hannah Arendt and the anthropologist Claude Lévi-Strauss. Koffka had emigrated to the United States in 1924, joining the faculty of Smith College. Köhler was soon forced to join his colleagues. By the end of the terrible year of 1933 some 196 professors, including at least twenty-seven psychologists, had been dismissed from German universities.

During the raids on German universities and the dismissals of Jewish professors, the majority of German academics and scientists kept silent. Many of them, including some psychologists, supported the Nazis (Wyatt & Teuber, 1944). Martin Heidegger was the most advanced and celebrated philosopher in Germany in the 1930s. He was a member of the Nazi party, actively supported Hitler, and dutifully enforced anti-Jewish regulations (Farras, 1988). Under the leadership of an avowed Nazi, Felix Kreuger, Wundt's Institute of Psychology at the University of Leipzig (Chapter 5) became "a folk-cell, that is a germinating center for ultra-nationalistic activities" (Wyatt & Teuber, 1944, p. 232). In contrast, Köhler vigorously opposed the Nazis (Henle, 1978a). Clarke Crannel, an American student at the Berlin Psychological Institute, described the atmosphere in 1933:

> The *Reichstag* had burned. Everywhere in Berlin the Star of David was
> being chalked on the windows of shops and the shingles of physicians whose
> misfortune was to be Jewish. A stroll down *Unter den Linden* was not to be
> enjoyed without encountering a parade of brownshirts, their boots a staccato
> beat to their chilling war song. (Crannel, 1970, p. 267)

On April 28, 1933, Köhler wrote an article critical of the regime for the Berlin newspaper *Deutsche Allgemeine Zeitung,* the German equivalent of the *New York Times.* This was the last anti-Nazi article to be published under the Nazis. Köhler's courage in writing it is shown by the expectation of his colleagues and students that he would be arrested. His prestige and reputation were such that he was not, but abuses soon came. In November 1933, a decree that professors must open their lectures with the Nazi salute was promulgated. Shortly thereafter Köhler gave a lecture to an audience of more than 200 people, including not only his students and colleagues but numerous Brownshirts and Nazi sympathizers. He began by flipping his hand in a caricature of the Nazi salute and went on to outline his opposition to national socialism. The audience responded with thunderous applause, but the authorities were outraged. The institute was repeatedly "inspected" by armed troops. In April 1934, Köhler resigned as the director, but his resignation was not accepted.

In October 1934, he was invited to Harvard University to deliver the William James Memorial Lecture. While he was in the United States Köhler received a letter demanding that he sign an oath of loyalty to Hitler. Köhler did not reply. Back in Germany in 1935 he continued to protest interference with the affairs of his institute and to demand reinstatement of his dismissed Jewish colleagues and assistants. In August of that year his resignation was finally accepted. Köhler immigrated to the United States and accepted a position as a professor of psychology at Swarthmore College. Thus by 1940 all three of the founders of Gestalt psychology as well as Lewin were in the United States. Unfortunately, three of them had short American careers: Koffka died in 1941, Wertheimer in 1943, and Lewin in 1947. Only Köhler had a long American career until his death in 1967.

Wertheimer and the University in Exile

Wertheimer was a member of a small group of émigré European scholars who found academic freedom and refuge from totalitarianism at the University in Exile at the New School for Social Research in New York City. During the seven years before he died, Wertheimer studied human thought and education. He had long been interested in these topics and had often given lectures and seminars on creative thinking and education. His book *Productive Thinking*, published posthumously in 1945, documents a small part of the material he presented in his lectures and seminars (Luchins & Luchins, 1970). The book is original and provocative but difficult to read, and it has been said that Wertheimer was a better lecturer and seminar leader than writer (Köhler, 1944).

Wertheimer adamantly opposed rote methods of instruction and problem-solving techniques that emphasized the mechanical application of principles or formulas. Instead, he recommended a Gestalt approach in which the problem is considered as a whole. To demonstrate this approach, he gave an example of teaching children to find the area of a parallelogram. One schoolteacher Wertheimer observed taught his children the conventional method:

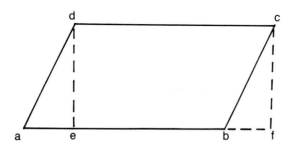

First the corners were labeled a, b, c, and d. Then perpendiculars were dropped from d to e and from c to f. Next, the base line was extended from b to f. Finally, the area of the parallelogram was found by multiplying the base by the altitude. With this method, pupils were able to find the area of various parallelograms and the teacher was well pleased with their progress. Wertheimer, however, suspected that the children had learned to apply the method mechanically, without a true understanding of the structure of parallelograms. With the teacher's permission Wertheimer asked the students to find the area of the following figure:

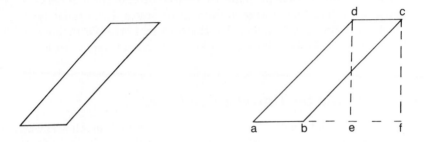

Some of the children realized that if they turned the figure 45 degrees, they could use the method they had been taught. Many others were not as flexible and became confused, protesting that the problem was unfair, for they had never seen a figure like that. They tried to apply the method they had learned but were uncertain about what constituted the base of the figure. The teacher said to Wertheimer with some indignation: "You certainly gave them a queer figure. Naturally they are unable to deal with it" (Wertheimer, 1945, p. 17). Wertheimer, however, believed that the children's failure showed the inadequacy of the method they had been taught. He suggested ways of teaching children to see the relationship between the parts of the parallelogram, to see it as a Gestalt, and to think productively. He demonstrated that any parallelogram can be broken into a number of parts:

When the parts of this parallelogram are reassembled, they form a rectangle whose area is easily computed. Once the children understood this, not only could they compute the area of any parallelogram regardless of its dimension and altitude, they could compute the area of even more irregular figures simply by realizing that such complex figures can be broken down into simple figures.

As an example of spontaneous productive thinking, Wertheimer recounted an episode in the life of the eminent mathematician Carl Gauss (Wertheimer, 1945, p. 90). When Gauss was six, his grammar school teacher asked the class: "Which of you will be the first to get the sum of $1 + 2 + 3 + 4 + 5 + 6 + 7 + 8 + 9 + 10$?" While his classmates were still thinking about this problem, Gauss came up with the solution: 55. "How the devil did you get it so quickly?" the surprised teacher asked, not realizing that he was dealing with a mathematical genius. Wertheimer reconstructed Gauss's thinking and decided that Gauss must have realized that the extreme numbers in the teacher's series always summed to 11:

$$1 + 10 = 11$$
$$2 + 9 = 11$$
$$3 + 8 = 11$$
$$4 + 7 = 11$$
$$5 + 6 = 11$$

There are five such numbers, so their sum or whole must be

$$5 \times 11 = 55$$

Wertheimer believed that it would be possible to develop such insightful, productive thinking in all children, not just in geniuses like Gauss.

Wertheimer also analyzed the thought processes Galileo Galilei might have used when he formulated the law of inertia governing falling bodies (Chapter 1) and the thought processes of Albert Einstein. The latter discussion was the result of the many hours Wertheimer spent in Einstein's study hearing from him how he came to formulate the general theory of relativity (Wertheimer, 1945, chap. VII). Wertheimer's discussion is too complex to summarize, but it is a unique analysis of the highest type of creative and productive thinking. Contemporary psychologists have also shown great interest in the definition of creativity and the ways in which it can be measured (Guilford, 1954; Flanagan, 1963; Barron, 1969). Like Wertheimer, they often emphasize flexibility and novelty in productive thinking—think of eight uses for a rubber ball, a toothpick, a paper clip, a brick, or a one-foot ruler—rather than conventional rules and methods.

Wertheimer challenged traditional methods of teaching children problem-solving skills. Though his work was innovative, it did not have the impact it merited either on the psychology of learning or on education. The major impact of Gestalt psychology resulted from the research on animal learning of Wertheimer's younger colleague Wolfgang Köhler. That research provided both different observations of animal learning and a different theoretical explanation of the process itself. Since animal learning was a central concern of American psychologists, Köhler made a major impression.

THE INSIGHT LEARNING EXPERIMENTS OF WOLFGANG KÖHLER (1887–1967)

Wolfgang Köhler obtained a Ph.D. with Stumpf (Chapter 6) in Berlin in 1909 and, as we have seen, served as a subject in Wertheimer's Frankfurt experiments. In 1913 Stumpf arranged for Köhler's appointment as director of the Anthropoid Research Station on Tenerife in the Canary Islands. The Prussian Academy of Science maintained a colony of apes on Tenerife, and Köhler went there to study their problem-solving abilities and general intelligence. He planned to stay just a few months but, because of the outbreak of World War I in 1914, found himself marooned on the island until 1920. Köhler put the time to good use doing his famous experiments on insight learning.

At the time, the prevailing view of animal learning was that of the American psychologist Edward Lee Thorndike (Chapter 10). After studying the learning of chickens, monkeys, dogs, and especially cats, Thorndike had concluded that learning is a trial-and-error process dependent on the selective action of reward and punishment. Köhler, however, was dissatisfied both with Thorndike's conclusion and with the experimental situations he had used. In particular, Köhler questioned Thorndike's general conclusion that his animals did not reason but rather learned mechanically through the selective action of reward and punishment. Köhler argued that Thorndike's animals might have been capable of reasoning but were unable to demonstrate it in the context of the types of problem situations he had used. Perhaps Thorndike's problem boxes forced animals to learn through trial and error, since more intelligent forms of problem solving were precluded. Köhler argued that in any test for higher levels of reasoning in animals all the elements necessary for an intelligent solution must be present. Thus debate was joined between Thorndike's connectionist, stimulus-response, trial-and-error view of animal learning and Köhler's field, Gestalt, or what he termed "insight" view. To prove the validity of his view Köhler devised problem-solving tasks that allowed an animal to perceive the elements of the solution and arrive at the solution through insight rather than trial and error.

Köhler's first experiments were done with a dog, a chicken, and a young child. He believed that one characteristic of intelligent problem solving is the ability to switch to an indirect solution when a direct solution is blocked. Kohler developed the *Umwege*, or *detour*, problem, in which direct access to a goal is blocked and the subject is forced to make a detour.

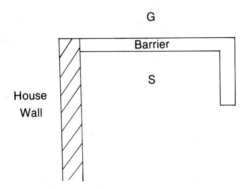

In his first detour experiment, a dog was placed at position S and food was placed at G. The dog ran smoothly and quickly around the detour to the food. Next, a one-year-old child was placed at *S* and saw her doll placed at *G*. First she tried to push through the barrier, but then Köhler reported that she "suddenly laughed joyfully, and in one movement was off at a trot around the corner to the objective" (Köhler, 1925, p. 14). Hens given detour problems were quite different. They rushed about in front of the barrier in a confused and unintelligent manner and never made the required detour. Therefore Köhler concluded that dogs and children are capable of the reasoning demanded by this situation whereas hens are not.

The situations Köhler used in his experiments with apes were more complicated. First he suspended a bunch of bananas in a basket from the wire roof of the animals' enclosure. The apes could not reach the bananas by jumping, the obvious direct solution, and so they were forced to develop an indirect way of reaching the food. A scaffold on one side of the enclosure was well within the arc of the swinging basket. When the apes first entered the enclosure they made futile attempts to jump up to the basket, but then one of them, Chica, "quietly surveys the situation, suddenly turns towards the scaffolding, waits with outstretched arms for the basket, and catches it. The experiment lasted about a minute" (Köhler, 1925, p. 19). Next the scaffolding was removed, making the problem more difficult, but another ape, Sultan, rose to the challenge and climbed on a roof beam within reach of the bananas as they swung past.

Köhler also gave his animals problems in which they had to use sticks as implements or tools. First bananas were placed outside the enclosure, out of the apes' reach. A number of sticks lay in the cage. One of the animals, Tschego, first tried unsuccessfully to reach the bananas with her hands, but after half an hour she gave up. She lay down quietly in the cage until a group of younger animals outside approached the fruit. Then, "suddenly Tschego leaps to her feet, seizes a stick, and quite adroitly pulls the bananas till they are within reach" (Köhler, 1925, p. 32). Apparently all Tschego needed was a little social motivation.

In another version of this test the animal had to use a short stick to rake in a longer one and then use the longer one to rake in the bananas. Again the animals were successful. In a still more complicated test, a banana lay outside the cage at such a distance that it could not be reached by either of two sticks left in the cage. However, if the two sticks were fitted together, their combined length was sufficient to reach the fruit. At one point Köhler demonstrated the solution by putting one of his fingers into the end of one of the sticks, but that did not aid Sultan. Köhler then left Sultan in the charge of a keeper, who later reported:

> Sultan first of all squats indifferently on the box, which has been left
> standing a little back from the railings; then he gets up, picks up the two
> sticks, sits down again on the box and plays carelessly with them. While
> doing this it happens that he finds himself holding one rod in either hand in
> such a way that they lie in a straight line; he pushes the thinner one a little
> way into the opening of the thicker, jumps up and is already on the run
> towards the railings, to which he had up to now half turned his back, and
> begins to draw a banana towards him with a double stick. (Köhler, 1925,
> p. 127)

This whole sequence took less than five minutes.

Next a banana was suspended from the roof, out of reach. First Sultan tried to knock it down with a stick. Then he dragged a box under the banana, climbed on it, and successfully knocked the fruit down. Subsequently, Sultan and a number of other apes built towers of as many as four boxes. On one occasion when fruit was suspended from the roof, no boxes were in the cage, so Sultan pulled a keeper under the fruit and climbed on his shoulders to reach it. Apes were also seen climbing on each other's shoulders or scaling a sturdy pole placed under the fruit until it fell down. One of Köhler's photographs shows Chica, at least four or five feet high on an almost vertical pole, grasping a suspended banana with one hand and holding the very end of the pole with the other.

In addition to allowing the animals to survey the whole problem, Köhler's experiments had the following characteristics. First, they were done in the animals' home enclosure or cages. Köhler believed that such situations were the ones in which the animals were most comfortable and so would be most likely to show intelligent behavior. Second, as we have seen, he often tested his animals in the presence of others. Köhler believed such a situation to be the most natural. He considered the behavior of animals tested alone to be abnormal. Incidentally, this group testing allowed Köhler to observe such social phenomena as observation learning and imitation. Third, Köhler reported his results descriptively with very few numbers and statistical interpretations. He believed that everything that was most valuable in his observations would be lost if they were handled in an abstract, statistical fashion.

Practically all of Köhler's remarkable observations were made during the first six months of 1914. Köhler spent his remaining years on Tenerife replicating and extending them. In doing so he caused some consternation among several British intelligence agents who could not believe a scientist would spend so much time finding out how an ape learns to get bananas. They were convinced that his reports of the experiments were part of an ingenious German espionage plan (Gleitman, 1981, p. 138).

Köhler first reported his results in a monograph of the Berlin Academy of Science in 1917 and then in a book published in Germany in 1921. However, their greatest impact followed their publication in English in 1925. Köhler termed the cognitive activity he had observed "insight learning" and said of it:

> We can, in our own experience, distinguish sharply between the kind of
> behavior which from the very beginning arises out of a consideration of the
> structure of the situation, and one that does not. Only in the former case do
> we speak of insight, and only that behavior of animals definitely appears to
> us intelligent which takes account from the beginning of the lay of the land,
> and proceeds to deal with it in a single, continuous and definite course.
> Hence follows this criterion of insight: *the appearance of a complete solution*
> *with reference to the whole lay-out of the field.* (Köhler, 1925, p. 190)

Köhler described the characteristics of insight learning. First, insight learning solutions are based on a perceptual restructuring of the problem. The animal "sees or perceives" the solution. It is characterized by a sense of "Ah, I have it" learning like that of Archimedes when he took his famous bath. In contrast, Thorndike's trial-and-error learning is slow and gradual. Second, insight learning does not depend on rewards. The fruits Köhler used provided incentives but were not responsible for the learning. The animals had solved the problems before they ever got to eat the fruit. Third, insight solutions are characterized by generalization, or large amounts of positive transfer, from one problem to another. Köhler's animals became test-wise or sophisticated; once they had solved one implement or stacking problem, they could quickly solve similar problems.

In 1925 Köhler visited the United States as a visiting professor at Clark University. He enjoyed the vastness and beauty of America and the friendliness of its inhabitants. Even the dogs, he is reported to have said, were friendly (Henle, 1986, p. 238). He gave numerous successful lectures on problem solving and insight learning in apes, but not in the South. Mary Henle explains why not:

> After all, 1925 was the year of the Scopes trial in Tennessee, the famous "monkey trial," in which a young high-school teacher was convicted of teaching evolution. Köhler subsequently learned that one of the best Southern universities would not invite him to speak on his work with the chimpanzees because it would "arouse a storm of indignation all over the state." (Henle, 1986, pp. 238–239)

Köhler's *Mentality of Apes* is a remarkable book which shows clearly the power of Gestalt principles in guiding and organizing a research program. In addition to descriptions of insight learning, the book contains many interesting observations of discrimination learning, memory, and emotion in animals. According to stimulus-response theorists such as Thorndike, what an animal learns in a discrimination experiment is to respond to a particular stimulus with a specific response; according to Gestalt theory, the animal learns to respond to the stimulus situation as a Gestalt or whole, especially in regard to relationships between stimuli. Köhler's elegant test of these different conceptions involved the *transposition* of stimuli. First, a chicken was trained to discriminate between two shades of gray. Pecking at a dark gray card (II) was always rewarded with food; pecking at a light gray card (I) never produced food.

I
Light
Gray

II
Dark
Gray

Chickens are not the most intelligent animals, but after between 400 and 600 trials they would peck consistently at card II and rarely at card I. But what had the chicken learned? Had it learned to peck at the gray stimulus card, the stimulus-response (S-R) view, or had it learned to inspect the relationship between the two cards and respond to the darker one? Köhler's test was ingenious. He transposed the stimuli so that the chicken had to choose between the original dark gray card (II) and a black card (III):

II
Dark Gray

III
Black

S-R theory predicts that since the original stimulus is present, the chicken should respond to card II; Gestalt theory predicts that the chicken should select the darker of the two stimuli and so peck at card III. The majority of Köhler's chickens chose card III on the transposition test. Similar experiments with apes and children using more complex stimulus dimensions such as color and form yielded similar results. On transposition, tests the subjects invariably chose the new stimulus, suggesting that they were responding to relationship between stimuli and to the field as a whole rather than to an isolated and specific stimulus. One test of the adequacy of a theory is its ability to suggest critical tests. The transposition experiment is an impressive demonstration of the capacity of Gestalt theory to provide such a test and also, of course, of Köhler's ingenuity as an experimenter.

A second major observation Köhler described concerned animal memory. He was convinced that an ape's memory is limited. In one experiment he covered a very large square of ground with several inches of sand. He made some marks and lines in the sand and a small hill to serve as landmarks. Then, while a restrained ape watched, Köhler buried food in the sand. When released after a short delay, the ape went immediately to the spot and dug up the food; when the delay lasted several minutes, the ape searched all over the ground before finding the food. This finding suggested to Köhler that an ape's memory is limited to recent events.

Finally, Köhler rejected empiricist accounts of emotion, which claimed that emotional reactions are acquired through experience (Chapters 2 and 12). How could such accounts explain the paroxysms of fear and terror his animals showed when they first saw a strange animal, such as a camel, walk past their enclosure? In one instance, the fear reaction was so intense that experiments could not be conducted for several days. Intense fear reactions were also elicited by mechanical toys, stuffed animals, a snake, and a mask. Köhler reported:

> One day, as I approached the stockade, I suddenly pulled over my head and face a cardboard copy of the mask of a Cingalese plague demon (certainly an appalling object), and instantly every chimpanzee, except Grande, had disappeared. They rushed as if possessed into one of the cages, and as I came still nearer, the courageous Grande also disappeared. (Köhler, 1925, pp. 322–323)

Köhler argued that such an immediate and intense reaction could not have been learned, as the mask had never been paired with punishment.

The research findings reported in *Mentality of Apes* convinced Köhler that trial-and-error learning cannot account for complex problem solving by animals and humans. Today, differences between insight and trial-and-error learning do not appear as clear-cut as they were to Köhler. Even in his own experiments, it is clear that solutions were often preceded by behaviors that resembled trial-and-error learning. Also, animals in trial-and-error situations sometimes show sudden, insightlike learning. The different experiments and interpretations of Köhler and Thorndike were a reflection of their conceptions of basic psychological processes: for Köhler, Gestalt; for Thorndike, functionalism.

Historically, Gestalt psychology has been associated with the work of Wertheimer, Koffka, and Köhler. Indeed, these three men laid the theoretical, conceptual, and empirical foundations for this new approach to psychology. One of their colleagues with a more applied bent, Kurt Lewin, was able to use the concepts and approach of Gestalt psychology to address broader psychological questions of personality development, worker efficiency, and various social behaviors and problems.

KURT LEWIN (1890–1947) AND THE APPLICATION OF GESTALT PSYCHOLOGY

Kurt Lewin's influence on contemporary psychology has not been widely acknowledged. Even psychologists who recognize the importance of his creative and innovative work are faced with an anomaly: nobody seems sure how to pronounce his name. Should it be *Loo-in* or *La-veen?* When he first arrived in the United States, Lewin used the German pronunciation, *La-veen.* Later he changed to the American pronunciation when his children were embarrassed by having to explain the German pronunciation to their American friends (Marrow, 1969). To the pedant's dismay, both pronunciations are correct.

Lewin's Early Life

Lewin was born September 9, 1890, in the village of Moglino in the German province of Posen, now part of Poland. His family had a small farm, but they lived above the general store they owned. He was the second child and first son in a family of four children and was raised in a warm and affectionate middle-class Jewish home, but that did not protect Lewin from the discrimination and anti-Semitism of life in Germany at the turn of the century. Lewin's educational, social, and eventually occupational opportunities were restricted. In 1905 Lewin's family moved to Berlin, and he finished his high school education at the Kaiserin Augusta Gymnasium. Until that time, his schoolwork had not been good and he had been best known for his fierce temper. Only during his last two years at the *Gymnasium* did his high intelligence become apparent.

After studying medicine and biology at the universities of Freiburg and Munich, Lewin transferred to the University of Berlin in 1910. Stumpf's Psychological Institute and the Berlin Department of Psychology (Chapter 6) were lively environments, and Lewin was intrigued by the possibility of a science of psychology. However, he found many of the department's courses in the "grand tradition" of Wundtian psychology irrelevant and dull. All too often it seemed psychologists performed small, disconnected studies that never formed a meaningful whole. Lewin spent three years at Berlin using nonsense syllables in a reaction time experiment before concluding that his research was pointless. He sought a new, more relevant psychology.

Lewin was one of a lively group of students concerned about the limited educational opportunities available to Berlin's working classes, the type of problem

Lewin felt psychologists could help solve. He organized a series of workers' courses to teach basic skills. The university authorities opposed such courses, considering them subversive, but this early "university without walls" was successful. All his life Lewin retained this commitment to applying psychology to the problems of society.

When World War I broke out in 1914, Lewin had completed all the requirements for a PhD and was about to graduate. He volunteered for the army and served four years, winning an Iron Cross before being wounded and hospitalized in 1918. His degree had been conferred in 1916 with Stumpf as his adviser, though Lewin later recalled that Stumpf did not once discuss his doctoral research with him (Lewin, 1937). Still, Lewin regarded Stumpf as one of the two most important German psychologists of the time, George Elias Müller (Chapter 6) being the other.

Lewin's Early Writings

While on furlough in 1917 Lewin published a remarkable paper, "The War Landscape," describing the soldier's experience of war. He referred to the soldier's "life space" and also used such terms as *boundary, direction,* and *zone,* all of which were to be central to his topological theory. Lewin stressed that a soldier's life space is very different from that of a civilian. For example, to a civilian, a shady path below some cliffs is an ideal place for a stroll or picnic; to a soldier, it is a dangerous place of possible ambush. Within the context of peace, actions such as burning furniture or books as fuel would be considered barbaric, but in times of war, they are understandable.

After his demobilization in 1918, Lewin returned to the Berlin Psychological Institute as a colleague of Wertheimer and Köhler and a professional friend of Koffka. Lewin found the Gestalt approach of these men appealing, but his professional interests stressed application more than theirs did. In 1919 he published two papers on the laborer in agriculture and industry in which he returned to the theme of his army paper. Despite the apparent similarities between agricultural and industrial workers—for example, their days involve hard physical labor—Lewin argued that their life spaces differ substantially. The industrial worker must develop a specialized skill to be used every day, whereas the agricultural worker must do many different things each day and in each season of the year. Lewin also felt that though an industrial worker often makes more money, agricultural work may be more satisfying. In his paper he also discussed the well-known time and motion studies of the pioneering American industrial engineer Frederick Winslow Taylor. Taylor had begun his studies of workers in machine shops in the 1880s. In 1911 he published *The Principles of Scientific Management,* which advocated a stopwatch and clipboard approach to factory life. Worker motions were to be timed and all unnecessary and inefficient motions were to be eliminated in the drive toward increased industrial efficiency and productivity. A common reaction to his approach among workers is shown by his nickname, "Speedy," but his time and motion studies were in vogue among managers. Lewin was more critical. He argued that work is something more than producing at maximum efficiency. Work has "life value" and must be enriched and humanized. We do not live to produce, Lewin argued; we produce to live. He was to return to this area of research later in his life.

In 1921 Lewin was appointed a *Privatdozent* at the University of Berlin, and even among the galaxy of stars at the university, he was able to attract students to his lectures and research programs. That was fortunate, for as a *Privatdozent*, much of his income depended on the number of students taking his courses. All his life Lewin enjoyed close relationships with his many students. Within the Berlin Psychological Institute they formed a close group and would often meet for informal discussions at the Swedish Café across the street. It was there that Lewin noticed that waiters recalled their customers' bills until they were paid and then forgot them, the observation that stimulated Zeigarnik's research mentioned earlier in this chapter. The ability to translate such everyday observations into important research was characteristic of Lewin all his life. However, he always conducted research within a theoretical framework, for as he often said, "There is nothing as practical as a good theory" (Lewin, quoted by Marrow, 1969, p. viii). What were some of Lewin's theoretical conceptions?

Lewin's Psychological Topology

Lewin thought of an individual as a complex energy field, a dynamic system of needs and tensions that directs perceptions and actions. Behavior (B) is a function (f) of a person (P) interacting with an environment (E). In his formula

$$B = f(P \times E)$$

each person moves in a psychological field Lewin termed the *life space*. A life space contains certain goals that have either positive or negative valence. They in turn create vectors that either attract or repel. To represent these concepts, Lewin borrowed from topology, a nonquantitative representational geometry. His aim was to develop a "topological psychology." To show a person's separation from the rest of the world, Lewin diagramed the life space as enclosed in Jordan curves—egg-shaped forms:

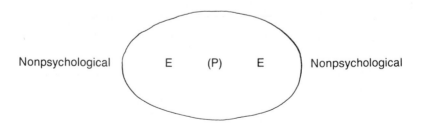

P and E form the individual's life space, and the curve separates the life space from the rest of the world. Lewin's papers are filled with diagrams like this. To his students at Berlin they were known as "Lewin's eggs," and to a later generation of students at the University of Iowa as "Lewin's potatoes" (Thompson, 1978). They symbolized his attempts to describe the dynamics of human behavior.

Lewin was a highly visual thinker, forever diagramming life situations with chalk on the nearest blackboard, with paper and pencil, or, if nothing else was at hand, with a stick in the dust or snow. In winter Lewin would often walk up and down in front of his house discussing problems in depicting life spaces with his students. After such discussions the snow was often covered by topological diagrams. Once at a convention Lewin gave a particularly impressive lecture. One skeptic was not convinced and asked how he took account of the complexities of individual differences in his life space diagrams. Lewin replied, "That's easy—I just use different colors of chalk."

Lewin's theory and research first became widely known to English-speaking psychologists following the publication by J. F. Brown, one of the first American students to study with him in Berlin, of "The Methods of Kurt Lewin in the Psychology of Action and Affection" in the 1929 *Psychological Review*. Brown outlined Lewin's concepts and described experiments by Zeigarnik and a number of other Lewin students. He emphasized Lewin's concern with total acts, or Gestalts. Brown warned psychologists not to dismiss Lewin because he had not discovered absolute psychological laws. Rather, Brown wrote, Lewin had been able

> to set up, measure and predict psychic energies with as much accuracy as the physicist used in the early days of dynamic concepts in his science. Like all pioneers, rather than dictate finished laws, Lewin's aim has been to indicate directions and open new paths for experiment from which laws must eventually come. (Brown, 1929, p. 220)

Also in 1929 Lewin presented a paper at the Ninth International Congress of Psychology at Yale University. He described his basic concepts and presented a film illustrating their application. The film showed an eighteen-month-old infant's attempts to sit on a marked spot on a stone. Clearly, she was not sure she would be able to sit on the spot if she once looked away from it. As a result, she circled the stone many times trying to work out a way of sitting on the spot without looking away from it. Finally, she put her head between her legs, backed over the stone, and was able to sit on the marked spot without ever taking her eyes off it—a wonderfully insightful solution. Lewin lectured in German, which many in his audience did not understand, but the film could be seen by all, and he was such a visual lecturer with his diagrams and illustrations that he was able to overcome the language barrier. A Harvard psychologist, Donald MacKinnon, recalled his lecture:

> He was a genius at being able to follow children around with his camera and get bits of behavior to illustrate the principles he was already developing. And he came across as a terribly exciting man—excited about what he was doing and about the presentation. (MacKinnon, cited by Marrow, 1969, p. 51)

Carl Murchison invited Lewin to contribute a paper to the forthcoming *Handbook of Child Psychology*. Lewin's "Environmental Forces in Child Behavior and Development," translated by Donald Adams, appeared in the 1931 *Handbook* along with papers by Mary Cover Jones (Chapter 12), Arnold Gesell (Chapter 9), Lewis Terman (Chapter 11), and Anna Freud (Chapter 8). In the paper, Lewin criticized statistical approaches to child behavior and conceptions of the "average child." Such a child, he said, was a "statistical myth." Rather, Lewin focused on the behavior of the individual child. For him it was much more useful to know a single case in depth than to know many cases in only a few aspects. The totality, or Gestalt, of the child's life space must be studied, and since each life space is different, that requires intense and concentrated effort.

According to Lewin, the infant's life space is small and undifferentiated. An infant is able to perceive and affect only a small portion of the environment. As he or she develops, the life space grows larger and more differentiated. To illustrate this change Lewin gave the example of a doll placed a few feet from an infant that can be taken away and even broken without any protest from the infant; the same action will elicit a violent reaction from a three-year-old. Lewin also described a number of experiments in which children had to solve detour problems (Lewin, 1931, p. 104). In one such problem chocolate is on the other side of a barrier from a child. The child (C) has to make a detour (D) around a barrier (B) to reach the positive valence chocolate (Ch).

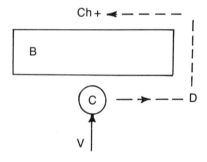

The problem is difficult because the child has to move counter to the positive vector (V). In another version of the problem, the child actually has to move in a direction opposite to that of the vector to obtain the chocolate (Lewin, 1931, p. 104):

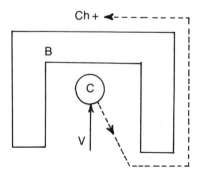

These problems were similar to the ones Köhler had used, and Lewin's explanation of the children's behavior was identical to that given by Köhler:

When the child finds the solution of such a detour problem it happens by
reason of a restructuring of the field. There occurs a perception of the total
situation of such a kind that the *path to the goal* becomes a unitary whole.
The initial part of the route, which "objectively" is still a movement away
from the goal, thereby loses psychologically that character and becomes
simply the first phase of a general movement toward the goal. (Lewin, 1931,
p. 105)

Lewin also presented descriptions and diagrams of constellations of forces in conflict. He diagramed the first type of conflict (Lewin, 1931, p. 109):

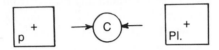

A child (C) must choose between playing with friends (P1) and going on a picnic
(P). Since both activities have a positive valence, the choice is easily made and the
conflict is resolved. However, Lewin pointed out that once such a choice is made,
the chosen activity often seems inferior. For instance, you must decide between two
brands of a product. Once you make a choice and purchase one of them, the rejected brand often appears increasingly attractive.

    Lewin diagramed a second type of conflict (Lewin, 1931, p. 110):

A child wants to climb a tree (Tr) but is afraid. Approach and avoidance vectors are
simultaneously present. Often in such a situation the child will approach the tree,
back away, and then approach again as the vectors wax and wane. A young child
at the ocean for the first time is a good example of this type of conflict. The child
runs to the water but then backs away as a wave rolls in, approaches again, and then
retreats as another wave appears.

    Lewin diagramed a third type of conflict (Lewin, 1931, p. 111):

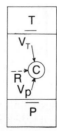

Now the child stands between two negative valences. An example of this would be when a parent uses a threat of punishment (P) to force a child to do something (T) the child does not want to do. Now two avoidance vectors are simultaneously active. The most common outcome, according to Lewin, is the "sideways resultant" of the two vectors (R), which leads the child to try to escape from the field.

Lewin in the United States

"Environmental Forces in Child Behavior and Development" secured Lewin's reputation as a brilliant and creative thinker. His field analysis of conflict situations is still a feature of contemporary psychology texts. American psychologists were eager to learn more about his work, and in 1932 Lewis Terman (Chapter 11) invited Lewin to spend six months as a visiting professor at Stanford University. Lewin enjoyed his stay in California, and though he was the friendliest and most informal of academics—it is characteristic of his students' recollections of their years with Lewin that they always refer to him as Kurt—he did enjoy being called "professor" for the first time in his life.

He returned home via the Pacific, visiting former students in Japan and Russia and giving lectures in both countries. On his way back to Germany on the Trans-Siberia Express, Lewin heard the terrible news that Hitler had become chancellor of Germany. He concluded that he had no future under the Nazis. In 1933 Lewin resigned from the University of Berlin, stating publicly that he had no wish to teach at a university that would not admit his children as students. He sought help from his American colleages, and they responded. Robert Ogden, whose work with Külpe was mentioned in Chapter 6, was dean of the School of Education at Cornell University. He respected the work of the Gestalt psychologists and had invited Koffka to Cornell as a visiting professor and had arranged for Köhler to give two series of lectures at the university (Ryan, 1982). Lewin had also lectured at Cornell in 1932, and Ogden admired both his research and his personal qualities. Ogden brought Lewin's desperate situation to the attention of Cornell's president, Livingston Farrand. Farrand was also a psychologist and was chairman of the Emergency Committee in Aid of Displaced German Scholars and Scientists, established to assist victims of Nazi persecution in finding positions at American universities (Freeman, 1977). Among the physicists this committee assisted were Enrico Fermi, who while fleeing Mussolini's Italy stopped in Stockholm on his way to New York City to receive a Nobel Prize; Leo Szilard, often called "the father of the atomic bomb"; Edward Teller, the director of the Los Alamos Laboratory, where the first atomic bomb was made; John van Neumann, who designed and built two of the first computers; and Albert Einstein (Rhodes, 1986). With the Emergency Committee's support Ogden was able to offer Lewin a faculty appointment at Cornell for two years (1933 to 1935) at a yearly salary of $3,000.

Lewin left Germany in August 1933, never to return. Two of his Berlin students, Tamara Dembo and Jerome Frank, joined him at Cornell, and together they began their research. Lewin's appointment was in the School of Home Economics, and so they decided to study a topic of prime interest to their new colleagues: the eating habits of children. However, they had a unique point of view and studied eating as it was influenced by the Gestalt of a child's social situation. Specifically, they investigated the effects of social pressure on children's choice of foods they either liked or disliked. When he arrived at Cornell, Lewin's English was not good and his language difficulties, frequent malapropisms, and misused colloquialisms created situations that his students, and Lewin too, found hilarious. One of his favorite ways of disagreeing was to say, "Can be, but I think absolute ozzer!" That phrase, in a heavy, mock-German accent, became a favorite slogan of his American students (Thompson, 1978).

His two years at Cornell were productive ones for Lewin. He published two major works, *A Dynamic Theory of Personality*, with Fritz and Grace Heider, and *Principles of Topological Psychology*, with Donald Adams and Karl Zener. Both books, especially the latter, were difficult works that did not receive the recognition they deserved. Lewin's topological analysis was still unfamiliar to most psychologists, and some of the reviews of these works were negative. In 1935 his appointment at Cornell ended, and as there was no chance of reappointment, Lewin was forced to seek another position. He had been involved in organizing a psychological institute he hoped to found at the Hebrew University of Jerusalem to conduct psychological research on the problem of Jews emigrating to Palestine from Europe and, more generally, on the roots of anti-Semitism and ways to combat it. Lewin was unable to secure adequate financial backing, and this visionary project failed, but he still considered leaving the United States and immigrating to Palestine. Fortunately for American psychology, a place was found for him at the Iowa Child Welfare Research Station at the University of Iowa. As this too was not a regular faculty appointment for the first three years, Lewin was supported by a grant from the Rockefeller Fund. At this stage in his career Lewin was still something of an outsider, and in fact he remained so all his life. It is a surprise to find, for example, that he was never elected president of the APA.

Lewin at the University of Iowa

Lewin's first years at Iowa City were happy and productive. The Rockefeller grant also provided fellowships for his faithful student Dembo and a number of postdoctoral fellows. As he had done at both Berlin and Cornell, Lewin quickly attracted students, and they too started an informal discussion group, "the Iowa, Tuesday-at-Noon, Hot Air Club." Once again Lewin was able to derive an important research topic from everyday observation. He noticed that people in cafeterias would often reach over pies in the front of a counter to choose pies at the back. One of Lewin's students, Herbert Wright, had the cafeteria staff place identical pies in ordered rows. People still usually chose the pies at the back. The more difficult the pies were to reach, the more attractive they seemed to be. Lewin concluded that the effort involved in reaching a goal affects the strength of its positive valence. Even a goal that objectively is of little value can be very attractive, and highly desired, if a great deal of effort must be expended to gain it. Lewin was not the first person to note this: Napoleon had once said that the secret of his success was the discovery that men would die for medals, while

Groucho Marx observed that he did not care to belong to any groups whose standards were sufficiently low to admit him.

Lewin and his Iowa students conducted a number of important and widely quoted experiments. Dembo, Barker, and Lewin (1941) studied the effects of frustration on the behavior of children. They used Lewin's dedifferentiation hypothesis, which predicted that under conditions of frustration, behavior should become dedifferentiated and the child should regress to earlier, more primitive, and less constructive behaviors. They tested children between the ages of two and six. First the children spent thirty minutes playing with conventional play materials. Their play was rated for its constructiveness. Then the experimenter lifted a wire screen in the center of the room and encouraged the children to play with some very attractive toys on the other side of the room. After they became totally absorbed with the new toys, the experimenter interrupted their play, led them back to the original part of the room, lowered and padlocked the screen, and observed the children's play with the original toys. Initially, most of the children tried to break through the screen or escape from the room. When these attempts failed, they would often play with the toys, but in a much less constructive manner. Their average play age regressed by seventeen months. Blocks that had been used to build towers were used as missiles, and a toy telephone that had been used to make calls was pounded on the floor; they cried, whined, and had tantrums, and some even sucked their thumbs. There was a 30 percent increase in hostile reactions to the experimenter and a 34 percent reduction in friendly approaches. Frustration led to both regression and aggression.

In another important series of experiments, Lewin and his students investigated the effects of authoritarian and democratic leadership styles on the behavior of children. In one study, ten-year-olds met eleven times after school to make theatrical masks (Lippitt, 1939). The children were divided into two groups for which Lippitt played different leadership roles. For one he was very authoritarian, exercising absolute authority, making all decisions, and imposing them on the children. For the second group he assumed a democratic role, allowing the children to select activities, accepting their decisions, and letting the majority decide. The different leadership styles and social climates produced striking differences in the two groups. In the autocratically led group, there was far more quarreling and hostility; the children blamed scapegoats for their problems and were less friendly than were the children in the democratic group.

In a second, more extensive experiment, Lewin, Lippitt, and White (1939) organized four clubs of ten-year-old boys. The boys engaged in various activities under different styles of adult leadership: authoritarian and democratic as before, but in addition a laissez-faire style in which the boys had complete freedom without any participation by the adult. Every six weeks each group of boys had a different leader and leadership style. Again autocratic leadership led to increased aggression, both overt aggressive acts and more subtle joking hostility; there was also a sharp increase in aggressive behavior when the autocratic leader left the room. Aggression was also common on the day following the transition from autocratic leadership to a freer atmosphere, and some of the boys became frightened and disturbed when the transition was made. However, with one exception, the boys preferred democratic leadership.

In 1939 Hitler, an authoritarian leader gone mad, led Europe into a terrible war. Lewin, Lippitt, and White's results confirmed Lewin's deep belief in the dangers of authoritarian leaders and the superiority of democratic systems of government. Lewin said later:

> There have been few experiences for me as impressive as seeing the expression on children's faces during the first day under an autocratic leader. The group that had formerly been friendly, open, cooperative, and full of life, became within a short half-hour a rather apathetic-looking gathering without initiative. The change from autocracy to democracy seemed to take somewhat more time than from democracy to autocracy. Autocracy is imposed on the individual. Democracy he has to learn! (Lewin, quoted by Marrow, 1969, p. 127)

Lewin's Applied Research

In 1939 Lewin had an opportunity to return to an earlier interest and conduct what he had come to call "action research" in an industrial setting. Albert J. Marrow consulted Lewin concerning problems his corporation had encountered in opening a new plant in rural Virginia. The 300 employees, mainly women, were eager workers, but management found it difficult to train them to meet the company's production standards. Even after a twelve-week training program the Virginia workers were only half as productive as were workers in northern plants. This was a problem in worker dynamics that appealed to Lewin. He visited the plant, consulted with the managers, and met the workers. They were well paid, especially in comparison to local wage rates, yet employee turnover was high.

Lewin organized group problem-solving sessions with the workers. He learned that the company's production standards were widely believed to be impossible to attain. The workers' failure to reach those standards decreased what Dembo had earlier labeled their "level of aspiration." In laboratory experiments one of Lewin's Berlin students, Ferdinand Hoppe (1930), had found that success or failure on any task increases or decreases the level of aspiration and that this change is general and not limited to the task alone. Lewin set out to make the workers succeed. They were organized into small groups and were allowed to set their own production goals; each group included at least one highly skilled worker to increase the chances of success. Production improved slowly, as did worker morale. The workers liked Lewin and were encouraged to discuss his suggestions before deciding to accept or reject them. Discussions between Lewin with his German accent and the Virginians with their southern drawls must have been wonderful to hear. Lewin's work in Virginia is an impressive demonstration of action research in industry (Marrow, 1969, pp. 141–152).

During World War II, Lewin had several opportunities for action research, this time within the American war effort (Marrow, 1969, pp. 153–159). He was intensely committed to the defeat of Nazi Germany and gloried in the fact that he had become an American citizen in January 1940, just in time to make a contribution. One of the first studies was done in collaboration with the anthropologist Margaret Mead. It was designed to advise government agencies on ways to alter the eating habits of the American people to take account of wartime shortages and surpluses. Groups of housewives and fraternity members at the University of Iowa discussed their use of such food items as whole-wheat bread—a nutritionally desirable food—and turnips, a vegetable available in abundance but widely disliked. First Mead, introduced as an eminent nutritionist from Washington, D.C., gave a lecture extolling whole-wheat bread and turnips. It was a dynamic performance but had no effect on the food-buying habits of her audience. Next the groups were urged to discuss different foods and the reasons for including whole-wheat bread and turnips in their diets. Both groups made a decision to eat more of these foods and followed through on their decision. A change in buying behavior followed a change in attitude, and Lewin and Mead concluded that attitudes were most effectively changed through group discussion and decision making.

During the war years Lewin also worked for the Office of Strategic Services on propaganda, military morale, leadership, and the rehabilitation of injured soldiers. During those years he founded the Society for the Psychological Study of Social Issues (SPSSI), serving from 1942 to 1943 as the society's president. Since its inception the SPSSI has been active in research and scholarly publications on such social issues as peace, war, poverty, prejudice, and more recently, family matters (Perlman, 1986). Lewin's frequent trips to Washington during the war years convinced him that his situation in Iowa was too restricted. He had spent nine productive years in the Midwest, but it was time to move on. Lewin concluded that he needed an independent action research institute. With characteristic confidence and energy, he organized the Research Center for Group Dynamics. Edward Tolman (Chapter 13) invited Lewin to locate his center at Berkeley, but despite the attractions of California, Lewin established it on the campus of America's major engineering and technological university, the Massachusetts Institute of Technology (MIT). He recruited a staff, all of whom were under thirty-five years of age, and attracted students from MIT, Harvard, and other universities in the area.

In 1945 Lewin and his group decided to work in four major program areas. First they sought to find ways of increasing group productivity and countering the well-known tendency for groups to be inefficient and stray from their original goals. Lewin did not want any of his groups setting out to design a horse and ending up with a camel. Second, studies of communication and the spread of rumor were designed. Third, areas of social perception and interpersonal relations were explored, along with studies of group membership and individual adjustment. Fourth, studies in leadership training were initiated, which led to the formation in 1946 of the National Training Laboratories in Bethel, Maine, and the beginning of training, or T, groups. These groups were designed to develop effective leadership, open lines of communication, and combat prejudice and destructive attitudes. They have been used widely in educational, counseling, industrial, and clinical settings.

Lewin was also involved in forming a second major research institution, the Commission on Community Interrelations (CCI), for the American Jewish Congress. Lewin had experienced anti-Semitism in Germany, and his mother had died in a Nazi concentration camp. He hoped to organize programs to combat racial and religious prejudice, confront social issues, study them objectively, and make recommendations for their solution. The commission, headquartered in New York City, conducted important research, including studies of discrimination in hiring and employment. At the time most department stores in the United States refused to hire black sales clerks because they believed their customers would not stand for it. Two CCI investigators, Gerhart Sanger and Emily Gilbert (1950), interviewed customers in one of the few New York City department stores employing clerks of both races after they had been served by either black or white sales clerks. They found that antiblack prejudice had no effect on sales. Sixty-four percent of the shoppers said they approved of black sales clerks being hired. A dozen respondents expressed extreme prejudice and said they would not shop in a store that employed black sales clerks, yet five of those people had been served by a black sales clerk and had continued to shop in that store. Lewin and his students found that what was crucial for the majority of shoppers was the knowledge and courtesy of the sales clerks, not their race. These findings were widely publicized in the 1950s to combat racial discrimination in employment.

A second CCI study investigated the effects of segregated and integrated housing on racial attitudes. Planned by Lewin, this study was actually carried out after his death by Morton Deutsch and Mary Evans Collins (Marrow, 1969, pp. 208–210). They interviewed 100 white and 25 black housewives and 24 teenage boys and girls living in four housing projects in New York City and Newark. The projects were physically identical, but two were completely integrated and two were partially segregated, that is, integrated in a "checkerboard" pattern, with whites and blacks living in alternate buildings. In the partially segregated projects prejudice against blacks was stronger and sharper than it was in the fully integrated projects, and the white residents in these projects expressed a strong preference for still more segregation. People in the more integrated projects had a greater sense of community; there was less prejudice and better morale. The white residents of integrated projects expressed pride in the open character of their buildings and were less suspicious and hostile than were people in the segregated buildings. Contrary to the popular belief that any building with a black occupancy rate above 50 percent would have trouble, the investigators found that the most cordial relations characterized an integrated project with 70 percent black occupancy. These were important and politically significant findings that would be central to debates in the 1950s and 1960s over equal occupational and housing opportunities for blacks in the United States.

Under Lewin's leadership the CCI was involved in a third significant educational and social development. In the early 1940s American universities and colleges used admission quotas that placed limits on the number of Jewish students allowed to enroll. Folk wisdom at the time held that "you can't legislate goodwill," but since Lewin had found in his research that attitudes can be changed by changing behavior, he encouraged the American Jewish Congress to challenge the quota system. It filed suit against the Medical School of Columbia University, charging discrimination in Columbia's admission procedures. The case became front-page news, was a great embarrassment to the university, and forced its administration to open its admissions records for inspection. Following Columbia's lead, other universities revised their admission procedures.

The CCI also supported a study of what Lewin, who was never one to mince words, called "Ways of Handling a Bigot" (Selltiz, Citron, Harding, Rosahn, & Wormser, 1950). They used role-playing in a series of playlets presenting different versions of an incident. In each case an actor expressed an extremely prejudiced or bigoted opinion. In the first playlet his remarks went unanswered, in the second they were answered quietly, and in the third they were answered angrily with an emotional, threatening reply. The calm answer was preferred 65 percent of the time, and significantly, 80 percent of the audience stated that they wanted to see the bigot challenged. When this happened, the audience usually supported the challenger.

Lewin died suddenly of a heart attack on February 1, 1947, having been hard at work up to the evening of his death. In a memorial address at that year's APA convention, Edward Tolman said of him:

> Freud the clinician and Lewin the experimentalist—these are the two men whose names will stand out before all others in the history of our psychological era. For it is their contrasting but complementary insights which first made psychology a science applicable to real human beings and real human society. (Tolman, 1947, in Marrow, 1969, p. ix)

When Heyduk and Fenigstein (1984) surveyed eminent psychologists, they found that Freud and Lewin were most frequently named as significant influences on their psychological development. This finding provided a striking confirmation of Tolman's prediction.

Gestalt Psychology and Gestalt Therapy

Gestalt therapy is often thought to derive from Gestalt psychology. This approach to therapy was first outlined by Frederick S. Perls in his 1951 book *Gestalt Therapy* and later in a number of works including *In and Out the Garbage Pail* (1969) and *The Gestalt Approach and Eyewitness to Therapy* (1973). Perls described his approach to therapy as radical and invited the reader to "invade" his or her "privacy" and through "self-discovery" observe "the self in action." In *Gestalt Therapy* Perls stated that in his approach, "For whatever help it can give us, we shall make use of terminology developed by gestalt psychology" (p. 25). In a later book he was to assert that his therapeutic approach and perspective derived "from a science which is neatly tucked away in our colleges; it comes from an approach called Gestalt psychology" (Perls, 1969, p. 61). In his last book, *The Gestalt Approach and Eyewitness to Therapy,* published posthumously in 1973, Perls continued to link his approach to that of the Gestalt psychologists.

The historical connection between Gestalt psychology and Gestalt therapy claimed by Perls must be rejected. Perls acknowledged that he was never accepted by the Gestalt psychologists and admitted to never having read their books. Nevertheless Perls dedicated one of his books on Gestalt therapy to Max Wertheimer. Wertheimer did not live to see the dedication, but Rudolf Arnheim described what his reaction might have been:

> I can see Max Wertheimer fly into one of his magnificent rages had he lived to see one of the more influential tracts of the therapeutic group in question dedicated to him as though he were the father of it all. (Arnheim, 1974, p. 570)

Ralph Franklin Hefferline coauthored *Gestalt Therapy* with Perls and Paul Goodman. Hefferline was a behaviorist (Skinnerian) psychologist best known for his 1959 report on escape and avoidance conditioning of minute muscle movements in the thumb (Hefferline, Keenan, & Harford, 1959). Later Hefferline described *Gestalt Therapy* as "misleadingly entitled" and remembered that when a prepublication copy of the book had been presented to Köhler, he had disavowed the idea that it was in any way a legitimate descendant of Gestalt psychology (Knapp, 1986, p. 54). Finally, Mary Henle, herself a Gestalt psychologist and historian of psychology, examined the relationship between Gestalt psychology and Gestalt therapy. Henle concluded:

> What Perls has done has been to take a few terms from Gestalt psychology, stretch their meaning beyond recognition, mix them with notions—often unclear and incompatible—from the depth psychologies, existentialism, and common sense, and he has called the whole mixture gestalt therapy. His work has *no* substantive relation to scientific Gestalt psychology. To use his own language Fritz Perls has done "his thing," whatever it is, it is *not* Gestalt psychology. (emphasis in the original; Henle, 1978b, p. 31)

More recently Henle stated:

> The most grotesque misunderstanding of Gestalt psychology is the notion that it has some relation to gestalt therapy....[I] will merely state that there is nothing in common between these two developments. (Henle, 1986, p. 121)

Whatever its merits as an approach to psychotherapy, Perls's Gestalt therapy should not be considered a clinical application or development of Gestalt psychology.

GESTALT PSYCHOLOGY IN PERSPECTIVE

Despite Tolman's praise of Lewin in 1947, field theory has not received nearly the same amount of attention as Freud's psychoanalytic theory has. Nor has Gestalt psychology, the conceptual basis of field theory, ever become a major school of American psychology. Köhler felt that Gestalt psychologists' impact was limited since they were interested primarily in perception while American psychologists were interested primarily in learning (Wallach, 1976). To some extent that is true, since Gestalt psychology is often presented within the framework of perceptual theory. However, Köhler was obviously interested in learning, albeit a qualitatively different type of learning from that being studied by American psychologists (Chapters 11 and 12). Also, Wertheimer's book *Productive Thinking* concerned itself entirely with the process of teaching complex concepts to children, and so it would not be inaccurate to say that he was interested in learning and cognition as well. Today, with the rising interest in cognitive psychology, the research of Köhler and Wertheimer has become relevant again. Also, ideas spawned by Lewin's diverse and innovative Gestalt approach are echoed in much contemporary research in social, industrial, and developmental psychology.

Sigmund Freud. (National Library of Medicine)

8

The Early History of Clinical Psychology and the Development of Psychoanalysis

In this chapter we turn from trends and developments in experimental psychology to the early history of clinical psychology. In 1969 the National Science Foundation surveyed 19,027 members of the American Psychological Association and found that 37 percent were clinical psychologists. Today the percentage would be even higher. From 1975 to 1980 all five presidents of the APA were clinical psychologists, and certainly the clinician's role is most often associated in the public mind with psychology. In this chapter the early development of clinical psychology will be presented, with particular attention to the revolution in the care and treatment of the mentally ill that occurred in the nineteenth century. The life and work of Sigmund Freud, the founder of psychoanalysis, will also be discussed.

EARLY VIEWS OF MENTAL ILLNESS

During most of recorded history the plight of the mentally ill has been desperate. While some Greek and Roman physicians made an attempt to understand mental illness scientifically (Chapter 1), the decline of Greco-Roman civilization saw a retreat from the relatively enlightened views of such men as Hippocrates and Galen. People who today would be diagnosed as mentally ill were treated as wicked sinners and punished for their sins. Martin Luther in his *Table Talks* (1652) described the feebleminded as godless people, possessed by the devil. Having neither reason nor souls, they were permanently doomed. Furthermore, since the mentally disturbed did not behave like normal people, for centuries they were regarded as nonhuman and were subjected to barbaric abuses. Luther personally recommended that one retarded twelve-year-old boy be drowned. Such individuals also served as convenient scapegoats when inexplicable calamities such as plagues befell communities.

Delusions of grandeur, hallucinations, and other pathologies undoubtedly underlay the behavior of the "mad" Popes, kings, and tyrants of these centuries. The Maid of Orleans, Joan of Arc, heard voices that inspired her military adventures but that, after her defeat, led to her trial by the English on charges of witchcraft, heresy, and sorcery. Joan of Arc was found guilty and burned at the stake in 1431. The equation of witchcraft with mental disorders was a tragic aspect of life in the Dark Ages and Middle Ages.

Witchcraft in Europe

The definitive work outlining the characteristics, identification, and punishment of witches was the *Malleus Maleficarum* (Hammer of the Witches), first published in 1510. An excursion into a terrifying world of sadism and cruelty, the book became an incitement to torture and mass murder. In the nineteenth century Carl Binz described this book:

> It is a heavy volume in quarto, so insane, so raw and cruel, and it leads to
> such terrible conclusions, that never before or since did such a unified
> combination of horrible characteristics flow from a human pen. (Binz, 1885,
> p. 10)

Yet the book was written to improve society and protect people from the wickedness and depravity of witches. Its authors were two German Dominican priests, Johann Sprenger and Heinrich Kraemer. Before publishing their book they obtained the backing of the Pope in December 1484; the support of Maximilian, the king of Rome, in 1486; and finally endorsement from the faculty of theology of the University of Cologne in 1487. With these papal, regal, and academic imprimaturs, *Hammer of the Witches* became a textbook of the Inquisition. Zilboorg and Henry described its impact:

> It went through ten editions before 1669 and through nine before another
> century passed. Bookmaking was not as efficient in those days as it is in
> ours, nor was literacy a characteristic of the age; thus, nineteen editions
> stand out as imposing and incontestable testimony not only of the popularity
> of the book but to the great need of the time which it undoubtedly filled.
> (Zilboorg & Henry, 1941, p. 152)

A translation of the *Malleus* by the Reverend Montague Summers was published in 1928, and a *Compendium Maleficarum* edited by Francesco Guazzo appeared as recently as 1970.

The *Malleus* had three main sections. The first section provided proof that witches exist. To question these proofs was heresy, punishable by the full authority of the church in this world and the next. The second section provided descriptions of the characteristics and actions of witches. From a psychological point of view this is the most interesting section. It is clear from the text and from the evidence presented at the trials of accused witches that many of them were mentally ill. Descriptions of delusions, hallucinations, manic and melancholic behavior, catatonia, and paranoia were frequent. Often these precise descriptions were based on careful observation, but that did not lead to accurate explanations of the behavior. The *Malleus* decreed that witchcraft springs from carnal lust, which is never satisfied in women, and so it is no surprise that girls and women were almost always the accused. Some women, who hungered after ever more intense gratification, sought it from the devil and were bewitched.

The third section of the *Malleus* outlined the forms of examination of witches and ways of ensuring full confessions. Accused witches were tortured first with "more gentle" techniques and then, if they resisted, with techniques of extreme cruelty and sadism. Having chosen of their own free will to consort with the devil, these women were to confess their witchcraft both in the torture chamber and in a place removed from the instruments of torture. This double confession constituted the final proof of guilt. Since it was believed that witchcraft could not be overcome by any natural power, the usual outcome of such a confession was death. From the early decades of the fourteenth century until the middle of the seventeenth, between 200,000 and 500,000 witches, 85 percent of whom were girls and women, were executed in Europe (Harris, 1975; Ben-Yehuda, 1980).

Witchcraft in the New World

Belief in demonology and the persecution of witches were not limited to Europe but spread to the New World. The best-known American witch trials were held in the village of Salem (now Danvers), near Boston, Massachusetts, in 1692. Before the Salem trials, accusations of witchcraft were common in New England, but the outcomes of witch trials usually favored the accused, and there were only five executions of accused witches in Massachusetts before 1692 (Kittredge, 1929).

The crisis in Salem began suddenly in December 1691, when eight young girls developed disorderly speech, hallucinations, odd postures, bizarre gestures, and convulsive fits. Physicians were unable to explain or cure their illness, which was diagnosed finally as being due to bewitchment of the girls. The girls accused a Barbadian slave living in Salem and two elderly women of ill repute as the ones who had bewitched them. A month later the girls' condition had not improved, and they made further accusations against two Salem women of good standing and reputation. All these women were tried as witches in the spring and early summer of 1692. The first woman condemned as a witch was hung in June, and by September nineteen men and women had been sent to the gallows. One man who defied the magistrates and refused to admit his guilt was pressed to death with stones. The girls participated in the trials, testifying against the accused witches and creating an uproar with their wild and disordered behavior. Their behavior in court was seen by the magistrates as "spectral evidence" of their bewitchment. Many of the people they accused of witchcraft were respectable and upstanding citizens of the village, including a former minister of Salem.

The madness at Salem ended as suddenly as it had begun, and by the end of 1692 the witch trials were over. The following spring, the governor of Massachusetts ordered 150 accused witches who had been imprisoned to be released. The witchcraft laws were rewritten, and witchcraft became a crime that was almost impossible to prosecute. What caused this outbreak of community madness in Salem? A number of explanations have been proposed. The girls might have behaved as they did to gain attention and notoriety or to take revenge on people they did not like. Once they began, they could not escape from the terrible trap they had created. One advocate of this position has suggested that the young girls of Salem were "no more seriously possessed than a pack of bobby-soxers on the loose" (Starkey, 1950, p. 29). On the other hand, some authors explain the outbreak as having been due first to hysteria on the part of the girls and then to a more general community hysteria.

Linnda Caporael (1976) claimed that convulsive ergotism might have been the physiological basis of the girls' behavior. Ergot poisoning is caused by a fungus which grows on damp grain crops, especially rye. Lysergic acid is a natural product of the ergot fungus. Convulsive ergotism produces symptoms that match closely those exhibited by the young girls of Salem: convulsions, sensations of being pricked or bitten, temporary blindness or deafness, and speechlessness. Rye was a staple of the early New England diet, and Caporael found that the cool, damp weather conditions of the summer and autumn of 1691 had been ideal for the development of the ergot fungus. The geographical distribution of the afflicted girls' homes, their symptoms, and the timing and duration of the crisis were all regarded by Caporael as indicating ergot poisoning. Having implicated ergot at Salem, Caporael went on to suggest that it might have been involved in other outbreaks of witchcraft. Her conclusions were challenged by Nicholas Spanos and Jack Gottlieb (1976), who claimed that the girls had been role-playing. However, more recently, Mary Matossian (1982), after examining the court records of the Salem trials along with climate and crop records, supported Caporael's conclusion that an outbreak of ergotism had been responsible for the behavior of the girls of Salem.

EARLY INSTITUTIONS AND "CURES" FOR MENTAL ILLNESS

When not tried as witches, many retarded and mentally ill people before the nineteenth century were treated as common criminals and thrown into prisons and jails or locked up in "fools' towers," "fools' homes," or "lunatic asylums." In 1547 a place to house mentally deranged people was established at St. Mary of Bethlehem Hospital in London. This institution became known to the Cockneys of London as "Old Bedlam" through a corruption of its name, Bethlehem to Bethl'em and then Bedlam. The modern meaning of the world *bedlam*—"a scene of wild uproar and confusion" (Stein, 1967)—describes the prevailing conditions at the hospital. Inmates were chained, whipped, and beaten; fed only slop; given purges and emetics; and subjected to bloodletting. Their keepers were not paid but earned small fees by displaying their charges for the entertainment of the general public. A visit to Old Bedlam to see the mad men and women was considered a pleasant outing and was chronicled by William Hogarth in a painting of a scene from the *Rake's Progress* in which two elegantly dressed and coiffed ladies visit Bedlam to see the sights. (Before the nineteenth century, wild animals were considered too frightening for members of the general public to see and so were kept in private collections. Today, mentally ill people are secluded and animals are displayed in zoos.) Melancholic and depressed patients whose behavior did not make a good show were sent out into the streets of London wearing badges that authorized them to beg for their keep. These "Toms of Bedlam" were well-known features of London life. In William Shakespeare's *King Lear,* Edgar enters

> like the catastrophe of the old comedy: my cue is villainous melancholy,
> with a sigh like a Tom o' Bedlam. (Act I, scene 2)

This picture of conditions at St. Mary of Bethlehem Hospital was recently challenged by a group of British historians (Bynum, Porter, & Shepherd, 1985) who claimed that conditions were not as bad as they are often described and that inmates were seldom exploited or abused. These authors considered the charge for admission to have been a collection of Christian alms rather than the price of admission to an entertainment. Restraint, manacling, and chaining, these historians claimed, were used with violent and assaultive inmates only when all else failed. James Norris was restrained with an iron collar and chained to the wall behind his bed only after four years of milder treatments had failed. These historians also point out that Norris was given books and newspapers to read and was allowed the company of a pet cat. Their critiques are lively and often acerbic but finally unconvincing. The back wards of the Central Ohio Lunatic Asylum, opened in 1877 and typical of

James Norris shackled in his cell in Bedlam. (Mary Evans Picture Library/Photo Researchers)

American institutions of that time, were fitted with iron bars and chains to restrain and manacle inmates. Such conditions were in fact common both in the United States and in England. In 1814, Ebenezer Haskell forced his way into St. Mary of Bethlehem and reported to the British House of Commons what he had seen:

> In the women's galleries, one of the side rooms contained about ten patients, each chained by one arm or leg to the wall, the chain allowing them merely to stand up by the bench or form fixed to the wall, or to sit down on it. The nakedness of each patient was covered by a blanket, made into something like a dressing gown, but with nothing to fasten it in front. This was the whole covering, the feet being naked. In another part I found many of the unfortunate women locked in the cells, naked and chained on straw, with only one blanket for covering. In the men's wing, in the side room, six patients were chained close to the wall, five handcuffed and one locked to the wall by the right arm, as well as by the right leg; he was very noisy; all were naked except as to the blanket-gown or small rug on the shoulders, and without shoes—their nakedness and their mode of confinement gave this room the complete appearance of a dog-kennel. (Haskell, cited by Roback & Kiernan, 1969, p. 192)

At times, inmates were starved, with the impact being increased by suspending the victim in a basket over the table at which others ate. Water "cures" were given in which as many as 100 buckets of ice-cold water were thrown over a chained inmate. In the "whirling cure" the person was strapped to a bed or chair that was rotated rapidly at speeds up to 100 rpm. This technique was popular both in England and in the United States. In 1811, an American physician, Joseph Mason Cox, published *Practical Observations on Insanity and Some Suggestions Towards Improved Mode of Treating Diseases of the Mind*. Cox was an enthusiastic advocate of whirling, swinging, and rotation in treating mania. He reported that when given in the dark,

> A very few circumvolutions [rotations] produces soothing, lulling effects, tranquilizing the mind and rendering the body quiescent; a degree of vertigo has followed, which has been succeeded by the most refreshing slumber; an object the most desirable in every case of madness, and with the utmost difficulty procured. (Cox, 1811, p. 1)

While Cox reported that some patients violently resisted being placed in the swing, he had used it with numerous manic patients and had seen "very surprising changes." In one "most miserable patient" a single application of swinging produced "the most complete revolution in the mind, changing the whole train of ideas" (Cox, 1811, p. 12).

Until the twentieth century many illnesses were thought to be caused by disorders of the blood, and so a common procedure was to let or remove blood by the application of leeches or through venous incisions done by physicians or barber-surgeons. The red and white barber's pole was originally the sign of a bloodletting barber-surgeon. In 1667 a physician named Denis withdrew ten ounces of blood from a melancholic patient and replaced it with six ounces of blood from a calf. Denis reported that the patient's mind cleared and he recovered from his melancholy (Zilboorg & Henry, 1941, p. 275). At St. Mary of Bethlehem, patients were bled routinely in the spring and autumn every year.

Benjamin Rush (1745–1813), the father of American psychiatry and a man whose silhouette appears on the seal of the American Psychiatric Association, was an enthusiastic advocate of bloodletting. In 1793 a severe yellow fever epidemic struck Philadelphia. More than 4,000 people died, and at one point Rush was one of only three physicians remaining in the city. He showed great courage in staying with his patients, but the purgings and bleedings he administered undoubtedly killed many of them. When Rush himself was struck with a violent fever, he instructed his assistants to bleed him plentifully. They did, and Rush almost died, but when he, along with some of his patients, recovered, Rush recalled:

> Never before did I experience such sublime joy as I now felt in contemplating the success of my remedies—the conquest of a formidable disease through the triumph of a principle of medicine. (Rush, quoted by Eisenberg, 1977, p. 1106)

Rush's principle was derived from the Brunonian system of medicine, which taught that excessive stimulation and excitement of the blood produce both physical and mental illness. Thus bloodletting was used to "quiet the blood" of both the physically and mentally ill. Rush, however, was not without critics. The English journalist William Cobbett likened bloodletting to "one of those great discoveries which have contributed to the depopulation of the earth." Rush sued for libel, and Cobbett was forced to pay damages of $8,000 (Middleton, 1928, p. 434).

REFORMATION OF INSTITUTIONS FOR THE MENTALLY ILL

Phillipe Pinel (1745–1826)

Pinel is often described as the father of scientific psychiatry. He was a quiet, shy person who lived before, during, and after the French Revolution and provoked a revolution in the care and treatment of the insane. Pinel's was a family of physicians, and he received a medical degree in 1773 from the University of Toulouse. He worked as a tutor and took additional courses in medicine, history, and Greek philosophy while obtaining a second degree in philosophy from the University of Montpellier. He then practiced medicine but was disenchanted with what he saw as the greed, meanness, and intrigues of his fellow physicians. He moved to Paris and served the city's poor people rather than the wealthy bourgeoisie he despised (Reisman, 1966).

Pinel also became progressively more interested in insanity, an interest that was stimulated in 1783 when a close friend, a young man of twenty-four, consulted him for help with his nervous condition. The man was a law student in Paris who had frequent periods of mania and depression. One day he would excitedly describe his plans for a brilliant career at the bar, and the next he would fall into a deep depression during which he was unable to leave his room, eat, or sleep. Pinel tried to help him, but one night in a fit of despair the young man fled from his father's house wearing nothing but a shirt, got lost in a nearby forest, and was attacked and killed by wolves. This dreadful accident moved Pinel deeply. Why had he, a physician, been unable to comfort and heal this poor man? What caused such behavior? What could be done to overcome such attacks of insanity?

Pinel resolved to take every opportunity to study the insane. He consulted with experts and read the literature on insanity. He found most of the opinions of the experts worthless, but the works of Joseph Daquin (1733–1815) struck a responsive chord. Daquin believed insanity to be a disease which must be understood and treated by the methods of natural science. The insane were not depraved animals but sick people who needed treatment. "To look at a madman and be amused," Daquin said, "was to be a moral monster" (Daquin quoted by Zilboorg & Henry, 1941, p. 318). Pinel and Daquin became mutual admirers, and when Daquin published the second edition of *Philosophie de la folie* (Philosophy of Madness) in 1793, he dedicated it to Pinel.

With Daquin's encouragement, Pinel began to write articles on insanity and entered an essay in a contest sponsored by the Royal Society of Medicine entitled "The Best Method of Treating Patients Who Become Insane Before Old Age." In it he argued that such people need humane treatment, sympathy, and guidance, not the beatings, imprisonment, and ridicule they so often suffer. His paper received honorable mention and brought his name to the attention of one of the judges, Thouret, the prefect of the Faculty of Medicine of Paris. After the revolution, Thouret was appointed to a board to oversee Parisian hospitals. Knowing Pinel's interest and enlightened views on insanity and the parlous state of his medical practice, Thouret arranged for his appointment as director of the Bicêtre Asylum in Paris beginning in 1793. Originally a prison, the Bicêtre had become a home for the poor and then in 1660 a retreat for the insane. The position as director was far from desirable, but Pinel accepted it with enthusiasm. First he reviewed the commitment papers of all the inmates, and then he toured the building, meeting the inhabitants individually and observing their behavior. Most were manacled, and archers patrolled the Bicêtre's walls to prevent escape. Pinel described what he saw:

> On my entrance upon the duties of that hospital [the Bicêtre], everything
> presented to me the appearance of chaos and confusion. Some of my
> unfortunate patients laboured under the horrors of a most gloomy and
> despondent melancholy. Others were furious and subject to the influence of
> perpetual delirium. Some appeared to possess a correct judgment upon most
> subjects, but were occasionally agitated by violent sallies of maniacal fury;
> while those of another class were sunk into a state of stupid idiotism and
> imbecility. (Pinel, 1801, pp.1–2)

Pinel decided that his first act would be to remove the physical restrictions from many of the inmates. Before taking such a step he had to gain the permission of the Revolutionary Council in charge of the Paris Commune. He stated his case and described his plan before the council and its president, a crippled revolutionary named Georges Couthon. After Pinel completed his presentation, Couthon said,

Phillipe Pinel orders the removal of an inmate's chains at the Bicêtre. (The Bettmann Archive)

"Citizen, you must be crazy yourself to let those brutes loose," and sarcastically remarked that Pinel's next step would be to go to the zoo and liberate the lions and tigers (Roback & Kiernan, 1969, p. 194). Pinel persisted, and finally Couthon agreed to visit the Bicêtre. His attempts to question the inmates met only curses and threats of violence. Couthon concluded that Pinel must have been mad himself to consider unchaining such people but gave him permission to do what he thought best. He felt sure that Pinel himself would be the first victim of this action.

Pinel's dramatic move was depicted in a famous painting by Charles Muller showing him ordering removal of the chains. This painting is somewhat misleading, for Pinel actually proceeded in a cautious and systematic manner. Starting in 1793 with a small number of inmates, he observed carefully the effects of removal of their fetters. The first man unchained was an English officer who had been at the Bicêtre for forty years, a vicious and violent man who had crushed a guard's head with his manacles. Pinel spoke quietly to him, asking if he would promise to be calm and not hurt anyone. The man agreed, and after his chains were removed he walked into the courtyard, gazing in ecstasy at the sky he had not seen all those years. He lost all his violence, helped care for the other inmates, and was released after two years. Another man unchained that dramatic day was Charles Chevigné, a former soldier kept in chains because of his legendary strength and violent nature. Ten years earlier Pinel had seen him being taken in a cart through the streets of Paris to the Bicêtre. Pinel calmly explained what he was going to do, and Chevigné too became a changed man. Some years later he saved Pinel's life when a mob attacked the Bicêtre and seized Pinel, accusing him of harboring members of the bourgoisie, turning dangerous lunatics loose, and even poisoning the wells of Paris and causing a cholera epidemic. They were about to hang Pinel when the giant Chevigné burst through the crowd to rescue him and rout the mob (Zilboorg & Henry, 1941, p. 324).

In four months Pinel ordered the chains removed from fifty-three inmates, and slowly their behavior and the atmosphere at the Bicêtre changed. Pinel always observed his charges with care, for their behavior, he said, is "the physician's best text-book." He improved the quality of the inmates' rations and ended all whirling and water "cures," emetics, and bloodletting. Pinel wrote of the latter:

> The blood of maniacs is sometimes so lavishly spilled, and with so little
> discernment, as to render it doubtful whether the patient or his physician
> has the best claim to the appellation of madman. (Pinel, 1801, p. 251)

Pinel also used the minimal restraint necessary for safety and order. He believed that

> a degree of liberty, sufficient to maintain order, dictated not by weak but
> enlightened humanity, and calculated to spread a few charms over the
> unhappy existence of maniacs, contributes in most instances, to diminish the
> violence of the symptoms, and in some, to remove the complaint altogether.
> (Pinel, 1801, p. 90)

Under Pinel cruel treatments were forbidden. The mentally ill, he taught, are not guilty people deserving punishment but sick people needing treatment. His regime had an immediate effect. In 1792, of 110 maniacs admitted to the Bicêtre, 57 died within a year; in 1793, 95 out of 151 died. In the first two years of Pinel's directorship the proportion of deaths to admissions was 1 to 8. His successes at the Bicêtre Asylum led to his appointment in 1795 as head of La Salpêtrière, the Parisian asylum for insane women.

La Salpêtrière, as the name implies, was located on the site of an old gun-powder factory. The building had been used as an arsenal and then as an asylum for the poor people of Paris. In 1795 it was the largest asylum in Europe, with some 8,000 inmates. Pinel found conditions there to be as bad as they had been at the Bicêtre, but in addition there was sexual abuse of the women inmates by their guards. He began to unchain the women of the Salpêtrière just as he had unchained the men at the Bicêtre. He again had many dramatic successes, and his fame spread throughout Europe. Afflicted people from many countries wrote to him for help. Letters addressed only to "Dr. Pinel" were delivered. He became a respected member of French medical and intellectual circles. In his many public lectures Pinel outlined his gospel of humane conditions for the mentally ill and scientific treatment of their condition. Pinel became an effective public speaker and also something of a quiet wit. When the astronomer Joseph Lalande, knowing Pinel's deep religious feelings, twitted him by saying that he was including Pinel in a new edition of his *Dictionary of Atheists*, Pinel replied that he was preparing a new edition of his *Philosophy of Madness* and would include Lalande in *it*.

Pinel died of pneumonia in October 1826 in his living quarters at La Salpêtrière. His funeral was a grand state occasion attended by ministers of state, physicians, students, and scientists but also by hundreds of ordinary people, including some whose attendance surely would have meant the most to Pinel—former inmates of the Bicêtre and the Salpêtrière.

The Wild Boy of Aveyron

One other episode in Pinel's life has proved to be of great importance: the case of the wild boy of Aveyron. Pinel was asked to examine a wild boy, believed to be about twelve years old, who had walked out of the woods of Saint-Serin in the department of Aveyron in southern France on January 9, 1800. From the reports of hunters who had caught glimpses of him, it was believed that he had lived in the woods for some years. He was virtually naked, covered with scars, dirty, and inarticulate. Apparently he had survived on a diet of acorns and roots. He walked on all fours much of the time and grunted like an animal. News of the capture of the wild boy caused a sensation in Paris. The newly formed Society of Observers of Man arranged for him to be brought to the capital for study.

A prevailing view was that the pure nature of men and women had been corrupted by civilization and that a natural life is the best possible life. Jean-Jacques Rousseau was an active proponent of such views. In 1749 an essay contest was held on the question of whether science or the arts had improved morals more. Rousseau won the contest with an essay arguing passionately against science and claiming that modern scientific society had corrupted and debased the innate goodness and purity of humans. In his books, Rousseau (Morley, 1915) described the natural state of humans as one of harmony and beauty, but this natural state, he claimed, had been corrupted by modern civilization. Such views were further strengthened by reports from European explorers of the seemingly idyllic societies of the South Seas. The wild boy of Aveyron had grown up *sub natura* (under nature), and so there was great interest in his behavior. Was he indeed a "noble savage"?

The answer was a resounding no. Taken to Paris in 1800 and exhibited in a cage, the wild boy sat rocking back and forth and was completely apathetic. He was a great disappointment to the hordes of curious spectators and to Rousseau's followers:

> A disgusting dirty child affected with spasmodic movements and often convulsions who swayed back and forth ceaselessly like certain animals in the menagerie, who bit and scratched those who opposed him, who showed no sort of affection for those who attended him and who was in short, indifferent to everything and attentive to nothing. (Itard, 1894, p. 4)

After examining him, Pinel concluded that far from being a noble savage, the boy was an incurable idiot. Despite this conclusion, one of Pinel's assistants, Jean Marc Gaspard Itard (1744–1835), undertook to care for the wild boy and try to educate him. He gave him a name, Victor, and then made a working assumption that Victor's problems were due to his social isolation rather than being the result of brain damage or another organic condition.

Itard undertook Victor's rehabilitation. With the assistance of Madame Guérin, Itard succeeded, after truly heroic efforts, in teaching Victor to pay attention, keep clean and dress himself, eat with his hands, play simple games, obey some commands, and even read and understand simple words. However, despite all their efforts Victor never learned to talk. At times he showed signs of affection, but often, especially under stress, his behavior was erratic, unpredictable, and violent. Victor learned simple discriminations, but when they were made more difficult, he became destructive, biting and chewing his clothes, the sheets, and even the chair and mantelpiece. After working with Victor for five years, Itard gave up hope of rehabilitating him. Victor's background and the "passions of his adolescence" could not be overcome. Victor lived with Madame Guérin until 1828, when he died at the age of forty, an almost forgotten half man. Itard told his story in *The Wild Boy of Aveyron;* more recently it has been dramatized in François Truffaut's film *The Wild Child* and in books by Harlan Lane (*The Wild Boy of Aveyron,* 1976) and Roger Shattuck (*The Forbidden Experiment,* 1980).

Itard considered his work with Victor to have been a failure, but an official report of the French Academy of Science applauded his efforts and pointed out that much progress had been made in helping Victor. Perhaps there was hope for remedial education of children from less deprived backgrounds who were classified as retarded.

The Remedial Efforts of Johann Guggenbühl (1816–1863)

In 1836 a young Swiss physician, Johann Jacob Guggenbühl, was traveling through the country when he saw a "dwarfed, crippled cretin of stupid appearance" (Kanner, 1964, p. 17) praying at a roadside shrine. At the time a combination of physical deformity and idiocy was thought to be endemic in certain Alpine valleys. Guggenbühl wondered if such an unhappy state was permanent and resolved to devote the rest of his life to the "cure and prophylaxis of cretinism" (Kanner, 1964, p. 221). On a tract of Alpine land on the Abendberg, near Interlaken, he established a residential and training center for mentally retarded children.

Guggenbühl believed that pure mountain air, the beauty of the Alps, a good natural diet, exercise, and "natural medications"—vitamins, minerals, and salts— would cure cretinism. At first his work was hailed as a major reform, and visitors to Abendberg reported many dramatic cures. Slowly, though, skeptics began to wonder how many children had actually been helped. Rumors of poor conditions and even abuse of the children spread. The British ambassador to Switzerland visited Abendberg to review the treatment of some British children. He found them in a neglected condition and the whole institution in a state of gross disorder. An official commission of inquiry investigated and concluded that not a single cretin had ever been cured at Abendberg. Guggenbühl went into exile—he had somehow accumulated a large fortune—and died in 1863 at the age of forty-seven. An obituary gave him credit only "for having effectively raised interest in the care of idiots" (Kanner, 1964, p. 29), but he deserves something more, for as Leo Kanner pointed out:

> Guggenbühl must be acknowledged as the indisputable originator of the idea
> and practice of the institutional care for feeble-minded individuals. The

hundreds of institutions now in existence derive in direct line from the Abendberg. (Kanner, 1964, p. 30)

William Tuke (1732–1822)

For our next reformer we cross the English Channel to consider a Quaker gentleman who at first sight seems a most unlikely agent of change. Late in the eighteenth century, William Tuke, a prosperous retired tea merchant, heard a very disturbing story. Friends told him that when they had tried to visit a relative committed to the Lunatick Asylum in the nearby city of York, the asylum's overseer had not allowed them to enter. A few days later they were told that their relative was dead. They suspected foul play and appealed to Tuke for help. Tuke visited the asylum and was horrified by what he saw. With support from the Society of Friends (the Quakers), who preached that God dwells within all people, Tuke devoted the remaining thirty years of his life to establishing an alternative place or retreat where "the unhappy might find refuge." In 1796 Tuke established near York a retreat where inmates would never be fettered, chained, or manacled but instead were given freedom, respect, good food, recreation, exercise, medical treatment, friendly support, and religious instruction. Tuke's York Retreat was purposely set up to resemble a farm rather than a prison. There were no bars or gratings on the windows, and gardens and farm animals were maintained (Reisman, 1966, p. 13). Tuke lived to be ninety years old and saw his York Retreat succeed and serve as a model for other enlightened institutions for the housing and care of the mentally ill. Both his son and his grandson devoted their lives to the York Retreat.

A Philadelphia Quaker, Thomas Scattergood, visited the York Retreat and was so moved that he "vented a few tears" (Price, 1988, p. 29). Inspired by his report, the Quakers of Philadelphia in 1813 founded the first private psychiatric hospital in the United States, the Friends Asylum for the Use of Persons Deprived of the Use of Their Reason. Friends Hospital of Philadelphia is still in operation. A second institution modeled on the York Retreat was established at Hartford, Connecticut, by Dr. Eli Todd (1762–1832) in 1824. Todd served as the physician in chief. He believed in "moral management" and giving patients the maximum amount of freedom and responsibility compatible with their conditions. Institutions modeled on Friends Hospital and Tuke's Hartford Retreat were established in Massachusetts, Vermont, and New Jersey. Patients were trained to lead a prudent life in harmony with what were seen as natural laws. Early admission was encouraged, and the typical stay was for six months. The best of these institutions apparently provided enlightened and humane treatment of the mentally ill.

Dorothea Lynde Dix (1802–1887)

Dorothea Lynde Dix was the child of an unhappy home. When she was ten years old, the religious fanaticism of her father forced her to leave home, and at fourteen she began a career as a schoolteacher. She also wrote a number of popular books for children and adolescents. When her health failed as a result of tuberculosis, Dix

Dorothea Lynde Dix. (The Bettmann
Archive)

was forced to give up full-time teaching and to take up an assignment teaching a
class of women prisoners in a Boston prison. She was distressed by what she saw,
especially by the fact that many people who were clearly mentally ill were treated
as common criminals and thrown into prison. For the remaining forty years of her
life Dix campaigned for improved conditions for the insane. She traveled to every
state east of the Mississippi, and although she was a quiet, dignified, and proper
lady, her tactics were overwhelming. First she would obtain facts about conditions
in a particular state, and then she would shrewdly and effectively publicize the
abuses and mistreatment she had found. She would enlist public support and that
of key legislators. In a *Memorial* to the United States Congress, Dix described how
she had seen

> more than 9,000 idiots, epileptics and insane in the United States, destitute
> of appropriate care and protection...bound with galling chains, bowed
> beneath fetters and heavy iron balls attached to drag-chains, lacerated with
> ropes, scourged with rods and terrified beneath storms of execration and
> cruel blows; now subject to jibes and scorn and torturing tricks; now
> abandoned to the most outrageous violations. (Dix, quoted by Sargent &
> Stafford, 1965, p. 276)

Always Dix preached her gospel of humane treatment and adequate facilities
for the insane and retarded. Within three years she had visited eighteen states and
stimulated reforms in most of them. During the Civil War Dix served as the chief
of hospital nurses. After the war was over she visited Europe on a lecture tour. In
an audience with Queen Victoria the doughty Miss Dix lectured the queen on the
need for continued reforms in England. This was probably the only time during her
reign that Queen Victoria was lectured. The experience made such an impression
that she appointed a royal commission to investigate British insane asylums. In an

audience with Pope Pius IX, Dix described Rome's insane asylums as a scandal and disgrace, prompting the pope to promise the establishment of a new asylum in Rome (Reisman, 1966).

Institutions for the Insane and the Retarded in the United States

The first public institution in the United States devoted to the care and treatment of the insane opened in Williamsburg, Virginia, in October 1773 (Zwelling, 1985). It was part prison and part infirmary. Windows were barred, doors were bolted, and the inmates were restrained with leg irons and straitjackets. The institution's first keeper, James Gault, had formerly headed the Public Gaol in Williamsburg. This institution has been restored as a museum open to the public (Turkington, 1985).

The early and middle decades of the nineteenth century saw the establishment of many large state-run asylums and institutions in the United States. At first they were modeled on private institutions such as the Friends Hospital of Philadelphia and the Hartford Retreat. Often located in rural settings, their goal was to provide the insane from all classes with moral treatment and education. Some well-run institutions achieved cure rates of 50 percent (Dain, 1971), but sadly, within months of opening, these institutions were inundated with great numbers of chronically disturbed people, many of whom had resided for years in almshouses, poorhouses, jails, and prisons. "Moral treatment" was not effective with these people, many of whom were chronically mentally disturbed. In addition, disproportionately large numbers of immigrants were committed, and the staff members were totally unprepared to deal with their different ethnic and cultural backgrounds. Large custodial institutions run by the states were then established. With the economic difficulties of the years following the Civil War, funding for these public institutions was uncertain, and so the physical facilities deteriorated and standards of care fell. Williams, Bellis, and Wellington reviewed these years:

> Increasingly, the major task of the asylum staff became the control of what was seen as deviant and dangerous behavior. The humane authoritarianism of moral treatment was transformed into rigid authoritarian control of people of whom little was understood or expected. Within a few years of their founding, the public asylums had become repositories for the custodial care of the poor and immigrant classes. (Williams et al., 1980, p. 57)

Early in the twentieth century Clifford W. Beers founded the mental hygiene movement. Beers had been a patient in a mental hospital. He recovered and wrote a book, *A Mind That Found Itself* (1908), describing his experience with mental illness. Beers enlisted the support of many influential people, including Theodore Roosevelt and America's leading psychologist, William James (Chapter 11). He was able to cite his own case to counter the pessimism which so often surrounded mental illness and the mentally ill. However, despite his efforts and those of others of similar views and persuasion, conditions for the care and treatment of the mentally ill went into a decline. The Great Depression and World War II diminished both the number of staff members and the financial support for mental institutions. In 1949 Albert Deutsch surveyed over two dozen state mental hospitals and found

> scenes that rivaled the horrors of the Nazi concentration camps—hundreds
> of naked mental patients herded into huge barnlike, filth-infested wards, in
> all degrees of deterioration, untended and untreated, stripped of every
> vestige of human decency, many in stages of semi-starvation. (Deutsch,
> 1949, p. 449)

In 1949 no state mental hospital met the minimal standards of operation set by the American Psychiatric Association (Williams et al., 1980, p. 61). While there has been progress since then, highlighted by the creation of the National Institute of Mental Health (NIMH) and the Community Mental Health Center Act of 1963, a visit to many contemporary institutions for the mentally ill and retarded shows that progress has been slow and that much needs to be done. A recent report described the Dorothea Dix Hospital in Raleigh, North Carolina, as a dangerous place where "wolves and lambs create a volatile mix," escalating violence includes beating and rape, and patients are crowded five to a room (Overton, 1986). Although policies of deinstitutionalization in the 1970s led to the release of many former patients, all too often they were left without adequate supervision and support and simply swelled the numbers of the urban homeless.

Radical Physical and Pharmacological Treatments of Insanity

Given the overcrowded and atrocious conditions in institutions for the insane, "great and desperate cures" that promised successful treatment of insanity were enthusiastically received (Valenstein, 1986). The most desperate of these cures was psychosurgery. In December 1935, Egas Moniz (1874–1955), a Portugese neurologist trained at La Salpêtrière, drilled holes into the skull of a mental patient and used a specially constructed instrument to cut or crush the nerve fibers in its path. Moniz named his procedure *prefrontal leucotomy*, since its target was the brain's frontal lobe and a *tome* (Greek for knife) was used to cut or crush nerve fibers (in Greek *leuco*). Four months later Moniz presented the results from twenty such operations. Seven patients were said to have recovered, seven were improved, and six were unchanged (Valenstein, 1986, chap. 6). In January 1937, Moniz reported successful outcomes in eighteen additional patients. Moniz's reports of success were often exaggerated, ignored side effects, and were based on vague and subjective data. Nevertheless, his procedures were widely used. For his work Moniz shared the 1949 Nobel Prize for medicine.

Walter Freeman (1895–1927), an American neuropathologist and neuropsychiatrist, was largely responsible for the worldwide adoption of psychosurgery as a treatment for mental illness. Freeman performed 3,500 such operations. Between 1948 and 1952 neurosurgeons in the United States performed 5,000 prefrontal leucotomies a year. Ultimately, controlled, long-term studies of the outcomes of such operations contraindicated their use. The beneficial effects had been grossly exaggerated by Moniz and Freeman, and such devastating side effects as lack of emotion, retarded movements and inertia, loss of initiative, mutism, and negativism had been minimized and neglected. At an International Mental Health Conference in Vienna in 1953 lobotomy was described as "turning a human being into a vegetable," as making "idiots out of madmen," and as an act of "therapeutic nihilism" (Oserezski, in Gerow, 1988, p. 38). In 1970 the number of psychosurgical procedures done in the United States was about 300. In these operations stereotaxic instruments (Chapter 3) were used to direct electrodes to brain targets. Before such procedures were developed tens of thousands of people all over the world had been lobotomized, often with devastating results.

Other radical treatments of mental illness involved the induction of coma or convulsions of the brain. With little theoretical justification or evidence from animal research, such cerebral insults were expected to have beneficial effects. Manfred Joshua Sakel, a Viennese physician, claimed in 1933 that 88 percent of the schizophrenics he treated improved after recovering from a deep insulin-induced coma. Shock therapy using pentylenetetrazole (Metrazole) to induce a convulsion was introduced by Joseph Ladislau von Meduna in 1935. Meduna's rationale was that since people with epilepsy rarely suffer from schizophrenia, a massive convulsive seizure might be effective in treating schizophrenia. This method was widely used in the United States to treat schizophrenia. Convulsive treatments, using electric shock, were developed by two Italians, Ugo Cerletti and Lucio Bini. They first used the technique in 1938 with schizophrenic patients but later found it to be most valuable in treating depression. Of these convulsive treatments only electroconvulsive therapy (ECT) continues to be used with any frequency today. The theoretical justification for convulsive treatments was never convincing, and there is always a distinct possibility of permanent brain damage with such treatments. ECT has been found effective for a sizable number of patients who do not respond to other therapies including antidepressant drugs (Cole & Davis, 1975). One way to decrease the possibility of brain damage is to limit the convulsion to one cerebral hemisphere, typically the nondominant side of the brain, and to restrict the number of treatments.

The second class of radical treatments involves the use of drugs having psychological effects. In the middle decades of this century psychoactive drugs were developed that provided not a cure but relief for some forms of mental illness. In the 1950s chlorpromazine was widely used in Europe and the United States to treat schizophrenics, many of whom were able to return to work and lead almost normal lives in the community. But there were problems. Required doses of chlorpromazine varied greatly from patient to patient; at high doses patients developed rigidity, difficulty moving, and tremors. Arvid Carlsson, a Swedish pharmacologist, speculated that chlorpromazine acts by blocking dopamine systems in the brain. More recently phenothiazines, drugs that block synaptic receptors in the brain that are sensitive to dopamine, have been reported to reduce the symptoms of schizophrenia (Snyder, 1984).

The usefulness of lithium in treating depression has been known since the mid-1960s. But since lithium is a common salt that cannot be patented, major pharmaceutical companies were unwilling to invest in its clinical trials, and so its widespread use was delayed (Snyder, 1984, p. 142). Paradoxically, lithium has been found to be effective in treating both the mania and the depression seen in bipolar affective disorders. Finally, a class of drugs known as antidepressants has been widely used.

These psychoactive drugs have had an enormous impact. In 1955 there were 560,000 patients in mental hospitals in the United States, with over half diagnosed as schizophrenics; by 1970 the number of patients had declined to 340,000, and by 1984 to less than 150,000 (Rothman & Rothman, 1984).

OTHER SYSTEMS OF DIAGNOSIS AND TREATMENT OF MENTAL ILLNESS

Thus far we have considered changes in the conditions under which mentally ill and retarded people were housed in institutions and the development of radical physical treatments. Of equal importance were changes in conceptions of mental illness and the development of psychological therapies.

Jean Esquirol (1772–1840), Pinel's assistant and his successor as head of La Salpêtrière, was the first person to establish relative frequencies of different mental conditions, their average durations, and their usual prognoses. His was a descriptive, statistical approach to mental illness. He also used case histories to establish the most frequent causes of different conditions. Esquirol believed that financial anxieties, disappointments in love, and bereavement were the most common precipitating factors. He distinguished between hallucinations—associated with mental illness—and illusions, which are incorrect but common misperceptions of no clinical significance. Before Esquirol, seeing an illusion had often been considered indicative of mental disorder. Since most people see illusions, this equation must have produced much lying and distortion. Esquirol was the first to propose that some forms of criminal behavior result from mental illness and that a mentally disturbed person is not responsible for his or her actions (Kanner, 1964). The insanity plea is still very controversial today.

Mesmerism and Hypnosis

Mesmerism and later hypnosis were used widely to treat a variety of physical and mental illnesses during the eighteenth and nineteenth centuries. The interest of French scientists and physicians in hypnosis dated back to the work of Franz Anton Mesmer (1734–1825). Mesmer qualified as a physician at the prestigious Medical School of Vienna. He was a man of high social class, a well-known physician, and a friend of artists and musicians, including Wolfgang Amadeus Mozart. Mesmer believed that planets generate celestial forces that can be focused through magnets to affect the human body, just as the moon affects the oceans through the tides. He lived at a time when magnetism and electricity were mysterious forces recently introduced to scientific thought (Chapter 2). Mesmer found that his patients would sometimes fall into a trance when stroking passes were made with a magnet over their bodies. He also reported magnetic cures of sickness and disease and went so far as to claim in 1766 that in his work with this magnetic method, "the art of healing reaches its final perfection." His medical colleagues, however, rejected his claims, and in 1777 Mesmer was expelled from the medical faculty of the University of Vienna and ordered to cease the practice of medicine. He found exile in Paris, a city which

> seemed to attract and nourish an assortment of confidence men, fakers, and adventurers rarely equalled in history. The success of science had produced a fertile ground for almost any idea in Paris (perhaps augmented by pre-Revolutionary restlessness) and the resulting picture was a kaleidoscope of popular science, buffoonery and outright charlatanism. (Hoffeld, 1980, p. 378)

Mesmer established a fabulously ornate clinic on one of the most fashionable streets in Paris. His reputation spread, and day after day large crowds gathered. They waited in a dimly lit room as Mesmer's assistant, Charles Deslon, removed a wooden cover from a large oaken tub, the *baquet*, and added water and chemicals to cover a layer of iron filings. The cover was then replaced, and jointed iron rods were inserted through openings in the tub's sides. Then the "great healer" would make his entrance. Perhaps dressed as a magician, Mesmer would walk in silence around the room, touching each person in turn with a long iron wand. Often when he stared into a person's eyes and gave the command *"Dormez"* (sleep), the person would fall into a trance. He or she had been mesmerized. Thousands of people flocked to the clinic. Mesmer's popularity was immense, but he was not without critics. The French clergy swore that Mesmer had sold his soul to the devil, while the medical profession described him as an impostor, charlatan, and quack. Unintimidated, he challenged the French Academy of Medicine to choose twenty patients, assign ten to him for treatment and ten to members of the academy, and compare the outcomes. The academy rejected the challenge.

In 1781, at the urging of Queen Marie Antoinette, one of Mesmer's most ardent supporters, the French government offered him a chateau and a lifetime pension if he would reveal his methods. Mesmer refused. In 1783, the French Academy of Science appointed a royal commission to investigate Mesmer and his claims. The commission, headed by the American ambassador, Benjamin Franklin, included the chemist Antoine Lavoisier, the discoverer of oxygen; Joseph Guillotin, whose invention was soon to be used widely; and the astronomer Jean Bailly. In its report of August 1874, the commission condemned the practice of mesmerism as dangerous and useless and branded Mesmer a mystic and fanatic. In addition to the public report the commission wrote a secret report for the king. This report had a sexual theme, stressing that Mesmer often treated young, attractive women who were not really ill but went to him out of idleness and a desire to be amused. Undaunted, Mesmer continued to practice, and his notoriety grew. In 1786 Deslon died while in a trance; a popular play, *The Modern Doctors*, performed in Paris, satirized Mesmer with frequent sexual innuendos. In 1792 Mesmer was forced to leave Paris, going first to London and then to Germany. Several years before his death in 1815 he moved back to Paris, but by that time the passions surrounding mesmerism had cooled, and he spent his final years in quiet retirement in the countryside near Versailles (Tatar, 1978).

Mesmer attributed his cures to the vivifying powers of a subtle fluid which can be transferred from a healthy to a sick person. When this vital energy flows, the recipient feels agreeably warm, with the head becoming lighter and clearer, the disposition improving, and certain ailments of nervous origin possibly disappearing. Cures of headaches, epileptic "fits," fainting, and rheumatism were believed to be especially likely.

While a small number of Mesmer's procedures bear at least some resemblance to those of a modern hypnotist and while it seems likely that he did cure some people, many of his other claims, beliefs, and procedures are well beyond the realm of reason. For example, Mesmer believed that trees could be "magnetized." He would then have his patients touch them to be cured. However, the investigating committee discovered that many of his patients touched "unmagnetized" trees and yet were said to have been cured. Mesmer also believed that a nickel disk he used had special magnetic powers. When the committee members examined the disk, they found that it was lead (Tatar, 1978).

Mesmerism in England

John Elliotson was Mesmer's foremost follower in England. He was an established member of the English medical profession, a past president of the Royal Medical and Surgical Society of London, and a professor of medicine at University College in London, a college he had helped found. Elliotson was also something of a radical. He introduced many new drugs to medical practice and was the first person in England to use a stethoscope, an instrument invented in 1816 by a French physician, René Laennec. Up to that time diagnoses were made at a distance, based on the patient's self-report and the physician's unaided observations (Reiser, 1979). The stethoscope required direct contact with the patient, and so its use was controversial.

Elliotson's interest in mesmerism was aroused when he saw demonstrations of induced trances and apparent cures of various illnesses. He became an advocate of mesmerism, giving many demonstrations and even performing surgery on mesmerized patients. His colleagues were scandalized. In 1837 the council of University College passed a resolution forbidding the practice of mesmerism in the hospital. Elliotson resigned and never entered the college again.

Elliotson and other mesmerists apparently did have some successes. Their most spectacular and well-publicized cure was the case of Harriet Martineau, an ardent feminist who believed herself to be dying of cancer. She was mesmerized with such striking results that the next day she was able to walk fifteen miles and write fifteen pages of text without any fatigue. She described her case in an article in the *Athenaeum* of November 1844, but even this dramatic case was greeted with scorn by Elliotson's critics. Martineau was said to be a hysterical woman, and the claim of a cancer cure was dismissed (Bailey, 1981).

James Esdaile (1808–1859), a surgeon with the British Army in Calcutta, India, read a description of Elliotson's use of mesmerism in surgery and began to use the procedure in his operations. To his surprise and pleasure, he found that his patients not only survived such operations but also reported that they had not experienced pain. By 1846 he had used mesmerism successfully in more than 300 operations (Esdaile, 1846). During the operations patients lay relaxed and quiet. People were less frightened, and many Indians came to him instead of conventional surgeons. However, he too was criticized by his medical colleagues and had difficulty publishing descriptions of his work.

Esdaile's was not the only successful use of mesmerism in surgery. In 1829 a French physician, Jules Cloquet, described the successful removal of a diseased breast in a mesmerized patient. In 1842 an English surgeon named James Ward amputated a leg in a patient under a mesmeric trance. However, interest in mesmerism as an anesthetic procedure quickly diminished with the development of chemical agents. In 1844 an American dentist named Horace Wells had one of his own teeth extracted while under the influence of nitrous oxide; in 1846 ether was first used as a general anesthetic in an operation at the Massachusetts General Hospital. The operation was a success, and Henry Bigelow, one of the surgeons who observed it, announced afterward, "I have seen something today that will go around the world" (Cohen & Dripps, 1970, p. 44). In 1847 chloroform was used to reduce the pain of childbirth. Somehow these chemical anesthetic agents seemed more acceptable than the mysterious mesmerism, but in recent years hypnosis has again been used as an anesthetic procedure, especially for dental surgery.

Hypnosis in England and France

The term *hypnosis* was introduced in 1843 by James Braid (1795–1860). Two years earlier, while practicing as a physician in Manchester, England, Braid attended a demonstration by an itinerant mesmerist. He was highly skeptical of the mesmerist's claims but did notice that the mesmerized subject's eyelids became heavy, drooped, and closed. At home he tried to mesmerize his wife and a friend. They stared at a slowly moving, bright metallic object while Braid suggested that their eyelids were becoming heavy. They both closed their eyes and fell into a trance. With this demonstration Braid ended the long, acrimonious debate over the role of magnetism and showed the importance of fixation and suggestion in inducing a trance. Braid concluded that hypnosis is a form of sleep induced by suggestion and a narrowing of attention. In 1843 he described numerous cases in which hypnotism had relieved illness and suffering. Braid, however, was always an empirical observer. His goal was scientific description and understanding, not the advocacy of Mesmer and Elliotson.

Mesmer's two most immediate successors in France were Ambrose-Auguste Liébault (1823–1904) and Hippolyte Bernheim (1837–1919). In 1864 Liébault began practicing as a hypnotist in Nancy. He claimed a number of cures of physical illness and convinced the initially skeptical Bernheim of the value of the procedure. With the assistance of a chemist, Emil Coué, he combined hypnosis with drugs, and Nancy became an important center for the treatment of psychosomatic illness. A second French hypnosis clinic was that of Jean Martin Charcot (1825–1893) in Paris. It was to Charcot's clinic that a young Viennese physician traveled in 1885, hoping to learn how to use hypnosis in treating hysterical patients. The young man's name was Sigmund Freud, and his theories and treatments were to change forever our conception of the human condition.

SIGMUND FREUD (1856–1939)

Freud's Early Life

Sigmund Freud was born in Freiberg, Moravia, on May 6, 1856, the first child of Jacob Freud's third wife. At the time Freiberg was part of the Austrian Empire; today it is part of Czechoslovakia. Freud was raised in the traditions and beliefs of the Jewish religion, his great-grandfather having been a rabbi. Though he later described his attitude to religion as "critically negative," Freud always considered himself a Jew. His family traced its heritage back to the fourteenth century and had originally fled from Cologne to escape anti-Semitic persecution. Freud's father was a wool merchant, a hardworking but often impoverished man. In 1859, when Freud was three years old, his family moved to Vienna. Since the Jews of Austria had been emancipated only in 1848, there was still much anti-Semitism, and their early years there were difficult financially. Freud did well at school, was graduated from high school summa cum laude, and was rewarded by his father with a trip to England, the family's finances having improved. Freud had always been a serious student with a deep need for recognition by his father and other authority figures. He had a love of literature—Shakespeare was his favorite author—and he was proficient in German, French, English, Italian, Spanish, Hebrew, Latin, and Greek (Jones, 1953).

Freud's Education

When the time came for Freud to prepare for a profession, his dreams of being a great general like his boyhood heroes Hannibal and Napoleon or a minister of state like another of his heroes, Oliver Cromwell, were wrecked by the harsh realities of anti-Semitism. In late nineteenth-century Vienna a Jewish boy's choices were restricted. Freud considered a career in law but found legal affairs dull, and so, though he later admitted to "no particular predilection for the career of a physician" (Freud, 1935, p. 13), he chose a medical career. He entered the University of Vienna in 1873 but did not graduate until 1881. Given his drive and dedication, it is surprising that Freud took three years longer than the average medical student to obtain his degree. The delay was caused by a year's military service in 1879, time spent translating and editing a German edition of John Stuart Mill's works (Chapter 2), and the biological research he did under Vienna's professor of physiology, Ernst Brücke. Freud did important research on the gonadal structure of eels and the nerve cells of crayfish and developed an important gold chloride method for staining nerve cells. In all, six productive years were spent at Brücke's research institute. Freud left reluctantly when it became clear that he would not be appointed to one of the institute's two research assistantships, both of which were held by young men.

Freud spent the next three years working his way through the various departments of the Vienna General Hospital, including five months in the psychiatric clinic of Theodor Meynert (1833–1892). Meynert had a great influence on Freud, who regarded him as the most brilliant man he had ever met. In Meynert's clinic Freud saw his first hysterical patients. This experience was important, but even more critical in developing Freud's interest in hysteria was a case seen by his colleague Josef Breuer (1859–1936).

Josef Breuer and the Case of Anna O.

In late nineteenth-century Vienna, Josef Breuer was known as the "doctor with the golden touch" because of his successful treatment of hysteria. He was a distinguished neurologist, who as a young man had established that the vagus nerve controls breathing and that the semicircular canals affect equilibrium. Freud described Breuer as a man of

> striking intelligence and fourteen years older than myself. Our relations soon became more intimate and he became my friend and helper in many circumstances. (Freud, quoted by Eissler, 1978, p. 13)

From November 1880 to the summer of 1882 Breuer treated a young, bright, attractive woman, Bertha Pappenheim. She presented him with a variety of hysterical symptoms: a nervous cough, *absences* during which she would stare into space, anorexia, paralyses, anesthesias, a double personality, and speech disorders, including an inability to speak her native German but an unchanged proficiency in English. Not surprisingly, Breuer found Pappenheim fascinating, and he became intensely preoccupied with her case. Each evening they would discuss her memories of the first occasion when a symptom had appeared. Many of the memories related to her father's final illness and to the intense emotions she had experienced while caring for him. Paralysis of her arm had first appeared when she hallucinated a large, black snake in her father's bed. She tried to ward off the snake with her right arm but found she could not move it. From that time her arm had been paralyzed. Pappenheim was highly susceptible to hypnosis, and often the trance helped her recall such memories. Those recollections were intensely emotional, but afterward she felt calm and cheerful. Breuer referred to this release of tension as *catharsis*, a term first used by Aristotle (Chapter 1). He found the effects of catharsis totally surprising but very real. Breuer began to describe his treatment of Pappenheim as "the talking cure," while she referred to it as "chimney sweeping" (Clark, 1980, p. 102).

Breuer's treatment of Bertha proceeded, but he was devoting an unusual amount of time to her case, often seeing her twice a day. Breuer's wife was unhappy and depressed about their relationship and insisted that Breuer end his treatment of Pappenheim. Bertha Pappenheim's reaction was to go into hysterical childbirth and to accuse Breuer of fathering her child. She was institutionalized for a year, but when she fell in love with the institution's superintendent, her mother intervened and took her back to Germany. There she recovered and went on to a successful career as Germany's first social worker and a zealous champion of women's rights.

Pappenheim was understandably sensitive about her relationship with Breuer and all her life refused to comment on her illness and treatment. When Breuer discussed her case with Freud, he respected her feelings by referring to her as Fraülein Anna O., the name by which she has come to be known. Freud was fascinated by her case and was to discuss it later in Paris with the leading nineteenth-century expert on hysteria, Jean Martin Charcot, who, however, showed little interest. Anna O. and Josef Breuer both played important roles in Freud's developing interest in hysteria and the formulation of psychoanalysis. She has been described as the "best-known of all psychotherapy patients" (Hollender, 1980, p. 797).

Freud's Personal Use of Drugs

In the spring of 1884 Freud began to experiment with cocaine. He found that the drug relieved his feelings of depression, turned bad moods into cheerfulness, and helped him work. He became an enthusiastic advocate of the drug and published six papers in the next two years describing its beneficial effects (Bernfeld, 1953). Cocaine seemed "a magical substance," and for the first time Freud felt himself to be a "real physician." He gave cocaine to his sister and sent some to his fiancée, Martha Bernays, "to make her strong and give her cheeks a red color" (Jones, 1953, p. 81). Freud himself took larger and larger doses and was fortunate not to become addicted. One of his friends for whom he prescribed the drug was not so fortunate: Ernst von Fleischl died a cocaine addict in 1891. At first Freud's enthusiasm for cocaine was widely shared, but by 1885 numerous cases of cocaine addiction and intoxication had been reported, and alarm spread through the medical community. As an advocate of the drug, Freud was censured and rebuked by his colleagues. His most severe critic, Albrecht Erlenmeyer, labeled cocaine, with alcohol and morphine, "the three scourges of humanity." Freud was deeply scarred by this "cocaine episode."

Though Freud was fortunate to have escaped cocaine addition, all his life he fought a losing battle against his addiction to another drug, nicotine. In 1894, when he was thirty-eight years old, Freud was told by his physician that his heart arrythmias were due to smoking and was advised to stop. He continued to smoke heavily, often twenty cigars a day. During World War I, when the cigars he favored were scarce, Freud traded his wife's needlework for a supply. As a physician he was well aware of the risks he was taking, and many times he tried desperately to stop smoking, but always without success. When he was sixty-seven years old Freud noticed sores on his palate and jaw that failed to heal and were found to be cancerous. Yet he continued to smoke, rationalizing his decision by quoting George Bernard Shaw's warning, "Don't try to live forever, you will not be successful." Freud underwent a series of thirty-three operations on his mouth, throat, and palate. His jaw was almost completely removed and replaced with an artificial jaw Freud called "the monster." When he was in his seventies a cancer specialist again advised him to stop smoking, but Freud refused to accept what he termed his "nicotine sentence" (Jones,

1957, p. 159); he continued to smoke heavily, for as he said, "I have never been able to put up with having only a couple of cigars in my cigar-case" (Freud, quoted by Jones, 1957, p. 121). Freud's forty-five-year struggle makes him a tragic prototype of addiction to nicotine (Brecher, 1972, p. 215).

Freud and Charcot

The year 1885 was a good one for Freud. He was able to overcome the notoriety of the cocaine episode and was appointed a *Privatdozent* at the University of Vienna. He applied for a grant to study hysteria and hypnosis under Charcot in Paris. Such grants were very competitive, and their award was often political. Fortunately, Freud had Brücke's support and was successful. He traveled to Paris in October 1885 and remained there until February 1886, five months that changed his life forever.

Charcot was then at the peak of his fame and influence, and his stature in French medicine equaled that of Louis Pasteur in chemistry. He was acknowledged to be the "world's greatest neurologist," and his La Salpêtrière clinic was the "Mecca of neurology," to which students flocked from many countries. The great attractions were Charcot's Tuesday demonstrations of hysterical phenomena and his lectures on hypnosis and hysteria. Freud saw Charcot's demonstrations of the induction and removal of hysterical symptoms through hypnotic suggestion and heard Charcot's claim that these symptoms were organically based but had psychological causes. Patients at the Salpêtrière showed "checkerboard" anesthesias, or paraly-

Jean Charcot demonstrates hypnosis with his patient "Wit." (The Bettmann Archive)

ses, which came and went and did not follow anatomic principles. After just a month in Paris, Freud described Charcot in a letter to his fiancée, Martha Bernays:

> Charcot, who is one of the greatest physicians and a man whose common sense borders on genius, is simply wrecking all my aims and opinions. I sometimes come out of his lectures as from out of Notre Dame, with an entirely new idea about perfection. But he exhausts me. When I come away from him I no longer have any desire to work on my own silly things....My brain is sated as after an evening at the theater. Whether the seed will ever bear any fruit, I don't know, but what I do know is that no other human being has ever affected me the same way. (Freud, November 14, 1885, in Freud, Freud, & Grubrich-Simitis, 1978, p. 114)

The most significant episode during Freud's time in Paris occurred neither at the Salpêtrière clinic nor in one of Charcot's lectures but rather at one of the fabulous parties for which Charcot was well known. There Freud overheard Charcot describing the case of a young married couple; the wife was a confirmed invalid, and the husband was impotent. Charcot stated adamantly, *"Mais, dans ces pareils, c'est toujours le chose genitale—toujours—toujours—toujours—toujours"* (But in such cases it is always a matter of sex—always—always—always—always). If that were the case, Freud wondered, why did Charcot not say so in his lectures and writings? Still, he was impressed that a neurologist of Charcot's stature should hold such a view (Clark, 1980, chap. 4).

When Freud returned to Vienna he translated one of Charcot's books, and in October 1886 he delivered a paper, "On Male Hysteria," to the Vienna Society of Physicians. Freud enthusiastically presented and endorsed Charcot's views, including his description of hysterical symptoms in males. Forty years later in his autobiography, Freud recalled bitterly the hostile reaction to his presentation. The chairman described his views as "incredible," and one critic even asked sarcastically whether he was aware that the word *hysteria* had its root in the Greek word for uterus, *hysteron*. Male hysteria was described by some as an impossibility, and Freud was challenged to find a case of male hysteria in Vienna. He was able to meet this challenge and present such a case a month later.

This episode often has been described as the first of a number of occasions on which Freud's views were rejected by the medical establishment. Sulloway (1979) claimed that accounts of this hostile reception are largely a myth created by Freud's misperceptions and his followers' view of him as a bold, courageous innovator. According to Sulloway, Freud's role as the self-appointed messenger from Paris was unnecessary, as Charcot's views on hysteria were well known in Vienna. Also, Freud's view of Charcot was far too positive and uncritical. Many in the audience had a more realistic view of Charcot than did the uncritical Freud. Furthermore, a description of male hysteria was not as novel or revolutionary as Freud had implied, since descriptions of hysterical symptoms in males had been given previously. The old uterine theory of hysteria had been widely discarded, and the baiting question about the origin of the word *hysteria* had been asked by a very old member of the society. The general reaction to Freud's presentation was probably not as hostile as he remembered it. According to Sulloway (1979), historically questionable accounts of this and similar episodes have contributed to the myth of Freud as a hero and revolutionary.

Freud's Medical Practice in Vienna

Freud established a private medical practice in Vienna in 1886, with the treatment of hysteria as his specialty. At first he used conventional treatments—baths, massage, electrotherapy, and rest cures—but by 1889 he concluded that these procedures were not effective. He turned to hypnotism and returned to France to study the techniques of Liébault and Bernheim of the Nancy School of Hypnosis. Freud also translated Bernheim's 1888 *De la Suggestion et de ses applications à la therapeutique* (Suggestive Therapeutics). After his return to Vienna, Freud used hypnosis in the case of Frau Emmy von N., an intelligent forty-year-old woman (Macmillan, 1979). Her most striking symptom was periodic interruptions of conversation during which she stretched her hands out in front of her face, which contorted with horror and disgust, and would say, "Keep still—don't say anything—don't touch me." Under hypnosis Freud found that many of her fears related to childhood events. Some of her symptoms were alleviated by recalling such memories and some by direct hypnotic suggestion, but Freud did not consider her case a success. He became more and more dissatisfied with hypnosis as a therapeutic technique. Not all patients could be hypnotized, and those who could submitted to different degrees. Some symptoms were unaffected, and some were relieved only temporarily. Freud concluded that his relationship with each patient was of more importance than any of the techniques he used. How could he improve this relationship and encourage patients to release pent-up memories without hypnosis?

Psychoanalytic Techniques

Freud began to instruct his patients to try to remember events associated with the first appearance of hysterical symptoms. He found that some patients were able to recall and describe memories that had been repressed for years. Often this recall was beneficial to them, just as it had been to Anna O. Freud began to rely more and more on a method of free association in which patients were asked to describe everything that came into their minds. He described this method as allowing the depths of the human mind to be probed like an archaeologist's excavation of a buried city. At first he referred to this procedure as "Breuer's method," then as "physical analysis," and finally as "psychoanalysis."

Freud begged Breuer to publish a description of Anna O. and his use of the "talking cure" to produce catharsis. The cautious and conservative Breuer was reluctant to do so. As he had an established reputation, his caution is understandable. Finally, he agreed and published *Studien über Hysterie* (Studies in Hysteria) with Freud in 1895. They described Anna O. and four other hysterical patients. Even as they wrote this book their views began to diverge. Breuer believed the crucial factor in a successful treatment of hysteria to be the relationship between the physician and patient. The patient describes his or her symptoms, the therapist listens with care and attention, and what Breuer termed *transference* develops; that is, the patient transfers earlier feelings about authority figures, especially parents, to the therapist. Freud agreed that transference is important, but remembering Charcot's statement about the origins of hysteria, he concluded that sexual problems and repressed sexual memories are the fundamental causes of hysterical symptoms. This conclusion was unacceptable to Breuer, and their professional relationship ended. Freud recalled:

> The development of psychoanalysis afterward cost me his [Breuer's]
> friendship. It was not easy for me to pay such a price, but I could not
> escape it. (Freud, quoted by Eissler, 1978, p. 33)

Freud always acknowledged Breuer's influence on his thinking, Breuer's first description of catharsis being especially important. Breuer also served as an important role model, collaborator, and source of support for Freud. In return, Breuer described his feelings of awe and admiration for Freud and recalled that "he gazed after his soaring intellect as a hen at a hawk" (Jones, 1953, chap. XI).

Freud's Seduction Theory

The years from 1887 to 1910 were Freud's great period of creativity and discovery. He corresponded frequently with a Berlin ear, nose, and throat specialist, Wilhelm Fliess (1858–1928), who took Breuer's place as his confidant. They exchanged manuscripts and papers, and their correspondence provides an invaluable record of their relationship and of Freud's creative genius. In 1950 a selection of 168 letters from Freud to Fliess was published. Earlier Freud had been astonished to learn that the letters had been preserved and begged their owner, the analyst Marie Bonaparte, not to permit their publication. They show an intense emotional relationship between the two men. Freud refers to Fliess as "my supreme arbiter." Fliess "panted after our congresses together," and Freud found his praise "nectar and ambrosia" (Jones, 1953, chap. XIII). Freud would have named either of his two youngest children Wilhelm, but they were both girls.

Fliess believed that there are two fundamental life cycles: a male cycle of twenty-three days and a female cycle of twenty-eight days that should not be confused with the menstrual cycle. These cycles are present in every living cell. Within each cycle there are peaks and valleys in physical and mental vitality. Fliess believed that both cycles are intimately connected with the mucous lining of the nose. He thought that he had found a relationship between nasal irritation and various neurotic symptoms and sexual irregularities. Fliess diagnosed these ills by inspecting the nose and treated them by applying cocaine to "genital spots" on the nose's interior. On two occasions he operated on Freud's nose. In 1895, Freud also arranged for Fliess to operate on one of his hysterical patients, Emma Eckstein. Fliess bungled the operation, leaving a gauze pad in the wound. The pad festered until it was discovered and removed by another surgeon a month later (Robinson, 1984, p. 32). Freud repeatedly reassured Fliess that he should not feel responsible for what had happened to Eckstein and characterized the continued nasal hemorrhaging she had experienced as psychosomatic.

According to Fliess's numerological theory, both life cycles are present in men and women, but one or the other is suppressed by the dominant cycle. Thus humans are inherently bisexual. Fliess also held that both cycles start at birth, and so events early in life may have lasting effects. Freud believed that such events are often sexual. He told Fliess of his shock at hearing many of his patients recall childhood sexual indignities and harassments, often by parents. Freud believed that such episodes were widespread. Patients with obsessional neuroses often reported prepubertal seductions by parents, most often the father. Those patients, unlike the hysterics, reported that the sexual experience had been pleasurable. In April 1896, Freud described eighteen fully analyzed cases at a meeting of the Vienna Society of Psychiatry and Neurology. In all these cases there had been one or more occurrences of premature sexual experience in childhood. Freud was convinced that such experiences were critical in the etiology of hysteria. Freud's paper was not well received by many members of the audience. Richard von Krafft-Ebbing was an authority on sexuality, and his *Psychopathia Sexualis* (1886) was a definitive text on sexual pathologies. He described Freud's presentation as "a scientific fairy tale," while another critic labeled it "horrible old wives' psychiatry" (Clark, 1980, p. 158). Freud, however, was undeterred and published his paper describing the seduction theory of hysteria.

By September 1897, however, in a letter to Fliess, Freud was expressing doubts about whether his seduction theory was true. Perhaps he had suggested to his patients what he was looking for and they in turn had reported sexual seductions back to him. Perhaps the episodes of sexual seduction had not actually taken place but rather were fantasies. Perhaps his patients had described imaginary or wished-for rather than real events. Despite his humiliation, Freud had arrived at two important conclusions: the reality of infantile sexuality and the realization that when a patient recalls such sexual memories, the unconscious mind does not distinguish between truth and "emotionally charged fiction." These patients' sexual memories, though fantasies, were critical determinants of their psychological state. In that sense they were as real and important as any actual event. There are thus two kinds of reality: actual and psychic. When actual reality is too frightening or harsh, psychic reality may take its place. More and more Freud aimed to liberate his patients from psychic reality and to give them knowledge and an understanding of actual reality.

In 1984, Jeffrey Moussaieff Masson published *The Assault on Truth*, in which he asserted that Freud had dishonestly disavowed his discovery of infantile seduction in order to placate public opinion and reestablish himself with the Viennese medical establishment. Masson also charged that had Freud remained faithful to his original seduction theory, the entire history of psychoanalysis would have been different. Instead of exploring the imaginary sexual lives of children, real sexual abuses of children would have been acknowledged (Crewdson, 1987). Masson depicted Freud's change as emblematic of the course of psychoanalysis to the present: real social evils, such as child molestation and sexual abuse, were explained away as fantasies. Freud's defenders have challenged Masson's account, stressing the importance of the self-analysis Freud began in the summer of 1897 (Storr, 1984). Freud discovered his own sexual desires toward his mother and his desire to be rid of his father. He knew that in his own case no actual incest had taken place. What he was later to term the Oedipus complex was based on fantasy, not reality. What was true of himself was also true of his patients. Although incest does occur, Freud concluded that it is not generally the cause of hysteria or other neuroses. Storr also found Masson's description of Freud's motivations unconvincing. He wrote:

> Although Freud was often dogmatic and sometimes wrong, he was far too proud, too used to isolation and too honest to discard a theory because it was unacceptable to the medical establishment. Everything we know about his character makes Mr. Masson's accusation wildly unlikely. (Storr, 1984, p. 35)

Further, as Robinson (1984) pointed out, Masson's description makes no sense because

> the position to which Freud "retreated"—i.e. the theory of infantile sexuality—was incalculably more objectionable to the Victorian prejudices of the medical establishment than the seduction theory ever could be. (Robinson, 1984, p. 30)

The Interpretation of Dreams

During these years Freud also discovered dreams as a *via regia* (royal road) to the unconscious (Jones, 1953, p. 351) and an invaluable tool in probing the unconscious mind. He distinguished between the manifest content of dreams—the events, situations, things, and people we dream about—and the dream's latent content—the underlying meaning of the manifest dream elements. Typically, for Freud, the latent content represents repressed wishes and desires. To understand latent content, the special language of dreams must be deciphered and interpreted, hence the title of Freud's *The Interpretation of Dreams* (1900). While this book is now considered a classic and is read widely, when first published it was not a success. After two years only 351 copies had been sold, and it took six more years before the entire first printing of 600 copies was sold. In later years, though, it sold well, and eight editions were published in Freud's lifetime. The book had the power to influence many readers. Hanns Sachs, a German analyst, wrote:

> My first opening of the *Traumdeutung* [Interpretation of Dreams] was the moment of destiny for me—like meeting the "femme fatale," only with a decidedly more favorable result. Up to that time I had been a young man who was supposedly studying law but not living up to the supposition—a type common enough among the middle class in Vienna at the turn of the century. When I had finished the book, I had found the one thing worthwhile for me to live for. (Sachs, 1944, quoted by Momigliano, 1987, p. 375)

The Interpretation of Dreams is Freud at his most intriguing and stimulating, and he considered it the most important of all his works (Clark, 1980, p. 181).

The Psychopathology of Everyday Life

While writing *The Interpretation of Dreams*, Freud discovered another "road to the unconscious" in such everyday events as slips of the tongue and pen, temporary failures of memory, and trivial mistakes. These psychopathologies of everyday life were described in another classic book published under that title in 1901. Freud gave many examples of slips of the tongue he believed to be symptomatic of unconscious dynamics. For example, the president of the lower house of the Austrian Parliament, expecting a stormy debate, opened the session with the declaration, "Gentlemen, I notice that a full quorum of members is present and hereby declare the meeting closed" (Freud, 1901, p. 77). When one of his patients returned from visiting her uncle, Freud asked how he was. She replied, "I don't know, I only see him now *in flagranti*." The next day she corrected herself, explaining that she had meant to say *en passant* (Freud, 1901, p. 83). A Jewish man who had recently converted to Christianity told his children to go into the garden but called them *Juden* (Jews) instead of *Jungen* (children) (Clark, 1980, p. 206). Such seemingly trivial accidents and everyday mishaps as the Oxford don who toasted his "queer dean" rather than "dear queen" and husbands who repeatedly lose their wedding rings or misplace their car keys before driving to an important event were for Freud indicative of unconscious conflicts and wishes.

Freud's Theory of Personality Development

In the first decade of the twentieth century, Freud also developed his psychosexual theory of personality development, in which an individual is seen to progress through a number of stages—oral, anal, phallic, latent, and genital—each characterized by a conflict between the gratification of instincts and the limitations of the external world. If the child receives too little or too much satisfaction at any stage, he or she may not be able to move easily to the next stage of development. Under- or overgratification may also result in *fixation*, or an investment of a portion of libidinal energy at that stage, leading to behaviors later in life that are characteristic of the conflict during that particular stage. Freud's postulation of libido and sexual feelings and satisfaction in children caused a furor. Young children were said to be pure and unadulterated. To suggest such motivations was beastly.

One of the most controversial ideas in Freud's theory of personality development was that of the *Oedipus complex*. During the phallic stage of a boy's development he is said to experience sexual longing for his mother and hostility toward his father. Resolution of this situation occurs when the boy experiences fear of castration by his father and overcomes this fear by identifying with him. The term *Electra complex* was used by Freud to describe the experience of a young girl during the phallic stage. Later, Freud argued against its introduction in his paper "Female Sexuality" (Strachey, 1966, p. 194), because it emphasized analogous development in the two sexes, a view Freud could not endorse. He preferred the term *castration complex* for the female, as her trauma was said to center on her disappointment in discovering that she already had been castrated, presumably by her mother. Also, unlike development in the boy, which generally follows only one course, development in girls, Freud suggested, may follow one of three possible lines. The first results in a general revulsion against sexuality. The second leads the girl to cling to the hope of obtaining a penis and the fantasy of being a man. Freud suggested that this "masculinity complex" may also result in a manifest homosexual choice of love object. In the third line of development, the girl surmounts her pre-Oedipal attachment to her mother and takes her father as her love object, thus developing a feminine attachment to the father and a feminine sexual orientation (Strachey, 1966, pp. 229–243).

Freud believed that his theory of personality, his "scaffold of the mind," was his most important contribution. He conceived of the mind as consisting of three separate but independent structures: the id, ego, and superego. The id is completely unconscious and is the source of basic impulses and drives; it is the biological reservoir that underlies all actions. The id operates in accordance with the "pleasure principle" and seeks immediate gratification and satisfaction. The ego derives its energy from the id, but it is the instrument of reason and sanity. It attempts to meet the id's demands within the limitations of reality; hence, it operates in terms of the "reality principle." Much of the ego is conscious, and it uses memory, perception of the environment, and habits to perform the role of a rational executive. Finally, the superego incorporates absolute standards of morality and ethics and plays the role of the "great nay-sayer and prohibitor." Certain avenues of satisfaction are not allowed, and so, loosely speaking, the superego plays the role of the conscience.

Freud saw the ego as serving three masters: the id, with its demands for immediate gratification and release of tension; the superego, with its prohibitions and restraints; and the reality of the world in which the person lives. At other times Freud compared the relationship between the ego and the id to that between a charioteer and his horses: the horses provide the energy and drive, and the charioteer provides direction. In the healthy personality the three components work together in harmony, largely as a result of a strong ego; in the hysterical or neurotic personality, they do not. At times Freud wrote as though the id, ego, and superego were real entities resident somewhere within the person, and it is important to remember that they are only metaphors.

Freud and His Followers

With his increasing fame and importance, Freud attracted followers. He saw himself as their leader, teacher, and prophet. Starting in 1902 a small group of five men, including Freud and Alfred Adler, met on Wednesday evenings in his waiting room in Vienna. They came to be known as the Wednesday Psychoanalytical Society. By 1908 this group had expanded to twenty members and changed its name to the Vienna Psychoanalytical Society. When Alfred Adler (1870–1937) developed critiques of Freud's sexual theory of hysteria and hypnosis, the two men became estranged. By 1911 Adler had been forced to resign from the Vienna Psychoanalytical Society and had taken nine of his followers with him. Adler then founded a school

Carl Jung. (Henri Cartier Bresson/
Magnum)

of "individual psychology" that emphasized social factors and the unity of health
and harmonious behavior (McGee, Huber, & Carter, 1983). Adler's school of individual psychology competed with Freud's orthodox psychoanalysis.

An estrangement even more bitter developed between Freud and Carl Jung
(1875–1961). Their correspondence began in 1906 after Jung sent Freud a copy of
his book describing his research on association tests. During the next seven years
they exchanged frequent letters, 360 of which have survived (McGuire, 1974). Freud
and Jung's correspondence shows a clear change in their relationship. At first Jung
is the submissive student, eager to learn from Freud; then he is the "crown prince"
and ordained successor. Seven years later, after Jung had immersed himself in my-
thology and had developed concepts such as the collective unconscious, which were
unacceptable to Freud, correspondence between the two men ended with this terse
letter (McGuire, 1974, p. 94):

> Dear Professor Freud,
>
> I accede to your wish that we abandon our personal relations, for I never thrust
> my friendship on anyone. You yourself are the best judge of what this moment
> means to you. The rest is silence. . . .
>
> > Yours sincerely,
> > Jung

Jung and his Swiss colleagues were expelled from the psychoanalytical movement
in 1914.

Freud was authoritarian, paternalistic, and dogmatic. He was unable to tolerate disagreements—his friendship with Fliess ended in a violent quarrel—or accept challenges from his followers. They were his children, his disciples, and they
were to accept what he said without question. Disagreements were acts of treason,

Freud with members of the "Committee." (The Bettmann Archives)

and dissenters were often vilified (Roazen, 1975). In reaction to the defections of Adler and Jung, Freud established in 1912 a secret committee of loyal adherents to ensure purity and orthodoxy. This 1912 photograph of the committee hung in Freud's waiting room.

From left to right, Otto Rank, Karl Abraham, Max Eitington, and Ernest Jones stand in the back row. Freud sits at the left front with Sandor Ferenczi and Hanns Sachs to his left. Freud gave each of these men a special ring, and the committee continued to meet in secret to plot the course of the psychoanalytical movement and repulse critics until 1927, when it merged with the official board of the International Psychoanalytical Association. Rank, Abraham, Ferenczi, and Sachs became well-known psychoanalysts, while Jones is best known for his biography of Freud. Max Eitington is an intriguing figure. He was a wealthy businessman who was analyzed by Freud and acted as his social secretary from 1925 to 1937. In a history of the Soviet secret police, the KGB, the historian John J. Dziak made the startling charge that Eitington was an active member of the KGB throughout this period and was involved in Stalinist purges and executions (Schwartz, 1988).

Though not part of Freud's inner circle, women analysts rose to high positions within the psychoanalytical movement and were successful theorists and highly regarded therapists (Thompson, 1987). Freud's daughter Anna Freud (1895–1982) was the most loyal of his followers. She described her analytical training by her father as "thoroughly irregular if not disorganized" (Anna Freud, quoted by Fine,

1985, p. 230). Anna Freud developed psychoanalytical techniques for children and such innovative methods as play therapy. She established the first day nursery in Vienna. Anna Freud dedicated her life to her father and was his confidante, secretary, and companion. She went into exile with Freud in 1938, and in 1947 she established the Hampstead Child Therapy Clinic in London. That center was largely supported by American funds, which was ironic, as Anna Freud is reported to have hated America (Fine, 1985, p. 230). One consequence of that support was that American students were given preference at the center, and so many American students were trained there. The clinic is now the site of the Freud Museum in London.

Karen Horney (1885–1952) taught at the Berlin Psychoanalytical Institute and in 1934 became a staff member at the New York Psychoanalytical Institute (Quinn, 1987). Between 1922 and 1935 Horney wrote fourteen papers in which she challenged Freud's antifeminist bias and stressed social rather than biological determinants of sex differences and "feminine psychology." According to Horney, it is not that women envy men their anatomy but rather that they envy the opportunities and power open to men but so often denied to women. Horney wrote that

> the assertion that one half of the human race is discontented with the sex assigned to it and can overcome this discontent only in favorable circumstances is decidedly unsatisfying. (Horney, quoted by Dinnage, 1987, p. 11)

Horney's emphasis on the social determinants of neuroses and her rejection of such Freudian cornerstones as the Oedipus complex were important modifications (Quinn, 1987). Other important women analysts included Melanie Klein, Helene Deutsch, and Marie Bonaparte (Bertin, 1982).

Recognition and Success

Freud's position within the intellectual world was assured by the end of this century's first decade. His invitation to the Clark Conference (Chapter 9) signified his developing international reputation. It is said that he first realized that he was becoming an international figure when he saw a ship's steward reading a copy of *The Interpretation of Dreams*. After World War I, Freud's fame and importance continued to grow, and he was in great demand as a therapist. He attracted large numbers of patients, many from America, and was able to command hourly fees that were two or three times those of his colleagues in Vienna. But Freud admitted that he had "never been a therapeutic enthusiast" (Roazen, 1975, p. 133) and had "become a therapist against my will" (Roazen, 1975, p. 134). Freud had no desire to be the savior of humanity and always acknowledged that his aim was to understand humanity rather than to help individuals. "I prefer a student to a neurotic ten times over," Freud is reported to have said (Freud, quoted by Momigliano, 1987, p. 376). Freud's expectations for therapy were limited, yet he continued to see large numbers of patients because he needed the money, wanted to confirm his theoretical speculations, and wanted to maintain his grip on the psychoanalytical movement through his analyses of analysts in training.

Roazen also shows that some Freudian orthodoxies are nothing more than shibboleths. Freud was quite dismissive of the need for analysts to have a medical degree and did not have a high opinion of the medical profession. He believed that "lay analysts" who were not medical doctors could function quite adequately. He adopted the classic position of the Freudian analyst, sitting behind the patient's couch, only because he disliked being stared at all day; he often analyzed his friends and relatives and socialized with his patients, behaviors considered taboo by later analysts. Analysis with Freud usually lasted only a few weeks, rarely more than two months. Later it was to become a process that often lasted years. Freud also had a strong interest in the occult and a low opinion of America and Americans. His daughter Anna Freud insisted that her father's anti-American opinions be excised from the authorized biography of Freud (Jones, 1953), since by that time New York City was the psychoanalytical capital of the world. It also comes as a surprise to learn from Roazen that Freud, the discoverer of infantile sexuality, sent his own sons to the family doctor to learn the facts of life (Roazen, 1975, p. 58). It was Freud, the world authority on human motivation, who wrote to Marie Bonaparte that "the great question that has never been answered and which I have not yet been able to answer, despite my thirty years of research into the feminine soul, is 'What does a woman want?'" (Freud, 1966, p. 244).

Freud in Exile

Following the Nazi occupation of Austria in March 1938, Freud's position and even his life were threatened. At the Leipzig Congress of Psychology in 1933 psycho-analysis had been branded "Jewish science," and it was subsequently banned in Germany. The Berlin Psychoanalytical Institute, founded in 1921, was closed. When Nazi soldiers came to their home, Freud's wife, Martha, asked them to leave their rifles in the hall. They searched the apartment, and when they had left, Martha informed her husband that they had taken an amount of money worth about $840. "Dear me," Freud remarked, "I have never taken that much for a single visit" (Hofmann, 1988, p. 21). While Hitler and his cohorts had probably never read a word of Freud's books, they considered them a slur on their civilization. Freud's personal library and that of the Viennese Psychoanalytical Society were destroyed. The Nazis made a public bonfire of all the books on psychoanalysis from the Vienna Public Library. Freud commented, "What progress we are making. In the Middle Ages they would have burnt me; nowadays they are content with burning my books" (Eissler, 1978, p. 21). Freud was a sick man at the time, but he was determined to remain in Vienna. Only after Anna Freud was interrogated by the Gestapo were friends and colleagues able to persuade Freud to seek refuge in exile. Marie Bonaparte paid a ransom for his release, but the Nazis insisted that he sign a statement that he and his family had been treated well. To this statement Freud added the ironic comment, "I can recommend the Gestapo to anyone" (Clark, 1980, p. 511). In 1938 Freud left the home at Berggasse 19 he had occupied for nearly forty-seven years. An American, Sanford Gifford, a student at the Psychoanalytical Institute, described Freud's situation:

> I understand that there were lengthy negotiations with the Nazis concerning his departure from the country. The exact nature of these negotiations I do not know but finally they were worked out and the family was granted a permit to leave. A permit to leave, however, was not always what it pretended to be. In many cases, so it was alleged, many prominent persons were granted such permits and allowed to board the train for their intended destination. When they reached the border, however, Nazi officials boarded the train to check thoroughly the possessions that the émigré was taking with him. This frequently led to a great deal of harassment and often resulted in a rescinding of the permit and the émigré's removal from the train. This was a very real danger in the case of the Freuds. (Langer & Gifford, 1978, p. 44)

President Roosevelt had been instrumental in pressuring the Nazis to issue exit permits for Freud and his family (Hofmann, 1988, p. 21). The American journalist and historian Walter Langer volunteered to accompany them on the train. At the German-French border Nazi officials boarded the train to interrogate the emigrants. Langer stationed himself outside the Freuds' compartment, making it clear that he, an American, was keeping a close eye on the officials' behavior. Some people were removed from the train, but Freud and his daughter Anna were not. They arrived safely in Paris, where they were received by Marie Bonaparte and Freud's son. Some of Freud's family remained in Vienna, and four of his sisters were murdered at Auschwitz. After a few days in Paris, the family journeyed to London, where, through the good offices of Ernest Jones, they found refuge at 20 Maresfield Gardens in Hampstead, the future site of Anna Freud's Hampstead Child Therapy Clinic, now the excellent Freud Museum. Freud was able to attend occasional meetings and seminars at the London Psychoanalytical Society and saw patients until a few weeks before his death. However, he was in great pain and died of cancer at the age of eighty-three.

Freud's Biographers

A vast literary and scholarly genre is devoted to Freud, but he has been most fortunate in his biographers. Ernest Jones published the authorized biography (Jones, 1953–1957). The three-volume work is a flattering and even heroic portrait of Freud. As one reviewer said of the Jones biography, "It reveals to its readers everything about Freud that Anna Freud thought fit to print" (Wollheim, 1988, p. 3). Paul Roazen in 1975 stressed the conflicts and dissensions swirling around Freud, while Frank Sulloway (1979) sought to debunk what he considered the historical myth of Freud as victim and hero. Ronald Clark (1980) wrote a detailed life of Freud, paying special attention to the social and scientific background of his work. Peter Gay (1988) presented Freud as a great thinker and a man who had a profound influence on Western thought and civilization. All these are excellent biographies, but it is Freud's own writings that show his powerful and subtle mind grappling with the imponderables of human experience.

CONCLUSION

Over many centuries demonological, satanic conceptions of mental illness slowly gave way to the realization that mentally disturbed people are ill and need special care and treatment. Parallel to this realization were changes in institutions for the mentally ill. At first such institutions were nothing more than barbaric prisons, but in the eighteenth and nineteenth centuries the efforts of such enlightened reformers as Pinel, Guggenbühl, Tuke, and Dix led to reforms and the establishment of relatively enlightened institutions. Unhappily, early in the twentieth century these institutions found themselves overtaxed by the large numbers of people committed to them. There was all too often a regression to a custodial function in such institutions. Only in recent decades has further progress been made.

In the history of approaches to the treatment of mental illness we see a similar progression from punitive and physical procedures to more enlightened attempts at understanding and treating mental illness. Freud's development of psychoanalysis and later modifications of his approach by his successors, together with the development of psychoactive agents (drugs) and other approaches to therapy, have revolutionized the treatment of mental illness.

William James. (Brown Brothers)

chapter

9

Forerunners of Functionalism in England and the United States

The functionalists formed the first major non-German school of psychology; they will be discussed in Chapter 10. Like the Gestalt psychologists (Chapter 7), the functionalists sought a new, more dynamic psychology, but in their case it was to be a psychology that would study the functions of the mind and the adaptive value of consciousness. Such interests and concerns were a product of the intellectual climate of the nineteenth century, which was dominated by Charles Darwin's theory of evolution.

CHARLES DARWIN (1809–1882)

Darwin's Early Life

Charles Darwin was born in England on February 12, 1809, the day Abraham Lincoln was born in Kentucky. The exciting story of Darwin's life and the events surrounding his formulation of the theory of evolution has been told many times: by Darwin himself in an autobiography edited by his granddaughter Nora Barlow (Barlow, 1958), by Alan Moorehead in a series of articles and a book (Moorehead, 1969a, 1969b), in a major biography by Ronald Clark (Clark, 1986), and by Irving Stone in a best-selling novel (Stone, 1980). The pivotal experience of Darwin's life was his five-year stint as the naturalist on the round-the-world voyage of the Royal Navy ship H.M.S. *Beagle*. Darwin embarked on this voyage on December 27, 1831, shortly after receiving a B.A. degree at Cambridge. His undergraduate record was undistinguished. First Darwin studied medicine at Edinburgh University, but observing surgical operations done without anesthesia dissuaded him from following his father in a medical career. At Cambridge he was described as being "of the most placid, unpretending and amiable nature" but also as "a fellow who was forever asking questions" (Clark, 1986, p. 15). After graduating, Darwin had vague plans to be a country parson and naturalist, hoping to emulate the one Cambridge man he did admire, Professor John Stevens Henslow, a clergyman and botanist whom Darwin accompanied on many field trips. Through a combination of chance and happy circumstance Darwin was offered a position as naturalist on board the *Beagle*. The position was unsalaried, and the voyage would cost Darwin £2,000. His expenses were met by his uncle Josiah Wedgwood II, the head of the famous pottery family. It is ironic that the Wedgwoods were devout Christians. The *Beagle*'s captain was Robert Fitzroy, a staunchly religious man who believed in the historical accuracy of the account of creation given in the Book of Genesis. Fitzroy, hoping that a trained naturalist would be able to find evidence at the *Beagle*'s many landfalls around the world to prove that the biblical account was true, arranged for Darwin's appointment. When he sailed on the *Beagle*, Darwin too was a firm believer in the biblical account of creation. He later recalled that early in the voyage the more worldly ship's officers often laughed at him when he quoted the Bible as an absolute and final authority. What Darwin saw during the *Beagle*'s five-year voyage changed his mind and altered forever conceptions of the human condition.

The Voyage of the *Beagle*

As Fitzroy had planned, Darwin left the *Beagle* and traveled inland at the ship's many landfalls. Because he was often seasick Darwin welcomed these excursions and spent weeks away from the ship. He traveled extensively in South America and also in Australia, New Zealand, the Cocos Islands, and Mauritius. In South America Darwin saw an abundance of new species. Why, he wondered, had God created so many different species? He also found fossils of very large extinct animals. Why had God created such animals and allowed them to become extinct? Where on Noah's ark could there have been space for pairs of such large animals? And what of their age? James Ussher, the Archbishop of Armagh, had calculated in 1650 that the creation of the earth began at 9 A.M. on October, 22, 4004 B.C., and that all creatures were created on the following six days. Fitzroy believed the date to be accurate, but both geological and fossil evidence convinced Darwin that the earth is much older.

For Darwin the voyage's most significant event was the *Beagle*'s stay on the Galápagos, a group of islands 600 miles off the coast of South America. The Galápagos were known as the "Enchanted Isles" because of their rugged beauty and abundant wildlife. Contemporary photographs show many of the scenes Darwin must have seen (Moore, 1980). He was especially fascinated by the giant tortoises after whom the islands had been named, *galápago* being the Spanish word for saddle horse, referring to the carapace of the giant 400-pound centenary tortoise. Nicholas Lawson, the English vice governor of the Galápagos, told Darwin that he could recognize at a glance which island a tortoise came from by looking at its shell. Tortoises from islands as little as fifty or sixty miles apart were clearly different. Darwin observed thirteen species of finches on different islands. They ate different foods and had

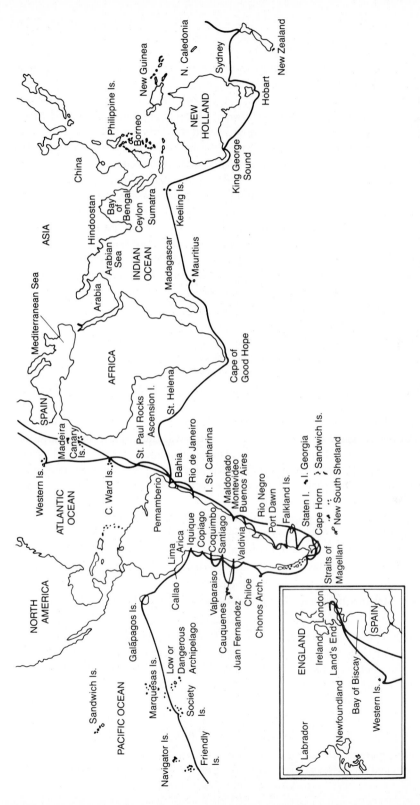

The five-year voyage of H.M.S. *Beagle*, 1831–1836. Place names are as they appear in *The Voyage of the Beagle*. Adapted from *The Voyage of the Beagle* (frontispiece) edited by L. Engel, 1962, New York: Doubleday.

beaks that allowed them to eat those foods with ease. On one island the finches had strong, thick beaks which they used to crack nuts and seeds; on another island they had smaller beaks and fed mainly on insects; on a third island they had beaks that allowed them to eat mainly fruits and flowers. Moore's photographs of contemporary Galápagos tortoises and finches, now known as Darwin's finches, show how striking these differences are. Darwin wondered how they had developed. The islands are separated by strong ocean currents and powerful winds. Perhaps living on those isolated islands, with their different food supplies, had forced animals to change. Perhaps species are not fixed and immutable but are able to adapt and change. The change must have occurred slowly over thousands of generations, but its results were clear. In these thoughts and speculations we see the beginning of Darwin's theory of evolution with its three fundamental assumptions: that the world is not static but ever-changing, that the process of change is slow but continuous, and that this process results in marked changes. There were to be many long and difficult years before Darwin finally published his theory of evolution.

Darwin's Theory of Evolution

The voyage of the *Beagle* ended in October 1836. Darwin then began the demanding task of writing the five-volume *Zoology of the Voyage of H.M.S. Beagle*, editing his journals for publication, and organizing the vast collection of specimens he had shipped back to England from all over the world. He also had time for further study and thought. During the voyage Darwin had observed that species can adapt and change, but one puzzle was why they did so. What was the impetus for adaptation and change? Why should species evolve? Answers began to emerge after Darwin read a review in the *Athenaeum* of *Sur l'Homme et le développement de ses facultés* (A Treatise on Man and the Development of His Faculties), published in 1842, by the Belgian scientist Lambert Adolphe Quetelet. In this book Quetelet summarized Thomas Malthus's view of population growth published originally in 1798 in his *Essay on the Principle of Population as It Affects the Future Improvement of Society*. Stimulated by this review, Darwin read Malthus's essay with its assertion that when it is unchecked, the population grows in a geometric progression:

$$1–2–4–8–16–32–64–128–256…$$

In contrast, Malthus believed that resources grow in an arithmetic progression:

$$1–2–3–4–5–6–7–8–9…$$

As an arithmetic progression is no match for a geometric series, Malthus predicted an increasingly severe struggle for existence. Darwin came to think of such ever-increasing populations and limited resources as "a force like a hundred thousand wedges trying [to] force every kind of adapted structure into gaps in the economy of nature, or rather forming gaps by thrusting out weaker ones" (Darwin, 1839, in De Beer, Rowlands, & Skramovsky, 1967, p. 129). Here was an answer to the questions and puzzles of the Galápagos. In *The Origin of Species* Darwin wrote:

> As many more individuals of each species are born than can possibly
> survive; and as, consequently, there is a frequently recurring struggle for

existence, it follows that any being, if it vary however slightly in any manner profitable to itself, under the complex and varying conditions of life, will have a better chance of surviving, and thus be *naturally selected*. (Darwin, 6th ed., 1899, pp. 3–4)

Increasing numbers of any population lead to a "struggle for existence" in which only the fittest animals survive. In this struggle animals having characteristics that allow them to adapt to a particular environment are favored and live to pass on those characteristics to their offspring. Therefore, over many generations species change or evolve. Darwin believed the results of this natural selection to be just as marked as those of the artificial selection practiced by breeders of domestic animals and plants. By 1840 Darwin was committed to these views and even wrote an outline of the theory of evolution that he gave to his wife, instructing her to publish it in the event of his sudden death. He was, however, to delay for nearly twenty years before publishing his theory. Why did he wait so long?

One answer was that he was busy with other things. In 1839 his journal, *The Voyage of the Beagle*, had been published successfully. It quickly went through two printings and a second edition in 1845. Darwin wrote in his autobiography, "The success of this my first literary child always tickles my vanity more than that of my other books" (Darwin, 1887, in Barlow, 1958, p. 116). *The Voyage of the Beagle* was a popular success because, as the editor of a modern edition said, "It is one of the greatest scientific adventure tales ever written" (Engel, 1962, p. ix). Darwin also devoted much time and effort to organizing his collection of specimens, work that was made difficult by a debilitating and mysterious illness. Darwin, who as a young man had been full of energy and vigor, now suffered constant ill health which "annihilated several years of my life" (Darwin, 1887, in Barlow, 1958, p. 122). What was the cause of his ill health? Some have speculated that it was a psychosomatic manifestation of Darwin's anxiety about the consequences of publishing his theory of evolution (Colp, 1977). Another explanation was proposed in 1957 by S. Adler. As an expert in tropical diseases, Adler recognized Darwin's symptoms as those of Chagas' disease, a prolonged, debilitating disease endemic to the areas of South America Darwin had visited as a young man (Engel, 1962, p. xx). By the summer of 1858 Darwin was ready to present his theory in public, but there was one more reason for delay. Unexpectedly Darwin received a letter from a British naturalist, Alfred Russel Wallace (1823–1913), asking him to look over Wallace's paper "On the Tendency of Varieties to Depart Indefinitely From the Original Type." When Darwin read this paper, he saw that Wallace had outlined a theory of natural selection almost exactly like his own and that "it was admirably expressed and quite clear" (Darwin, 1887, in Barlow, 1958, p. 122). His first generous impulse was to withdraw and yield priority to Wallace, but he was persuaded by his friends to present his theory and Wallace's paper jointly at the August 1858 meeting of the Linnean Society. This joint presentation of the theory of evolution elicited little interest. At the end of 1858 the president of the society concluded in his annual report "that the year had not been marked by any of those striking discoveries which at once revolutionize, so to speak, the department of science on which they bear," while a Professor Haughton of Dublin concluded that "all that was new in their joint presentation was false, and what was true was old" (Darwin, 1887, in Barlow, 1958, p. 122).

In November 1859 Darwin published *Origin of Species*, and the reaction was intense. Legend has it that the first edition of 1,250 copies sold out on the day of publication. In fact they were all ordered by booksellers anticipating a lively reaction to the book. They were correct and Darwin's theory was hotly debated. The reaction reached a climax in a debate at the June 1860 meeting of the British Association held in Oxford. Before this debate the Bishop of Oxford, Samuel Wilberforce, known to his students as "Soapy Sam," announced in public that he would "smash Darwin." He accused Darwin of expressing sensational opinions that were unfounded in science and heresies that were contrary to the Bible's divine truths. Darwin did not attend the debate but had an able champion in the biologist Thomas Henry Huxley (1825–1895). In his peroration Wilberforce turned to Huxley and demanded to know if it was through his grandfather or his grandmother that Huxley claimed to be descended from the apes. "The Lord," said Huxley in an undertone, "has delivered him into my hands," and replied that he would prefer to be descended from an ape than from a man like Wilberforce, who showed only prejudice and false faith (Clark, 1986, p. 155). Huxley's riposte was cheered by the undergraduates but condemned by members of the clergy, who demanded an apology. Huxley refused to yield. One cleric went home to tea and told his wife that the horrid Professor Huxley had shown that man was descended from the apes. "My dear," the good lady exclaimed, "do let us hope that it is not true, but if it is, let us pray that it will not become generally known" (Montagu, 1977, p. 23). Of course, Darwin's theory of evolution did become widely known and forms one of the underpinnings of modern science.

Mental Continuity

Darwin had made a resounding case for the continuity of species and had placed humans firmly with other animals as far as physical characteristics are concerned. But what of mental characteristics? Do we share mental characteristics with other species or is there a discontinuity between humans and all other animals? In *The Descent of Man* Darwin asserted that "there is no fundamental difference between man and the higher mammals in their mental faculties" (Darwin, 1871, p. 446). This topic was largely bequeathed by Darwin to his followers: George John Romanes (1848–1894), who used mainly anecdotal methods; Douglas Spalding (1840–1877), a pioneering experimentalist; and C. Lloyd Morgan (1852–1936), whose canon or principle of parsimony became a critical methodological guide. These three men were among the most important founders of comparative psychology, the division of psychology dealing with comparisons of different species (Dewsbury, 1984).

Darwin's Psychology

Darwin's *The Descent of Man* (1871) and *The Expression of the Emotions in Man and Animals* (1872) contain much psychological material. For example, Darwin had a great interest in the insane and used both his own observations of the insane and descriptions and photographs by others. He believed that raw emotions exist in humans just as they do in other animals and that such emotions are often given "uncontrolled vent by the insane" (Darwin, 1872, pp. 13–14). According to Sander Gilman:

> The insane, for Darwin, were those individuals who, through their illness, lost the protective structure by which civilized man controls his expression of emotion. In a way the insane and idiotic form a "missing link" to our emotional past. (Gilman, 1979, p. 261)

In July 1877, Darwin published "A Biographical Sketch of an Infant" in the journal *Mind*. In this paper, later expanded to a book, Darwin reported his observations of his own children. For the developmental psychologist the book provides a rich record of observations of children by perhaps the greatest observer of nature of all time. In the twentieth century Darwin's example of observing his own children has been followed by observers as different as the animal behaviorist Jane Goodall raising her son among the chimpanzees of Africa's Gombe Reserve (Goodall, 1971), the cognitive developmental psychologist Jean Piaget studying problem solving by his own children (Piaget, 1954), and the behaviorist psychologist B. F. Skinner (Chapter 13) using operant conditioning principles in raising his daughters. Darwin was also a careful observer of his own behavior. He found his use of snuff excessive and attempted to check the habit by keeping his snuffbox in the hall of his home rather than in the study. Unhappily, this attempt was largely unsuccessful.

Darwin died at Down House on April 19, 1882, and was buried in Westminster Abbey a few feet from the grave of Isaac Newton. The high honor of burial in the Abbey was less incongruous than it first appears. Though Darwin thought that the description *agnostic* fitted him best, he was never bigoted or prejudiced in his views on religion and enjoyed close friendships with religious people. The Vicar of Downe was a lifelong friend of Darwin. After Darwin's death the Vicar erected a commemorative plaque in Darwin's honor in the graveyard of his church. Down House is now the property of the Royal Society and is open to the public. Located twenty miles south of London in the county of Kent, a short walk from the village of Downe, it is off the beaten track but well worth a visit. No remnant of H.M.S. *Beagle* survived, and her last resting place was probably a ship's graveyard (Thompson, 1975).

Darwin's theory of evolution provided, and still provides, a framework for all the life sciences. Questions of the adaptive value of consciousness and of the contribution of the mind to human adaptation and survival were to be fundamental concerns of the functionalist psychologists. An immediate expression of such concerns is seen in the writings and research of the second forerunner of functionalism considered in this chapter, another nineteenth-century Englishman, Darwin's cousin, Francis Galton.

SIR FRANCIS GALTON (1822–1911)

Galton was a man of wide interests and diverse talents who made impressive contributions to many fields of knowledge. To psychologists Galton is best known for his development of mental tests and his research into human heredity. However,

Sir Francis Galton. (Brown Brothers)

he was also a meteorologist who pioneered daily weather reports and coined the term *anticyclone;* a student of perception who experimented with stereoscopic photographs and developed the method of composite portraiture, in which individual photographs are superimposed to form a composite accentuating their common features; a student of people's physical characteristics who developed fingerprinting as a method of identification; an experimentalist who used blood transfusions in rabbits to test Darwin's pangenesis hypothesis, which holds that unformed cells throw off freely circulating granules; an inventor of an early teletype machine; and an anthropologist and explorer. Galton pursued all knowledge with energy and enthusiasm. He wanted "to know the worst of everything as well as the very best" (Galton, quoted by Newman, 1956b, p. 1170). His passion for science was such that he expected that in the future delegates to scientific meetings would join in a type of pilgrimage, united by their devotion to science and the advancement of knowledge.

Galton's Early Life

Galton was born in Warwickshire, near Birmingham, England's second largest city. His family was well-to-do, having made its fortune during England's industrial revolution. Galton was a precocious child who learned to read at age two and a half, wrote a letter at age four, and could read any book in the English language by age five. Galton himself summarized his achievements in this remarkable letter to his tutor and older sister Adele:

My dear Adele:

I am four years old and I can read any English book. I can say all the Latin Substantives and Adjectives and active verbs besides 52 lines of Latin

poetry. I can cast up any Sum in addition and can multiply by 2, 3, 4, 5, 6, 7, 8, , 10,   . I can also say the pence table. I read French a little and I know the Clock.
(Galton in Pearson, 1914, Vol. 1, p. 66)

Galton had originally written the missing numbers 9 and 11 into the sequence. Apparently realizing that he had claimed too much, he scratched out one numeral with a penknife and pasted over the other with a blank piece of paper (Fancher, 1985, p. 20). However, his scholastic record was undistinguished, and Galton had difficulty passing his university examinations at Cambridge. As an adult he exemplified Virginia Woolf's suggestion that independent thought is often the result of independent means. Galton's inheritance allowed him to pursue whatever interests he wished. First he studied medicine. Robert Watson (1968) reported that as a medical student the characteristically curious Galton tested the effects of different substances by taking them himself. His intention was to work through the pharmacopoeia from A to Z, but understandably he stopped at the letter C after taking croton oil, a powerful purgative.

Galton's first professional interest was exploration. In 1845 and 1846 he traveled to Egypt, the Sudan, and Syria, and in 1850 he visited a vast area of South West Africa (present-day Namibia). He penetrated more than 1,000 miles into the interior, mapped and explored the land, and made contact with the indigenous peoples: the nomadic Bushmen living under the harsh conditions of the Kalahari Desert, the cattle-worshiping Damara, the Ovambos, and the Hottentots. Galton was unusual among nineteenth-century English explorers in that he did not feel superior to the people he met. To some of his contemporaries native people were closer to animals than to humans. A Bushman captured on an earlier expedition had been exhibited in the primate section of the London Zoo until his death at the turn of the century (Kiley, 1987). But Galton was impressed by how well the people he met had adapted to their harsh desert environment and how much better they were able to survive than he was. Galton resolved to study such human adaptations further.

After returning to England from Africa, Galton found himself "rather used up in health" (Newman, 1956b, p. 1168), but in 1855 he published *Francis Galton's Art of Travel*, subtitled *Shifts and Contrivances Available in Wild Countries*. He hoped the book would help future travelers, especially soldiers in the British Army, adapt to foreign climates. At the time British soldiers were hopelessly ill equipped for service in the tropics with their heavy woolen red coats, and so Galton's advice was sorely needed. His book was published in eight editions and became an indispensable companion of nineteenth-century travelers and explorers. It is an exhaustive collection of hints, maxims, plans, descriptions, and diagrams, a nineteenth-century *Whole Earth Catalogue*. Galton told the reader how to use local materials to make gunpowder, ink, louse powder, pemmican, needles, glue, and a host of other things. Much of his advice is practical, indeed. Need a nutritious sandwich? Try two slices of bread and cheese sprinkled with sultana raisins. Have to cross a deep river with a horse? Hold on to his tail and splash water in his face with the right hand to steer left and with the left hand to steer right. This hint is illustrated with a drawing of a top-hatted gentleman crossing a stream. Want to find honey? Catch a bee, tie a feather or straw to its leg (Galton reports that this can be done easily), throw the bee into the air, and follow it as it flies slowly to the hive. Want to stop an ass from braying? Lash a heavy stone to the beast's tail. Before braying, an ass elevates the tail. If the tail is weighted down, the ass does not bray (Middleton, 1971).

Galton's Measurements of Individual Differences

After his return to England, Galton pursued his interest in human characteristics, both physical and mental. His travels had produced a fascination with differences between people, and he was especially intrigued by the workings (functions) of the human mind. One of Galton's favorite maxims was "Whenever you can, count" (Newman, 1956b, p. 1169), and count he did. His counting of the number of fidgets per minute during lectures showed that children were rarely still, middle-aged persons were medium fidgets, while elderly philosophers sometimes remained rigid for minutes at a time (Newman, 1956b, p. 1169). He made a "beauty map" of Britain in which the women of London ranked first, those of Aberdeen last. Galton went to the English Derby, but rather than watching the horses, he studied changes in the prevalent tint of spectators' faces as the horses neared the finish.

To make more formal and controlled measurements Galton established in 1884 an anthropometric laboratory at the International Health Exhibition in London "for the measurement in various ways of Human Form and Faculty" (Galton, quoted in Pearson, 1924, p. 359). In twelve months data were collected on 9,337 individuals (Johnson, McClearn, Yven, Nagoshi, Ahern, & Cole, 1985, p. 875). In 1888 a similar laboratory was established in the science galleries of the South Kensington Museum. In those laboratories the people of London could, for a fee of three pence for the first examination and two pence for second and later testings, have their physical and mental powers tested—the world's first psychometric clinic. Some 17,000 individuals were tested in Galton's laboratories in the 1880s and 1890s. Some 7,500 individual data records still exist at the Galton Laboratory in London and have recently been reanalyzed (Johnson et al., 1985, p. 876). A variety of physical measurements were made: height, weight, girth, arm span, strength, rate of movement, visual acuity, and lung capacity. To measure mental abilities Galton relied heavily on such physical measures as visual and auditory reaction times and the highest audible tone, since he believed that there is a consistent relationship between sensory and mental acuity. He believed that they were co-related, and in 1888 he published a paper describing a method for quantifying this co-relation. Some years later, in 1895, Galton's student Karl Pearson derived a formula for the product moment correlation coefficient that allows such relationships to be expressed mathematically. Galton also developed a simple device that produced a series of whistles of different frequencies: the Galton whistle. He tested auditory acuity and found a remarkable falling off in acuity for high notes with age. Most older people were quite unaware of this decline, and Galton took a certain delight in demonstrating it to the more haughty among them.

Galton developed a series of weights arranged in a geometric series so as to produce sensations that increased arithmetically and a set of color, taste, and touch discrimination tests. A large proportion of the Quaker families he tested were color-blind. Galton compared men and women on these tests and concluded that men have more delicate powers of discrimination. Everyday experience, Galton suggested, confirms this conclusion:

> The tuners of pianofortes are men, and so I understand are the tasters of tea and wine, the sorters of wool and the like. These latter occupations are well salaried, because it is of the first moment to the merchant that he should be rightly advised on the real value of what he is about to purchase or sell. If the sensitivity of women were superior to that of men, the self-interest of merchants would lead to their being almost always employed: but as the reverse is the case, the opposite supposition is likely to be the true one. (Galton, 1883, p. 30)

Galton also pointed out that most *men* agree that women rarely recognize a good wine or make a successful cup of tea or coffee. His conclusions and arguments were definitively sexist.

In addition to these physical tests Galton made extensive use of questionnaires in what he termed his psychometric studies and experiments. One of his best-known studies concerned mental imagery. He asked people to recall scenes from memory, for example, the scene at the breakfast table that morning, and then to answer a series of questions about the illumination, coloring, extent, detail, reality, and persons in the scene. Most people were able to recall clear and distinct mental images, but to Galton's astonishment he found that the great majority of scientists and mathematicians were unable to do so. Indeed, many of them thought him "fanciful" for thinking they might be able to recall such scenes. They reported that such mental imagery was as unknown to them as colors to a blind person. Galton concluded that such people had been trained to think in largely abstract terms. Others, though, were able to describe their images in minute detail, almost as if describing a scene that lay before their eyes: chess players who could play the game blindfolded, pianists who read a mental score while playing, orators who followed a mental text while speaking, and a Mr. Flinders Petrie, who habitually solved arithmetic problems using a mental slide rule. Petrie would "set" the slide rule's cursor to the appropriate position and then read off the answer from the scales. Such clear mental images were rare, but Galton believed that gradations of imagery are present in all people and that in general they are more distinct in women than in men; this was one of the few good things the generally misogynistic Galton had to say about women.

Galton also developed and used two forms of association tests. In the first a subject was asked to respond with an association to a stimulus word. The latency of each association was used as a measure of the alacrity of the subject's mind. In studying the origins of individual associations, he found that 40 percent of them derived from childhood experiences, an empirical conclusion strikingly consistent with Freud's emphasis on the importance of the early years as determinants of adult behavior (Chapter 8). In his second association test Galton simply asked the subject to allow the mind to play freely for a brief period and then to arrest and carefully scrutinize the ideas that had been present. In such a test on himself Galton strolled along Pall Mall, one of London's most fashionable avenues, scrutinizing everything that caught his eye and examining his associations for each object (Galton, 1883, pp. 185–203). In walking 450 yards he saw 300 objects and found that they led to numerous associations. His mental life seemed rich and diverse. A few days later he repeated the walk and found to his surprise that many of the original associations recurred. He wrote:

> The actors in my mental stage were indeed very numerous, but by no means as numerous as I had imagined. They now seemed to be something like the actors in theatres where large processions are represented, who march off one side of the stage, and, going round by the back, come on again on the other. (Galton, 1883, p. 188)

Galton was intrigued by all the phenomena of the human mind, especially memory. His view of the basis of memory was very much a product of the views of the British empiricists (Chapter 2): brain elements simultaneously excited become liable to be thrown into a similar state of excitement in the future. Galton studied various techniques for improving memory: the use of concrete imagery, the formation of strings of associations, and mnemonics. While some people were able to use mnemonics, Galton found them confusing and not worth the mental effort.

Abnormal mental functioning, seen in its extreme in the insane, intrigued Galton, just as it had Darwin. Galton spent much time studying the inmates of a number of asylums, including the large Hanwell Asylum near London. He observed disordered sexual behaviors and described delusions and hallucinations—patients who thought that their bodies were made of glass, that their brains had melted or disappeared, or that their souls had been taken over by others (Galton, 1883, p. 67). Galton commented on the "gloomy segregation" (Galton, 1883, p. 67) of the insane, with each person "walking alone buried in his own thoughts" (Galton, 1883, p. 67). To better understand their mental world Galton set out to make himself paranoid. He was so successful that after a while "every horse seemed to be watching, either with pricked ears or disguising its espionage" (Galton, 1883, p. 68). The road from sanity to insanity seemed alarmingly short. In a moving description Galton pictured sanity as a tableland with unfenced precipices on all sides over which any of us can fall at any time.

Galton as a Hereditarian

In *Hereditary Genius*, first published in 1869, with a second edition in 1878 and an American edition in 1880, Galton reported his investigations of the relative importance of hereditary and environmental influences on our abilities and capacities. In the first sentence of the book he stated his position in unequivocal terms:

> I propose to show in this book that a man's natural abilities are derived by inheritance under exactly the same limitations as are the form and physical features of the whole organic world. (Galton, 1880, p. 1)

Galton had no patience with the "fairy tale" that babies are born pretty much alike and objected "in the most unqualified manner to pretensions of natural equality"

(Galton, 1880, p. 14). Humans are inherently different, and differences in such areas as level of mental ability are inherited and distributed on a continuum, with the frequency of occurrence of individuals at each level being in accordance with "the very curious theoretical law of deviation from the average" (Galton, in Newman, 1956b, p. 1181). That law had been proposed by Adolphe Quetelet, the astronomer royal of Belgium and the greatest authority of the time on vital and social statistics. Quetelet's aim had been to create a numerical social science that would bring order to social chaos (Porter, 1986). He studied the rates of birth and death and of marriage and divorce and the relationship between crime and poverty. Quetelet found order and predictability in these numbers. He also found that many physical characteristics were distributed in populations according to his law: the greater the distance from the average, the fewer the number of cases. In a regiment of Scottish soldiers Quetelet found 1,882 men with forty-inch chests, 160 men with forty-four-inch chests, and only 2 men with chests of forty-eight inches. A similar distribution held for smaller chest sizes. In both cases, as the distance from the average increased, the number of cases decreased. Galton found that many physical and behavioral characteristics were similarly distributed: weight and height, hair color, the examination marks of university students, and the spread of shots around a target.

Galton was the first person to propose that mental characteristics and capacities are similarly distributed. He suggested that the distribution of a mental characteristic such as intelligence would follow what we now term a normal curve, with most people falling close to the average and extreme deviations from the average becoming increasingly infrequent. The application of the normal curve model has been of great importance in psychological testing.

Quetelet and Galton developed the concept of the "average man" as a statistical and probabilistic concept. While the physical, social, and mental characteristics of an individual were difficult to predict, they found regularities and predictability in the characteristics of populations, and these regularities could be described statistically. Galton invented the median and percentiles as ways of expressing the central tendency and variations in the distribution of scores. This approach was not without critics. To some it was a dehumanizing and deadly type of social physics. Charles Dickens described people such as Quetelet and Galton who see nothing but figures and averages as "addled heads." Nevertheless, their concept and approach have been of great importance for all the social sciences, including psychology.

Galton's Eminent Families

Galton also gathered data on the accomplishments, honors, awards, high offices, and other marks of intellectual quality of 200 or so members of forty-three families, including his own. He reported that high levels of intellectual achievement were found above predicted frequencies in these families. In *Hereditary Genius* Galton presented an expanded list of 977 members of 300 different families he judged to be eminent. Since he calculated eminence to be ordinarily achieved by one person in four thousand in the normal population, Galton's families showed a disproportionate concentration of eminence. The occurrence of such high levels of achievement in certain families was for Galton definitive proof that such abilities are inherited. He also reported that 31 percent of the fathers in his sample were judged to be eminent, while 48 percent of their sons were so judged. Galton concluded that "genius" is hereditary and runs in certain families.

Criticisms of Galton's conclusions were soon forthcoming. Ironically, the most telling came from Alphonse de Candolle (1806–1893), a Swiss scientist whose family had been one of the forty-three studied by Galton (Fancher, 1983). Candolle (1873) studied over 300 foreign members of the French and German Academies of Science and the British Royal Society. Election as a foreigner to those prestigious societies was considered a true mark of distinction for a scientist. In studying their backgrounds Candolle drew up a list of environmental *causes favorables* (favorable influences). Temperate climates nurtured more scientists than did hot ones; scientists who spoke the dominant scientific languages of German, French, and English enjoyed an advantage; the *absence* of a dogmatic and authoritarian religious establishment dispensing preconceived notions of truth and the *presence* of teachers promoting a spirit of free inquiry were important favorable causes; and finally, eminent scientists tended to come from countries with relatively high standards of living offering libraries, universities, and laboratories—and people with sufficient free time to make use of them (Candolle, 1873, in Fancher, 1983, pp. 343–344).

Candolle's conclusions and his claims to have a larger and more complete set of information than did Galton prompted Galton to conduct a more extensive study. Galton's new sample consisted of 200 members of the British Royal Society, who were asked to respond to a long series of questions about their background, education, and scientific interests. The majority agreed with Charles Darwin, who responded that his interest in science was "certainly innate." Galton summarized his findings in *English Men of Science: Their Nature and Nurture* (1874). This was the first use of the phrase *nature and nurture* to describe innate and environmental influences on development. Though Galton admitted that at times hereditary influences could be augmented or thwarted by influences such as those described by Candolle, he continued to insist on the supreme importance of nature and the dominant role of heredity.

Galton's methodology can certainly be criticized. He relied heavily on self-reports, supplemented at times by the reports of families and friends. He paid little attention to the fact that his subjects generally came from the wealthy and aristocratic classes of England, a highly advantaged group with the best educational, occupational, and professional opportunities. He discounted these differences and attributed the performance of these men largely to their nature.

Galton's impressive scientific creativity continued with his chapter "The History of Twins, as a Criterion of the Relative Powers of Nature and Nurture" in *Inquiries into Human Faculty and Its Development* (1883). He stated that identical twins raised in different environments provided an ideal way of investigating the relative contributions of nature and nurture. Galton collected information on eighty pairs of identical twins separated shortly after birth and raised apart, often in very different environments. Galton's conclusion was that as adults these identical twins were more alike in their physical and mental characteristics than were siblings raised together. Hereditary influences ruled.

Galton's identical twin paradigm has often been used in attempts to assess the relative contributions of heredity and environment to human behavior. One of the most extensive of these investigations was that of Thomas Bouchard and his co-workers at the University of Minnesota's Center for Twin and Adoption Research (Bouchard, 1981). Ninety sets of identical twins were given an extensive series of physical, medical, and psychological tests over the six days they spent in Minnesota. While many of the data from this project have been published (Bouchard, 1984; Tellegen, Lykken, Bouchard, Wilcox, Segal, & Rich, 1988), any final conclusions would be premature. However, such research demonstrates the usefulness of the identical twin paradigm introduced by Galton.

Galton's hereditarian position was accepted by many of the first generation of psychologists but was then largely rejected by the behaviorists and neobehaviorists, only to be revived with much controversy by Jensen (1969) and Eysenck (1979). The historical lineage from Galton to these contemporary hereditarians can be traced:

1. Galton, though never holding a university appointment, was a resident of London and was active professionally in that city.
2. Charles Spearman received his Ph.D. with Wilhelm Wundt in 1904, accepted an appointment at the University of London, and held the Grote Chair of Mind and Logic until 1928. He was an eminent statistician, greatly influenced by Galton, and worked in the Galtonian tradition.
3. Spearman's successor was Cyril Burt, who held the Grote Chair from 1932 until 1950. As a boy Burt met Galton, for his father was the Galton family's physician. His well-known, now extremely controversial studies on the genetic determinants of intelligence will be reviewed in Chapter 11. In both his research and his theoretical conceptions, Burt was very much a Galtonian.
4. Hans Eysenck received his Ph.D. at the University of London with Burt as his adviser. For many years he has directed the Psychological Laboratory of the Maudsley Hospital in London. He too has studied the inheritance of intelligence, adopting a hereditarian position; he has been one of Burt's most vigorous defenders (Eysenck, 1977).
5. Arthur Jensen, after receiving his Ph.D. in the United States, held a two-year postdoctoral fellowship in London, working with Eysenck. His article "How Much Can We Boost IQ and Scholastic Achievement?" (Jensen, 1969) precipitated the current controversy over the relative importance of genetic and environmental factors as determinants of intelligence. In answering his own question "Not very much," Jensen took a hereditarian position.

Galton and Eugenics

Throughout his life Galton was fascinated by the prospect of human improvement through genetic control. In 1901 he published in *Nature* a paper in which he introduced the term *eugenics*, from the Greek word *eugenes*, meaning "well born."

Galton argued that "the possibility of improving the race of a nation depends on the power of increasing the productivity of the best stock" (Galton, 1901, p. 663). He proposed that a systematic attempt be made to improve the nation's genetic quality by "1) encouraging marriage between a selected class of men and women; 2) encouraging earlier marriage between them; and 3) providing healthy conditions for their children, including good food and housing" (Galton, 1901, p. 664). In 1908 Galton founded the Eugenics Society of Great Britain, and the following year he started a monthly journal, *The Eugenics Review*. Galton promoted eugenics enthusiastically and left £45,000 in his will to endow a chair of eugenics at the University of London.

During the 1920s and 1930s eugenics was influential in England, the United States, and Germany. At the University of London the chair of eugenics was held from 1912 to 1933 by the eminent statistician Karl Pearson and from 1933 to 1943 by Ronald A. Fisher, a mathematician and geneticist. In England class-based discrimination in education and employment was common. In the United States segregation and sterilization of the mentally retarded and restrictive immigration laws were often "justified" by scientific eugenics (Chapter 11). In Germany the Kaiser Wilhelm Institute for Anthropology, Human Heredity and Eugenics was established in 1927 (Weindling, 1985) as a national eugenics institute. With the rise of the Nazis, mass deportations and murders of European Jews and gypsies were justified as necessary to preserve the purity of the "Aryan race." On January 20, 1942, fifteen senior officials of the Gestapo, government, and Nazi party met in conference to consider the "final solution to the Jewish question" (Schmemann, 1987, p. 23). This conference led to the deaths of 6 million people in Nazi concentration camps in the next three years.

Thus eugenics came to have a very bad reputation. Recently, while acknowledging the abuses of eugenics, Daniel Kevles (1987) asked if eugenics must always be a dirty word. He argued that eugenics and conservation of natural resources are similar. Both can be practiced foolishly so as to abuse individual rights, but both can be practiced wisely. Sandra Scarr asserted that contemporary research paradigms allow both genetic and environmental factors to be investigated (Scarr, 1987).

Galton's Inquiries into Human Faculties

In his book *Inquiries Into Human Faculty and Its Development*, originally published in 1883, with a revised edition in 1907, Galton examined a number of different human faculties, including the faculty for prayer. Given that so many people pray, Galton asked why. Are prayers efficacious? Do they have any effect? He believed that such questions could be answered using statistical techniques. Simply stated, the question is: Are prayers answered or are they not? Galton considered the longevity of both people who were publicly prayed for and those who were not so fortunate. The sovereigns of England were the subjects of much prayer; every English schoolchild began each school day with a prayer for Queen Victoria that God grant her "in health long life to live." In Queen Victoria's case the prayers certainly appeared to have been effective, but was this generally true? Galton cited a study by

Dr. Guy, who had compared the longevity of the kings and queens of England with that of other aristocratic and upper classes of people. Dr. Guy found that the sovereigns, with an average life span of sixty-four years, were the shortest-lived of all these groups. Prayer had apparently not been beneficial. However, Guy also found that clergymen were second only to the country gentry in longevity. Was that because they spent so much of their time in prayer? No, said Galton, it was not, but rather was a result of "the easy country life and family repose of much of the clergy" (Galton, 1883, p. 282).

Galton also studied insurance claims filed with Lloyds of London by people who were clearly about God's business (missionaries) and people who equally clearly were not (traders in slaves). There was no evidence that the missionaries' voyages were safer. Insurance companies paid attention to the class of the ship and the experience of the crew but ignored completely whether the success of the voyage was prayed for. This and similar evidence led Galton to conclude that the question of the efficacy of prayer was at best still open.

To provide a definitive answer Galton proposed that Parliament pass a law requiring all the churches of England to hold services only on alternate Sundays. By comparing the course of history and the nation's welfare on weeks which began with or without church services, a test of prayer could be made. Predictably, his proposal was never accepted. In alternate weeks Galton prayed to an idol he mounted on his mantelpiece and ignored it completely. He found no difference in the quality of his life. Galton's proposals and studies were roundly criticized. He was said to be weakening people's faith, assailing religion, and tampering in areas where science did not belong. Such criticisms were effective, and it is significant that his chapters "Theocratic Intervention" and "Objective Efficacy of Prayer" were the only two omitted from the second edition of the *Inquiries*.

Galton's Far-Reaching Interests

Inquiries also contains much information about animals, a product of Galton's wide interests. He tested animal sensory acuities by walking through the streets of London and the London Zoo with a whistle hidden in his walking stick. When he sounded the whistle, dogs would turn and look around and animals in the zoo would often walk to the front of their cages. His knowledge of the countryside led Galton to speculate about the cuckoo. Cuckoos, like cowbirds in the United States, lay their eggs in the nests of other birds, and so their young are reared by a host species. Why does the cuckoo not adopt the song and habits of its parents and nest mates? It does not, Galton answered, because such behaviors are controlled by the bird's heredity.

For his many contributions to science Galton was knighted Sir Francis in 1909. He died on January 17, 1911, having been socially and professionally active until his last days. Galton was truly a Renaissance man living in the age of Queen Victoria. Like some of the people he studied, Galton appears to have been a genius. His hereditarian position is still important in contemporary psychology, and the paradigms he developed to investigate the relative contributions of nature and nurture to human behavior are still used.

JAMES MCKEEN CATTELL (1860–1944)

Cattell's Early Life

James McKeen Cattell studied under both Wundt and Galton but all his life was a Galtonian in the United States. In Cattell's autobiography he described himself as having had "a birthplace in the sun" (Cattell, 1936, in Sokal, 1971, p. 629). He was born in May 1860 in Easton, Pennsylvania. His father, William Cattell, was a Presbyterian clergyman, a professor of Greek and Latin, the president of Lafayette College for twenty years, and a man described by his son as having "wondrous winning ways" (Cattell, 1936, in Sokal, 1971, p. 632). Cattell's mother, Elizabeth McKeen, came from a wealthy and prominent family of Irish-Americans. Cattell was admitted to his father's college at the age of fifteen in 1875 and was graduated in 1880. Later that year he left for Europe, using the dividends from his inheritance— at the time 50 percent per year on his grandfather's original investment—to pay for his travels. In 1881 he visited Leipzig, where he heard Wundt lecture. Returning to the United States, he won a fellowship to Johns Hopkins University to study with G. Stanley Hall, recently appointed the first professor of psychology at an American university. Cattell helped Hall establish his laboratory and spent the years 1882 and 1883 with him.

At Johns Hopkins, Cattell studied the effects of various drugs by taking them himself, just as Galton had done at Cambridge. Until that time he had never used wines, spirits, coffee, or tobacco—his father had promised him $1,000 if he did not smoke until he was twenty-one—and the effects were dramatic. His first cup of coffee reduced his pulse rate to forty-eight beats per minute, and as he drank a bottle of wine his handwriting showed dramatic change. Under the influence of hashish he wrote musical compositions apparently grander than those of Bach and verse more beautiful than Shelley's; unhappily, the verse turned out to be

> In the Spring,
> The birds sing.

Fifty years later Cattell looked back on his youthful dabbling with drugs and concluded that his drug doses had been "perhaps the largest ever taken without suicidal intent" (Cattell, 1936, cited by Sokal, 1971, p. 632). He remained intensely curious about his own behavior and reactions throughout his life and never neglected an opportunity to collect data. In his address as president of the International Congress of Psychology (Cattell, 1929) he presented curves showing his own times walking and running a mile each day for many months, heart rate measurements after each mile of many three-mile runs, and practice curves for learning to type and play bridge, chess, billiards, and tennis. The similarity to Galton is striking.

Cattell's Psychometric Investigations

While at Johns Hopkins, Cattell began what he termed his "psychometric investigations," timing different mental processes. In 1883 he took his data and apparatus designs to Wundt's Leipzig laboratory. Edwin G. Boring (1957) reported that the brash young Cattell informed Wundt that Wundt needed a research assistant and that he, Cattell, was the man. Perhaps taken aback by Cattell's boldness, Wundt appointed him to a research position in his laboratory. Cattell's journal and letters from Germany have been published (Sokal, 1980b). They provide a firsthand account of what it was like to be one of the many American students who traveled to Europe in the late nineteenth century seeking a graduate education in psychology, not then available in the United States. At Leipzig, Cattell worked incredibly hard. Even the laboratory hours set by Wundt were not long enough for him; he set up his apparatus at home so that he could work when the laboratory was closed. Unlike most of Wundt's students, Cattell worked on a research problem of his own choosing: psychometric studies in which reaction time was used to measure such processes as perception, choice, and association. Cattell's use of reaction times was based on earlier research.

Early Measurement of Reaction Times

In 1796 the Reverend Nevil Maskelyne, the fifth astronomer royal of England, and his assistant, a young man named Kinnebrook, were observing transits of stars at the Greenwich Observatory near London. They followed the transit of a star across the sky, looked away from the telescope to record the time when the star crossed the first of two parallel lines on the telescope reticle, looked back through the telescope to track the star until it crossed a second line on the reticle, and then recorded a second time. The interval between the two times was the star's transit time. In a second procedure, the "eye and ear method," they listened to the beats of a metronome while observing the star, counting the number of beats until it crossed the first line, making a mental note of this number, and continuing to count until the star crossed the second line. In retrospect these techniques appear difficult and prone to error. It is not surprising that Maskelyne and Kinnebrook's observations differed, at times by as much as a second. But to Maskelyne the difference was due to error, and since he was the astronomer royal, the conclusion as to who was in error was inescapable: Kinnebrook was dismissed from his position at the observatory. Maskelyne went on to a distinguished career—perhaps his most important contribution was founding the *Nautical Almanac*, which is still the standard yearly reference book for astronomers and navigators—but it is clear that he did an injustice to Kinnebrook. The "errors" were due to the observational procedures and differences in the observers' reaction times rather than to ineptitude on Kinnebrook's part.

Ten years later a German astronomer, Friedrich Bessel, read an account of this incident in a history of the Greenwich Observatory. He concluded that no error had been involved but rather that Maskelyne and Kinnebrook had differed in their reaction times. He measured the reaction times of many astronomers and found consistent individual differences. To allow for such differences Bessel and other astronomers worked out personal equations to correct for differences in reaction times between observers. Using these personal equations, pairs of astronomers could work together.

In the 1860s the Dutch physiologist Fransiscus C. Donders developed a number of experimental paradigms for the systematic study of reaction times. In his *simple* reaction time procedure a person had to respond to one stimulus (S1) with a particular response (R1); in Donders's *choice* reaction time procedure a number of stimuli (S1, S2, S3 . . .) were presented, and different responses (R1, R2, R3 . . .) were required for each one. Finally, in his *discrimination* reaction time procedure a large set of stimuli was presented in a random order and the person was asked to respond to only one of them.

Donders found that simple reaction times were consistently shorter than either choice or discrimination reaction times. Subtraction gave Donders a measure of the time it had taken to discriminate or choose. In his paper "On the Speed of Mental Processes" (1868), Donders described a stage theory of mental processing. He believed that the stimulus-response interval in a reaction time experiment is filled with a series of mental processing stages that are arranged so that one does not begin until the preceding one is complete: the stimulus is perceived, the response is selected, and then the response is made. According to Donders, a measured reaction time is the sum of the times for each of these mental stages. An impressive contemporary formalization of this approach is the additive factors technique developed by Saul Sternberg (1969). Donders's research provided the background for Cattell's research on reaction times.

Cattell's Reaction Time Research

Cattell was interested in individual differences in reaction times and other mental processes. His first psychological paper was published in Wundt's journal, *Philosophische Studien*, in 1885. The following year he published four papers on aspects of human mental activities. These five papers, collectively titled "The Time Taken Up by Cerebral Operations," filled seventy-two pages of *Philosophische Studien* (Moulton, 1944, p. 250). In 1886 a shorter version, "The Time It Takes to See and Name Objects," was published in the British journal *Mind*. In it Cattell described two of the most important experiments to be done in Wundt's laboratory.

In his first experiment Cattell mounted letters on a rotating drum, and an observer named them as they passed through a narrow slit. With a single letter, Cattell found the naming time to be about half a second. When the slit was made wider so that a second letter came into view before the first one disappeared, the naming time dropped to one-fifth of a second. Naming times continued to decline as the slit was widened so that more letters could be seen. In a second experiment Cattell presented either connected or unconnected words and letters and asked observers to read them aloud. He found that reading times for unconnected words and letters were twice as long as times for connected ones. Such results supported the "whole word" approaches to reading instruction then coming into vogue. They are still quoted in contemporary papers on reading (Venezky, 1977).

Cattell received a doctoral degree from Wundt in 1886. On his way home Cattell stopped in England and met Galton. From that time on Cattell was a self-proclaimed disciple of Galton. As Galton's approach to the measurement of individual differences was very similar to his own, Cattell returned to England in the autumn of 1886 to study and lecture at Cambridge University. Cattell was convinced that individual differences and mental functions can be measured, but such views were not acceptable at Cambridge. In 1877 James Ward's proposal that a psychophysical laboratory be established at Cambridge had been rejected by the university senate because such experiments would "insult religion by putting the human soul in a pair of scales." (Sokal, 1971, p. 631). Cattell sought an academic position elsewhere and at the end of 1888 was named professor of psychology at the University of Pennsylvania. He established a laboratory there and used reaction time tests and other Galtonian measures with students taking the laboratory course in psychology. In a paper published in 1890 in *Mind*, Cattell described these tests and used the term *mental test* for the first time. Such tests, he argued, would allow mental processes to be measured and understood. In 1891 Cattell moved to Columbia University and there established a laboratory and department of psychology he headed until 1917. He continued his testing, eventually giving a battery of ten tests to fifty or more volunteers from each year's freshman class; this came to be known as the "Freshman Test," though it had nothing to do with admission to the university. His tests included measures of strength, rate of movement, sensation and perception, span of attention, reaction times, time estimation, and memory for letters. Cattell's tests were a culmination of attempts to assess psychological processes using physical measurements. Such attempts had been made previously in Germany by Griesbach (Chapter 6) and in England by Galton. They were all to be superseded by psychological measures of psychological processes developed by Alfred Binet, Lewis Terman, and many others (Chapter 11). Cattell found disappointingly low levels of correlation between his different measures and saw his method of testing abandoned.

Cattell's Other Research

In an 1895 paper published in *Science*, Cattell reported the results of experiments in which he asked students about distances on campus, the weather a week before, the dates of important historical events, and the content of a lecture given the previous week. Recall was often disconcertingly poor. In the case of the lecture, students often recalled fanciful and extraordinary material that had not been presented. Cattell concluded that our memories are often much less reliable than we think.

Cattell also conducted experimental research on judgments of relative rank. First he produced a series of 200 shades of gray, which changed in subtle steps from black to white. Students were asked to order them on the basis of brightness and their rankings were compared with photometric brightness measurements. The students' rankings and photometric measures correlated well. Cattell then used a similar procedure to establish relative rankings of scientists. For psychologists, for example, Cattell (1903) first prepared a list of contemporary psychologists and then asked leading psychologists to rank the listed individuals. It is one thing to rank shades of gray and quite another to rank one's contemporaries. Discreetly, Cattell did not publish the psychologists' rankings until 1929, when he made them available in conjunction with his presidential address to the Ninth International Congress of Psychology (Cattell, 1929). His "top ten" psychologists in 1903 were

>   James—Cattell—Münsterberg—Hall—Baldwin—
>   Titchener—Royce—Ladd—Dewey—and Jastrow.

Similar rankings of other scientists were published by Cattell in *American Men of Science* (1906). In the Galtonian tradition he also studied the family backgrounds and education of the men he ranked. Cattell's conclusion was that a person who aimed to become a scientist had the best chance if he had a professor or a clergyman for a father; Cattell himself had had both. Given such studies and his Galtonian heritage, it is no surprise that Cattell was a eugenicist. He argued forcefully for the importance of inheritance and proposed that "incentives be given to the best elements of all the people to intermarry and have large families" (Cattell, 1909, in Sokal, 1971, p. 360). Cattell had seven children and offered each of them $1,000 if they married the child of a college professor. None of his children attended public schools but were educated at home by tutors, often Cattell's graduate students, working under his supervision. All seven of them became either scientists or science editors, with McKeen and Psyche (!) Cattell following their father into psychology.

   More than fifty students took Ph.D. degrees with Cattell during his twenty-six years at Columbia University. Three of the best known were Edward Lee Thorndike, whose experiments on instrumental learning by cats are still widely quoted (Chapter 10); Robert S. Woodworth, a prominent experimental psychologist who succeeded Cattell as head of the Department of Psychology at Columbia (Chapter 10); and Edward K. Strong, a well-known industrial and vocational psychologist who developed the Strong Vocational Interest Test. Despite Cattell's reputation as a difficult, prickly, and aggressive personality (Sokal, 1971), his students were warm and appreciative in their recollections of him (Conklin et al., 1944). Woodworth, for example, remembered Cattell as a man at whose home "the latch-string seemed to be always out for his colleagues" (Woodworth, 1944b, p. 9).

The Controversial Cattell

In 1917 Cattell's career at Columbia came to an abrupt end when he was dismissed from the faculty for his vehement opposition to American involvement in World War I. In May 1917, one of his sons, Owen Cattell, was arrested and convicted of distributing literature opposing conscription. In August, Cattell wrote an open letter to Congress supporting his son and protesting the government's decision to send conscripts to fight in Europe. His letter caused a storm of controversy. In announcing Cattell's dismissal, the president of Columbia, Nicholas Murray Butler, stressed that with America at war:

What had been tolerated before becomes intolerable now. What had been wrongheaded was now sedition. What had been folly was now treason. There is and will be no place in Columbia University for any person who opposes or counsels opposition to the effective enforcement of the laws of the United States, or who acts, writes or speaks of treason. The separation of any such person from Columbia University will be as speedy as the discovery of his offense. (P. Smith, 1985, vol. 7, p. 551)

Cattell sued the university and was awarded damages but was never reinstated and never again held an academic position.

Cattell as an Editor and Publisher

After his dismissal Cattell turned to editing and publishing. In 1894 he had established with James Mark Baldwin of Princeton the *Psychological Review*. He edited the review in alternate years until 1904. Cattell also had a long association with the journal *Science*. Founded in 1880, *Science* had been supported financially by Thomas Edison and Alexander Graham Bell, but despite this auspicious backing the magazine lost large sums of money and ceased publication in 1894 (Kohlstedt, 1980). Cattell bought the rights to the defunct magazine for $25 and in January 1895 published the first of a "new series" of *Science*. Early in 1896 he had the good fortune to score a journalistic coup with a paper describing x-rays. X-rays had been discovered in November 1895 by Wilhelm Roentgen and had been described in a German journal article published in December of that year. Hugo Münsterberg wrote a description of Roentgen's discovery that Cattell published in *Science* on January 15, 1896. X-rays were exciting and controversial—the eminent British physicist Lord Kelvin had predicted that they would prove to be a hoax—so the first English-language description was an important paper. In 1900 Cattell made an agreement with the American Association for the Advancement of Science (AAAS) by which *Science* became the official journal of the association. Cattell agreed to provide each AAAS member with a subscription to *Science*, for which the AAAS would pay him $2. The agreement was mutually beneficial, for Cattell gained a guaranteed circulation and a source of papers for publication, while the AAAS could attract members by providing them with a subscription to *Science*. In 1944 the AAAS bought the rights to *Science* from Cattell. When the final payment was made in 1954, $270,000 had been paid to Cattell's heirs (Boffey, 1971). At one time or another Cattell published seven journals, including *Popular Science Monthly*, *American Men of Science*, and *The American Naturalist*. He was psychology and science's first great publisher and businessman.

Cattell's Involvement in Professional Affairs

Cattell was one of the founding members of the APA in 1892, a member of the APA's council from the beginning, the association's third secretary in 1894, and its president in 1895. In 1901 Cattell was the first psychologist admitted to the National Academy of Sciences; he was president of the American Association for the

Advancement of Science in 1924 and presided at the Ninth International Congress of Psychology held at New Haven in 1929. In 1921 Cattell established the Psychological Corporation to apply psychological knowledge to industry and education. The corporation was a success and is still active in marketing such psychological tests as the Wechsler Adult Intelligence Scale (WAIS), the Wechsler Intelligence Scale for Children (WISC), the Thematic Apperception Test (TAT), and the Beck Depression Scale.

Cattell died in 1944. His was a rich and diverse professional life, very different from that of his contemporary Titchener. It seems appropriate to describe Cattell's life and career as truly Galtonian.

WILLIAM JAMES (1842–1910)

During the late nineteenth and early twentieth centuries William James was widely recognized as America's foremost psychologist. In Cattell's 1903 ranking, James was the most distinguished contemporary psychologist, but even more impressive, all Cattell's rankers placed James first. James also had an international reputation and was regarded by many in Europe as the pope of American psychology. Who was William James and how did he come to have such a distinguished reputation?

James's Early Life

James was the child of a wealthy and cultivated Irish-American family. He was born on January 11, 1842, in the Astor House, the busiest and most luxurious hotel in New York City. One of James's biographers, Gay Wilson Allen, described his early years as a "transatlantic infancy" (Allen, 1967, chap. 2). James made a trip to Europe in 1843, the first of many such journeys and tours. He attended schools in the United States, England, France, and Switzerland, encouraged by parents who took an active interest in their children's education. James was truly cosmopolitan, speaking French, German, and Italian fluently and feeling thoroughly at home anywhere in Europe. Later in life he claimed to know every important European psychologist and philosopher.

As a young man James met many of the great people of his time. In the United States Ralph Waldo Emerson, Henry Thoreau, and William Thackeray, among others, visited his home; in England, Thomas Carlyle, Alfred Lord Tennyson, and John Stuart Mill (Chapter 2) were frequent visitors. He grew up in a liberal, enlightened, stimulating environment. On their many tours abroad the James family always traveled in high style; on a trip to England they lived in a house adjoining Windsor's Great Park, next door to the duchess of Kent and within sight of the queen's Windsor Castle. James had three brothers and one sister, Alice, with whom he had an especially affectionate relationship. In her biography of Alice James, Jean Strouse (1980) described her as a brilliant woman whose family did not allow her to build a career as a writer. Rather, she was expected to fulfill what they saw as her destiny: to marry and have children. Alice James was unable to meet those demands. She had a long series of illnesses characterized by serious neurasthenic symptoms and died in 1892 at the age of forty-four. Her death was a devastating blow to William James. Henry James, Jr., the writer, was another son in this extraordinary family. Unlike Henry, who always wanted to be a writer, William's career plans were vague. First he studied painting, but in 1861 he was forced to give it up when he had trouble with his eyes. In 1864 he began an erratic course of premedical studies at Harvard University, but not without reservations. In a typically Jamesian letter he wrote:

> I embraced the medical profession a couple of months ago. My first impressions are that there is much humbug therein, and that, with the exception of surgery in which something positive is sometimes accomplished, a doctor does more by the moral effect of his presence on the patient and family, than by anything else. He also extracts money from them. (James, 1864, in Allen, 1967, p. 98)

James also quoted with approval a quip by a former dean of the Harvard Medical School, Oliver Wendell Holmes, that "if the whole *materia medica* excepting only opium and ether as now used was sunk to the bottom of the sea it would be all the better for mankind and all the worse for the fishes" (Holmes, 1853, in Allen, 1967, p. 99).

As a premedical student James took courses in chemistry, comparative anatomy, and physiology, all with the hope of understanding the workings of the body and mind, especially mind-body interactions. He concluded that the human mind and consciousness cannot be reduced to physiology, chemistry, or anatomy, an antireductionist position he maintained throughout his life.

In 1865 James went with Louis Agassiz as an unpaid research assistant on a collecting trip to the Amazon. Agassiz was a Harvard luminary, a famed biologist and an active proponent of the view that all forms of life are separate, immutable, fixed species created by God. He considered Darwin's theory of evolution to be wrong, unscientific, and sacrilegious. Though Agassiz was a genial professor much loved by his students, for James the expedition was far from successful. He was terribly seasick on the voyage to South America and developed a severe stomach disorder that delayed his departure for the interior. James had to remain in Rio de Janeiro with the dull job of preserving and classifying specimens sent back by the expedition. He was very homesick, and though he found the sights of Rio intoxicating, he was still more of an artist than a scientist, and his first impulse was to sketch the things he saw. When he finally joined the expedition on the Amazon, James loved the beauty and abundance of the plant and animal life but hated the ferocious insects and debilitating climate. He also became disillusioned with Agassiz, whom he came to regard as a great teacher of scientific observation but a man with fixed and rigid views. James left the expedition in December 1865 and sailed home, convinced that the life of a systematic collector was not for him. His interests were more speculative—he characterized them as "lightweight"—but they allowed him to make major contributions to psychology and philosophy.

He returned to Harvard, but before receiving his medical degree the restless James spent 1867 and 1868 traveling in Europe to visit the laboratories of Gustav

Fechner, Hermann von Helmholtz, Wilhelm Wundt, and Emil du Bois-Reymond (Chapter 3). He received an M.D. degree in 1869, but firmly resolved never to practice medicine—a resolution he kept for the rest of his life. As a medical student James had been plagued by numerous illnesses—back pains, eye troubles, insomnia—many of which he accepted as psychosomatic. He also suffered exhausting bouts of anxiety and depression and at times even contemplated suicide (Myers, 1986). James was far from the "adorable genius" of some depictions. At the age of twenty-eight, in 1870, James reported in his diary a crisis in his life. He decided to accept the view of Charles Renouvier that we have free will since we can sustain a thought because we choose to, when we might have other thoughts instead (Myers, 1986). James was later to label such assertions "pragmatic," and he found them most encouraging. He announced in his diary that he would assume that he had free will in Renouvier's sense and that his first act of free will would be to believe in free will. James also resolved that for the rest of his life he would take philosophy seriously.

James Enters Psychology

In 1872 James was offered a position as an instructor in physiology and anatomy at Harvard at an annual salary of $600. Melvin Maddocks described Harvard at the time as "unimaginably small and humble" (Maddocks, 1986, p. 140), but under the presidency of Charles William Eliot, Harvard was about to enter its golden age. James procrastinated for a year before accepting and then in 1874 offered his first Harvard course on the relationship between physiology and psychology. James had taken courses in physiology but not in psychology for the simple reason that none were offered at Harvard. Where, then, did he learn his psychology? From studying his own consciousness and observing the behavior of people around him; he was self-taught. In a characteristically charming way James once recalled that the first lecture on psychology he ever heard was the first lecture he gave himself. In 1875 James used $300 from the Harvard Corporation to set up an improvised demonstration laboratory that allowed students to observe some of the experiments he described in his lectures. James was as far from an autocrat as a professor could be. When Gertrude Stein took one of his courses at Radcliffe, she showed up for the final examination, but after reading the questions, she wrote in her blue book: "Dear Professor James, I am sorry but really I do not feel like an examination paper in philosophy today." Then she left. The next day she received an answer: "Dear Miss Stein, I understand perfectly how you feel. I often feel like that myself." With the reply went the highest mark in the class (Maddocks, 1986, p. 150). His courses were a success, and in 1876 James was appointed to the rank of assistant professor at a salary of $1,200 a year.

In 1882 James took a leave of absence from Harvard and traveled to Europe, renewing his contacts with many European psychologists, philosophers, and physiologists. Returning to Harvard, he was appointed a professor of philosophy in 1885 and a professor of psychology in 1889. It appears that these promotions were based almost entirely on his obvious promise and brilliant teaching reputation rather than his research contributions. However, James was well known in Europe and in 1889 was invited to preside at the opening session of the International Congress of Psychology held in Paris. James reported after the congress that he had been greatly encouraged by the sight of 120 men actively interested in psychology. However, his views of some of those men and of others he met in Europe were not always positive. In a letter to Stumpf (Chapter 6), James (1887) described Wundt as "the model of a German Professor" but as "the finished example of how much mere *education* can do for a man." Müller was described as "brutal," and Fechner was considered to be a man whose careful work in psychophysics would produce "just *nothing*" (James, 1890, vol. I, p. 534). In a letter to the Harvard historian George Santayana, James described Ebbinghaus as one of the Europeans' "best," and "the good and sharp-nosed Stumpf the most profound and philosophical of all the writers," to whom he owed much (James, 1888, in Perry, 1935, vol. II, p. 60).

James's *Principles of Psychology*

James's successful teaching career at Harvard and the recognition he had received in Europe increased his self-confidence and sense of well-being. But he was still unable to assert his complete independence from his father. In 1876, when James was 34, his father informed him that he had just met William's future wife, Alice Gibbons, a Boston schoolteacher (Allen, 1967, p. 214). It was up to him to meet, court, and marry Miss Gibbons, which William James dutifully did in 1878. James was fortunate in his father's choice, for his wife shared many of his interests and was untiring in her devotion to him. Also in 1878, James signed a contract with the publisher Henry Holt for a book on psychology. James hoped to write the book in two years and began it on his honeymoon, but it actually took twelve years to complete. For James, writing was a painstaking task, requiring constant revision and reworking. In a letter to his publisher accompanying the final manuscript James described the *Principles* as

> a loathsome, distended, timified, bloated, dropsical mass, testifying to nothing but two facts: first, that there is no such thing as a *science* of psychology and second that W.J. is an incapable. (James, 1890, in Murphy & Kovach, 1972, p. 195)

Published in 1890, the two-volume, 1,393-page *Principles of Psychology* was an immediate success and is often cited as a classic among classics. Much of the writing seems so effortless that it is hard to remember that great emotional turmoil and sheer hard work went into the book. With an eye to a major commercial success Henry Holt in 1892 published a 478-page abridgement of the *Principles* entitled *Psychology: A Briefer Course*. This book was a popular success. For many years James's two books were the standard psychological texts not only in the United States but also in England, France, Italy, and Germany. They were even translated into Russian. A whole generation of psychologists learned from these books, referring to them affectionately as "the James" (*Principles*) and "the Jimmy" (*Briefer Course*). Ralph Barton Perry recalled their impact:

> The *Principles of Psychology* was successful in a sense that is unusual for a
> book of science—it was widely read, not only by other psychologists, or by
> students of psychology, but by people who were under no obligation to read
> it. It was read because it was readable, and it was read by people of all sorts,
> often because of the very qualities which condemned it in the eyes of some
> professional psychologists. It was a tolerant, curious book; and because its
> author saw so wide a range of possibilities, and was so promiscuously hospi-
> table to them, almost any later development in psychology can trace a line
> of ancestry there. (Perry, 1948, p. 196)

These two books established James as America's foremost psychologist. He
was also a superb lecturer, famous for his brilliant style, striking metaphors, and
lively presentation. James delighted in questions—he was one of the few Harvard
professors at the time who allowed students to ask them—and it was said that students were able to see his mind at work while he was framing his answers. One of
the great joys of university teaching is following the careers and achievements of
former students. One of James's most famous students was Theodore Roosevelt.
James was also interested in addressing a wide audience. He developed a series of
lectures for teachers which grew into his popular book *Talks to Teachers*, published
in 1899. This book is practical and down to earth, a delightfully written collection
of hints and advice for the teacher.

James was not suited by temperament or inclination to be a research worker.
He was a gentleman psychologist. For him the results of laboratory investigations
in psychology were simply not commensurate with the effort involved. James described Wundt's method of introspection and precise laboratory investigation as "a
method which taxes patience to the utmost, and could hardly have arisen in a country whose natives could be bored." Similarly, what he termed the "brass-instrument"
and "algebraic-formula filled psychology" of Fechner filled him with horror (James,
1890, vol. I, p. 549). For James, laboratory research was a psychological tool to be
regarded with suspicion. His forte was broad thoughts and insights. Given such
views, it comes as no surprise that following the success of his books James withdrew from experimental research and, as we have seen (Chapter 5), sought a successor to head the psychological laboratory at Harvard. In 1892 he chose Hugo
Münsterberg, a twenty-eight-year-old German psychologist trained in orthodox introspective methodology by the master himself, Wilhelm Wundt.

James as an Eclectic

During the 1890s James became increasingly interested in mind-body relationships
and psychical phenomena. Since he had a long history of psychosomatic illness, he
was interested both personally and professionally in what were called "mind cures."
He took claims for such cures seriously, investigating them scientifically and even
defending their advocates against orthodox medical practitioners. This, of course,
did not endear him to his medical colleagues. James believed that the whole realm
of psychological experience, including psychical experiences, must be studied by
psychologists. He was active in both the American and British Societies for Psychical

Research. He personally studied automatic handwriting, telepathy, clairvoyance, fortune-tellers, and a famous Boston medium, Mrs. Piper. His conclusion was that in Piper's case, some external will to communicate probably was there, but he rejected many of her claims. In searching for facts in this tremendously difficult area of psychological inquiry, James was both skeptical and open-minded. He was also interested in the effects on human consciousness of religious experiences. He defined such experiences very broadly as ones in which some sort of energy flows into consciousness. Such an energy flow could occur in both conventional and unconventional religious settings. His book *Varieties of Religious Experience* (1902) was very popular. James was also fascinated by the possibility of life after death and promised that after his death he intended to return to the world of the living if he could possibly manage it.

James as a Philosopher

During the last decade of his life and career James turned away from psychology toward philosophy and established a reputation as America's best-known philosopher since Emerson. In *Pragmatism* (1907) and *The Meaning of Truth* (1909) James presented a practical, down-to-earth pragmatic philosophy he had described in a letter to Theodore Flournoy in 1907 as a "philosophy without humbug" (James, 1907, in Allen, 1967, chap. 23). This philosophy was well suited to the spirit of the times in the United States. The central tenet of pragmatism is that pragmatic criteria may be applied in establishing truth. Beliefs do not work because they are true; they are true because they work. If, for a particular person, a belief in God works—that is, produces practical benefits in terms of happiness, personal adjustment, and psychological health—then for that person the existence of God is a pragmatic truth. If a person believes that bathing in a particular mineral bath—something James himself did—will relieve back pain, and it does, then that is a truth for that person. However, such beliefs or truths are not absolute and should not be imposed on others. Each person's system of beliefs must be established using pragmatic criteria. Pragmatic philosophy therefore is an individual and relative system. The pragmatist judges all beliefs by their consequences in action: the statement that John is six feet tall means nothing more than that a one-foot rule can be turned end-over-end six times alongside John; the statement can be defined operationally. James believed that pragmatic criteria can resolve the seemingly eternal clash within philosophy between rationalism and empiricism. James believed rationalists to be intellectualistic, idealistic, optimistic, religious, free-willed—in summary, "tender-minded," and empiricists to be sensationalistic, naturalistic, pessimistic, irreligious, fatalistic—in summary, "tough-minded."

James is describing a personality typology. Typologies such as introversion/extroversion, dominant/submissive, and liberal/authoritarian, with their descriptions of ideal personality types, have been common in psychological studies of personality. However, no other psychologists have come up with such a perfect summary description as James's "tender-" and "tough-minded" characterizations.

As we have seen, the work that established James's reputation was the *Principles*, and it is to that book we turn in considering his specific contributions to the development of psychology.

James as a Psychologist

James defined psychology as "the description and explanation of states of consciousness as such" (James, 1890, vol. I, p. 1). He studied consciousness by means of informal introspective analysis of his own conscious experience. James opposed the Wundt-Titchener approach to the study of consciousness and outlined his objections in a forceful and convincing manner in an important article entitled "Some Omissions of Introspective Psychology" (James, 1884). According to James, their method assumed consciousness to be a synthesis of basic elements and so searched for its elements. James believed that this approach was unnecessarily restrictive, sterile, and artificial. It robbed psychology of most of the phenomena of consciousness James found important and interesting. James compared the structuralists' approach to that of a person who assumes that a house is a synthesis or agglutination of bricks and sets out to learn about the house by studying each brick. James proposed instead an analytical approach which studies the functions of consciousness and analyzes its characteristics, which studies how the mind works rather than what its structure is. For James the outstanding feature of human consciousness is that it is adaptive; that is, it allows us to adapt and adjust to our environment. Consciousness also has a number of other characteristics (James, 1890, vol. I, p. 225):

1. It is *personal*. My consciousness is mine alone; it is individual, not part of a general consciousness or group mind. My thoughts are mine, and yours are yours.
2. It is *ever-changing*. We are constantly seeing, hearing, reasoning, willing, recollecting, longing, etc., and so consciousness is not static but is a stream.
3. It is *continuous*. Consciousness does not appear chopped up into bits or quanta for the convenience of introspectionist psychologists. It is a continuous stream.
4. It is *selective*. We are born into a world that James described in a famous metaphor as "one great blooming, buzzing, confusion" (James, 1890, vol. I. p. 488) in which "sounds, sights, touches, and pains form probably one unanalyzed bloom of confusion" (James, 1890, vol. I, p. 496). As we grow up, this confusion is analyzed and consciousness becomes selective.

Given such characteristics James believed that attempts by the structuralists to develop general laws or principles of consciousness, to freeze consciousness and find its elements, were doomed to fail.

James made another major contribution to psychology with his formulation of a theory of emotion. This theory has come to be called the James-Lange theory since a very similar hypothesis was formulated at about the same time by the Danish physiologist Carl Lange. James first described the theory in a paper published in 1884 in the journal *Mind*. According to this theory, there are certain innate or reflex adjustments of the nervous system to external stimuli, and it is the perception of these changes that constitutes the emotion. In the presence of emotional stimulation our heart rate increases, we breathe more rapidly, we perspire, and the like, and we label the perception of these changes "emotion." To quote James's famous examples, we see a bear, certain physiological responses occur, and we experience fear; we lose our fortune, other changes occur, and we feel sad. James wrote:

> My theory...is that the bodily changes follow directly the perception of the exciting fact, and that our feeling of the same changes as they occur IS the emotion. Common-sense says, we lose our fortune, are sorry and weep; we meet a bear, are frightened and run; we are insulted by a rival, are angry and strike. The hypothesis here to be defined says that this order or sequence is incorrect, that the one mental state is not immediately induced by the other, that the bodily manifestations must first be interposed between, and that the more rational statement is that we feel sorry because we cry, angry because we strike, afraid because we tremble, and not that we cry, strike, or tremble because we are sorry, angry, or fearful as the case may be. (James, 1890, vol. II, pp. 449–450)

Thus physiological changes are the "mind-stuff" that constitute emotions. A direct corollary of such a view of emotion is that arousing the physiological changes of a special emotion should give rise to the emotion itself, and James pointed out that this is often the case. Giving way to grief or anger makes the emotion more intense; sobbing makes sorrow more acute; in a rage we work ourselves up to a climax. On the other hand, controlling the physiological response by, for example, counting to ten in the face of a provocation or whistling to keep up our courage, in turn affects the emotions of anger and fear. In the two years preceding the formulation of his theory of emotion James had lost both of his parents. Perhaps his awareness of his own response to that loss and the ways in which he had been able to control his grief influenced his formulation of this theory.

One way to attempt to control undesirable emotions would be to learn to control the physiological changes which accompany them, an approach adopted by many modern clinicians. Thus one might be trained to relax in the presence of a fear-eliciting situation such as taking an exam, riding in an elevator, or taking radiation treatment. If the physiological responses can be countered by relaxation, fear can often be overcome. In an even more direct approach, modern biofeedback techniques can be used to develop some control over these physiological changes.

James's theory of emotion was an original and novel contribution, one which was and still is highly regarded by psychologists but that has been less appealing to physiologists. In 1927 Walter B. Cannon (1871–1945) cited several pieces of evidence he considered to be in conflict with the James-Lange theory. First, emotions continue even though awareness of internal bodily changes is reduced or even eliminated. Cannon described the case of a woman with a broken neck who received no sensations from the viscera below her neck yet after the accident continued to experience a full range of emotions. Second, there are many different emotions with a common set of visceral reactions. Where does the specificity come from? When we are angry, happy, or fearful, the heart rate speeds up, the blood pressure increases, and so forth, yet these are clearly different emotional experiences. Attempts to associate discrete bodily reactions with different emotions are generally unsuccessful. Third, visceral reaction times are relatively slow, whereas emotional reactions are often immediate. How can responses in a relatively "sluggish" system cause rapid emotional responses? Finally, Cannon pointed out that when visceral changes are produced artificially, for example, by adrenaline, which causes an increased heart rate and similar responses, people report that they feel "as if" they were afraid but say that the emotion is not the "real thing." While all these points are well taken, the James-Lange theory has survived well. It is still presented in most introductory psychology texts, and the famous examples of seeing the bear and losing a fortune are familiar to many psychology students.

The most often quoted chapter of the *Principles* was undoubtedly Chapter IV of Volume 1, the chapter on habit. According to James, the nervous system has the property of plasticity and can be modified by experience. Habits are established when pathways form between nerve centers in the brain. If a habit requires a series of actions A, B, C, D, etc., there occur "concatenated" discharges in the nerve centers underlying these actions which become associated. James stressed that many well-rehearsed habits are performed in an almost reflex manner and quoted with approval the statement of the Duke of Wellington that habit is ten times nature. Thus soldiers must be drilled over and over again to obey commands. James told the story of a prankster who, seeing a discharged veteran carrying home his dinner, suddenly called out, "Attention!" The veteran instantly brought his hands down and lost his mutton and potatoes in the gutter. The habit had become second nature. The great task of all forms of education is to make the nervous system an ally instead of an enemy. For James, habit is a pervasive force of great importance. It is

> thus the enormous fly-wheel of society, its most precious conservative agent.
> It alone is what keeps us all within the bounds of ordinance, and saves the
> children of fortune from the envious uprisings of the poor. It alone prevents
> the hardest and most repulsive walks of life from being deserted by those
> brought up to tread therein. It keeps the fisherman and the deckhand at sea
> through the winter; it holds the miner in his darkness, and nails the
> countryman to his log-cabin and his lonely farm through all the months of
> snow; it protects us from invasion by the natives of the desert and the frozen
> zone. It dooms us all to fight out the battle of life upon lines of our nurture
> or our early choice....(James, 1890, vol. I, p. 121)

James believed that most habits are formed by nurture early in life and that by the age of thirty in most people they are "set like plaster," an ancient but effective metaphor. As we settle into new habits, we come to them with a stock of old habits that may block or facilitate the new ones. Given such a position, principles of habit formation and maintenance are of central importance for psychology. Their formulation was to be a primary concern of psychologists for many decades in the twentieth century.

James hoped that once psychologists understood how habits are formed and maintained they would be able to apply their knowledge to the creation of a better world, a world in which people would be trained in the habit of working together to eliminate such common scourges as war, pestilence, famine, and ugliness. James presented his views in 1910 in a widely acclaimed speech in San Francisco entitled

"The Moral Equivalent of War." He recognized the appeal of war—the challenge, excitement, and camaraderie—and the value of such martial virtues as courage, loyalty, self-sacrifice, and bravery. James believed that the activities of everyday life give few outlets for those qualities. While making a living, holding a job or following a career, and supporting a family require courage and tenacity, they have few heroic qualities. James speculated that the unexpressed martial qualities accumulate like water behind a dam until they burst out in violent and destructive behavior, often in war. Given the terrible destructive power of twentieth-century war, James saw a compelling need for a "moral equivalent of war" that would provide an outlet for those impulses. He proposed that young people be drafted in service to the nation not only as soldiers but also to serve the needs of the society as a whole. Such work, he believed, would have exemplary effects on both poor and disadvantaged people, who would have the opportunity to work in dignity and learn useful skills, and also on the "gilded youth of the upper classes," who would learn about society's foundations and the difficult lives of others.

Once a habit is formed, a related question concerns how it is retained or remembered—the question of *memory*. James devoted a chapter of his *Principles* to memory, which he defined as "knowledge of an event or fact, of which meantime we have not been thinking, with the additional consciousness that we have thought or experienced it before" (James, 1890, vol. I, p. 648). Memory allows a previous event or fact to be restored to consciousness after a period of time and thus to be recollected, reproduced, or recalled. Memory retains some of our past experiences. James believed that events and facts leave paths—vestiges or traces—between nerve centers in the brain. When these paths are excited, a particular memory results.

James held that the strength of a person's memory depends on the quality of the structure of the brain, an innate physiological characteristic which is not affected by experience. No amount of trying can improve this native capacity for memory. Experience acts to affect the number of paths underlying a particular memory; the more paths involved, the prompter and more secure the memory. James believed that it might be possible to improve memory by improving one's habitual methods of recording facts so as to increase the number of brain paths involved. Systematically linking facts or events together might improve memory. James further argued that such linkages might be possible with similar material but were most unlikely with dissimilar material such as, for example, English prose and chemical formulas. His views contradicted proponents of the most influential educational doctrine of the time, the doctrine of formal discipline. According to this view, the mind can be exercised and developed so as to improve a general intellectual faculty that can then be used in a variety of tasks. The conflict between these different views of memory was so clear that it stimulated James to conduct research on the effects of memorizing one type of material on one's ability to memorize a second type. First James memorized 158 lines of Victor Hugo's poem "Satyr," finding that he could memorize it at the rate of a line every fifty seconds; next he memorized the entire first book of Milton's *Paradise Lost* and then returned to the "Satyr" and learned an additional 158 lines. In this second memorization his learning rate dropped to a line every fifty-seven seconds. James attributed his difficulty to the intervening memorization of *Paradise Lost*. He persuaded a number of friends to make similar tests, and their results were similar to his. James did meet one clergyman who had developed a very functional ability to memorize sermons: as a young man he had needed three days to commit an hourlong sermon to memory, then two days, then one, then half a day, and finally one slow "adhesive" reading. In general, though, James concluded that the doctrine of formal discipline was wrong.

Despite these contributions, James's reputation, and his acknowledged influence on the development of psychology—Cattell's 1903 poll ranked James first— in 1970, 1,000 members of the APA ranked James as the sixth most important influence on the development of psychology (Wright, 1970), while another poll a few years earlier ranked James the greatest American psychologist, he remains something of a paradox. James was never committed to psychology. In a letter to his brother Henry he expressed a desire to be known as a philosopher rather than a psychologist. Allen (1967) reported that when Harvard awarded James an LL.D. degree in 1903, he feared that he would be introduced as William James, psychologist, and was greatly relieved when he was introduced as a philosopher. James did not found a school of psychology and in fact regarded the schools of others as premature, ill-considered, and harmful influences on the development of psychology. There were no Jamesians in the sense that there had been Wundtians and there later were to be Freudians, Hullians, and Skinnerians, among others. James had a very small group of students, but their number included James Angell, Edward Lee Thorndike, Robert Woodworth, and Mary Calkins, who completed all the requirements for the Ph.D under James at Harvard but was denied a degree because she was a woman. Despite such discrimination Calkins was able to build a career as a psychologist. She held the first chair in psychology at Wellesley College and in 1905—the year after James's second term—was elected the first woman president of the APA (Furumoto, 1979).

James was not a research psychologist and is not remembered for any outstanding research contributions. He was active in the professional affairs of psychology and served as president of the APA in 1894 and again in 1904 but was not a founder of psychological institutions, unlike G. Stanley Hall, the only other person elected president of the APA twice. James's reputation rests on his writings, especially his *Principles of Psychology*. Even with his writings it is difficult to assess how much James's reputation is due to the content of his works and how much to his brilliant writing style. As in his lectures, his metaphors and vivid examples are often remembered long after the substantive points they illustrate have been forgotten. The stream of consciousness, habit as the great flywheel of society, the blooming, buzzing confusion of the infant's world, the moral equivalent of war, tender-minded and tough-minded approaches—these vivid metaphors and phrases have become part of everyday language.

After a twelve-year struggle with a weak heart, James died of a heart attack in the summer of 1910. In one of many posthumous tributes to James, Bertrand Russell described him as "the most eminent, and probably the most widely known of contemporary philosophers" and stated that "the high value of his work on psychology is widely admitted" (Russell, 1910, cited by Allen, 1967, p. 494). Few would dispute Russell's judgment today.

GRANVILLE STANLEY HALL (1844–1924)

G. Stanley Hall was a forerunner of functionalism and an influential pioneer in American psychology. Despite these similarities to James, the two men were very different in their backgrounds, approach, contributions, and relationships with their contemporaries. Unlike the patrician James, Hall was born into a family of New England farmers. On his mother's side he could trace his "roots" back eight generations to one of the signers of the Mayflower Compact; on his father's side he could go back nine generations to John Hall, who had left England in 1630 and settled in Massachusetts. Hall's mother was a pious, hardworking woman. She had been a schoolteacher and was intensely interested in the development of her children. For many years she kept detailed records of their progress. Perhaps one can see in his mother's interest the seed of Hall's professional interest in developmental psychology. Hall's father, who had also been a schoolteacher for a short period, was elected to the state legislature on the Know Nothing ticket and served from 1855 to 1856 but earned his living primarily as a farmer. Hall later described him as the best of fathers and a creative person who invented a machine for sowing carrots but also as a man whose life was full of disappointments.

Hall grew up in the country, near the village of Ashfield, Massachusetts, in touch with the fascinating world of animals and plants—very different from the cosmopolitan world of James's childhood. Hall retained an interest in animals all his life and always made a point of exploring the zoo in any new city he visited. We can imagine a cameo of James and Hall in a new city: James visits the art galleries and museums; Hall goes to the zoo. On rainy days the young Hall would often visit Ashfield, watching the cobblers, tanners, wool carders, and saddle and basket makers at work and eavesdropping on the gossip of the old men—gossip which he later described as one of the foreschools of psychology. From his Puritan family heritage

G. Stanley Hall. (National Library of Medicine)

Hall derived admiration for hard work, belief in duty and obligation, and a powerful respect for education as a way of improving oneself.

After finishing school Hall was employed as a village schoolteacher, instructing a number of his former classmates, boys who were often bigger and stronger than he was. He enrolled in Williston Seminary and then Williams College, which he attended as an undergraduate from 1863 to 1867. After his graduation, Hall entered the Union Theological Seminary in New York City. Hall was fascinated and thrilled by the big city and spent much of his time exploring its wonders: the theaters, musical events, concerts, shows, the sights and sounds of Harlem. Hall attended a séance and even paid $5 to have his "bumps" read at the phrenological emporium of Fowler and Wells (Chapter 3). It is not surprising that his theological studies suffered. After preaching his trial sermon before the faculty and students of the seminary, Hall was called to the president's study for the customary critique. When Hall entered, President Skinner knelt and prayed that Hall might be shown the true light and saved from mortal errors of doctrine. He then excused Hall without a word (Hall, 1924; Ross, 1972).

Hall's Professional Education

In 1868, Hall left for Europe, where he traveled widely visiting universities and taking an occasional course, including one with the physiologist du Bois-Reymond (Chapter 3) at the University of Berlin. Hall returned home in 1871 and accepted a position at a large midwestern state university. As a last formality the university's president asked Hall for a letter giving details of his experience overseas and the courses he proposed to teach. When Hall replied that he planned to teach a course defending evolutionary thinking, his appointment was abruptly canceled. He was forced to earn a living as a private tutor in New York City before finally securing an appointment to the faculty of Antioch College in Yellow Springs, Ohio. Hall spent four years there teaching courses on religion and philosophy. In addition he offered occasional courses for black students at the nearby Wilberforce University. During these years Hall read the first edition of Wundt's *Physiological Psychology* and decided to resign his position, travel to Leipzig, and resume his studies with Wundt.

On his way to Europe, Hall stopped in Cambridge, Massachusetts, and accepted a position as an instructor in English at Harvard University. He quickly found that the position involved endless recitations and grading of themes. However, he did meet James and worked in the laboratory of the Harvard physiologist Henry P. Bowditch. Hall was awarded a Ph.D. degree by Harvard in 1878, the first such degree in psychology awarded at an American university. The degree was awarded by the Department of Philosophy, but that was an administrative convenience. Hall was a Ph.D. psychologist.

Shortly after receiving his degree, Hall left for Leipzig. At the time Wundt's laboratory was barely organized, and Hall seems to have profited most from his contact with his fellow students, including Emil Kraepelin and Oswald Külpe (Chapter 6). He also met Gustav Fechner, at the time a very old man and almost blind but still assiduously preparing his final book on psychophysics. Hall spent his second year in Berlin working in Hermann von Helmholtz's laboratory on a number of his research projects, including the famous ones in which the speed of the nervous impulse was measured (Chapter 3).

Hall's Early Academic Career

Hall returned to America in 1880 with a new bride, heavy debts, and no prospects of an academic appointment. Fortunately, President Eliot of Harvard asked him to give a series of public lectures on education under the auspices of the university. The lectures were a popular success, and Hall was invited to give a similar series of lectures at the recently founded Johns Hopkins University in Baltimore. His lectures there were also a success, and Hall was offered a position as a lecturer. In 1884 he was given a five-year appointment at Johns Hopkins University as a professor of psychology and pedagogy at an annual salary of $4,000. The only opposition to his appointment came from the professor of physiology, who felt that in studying sensory functions Hall would encroach on his department's territory, and from the professor of philosophy, who questioned Hall's teaching Aristotle and Plato in English translation.

Dan Coit Gilman, the president of Johns Hopkins, was determined to make his university an outstanding center of graduate education in the United States. He believed in the importance of research to graduate students and so established research laboratories, including one for Hall—the first laboratory for psychological research in the United States (Hulse & Green, 1986). Another of Gilman's innovations was the establishment of fellowships for graduate students. These fellowships attracted some excellent graduate students, including John Dewey (Chapter 10) and James McKeen Cattell. Hall, like James, saw one of his former undergraduate students, Woodrow Wilson, elected President of the United States.

Hall and the *American Journal of Psychology*

Hall was one of the great founders of psychology departments, laboratories, institutes, and journals and an organizer of American psychologists. While at Johns Hopkins, he founded the first of his journals, the *American Journal of Psychology*. A misunderstanding allowed this journal to be founded. One afternoon in 1887 Hall received a call from a wealthy stranger who said that he had heard about the new department of psychology at the university and felt it should have a research journal. He gave Hall a check for $500 to start a journal and intimated that additional financial support would be forthcoming. In the journal's first number Hall criticized psychical research, which turned out to have been the stranger's main interest. No further funds were forthcoming. This loss was a severe blow to Hall, who had to make up a deficit of $1,000 from his savings. The *American Journal of Psychology* was the first English-language journal to be devoted exclusively to psychology, the earlier journal *Mind* being largely philosophical. Hall's journal was open to the work of all psychologists and published papers on a wide range of topics, including the first English translations of papers on psychoanalysis by Freud and Jung. The first issue included papers on the estimation of star magnitudes, the relation of neurology to psychology, insistent and fixed ideas, the legibility of small letters, paranoia, and the winter roosting of crows. It reflected Hall's wide-ranging interests and enthusiasms. However, it was not to all psychologists' liking. Cattell described Hall's editorial work as a disgrace, and a major motive in his founding of the *Psychological Review* with James Mark Baldwin was to provide an alternative journal. Hall edited the *American Journal of Psychology* and supported it with $10,000 of his own money before selling it in 1920 to Titchener.

Hall and Clark University

In 1888 Hall was surprised by an invitation to become the president of a new university to be established in Worcester, Massachusetts—Clark University. This university was founded by Jonas Gilman Clark, who, having made his fortune selling mining tools and equipment, had decided to establish a university modeled on Johns Hopkins in his hometown. His original gift was $1 million. Clark commissioned Hall to visit Europe, study European universities, discuss the concept of the new university with European academicians, and recruit senior professors. Hall spread the word with great enthusiasm, visiting most of the European countries and Russia. However, his attempts to recruit three European professors were vetoed by Clark in the first of what was to be a long series of misunderstandings and disagreements.

Clark University opened in October 1889 with Hall as its president and five academic departments: mathematics, chemistry, biology, physics, and psychology. Clark's fortune was $20 million, but he badly underestimated the cost of founding and supporting a university. Income from student fees fell far short of expenses, and Clark found it difficult to maintain a sympathetic and supportive relationship with Hall, the faculty and students, and even the board of trustees. He withdrew from the situation, becoming secretive about his plans for the future and especially about any bequests he planned to make. Finally, the local newspaper accused the university of cruelty to animals in experiments allegedly being conducted in the biology department. A final blow fell at the end of that first terrible year when Hall caught diphtheria, went to the country to recuperate, and while there learned that his wife and child had been killed in an accident.

Despite these misfortunes the indomitable Hall carried on, but in 1892, as prospects of continued support from Clark appeared ever more dim, the faculty Hall had recruited called for his resignation. The university's trustees supported Hall, but the same year President William Harper of the University of Chicago visited Clark University and made attractive offers to many of the faculty members, including Hall. Hall refused to join what he termed a "Standard Oil institution"—a reference to the source of the University of Chicago's financial backing—but two-thirds of the faculty members and half the graduate students left for Chicago. In his autobiography some thirty years later, Hall's bitterness over what he called this "act of wreckage" was still clear. He compared Harper's behavior to that of a "housekeeper who steals in at the back door to engage servants" (Hall, 1924, p. 296) and termed the flight of much of the faculty "the hegira" (Hall, 1924, p. 296).

In the following years Hall and the remaining faculty members carried on and, having been through the fire together, were all intensely loyal to the university. During the twenty-one years following Harper's raid, not a single original faculty member resigned. Hall remained at Clark for thirty-one years.

Despite the chaos and uncertainties of those years Hall was able to continue his role as the founder of psychological institutions. In 1891 he established the Pedagogical Seminary for the scientific study of education. In 1893 Hall founded a second journal, the *Pedagogical Seminary*, again using his own money. With its name changed to the *Journal of Genetic Psychology*, the journal is still published.

Hall and the American Psychological Association

Hall was also instrumental in founding the APA. The first organizational meeting for the new association is often said to have been held in Hall's study on July 8, 1892. The psychologists who were present, in addition to Hall, included Fullerton, Jastrow, James, Ladd, Cattell, and Baldwin (Fernberger, 1932, p. 2). At that meeting twenty-six additional psychologists were invited to become charter members of the APA, including Dewey, Scripture, Witmer, Wolfe, Münsterberg, and Titchener (Fernberger, 1932, p. 4). Hall was definitely the leader. He issued the invitations, acted as host, and was, as Cattell later acknowledged, "our Socrates and midwife" (Cattell, 1929, p. 9). Hall was elected the first president of the APA, and Joseph Jastrow, an active experimental psychologist, became its first secretary. The group also accepted an invitation to hold its first annual meeting at the University of Pennsylvania on December 27, 1892. The psychologists attending that first annual meeting of APA are shown in the following table.

Affiliation	Members
Clark	W. H. Burnham, B. I. Gilman, E. H. Griffin, G. S Hall, W. O. Krohn, E. C. Stanford
Harvard	W. James, H. Münsterberg, J. Nichols, J. Royce
Columbia	J. McKeen Cattell, J. H. Hyslop
McLean Hospital	E. Cowles, W. Noyes
Pennsylvania	G. S. Fullteron, L. Witmer
Toronto	J. M. Baldwin, J. G. Hume
Yale	G. T. Ladd, E. W. Scripture
Brown	E. B. Delabarre
Catholic	E. A. Pace
Cornell	E. B. Titchener
Indiana	W. S. Bryan
Iowa	G. T. W. Patrick
McGill	T. W. Mills
Michigan	J. Dewey
Nebraska	H. K. Wolfe
Princeton	A. T. Ormond
Stanford	F. Angell
Wisconsin	J. Jastrow

Hilgard, 1987, p. 739, after Dennis & Boring, 1952.

Hall's 1892 presidential address to APA was never published, but one can see his enthusiasm and vigorous advocacy of psychology in an article he published in 1894:

> It [psychology] is already represented in two score of the best institutions. It has already a voluminous literature; several hundred standard, new experiments...it studies the instincts of animals from the highest to the lowest...it studies the myths, customs and beliefs of primitive man...it devotes itself to the study of sanity and nervous diseases and has already begun to introduce new methods and utilize new results...it has transformed and shaped the problems of logic and ethics; is slowly rewriting the whole history of philosophy and, in the opinion of many of its more sanguine devotees, is showing itself not only to be the long hoped for, long delayed science of man, to which all other sciences are bringing their ripest and best thoughts, but is introducing a period that will be known hereafter as the psychological era of scientific thought even more than a few recent decades have been marked by evolution. (Hall, 1894, quoted by Woodworth, 1943, pp. 17–18)

At this stage of his career, Hall considered himself one of the "sanguine devotees" of psychology. With his enthusiasm, formidable organizational abilities, and compelling lecturing style, he was able to contribute much to the development of psychology.

The establishment of the APA was an important step for psychology. It marked a coming of age of the new discipline, and the APA's annual meetings gave psychologists an opportunity to present and discuss their work. In recent decades the growth in the APA's membership has been spectacular:

Year	Members	Year	Members
1892	31	1950	9,500
1900	127	1960	19,200
1910	228	1970	30,652
1920	393	1980	50,933
1930	1,113	1985	75,545
1940	3,100		

Fernberger, 1943; APA membership directories for 1950, 1960, 1970, 1980; Fowler, 1987.

In 1893 the APA's budget was $63; in 1986 the APA's revenues were over $35 million (Fowler, 1987, p. 632).

Hall as a Developmental Psychologist

In addition to these organizational contributions to psychology, Hall did significant research and wrote a number of important books. His dissertation research with James in 1878 concerned the role of muscle cues in space perception, the classic problem originally addressed by George Berkeley (Chapter 2). In the following years Hall published papers on hypnotism, moral and religious training, optical illusions, and reaction time measurements of attention. He was eclectic, a man of many and ever-changing interests. To some, however, he was a dabbler, a man with many enthusiasms but little depth, an eclectic with his feet firmly anchored in midair.

In 1883 Hall began his most valuable studies. He developed a number of questionnaires that were given to Boston kindergarten children. The children were asked about their conceptions of nature, including animals, plants, stars, and the sun and the moon; their own bodies; their ideas of number; stories they knew and games they played; things they could do; and their notions of religion, immortality, and death. Hall tried to establish empirically the "contents of children's minds" (Hall, 1893). He found that 80 percent of these Boston children did not know what a beehive was, while 50 percent could not describe a frog. Even more interesting is the narrative account Hall gave of his findings:

> Many children half believe the doll feels cold or blows, that it pains flowers to tear or burn them, or that in summer when the tree is alive it makes it ache to pound or chop it. . . . Children who are accounted dull in school are more apt to be imaginative and animistic. The chief field of such fond and secret childish fancies is the sky. About three fourths of all questioned thought the world a plane, and many described it as round like a dollar, while the sky is like a flattened bowl over it. . . . Some thought the sun went down at night into the ground or just behind certain houses, and went across, on, or under the ground to go up or out of, or off the water in the morning; but 48% thought that at night it goes or rolls or flies, is blown or walks, or God pulls it up higher out of sight. He takes it into heaven, and perhaps puts it to bed, and even takes off its clothes and puts them on in the morning, or again it lies under the trees where the angels mind it. (Hall, 1893, pp. 36–37)

By 1915 Hall and his coworkers had developed 194 questionnaires on such topics as anger, play, crying and laughter, fears, humor, affection, prayer, envy, jealousy, and dreams. The questionnaires produced a wealth of information that was presented by Hall in his monumental 1,373-page *Adolescence* (1904). Hall was the first psychologist to describe adolescence as a distinct stage in the life cycle. His description of the Sturm und Drang (storm and stress) of adolescence was echoed in many later works. This book is often said to mark the formal beginning of child or developmental psychology. In 1910 Hall organized the Child Study Institute at Clark University, including a Pedagogical Museum housing a collection of objects from all over the world relating to children and child rearing.

Hall's theoretical orientation was that of a genetic psychologist, and he stressed the importance of genetics and evolution in human and animal development. He recalled: "As soon as I heard it in my youth I think I must have been almost hypnotized by the word *evolution,* which was music to my ears and seemed to fit my mouth better than any other" (Hall, 1924, p. 357). Hall considered psychological questions within a framework of evolutionary theory and sought an understanding of the adaptive value of behavior and consciousness. He developed a version of recapitulation theory in which the developing child is seen as recapitulating the development of the human species. Recapitulation theory had been formulated in 1866 by Ernst Haeckel, a German anatomist. Haeckel believed that embryological development recapitulates the developmental history of the species; in Haeckel's euphonious phrase, "ontogeny recapitulates phylogeny" (K. S. Thompson, 1988). In human intrauterine development the fetus was said to go through stages very much like fish, reptiles, and nonprimate mammals before becoming recognizably human. Hall extended this theory to child development: A child first crawls on all fours and then walks upright. Children's play, art, and social behavior were seen as recapitulations of earlier stages of human development.

Hall was no ivory tower theorist and wrote many articles on children and adolescents for the popular magazines of the time. Among them are the following: "How and When to Be Frank with Boys" in the *Ladies Home Journal*, 1907; "Must Your Child Lie?" in *Appleton's Magazine*, 1908; "The Boy That Your Boy Plays With" in *The Circle*, 1908; "The Awkward Age" in *Appleton's*, 1908; and "The Budding Girl" in *Appleton's*, 1909.

As Hall grew older, his interests moved to the last third of life. In 1922 he published another major work, *Senescence*, describing the psychology of the later years. Interest in aging was unusual for the time, and Hall's work was both pioneering and for many years unique. Children have been studied extensively by psychologists, but until very recently older people have hardly been studied at all. Why? Possibly, as Sidney Pressey speculated, "because as adults we have all been children and so feel that we understand them; perhaps subconsciously we do not expect ever to be old, and so have less interest in older people" (Pressey, 1976, p. 7).

Hall and Eugenics

Given Hall's theoretical position, we should not be surprised that he was interested in eugenics. He was in fact an enthusiastic proponent of eugenic controls and bequeathed $300,000 to Clark University with instructions that a chair of genetic psychology be established (Rosenzweig, 1984). Hall was a firm believer in "higher" and "lower" human races (Hall, 1903). He believed the "Negro races" to be at an earlier stage of human development (Hall, 1906b), dependent on the "higher" white races for their development and supervision (Hall, 1911c). Hall saw it as his responsibility to educate black students, and more black psychologists received their doctorates from Hall during the early decades of this century than from any other adviser (Guthrie, 1976).

Hall's Students

Hall was *the* great teacher of graduate students during the first decades of American psychology. Robert Watson (1968) reported that by 1893 eleven of the fourteen American Ph.D. degrees in psychology had been granted under Hall's supervision. By 1898 the number had increased to thirty of fifty-four. Hall was an inspirational teacher. Lewis Terman (Chapter 11) stated: "For me, Clark University meant briefly three things, freedom to work as I pleased, unlimited library facilities, and Hall's Monday evening seminar." Arnold Gesell earned his Ph.D. with Hall in 1906. He continued Hall's developmental studies and summarized them in *Infant and Child in the Culture of Today* (1943) and *The First Five Years of Life* (1954). Hall considered the great themes of life: the influence of the childhood years, adolescence, aging, insanity, religion, sex, death, and immortality. It is not surprising that students found their studies with this brilliant, far-ranging man stimulating and memorable.

The Clark Conference

Hall also organized the first opportunity for most American psychologists to meet Sigmund Freud and hear him lecture (Evans & Koelsch, 1985). Hall had seen sexual interests in the children he studied and so was more sympathetic to Freud's views than were many of his contemporaries. He was convinced that "sex plays a leading role in life's drama" (Hall, 1924, p. 570), he had established a weekly course on sex at Clark in 1904, and in 1907 he was the first to propose teaching sex education in the schools (Ross, 1972, p. 384). His lectures on sex attracted large, enthusiastic audiences, but it proved impossible to keep "outsiders" out, and so the lectures were abandoned. Hall, as he wrote in his autobiography, welcomed Freud's views:

> Human life has its night as well as its day side and the Freudian mechanisms enable us to explore the vast regions of the psychic life below the conscious surfaces. Nothing since Aristotle's categories has gone deeper or, in my opinion, is destined to have such far-reaching influence and results. (Hall, 1924, pp. 11–12)

Clark University's twentieth anniversary was to be celebrated in 1909 with a series of conferences held at the university. Hall invited two foreign savants to the psychology conference: Wundt, representing experimental psychology, and Freud, representing clinical psychology. In December 1908, Hall offered Wundt a fee of $750 and an honorary degree. Wundt declined, citing his age and reluctance to travel. Hall then invited Ebbinghaus, who accepted but died in late February 1909. William Stern of Breslau finally accepted and attended the conference. Hall's invitation to Freud included an offer of a fee of $400. Freud declined, citing the demands of his practice. Hall reissued the invitation under the same terms offered to Wundt. Encouraged by Jung, who saw the conference as an opportunity to present psychoanalysis in America, Freud accepted (Evans & Koelsch, 1985). He traveled to America with two of his colleagues, Sandor Ferenczi of Prague and Carl Jung of Zurich. Two other psychoanalysts, A. A. Brill and Ernest Jones, met them in New York Harbor, and together they spent four days touring the city: Central Park, Chinatown, the Metropolitan Museum, Columbia University, and Coney Island, where they all took a ride through the tunnel of love.

Forty American psychologists were among the 175 people attending the conference. Hall presided, arranged the order of the lectures, and even made the social arrangements. Freud and Jung stayed at his home and were flabbergasted by Hall's high style of living. The conference lectures, especially those by Freud, were reported and discussed in the daily papers and in an article in *The Nation* (Cromer & Anderson, 1970). There was little criticism and much praise for Freud and his ideas. The *Boston Transcript* reported "an enthusiastic reaction to Freud's lectures," while the *Worcester Telegram* regretted that "the lectures were not given in English so that they could be taken in by more people" (Doorley, 1982, p. 75).

Freud described his use of free association, his work with Josef Breuer on the "talking cure" treatment of hysteria, his theory of the unconscious, slips of the tongue, and dream analysis. In his fourth lecture Freud discussed infantile sexuality and its importance in personality development. His last lecture dealt with defense mechanisms, transference, and sublimation (Chapter 8).

The audiences were eager and responsive, but Freud's views were too much for some people. An eminent physician, Dr. Weir Mitchell, called Freud "a dirty filthy man" (Doorley, 1982, p. 75). Titchener left the conference early, and a dean from the University of Toronto wrote: "An ordinary reader would gather that Freud advocates free love, removal of all restraints and a relapse into savagery" (quoted by Jones, 1955, p. 59). Others were more supportive. James was gravely ill but courageously attended the lectures. "I want to see what Freud is like," he said before the first one. When they were over, Jones remembered that "James, with his arm around my shoulder, said, "the future of psychology belongs to your work" (Jones, 1955, p. 57). However, James did have some reservations and said in a letter to a friend:

> Freud and his pupils must push their ideas to their utmost limits...but I
> must confess that he made on me personally the impression of a man
> obsessed with his own ideas. (James, quoted by Doorley, 1982, pp. 143–144)

At the end of the conference the European visitors were awarded honorary degrees: Jung in education and social hygiene, and Freud a doctor of laws in psychology. The *Worcester Gazette* said that Freud was cited as

> the founder of a school of phychology [*sic*] already rich in new methods and
> achievements; a leader today among students of the phychology [*sic*] of sex,
> and of psychotherapy and analysis. (Cromer & Anderson, 1970, p. 350)

Freud was deeply grateful for the recognition.

Hall arranged for the conference lectures to be published in the *American Journal of Psychology*, thus enlarging the audience. For a number of years Hall was an ardent supporter of Freud and an advocate of psychoanalysis. At one time he went so far as to propose universal psychoanalysis. In *Educational Problems* Hall said of Freud:

> [He] has brought more unity and insight into the very nature and operations
> of the soul, and the mechanisms of the conscience than any other in our
> generation. It marks the end of the old and the dawn of a new era. It is the
> most triumphant vindication of the genetic mode of conceiving the mind.
> (Hall, 1911d, vol. I, p. 445)

Later, as was often the case with Hall, his enthusiasm for Freud cooled, but his organization of the Clark Conference was a major contribution to the development of psychology. As Dorothy Ross said in the first lines of the preface to her biography of Hall:

> G. Stanley Hall is remembered best, perhaps, for bringing Sigmund Freud
> and Carl Gustav Jung to America in 1909 to lecture to an influential group
> of psychologists and scholars at Clark University. (Ross, 1972, p. xiii)

Hall's Life and Confessions

Toward the end of his life Hall seems to have been a rather bitter and disenchanted man. His autobiography, *Life and Confessions of a Psychologist* (1924), is a remarkably honest and open account of his life but has a bitter and defensive tone. In it he described (Hall, 1924, pp. 9–21) what he considered to be impediments to the progress of psychology, including the James-Lange theory of emotion, dubbed by Hall "the sorry because we cry theory"; the classical introspectionist psychology of Titchener and mental testing (Chapter 11); psychophysics, descriptions of mind-body parallelisms or interactions, and the controversy between structuralism and functionalism, which he thought were absurd; and extreme behaviorism, which was also unsatisfactory (Chapter 13). Hall was unable to accept many developments in psychology and became increasingly disenchanted with the field, but one final honor came his way. In 1924, just months before his death, he was reelected president of the APA, becoming the second person to hold the presidency twice, James having been the first.

THE FORERUNNERS OF FUNCTIONALISM IN PERSPECTIVE

A common concern with function characterizes the men discussed in this chapter. For Darwin, different structures and behaviors allow animals to adapt to a particular environment. Through natural selection, the frequency of such structures and behaviors changes, and the species evolves. Galton extended Darwin's concepts and approach to the study of human consciousness. He asked: How do such mental functions as memory, association formation, attention, and prayer work? What do they accomplish? Galton tried to answer these questions with careful observations inside and outside his London clinics.

Cattell also studied and measured mental functions. He measured reaction times and a number of other physical responses before concluding that they did not in fact provide the measures of mental functions he sought. Another approach was needed: psychological measures or psychometric assessment of mental functions.

James's recurrent concern was human consciousness. How do we remember, attend, learn, feel emotions, and have religious experiences? With such questions James created a broader, more lively psychology and challenged restrictive approaches to consciousness. Hall pioneered studies of children, adolescents, and older people—today's life-span developmental psychology. Hall was a genetic psychologist, and his fundamental questions always concerned adaptive value and significance.

Cattell and Hall founded, edited, and contributed to the first psychology journals. They were both active in the APA. The psychology departments they headed—Cattell at Columbia University and Hall at Clark University—provided an education in psychology for many students. James's *Principles of Psychology* quickly became *the* textbook of psychology. It was read by generations of students, some of whom were stimulated to become psychologists themselves.

Following the theoretical approaches of Darwin and Galton, Cattell, James, and Hall established a functionalist approach to psychology in the United States. Many of their interests and research topics were taken up by the functionalist psychologists discussed in the next chapter. Through them, they continue to influence contemporary psychology.

Edward Thorndike. (Brown Brothers)

Functionalism at the University of Chicago and Columbia University

Functionalism was the first truly *American* school of psychology. Structuralism and Gestalt psychology were influential schools in the United States, but they were imports from abroad. Functionalism was American in origin, approach, and character, though it was never a formal school of psychology, and some question whether it was a school of psychology at all. However, there is no debate about the importance and influence of the psychologists, loosely described as functionalists, to be presented in this chapter.

Functionalism began at the University of Chicago and developed there and at Columbia University, in America's two largest cities. Three psychologists from Chicago and two associated with Columbia will be discussed in this chapter.

JOHN DEWEY (1859–1952)

Dewey's Early Life

John Dewey was one of America's foremost philosophers, an influential educational innovator and reformer, a social critic and commentator, and a psychologist whose writings formed the foundation of functionalism. He was born in the beautiful Vermont town of Burlington on October 20, 1859, the third of four sons of a middle-class family. Dewey grew up in a family and society that reflected the classic New England virtues: respect for personal liberty and individual rights, love of simplicity, disdain for ostentation, and dedication to democracy. Both his mother's and father's families traced their ancestry to the early New England settlers. Though he moved away from Vermont when he was a young man, Dewey remained forever a New

Englander. His portraits show a craggy, flinty type of man who as he grew older—Dewey lived to be ninety-two—grew ever more craggy and flinty (Schilpp, 1939).

Dewey's father was a grocer. A man of modest ambition for both himself and his sons, he often said that he hoped one of his boys would become a mechanic. The friendship of his customers was more important to him than their money, and no merchant in Burlington was said to have sold more goods and collected fewer bills. His wife provided the family's drive and ambition. She was determined that her sons would attend college, and all of them did.

John Dewey found his years at public school dull and tedious. He felt that he discovered more with his brothers and friends on their adventures in the Vermont countryside than he learned in school. He graduated from high school at age fifteen and entered the University of Vermont. There, of necessity, he received a broad education. The university had only thirteen faculty members, and he took at least one course with each of them. At Vermont, Dewey learned easily, found much of the work interesting, received good grades, and graduated Phi Beta Kappa in 1879. His graduating class of seventeen included two of his brothers. Dewey's mother's cousin, the principal of a high school in Pennsylvania, offered Dewey a teaching position, and Dewey taught there for two years before returning to Vermont and teaching in a Burlington high school for a year. In both schools Dewey was required to teach all subjects. His experience convinced him of the need for educational reform. At the time there were no national or state educational requirements or policies. Teachers were either political appointees or friends or relatives of the school authorities; they were said to "keep" rather than to "teach" school. Discipline was maintained through physical force, and children were required to sit silently at their desks until called on by the teacher. Rote learning was the rule, and most teachers would not tolerate questions (Schilpp, 1939).

Dewey at Johns Hopkins University and the University of Michigan

Three years of teaching was enough for Dewey. Having heard of President Daniel Coit Gilman's plan to make Johns Hopkins an outstanding graduate university, he borrowed $500 and traveled to Baltimore to enroll as a graduate student. At Johns Hopkins, Dewey studied philosophy and psychology, the latter under G. Stanley Hall. One of his fellow students was James McKeen Cattell. Cattell held the department's only fellowship, but at the end of his first year Hall recommended that his appointment be terminated and Dewey be appointed in his place. At the end of Dewey's first year Hall recommended that he too be denied reappointment because of his allegedly unsatisfactory work. Dewey, unlike Cattell, could not afford to leave Hopkins, and, being close to attaining his degree, he carried on, writing a thesis entitled *The Psychology of Kant;* he received a Ph.D. degree with Hall as his adviser in 1884. Their relationship, however, was never close, and when Gilman suggested some years later that Dewey be brought back to Hopkins to teach philosophy, Hall vetoed the suggestion, declaring that Dewey was not competent to do so (Ross, 1972, p. 146).

Following his graduation, Dewey accepted a position as an instructor in the Department of Philosophy at the University of Michigan. His annual salary was $900. Dewey spent his first years at Michigan teaching courses on philosophy and psychology and writing a number of papers and books, including his *Psychology*, published in 1886. In this book Dewey tried to blend philosophy and the new psychology, but the book was far from successful; its brief use as a psychological text ended in 1890 with the publication of James's *Principles*. Dewey acknowledged the superiority of James's text and often described it as a classic.

In 1894 Dewey published one of his only empirical studies, an assessment of language development in two young children. Dewey counted relative frequencies of word usage and found that the majority of words the children used were nouns (Dewey, 1894). The subjects were not identified, but their ages and the fact that they were observed continuously for some time suggest that they were Dewey's children.

Dewey's Functionalism

In 1894 Dewey was offered a position at the University of Chicago. The university had opened in October 1892, but faculty members were still being recruited. President William Harper, with the backing of John D. Rockefeller, who eventually gave $80 million to the university, was able to offer high salaries and attractive conditions (Chapter 9). Dewey was appointed head of the Department of Psychology at Chicago. There he wrote a paper that has become a classic in psychology and which marks the formal beginning of functionalism, "The Reflex Arc Concept in Psychology," published in the *Psychological Review* of 1896. Dewey introduced his paper with a discussion of the need for a unifying principle or hypothesis in psychology and proposed the reflex arc concept, borrowed from physiology (Chapter 3), as perhaps coming closest to meeting that need. However, his conception of the psychological reflex arc was not as a patchwork of disjointed parts but as a coordinated unit to be viewed as a whole. Dewey criticized stimulus-response and sensation-idea dichotomies, since they suggest distinct psychical entities rather than coordinated wholes. He stressed that responses and ideas always occur in a functional context and used as an illustration a child reaching toward a candle flame. That example had previously been used by John Locke (Chapter 2) and William James (James, 1890, vol. I, p. 25), among others. According to conceptions of this situation that analyze it into stimulus and response elements, the child sees the bright flame (the stimulus), reaches for it (the response), feels the burning pain (stimulus), and withdraws the hand (response). In this elementist analysis behavior is seen as a series of reactions to stimuli. Dewey argued that this conception is artificial in that it begins and ends at arbitrary points and ignores the role of behavioral adjustments to the environment. Before the child sees the flame, a whole series of responses must occur; after the sequence is supposedly over, many responses and other changes persist. Reaching for the flame is transformed by the painful experience, and so in the future the child will probably not respond that way. This behavioral sequence, according to Dewey, does not begin with perception of the candle or end with withdrawal of the hand. The lesson Dewey drew for psychology is that behavior and consciousness cannot be broken down into parts, bits, or elements. They must be understood in terms of their role in allowing the organism to adjust to the environment. In taking this position Dewey found himself in agreement with William James (Chapter 9) and at odds with Edward Titchener (Chapter 5). The similarity between his position and that of the Gestalt psychologists (Chapter 7) is also clear.

In addition, Dewey argued that any conception of behavior as a series of reactions to stimuli ignores one of the most important characteristics of a stimulus: it occurs in a context and is perceived by a particular individual with certain characteristics. A sudden loud noise elicits totally different reactions from a scholar working in a library and a sentry on patrol. In the two situations the stimulus has different "psychical value." Twenty years later Kurt Lewin was to give similar examples in his discussion of the "life spaces" of people in different situations (Chapter 7). Dewey also pointed out that some stimuli fall below the threshold for perception by a particular person at a specific time and so do not affect behavior. Therefore, stimuli must be seen as psychological events, not simply as physical energies from the environment. In a similar vein Dewey saw the final component of the psychological reflex arc as much more than a disjointed reaction; it too always has a context. Thus, although Dewey's concept of the psychological reflex arc was very different from that of the physiologists, he still argued that the model is a useful one for psychology.

Dewey's Views of Education

Dewey, influenced by Darwin's theory of evolution, described himself as a democratic evolutionist. He accepted Darwin's descriptions of finite limited resources and an increasingly competitive struggle for survival but saw culture and systems of government as differentiating the human species from others. Schools are part of a society's culture, and Dewey believed that education is a crucial means of ensuring that in the struggle for survival people have an opportunity to function and compete to the best of their abilities. He was opposed to divine right, inherited aristocracies, and undemocratic systems of government. All people should have an equal chance, and one way of seeing that they do is to provide equal educational and occupational opportunities. Dewey's views were attuned to the climate of his time. At the turn of the century America was a land of opportunity where people of talent could thrive and fortunes could be made. Andrew Carnegie, the son of a poor Scottish hand weaver, immigrated to the United States in 1848. In 1901 Carnegie was said to be the richest man in the world. John D. Rockefeller, the son of a small-time businessman and peddler of cancer "cures," was to build his Standard Oil Company into the "colossus of Cleveland," the largest and richest oil company in the world (Heilbroner, 1985). It was also the era of Henry Ford, Thomas Edison, the Wright brothers, and Alexander Graham Bell. Perhaps the twentieth century would indeed be the "American century," but if that promise was to be fulfilled, Dewey was convinced that educational reform was critical.

Dewey was no ivory tower theorist but a person who believed in testing his views and theories in the rough and tumble of the classroom. One of the attractions of his appointment at Chicago had been the inclusion of pedagogy in the department with philosophy and psychology and the opportunity to work with children. Dewey was convinced that the existing educational methods, particularly as used in elementary schools, were not psychologically sound. He aimed to establish a different type of school, one in which children would not be taught by rote methods but rather would be stimulated to think, to explore, and thus to learn.

With the aid of a small group of Chicago parents interested in a different type of education for their children, Dewey started a "laboratory school" for elementary-age children under the auspices of his department. He intended the relationship between the university's departments of psychology, philosophy, and pedagogy and this school to be similar to that between the departments of physics and chemistry and their laboratories. Dewey's laboratory school was not intended to be a teacher training school but rather a laboratory to study how children think and learn and how they can best be taught. At Chicago the school became known as "Dewey's School." It served as a model for similar schools, often on university campuses. Dewey also had an international influence, serving as an adviser to the governments of China and Japan when they reorganized their school systems. He also attracted many foreign students, who carried his educational philosophy back to their native countries.

Dewey was convinced that education must foster growth, keep the mind limber, and allow children to participate in the educational process. He was totally opposed to rote and drill learning. To Dewey such sledgehammer approaches made it likely that a child who learned only to use a sledgehammer would treat everything as a spike. For him the task of education was not to pass on conventional knowledge—such knowledge was often incorrect in any event—but rather to develop creative intelligence and versatility. The educator's function was not to transmit dogma but to foster divergent thinking. These were revolutionary ideas, and though Dewey had enthusiastic supporters, he also had critics. His school received only a small budget from the university and was supported almost entirely by fees and donations. It was a special annoyance to members of the faculty of education that Dewey refused to allow formal teacher training in his school. Unfortunately, these critics were eventually able to convince the university's president that Dewey's school should be merged with the Teacher Training Institute operated by the department of education. The merger was arranged without consulting Dewey and without his consent. Dewey and his supporters were outraged, and though he was offered the directorship of the School of Education, Dewey refused and in 1904 resigned from the University of Chicago faculty. Through the efforts of his friend Cattell, he was offered a position at Columbia University, where he remained for the rest of his life. In education Dewey continued to lead the "progressive movement," which in later years became almost a parody of what Dewey intended it to be but which in its first decades was a significant influence on the educational system of the United States.

Dewey's Later Life

Dewey was elected a charter member of the APA in 1892 and served as the association's president in 1899. In 1910 he was the fourth psychologist elected to the

National Academy of Science. However, after leaving Chicago he turned more and more to philosophy and to educational and social commentary. Dewey was a prolific writer. One listing of his bibliography covers seventy-five pages (Schilpp, 1939). Many books have been written about Dewey, and there is even a *Dewey Newsletter* that allows "Dewey scholars" to keep in touch. Dewey was one of the founding members of the first teachers' union in New York City, and the union's motto, "Education for democracy and democracy for education," could well have been his personal creed. With Cattell, he was actively involved in establishing and organizing the American Association of University Professors and served as its first president. At the age of seventy Dewey became interested in art; such was the versatility of his mind that he developed into an authority on the subject, writing books on art and aesthetics that were widely read and critically acclaimed. He was regarded as one of America's most important intellectuals—America's philosopher—yet he remained a modest, delightful person. One interviewer described Dewey at the age of ninety:

> The widespread power of Dewey's thinking is all the more remarkable to look back upon when one considers its modest, personal source. John Dewey is a homespun, almost regional, character. To this day, on meeting him, one would imagine himself talking with a Vermont countryman, as seven generations of his forebears were. At many an academic gathering over the last fifty years, those who had come a long distance to see and hear the great John Dewey have been pleasantly discomfited to find that he was none other than the modest, gray-haired, stoop-shouldered man with a Green Mountain drawl and a chuckle and a grin to whom they had been speaking for the past ten minutes. (Edman, 1970, pp. 101–102)

Dewey's career as a psychologist essentially ended in 1904, yet he remains an influential figure in the history of psychology. He never did a controlled experiment, rarely conducted empirical studies, never designed or administered a psychological test, and certainly did not set out to found a school of psychology, yet he was one of the founders of American psychology.

ANGELL AND CARR: FUNCTIONALISM AT THE UNIVERSITY OF CHICAGO

James Rowland Angell (1869–1949)

When Dewey left the University of Chicago, leadership of the Department of Psychology and of the Chicago school of functionalism was assumed by his student James Rowland Angell. The two men had much in common. They had both been born in Burlington, Vermont—Angell on May 8, 1869—and could trace their ancestry to the original New Englanders—in Angell's case to the *Mayflower* settlers. Angell's father was president of the University of Vermont and later of the University of Michigan. At Michigan, Angell took a course in psychology taught by Dewey, using his *Psychology* as the text, and was fascinated by both the course and the instructor. He received an A.B. degree in 1890 and was encouraged by Dewey to stay on for a master's degree in philosophy. In his autobiography, Angell recalled his student years with Dewey and paid his former teacher this warm tribute:

> I am under the deepest obligation to John Dewey whose simplicity of character, originality and vitality of mind brought him the unqualified affection and devotion of thousands of students. (Angell, 1936, p. 6)

In 1891 Angell entered Harvard, where he studied under William James, George Palmer, Josiah Royce, and the historian George Santayana. James put him to work analyzing a great mass of material gathered by the American Society of Psychical Research. Angell was unable to draw any firm conclusions about the reality of psychical phenomena but did have the experience of working closely with James. After earning a second master's degree at Harvard, Angell was encouraged by his cousin Frank Angell to travel to Europe to work in Wilhelm Wundt's laboratory. Frank Angell had just returned from Leipzig and so was able to provide a letter of introduction. Unfortunately, when James Angell arrived at Leipzig, he found the laboratory full, and the only thing Wundt could offer was an opportunity to attend his lectures. Angell had read Wundt's text and was already familiar with his psychology, and so he decided to move on. He spent some time with Hermann Ebbinghaus and was impressed with his memory research but not with his style as a lecturer. He also met Hermann von Helmholtz. Finally he enrolled at the University of Halle, where he worked under Benno Erdmann, writing a Ph.D. dissertation on Kant's treatment of freedom in his *Critique of Pure Reason* (1781) and *Critique of Practical Reason* (1788). The dissertation was accepted contingent on its being rewritten in better German. Angell planned to spend the next months revising it but unexpectedly received an offer of a position as an instructor in philosophy at the University of Minnesota that required him to return immediately for the start of the autumn quarter. The position carried a salary of $1,500, a strong attraction for a young man who had been engaged for four years and was keen to marry. Angell abandoned his dissertation and traveled to Minnesota. Later, as a university president, Angell conferred hundreds of doctoral degrees, but he never earned a Ph.D. himself.

After one year at Minnesota, Angell was offered an assistant professorship in Dewey's Department of Philosophy at the University of Chicago. At Chicago Angell rose through the academic ranks to a position as the university's acting president in 1918.

Angell's Functionalism

In 1906 Angell served as president of the APA, and in his presidential address, "The Province of Functional Psychology," he gave a clear outline of his functionalist position. Angell began:

> Functional psychology is at the present moment little more than a point of view, a program, an ambition. It gains its vitality primarily perhaps as a protest against the exclusive excellence of another starting point for the study of the mind, and it enjoys for the time being at least the peculiar vigor

which commonly attaches to Protestantism of any sort in its early stages
before it has become respectable and orthodox. (Angell, 1907, p. 61)

Despite this modest beginning, the paper illustrates Angell's perception of functionalism as more than simply a protest against "another starting point for the study
of the mind," namely, structuralism. He saw functionalism as an approach that
differed in crucial ways from that of the structuralists. First, Angell described functionalism as the psychology of mental operations or functions, while structuralism
is the psychology of mental elements. Functionalism is the psychology of the *how*
and *why* of consciousness; structuralism, the psychology of the *what* of consciousness. The structuralist asks, "What is the mind?"; the functionalist asks, "What is
the mind for?" Second, the functionalist describes the operations of the mind and
the functions of consciousness under actual life conditions. Consciousness is adaptive in that it allows people to function and adapt to the demands of their environment. Consciousness mediates between the environment and the needs of the
organism. It is active and forever changing. Consciousness cannot be stopped for
an analysis of its structure. According to Angell, the moment of consciousness per-
ishes but mental functions persist. Psychology must study thinking, not thoughts.
Third, the functionalist assumes a constant interplay between the psychological and
the physical. There is no real distinction between the two; they are one.

Angell's address was given when functionalism was at the peak of its importance and influence, a mature system of psychology. With that maturity came tol-
erance for diverse areas of psychology. One of the areas that achieved rapid growth
at Chicago was comparative psychology. Angell supported this development. He
had a thorough understanding of Darwin and wrote a number of papers describing
his theory of evolution and its psychological significance (Angell, 1909). Angell
listed three primary contributions of Darwin to psychology: his doctrine of instinct,
the notion of continuity among the minds of animals, and the study of the expression of the emotions. Angell was especially interested in the evolution of intelligence
and the history of instinct. He did a number of experiments on maze learning by
rats, investigating the sensory cues a rat uses in running through a maze. That topic
was to be further investigated by his student John B. Watson (Chapter 12). Another
of Angell's students, Walter S. Hunter (1889–1954), developed a delayed response
test often used in experiments on animal memory.

During World War I Angell served on the Committee for the Classification
of Personnel, and when the war ended he concentrated on administrative work at
the University of Chicago. In 1919 he was elected president of the Carnegie Corporation, and the following year as president of Yale University. He served as an
educational adviser to the National Broadcasting Company (NBC). When Angell
left Chicago, the chairmanship of the Department of Psychology was assumed by
another of his students, Harvey A. Carr.

Harvey A. Carr (1873–1954)

Harvey A. Carr—the initial did not signify a middle name but was added by Carr
to round out his signature—was born on an Indiana farm, went to Indiana public

schools, and then, after working on his family's farm, enrolled at the age of twenty-six at the University of Colorado. He received bachelor's and master's degrees at Colorado and in 1901 entered the University of Chicago as a graduate student. He worked as Watson's assistant in his courses on comparative psychology and studied with Angell. Later Carr recalled Angell's personality:

> There was the keen and incisive intellect, the judicial attitude towards controversial questions, the delightful idiosyncrasies of manner and expression, the bubbling humor which ran the gamut from good-natured levity to brilliant wit, and the free and easy flow of choice diction which always seemed so well adapted to the illumination of the topic under discussion. (Carr, 1936, p. 75)

Carr's dissertation at Chicago was entitled *A Visual Illusion of Motion During Eye-Closure,* a line of research which led to studies of autokinetic effects similar to those of Max Wertheimer (Chapter 7). Carr graduated in 1905 with the third doctoral degree in psychology awarded at Chicago. As there were no academic positions available, he taught for a couple of years in a Texas high school. In 1908 Watson left Chicago for Johns Hopkins, and Carr was appointed as his replacement. He taught the introductory, experimental, and comparative psychology courses. From 1920 to 1926 Carr directed the animal laboratory Watson had established. In 1926 he was appointed chairman of the Department of Psychology at Chicago, a position he held until 1938. In his autobiography Carr (1936) reported that 130 doctorates were conferred during his years at Chicago and that he had had considerable contact with all those students.

In 1927 Carr was elected president of the APA. In his presidential address, "Interpretations of the Animal Mind," Carr considered the evidence for assuming consciousness in animals and concluded that the only evidence for a positive conclusion lies in the similarity of the responses of humans and animals—a behavioral criterion. In studying animals Carr was a thoroughgoing behaviorist, but in studying humans he refused to classify himself as a behaviorist, preferring a more flexible and wide-ranging approach. Carr was always suspicious of dogmatic, restrictive positions. For example, in considering depth perception, he concluded that both nativist and empiricist positions were of value. Although Carr was a careful and precise experimenter, he also saw that much important psychological work could be done without the use of experimental methods. Carr's major books were *Psychology: A Study of Mental Activity* (1925), a widely used introductory text, and *Introduction to Visual Space Perception* (1935).

Carr's was a mature functionalist position that developed some years after the initial polemics and controversies had died down. Titchener had insisted that psychology study the world with man left in; Carr's psychology would study "man left in the world" (Heidbreder, 1961, p. 230). His was a broad psychology rooted in the world of everyday affairs. In 1936 Carr ended his autobiography with these words:

> I sometimes wish that I might be vouchsafed a glimpse of the Psychology—or Psychologies—of 1990, but perhaps it is just as well for I might be woefully disappointed. (Carr, 1936, p. 82)

He always protested against being labeled with any particular tag, even that of a functionalist, considering such labels unnecessarily restrictive. Perhaps Carr would not be disappointed to know that as we approach 1990 functionalism as a formal school of psychology no longer exists. It surely would be encouraging for him to learn that the basic attitudes and approach of the functionalist psychologists are an important influence on contemporary psychology. It may not be too strong a statement to say that the majority of contemporary psychologists are functionalists even though they do not use the term.

WOODWORTH AND THORNDIKE: FUNCTIONALISM AT COLUMBIA UNIVERSITY

The Department of Psychology at Columbia University was the setting for the careers of the next two psychologists we will consider, Robert Woodworth and Edward Thorndike. Neither man was formally a member of the functionalist school, but in their approach to psychology they were clearly sympathetic to the Chicago psychologists. Woodworth and Thorndike first met as students, were lifelong friends and coresearchers, and for many years were colleagues at Columbia.

Robert Sessions Woodworth (1869–1962)

Woodworth's Early Life Robert Sessions Woodworth was born on October 17, 1869, in Belchertown, Massachusetts. His family was of old New England stock,

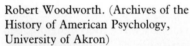

Robert Woodworth. (Archives of the
History of American Psychology,
University of Akron)

and one of his ancestors, Robert Sessions, had participated in the Boston Tea Party. Woodworth's father was a Congregationalist minister, and his mother was a college graduate and teacher. During Woodworth's childhood his father held pastorates in New England, with shorter stays in Iowa and Ohio. Woodworth's mother was his father's third wife. Children had been born of each marriage, and so Woodworth grew up in a large family. His father was fifty-five years old at the time of Woodworth's birth, a stern, unyielding man who believed in firm discipline.

Woodworth attended high school in Newton, Massachusetts, and graduated with the intention of becoming a minister. He enrolled at Amherst College and gained an A.B. degree in 1891. His main course work was in religion, classics, mathematics, science, and history. It was not until his senior year that Woodworth took a course in psychology. During his undergraduate years, his religious vocation weakened and he decided to become a schoolteacher. Woodworth taught science and mathematics for two years in a high school and then was an instructor for two years at a small college in Topeka, Kansas. During this period he had two experiences that changed his career plans. First he heard G. Stanley Hall lecture. Woodworth was impressed by Hall's description of the new science of psychology and his emphasis on the importance of finding things out through investigation. When he returned home after Hall's lecture, Woodworth printed the word *INVESTIGATION* on a card and hung it over his desk. The second experience was reading James's *Principles of Psychology*. As did many other students of his generation, Woodworth found the book captivating.

In 1895 Woodworth enrolled as an undergraduate student at Harvard University. He studied philosophy with Royce, psychology with James, and history with Santayana. At Harvard he also met Edward Lee Thorndike and Walter B. Cannon and began lifelong friendships with both. James directed his research on time perception, thought, and language. At the time James was also interested in the content of dreams and encouraged Woodworth to keep a dream diary. They tried unsuccessfully to correlate the content of his dreams with specific events during the day but did notice that Woodworth often dreamed about matters that had been interrupted during the day, an unconscious manifestation of the effect Bluma Zeigarnik was to report some thirty years later (Chapter 7).

In 1896 Woodworth received a second bachelor's degree from Harvard, and from 1897 to 1898 he was an assistant in psychology at the Harvard Medical School. There he saw Cannon's experiments on stomach movements and hunger and on visceral processes in emotion (Chapter 9). At the end of that year Cattell offered him a graduate fellowship at Columbia. Cattell's approach to psychology, with its emphasis on precise testing of psychological functions, appealed to Woodworth, and he accepted. He received a Ph.D. under Cattell in 1899. In his dissertation research Woodworth studied the accuracy of voluntary movements under the control of different sensory systems. He visited Europe in 1900 and attended the Second International Congress of Psychology, where he met a number of well-known European psychologists, including Hermann Ebbinghaus, Pierre Janet (Chapter 8), and Karl Pearson (Chapter 9).

Woodworth's Early Research Thorndike had accepted a position at Columbia in 1899. With him, Woodworth conducted a series of experiments on the transfer of training, that is, the effects of improvement in one mental function on the efficiency of other functions. They first described their results in a paper presented at the December 1899 meeting of the APA and then in three papers published in the 1901 *Psychological Review*. The background to their experiments was the educational doctrine of *formal discipline*. As we saw in discussing James's research (Chapter 9), according to this popular doctrine, it is possible to exercise and discipline the mind. Through hard work and study of the "disciplinary subjects," especially Latin, Greek, and mathematics, the mind's fibers were said to become more active, agile, facile, and powerful. This muscular doctrine was widely accepted and formed a cornerstone of much of the educational philosophy of the time. The following statement by Joseph Payne, a respected nineteenth-century educational theorist, is representative of views that were current at the time:

> My first proposition is that the study of the Latin language itself does
> eminently discipline the faculties, and secures to a greater degree than that
> of other subjects we have discussed, the formation and growth of those
> mental qualities which are the best preparatives for the business of
> life—whether the business is to consist in making fresh mental acquisitions,
> or in directing the powers thus strengthened and matured, to professional
> and other pursuits. (Payne, 1883, p. 264)

Children were taught Latin, Greek, and other "disciplinary subjects" not for their intrinsic value but to exercise and develop their minds. Sadly, such children often learned only to hate these subjects and exercised their minds with chants such as the following:

> Latin is a language, dead as dead can be.
> It killed the ancient Romans and now it's killing me!

Woodworth and Thorndike's experiments were more elaborate than those of James. First they studied such mental functions as area estimation and judgment of length or weight; then they gave their subjects training either on the function tested or on another function; finally, the subjects were retested on the original task. Even with tasks that superficially looked alike there was often little positive transfer, and at times the effect was negative. Their results gave no support to the doctrine of formal discipline, for when positive transfer occurred, it did so on the basis of specifically similar work methods. In these experiments Woodworth and Thorndike established a paradigm that has been used in hundreds of transfer experiments over the last eighty years.

Transfer can be a powerful influence on our lives. When it is positive—learning to drive a truck after having learned to drive a car—the effect is welcome. When it is negative—driving in England on one side of the road after having learned to drive in America on the other side—the effect can be disastrous not only for drivers but also for pedestrians. On his first visit to the United States, Winston Churchill stepped off a curb, looked the wrong way for approaching traffic, and was hit by an automobile—all within an hour of his arrival. When Christopher L. Sholes invented the modern typewriter in 1867, his machine had a sluggish mechanism, and so he deliberately scrambled the letters on the keyboard to prevent rapid typing. Today, on machines that are capable of high rates of typing and even on the keyboards of computers, we still use the scrambled arrangement of letters Sholes introduced. It is, however, possible to design a more efficient keyboard. In 1932 an American educator, August Dvorak, designed a keyboard in which all the vowels and major consonants are grouped together in the middle row. With this keyboard the speeds of novice typists increase by 30 to 50 percent, but imagine the massive negative transfer skilled conventional keyboard typists would experience if they tried to use the new keyboard.

Woodworth was interested in physiology and spent 1902 on a fellowship in the laboratory of Charles Sherrington (1857–1952) at the University of Liverpool in England. At the time Woodworth's aim was to make "his psychology contribute to a career in brain physiology, rather than vice versa" (Woodworth, 1932, p. 368). Sherrington offered him a position in his laboratory, as did Cattell. Woodworth decided to accept Cattell's offer and returned to Columbia and to psychology. He remained there for the rest of his life.

Woodworth's Psychometric Studies As we have seen, Cattell had established a strong tradition of psychological testing at Columbia (Chapter 9). The organizers of the 1904 St. Louis Exposition asked him to conduct tests with people of many different races who would be attending the fair. Cattell saw this as a valuable opportunity to collect anthropological and psychological data. He put Woodworth in charge of the project, and under his supervision nearly 1,100 people were tested. Woodworth presented his results in his vice-presidential address to the AAAS in 1909. Woodworth took a remarkably sensible and fair-minded position on racial differences in test performance. He acknowledged that scientists hope to discover an orderly universe and often try to develop classifications. However, he also pointed out that anthropological and psychological classifications are often based on physical (light-skinned versus dark-skinned), physiological (large-brained versus small-brained), or psychological (intelligent versus dull) characteristics. Woodworth stressed that such characteristics are not equally measurable, and even if they were, they are always distributed within a population. They vary from person to person within the population, and this variation is often greater than between-population differences. Claims of clear-cut racial differences are misleading, Woodworth stressed, because they emphasize differences between the averages of groups and neglect the large degree of overlap (Woodworth, 1910).

At St. Louis, Woodworth and his coworkers also used tests of sensory acuity. They found that, on the whole, sensory acuity is about the same in different races. They did find some striking examples of acute vision, hearing, taste, touch, and smell, but these characteristics were found among all racial groups. When he considered the question of racial differences in intelligence, Woodworth foresaw clearly the problems of comparing racial groups. He was pessimistic that such comparisons could ever be made. Woodworth also criticized the then-popular way of assessing the intelligence of groups of people by studying their cultures. He pointed out that the German culture of his time was often judged to be more advanced than that of the Romans. Did that mean that contemporary Germans were mentally more advanced than the Romans? Since on an evolutionary time scale the distance between the Romans and Germans was small, it would be extraordinary indeed if such a change in mental status had occurred. Woodworth criticized those who would label one group of people as being more "primitive" or "advanced" than others. Each group must be considered in terms of its habitat, group size, migration opportunities, and customs. Woodworth's views were judicious and prescient, and it is unfortunate that his warnings and admonitions were not widely heeded.

In 1906 the APA appointed a committee to study tests and measurements. Woodworth served on a subcommittee that developed and studied specific tests: color and form naming tests, a logical relation test, and a test of ability to follow instructions. When the United States entered World War I in 1917, Woodworth was asked by the APA to develop a test of emotional stability that would detect a soldier's tendency to develop "shell shock" or "war neurosis." He collected a list of hundreds of symptoms of shell shock from case histories and arranged them in a questionnaire. Single questions were to be answered yes or no. This personal data sheet was tried out on 1,000 recruits and a smaller number of men suffering from shell shock and battle fatigue. The aim was to develop an instrument that would show a need for more intensive counseling or psychological help for a recruit who might otherwise experience serious problems in combat. The war ended before the data sheet could be used extensively, but it later formed the basis of a number of personal data inventories for the measurement of neuroticism.

Woodworth was an active author. He published an extensive evaluation of G. T. Ladd's *Physiological Psychology* (Ladd & Woodworth, 1911) and after the war began a task that was to take nearly twenty years—writing his monumental *Experimental Psychology*. This book was finally published in 1938 and quickly became a definitive text. Published in a revised edition coauthored by Harold Schlosberg (1954), this book taught experimental psychology to thousands of students. In the 1920s Woodworth began work on a history of psychology published in 1931 as *Contemporary Schools of Psychology*. Woodworth presented the different schools of psychology as being complementary to one another. He denied that any one approach to psychology was *the* approach; his was a tolerant, open-minded view. In writing this book Woodworth was in a unique position, for the fifty years of the history of psychology he described were his own years as a psychologist. In a quiet, unassuming way he had emerged as the dean of American psychology. The last chapter, "The Middle of the Road," ends with these typically Woodworthian words:

> Every school is good, though no one is good enough. No one of them has the full vision of the psychology of the future. One points to one alluring prospect, another to another. Every one has elements of vitality and is probably here to stay for a long time. Their negative pronouncements we can discount while we accept their positive contributions to psychology as a whole. (Woodworth, 1948, p. 255)

Imageless Thoughts In 1914 Woodworth was elected president of the APA. In his presidential address he discussed the question of imageless thoughts, a topic that he had first studied in his dissertation experiments. He found that some voluntary movements occur without images and sensations. Similar results had been reported by Oswald Külpe and Alfred Binet (Chapters 6 and 11), and Woodworth spent the summer of 1912 working in Külpe's laboratory. Claims of imageless thoughts had been criticized by Titchener, who held that sensations and images are always present in thinking (Titchener, 1921c, 1922a). Woodworth was prepared to admit that they are present in many and perhaps even in most thoughts, but not in all: some thoughts occur without sensations and images. To study these imageless thoughts Woodworth introspected at the times when new ideas came to his mind. Rather dryly he pointed out that observational opportunities were limited, for new thoughts did not come to mind as often as he would have liked, but when they did, his introspections did *not* show sensations and images. New thoughts seemed to "come to mind" without specific content. Woodworth concluded that such new ideas are determined by memories of past experiences. Woodworth described an experiment he did with Thorndike in which subjects were asked to recall a scene, for example, the front of the United States Supreme Court building. Most people had seen the building or photographs of it and so were able to recall its appearance. However, when asked how many columns the building's portico had, they were unable to say unless they had previously counted them and remembered the fact.

In his research on imageless thoughts (Woodworth, 1915), we see Woodworth's willingness to use whatever approach was best. He was never doctrinaire. At times he considered behavioral approaches most appropriate; at other times, such as in the study of imageless thoughts, introspection was best. Woodworth always opposed narrow, restrictive approaches to psychology. The proponents of such approaches—Titchener and Watson—he called his "bogeymen," and he vowed never to accept their "epistemological tables of commandments" (Woodworth, 1932, p. 376). In studying the workings of the mind, Woodworth saw the need for different approaches. He realized that his middle-of-the-road approach ran the danger of being called "merely eclectic" but was prepared for such criticism.

Woodworth's Motivational Psychology In accord with the Chicago functionalists, Woodworth could not accept mechanistic stimulus-response (S-R) conceptions of behavior. For him stimuli do not cause responses; they excite the response, but its form and energy may be independent of the stimulus. An example Woodworth gave is that pulling a trigger causes a gun to fire but that the bullet's velocity is determined by the characteristics of the gun and the bullet, not by how hard the trigger is pulled. Woodworth also pointed out that the same behavioral response can be elicited by many stimuli. Sherrington (1906) had referred to the "receptive field" of a reflex; a cat's scratch reflex can, for example, be elicited by stimuli on many parts of the body. Woodworth also stressed the state or condition of the organism receiving the stimulus. Rarely does a stimulus reach an organism at rest, and the organism's activity often affects the response. Motivational variables are important determinants of this background activity. Throughout his career Woodworth stressed the effects of drives. In fact, he introduced and popularized the term *drive*. Why do we do one thing rather than another? Why do we put different energies into different activities? These questions were answered by Woodworth in his book *Dynamic Psychology* (1918) and forty years later in *Dynamics of Behavior* (1958). Woodworth described various drives. Basic drives arise from the organism's biological needs; they include the drives for food, water, and sexual contact. Other drives consist of neuromuscular preparations for stimuli. This is exemplified by an athlete at the starting blocks who is motivated to respond to the starter's gun. Other drives may be personal ambitions or professional interests. Woodworth believed that all of them are important influences on behavior and mental processes. Any psychology that ignored them, he thought, would necessarily be incomplete.

To emphasize the importance of motivation Woodworth modified the S-R formula to include the organism (O). His modified formula was S-O-R. Woodworth wrote of this revised formula:

> The O inserted between S and R makes explicit the obvious role of the living and active organism in the process; O receives the stimulus and makes the response. This formula suggests that psychologists should not limit their investigations to the input of stimuli and the output of motor responses. They should ask how the input can possibly give rise to the output; they should observe the intervening processes if possible or at least hypothesize them and devise experiments for testing the hypotheses. (Woodworth, 1958, p. 31)

Woodworth also addressed a vexing problem psychologists have in describing the phenomena they study. The technical vocabulary of psychology consists of terms such as *intelligence, habit, drive, feeling,* and *emotion* that have everyday meanings. However, much as psychologists may wish to restrict these terms to a particular technical meaning, it is often difficult to do so; the everyday meanings persist. Sciences such as physics and chemistry do not have this difficulty because they have developed their own technical vocabularies. Today, though, this may be changing; particle physicists refer to the "behavior of atoms" and to five known quarks—up, down, strange, charm, and bare bottom. Not to be outdone, physicists studying superfluidity have offered "the boojum" (Waldrop, 1981). At times psychologists have resorted to operational definitions—intelligence is what an intelligence test measures, hunger drive is the result of so many hours of food deprivation—but such definitions are not completely satisfactory. In his presidential address to the APA, Woodworth suggested that psychologists consider inventing a technical vocabulary. Even the term *psychology* seemed so overloaded with connotations of soul and psyche as to be worthless. Woodworth proposed that it be replaced with the term *motivology.* He also made two other suggestions. Rather than *conscious attitudes*, psychologists should refer to *marbs* in honor of Marbe, the psychologist who had studied them (Chapter 6); thoughts might be referred to as *kulps* in honor of Külpe. Woodworth's suggestion was never followed, but some additional examples come to mind. Nonsense syllables might be *ebbs* in honor of Ebbinghaus; reinforcers might be *burrhuses* in honor of Skinner; intelligence testing might be *bineting* in honor of Binet; finally, drives would certainly have to be *woodworths*.

Woodworth had no wish to develop or lead a school of psychology. He was always a modest man and seems to have consistently underestimated his many contributions to psychology. In his autobiography he mentioned that he had participated in activities of the National and Social Research Councils but characteristically did not mention that he had been chairman of the National Research Council's Division of Anthropology and Psychology and president of the Social Research Council. Fortunately, his many contributions were recognized and Woodworth was awarded many honors: the presidency of the APA in 1914 and election to the first board of directors of the Psychological Corporation in 1921, a position he held until 1960. In 1956 he was awarded the first gold medal of the American Psychological Foundation for his

> distinguished and continuous service to scholarship and research in psychology and for contributions to the growth of psychology through the medium of scientific publication. (Poffenberger, 1962, p. 689)

Woodworth officially retired from Columbia on his seventieth birthday, but he continued to lecture until he was eighty-nine years old and to write until he was ninety-one. He died on July 4, 1962, and with his death one of the last links to the founders of psychology was broken.

EDWARD LEE THORNDIKE (1874–1949)

Thorndike's Early Life

Thorndike, Woodworth, Angell, and Dewey were all sons of old New England families, in Edward Lee Thorndike's case a family that could trace its ancestry back to 1630 and included farmers, lawyers, and storekeepers. Thorndike was born on August 31, 1874, in Williamsburg, Massachusetts. His mother was a resolute Victorian housewife, and his father was a Methodist minister. Ministerial appointments in the Methodist church of the late nineteenth century were for short periods, rarely more than three years, and so Thorndike grew up in a succession of New England towns. He was strongly motivated to succeed, found schoolwork easy, and was a brilliant student. He was also painfully shy, often lonely, and very conscious of being a "minister's kid." Thorndike graduated in 1891, having ranked first or second in all his high school courses.

In 1891 Thorndike entered Wesleyan University, a school founded by the Methodist church and where his older brother Ashley was a student. Thorndike had a brilliant academic record there and each year won at least one major academic prize. He also edited the college newspaper and played competitive tennis. However, he was still very shy and envied his older brother, who in addition to being a brilliant student was poised and popular. At Wesleyan, students in their junior year were required to take psychology, a course that Thorndike found dull. However, as a candidate for an academic prize he was required to read James's *Principles of Psychology.* Forty years later Thorndike remembered the James book as more stimulating than any book he had read before or since. As an undergraduate he bought the book, the only nonliterary work he purchased, and even went so far as to reproach the faculty member who taught the psychology course for not using *Principles of Psychology* as his text. Thorndike graduated in 1895 with Phi Beta Kappa honors, having earned the highest academic average achieved at Wesleyan in fifty years (Joncich, 1968).

Thorndike at Harvard University: Animal Learning Experiments Thorndike then entered Harvard University, where he planned to study English, philosophy, and psychology. His interest in English and philosophy soon waned, but his contacts with James strengthened his interest in psychology. In 1896 he began his first piece of independent research. This work was inspired by James's belief that in mind-reading demonstrations, subtle facial movements made unconsciously by the person whose mind is supposedly being read may provide cues for the "mind reader." The hypothesis of the experiment was that such subtle movements may be seen more easily by children than by adults, and so Thorndike studied three- to six-year-old children. He sat facing a child and thought of a number, letter, or object while the child tried to guess what he was thinking. His results showed no support for the hypothesis, but the experimental procedure had one significant detail: for each correct guess the child received a piece of candy. This was Thorndike's first use of an explicit reward. While the children enjoyed the experiments, the school authorities became suspicious of Thorndike's "mind reading" and refused to allow them to continue. Therefore, Thorndike was forced to consider other research possibilities. He turned to animal learning and conducted some of the best known experiments in the history of psychology.

In his autobiography Thorndike described how he began his experiments on learning in chickens:

> I then suggested [to James] experiments with the instinctive and intelligent behavior of chickens as a topic, and this was accepted. I kept these animals and conducted the experiments in my room until the landlady's protests were imperative. James tried to get the few square feet required for me in the laboratory, and then in the Agassiz Museum. He was refused and with his habitual kindness and devotion to underdogs and eccentric aspects of science, harbored my chickens in the cellar of his own home for the rest of the year. (Thorndike, 1936, p. 264)

Using stacked books as walls, Thorndike built a number of pens for the chickens. With the assistance of two neighborhood children, he ran an experiment in which a chicken had to find its way out of the pen through an exit to a surrounding enclosure containing food, water, and other chickens. First the chicken would run up and down peeping loudly and showing clear signs of distress. After many unsuccessful attempts the chicken would finally find the exit and leave the pen. When a chicken was repeatedly placed in the pen, it ran to the exit more and more rapidly. Thorndike found that

> the chick, when confronted by loneliness and confining walls responds by those acts which in similar situations in nature would be likely to free him. Some one of these acts leads him to the successful act, and the resulting pleasure stamps it in. Absence of pleasure stamps all others out. (Thorndike, 1911, p. 64)

The chickens had learned to escape from the pen.

In view of their significance, it is important to consider the background of these experiments. Thorndike gave the following practical reasons for conducting them:

> The motive for my first investigations of animal intelligence was chiefly to satisfy requirements for courses and degrees. Any other topic would certainly have served as well. I certainly had no special interest in animals and had never taken a course in biology until my last year of graduate work, when I worked hard at it and completed a minor for the doctor's degree. (Thorndike, 1936, p. 165)

Certainly such practical considerations were important, but the question remains: Why did Thorndike choose to experiment with chickens? At the time there was no tradition of such research at Harvard. Any influence must have come from elsewhere. It seems likely that one source was the work of one of the British followers of Charles Darwin, C. Lloyd Morgan (Chapter 9). In 1894 Morgan had published *Comparative Psychology*, which included descriptions of experiments in which chickens had learned to discriminate between different-colored kernels of corn. Some kernels were dipped in quinine to make them taste bitter, others in sugar water to make them taste sweet. The chickens learned quickly to peck only at the sweet-tasting kernels. Lloyd Morgan gave the Lowell Lectures at Harvard in 1896, describing his approach to comparative psychology and his learning experiments with chickens. It is probable that Thorndike attended these lectures and heard Morgan's description of what he called trial-and-error learning.

Thorndike at Columbia University: Cats in a Puzzle Box Despite the success of the learning experiments with chickens and his admiration for James, in 1897 Thorndike decided to leave Harvard. He wished to leave New England for a personal reason—the rejection of a marriage proposal he had made. Thorndike accepted Cattell's offer of a graduate fellowship at Columbia University and moved to New York City, taking with him in a basket his two most highly trained chickens. Originally he intended to study the inheritance of acquired characteristics with these chickens, but Thorndike, a young man in a hurry, soon realized that such a study would take time and abandoned it. Cattell, perhaps in reaction to his own experiences in Wundt's laboratory, insisted that his students develop their own thesis plans. Thorndike proposed to study the formation of associations by extending his experiments with chickens to other species. His plan was accepted. At first he kept chickens and a kitten in his apartment—his neighbors thought he was a circus animal trainer—but after a near fire in an incubator his landlady insisted that the chickens be removed. Cattell was able to find some space for him in the attic of a building at Columbia, and there Thorndike established his animal laboratory. He acquired seven kittens and six young cats, the subjects for his most famous experiments.

Thorndike built fifteen puzzle or problem boxes. A hungry cat placed in a box was required to learn to escape and obtain food by making a specific response, such as pushing a pedal or pulling on a looped rope. When the response occurred, Thorndike opened the box door and allowed the cat to escape. When first placed in these boxes cats showed a great deal of hit and miss, or what Thorndike called "trial-and-error" behavior: scratching at the walls, attempting to squeeze through small openings and gaps, clawing at the wire netting, and the like. Eventually, apparently by accident, the correct response would occur and the cat would escape and reach the food. With training, the amount of trial-and-error behavior decreased so that eventually the cats could escape from the boxes quickly and smoothly.

Thorndike considered the learning he had observed to be governed by what he called the "law of effect." He saw the problem box as a stimulus situation in which a hungry cat makes a variety of responses. Most of the responses are followed by "annoyers," that is, failures to escape from the box and gain food, and so the connection between the responses and the stimulus situation is weakened. A much smaller number of responses lead to "satisfiers," that is, escape from the box and access to food, and so the connection between the responses and the stimulus situation is strengthened. According to Thorndike, satisfiers and annoyers act selectively to "stamp in" certain stimulus-response connections and to weaken others. Responses that produce satisfiers have their connection to the situation "glued" more strongly than do responses that produce annoyers, which have their connection weakened. Thorndike gave an elegant explanation of the learning he had observed. For more than forty years his explanation was central to psychologists' conceptions of animal learning. Explanations of learning were almost always a matter of either agreeing or disagreeing with Thorndike. His classic experiments had a number of other characteristics that are important. First, Thorndike included only one illustration in his monograph describing the results of his experiments (Thorndike, 1898a). His drawing of Box K shows a neat, tidily constructed box that has been reproduced in numerous psychological texts as an example of the type of box Thorndike used. It is, however, a misleading example. Photographs of the boxes Thorndike used (Burnham, 1972) show that they were very different from this tidy drawing. Odd pieces of lumber protrude at various angles, unhammered nails stick out, and the walls, floors, and roofs are often crooked. In general the boxes have a rickety, thrown-together appearance, and a number of labels show their origin as fruit and vegetable crates. Thorndike disliked tools and machines—as an adult he was never able to learn to drive a car—and it is clear that his carpentry skills were limited. Thorndike's elegant research was done using the crudest apparatus. Second, Thorndike used fifteen different boxes in his experiments. They required different escape responses, and one of his most important findings was that these responses were not learned with equal ease. All the cats learned to escape from five boxes that required discrete, single responses: clawing or pulling a string, pushing a button, pawing a lever. However, four of the ten cats tested in a box requiring a multiple response of pulling a loop and then moving a stick or two bolts did not learn to escape; five of the eight cats tested in a box requiring that a thumb latch be moved with a force of at least 400 grams were also unsuccessful. Thorndike believed that the cats had difficulty learning to make these escape responses because the responses lacked simplicity and definitiveness. Third, some of the most interesting results Thorndike reported came from his observations of the behavior of cats in Box Z, which was entirely closed except for a small opening in the left-hand corner. To escape from this box the cats had to lick or scratch themselves. In their home cages they often made these responses, but they had difficulty learning to make them to escape from Box Z. While every cat eventually learned to escape from the box, the formation of the association was slow and difficult. Unlike the smooth, coordinated responses made in the other boxes, licking and scratching were labile and tended to diminish so that they eventually became mere vestiges of the original acts, for example, a rapid waving of the paw up and down rather than a hearty scratch. If the door was not opened immediately after a lick or scratch, the response was not repeated, unlike the vigorous repetitions of other responses. Responses were not equally easily learned. Thorndike's results clearly anticipated modern experiments on "biological constraints upon learning" and their finding that not all behaviors can be modified equally readily by reinforcement (Hinde & Stevenson-Hinde, 1973; Shettleworth, 1973). Fourth, Thorndike found that when cats were tested in a number of boxes they became progressively better at learning to escape from them. They became "box-wise" and able to learn new escape responses with a minimum of difficulty. They had developed what Harry Harlow (1905–1982) many years later was to call "learning sets" (Harlow, 1949). Fifth, Thorndike observed no beneficial effects of imitation (seeing another cat solve the problem) or being "put through" the problem by having the human experimenter move the animal's limbs through the requisite motions.

These are all classic results, and it is extraordinary that Thorndike did the experiments in less than a year. He first described his results in "Experiments on Comparative Psychology," a paper presented at the January 1898 meeting of the New York Academy of Science, and then in "Some Experiments in Animal Intelligence," published in *Science* in June 1898. His thesis, *An Experimental Study of the Associative Processes in Animals*, was accepted by Columbia in 1898 and published as a monograph supplement in the *Psychological Review* of that year. Finally, at the end of an incredible year, Thorndike described his results at the December 1898 meeting of the APA. Thorndike's ambition was to make it to the top of psychology within five years; he was well on the way to doing so.

Many psychologists, including James and Cattell, regarded Thorndike's learning experiments as a major step forward in the study of animal intelligence. However, Thorndike did have critics. After the APA meeting Thorndike wrote to his fiancée that his paper had been severely criticized by an "old oak" (Joncich, 1968, p. 146). He was not disturbed by the criticism and welcomed the controversy. The "old oak" was T. Wesley Mills (1847–1915), a comparative psychologist from McGill University in Montreal. The following year Mills renewed his criticism of Thorndike's experiments in a long paper entitled "The Nature of Animal Intelligence and the

Methods of Investigating It," published in the May number of the *Psychological Review* (Mills, 1899). Mills criticized Thorndike for neglecting the work of previous investigators:

> Dr. Thorndike has not been hampered in his research by any of that respect for workers of the past of any complexion which usually causes men to pause before differing radically from them, not to say gleefully consigning them to the psychological flames. For Dr. Thorndike the comparative psychologists are readily and simply classified—they are all insane—the only difference being the degree, for he speaks of one of them as being the "sanest" of the lot. (Mills, 1899, p. 263)

This neglect of previous work was entirely intentional on Thorndike's part. He hoped to sweep away the entire fabric of comparative psychology and start anew. Comparative psychology must reject the anecdotal reports of such investigators as Romanes (1912) (Chapter 9) and replace them with objective experiments. Romanes had made much of the "homing instinct" of dogs and had included reports of lost dogs finding their way home over many miles, but as Thorndike noted:

> Dogs get lost hundreds of times and no one ever notices it or sends an account to a scientific magazine. But let one find its ways from Brooklyn to Yonkers and the fact immediately becomes a circulating anecdote. (Thorndike, 1898a, p. 24)

The only earlier work of any value was that of Lloyd Morgan, the man Thorndike called the "sanest of an insane lot."

Mills also criticized Thorndike for the type of situation he had used in his experiments. He stressed that

> when animals are removed from their usual, not to say natural, surroundings, they may be so confused or otherwise disordered that they fail to act normally, and this I have illustrated by experiments. (Mills, 1899, p. 266)

Mills claimed that Thorndike's animals had been in a state of panic and so had failed to act intelligently. Their situation, Mills said, was like that of "a living man in a coffin" (Mills, 1899, p. 266). His own experiments with dogs in field and farm situations had shown them to be capable of highly intelligent behavior. Mills claimed that if Thorndike had observed the behavior of these animals,

> even one so fast bound in the grip of his own experience as he, would have altered his opinion on this and many other subjects. (Mills, 1899, p. 266)

In the June 1899 number of the *Psychological Review*, Thorndike replied to Mills's criticism in a harsh rebuttal. He admitted that Sir John Lubbock had used a method similar to his own in experiments with insects and acknowledged the value of his contribution. At least one additional earlier worker was now seen to be quite sane. Thorndike also admitted that at times his animals did panic and show signs of violent behavior. However, these reactions had occurred only on the early trials and had not, according to Thorndike, interfered with formation of the association. Rates of learning were similar in animals that did and did not show this early panic. Thorndike reported that his cats went into the boxes freely and of their own accord over and over again. Surely they would not have done so if they had been panic-stricken. He also accepted Mills's description of his situations as unnatural but pointed out that that was exactly what he had intended them to be. His aim was to have his cats learn a novel and unfamiliar action; he did not want to study natural or instinctive reactions. Thorndike questioned Mills's description of his situations as artificial. His cats had spent most of their lives living in a laboratory, so for them the situation was not artificial. It was as natural for them as a farmyard was for a farm cat. This Thorndike-Mills debate had its share of *ad hominem* arguments but is fascinating because of the speed with which it was joined and the fact that the issues they debated have recurred repeatedly in the twentieth century.

Thorndike and Education After he earned a Ph.D., the best position Thorndike could find was one as an assistant professor of pedagogy at the College for Women of Western Reserve University in Cleveland, Ohio. As his brother Ashley was on the faculty, Thorndike went to Cleveland with high hopes, but the year turned into a time of unhappiness in what he considered academic exile. He knew very little pedagogy and had to spend a frantic six weeks becoming familiar with the literature. Much of the time he was only one step ahead of his students, and in his lectures he often had to rely on "bluff." Thorndike wanted most to continue his experiments, which he called his "stunts," but there were no facilities for animal research on campus. At the end of a year he was delighted to receive a call from Cattell to move to Teachers College at Columbia. He returned to New York in 1899, joining two of his brothers who were faculty members in the departments of English and history. The students chanted:

English, history and psych,—each has its own Thorn-dike.

Thorndike remained at Teachers College for the rest of his academic career, forty-three years during which he averaged ten publications a year. Many of these publications were major works. His *Educational Psychology*, for example, published in 1913, was a three-volume book. Thorndike described his publications as "opportunistic," in that many of them were written as adjuncts to the courses he taught. He distrusted students' ability to take accurate notes and so wrote books for them to read. His approach led to some criticism. Following the publication of Thorndike's *Elements of Psychology* (1905), Titchener issued this stinging rebuke:

Professor Thorndike finds it necessary, or profitable, to publish his lecture courses as soon as the lectures have been delivered. Work put out in this way may very well be clever and original and suggestive, but it must inevitably show marks of hasty preparation and of immaturity of judgment. (Titchener, 1905, p. 552)

Such criticisms, however, were passing setbacks, and Thorndike's career developed apace. Cattell supported him enthusiastically, and within five years Thorndike was promoted to the rank of professor at more than double his starting salary. Initially he continued experimental research with both animals and humans, but then he extended his learning experiments to dogs and also studied the mental life of monkeys. Thorndike spent the summers of 1899 and 1900 at the Biological

Sciences Research Station at Woods Hole, where he conducted one of the earliest studies of learning in fish. At Woods Hole, Thorndike also met the renowned biologist Jacques Loeb (1859–1924) and the young comparative psychologist Robert Yerkes (Chapter 11). In 1899 Thorndike also collaborated with Robert Woodworth on the transfer in training experiments discussed earlier in this chapter (Thorndike & Woodworth, 1900). As the years passed Thorndike's interest centered more and more on education. Perhaps the nature of his academic home influenced him, for Thorndike made it his custom "to fulfill my contractual obligations as a professor before doing anything else" (Thorndike, 1936, p. 270). But it surely was comparative psychology's loss that he did not do more animal experiments. Instead, he devoted his time to education, becoming an authority on educational measurement and, with John Dewey, one of the leaders of the progressive education movement.

Thorndike's Development of Mental Measurements Thorndike recognized the reality and importance of individual differences. He believed that one of the great tasks of psychology was to develop techniques that would allow such differences to be measured. He published a monograph entitled *Heredity, Correlation and Sex Differences in School Abilities* in 1903 and *Introduction to the Theory of Mental and Social Measurements* in 1904. He opposed conceptions, such as that of Charles Spearman (1904), that emphasized "general intelligence." Thorndike thought of intelligence as a combination of a number of specific skills and abilities. He developed an intelligence test consisting of subtests to measure sentence completion (C), arithmetic (A), vocabulary (V), and ability to follow directions (D). This CAVD test was widely used at Columbia and many other institutions to measure students' skills and abilities. Thorndike believed that these subtests could tap or measure different abilities that might or might not be correlated in a particular person.

With regard to the question of the origin of individual differences, Thorndike was a convinced hereditarian (Thorndike, 1913), believing that genetic factors are of primary importance and that systematic eugenics is the only hope for the improvement of the human population. Genetic determination of individual differences in intelligence, he argued, must be accepted as a fact. Thorndike opposed educational egalitarianism. He proposed that different educational opportunities be provided for children of different levels of ability, since schools can do very little to modify a child's intellectual standing. On the other hand, he considered high intelligence a precious resource that should not be wasted through poor schooling. He often used dramatic examples to illustrate his points. Send 1 million English schoolboys on a voyage like that of H.M.S. *Beagle*, and how many of them, he asked, would make the discoveries Charles Darwin made? Not 1,000, not 100, not 10, perhaps not even 1. In these views he was very much a product of his times.

Thorndike's Applied Research During his years at Teachers College, Thorndike also worked on a number of industrial problems: development of employee examinations for applicants for positions with the American Tobacco Company and selection tests for clerical workers. During World War I, he did much of the statistical analysis for the Army Testing Project (Chapter 11) and worked on the development of selection techniques for aviators. After the war Thorndike was elected to the board of directors of the Psychological Corporation as a charter member.

As did Cattell, Thorndike favored a precise, quantitative approach to the assessment of psychological phenomena. Two examples of his work will illustrate his approach. With support from the Carnegie Corporation, Thorndike undertook to survey the quality of life in American cities. His results for 310 large cities were published in *Your City* (1939), and those for 144 smaller cities in *One Hundred Forty-four Smaller Cities* (1940). He assembled a multitude of facts about each city's population, its educational and recreational facilities, the health of its inhabitants, and their occupations; per capita expenditures for schools, libraries and museums; incomes; crime rates, and other factors. These facts were then combined to yield a general G score reflecting the city's general quality of life. Thorndike also combined a number of other measures—including number of high school graduates, literacy rate, library circulation, and homicide rate—to arrive at a P score for each city. He regarded P as a reflection of the intelligence, character, and personal qualities of the city's citizens. Thus, G was considered a measure of the quality of the environment, and P a measure of the genetic quality of the population.

A second line of investigation was inspired by one of Thorndike's children's difficulty learning to spell, which led Thorndike to become interested in word usage. First he made counts of word frequencies in literature, textbooks, the Bible, newspapers, correspondence, and other written materials. From fifty different sources Thorndike compiled a list of the 10,000 words that occurred most frequently (Thorndike, 1921). This list was expanded in 1932 to 20,000 words (Thorndike, 1932). Among the 500 most used words were *and, apple, big, but, I, dead, man, most, near, no, now, open, pass, top,* and *sister.* Thorndike urged that teachers pay particular attention to teaching children to use and spell these words.

In 1931 Thorndike published a *Junior Dictionary*, and in 1940 the *Thorndike Senior-Century Dictionary*. In these dictionaries he followed a rule of always making a word's definition simpler than the word itself. His dictionaries enjoyed great success, with the *Junior Dictionary* selling more than 1 million copies. Thorndike was also interested in the more general question of language acquisition and formulated what he termed the "babble-luck" theory to explain how a child learns a particular language. According to this theory, the child first makes a wide range of babbles. Some of the sounds are recognized by the parents and rewarded. This is satisfying to the child, and so language is learned through trial and success (Thorndike, 1913).

Thorndike's Honors Thorndike received many honors and awards. In 1912 he turned down an offer of a professorship at Harvard University and that same year was elected president of the APA. In 1917 Thorndike was elected to membership in the National Academy of Science, and in 1921 he was appointed research director of the Institute for Educational Research at Teachers College. In a 1921 poll of psychologists for his *American Men of Science*, Cattell found that Thorndike ranked first; in 1925 the board of trustees of Columbia University awarded Thorndike the gold Butler Medal in recognition of his contributions to education; in 1933 he served as president of the American Association for the Advancement of Science.

Thorndike attracted many students and was often kind and generous with them and his coworkers. One of his students, Herbert Toops, named his first son Edward L. Toops and his second son Thorndike Toops (Meyer, 1983, p. 2). Others, however, found him aggressive, abrasive, and domineering—behaviors that Thorndike himself described as the "bluff" he used to mask his shyness. He made a great deal of money from his books; in 1924 his royalties were five times his professorial salary, and he prospered even during the Depression years. His life as a psychologist seems to have been deeply satisfying. He retired in 1940, but his retirement years were often filled with sadness and melancholia. Thorndike suffered from arteriosclerosis, was deaf, and much of the time thought of himself as a "tired old man." He published nearly fifty psychological works after his retirement, but the joy and satisfaction had gone out of publishing. The habit persisted, but the satisfiers had lost their value. Thorndike died at the age of seventy-four on August 9, 1949, from a massive cerebral hemorrhage. His name is known to most contemporary psychologists, but most often for the animal learning experiments he did at the very beginning of his career.

CONCLUSION

Thorndike's death ends our consideration of functionalism. Today functionalism no longer exists as a formal school of psychology, and it would be impossible to point to a university as the home of functional psychology. However, the functionalists' point of view has been widely accepted and is now part of the frame of reference of nearly all psychologists. Paradoxically, while there are few, if any, formal functionalists, nearly all psychologists are functionalists in that they are interested in mental functions as adaptations and adjustments to the environment. As a formal school of American psychology, functionalism was displaced early in the twentieth century by a more radical and aggressive movement—the behaviorism of J. B. Watson. Before we consider Watson's behaviorist revolution (Chapter 12), we will describe the development, use, and occasional abuse of intelligence tests by psychologists during the early decades of the twentieth century. The story of attempts to measure this particular function of the human mind is fascinating and at times very sad.

Alfred Binet. (National Library of Medicine)

Historical Uses and Abuses of Intelligence Testing

The early decades of the twentieth century saw the first attempts to measure one particular function of the human mind: intelligence. While the development of intelligence tests was primarily an American undertaking, the first tests were developed in France, where an interest in the measurement of mental capacities dated back to Pierre Broca.

PIERRE BROCA'S CRANIOMETRY

In addition to his outstanding work on the localization of speech (Chapter 3), Pierre-Paul Broca undertook extensive measurements of the human body, including the head, in an attempt to understand its functions. Broca believed that brain size is a good general index of intelligence. He concluded that men are on average more intelligent than women and that this difference is greater in contemporary men and women than it was in the distant past. Broca's conclusions were based on two sets of data:

1. The results of his own autopsies in four Parisian hospitals. He collected data on 292 brains of men and 140 brains of women. The average weight of the men's brains was 1,325 grams and that of the women's was 1,144 grams, a difference of 181 grams, or 14 percent of male brain weight.
2. Measurements of the cranial capacities of a number of prehistoric skulls. In those skulls Broca found a difference of 99.5 cubic centimeters between male and female brains, with male brains being larger. His measurements of contemporary brains showed volume differences ranging from 130 to 221 cubic centimeters. Broca concluded not only that brains of primitive people were smaller

than brains of modern people but that sex differences in brain volume were increasing over time.

From such data, Broca concluded that

> in general, the brain is larger in mature adults, than in the elderly, in men than in women, in eminent men than in men of mediocre talent, in superior races than in inferior races....Other things being equal, there is a remarkable relationship between the development of intelligence and the volume of the brain. (Broca, quoted by Gould, 1978, p. 44)

Broca's conclusions can be questioned. He simply assumed that mature adults are more intelligent than the elderly, that "primitive" people were less intelligent than modern people, and that men are more intelligent than women. Each one of these assumptions was unsupported, but once he accepted them, it seemed logical to Broca that any differences he found in the brain sizes of these groups would be a reflection of their intellectual capacities. His reasoning was surprisingly circular for a scientist of his stature. Why did he not question his original assumptions? The answer may lie in an examination of his social context. Broca's basic assumption that men are more intelligent than women was a prevailing one of the time. We saw Galton's views of male superiority in Chapter 9. Such views were also common in France, as is shown in the following attack on women by one of the leaders of nineteenth-century French psychology, Gustave Le Bon:

> In the most intelligent races, as among the Parisians, there are a large number of women whose brains are closer in size to those of gorillas than to the most developed male brains. This inferiority is so obvious that no one can contest it for a moment; only its degree is worth discussion. All psychologists who have studied the intelligence of women...recognize today that they represent the most inferior forms of human evolution and that they are closer to children and savages than to an adult civilized man. They excel in fickleness, inconstancy, absence of thought and logic, and incapacity to reason. (Le Bon, quoted by Gould, 1978, p. 46)

A second aspect of his cultural and intellectual environment might also have influenced Broca's thinking: the rise of Charles Darwin's theory of evolution. Broca was the founder and leader of a small group of French "freethinkers" who accepted Darwin's theory of evolution. "I would rather," Broca said, "be a transformed ape than a degenerate son of Adam" (Sagan, 1979, p. 6). Broca developed a primitive form of social Darwinism to account for the apparently increasing difference in brain size between men and women over time. Men were said to be involved in a struggle and competition for survival; they are active in meeting the demands of their environments and protecting their families, and so bigger brains have been selected for in men. Women were said to have been protected, passive, largely sedentary, and restricted to the family situation, and so they were not subject to the same selection pressure.

Broca's works were regarded by many as jewels of nineteenth-century science. Thomas Huxley, the man known as "Darwin's bulldog" for his tenacity in defending the theory of evolution, said that the mere mention of Broca's name filled him with a sense of gratitude for what Broca had accomplished. Broca's work measuring brain size was often cited in opposition to the extension of higher education and the right to vote to women. After all, if women are the most inferior forms of human evolution, with brains more similar to gorillas' than to men's, why should they be allowed to enter universities or vote? Yet even before Broca the role of women had begun to change. In America women participated fully in the revolution and began to question their status (Smith, 1976, vol. 2, chap. 19). In 1776 Abigail Adams urged her husband John to lead Congress in considering the question of the independence and education of women (Smith, 1976, vol. 2, p. 1809), although it was only in the middle decades of the nineteenth century that the first women's colleges were established and in the 1880s and 1890s that state universities became coeducational. The struggle for women's right to vote began early in the 1800s and continued under the leadership of Carrie Chapman Scott and Susan B. Anthony. Final success came on August 18, 1920, with ratification of the Nineteenth Amendment to the Constitution affirming:

> The right of citizens of the United States to vote shall not be denied or
> abridged by the United States or by any State on account of sex.

The battle had been won, but the struggle had been long and difficult. All too often assumptions of male superiority and prejudice against women had blocked progress. Broca's findings and conclusions supported such prejudice. The pathos of that situation is further heightened by the falsity of his conclusions.

A modern biologist and historian of science, Stephen Jay Gould, questioned the validity of Broca's widely accepted conclusions (Gould, 1978). Gould pointed out that one of the most important determinants of brain weight is age; brain weights generally decrease with age. The women whose brains were studied by Broca were older than the men, but Broca did not take account of that fact in analyzing the differences in brain weight he found. When Gould reanalyzed Broca's data and controlled for differences in age, he found that the difference in brain weight between the male and female brains was reduced from 181 to 113 grams. Other important influences on brain weight are cause of death and body size. After taking these factors into account, Gould concluded:

> Thus, the corrected 113-gram difference is surely too large: the true figure is
> probably closer to zero and may as well favor women as men. And 113
> grams is exactly the average difference between a 5 foot 4 inch and a 6 foot 4
> inch male in Broca's data.... They certainly don't permit any confident
> claim that men have bigger brains than women. (Gould, 1978, p. 48)

Gould was also able to demonstrate the invalidity of Broca's claim of a larger difference in volume between contemporary male and female brains than can be seen in brains from prehistoric times. Gould found that it was based on only seven male and six female prehistoric skulls. To draw conclusions on the basis of such a small sample was a serious error of judgment by Broca.

Pierre-Paul Broca died in 1880. The brains he had studied became part of the Musée Paul Broca (Broca's Museum), which later merged with the Musée de l'Homme (Museum of Man) in Paris. In a musty back room of the Museum of Man,

Carl Sagan (1979) found shelf upon shelf of bottles containing human brains. The label on one of them read "P. Broca." Broca's brain had been preserved as part of the collection he had established more than 100 years earlier.

True progress in measuring intelligence would not come from Broca's pseudo-scientific craniometry or from attempts such as those of Galton and Cattell to use physical measures of mental functions (Chapter 9) but from the work of another Frenchman, Alfred Binet. In 1984 the editors of *Science 84*, a journal published by the AAAS, included Binet's method of testing intelligence among the twenty discoveries of the twentieth century that changed our lives (Miller, 1984).

ALFRED BINET (1857–1911)

Binet's Early Life and Education

Binet's greatest contribution to psychology was developing the first psychological scales to measure intelligence. His scales quickly supplanted earlier attempts using physical measures and replaced subjective judgments and characterizations. We often assume that people we know differ in their mental abilities, but it is difficult to specify the criteria we use in making such judgments. Some people just "look" bright or dull, or perhaps they have the "right" shape of head (shades of the phrenologists discussed in Chapter 3). However, scientific attempts to use such criteria to assess intelligence have always proved futile. Many people whose professions involve evaluations of others—teachers, personnel directors, and the like—develop their own informal ways of evaluating intelligence. Some of their judgments may be acute, but they are also prone to error and prejudice and are especially troublesome when the person making such judgments has total confidence in them. Binet's great contribution was to replace such informal, subjective appraisals of intelligence with standard, uniform, objective methods.

Alfred Binet was born in Nice, France, on July 11, 1857, the only child of a physician father and a mother who had modest artistic talents (Wolf, 1973). Binet's parents separated when he was young, and he was raised by his mother. Binet first studied law and then followed the family tradition of medicine, both his grandfathers having been physicians. However, Binet did not complete his medical studies, instead deciding to concentrate his reading on psychological works. He had an independent income and so was able to pursue his interests without the pressure of earning a living. He read Francis Galton's *Hereditary Genius* (1869), Charles Darwin's *The Expression of the Emotions in Man and Animals* (1872), and the works of Alexander Bain and John Stuart Mill (Chapter 2). Binet was a self-taught library psychologist, and these books were his tutors. Such an education suited Binet, for he was an introverted person who had few friends and did not enjoy meeting people. Its disadvantage was that it deprived Binet of one of the advantages of a university education: training in critical thinking. Interaction with other students and with skilled faculty members weakens the power of the printed word and teaches a student to test and evaluate ideas, approaches, and assumptions. In the careers of many psychologists we see the influence of great teachers. In his solitary education Binet was denied such influences. Within a few years he was to pay a very heavy price for uncritically accepting the views of others (Wolf, 1973).

Binet's Early Years with Jean Charcot at La Salpêtrière

The years of solitary reading and study ended in 1883 when Binet's former schoolmate Joseph Babinski, the man who thirteen years later was to discover the infant reflex that bears his name, introduced him to Charles Féré. Féré in turn introduced Binet to his supervisor and the director of La Salpêtrière, Jean Charcot (Chapter 8). Binet was pleased to accept Charcot's offer of a staff position at the clinic and spent seven years there with Charcot as his mentor and Féré as his coworker.

Charcot was world-famous for his demonstrations of neurological and hypnotic phenomena. His clinic at La Salpêtrière was known as the "Mecca of neurology and hypnosis." Binet was dazzled by Charcot's reputation, called him the "master," and accepted without question his views on hypnosis. Charcot had described three distinct hypnotic states: lethargy, somnambulism, and catalepsy. He also believed that persons who could be hypnotized had unstable or deteriorated nervous systems. How did Charcot know they had such nervous systems? He knew because they could be hypnotized. Why could they be hypnotized? Because they had unstable or deteriorated nervous systems. Binet never challenged such circular reasoning and accepted Charcot's views unconditionally.

Binet and Féré used hypnosis in their experiments at La Salpêtrière and claimed to have discovered a new and startling phenomenon they labeled *transfer*. They reported that in hypnotized patients an act—lifting an arm, for example—could be moved or transferred from one side of the body to the other by the action of a magnet. In a similar manner, visual, auditory, and tactile sensations could be magnetically transferred from one part of the body to another. They also reported what they called perceptual and emotional *polarization*. In perceptual polarization the polar opposite of an existing perception could be induced by a magnet: a red cross hallucinated on white paper would turn green when the magnet was brought near. In emotional polarization a magnet produced an opposite emotion: a hypnotized patient showing intense fear of a piece of rubber she had been told was a snake caressed and even showed affection for the "snake" under the magnet's influence. Fear and withdrawal had been polarized into affection and approach. Transfer and polarization were described by Binet and Féré as marvelous findings that had been totally unexpected, of capital importance and inexplicable by conventional neurological theories. They believed that such effects were produced by the magnet's field and claimed that they were as reliable and easily demonstrated as the magnetic phenomena of the physical world.

Other investigators, however, were not convinced. Ambrose-Auguste Liébault had practiced hypnosis in the French town of Nancy since 1864 (Chapter 8). He had cured some physical illnesses using hypnosis and accepted the reality of certain hypnotic phenomena, but not the ones reported by Binet and Féré. In December 1885, he visited La Salpêtrière and was appalled by what he saw. Patients in the experiments had full knowledge of the expected effects, and many of the demonstrations were done on the same patient, an attractive, compliant woman nicknamed "Wit." She was in fact Binet and Féré's "Exhibit A." The experiments were poorly controlled and carelessly conducted. Liébault returned to Nancy and tried many times to obtain transfer and polarization in his own patients, but always without success. The critical difference between his experiments and those at La Salpêtrière was that his patients did not know what was expected or when the magnet was moved. He was convinced that suggestion alone had accounted for Binet and Féré's results. Their patients knew what was expected and when the effect was supposed to occur, and they complied.

Liébault also disputed Charcot's claim of a link between hypnosis and disordered nervous systems and especially Charcot's dictum that hysteria and hypnosis are always associated with each other. Some of Liébault's hysterical patients were difficult to hypnotize; their hysteria was a barrier to hypnosis. On the other hand, many strong, robust, obviously sane patients were easily hypnotized. Thus Liébault concluded that susceptibility to hypnosis bore little relationship to hysteria.

Liébault alone was a formidable opponent, but the critical chorus grew louder in 1888 when Hippolyte Bernheim, the leader of the hypnotists in Nancy, published a second edition of *Hypnosis and Suggestibility in Psychotherapy*. He accused the Salpêtrière researchers of a series of errors, especially of ignoring the influence of suggestion in their experiments. Bernheim stated as a fact that transfer and polarization could *not* be demonstrated in patients who were unaware of the expected effects. He also rejected the belief in a link between hysteria and hypnosis.

Binet and Féré responded to these criticisms with a long series of tense, dogmatic, unyielding rebuttals. Failure to replicate their results, they said, was due to the general ineptness of the Nancy hypnotists and their inability to replicate the experimental conditions exactly. They claimed to have replicated their findings thousands of times under the most carefully controlled conditions. They stated confidently that there was no possibility that their results were due to suggestion. Rather, they were due entirely to the magnet's power, and to question them was to doubt all magnetic phenomena, including those of the physical world. Binet and Féré even disputed the ability of the Nancy workers to hypnotize their patients, leading Bernheim to reply sarcastically that it seemed only the Parisians had access to "profound hypnotism," while all others had to be content with a "petty hypnotism of the provinces."

The final blow to Binet and Féré came when the Nancy workers reported that they had been able to produce both transfer and polarization in nonhysterical patients simply through suggestion and without the use of a magnet. In a most painful and humiliating manner Binet and Féré were forced to admit that they had been wrong. In 1892 Binet wrote this anguished summary of his hypnosis experiments at La Salpêtrière:

> At first, when these studies on hypnosis were returned to an honorable place
> by M. Charcot, there was a great movement of enthusiasm. Since then, we

> may as well admit it, the enthusiasm has diminished; it has often been recognized that these studies present a host of causes of error, which very often falsify the results without the knowledge of the most careful and prudent experimenter, and no one can say that he has never made a mistake; one of the principle causes of unceasing error... is suggestion, that is the influence of the operator by his words, gestures, attitudes and even silences. (Binet, 1892, pp. 67–68)

Binet had staked his reputation on these results. His humiliation in having to admit that they were due to suggestion can easily be imagined. It is a pleasure to be able to report that he was able to salvage his career from the wreckage of these years at La Salpêtrière and to make many important contributions to psychology, including, of course, his intelligence tests. However, Wolf (1973) showed that Binet was scarred by this experience. His collaborator in developing the intelligence tests, Théodore Simon, recalled that Binet never spoke of his years at La Salpêtrière and rarely mentioned Charcot's name. His concern with the effects of suggestion became almost obsessive. Binet described suggestion as "the cholera of psychology" and often warned, "Tell me what you are looking for and I will tell you what you will find" (Tuddenham, 1974, p. 1072). His concerns and warnings were clear anticipations of later concerns among psychologists with experimenter effects (Rosenthal, 1966) and the demand characteristics of psychological experiments (Orne, 1962). Binet became increasingly withdrawn and rarely attended meetings of psychologists. G. Stanley Hall (Chapter 10) invited him to the 1899 (10th anniversary) and 1909 conferences at Clark University, but both invitations were declined. The dark side of his personality was expressed in writing and producing Gothic plays with melodramatic themes of terror, murder, and psychopathology; four of his dramas were staged in Paris, to modest success.

Binet's Research on the Development of Cognition

Binet resigned from the Salpêtrière clinic in 1890 and was then without a professional position. His interests turned toward his own family and especially to developmental studies of his children, Madeleine and Alice (Varon, 1935). At the time Madeleine was four and a half years old and Alice two and a half. Binet was struck by the individual differences between them: Madeleine always concentrated firmly, whereas Alice was more impulsive; Madeleine was often silent, cool, and controlled, whereas Alice was gay, usually laughing, giddy, and turbulent. In 1890 Binet published three papers describing his observations, using the pseudonyms Margeurite and Armande for the girls. He stated that the girls recognized things in simple line drawings and were able to describe the uses of everyday objects. Binet also devised a number of tests of his daughters' thinking. Madeleine was asked which of two piles of coins, beans, or tokens contained more. Binet found that Madeleine judged not in terms of the number of objects but in terms of the space on the table they covered; the more space covered, the greater the number of objects she would report. In another test Binet showed Madeleine a number of familiar objects and then took them out of sight. When more than five objects were shown, removed, and then brought back one by one, Madeleine always reported that there were more than there actually were. Binet's experiments with his daughters anticipated Jean Piaget's mid-twentieth-century research on the development of cognition in children. Binet's death in 1911 deprived Piaget of the opportunity of working with him. However, Piaget did work in 1920 in the laboratory school of Binet's collaborator Simon (Elkind, 1974, p. 14). There he analyzed the "wrong" answers that children regularly gave to questions on intelligence tests. Piaget was surprised to find that the responses fell into patterns that differed according to the children's ages. Returning to Geneva's Rousseau Institute, Piaget devoted his life to studies of the development of cognition (Gerow, 1988, p. 53).

Binet at the Sorbonne

In 1891 Binet joined the Laboratory of Physiological Psychology at the Sorbonne, working without salary until 1892, when he was appointed associate director. In 1894 he assumed the laboratory's directorship. At the Sorbonne, Binet conducted many research studies and published prolifically. One can only assume that his driving energy and dedication to psychology allowed him to do this, together with the fact that for Binet "one of my greatest pleasures is to have a piece of white paper to fill up. I work as naturally as a hen lays eggs" (Wolf, 1973, p. 34). His research can best be described as functionalist studies of individual psychology: the perception of inkblots; memory, imagery, and creative and imageless thought; handwriting; and the reliability of eyewitness testimony. He also described children's fears and the effects of fatigue on workers.

In addition to directing the Sorbonne laboratory and doing his own prolific research, Binet served during these years as director and editor in chief of the leading French journal of psychology, *L'Année psychologique,* founded in 1875. Binet solicited and edited the contributions of others, published hundreds of pages of his own writings, and even attended to the journal's often trying business affairs.

Binet's Tests of Intelligence

In 1899 Binet was invited to become a member of the newly founded Société Libre pour l'Étude Psychologique de l'Enfant (the Free Society for the Psychological Study of the Child). The word *free* in the society's name was significant, for the founding group of teachers, principals, and physicians hoped to free themselves from the old pedagogy and begin scientific studies of children. As a member of this society Binet had access to children in public schools, an important consideration since his notoriety after the Salpêtrière years had led to his being barred from many schools. That same year Théodore Simon, a young medical student, nominated himself to be Binet's research assistant. He became Binet's most important collaborator, working with him on the intelligence tests that bear their names.

In 1899 the members of this society launched a campaign to persuade the French Ministry of Public Instruction to do something about the problem of retarded children in the schools. In 1903 the ministry, as bureaucracies are prone to do, appointed a commission to study the problem. Binet and fifteen other people, many of them members of the society, were appointed to this Commission for the Retarded. In 1904 the commission resolved unanimously that children in the schools judged by their teachers to be "refractory to education" should be given a "medico-pedagogical examination" and, if found educable, placed in a special class annexed to a regular school or in a special establishment. But what should the "medico-pedagogical examination" consist of? Binet defined the problem as

> establishing scientifically the anthropometric and mental differences that separate the normal child from the abnormal: of making these differences exact, of measuring them in some way so that their assessment ceases to be a matter of tact and intuition, but rather becomes something objective and tangible. (Binet, 1904, p. 408)

Binet set out to measure such differences. He described his methods in 1903 in his masterful book *L'Étude experimentale de l'intelligence* (Experimental Studies of Intelligence). He had used a number of tests:

1. Association tests in which a child was given twenty-five to thirty words and asked to describe the idea each word aroused
2. Sentence completion tests similar to the ones used by Ebbinghaus (Chapter 6)
3. Themes on a given topic
4. Picture descriptions and memory tests
5. Object drawing and description
6. Digit repetition and other memory and attention tests
7. Tests of moral judgment

Binet and Simon developed twenty such tests and also investigated other possible measures of intelligence and the relationships between them. Simon wrote his thesis on Broca's craniometry and head measurements, concluding that such measures were of little value in assessing intelligence. Binet and Simon also considered graphology, concluding that it was of some value but that something more was needed to truly measure and evaluate intelligence.

In 1905 Binet and Simon published a number of papers in *L'Année psychologique* describing a new scale for the measurement of intelligence in children, the 1905 Binet-Simon scale. Their first paper gave what they described as a "rough sketch" of a way to diagnose inferior states of intelligence, and the second gave further details of their methods and the tests themselves. The scale was to be given under controlled conditions, which they were careful to specify, and was said to measure general intelligence, which Binet considered to be a "fundamental faculty" to make correct judgments, show initiative, and adapt to circumstances. The 1905 scale included thirty tests arranged in order of difficulty. Each child passed as many tests as possible. Though they had given the tests to many Parisian schoolchildren, Binet and Simon did not consider the scale in any way a final test of intelligence or a solution to the problem of diagnosing retarded children. Rather, it was a beginning, a first step in investigating the nature of intelligence. Between 1905 and 1908 Binet and Simon gave the tests to large numbers of schoolchildren, and arranged the children in a hierarchical order based on their performance.

In 1908 Binet and Simon described a revised scale. Fourteen of the original tests were retained, nine were dropped, and seven were modified; thirty-three new tests were added. In addition, the tests were arranged according to age levels from three to thirteen. In this arrangement Binet and Simon's guiding principle was that a child should test "at age"; that is, the average five-year-old should show a mental level of five, and so on. If a majority, usually 75 to 90 percent, of the children in a particular age group passed a test, it was assigned to that age level. It is important to note Binet and Simon's use of the term *mental level* rather than the later, more common term *mental age*. The latter term was introduced in 1911 by a German psychologist, Wilhelm Stern, but was firmly rejected by Binet and Simon. To them mental age implied something endogenous, fixed, and similar to chronological age. They used the term *mental level* to emphasize change and fluctuation. A child's mental level, as measured by their tests, could change. They believed that even the mental level of retarded children could be raised and devised a system of orthopedic training for the retarded that rivaled that of Maria Montessori for normal children. It was also Stern who introduced the *mental quotient* as a ratio of mental age to chronological age. Scores below and above 1 were indicators of retardation and superior intelligence, respectively. When multiplied by 100, the mental quotient yields an intelligence quotient (IQ). Binet and Simon strongly opposed the use of IQ, feeling that it would be misleading and even dangerous. Despite their opposition, the simple-to-compute and easily understood IQ quickly became the standard way of describing performance on intelligence tests. However, Binet and Simon always opposed its use. When the eighty-six-year-old Simon was interviewed in 1959, he passionately described the IQ as "a betrayal of the scale's objectives" (Wolf, 1973, p. 203). Shortly before Binet's death in 1911 a third "still unfinished" revision of the Binet-Simon scale was published, which differed from the earlier ones only in its details. The tests were now arranged for mental levels from three to fifteen years, and there were five tests for adults. Scoring was modified to allow credits for each test a child passed above a basal year, a change that Binet accepted reluctantly, as he was too sophisticated to believe that intelligence could be parceled into fractions of mental levels.

The Binet-Simon scales provided what had long been sought: a way to measure intelligence that was easy to administer and reasonably brief. The scales were an immediate success. Twenty-two thousand copies of the 1908 scale were distributed in three years, and 50,000 copies of the 1911 revision were distributed in five years. At the outbreak of World War I in 1914 the tests were being used in at least a dozen countries. Often the scales were simply translated without an attempt to standardize them for the new setting. Intelligence testing was an idea whose time had come, and the imperative to use the scales was overwhelming. Binet's death at the age of 54 in 1911, together with the disruption caused by the war, prevented the later revisions of the scales Binet and Simon would certainly have made.

Instead of careful revisions of the original scales, intelligence testing developed in a way Binet did not anticipate and certainly would not have welcomed: mass testing of large numbers of adults and children. Before the end of the war, 1,700,000 inductees to the United States Army had been tested; within thirty months of Lewis M. Terman's introduction of the Binet-Simon test in the United States, some 4 million children had been tested. The time lag between Binet and Simon's first scale in 1905 and these large-scale testing programs was very short. These developments will be considered later in this chapter. However, before leaving Binet, two post-humous recognitions that surely would have pleased him must be mentioned. In 1917 members of the Free Society for the Psychological Study of the Child voted to change their name to La Société Alfred Binet, a fitting and appropriate memorial to a great psychologist. In November 1984 the editors of the American Association for the Advancement of Science's journal *Science '84* selected Binet's development of the intelligence test as one of the twenty most significant developments or discoveries in science, technology, and medicine of this century (Hammond, 1984, p. 9).

HENRY H. GODDARD (1866–1957)

Henry H. Goddard was one of two men primarily responsible for introducing the Binet-Simon scales to the United States, Lewis M. Terman being the other. Goddard received a Ph.D in psychology at Clark University in 1899, having been encouraged and influenced by G. Stanley Hall (Chapter 9). He was an active and vigorous person who had climbed the Matterhorn as a young man and kept a photograph of the mountain above his desk (Burtt, 1980). In 1906 Goddard was appointed director of the Research Laboratory for the Study of Feeble-Mindedness at the Vineland Training School for the Feeble-Minded in New Jersey. There he became convinced of two critical needs: a reliable means of distinguishing between normal and feeble-minded children and a reliable way of distinguishing between different levels of mental ability in both normal and feebleminded children. Binet's scales promised to meet both needs. Goddard translated the 1908 scale into English and made some small alterations, such as changing the names of coins from sous to cents. However, all his changes were minor, and while his scales are sometimes called Goddard's revisions of the Binet-Simon scales, it is more correct to think of them as translations.

Goddard administered the translated scales to 400 children at Vineland and 2,000 children in the New Jersey public schools (Goddard, 1911b). They satisfied his psychometric needs. The scores of the children at Vineland and those in the public schools were usually very different, although he did discover that an alarming number of public school children tested below their age norms; he also found a wide range of scores in both the Vineland and the public school children. Goddard was convinced of the scales' value and from then on was an enthusiastic advocate of intelligence testing. He saw a need for testing in the public schools and began courses at Vineland in which teachers were trained to administer and score the tests. When Binet's 1911 scale appeared, Goddard immediately translated it. Until Terman's ambitious 1916 revision of the Binet scale, Goddard's 1911 translation was the standard test instrument in the United States.

The Kallikaks

Goddard also conducted a famous—some might say infamous—investigation of the inheritability of intelligence: his study of the Kallikak family (Goddard, 1912). He described his book *The Kallikak Family* as the real story of genuine people and subtitled it *A Study in the Heredity of Feeble-Mindedness.* The scientific background to this study of human inheritance consisted of experiments on plant inheritance conducted fifty years earlier by an obscure Austrian monk, Gregor Mendel (1822–1884). Mendel's experiments had produced a revolution in biology and provided the impetus for Goddard's work. Mendel came from a poor Austrian family, joined an order of monks to gain an education, and studied at the University of Vienna, intending to become a schoolteacher. He took the final examination twice but failed both times. The examiners found his knowledge of physical science adequate but concluded that he was not fit to teach natural history and biology. One professor said of Mendel that "he lacks insight and the requisite clarity of knowledge" (Bronowski, 1973, p. 380). Having failed to qualify as a teacher, Mendel was sent by his order to the monastery at Brno in Moravia, now part of Czechoslovakia, and was assigned to the kitchen garden. Mendel accepted the assignment willingly, for plants and animals had always fascinated him. The garden plants and animals became his "children," and he tended them with care and attention. Beginning in 1856 and continuing for eight years, Mendel conducted some of the most important experiments in the history of biology.

First Mendel worked with honeybees. He hoped to combine the gentleness of a race of Italian honeybees with the greater industriousness of a German race. Un-

Gregor Mendel. (The Bettmann Archive)

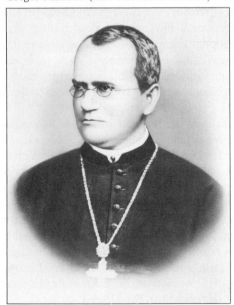

fortunately, what his breeding experiment produced was a colony of highly aggressive hybrid bees (Gould, 1982, p. 308), so Mendel turned to working with plants. His experiments were all done in the monastery's 120-foot by 20-foot vegetable garden. Mendel studied the characteristics of the most common of all kitchen garden plants, the pea: blossom color, smooth or wrinkled skin, shape, and most important, stem length. He performed numerous breeding experiments on the inheritance of these characteristics. The results of his experiments established for the first time a valid set of principles of genetic inheritance. To illustrate Mendel's methods and conclusions, let us consider his experiments on the inheritance of stem length. First, Mendel bred a hybrid of tall and short pea plants by artificially inseminating short plants from tall ones. The hybrid peas bore seeds that he then planted. Existing genetic principles predicted that the resulting plants would be a blend of the parental characteristics, that is, that they would be of medium height. Mendel's peas, however, were not of medium height—they were *all* tall. Next he bred the second generation by fertilizing the hybrids with their own pollen. Their peas were planted, and the resulting plants were measured. In this generation Mendel found a majority of tall plants but a significant minority of short-stemmed plants. He guessed that height in pea plants is controlled by two factors, one contributed by each parent. Today we call Mendel's "factors" genes. If the two parental factors are different, Mendel assumed that one would be dominant and one recessive. His first generation of peas had shown the tallness factor to be dominant. However, in the second generation one mating in every four should, on the basis of chance, have caused two recessive factors to come together and so produce a plant that was short. If tallness is represented by A and shortness by a, with A being dominant, then of the four possible combinations AA, Aa, aA, and aa, only the last (aa) produces a short plant: one out of four or a ratio of one to three pea plants should be short. Among the 1,064 second-generation plants Mendel measured, in 787 cases the stem was long and in 277 it was short, a ratio of 2.84 to 1. The numbers had come out right.

In fact the match between Mendel's theoretical predictions and the results was so close that the validity of his results has been questioned. The statistical geneticist R. A. Fisher asserted that the probability of results as close to the predicted values as Mendel's is less than one in 30,000 (Dunbar, 1984, p. 38). Other critics have claimed variously that Mendel deliberately doctored his data, that he was cheated by an assistant, that he counted only as many plants as were necessary to have the right ratio, that he saw what he wanted to see or, finally, that he was simply lucky. A recent alternative explanation is more convincing. Robert Root-Bernstein (1983) suggested that in sorting his peas Mendle used what are today called "fuzzy sets". When an attempt is made to classify a continuously variable quality into discrete categories, problems arise over intermediate or "fuzzy" cases at the boundaries. The qualities Mendel studied—height, stem length, and blossom color—are "fuzzy," and so Mendel may have used "fuzzy logic" in his sorting. Mendel recognized this problem in categorization and often set aside awkward cases to be assessed later. So the close match he obtained may have been to some degree the consequence of the categories being used.

In 1856 Mendel presented a study entitled "Experiments on Plant-Hybridization" at a meeting of the local Society for the Study of Natural Science. The audience was large and initially attentive, but there were neither questions nor discussion (Iltis, 1932, p. 179). Ten years later Mendel tried again, publishing his results in the *Journal of the Brno Natural History Society*, where they achieved instant oblivion. Shortly thereafter Mendel's career as an experimental biologist ended when he was elected abbot of his monastery. His administrative duties precluded further research, which was probably just as well, for his superiors were suspicious of his "tampering with nature." To be sure that his research would not have heretical results, his fellow monks burned all Mendel's research papers and notes after his death in 1884.

Mendel's paper remained in obscurity for over thirty years until it was discovered and republished by a number of scholars, including the Dutch botanist Hugo de Vries. Goddard read de Vries's 1900 account of Mendel's experiments and wondered whether Mendelian principles might account for the inheritance of feeblemindedness. The leap from pea length, color, and form to something as complex as human intelligence seems enormous, but to Goddard the possibility was quite reasonable. He was convinced that both high and low levels of intelligence are inherited, for he had read Galton's reports of hereditary genius (Chapter 9) and had also discovered that many of the brothers and sisters of the children at Vineland had themselves been judged feebleminded and often institutionalized. For further study he sought a family. Goddard called the people he found the Kallikaks.

In 1897 a young girl, Deborah Kallikak, was admitted to the Vineland Institute at the age of eight. Fourteen years later, in 1911, she was tested with the Binet-Simon scale and found to have a mental age of nine years, leading Goddard to classify her as a "moron," a term he introduced to psychology from the Greek *moros*, meaning "dull" (Burtt & Pressey, 1957). Goddard described Deborah as

> a typical illustration of the mentality of a high grade feeble-minded person,
> the moron, the delinquent, the kind of girl or woman that fills our
> reformatories. They are wayward, they get into all sorts of trouble and
> difficulties, sexually and otherwise, and yet we have been accustomed to
> account for their defects on the basis of viciousness, environment, or
> ignorance. (Goddard, 1912, p. 11)

Goddard investigated Deborah's family background and traced her ancestry back to the American Revolution, when a soldier of good family, Martin Kallikak, Sr., had a "casual intimacy" with a feebleminded barmaid which led to the birth of a boy, Martin Kallikak, Jr. After the war was over Martin Senior left the Army and became a wealthy and respectable citizen. He married a "worthy girl" from a Quaker family, and they had seven children—the "good" side of the Kallikaks. Martin Junior also married and had ten children—the "bad" side of the Kallikak family. Goddard investigated the children of both marriages, seeking evidence of their mental status. He concluded that none of the children of the Quaker woman was subnormal, while five of the children of Martin Junior were feebleminded. In later generations the difference between the two lines of the Kallikak family became even more striking. Among the descendants of Martin Junior, Goddard claimed to have found 46 normal people, 143 who were definitely feebleminded, 36 illegitimate births, 33 sexually immoral people, 3 epileptics, and 24 alcoholics. These people were horse thieves, paupers, convicts, prostitutes, criminals, and keepers of houses of ill repute—the riffraff of society.

The 495 descendants of the marriage to the Quaker woman were very different: only three "somewhat mentally degenerate people," two alcoholics, one sexually loose person, and no illegitimate births or epileptics. In this family line Goddard found doctors, lawyers, judges, traders, educators, and landholders—the pillars of society. The differences between the two family lines could not have been more striking, and to Goddard they provided overwhelming evidence for the inheritance of degeneracy along classic Mendelian lines. Goddard wrote that the Kallikaks provided

> as it were a natural experiment with a normal branch with which to compare
> our defective side. We have one ancestor giving us a line of normal people
> that shows thoroughly good all the way down the generations, with the
> exception of the one man who was sexually loose and the two who gave way
> to the appetite for strong drink. This is our norm, our standard, our
> demonstration of what the Kallikak blood is when kept pure, or mingled
> with blood as good as its own. Over against this we have the bad side, the
> blood of the same ancestor contaminated by that of the defective mentality
> and bad blood having been brought into the normal family of good blood,
> first from the nameless feeble-minded girl and later by additional contamina-
> tion from other sources.
>
> The biologist could hardly plan and carry out a more rigid experiment or
> one from which the conclusions would follow more inevitably. (Goddard,
> 1912, pp. 68–69)

Goddard's conclusion that feeblemindedness is inherited was quoted widely (J. D. Smith, 1985). The Kallikaks were indeed different, and these differences were highlighted by Goddard's graphic language: Martin Junior is referred to as "Old Horror," and the descriptions of the poverty, licentiousness, degradations, and general horror of the lives of his descendants are reminiscent of Dickens. Even the name Goddard chose for the family is significant. Goddard (1942) claimed that *Kallikak* meant "the nameless one," but a root in the Greek words *kalos* meaning "good" and *kakos* meaning "bad" is likely. The Kallikaks quickly became a feature of social science texts, with Goddard's results often being presented in highly simplified summaries. As recently as 1955 a *General Psychology* text by Henry Garrett, the chairman of Columbia's Department of Psychology for sixteen years and president of the APA in 1946, included a figure summarizing Goddard's results. Children in the "good" side of the family were depicted as worthy, Quaker types; children from the "bad" side were shown as little devils, complete with horns (Garrett, 1955, p. 65).

Obviously, the control Mendel had of his pea patch cannot be attained in studying the inheritance of human intelligence. In addition, Goddard's investigation had numerous methodological and procedural weaknesses:

1. The whole study took just two years, which seems very short for a study of this magnitude and detail.
2. The research assistants who worked with Goddard were people interested in social problems, but they had little training in genealogical research or interviewing. They were inspired by Goddard's crusading zeal, knew the aims of his study, and thus might have been biased.
3. There was little objective testing of the family members, and conclusions about a person's intelligence were often inferences from passing observations. In many cases the investigator was not even able to see the person, who could not be found, was uncooperative, or was dead. For these people reports from family members, friends, neighbors, associates, pastors, and others were used. At other times a person's occupation and standing in the community were used to estimate intelligence.
4. Criminal behavior and feeblemindedness were often equated. If a family member had a criminal record, he or she was classified as feebleminded.
5. Galton's assumption that feeblemindedness is caused by a single recessive Mendelian gene is implausible.
6. Finally, while the different environments of the two lines were described graphically, their influence was largely ignored. Goddard even went so far as to describe the environments of the two family lines as "practically the same." Clearly that was not the case. To cite two obvious differences, medical care and nutrition must have been very different. Such differences were reflected in the numbers of infant deaths: eighty-two in the "bad" family and fifteen in the "good" family.

In 1981 Stephen Jay Gould (1981) added another criticism of the Kallikak investigation with his assertion that Goddard had tampered with at least five photographs shown in *The Kallikak Family* by adding crude dark lines to accentuate the unfavorable facial features of members of the bad side of the family. A photographic expert who examined the photographs stated:

> The harshness clearly gives the impression of dark, staring features,
> sometimes evilness, and sometimes mental retardation. It would be difficult
> to understand why any of this retouching was done were it not to give the
> viewer a false impression of the characteristics of those depicted. (James H.
> Wallace, Jr., quoted in Gould, 1981, p. 171)

Gould concluded that Goddard had been guilty of "conscious skullduggery" (Gould, 1981, p. 171). Raymond Fancher in his history of the IQ controversy (Fancher, 1985, p. 114) reported that several of Goddard's Kallikak photos had been "doctored," but more recently he proposed an intriguing alternative explanation (Fancher, 1987). Fancher found a press photograph of a 1920s Canadian sportsman that had been retouched in much the same way as the Kallikak photos had. The retouching had been done before publication to avoid an impression of blank-facedness; that, rather than "conscious skulduggery," might have been the motive for Goddard's retouching. In addition, since Goddard believed that the feebleminded usually appear normal, he would have been unlikely to have retouched photographs so as to make the "bad Kallikaks" appear more depraved (Fancher, 1987, pp. 586–588). Fancher concluded:

> I would now suggest that any "evil," "sinister," or "retarded" qualities
> added to the Kallikak photos may lie more in the eye of the beholder than in
> the ulterior or dishonest motives of the retoucher. (Fancher, 1987, p. 588)

Eugenic Sterilization

Goddard's study of the Kallikaks spawned a host of similar studies of the Jukes, the Hill Folk, the Nams, the Ishmaelites, and the Zeros—families reportedly showing high levels of social and intellectual degeneracy. Such "bad seed" families were all reported to be reproducing at over twice the rate of normal families. Though Goddard had found 480 "bad" Kallikaks and 495 "good" Kallikaks, he did not hesitate to publicize what he considered to be a genetic threat to the American people. He served on the Committee for the Heredity of the Feeble-Minded, which recommended that mentally defective people be sterilized. Goddard described sterilization of males as being almost as simple as having a tooth pulled. He also served as the psychological consultant appointed by the Eugenics Section of the American Breeders' Association to report practical methods of eliminating "defective people" from the population of the United States. This committee recommended in 1914 that the "defective classes be eliminated from the human stock through sterilization." Such "defective classes" included the feebleminded, paupers, criminals, epileptics, the insane, and the congenitally handicapped (Van Wagenen, 1914, pp. 186–187).

These Draconian recommendations were made not by a fringe group of crackpots but by a committee advised by such luminaries as Alexander Graham Bell; Walter B. Cannon, the famed Harvard physiologist, (Chapter 9); and Robert Yerkes, Edward Lee Thorndike, and Lewis Terman, three of the most eminent psychologists of the day. This was the authentic voice of the scientific establishment, and it was heard.

The first state sterilization law was passed by Indiana in 1907. During the next twenty-one years twenty additional states were to pass laws permitting eugenical sterilizations (Karier, 1976, p. 345). Between 1924 and 1972 some 8,300 sterilizations were performed in Virginia. Many of these laws remained in place until the 1960s, and one survey of these operations concluded that "the numbers would be staggering to the imagination if we knew exactly how many [people] were sterilized nationwide" (Nelson, 1980).

Reports of sterilization appeared regularly in the psychological journals of the 1920s and 1930s. In general the articles described positive outcomes of the sterilization of mentally and socially "defective" people. Goddard reported that he had not observed a single bad consequence following sterilization. It was quickly becoming the procedure of choice for many mental and social problems. When the

German sterilization law was passed in 1933, an editorial in the American journal *Eugenical News* praised the Reich for leading "the great nations of the world in the recognition of the biological foundations of national character" and noted that the German sterilization law "constituted a milestone which marks the control by the most advanced nations of the world of a major aspect of controlling human reproduction, comparable in importance to the state's legal control of marriage" (editorial, quoted by Tucker, 1987, p. 288). Recommendations for "positive eugenical measures" were common in Europe and the United States. They included incentives and encouragements to the "best" people to marry at an early age and to have large families. Such recommendations are now seen as social planning at its worst. In one case they led to an amusing exchange. The beautiful American dancer Isadora Duncan suggested to George Bernard Shaw that together they could produce a baby with her body and his brain. Shaw reluctantly declined her invitation, wittily pointing out that their baby was just as likely to have *his* body and *her* brain.

Goddard at Ellis Island

A second threat to the integrity of the American genetic constitution was seen in the flood of immigrants entering the country in the decades before and after the turn of the century. America was perceived as the land of opportunity, and millions of

"Immigration Restriction Prop Wanted."
A 1903 *Philadelphia Inquirer* cartoon
supporting restrictive immigration laws.
(Courtesy of the New York Public Library)

people answered the call. Between 1905 and 1914 over 10 million immigrants entered the United States, primarily from Southern and Eastern Europe. For many of them America fulfilled its promise, but for many "native" or "old" Americans, that is, people whose families had been here for more than one generation, the flood of immigrants raised fears that the country was being swamped and undermined by socially and mentally defective people. Even immigrants who were able to work and find employment were feared, for it was claimed that they would provide an impetus for the development of unions, which would threaten the American economic system (Blum, 1978). Such views were based on prejudice and a gangplank view of immigration—"I'm ashore, so pull up the gangplank"—but they were widely shared and politically potent. With as many as 10,000 immigrants arriving every day, how were "defective people" to be recognized and deported? The immigration inspectors did in fact order the deportation of 10 percent of the would-be immigrants; tens of thousands of people were sent back to their native lands, but not enough to assuage fears that the country was being overrun. In 1882 Congress passed a law forbidding entry to the United States of lunatics and idiots, but how were they to be detected among the great mass of humanity arriving every day? Additional measures were needed to ensure that undesirables were not slipping through Ellis Island's golden door. One such measure was the use of psychological tests.

In 1913 the commissioner of immigration invited Goddard to Ellis Island to study immigrant screening procedures. His first visit was initially disappointing, since a fog in the harbor had delayed the ships and none of the expected 5,000 immigrants arrived. Goddard did see 100 earlier arrivals. They had completed their interviews, inspections, and medical examinations without being tagged with the dreaded chalk deportation X and were about to leave. Goddard asked that they be lined up for his inspection. He walked down the line and selected one young man he judged to be mentally defective. Through an interpreter Goddard gave him the Binet test. The man tested at the mental age of eight, apparently confirming Goddard's selection. The interpreter, however, protested that the test was unfair as the questions were unfamiliar. He argued that he would not have been able to answer them when he had first entered the country. Goddard firmly disagreed. The commissioner was impressed by Goddard's ability to pick out a mentally defective person and have his selection "confirmed" by a psychological test. Perhaps others could be trained to make such selections. The commissioner invited Goddard to return to Ellis Island the next week.

Goddard stationed one of his assistants to review the immigrants as they walked by, and she picked out nine people judged to be defective. On the Binet test all nine were below normal. Again the commissioner was impressed and invited Goddard and his coworkers to return for a more extended period. They spent a week on Ellis Island. Goddard claimed that they were able to detect 90 percent of the feebleminded immigrants by looking at them. In a small number of cases their selections were said to have been confirmed by psychological testing. Goddard concluded that psychological methods would

> be of tremendous value in the immigration problem. . . . Using the psychological method of examining, the percentage of immigrants that would be

picked out as defective would be much greater than now. (Goddard, 1913,
p. 107)

Goddard's prediction was soon confirmed. Immigration inspectors on Ellis Island
began to use "psychological methods," and the number of deportations of allegedly
feebleminded people rose dramatically. In 1913 and 1914, there were 350 percent
and 570 percent more deportations, respectively, than there had been in the preceding five years (Williams, 1914). Thousands of people were being refused admission to the United States because they appeared feebleminded or performed
below average on the Binet test.

The immigration officials welcomed Goddard's work as a scientific solution
of one aspect of the immigration problem. His funding was increased, and he was
asked to continue his work on Ellis Island. Three members of his staff spent three
months there in 1914, testing 178 people from a group of average steerage passen-
gers who were about to enter the United States. Through interpreters the immigrants were given the Binet and DeSanctis tests. In the latter the person was asked
such everyday questions as "What is Crisco?" and "Who is Christy Matthewson?"
They also used two board tests in which geometric forms had to be fitted together
to assess mechanical ability. The immigrants' performance was poor, especially on
the Binet and DeSanctis tests, perhaps not surprisingly, given the language difficulty and cultural differences. How many Hungarians used Crisco or followed the
New York Giants? Goddard drew a very different conclusion. He reported the results as showing that 83 percent of the Jews, 80 percent of the Hungarians, 79
percent of the Italians, and 87 percent of the Russians tested were feebleminded
(Goddard, 1917, p. 252). Such results seemed to confirm "that a surprisingly large
percentage of immigrants are of relatively low mentality" (Goddard, 1917, p. 269).
Restrictive immigration quotas were soon to be legislated, with Goddard's findings,
together with those of other psychologists to be considered later in this chapter,
providing scientific justification. Before considering this sorry and tragic aspect of
psychology's past we must briefly consider Goddard's later career and Lewis
Terman's contributions to the development of psychology, especially psychological
testing.

Goddard's Work with Gifted Children

Goddard left Vineland in 1918 for a position as director of the Ohio State Bureau
of Juvenile Research. He held that position until 1922, when he was appointed
professor of abnormal and clinical psychology at the Ohio State University, remaining there until his retirement in 1938. During his years at Ohio State, Goddard
studied the other end of the mental ability continuum: the intellectually gifted.
Early in 1922 a group of concerned and public-spirited women in Cleveland organized a committee to promote special education for the intellectually gifted. Goddard
served as the committee's consultant and adviser for the next five years. As a result
of the committee's efforts, in the 1920s the Cleveland public schools had one of the
most extensive and progressive programs for the education of gifted children in the
United States. In *School Training for Gifted Children* (1938), Goddard described the

Cleveland program. He advocated what he termed "enrichment," that is, expanded educational opportunities for gifted children, rather than rapid promotion schemes in which gifted children were promoted to higher grades. Goddard believed that gifted children would benefit most from being placed in special classrooms with other gifted children. Every effort should then be made to enrich their classroom experiences. Some 600 children from all grade levels participated in the Cleveland program. In his book Goddard described the children and many of their activities in detail. The activities are indeed impressive: full-scale productions of plays, elaborate sculptures, intricate mathematical games, publication of a school paper, and always equal participation by girls and boys. Seeing the children's photographs and reading about them, one wonders what became of them as adults. Terman was soon to begin his study of gifted children in California, described later in this chapter, but the Cleveland children were never followed up. It would be fascinating to know what sort of lives Goddard's children led, especially as they were young men and women during the years of the Great Depression. How did they manage in that harsh economic environment? Did they fulfill their intellectual promise? As adults how did they assess their school experience? Unfortunately, these questions remain unanswered for the Cleveland children, but similar questions were soon to be answered for Terman's children. However, before considering that famous investigation, we will outline Terman's other important contribution: the Stanford revisions of the Binet tests.

LEWIS M. TERMAN (1877–1956)

Terman's Early Life

Lewis M. Terman was born on an Indiana farm in 1877, the twelfth in a family of fourteen children. He entered school at the age of six and within six months was promoted to the third grade. Schoolwork came easily to the bookish Terman, but in most ways his life was no different from that of any other boy growing up in rural Indiana in the late nineteenth century. He was expected to help on the farm and spent summers working full time on the land until he was eighteen. Terman (1932) recalled that even as a boy he had been interested in personality differences among his friends and schoolmates. He also found that through monotonous repetition of a phrase he could lose entirely his sense of personal identity and his orientation in time and space. He would gaze fixedly at something and repeat "Is this me? Is this me? Is this me?" until he entered a mystical haze. Terman had discovered his mantra. When Terman was ten, a traveling book peddler sold his family a phrenology text. He spent a night with the Termans discoursing on the new science of phrenology (Chapter 3) and reading the bumps on their heads. He predicted great things for Lewis Terman, who remained interested in phrenology until he was fifteen. Thus a phrenology text introduced Terman to the measurement of individual differences.

    When Terman was fifteen his parents sent him to Central Normal College in Danville, Indiana, to prepare for a career as a schoolteacher. He was pleased to escape from the endless chores, arduous plowing, and dull routine of farm life. Terman graduated in 1895, taught in a number of rural schools, entered Indiana University, and obtained an M.A. degree in 1903. He was attracted by Hall's writings and approach to psychology (Chapter 9). With Hall's support, Terman obtained a fellowship that allowed him to enter Clark University in 1903. He delighted in Clark's free academic atmosphere: no majors or minors, no course requirements or formal lectures, no grades, and no examinations other than the final four-hour doctoral oral. At their first meeting Hall reassured Terman by referring to his "splendid training" at Indiana and the "fine reports" he had received from his former teachers. Only later did Terman learn that such reassurances were a favorite device of the crafty Hall.

At first Terman worked under Hall, but when he decided to use mental tests in his thesis research, Terman was forced to change advisers. As we have seen, Hall disapproved of mental tests, distrusting what he termed their "quasi-exactness," and so Edmund Sanford directed Terman's research. Terman graduated from Clark in 1905. During his years there he developed tuberculosis and so was forced to seek a position in a warm climate. At first he was the principal of a high school in San Bernardino, California; later he became a faculty member at the Los Angeles Normal School. He remained there for four years before joining the faculty of Stanford University in 1910. Thus the Indiana farm boy found himself "a member of the faculty of Stanford University, the university that I would have chosen before any other in the world" (Terman, 1932, p. 323). Terman remained at Stanford for the rest of his life, serving the university as one of its most distinguished teachers and researchers and, as chairman, helping to establish one of the finest psychology departments in the world.

Terman's Revision of the Binet-Simon Scales

At Stanford, Terman began an investigation of the strengths and weaknesses of the Binet-Simon intelligence test that led to his revising the original scale. Terman described his revision in *The Measurement of Intelligence* (1916) and dedicated it

> to the memory of Alfred Binet: Patient researcher, creative thinker,
> unpretentious scholar; inspiring and fruitful devotee of inductive and
> dynamic psychology. (Terman, 1916, p. v)

The book is a classic in psychology, although Terman was surprised by its favorable reception and psychologists' rapid acceptance of his revision. In revising the scale, Terman and his coworkers used a standardization sample of 2,300 people: 1,700 normal children, 200 defective and superior children, and 400 adults.

Terman's was by far the most extensive and varied standardization sample to have been used to that time. Besides the original Binet-Simon test items, Terman included ten additional items in the pool of potential test items from which the final revision items were selected. In selecting test items Terman's aim was to arrange the different tests so that the median mental and chronological ages of a group of unselected children would coincide: the average child of ten should test at the mental age of ten, the average child of twelve should test at the mental age of twelve, and so on. Terman found many of the test items from the original Binet-Simon scale too easy at the younger ages and too difficult at the older ones so that the average child of five would test above the mental age of five while the average child of twelve would test below the mental age of twelve. Sometimes a child's IQ would show a sudden decrease at adolescence as an artifact of the test items themselves. In revising the scale Terman constantly added and deleted test items until it yielded an average IQ of 100 for unselected groups of children of any age. Ninety tests were included in the final 1916 Stanford revision of the Binet-Simon scale. This revision quickly became the standard measure of children's intelligence. Terman considered its strengths to be

1. The large and varied standardization sample
2. The use of IQ to represent a child's performance
3. The clear, detailed, and well-organized instructions for administering the test

Given these strengths, the question of the validity of Terman's revision remains. How well did the scale measure what it was supposed to measure? How accurate a measure of a child's intelligence did it provide? Terman went to great lengths to assess the validity of the scale. He compared teachers' gradings of the schoolwork of 504 children with the children's IQ scores. Fairly close agreement was found, but in one case out of ten there was disagreement. He also found a correlation of 0.48 between teacher estimates of intelligence and IQ scores and a good correlation between grades and IQ scores. It is somewhat anomalous that much of the impetus for the development of intelligence tests came from dissatisfaction with teacher ratings and evaluations of intelligence, which now were being used to assess the validity of the tests themselves. However, Terman's difficulty is easily understood, since the selection of appropriate validity criteria for intelligence tests remains a problem today.

In the United States the 1916 Stanford-Binet scale remained the standard test instrument for measuring intelligence until 1937, when Terman and his coworkers published their second revision. For this they used a standardization sample of 3,000 people from all areas of the United States. The range of the 1937 scale was from age two, through adolescence, to four levels of adult intelligence. Two comparable forms of the 1937 revision were available, allowing a person to be tested twice. This second Stanford revision also enjoyed widespread acceptance and popularity.

Terman's Studies of Genius

In addition to the intelligence test revisions, Terman also conducted one of the best known of all psychological investigations, his intensive, long-term study of 1,500 gifted children. In his 1905 Ph.D. dissertation Terman had argued that psychology must connect itself with life. In his studies of these children of genius Terman connected psychology with their lives, and this connection yielded some of the most important data ever collected by psychologists.

The investigation began in 1921, when Terman was in his mid-forties and the average age of the children selected was eleven years old. Terman directed the investigation until his death in 1956, when it was continued by his coworkers. To date, data have been collected for more than six decades. Not only did Terman collect data and direct the study, he also supported it financially and maintained close and affectionate contact with the participants. Terman thought of the children as "his children" long after they had reached adulthood, always beginning his letters to them with the salutation "To my gifted children." To him they were special. The "children" returned his warmth and friendship to such a degree that in 1958, nearly forty years after the study began, 95 percent of the surviving members of the original group were still participating. Some years ago I saw the warmth and affection one of Terman's "children" felt for him. Curious about the gold termite lapel pin the wife of one of my colleagues often wore, I asked her about it. She told me that she had been one of Professor Terman's children, the "Termanites or Termites," and so was proud to wear her termite pin.

Terman's aim was to conduct a long-duration investigation of the physical, mental, and personality traits of a large group of gifted children. What sort of adults did children of genius become? His gifted children were selected from urban schools in California, many of them in the Stanford area. Each teacher in grades three to eight was asked to nominate the three brightest students and also the youngest student in his or her class. Some 250,000 children were given an intelligence test, and those with IQs over 135 were selected to participate in the study. In all, 857 boys and 671 girls were chosen. Their average chronological age was eleven years, with a range from eight to twelve years old, and a small number of younger children and teenagers were included. Their mean IQ was 151, and the range of their IQ scores was from 135 to 200, with seventy-seven children scoring above 170. Detailed information about family background, educational history, physique, health, interests, preoccupations, character, and personality was collected, allowing the first comprehensive portrait of the gifted child. This mass of information was summarized in 1926 in the first volume of a series of *Genetic Studies of Genius*. The children were described as typically the products of parents with a superior educational and cultural background; they were accelerated some 14 percent in grade placement; typically they learned to read early, read widely and well, and enjoyed a wide range of childhood activities. They were taller and broader-shouldered and had greater lung capacity than did the average child. Clearly the popular stereotype of the gifted child as a sickly weakling, a "brain" interested in nothing but books, did not apply to these children.

The first follow-up study was done in 1927 and 1928, when the average age of the children was sixteen to seventeen years and the majority of them were in high school. They were given a battery of psychological tests, and detailed biographies of their adolescent years were collected. This information was published in 1930 in volume 3 of the series (Burks, Jensen, & Terman, 1930); volume 2 was a retrospective investigation of the early mental traits of 301 men and women estimated to have had very high IQs (Chapter 2). The children's test scores had changed little, placing them among the top 1 percent of the general population; their schoolwork had been consistently excellent—two-thirds of the girls' high school grades and half the boys' grades were A's. They continued to have many varied interests and activities and to excel in nearly all of them.

A second follow-up was done in 1939 to 1940, when the average age of the subjects was twenty-nine to thirty years. They were tested, and information was collected about their early adulthood (Terman & Oden, 1947). Their test scores again placed them above the ninety-ninth percentile of the adult population. Their educational record was outstanding: 87 percent of the men and 83 percent of the women had entered college, and 70 percent and 67 percent, respectively, had graduated. At the time only 8 percent of the general population were college graduates. As undergraduates 40 percent of the men and 35 percent of the women won high academic honors; 56 percent of the men and 33 percent of the women continued their education and took one or more advanced degrees. Contrary to a common "early ripe, early rot" stereotype, they had not peaked too early.

The last follow-up in which Terman was directly involved was done between 1950 and 1952 (Terman & Oden, 1959). Contrary to the popular belief in "burnout" among gifted people in their middle years, the group continued to excel. Eighty-seven percent of the men were in the professions: lawyers, physicians, engineers, faculty members, or businessmen. Thirty percent of the group had incomes greater than $15,000, placing them in the upper 1 percent of American incomes in 1954. Remarkably for the time, 42 percent of the women held full-time positions. By their mid-forties the group had produced thousands of scientific papers, sixty nonfiction books, thirty-three novels, 375 short stories, 230 patents, and numerous radio and television shows, works of art, and musical compositions. Behind these percentages stood real people whose career biographies are impressive not only for their distinction but also for their variety. Terman's gifted group included a well-known columnist, a number of authors, an Oscar-winning motion picture director, a Walt Disney staff artist, jazz musicians, radio announcers, a linguist who mastered fifteen languages, a fox farmer, a dealer of rare stamps, a millionaire real estate developer, successful inventors, a number of judges, and the police chief of a major city. As mature adults they had maintained a breadth and range of interests.

After Terman's death in 1956 his coworkers continued to study the gifted group. M. H. Oden published volume 5 of the *Genetic Studies of Genius* series and conducted a follow-up in the 1960s, when the men and women were approximately fifty years old (Oden, 1968). In 1972 the gifted men were studied by Robert Sears and Lee Cronbach (Sears, 1977). Four hundred eighty-six men, or 75 percent of the living members of the original group, participated in this follow-up. A similar study of the gifted women was done by Pauline Sears and Ann Barbee (Sears & Barbee, 1977). In both studies emphasis was placed on sources of life satisfaction. Two-thirds of the group had married, and their divorce rate was below the national rate; their mortality and suicide rates were below the average, and they had fewer confinements in mental hospitals. They generally reported that they were content and satisfied with their lives, countering the stereotype of the "tortured genius" who can never be happy or content.

Terman's gifted men and women have now been studied for over sixty years, a remarkable achievement and a tribute to the creativity and perseverance of Terman and his associates. Inevitably a study of this magnitude has had its critics: First, the sample has been described as unrepresentative, which indeed it was. There were very few Mexican-American, black, or oriental subjects, while Jewish children were overrepresented. Most of the children were from professional, urban families. Second, Terman's group grew up during unusual times, the Great Depression and World War II. Third, simply having been chosen to participate in the study might have changed the way the children behaved. Fourth, Terman did not have a control group, and so comparisons are limited. Fifth, even their achievements have been questioned. *Time* magazine echoed such questions in Terman's obituary:

> His [Terman's] bright children grew up healthier, slightly wealthier and
> better employed than the average child, but the group contained no
> mathematicians of truly first rank, no university president...gives no
> promises of contributing any Aristotles, Newtons, Tolstoys. (*Time*,
> December 31, 1956, in Gerow, 1988, p. 45)

Finally, Terman has been said to have constructed a counter "myth" of the superachieving person of genius. Despite these criticisms, Terman's study was an outstanding contribution and is an example of psychological research at its best.

The last important development in the history of intelligence testing occurred in the context of the 1917 mobilization of armed forces for America's entrance into World War I. The pivotal role in organizing the contribution of psychology to this mobilization was that of Robert Mearns Yerkes.

ROBERT MEARNS YERKES (1876–1956)

Yerkes's Early Life

Robert Mearns Yerkes was born on a farm near Philadelphia in 1876. As children, both Yerkes and a younger sister contracted scarlet fever. His sister died, and Yerkes was left physically weak. Despite this, he was able to follow the classic American path of working his way through college. He attended Ursinus College while earning his board and a salary of $10 a month as a live-in handyman for his uncle, a physician. Yerkes graduated in 1897 and entered Harvard University, where Hugo Münsterberg (Chapter 5) encouraged him to pursue his interest in comparative psychology. Yerkes received a Ph.D. degree in 1902. As a graduate student he had an outstanding record and so was offered an appointment as an instructor in comparative psychology at Harvard. At first both he and Münsterberg wondered if he could afford to accept the position—the salary was only $1,000 per year—but he did and he never regretted his decision. Yerkes remained at Harvard until 1917, and his years there were among the most fruitful and happy of his life (Yerkes, 1932).

Yerkes's Comparative Research and Early Psychometric Investigations

At Harvard, Yerkes found himself in distinguished company. The university's three great philosopher-psychologists—William James (Chapter 9), Josiah Royce, and George Palmer—were still active members of the faculty. Yerkes, however, was far from being intimidated. Sidney Pressey, a Harvard student at the time, recalled that when Yerkes joined the faculty, he moved into an attic office in Emerson Hall that had on the wall a formal portrait of James, Royce, and Palmer. Yerkes took the portrait down and replaced it with photographs of three great apes, saying, "These are my philosophers" (Pressey, 1974). True to his boast, Yerkes began his studies of the mental life of monkeys and apes in collaboration with Ada Watterson, who later became his wife. These studies culminated in 1929 with their classic publication *The Great Apes*.

At Harvard, Yerkes also studied the physiology of the invertebrate nervous system, habit formation in vertebrates and invertebrates, problems of instinct versus individual acquisition of habits, observations of the behavior of dancing mice, and studies of savageness in wild rats. His coworkers included Edward Thorndike (Chapter 10). These were pioneer investigations in comparative psychology.

Yerkes also took advantage of an opportunity provided by Ernest E. Southard, professor of neuropathology in the Harvard Medical School, to work as a psychologist at the Boston State Psychopathic Hospital. There he became aware of the need for improved methods of psychological examination and measurement. With the assistance of James Bridges and Rose Hardwick, he developed a point scale for measuring intellectual ability, in which test items are arranged in order of difficulty and the testee's score in points depends on the number of items passed (Yerkes, Bridges, & Hardwick, 1915). Yerkes also developed a multiple choice test of idea formation. This experience in test construction and use was of great value to Yerkes when he directed a major part of the response of psychology to World War I.

The Army Alpha and Beta Tests

On April 6, 1917, the day President Woodrow Wilson signed a declaration of war and the United States entered World War I, the Society of Experimental Psychologists was meeting at Harvard (Chapter 5). Yerkes arranged a special session to discuss the contributions psychologists might make to the war effort. Titchener, the chairman of the meeting, excused himself from the planning session, and so Yerkes took the chair. Titchener's explicit reason was that as a British subject it was inappropriate for him to attend, but it also seems likely, as John O'Donnell (1979) speculated, that he might have feared that Yerkes and his colleagues were about to stray from "pure experimental psychology" and "trade a science for a technology" (Titchener, 1914, p. 14). At this planning session it was agreed that Yerkes, the current president of the APA, should visit Canada to study the psychological problems the Canadians had experienced during their years at war and the ways in which psychologists might best contribute to the war effort and then request an early meeting of the APA to discuss the response of psychology to the national emergency.

Yerkes responded with alacrity, traveling to Canada on April 10. There he met Carl C. Brigham, a psychologist attached to the Canadian Military Hospitals Commission. With Brigham as his guide, Yerkes visited Montreal, Ottawa, and Toronto, meeting the Canadian authorities and hearing their recommendations as to how psychological methods could best be used in selecting and grading recruits. The APA's council met in Philadelphia on April 21 and 22 and appointed a committee of nine psychologists, including James McKeen Cattell, G. Stanley Hall, Edward Lee Thorndike, J. B. Watson, and Yerkes, to study the role of psychology in the war effort.

They decided to concentrate on developing methods of psychological examination specially adapted to military needs. At Goddard's invitation, a group of psychologists including Terman and Yerkes spent two weeks at the beginning of June at the Vineland Training Institute. They prepared psychological tests and examinations that were tried out in a number of institutions and then on selected Army and Navy bases. On August 9, Yerkes was recommended for appointment as a major to organize psychological examinations for the Army. At his recommendation a group of forty psychologists was assembled and began to prepare tests for widespread use by the Army. On October 1, psychological examinations began in four Army camps. In a letter to the surgeon general of the United States Army written on November 16, Yerkes outlined the aims of these examinations: to aid in segregating the mentally incompetent, to classify men according to their mental ability, and to assist in selecting the most competent men for special training and responsible positions (Yerkes, 1921, p. 19).

On December 24 the surgeon general ordered that psychological examining be extended to the entire Army and that all newly drafted and enlisted men be tested. Yerkes organized a psychological service of 115 commissioned officers and 300 enlisted personnel. They used the following criteria in devising and selecting tests:

1. The test had to be a group test. Very large numbers of men were being inducted every day, and so individual tests were not possible.
2. The test was to measure "native wit" and to be as independent as possible of schooling.
3. The test was to be steeply graded in difficulty, hard enough to tax men of high intelligence but easy enough to be taken by those of lesser ability.
4. The test could not take more than an hour to administer and had to be simple to score objectively.

In the preliminary testing, they found that some 40 percent of the inductees were not sufficiently literate to be able to read and follow written instructions, so two forms of the test were constructed: the Army Alpha Test for men who were literate and the Army Beta Test for those who were illiterate or were not English speakers. Both tests were administered to groups of inductees with military precision. The

Army Alpha Test had eight individual tests:

Following directions	Disarranged sentences
Arithmetic problems	Number series completion
Practical judgment	Analogies
Synonyms-antonyms	General information

The Army Beta Test had seven individual tests:

Maze drawing	Number checking
Cube analysis	Picture completion
X-O series completion	Geometric constructions
Digit-symbol substitution	

During 1918 the testing program expanded rapidly, and by the autumn testing units were in place at thirty-five Army camps throughout the country. On November 11, 1918, the armistice was signed, ending the war. The psychological testing program ended officially on January 31, 1919, by which date 1,726,966 men had been tested. Under the most difficult and demanding conditions Yerkes had led the mobilization of psychologists. Judged in terms of the number of men tested, the program had been a success, and Yerkes's administrative and organizational abilities were clearly of the highest order. The Army Testing Project has often been described by psychologists as an example of how psychology can respond to a national emergency in a practical and useful way. Without doubt the Army Testing Project advanced the careers of many psychologists. In 1917, Yerkes was appointed chairman of an important division of the National Research Council (NRC) and James Rowland Angell was elected chairman of the council. The NRC supported the construction of the National Intelligence Test for Children. Within thirty months of its publication more than 4 million children were tested; during the 1920s it was given to 7 million American schoolchildren.

The war, and specifically the Army Testing Project, also had a great impact on psychology. All but one of the sessions at the December 1918 meeting of the APA dealt with war problems. Hall, the APA's president in 1918, commented:

> The war had given psychology a tremendous impulse. This will on the
> whole, do good, for psychology, which is the largest and last of the sciences,
> must not try to be too pure. . . . In a peculiar sense the future of the world
> depends upon American psychology. (Hall, 1919, pp. 48–49)

Other psychologists were equally optimistic. Cattell declared in 1922 that the war years had put psychology "on the map," and in his presidential address to APA Terman said:

> It is the method of tests that has brought psychology down from the clouds
> and made it useful to men; that has transformed the "science of trivialities"
> into the "science of human engineering." (Terman, 1924, p. 106)

Confident words, but given that the war did a great deal for psychology and psychologists, the question remains: What did psychology and psychologists do for the war effort? Franz Samelson examined the evidence and concluded that it is at best "rather equivocal" (Samelson, 1977, p. 274). Psychologists in the Army Testing Project recommended that some 7,800 men (0.005%) be discharged as mentally unfit to serve in the armed forces. This percentage is minute, and Samelson further pointed out that the psychologists' recommendations were often ignored. The Army had a war to fight, and the recommendations of a group of psychologists were of little consequence to the generals. The Army report includes favorable letters from commanding generals of the camps where the tests had been administered. However, these favorable evaluations are not convincing, for had the test program been a clear success, the Army would have continued it after the war. Such was not the case. Soon after the armistice, intelligence testing of soldiers was stopped. Perhaps the most conservative conclusion is to agree with Yerkes that while the Army Test Project *could* have increased the Army's efficiency and *could* have saved millions of dollars, it could have done so only if the information had been used. In the great majority of cases it was not (Yerkes, 1932).

Reaction to the Army Report

The results of the testing project were presented in Part 3 of the final report on the Army Testing Project in more than 300 pages of tightly packed data and analysis. Unfortunately, these pages were read by few but quoted by many. A man's score on the tests was obtained by adding subtest scores. Through a statistical procedure this combined score was then transformed into a mental age. While nearly all the results were reported as point scores, the authors chose to use mental age equivalents in answering the question "How intelligent is the Army?" They concluded:

> It appears that the intelligence of the principal sample of the white draft, when transmuted from alpha and beta examinations into terms of mental age, is about 13 years (13.08). (Yerkes, 1921, p. 785)

Thirteen years was claimed to be a reasonable estimate of the mental age of the white population as a whole. Since the adult mental age had previously been assumed to be sixteen years, this finding was disturbing. This reaction was exacerbated by the report's conclusions as to the percentage of mentally defective people in the general population. The Army report used Goddard's term *moron* to describe adults with a mental age below thirteen who were sufficiently retarded to be unable to pass beyond the sixth grade. It concluded:

> If this definition [of morons] is interpreted as meaning anyone with a mental age of less than thirteen years, as has recently been done, then almost half of the white draft (47.3 percent) would have been morons. Thus it appears that feeble-mindedness, as at present defined, is of much greater frequency of occurrence than had previously been supposed. (Yerkes, 1921, p. 789)

These conclusions were buried in a 900-page, half-million-word report, but they were so sensational that they were quickly popularized in newspaper and magazine articles and books. One wonders what the reaction of veterans must have been. They had been inducted into the Army, had fought and helped win a terrible war, and now they were being told by psychologists that half their numbers were moronic.

Racist, antidemocratic conclusions were often part of the popularized accounts. Some authors advocated an intellectual quasi-caste system in which a person's station in life would be determined by his or her score on an intelligence test. Goddard in *Human Efficiency and Levels of Intelligence* (1920) stated that the average mental age of the white population of the United States was thirteen years and that of the Negro population was "much lower." He concluded that 45 million whites had mental ages below thirteen and, given such numbers, questioned the possibility of a successful democracy in the United States. While Goddard was confident that people of lower intelligence would usually allow themselves to be ruled by people of higher intelligence, he raised the specter of a Russian-style revolution should the "unintelligent millions decide to take matters into their own hands" (Goddard, 1920, p. 97). As a solution to this problem, Goddard proposed that these people be disenfranchised and that America's democracy be replaced with a meritocracy based on tested intelligence levels.

Goddard believed equality to be a myth, a psychological impossibility. Millions of dollars, he said, had been wasted in futile attempts to improve the lot of the poor and disadvantaged. Society, he urged, must accept different levels of intelligence as a fundamental fact. Intelligence levels for different occupations must be determined, and only people at those levels should be allowed to perform those functions. He also recommended that such provisions be applied retroactively; that is, once an intelligence level had been established for a particular occupation or profession, all members of that group should be tested and only those men and women whose test scores were above the set level should be allowed to continue their careers. Goddard reassured his readers that this would work no hardship and might actually increase personal happiness, for there is nothing so uncomfortable, he said, as to be in a profession or career for which one is not intellectually suited.

Goddard's Draconian proposals were well received. In a review in the *Journal of Biology*, Paul Popenoe praised Goddard's books as a "real service to biology" (Popenoe, 1921, p. 233) and endorsed his proposals. Eugenicists and such groups as the Race Betterment Foundation of Battle Creek, Michigan, enthusiastically publicized and supported Goddard's recommendations.

In a sensational article Albert Wiggam declared that the Army report demonstrated that any belief in human equality is a "great sentimentality" (Wiggam, 1922, p. 645). He concluded that "slum-people make the slums" (Wiggam, 1922, p. 646) and that efforts to improve living standards and educational opportunities for the disadvantaged are folly, since they allow weak elements in a nation's genetic pool to survive. In 1923 Carl Brigham, the Canadian psychologist who had assisted Yerkes in the early days of the Army Testing Project, published *A Study of American Intelligence*. The book had a curious history. Charles W. Gould, a eugenicist and advocate of the superiority of "pure" races, had urged Brigham to write the book and had supported the project financially. As Brigham admitted in the foreword, Gould "read and re-read the ms. at all stages of preparation and was mainly responsible for the whole work" (Brigham, 1923, p. vii). Brigham reanalyzed the

Army data, paying special attention to the intelligence of immigrants to the United States. He drew these major conclusions:

1. The Army mental tests did indeed measure innate intelligence.
2. The average scores of native-born draftees were higher than those of foreign-born draftees.
3. The average intelligence of immigrants was declining, as shown in the following table.

Period	Number of Cases	Combined Scale Average (years)
1887–1898	764	13.82
1899–1902	771	13.55
1903–1907	1,897	12.47
1908–1912	4,287	11.74
1913–1917	3,576	11.41

Adapted from Brigham, 1923, p. 177.

This steady decline was attributed to the increasing proportion of immigrants from central European and Mediterranean countries. Brigham claimed that the mental ages of these immigrants were consistently lower than those of Nordic immigrants from western Europe.

Brigham accepted the doctrine of Nordic superiority originally proposed by Madison Grant in *The Passing of the Great Race* (1916). Grant wrote:

> The Nordics all over the world, a race of soldiers, sailors, adventurers and explorers, but above all of rulers, organizers and aristocrats are in sharp contrast to the essentially peasant and democratic character of the Alpines. The Nordic race is domineering, self-reliant, and jealous of their personal freedoms both in political and religious systems, and as a result they are usually Protestants. (Grant, 1916, p. 228)

Brigham's conclusion was that an uncontrolled influx of non-Nordic immigrants from southern and eastern Europe would lower native American intelligence and so recommended that immigration be restricted to those of Nordic stock.

Terman, in a 1923 address to the National Education Association, claimed that differential birth rates of "good," that is, northern European, and "bad," that is, Mediterranean, Mexican, and Negro, racial stocks were such that after 200 years an original group of 1,000 Harvard graduates (presumed to be "Nordic") would have 50 descendants, while an original group of 1,000 southern Italians would have 100,000 descendants (Terman, 1924, p. 113).

Such racist, antidemocratic views had credibility, since their authors were respected members of the scientific community. Brigham was a member of the Psychology Department at Princeton University. His book was introduced by Yerkes, who wrote:

> Mr. Brigham has rendered a notable service to psychology, sociology and above all to our law-makers by carefully re-examining and re-presenting with

illuminating discussion the data relative to intelligence and nativity first
published in the official report of psychological examining in the United
States Army. It behooves us to consider their reliability and their meaning,
for no one of us as a citizen can afford to ignore the menace of race deterioration or the evident relation of immigration to national progress and
welfare. (Yerkes, foreword to Brigham, 1923, p. vii)

The National Origins Act of 1924 established immigration quotas based on the
proportion of each nationality recorded in the 1890 census, that is, *before* the wave
of central and southern European immigrants. Congressmen expressed the hope
that such restrictions would restore the "genetic integrity" of the United States.
While the views of Goddard, Brigham, and Yerkes had been influential, they did
not go unchallenged.

The Challenge

In the 1920s the psychological community was divided in its evaluation of the Army
Testing Project and its reaction to the recommendations of Goddard, Terman, and
Brigham (Synderman & Herrnstein, 1983). In 1922 Horace B. English, a psychologist who had also participated in the Army Testing Project, asked the question "Is
America feebleminded?" He answered that America was not and stated that conclusions to that effect had been based on misreading of the Army data. E. G. Boring
(1923) stressed the need for more adequate and better data before legislative recommendations such as that of Brigham were made. F. N. Freeman in 1923 surveyed a number of leading mental testers, including Yerkes and Terman, and published their consensus that there was no logical way to judge the native mental
ability of groups that had dissimilar upbringings. Earlier Freeman had admonished
his colleagues for their descriptions of the average mental age of the population as
a whole (Freeman, 1922). Such averages, he said, were indefensible. He stressed
that it was time to stop talking nonsense about such matters (Freeman, 1923). However, the most vigorous attack came not from a psychologist but from a well-known
columnist and commentator, Walter Lippmann, a man described by his biographer
as "without doubt the nation's greatest journalist" (Steel, 1980, p. xvi).

In a series of articles in the *New Republic*, a magazine he had founded and
edited, published in 1922 and 1923, Lippmann lambasted Yerkes, Terman, and
Brigham, their assumptions, and their conclusions. He was especially critical of the
assumption that intelligence tests measure native intelligence and of claims that the
average intelligence of the white population was thirteen years. Lippmann stressed
the importance of differences in early environment and experiences and felt that
they were so great as to make comparisons of different classes and races meaningless. He argued that it was logically impossible for the intelligence of the average
adult to be that of an immature child:

> It is quite impossible for honest statistics to show that the average adult
> intelligence of a representative sample of the nation is that of an immature
> child in that same nation. The average adult intelligence can not be less than
> the average adult intelligence. (Lippmann, 1922a, p. 213)

Lippmann cited an earlier estimate of sixteen years based on the results of a group of people tested with the Stanford-Binet test. Thus the average intelligence was to be either sixteen or thirteen depending on which test was used. Obviously it could not be both, and Lippmann argued that all such claims were nonsense.

While he saw some potential usefulness for testing in school administration and acknowledged the importance of Binet's tests, Lippmann castigated the work of later psychologists:

> It leads one to suspect, after such a beginning, that the real promise and
> value of the investigation which Binet started is in danger of gross perversion
> by muddleheaded and prejudiced men. (Lippmann, 1922a, p. 215)

Lippmann wrote movingly and with foresight in describing the dangers of premature classification of children in terms of intelligence:

> If, for example, the impression takes root that these tests really measure
> intelligence, that they constitute a sort of last judgment on the child's
> capacity, that they reveal *scientifically* his predestined ability, then it would
> be a thousand times better if all the intelligence testers and all their
> questionnaires were sunk without warning in the Sargasso Sea. One only has
> to read the amount of literature on the subject, but more especially in the
> work of popularizers to see how easily the intelligence test can be turned
> into an engine of cruelty, how easily in the hands of blundering or
> prejudiced men it would turn into a method of stamping a permanent sense
> of inferiority upon the soul of a child. (Lippmann, 1922c, p. 297)

To Lippmann, labeling children with IQs or mental ages was contemptible. He ended his series of articles with this indictment of both tests and testers:

> The claim that we have learned how to *measure hereditary intelligence* has no
> scientific foundation. We cannot measure intelligence when we have never
> defined it, and we cannot speak of its hereditary basis after it has been
> indistinguishably fused with a thousand educational and environmental
> influences from the time of conception to school age. The claim that Mr.
> Terman or anyone else is measuring hereditary intelligence has no more
> scientific foundation than a hundred other fads, vitamins and glands and
> amateur psychoanalysis and correspondence courses in will power and it will
> pass with them into that limbo where phrenology and palmistry and
> characterology and the other Babu sciences are to be found. (Lippmann,
> 1922d, p. 10)

Four weeks later Terman replied to Lippmann's charges in an article published in the *New Republic* (Terman, 1922). His reply is uncharacteristically harsh and drips with venom and sarcasm. It is clear that he considered Lippmann an uninformed layman who had no right to question the scientific basis and findings of tests and testing. The title of his reply—"The Great Conspiracy: The Impulse Imperious of Intelligence Testers, Psychoanalyzed and Exposed by Mr. Lippmann"— shows its tone. Terman claimed that the validity of psychological tests was without question and that it would be pointless to debate the matter with Lippmann. Lippmann was said to be confused over the issue of the average mental age of the general population, although Terman did admit that there was some disagreement among psychologists as to how this finding should be interpreted. He parodied Lippmann's belief in the importance of early environment in the following savage passage:

> One wonders why Mr. Lippmann, holding this belief, did not suggest that
> we let up on higher education and pour our millions into kindergartens and
> nurseries. For, really and truly, high IQs are not to be sneered at.... And
> just to think that we have been allowing all sorts of mysterious uncontrolled,
> chance influences in the nursery to mold children's IQs this way and that
> way, right before our eyes. It is high time that we were investigating the IQ
> effects of different kinds of baby talk, different versions of baby talk,
> different versions of Mother Goose, and different makes of pacifiers and
> safety pins. If there is any possibility of identifying, weighing, and bringing
> under control these IQ stimulants and depressors, we can well afford to
> throw up every other kind of scientific research, until the job is accom-
> plished. That problem once solved, the rest of the mysteries of the universe
> would fall easy prey before our made-to-order IQs of 180 or 200. (Terman,
> 1922, p. 119)

Terman went on to suggest endowment of the "Walter Lippmann Bureau of Nurs-ery Research for the Enhancement of the IQ" (Terman, 1922, p. 119). He was an unwitting prophet. In recent decades psychologists have often studied the effects of various early enrichment experiences on intellectual performance. Think of the Head Start program, for example. Given the choice Terman proposed between sup-porting colleges and supporting nursery schools, Rhoda Kellogg, a distinguished contemporary developmental psychologist, responded that she would recommend supporting nurseries (Kellogg, 1972).

Terman's sarcastic, hostile response with its frequent *ad hominem* remarks—"it is evident that Mr. Lippmann has been seeing red; and also that seeing red is not very conducive to seeing clearly" (Terman, 1922, p. 119)—allowed Lippmann to respond in kind—"Mr. Terman's logical abilities are so primitive that he finds this point impossible to grasp" (Lippmann, 1923, p. 146)—and to aver that "a psychologist who sneers at the significance of early impressions and habits is too shallow to write about education" (Lippmann, 1923, p. 146). Terman had accused Lippmann of having an "emotional complex" about testing, a complex Lippmann freely acknowledged, for, as he said:

> I hate the impudence of a claim that in fifty minutes you can judge and
> classify a human being's predestined fitness in life. I hate the pretentiousness
> of that claim. I hate the abuse of scientific method which it involves. I hate
> the sense of superiority which it creates, and the sense of inferiority which it
> imposes. (Lippmann, 1923, p. 146)

Lippmann was a master of such exchanges, and the Terman who responded to his charges does not seem the same person whose enlightened work and writings were presented earlier in this chapter. Lee Cronbach cited Terman's role as an example of the way in which scholars involved in a public controversy lose their "composure, clarity and judgment" (Cronbach, 1975, p. 12).

The Lippmann-Terman debate ended, and the controversy faded. Research by psychologists continued and in at least one notable case produced a change of mind. In 1930 Brigham published a paper discussing intelligence testing of different immigrant groups. He concluded that such testing was invalid and that the results were of no value. The last paragraph of his paper is a remarkably open and honest admission of the error of his earlier views:

> This review has summarized some of the more recent test findings which show comparative studies of various national and racial groups may not be made with existing tests, and which show, in particular that one of the most pretentious of those comparative racial studies—the writer's own—was without foundation. (Brigham, 1930, p. 165)

LATER CONTROVERSIES

The decade of the 1920s was a period of great controversy surrounding mental tests. It is remarkable that just twenty years after the first individual test for children was published by Binet and Simon, nearly 2 million men had been tested in the United States Army and 7 million children had been tested in schools. Mental testing was an idea whose time had come, and the tests were widely used. Perhaps they were used *too* widely *too* soon. Much as psychologists might have wanted test results to be neutral, they were not. Had more time been available for the development and validation of these tests, psychologists might have been in a better position to respond to their critics. But history does not wait. Later writers, influenced by the spirit of the times, popularized the test results and stimulated much controversy.

Debates and controversies over testing during the 1920s were the forerunners of similar debates and controversies in later decades. In the 1940s, there were charges of social bias in the tests (Davis, 1949); in the 1950s in England, controversy erupted over a program organized in the 1940s by "Mr. British Psychology," Sir Cyril Burt, in which eleven-year-old children were given the eleven-plus examination and on the basis of their test scores were "streamed" into different types of schools—trade schools preparing students for apprenticeships in the trades, grammar schools preparing students for white-collar careers, and schools preparing students for university entrance and professional careers (Vernon, 1957). All of this at the age of eleven. Largely because of the inflexibility of its "streaming," the eleven-plus program was a social and educational disaster. Neil Kinnock, the leader of the British Labour Party and a man who had himself failed the eleven-plus examination, described it as the mark of Cain put on working-class children and went on:

> Nobody who has observed a community that operates a selective eleven-plus can doubt that on the morning of the results there are not faces of children wreathed in smiles but there are floods of tears in many homes. (Kinnock in Harris, 1984, p. 126)

The eleven-plus has been abandoned. Currently the British have a single national test of educational achievement given at age sixteen. Under a proposed plan, nationwide testing will occur at ages seven, eleven, fourteen, and sixteen (Bencivenga,

1987). In the 1960s there were charges of racial bias in intelligence testing (Williams, 1970) and Arthur Jensen's provocative *Harvard Educational Review* question: "How much can we boost IQ and scholastic achievement?" (Jensen, 1969). Jensen's answer—"not much"—and his conclusion that IQ scores are 60–90 percent determined by genetics echoed the past and provoked a still-unresolved debate over testing and the interpretation of test results. In the 1970s this debate over "Jensenism" continued with charges (Herrnstein, 1971) and countercharges (Kamin, 1974). Finally, toward the end of the 1970s allegations were made that one of the most eminent British intelligence testers, Cyril Burt, might have fabricated some of his test results, invented coworkers and coauthors of papers, and manipulated statistics: Burt had reported correlations between the IQ scores of identical twins reared apart that remained the same to the third decimal point as more and more twins were studied, an extraordinary and highly unlikely finding (Gillie, 1976; Dorfman, 1978; Hearnshaw, 1979). Today, Educational Testing Services (ETS), the largest developer and provider of psychological tests in the United States, employs more than 2,000 people and earns more than $100 million a year. ETS is often the center of controversy and the target of criticism. Our consideration of the history of intelligence tests shows that controversies have always been associated with mental testing and may always be (Gould, 1981; Fancher, 1985).

John Watson. (Culver Pictures)

The Behaviorism of John B. Watson and the Work of Ivan Pavlov

Of all the schools of psychology considered in this book, none is more closely associated with the name of one person than is behaviorism with John B. Watson. Watson defined behaviorism, established its subject matter and research methods, and for a dramatic decade was *the* American behaviorist. His life was one of great success and brilliant achievements but also one of personal and professional tragedy.

JOHN BROADUS WATSON (1878–1958)

Watson's Early Life

Watson was born near Greenville, South Carolina, in January 1878, the second of five children. His mother, Emma Watson, was a pious and religious woman who adhered strictly to fundamentalist prohibitions against drinking, smoking, and dancing. She made her son vow at an early age that he would become a minister (Creelan, 1974). In an appreciation of Watson written after his death, Robert Woodworth (Chapter 10) described Watson's father, Pickens Watson, as a "well-to-do farmer." Woodworth's description was characteristically kind but not accurate. Watson's father was in fact a ne'er-do-well, a violent man of unsavory and notorious reputation who in 1891, when Watson was thirteen years old, abandoned his wife and family to live with two Indian women on the outskirts of Greenville. Watson never forgave his father and, many years later, when Watson was rich and famous and his father was in his eighties, refused even to see him (Cohen, 1979).

As a young boy Watson attended small rural schools in Reedy River, White Horse, and Traveler's Rest—South Carolina towns and villages with pretty names but much poverty. In 1890 his family moved closer to Greenville, and there Watson attended high school. In his autobiography Watson (1936) looked back at his high school years with "few pleasant memories" and pictured himself as lazy, insubordinate, vicious, and violent. He was in fact a poor student, constantly in trouble with both school and civic authorities. Watson was arrested twice, once for illegally firing a gun and once for racial fighting, an activity that he remembered as one of his favorite pastimes. With his record of juvenile delinquency, nothing good might have been expected of the young Watson, yet he wanted desperately to attend college. All his life Watson faced what he called "life's little difficulties" realistically. He realized that his academic record precluded any chance of regular admission to college, and so took the extraordinary step of arranging for a personal interview with the president of Greenville's Furman College. Perhaps because of the influence of his mother's church connections (Karier, 1986, p. 115), his plea for admission was successful, and he entered Furman in 1894 as a sixteen-year-old "subfreshman."At the time Furman College was a small Baptist institution, and Watson's announced intention was to study for the Baptist ministry. Soon, though, whatever religious vocation he had weakened. In the classic American way Watson worked his way through college, holding a variety of menial jobs, including one as a janitor in the chemistry department. In his autobiography Watson gave a bleak picture of his years at Furman, claiming that college life had held little appeal, that his education had been worthless, and that he had had few friends and was asocial. In fact he was an honors student and was seen by many women as a handsome and attractive young man. Many years later an older lady of my acquaintance described Watson as the handsomest psychologist she ever met. At Furman, Watson took a full course load, including biblical studies, Greek, Latin, mathematics, and philosophy, which included psychology. His academic record was good, yet in his autobiography Watson downgraded his performance, reporting that in his senior year he was the only student able to pass the Greek exam, but only because he had crammed for hours before the exam, staying awake by drinking a quart of Coca-Cola syrup. At the time Coca-Cola contained cocaine. He also claimed to have passed his other subjects because he was able to manipulate his professors into practically writing his examination papers for him (Watson, 1936).

The material Watson liked best was the psychology in his philosophy courses. He was fortunate in having as a teacher Gordon B. Moore. Moore had spent a sabbatical at the University of Chicago in 1898 and was up to date on developments in psychology. Moore introduced Watson to the works of Wilhelm Wundt, Edward Titchener, William James, and the Chicago functionalists. Despite his respect for Moore, Watson, in his intransigent way, managed to cross him. One day Moore threatened to fail any student who handed in a paper with the pages backward. In his senior year Watson tested Moore's threat, and true to his word Moore failed him. Watson had to stay at Furman an additional year, graduating in 1899 with a master's degree. Watson described his emotions when Moore failed him:

> [I] made an adolescent resolve then to the effect that I'd make him seek me
> out for research some day. Imagine my surprise and real sorrow during the

second year of my stay at Hopkins, when I received a letter from him asking to come to me as a research student. Before we could arrange it, his eyesight failed, and he died a few years later. (Watson, 1936, p. 272)

After graduating Watson taught for a year at "Batesburg Institute," which was his contrived name for a one-room school in Greenville (Cohen, 1979, p. 19). His salary was $25 a month. Not only did the school have just one room, it had one teacher, one principal, one janitor, and one handyman—and Watson was all of them. He was a talented teacher, popular with the children and able to teach in a lively and interesting way. For his biology classes Watson trained a couple of rats to do tricks, his first encounter with the animals that were to figure so prominently in his early career as a psychologist. However, teaching was only a temporary diversion as he realized the need for more education at a "real university." Moore had moved to the University of Chicago and encouraged Watson to apply for admission as a graduate student. He was accepted and in 1900 traveled to Chicago with $50 in his pocket and vague plans to study philosophy and possibly psychology. Eight years later Watson was to leave Chicago for a chair in psychology at Johns Hopkins University in Baltimore. By that time he had a national reputation as a comparative psychologist, truly a remarkable achievement for a young man from Greenville.

Watson at the University of Chicago

At Chicago, Watson first majored in philosophy, taking courses with Moore and John Dewey (Chapter 10). However, he soon realized that philosophy was not for him:

> I passed my exams but the spark was not there. I got something out of the
> British school of philosophers—mainly out of Hume, a little out of Kant,
> and, strange to say, least of all out of John Dewey. I never knew what he
> was talking about then, and, unfortunately for me, I still don't know.
> (Watson, 1936, p. 274)

Nearly thirty years after taking his courses Watson was to describe Dewey's views on education as a "doctrine of mystery" (Watson, 1928b). The missing stimulus to Watson's intellectual development was provided by James Rowland Angell (Chapter 10), who seemed to Watson the "real psychologist" he sought and the very model of the erudite professional man he hoped to become.

At Chicago, Watson worked hard, supporting himself with a variety of jobs: waiter in a boardinghouse for his room and board, janitor in the department of psychology, and caretaker in the animal laboratory of the Chicago neurologist Henry H. Donaldson. Watson was always short of money and many weeks survived on $6 or less. In Donaldson's laboratory Watson not only cared for the rats but also learned some neurological and physiological testing procedures. Watson owed much to Angell and Donaldson and later dedicated his book *Behavior* (1914) to them. Watson also studied biology and physiology under Jacques Loeb. Loeb was an authority on *tropisms*, unlearned orienting reactions toward or away from stimuli. Some plants orient toward the sun, a heliotropic response; some insects crawl up a wall, a negative geotropism away from gravity; other species crawl down the wall, a positive geotropism. Loeb believed that much animal, and even some human, behavior consists of such mechanical responses.

Watson's Comparative Research

Watson's dissertation research was directed jointly by Angell and Donaldson. Beginning in 1901, Watson investigated the relationship between the increasing complexity of behavior in the growing rat and the development of its nervous system. He trained rats of different ages to run around a box, cross a plank, or run through a labyrinth. Rats as young as twelve days old could learn to find their way around a box or cross a plank to reach their mothers, but in the labyrinth they curled up and went to sleep. Older rats successfully learned to make their way through labyrinths with many entrances and exits. Watson concluded that there is a significant change in the rat's "psychical life" around the age of twenty-four days.

In the second phase of this research Watson investigated the relationship between this change in intelligence and changes in the brain. Rats aged one to thirty days were sacrificed, and their brains were examined. In rats twenty-four days old Watson observed a great increase in the number of medullated fibers in the cortex. He suggested that this might be the neurological basis for the more complex performance of older rats. Watson's experiments went well and his conclusions were important, but his research was very demanding. Watson was very much on his own, with no established literature of experimental techniques to which he could refer. He built his apparatus himself, ran the experiments, and even shared his food with the rats. When they found their way out of the labyrinth, Watson gave them a piece of bread dipped in milk; when they did not, he often ate the bread and drank the milk. He enjoyed working with rats and felt that he understood their behavior; they were "bright intelligent little fellows," often "playful" but at times "a picture of discouragement" (Watson, 1903). It is difficult for people who are not "rat runners" to understand how interesting and appealing rats can be. To the uninitiated they are smelly, nasty animals, but upon better acquaintance many people find, as Watson did, that the behavior of rats can be fascinating.

In the autumn of 1902 Watson suffered a serious mental breakdown. His compulsive work habits and subsistence level of existence had finally taken their toll. He found himself overwhelmed by feelings of depression, worthlessness, and anxiety. Watson had been afraid of the dark all his life and now found it almost impossible to sleep. Often he would walk eight or ten miles through the streets of Chicago in the early morning hours. He was forced to leave the university to recuperate. Watson recovered within a month, but his breakdown was a frightening experience, and he resolved to "watch my step" (Watson, 1936, p. 274). He completed his dissertation, *Animal Education: An Experimental Study of the Psychical Development of the White Rat, Correlated With the Growth of Its Nervous System*, in 1903, and the newly independent Department of Psychology at the University of Chicago awarded him its first Ph.D. degree. At twenty-five Watson was the youngest Ph.D. Chicago had graduated.

Watson hoped to bring his research to the attention of psychologists outside the University of Chicago and so arranged for his thesis to be published. Publication by the University of Chicago Press cost him $350, at the time a large sum of money. He borrowed it from Donaldson. His willingness to go into debt to publish his thesis shows his self-confidence and belief in the importance of his research. Reviews of *Animal Education* in the psychological journals were generally favorable, with note being made of his clear and interesting writing style and meticulous experiments (Yerkes, 1904). However, Watson was pilloried in articles in the popular press and in a mass-circulation magazine. Sacrificing baby rats to study their brains was described as barbaric, and Watson was depicted as a "mad killer of baby rats." This, his first brush with the press, must have been a jarring experience.

Despite the bad publicity Watson was offered a number of academic positions, one with Donaldson in the Department of Neurology at the University of Chicago and one in psychology at the University of Cincinnati. Angell did not want Watson to leave either psychology or Chicago and so offered him a position in psychology at the University of Chicago. Watson accepted Angell's offer. Had he decided to accept either Donaldson's offer or the position at Cincinnati, his career and possibly the history of psychology would have been very different.

Watson's main teaching responsibility involved courses on experimental psychology. He taught them in a conventional manner, using Titchener's manuals (Chapter 5) and training the students to analyze the contents of their minds by using introspection. However, he was never comfortable with Titchener's methods and was more at ease with animal than with human subjects, and so he studied the behavior of rats in a laboratory in the basement of the psychology building. His research there did much to define his approach to psychology and to undermine the structuralist approach he was teaching in the human laboratory on the floor above. His rats could not talk; they could not introspect to describe the contents of their minds. What they could do was behave. As early as 1904 Watson began to think that psychology should concern itself with behavior rather than with the mind. He concluded that he could "find out by watching their behavior everything that the other students are finding out by using human observers" (Watson, 1936, p. 276). The reactions of his instructors were not encouraging. When he presented this approach to Angell, the rebuttal was forceful. "Man," Angell said, "is not a mere animal but a thinking being." Angell never changed his conviction that the task of psychology is to study the functions of the mind. When Watson outlined his behaviorist position in 1913, Angell dismissed his views as "crazy" and "ignorant." Many years later Angell described Watson's behaviorism as having "developed in such an extravagant manner" (Angell, 1936, p. 26).

Watson was an ingenious and skilled animal experimenter. His books and papers often included drawings and photographs of the apparatus he designed and built, some of which would find a use in a modern laboratory of comparative psychology. Watson began to study the behavior of rats in mazes. The maze had been introduced to American psychology by Willard S. Small in 1899. Small believed the maze to be an ideal apparatus for rats because it appealed to their "propensity for winding passages" (Small, 1900–1901, p. 208). His original apparatus was modeled on a garden maze built at Hampton Court Palace near London by King Henry VIII. Small placed a hungry rat at the starting point and gave it a piece of food when it reached the center of the maze. Originally Small had planned to use wild rats in his maze-learning experiments, but he experienced what he termed "considerable difficulties" with them and instead turned to laboratory rats. Small believed that "restrained anthropomorphism was wholesome," and so his descriptions of the rats' actions in the maze were often subjective and mentalistic. For example, Small reported that in many cases a rat's selection of the correct path "was accompanied by a flick of the tail and a general abandon that said 'I've struck the right trail'" (Small, 1900–1901, p. 213). Such descriptions were to be criticized by comparative psychologists, including Watson, but Small deserves credit for introducing the maze to psychological research and thus giving psychologists a paradigm for studying animal learning.

Watson trained four rats to run through a miniature "Hampton Court maze" for food. Initially they took as long as thirty minutes, but after thirty training trials they required less than ten seconds. Having spent some time wandering around the Hampton Court maze in a futile search for the exit, I find the performance of Watson's rats impressive. Watson asked the obvious question: "How do they do it?" First he trained rats to run the maze in daylight; once they had learned, he tested them in darkness. Their performance was unchanged. Other rats trained in the dark ran just as well in daylight. Next Watson surgically blinded trained rats. After the operation there was a small falloff in performance, followed by rapid recovery. Watson concluded that vision was unimportant in the rats' maze behavior.

Next Watson investigated the importance of smell. Once rats learned the maze, it was washed and even boiled to remove olfactory cues. The rats' performance was unchanged. Rats that were anosmic, that is, unable to smell, learned the maze quickly and with few errors. Deaf rats and those with their vibrissae cut off ran through the maze as well as intact animals did. One rat made blind, anosmic, deaf, and whiskerless was still able to run the maze (Watson, 1907, p. 100). Watson concluded that kinesthetic cues or muscle sensations were most important. With Harvey A. Carr (Chapter 11) he designed an ingenious apparatus to demonstrate the role of such cues (Carr & Watson, 1908). This maze could be lengthened or shortened without changing the sequence of turns. Rats trained in one maze were tested in the other one. Animals trained in the longer maze often ran headlong into the walls at choice points; animals trained in the shorter maze would turn into the side wall before reaching the choice point. Similarly, rats trained in either a short or a long runway, when tested in the other one, would hesitate and stop halfway down the runway, apparently searching for food, or would run right past the food. Their muscles had learned the maze or runway. These were elegant experiments, and many years later Watson admitted that "thinking about them still gave a bit of a kick" (Watson, 1936, p. 276). Later experimenters trained rats to run or swim through mazes, pulled them through in trolleys, or carried cats through in their arms, but none of these ingenious experiments surpassed Watson and Carr's.

Watson's Field Studies of Animal Behavior

While at the University of Chicago, Watson began field studies of noddy and sooty terns on the Dry Tortugas Islands seventy-five miles west of Key West, Florida, in the Gulf of Mexico (Todd & Morris, 1986). He spent the summers of 1907, 1910, and 1913 there making naturalistic observations of the gulls' behavior, especially the exchange of signals that occurs when a foraging parent bird returns to the nest to feed the young. The young gulls pecked the parent's bill, and the adult would then regurgitate food for them to eat. Watson also studied nest building, egg incubation, territorial defense, and migration. He tested egg recognition by painting some of the eggs or substituting fake eggs. He found that birds would accept both painted and fake eggs and that placing an egg in the empty nest of a noddy tern would release a full range of nesting behavior in the bird. To study their homing behavior Watson sent birds away from the island in boats in all directions. He found that they could return from locations hundreds of miles away. He also noted that three-day-old sooty terns would run toward him and would answer his "peeps." Watson commented:

> The birds have formed a great attachment for me. They will follow me all around the room. It is becoming more and more difficult to keep them in any box. (Watson, 1908, p. 240)

Watson's description anticipated the later reports by Konrad Lorenz of what he termed *imprinting* (Lorenz, 1935). In general, Watson's work is best described as ethological studies of instinctive behavior. This description is somewhat ironic, since to contemporary ethologists such as Lorenz and Niko Tinbergen, Watson has often seemed an archenvironmentalist and he and other comparative psychologists have been criticized as being "ratomorphic," that is, unfamiliar with any animal other than the laboratory rat. In 1950 Lorenz stated:

> If J. B. Watson had only once reared a young bird in isolation, he would never have asserted that all complicated behavior patterns were conditioned. (Lorenz, 1950, p. 233)

Clearly, such a criticism could not have been applied to Watson early in his career. In his laboratory at the University of Chicago, Watson also did experiments with monkeys, chickens, dogs, cats, frogs, and fish. His was truly a comparative psychology.

Watson at Johns Hopkins University

Watson's years at Chicago were happy ones in both his personal and his professional life. He married Mary Ickes in 1903 and they had two children. In a letter, Watson wrote of his son John: "A baby is more fun to the square inch than all the rats and frogs in creation" (Watson, in Cohen, 1979, p. 38). Professionally, Watson had established a laboratory of comparative psychology and an interest in animal research that continued under Carr after he left Chicago. In 1907 Mark Baldwin, the head of the Department of Philosophy and Psychology at Johns Hopkins University, offered Watson an assistant professorship at his university. Both the salary of $2,500 a year and the rank were higher than what Watson had at Chicago. Angell countered by offering Watson a position as an assistant professor elect. The salary was lower, but Watson decided to stay at Chicago. The next year Baldwin made him an even better offer—the chair of psychology at Johns Hopkins at a salary of $3,500 a year—an offer Angell did not match and Watson could not refuse. He left reluctantly:

> I hated to leave the University of Chicago laboratory and Mr. Angell. I am
> sure I would not have gone had they offered me even an associate professor-
> ship. I had several researches going. I had wired the lab with my own
> hands, built the partitions, animal yards and much apparatus. (Watson,
> 1936, p. 275)

Watson was twenty-nine years old and had traveled a long way in a very short time. Twelve years later his academic career was to come to a sudden and dramatic end.

Watson's later difficulties were portended by a major scandal involving Baldwin that erupted at Johns Hopkins shortly after Watson's arrival:

> On March 6, 1909, he [Baldwin] was nominated by the mayor of Baltimore
> to the School Board. By the 11th he had been asked to resign from the
> University and had left the city.... In the summer of 1908 Baldwin had been
> caught in a police raid on a "colored house of prostitution." He gave a false
> name to the police and the charge was eventually dropped; although [Ira]
> Remsen [the president of Johns Hopkins] had information on the matter, he
> made no effort to pursue it. Only when the School Board nomination was
> announced did those who knew the secret feel called upon to act. (Pauly,
> 1979, p. 38)

Gossip and rumor spread quickly. President Remsen demanded Baldwin's resignation, and Baldwin left for Mexico. Previously Baldwin had been chosen to preside at the planned 1913 International Congress of Psychology, but his nomination was withdrawn and for the rest of his life Baldwin was an outcast from American psychology.

Baldwin's departure affected Watson in a number of ways. First, he lost Baldwin's support and guidance. Watson now had no academic superior and so was free to do what he wished and to steer the Department of Psychology in whatever direction he chose. Second, he inherited from Baldwin the editorship of the *Psychological Review*. He was now free to publish his views in the journal he edited. Third, Watson had seen firsthand the disastrous consequences that behavior considered immoral or unethical by the Johns Hopkins authorities could have on a career. This lesson he did not learn, and ten years later he too was forced to resign from the university on moral grounds.

In his first years at Johns Hopkins, Watson began to think more and more about the nature of psychology and his earlier views that it should become the science of behavior. Now there was no Angell to dismiss such ideas and no Baldwin to criticize them. Watson became convinced that descriptions of behavior without reference to consciousness were the only way in which psychology would become a true science. In 1910 *Harper's* magazine paid Watson $75 for an article entitled "The New Science of Animal Behavior," and in 1913 James McKeen Cattell invited him to give a series of lectures on his new psychology at Columbia University. The lectures attracted large audiences and were well received. The same year Watson published in the *Psychological Review* a detailed outline of his views—his behaviorist manifesto.

Watson's Behaviorist Manifesto

The forceful opening paragraph of "Psychology as the Behaviorist Sees It" left no doubt as to Watson's intent:

> Psychology as the Behaviorist sees it is a purely objective, experimental branch of natural science. Its theoretical goal is the prediction and control of behavior. Introspection forms no essential part of its methods, nor is the scientific value of its data dependent upon the readiness with which they lend themselves to interpretation in terms of consciousness. The behaviorist, in his efforts to get a unitary scheme of animal responses, recognizes no dividing line between man and brute. The behavior of man, with all of its refinement and complexity, forms only a part of the behaviorist's total scheme of investigation. (Watson, 1913, p. 158)

The challenge in this behaviorist manifesto was explicit, and Watson intended to force psychologists to choose between his behaviorism and older conceptions of psychology. There could be no middle ground.

In this paper Watson developed the following points. First, he stated that psychology had failed signally during the fifty-odd years of its existence to develop as an undisputed natural science. This failure, Watson asserted, had been caused by concentration on either the structure or the functions of consciousness. These two elements had proved equally unproductive, for no two psychologists could agree on a definition of consciousness or specify the methods to be used in its study. Consciousness for Watson was neither a definable term nor a usable concept. In the approaches of both the structuralists and the functionalists Watson found only confusion, and he rejected both of them. His new behaviorist psychology would abandon the "delusion" that consciousness can be studied. As the wags put it, "Psychology having first lost its soul to Darwin, now lost its mind to Watson."

Second, since consciousness would not be studied, there was no need for introspection, a method Watson believed had hindered the development of psychology as a science. Introspection led only to endless argument and debate over such "pseudo-issues" as the nature of attention and apprehension, sensory and motor reaction times, imageless thought, and stimulus error. Only appeals to an authority such as Titchener could resolve such disputes, and Watson was not one to accept the views of any such authority. Watson believed passionately that introspection is a faulty and defective method. All too often introspectionists had been criticized as poorly trained or incompetent if their reports did not agree with those of the teacher. Watson argued that the method itself was defective. Accordingly, introspection must be replaced with objective, experimental methods comparable to those of other sciences. If that was not done, Watson predicted that 200 years in the future psychologists would be engaged in the same futile disputes and arguments.

Third, psychology, according to Watson, was no longer the science of the mind and had no further use for introspection. What, then, are psychologists to do? Watson's answer was direct and simple: "They are to study behavior" (Watson, 1913, p. 159). Psychology must become the science of behavior, with observation, prediction, and control of behavior as its goals. The behavior of both animals and humans would be observed, for Watson regarded animal behavior as directly relevant to an understanding of humans. He saw no dividing line between the behavior of humans and that of other animals. A rat running a maze, a gull building a nest, a child playing, a teacher in a class, a businessman selling a product, and a politician making a speech are all behaving, and as such they provide grist for the behaviorist's mill. Having outlined his position, Watson ended his paper with the following call to the standard of behaviorism:

> What we need to do is to start work upon psychology making behavior, not *consciousness*, the objective point of our attack. Certainly there are enough problems in the control of behavior to keep us all working many lifetimes without ever allowing us time to think of consciousness as such. Once launched in the undertaking we will find ourselves in a short time as far divorced from an introspective psychology as the psychology of the present time is divorced from faculty psychology. (Watson, 1913, p. 176)

Action and Reaction

A growing cadre of psychologists, tired of the old disputes and problems that so often seemed lifeless and full of shadows, answered Watson's call to behaviorism. His approach seemed attractive, vital, dynamic, full of promise, and well suited to life in America at the beginning of a new century. While Boring's claim that "for a while in the 1920s it seemed as if all America had gone behaviorist" (Boring, 1957, p. 645) is an exaggeration, Watson's behaviorism did have wide appeal. His definition of psychology as "the science of behavior" had been proposed by William McDougall in 1905 and by Walter B. Pillsbury in 1911, but their definitions had had little impact. Watson had an aggressive personality and style. He wanted to create a revolution in psychology. He was a radical with a clear, simple, unambiguous proposal for change. Strong actions often provoke strong reactions, and reactions to Watson were soon forthcoming. One came from a predictable source: Edward Titchener.

Titchener defended introspective studies of consciousness and pointed out that psychology was still a young science in which progress had indeed been made. Watson, Titchener contended, was too impatient. His behaviorism was "ridiculously crude" and not part of psychology since it did not study the mind; rather, it was a technology for the control and manipulation of behavior. Titchener wrote to Yerkes:

> Watson is the kind of man, I think, who should never trust himself to write on general questions, but should stick to his concrete work. He has no historical knowledge, and no power of continuous thinking in the realm of concepts. (Titchener, in Karier, 1986, p. 129)

Despite such criticism Watson remained on cordial terms with Titchener throughout his life (Larson & Sullivan, 1965). Titchener's criticism of Watson might actually have stimulated support for the behaviorist position, since no psychologist likes to be told what he or she can and cannot do. Other psychologists, including Cattell, McDougall, Woodworth, Thorndike, Münsterberg, and Angell, attacked Watson's proposals as too extreme, but Watson remained true to his behaviorist position.

Behaviorism in Action

Having stated his position, Watson had to show that behaviorism would indeed work, that it was possible to have a science of behavior without recourse to consciousness and the mind. During the next ten years Watson worked assiduously to make good his claim. He was assisted by a number of colleagues at Johns Hopkins. Knight Dunlap, who had received his Ph.D. with Hugo Münsterberg, shared Watson's dissatisfaction with the "old Gods" of introspection, consciousness, sensation, and image. In 1912 Dunlap published "The Case Against Introspection," vigorously arguing for a new approach to psychology. Watson and Dunlap developed a close professional relationship.

In 1909 Robert Yerkes and Sergius Morgulis published a paper in Watson's *Psychological Review* describing Ivan P. Pavlov's experiments on conditioning glandular responses in dogs (Yerkes & Morgulis, 1909). This paper introduced Pavlov's research to American psychologists. The same year Yerkes moved to the Johns Hopkins Medical School, where he continued his experiments on conditioned glandular responses in dogs. He and Watson became good friends. At first Watson believed that Pavlov's conditioning method had limited applicability. In *Behavior: An Introduction to Comparative Psychology* (1914) Watson gave a detailed description of "Pawlow's [*sic*] salivary secretion method" but questioned its general usefulness. Watson pointed out that while dogs adapted well to this type of experiment, the method could not be used with birds, fish, reptiles, and primates. Later, under pressure of events and circumstances, Watson was to change his behavior, if not his mind.

A third man Watson met at Johns Hopkins also influenced his career. Karl S. Lashley enrolled as a graduate student in 1912 and took a Ph.D. in zoology with a minor in psychology under Watson. Lashley and Watson worked on a wide range of comparative behaviors: homing in pigeons, imitation in parrots, color vision in hens, the effects of strychnine and caffeine on learning in rats, handedness in monkeys, and skill acquisition in humans. However, from Watson's point of view, their most important research concerned the nature of thought. In his 1913 paper Watson had considered how a behaviorist could study thought and thinking. Since mental events are not directly observable, how can they be studied? Watson's answer was characteristically direct and simple. Thinking is nothing more than subvocal speech, and this activity would be associated with "faint contractions of the musculature involved in speech" (Watson, 1913, p. 174). If these "faint contractions" of the speech muscle systems could be observed and recorded, thought would be accessible to the behaviorist. Watson believed that such recordings would bear a relationship to thought similar to that of a phonograph record to a symphony concert. Making such recordings would be a triumph for behaviorism and would deal a telling blow to introspective approaches to thought.

In 1915 Watson was elected president of the APA. In his presidential address he planned to restate his views on the nature of thought and show records of subtle movements of the tongue and larynx associated with thinking. Watson had always been a technically adept experimenter and was confident that such recordings could be made. He and Lashley spent the summer of 1915 trying to make them, but their efforts were unsuccessful. They continued to try well into the autumn months, but always without success. To add to Watson's unhappy state his wife was gravely ill, and during these months he nursed her back to health. No matter how desperately Watson and Lashley tried to record the "faint contractions," they failed. Just two weeks before his scheduled address Watson, at Lashley's suggestion, finally abandoned the attempt and changed the title of the address to "The Place of the Conditioned Reflex in Psychology" (Watson, 1915).

Watson told his audience that having rejected introspection, he felt a responsibility to suggest a new method for psychology. Without mentioning subvocal speech or his unsuccessful attempts to record the faint contractions he had believed accompany thinking, Watson described the conditioned reflex as an objective, experimental technique that held great promise. He described the conditioning experiments he and Lashley had done with humans, dogs, and owls. Watson showed photographs of a dog and an owl resting comfortably in the conditioning apparatus. Such methods held great promise, and he predicted that the conditioned reflex method would take a "very important place" among the methods of psychology and would prove to be a technique of "wide generality." In conclusion, Watson admitted to "a bias in favor of this method." From that time on, the conditioned reflex held a central position in Watson's behaviorism. It had been a close call, but the resourceful Watson had overcome another of "life's little difficulties."

Watson and World War I

When the United States entered World War I in 1917, Watson tried to enlist as a line officer but was turned down because of poor eyesight. Instead, the committee on Classification of Personnel in the Army gave him the task of organizing and running the boards that screened applicants for pilot training. The military authorities were especially interested in rating would-be aviators' endurance under conditions of reduced oxygen similar to those which might be encountered in flight. Watson devised a number of perceptual and motor tests which were given under conditions of progressive asphyxiation. However, in his opinion they proved nothing and were worthless as selection devices. He also questioned the value of the rotation test, a great favorite of the military as it was said to measure the critical senses of equilibrium and balance. However, on this test circus acrobats, trapeze artists, and successful pilots scored below the selection criterion established for would-be aviators. Watson was convinced that the test was invalid and wrote a report expressing his opinion. He was nearly court-martialed for doing so, and thereafter his military record carried the notation that "he not be allowed to serve his country in his scientific capacity but be sent to the line" (Cohen, 1979, p. 110). Fortunately, the war ended before this transfer could be made, and Watson ended what he termed his "Army nightmare" and returned to Johns Hopkins.

Watson's Research with Children

In 1916 Watson began research with children at the Phipps Psychiatric Clinic in Baltimore. The clinic's director, Adolf Meyer, the founder of a psychobiological approach to mental illness, was sympathetic to Watson's behaviorism and invited him to create a research laboratory for the study of child development. Watson had long been interested in the behavior of children. At Phipps he began a series of studies of newborn infants that continued after the war was over. At the time forty to fifty babies were born at Johns Hopkins University Hospital each month. Watson and his students observed the neonates while they were in the hospital and followed a small number of infants after they had gone home. In all, more than 500 infants were studied.

First an infant's reflex and emotional reactions were observed. The newborn infant was seen to have a number of reflexes: sneezing, hiccuping, yawning, coughing, grasping, swallowing, and sucking. In addition to these reflex responses Watson believed that three main classes of emotional response could be distinguished in the human neonate: fear, rage, and love. Each of these basic emotions was elicited by a restricted set of stimuli: fear by a sudden loud noise or loss of support, rage by restraint and hampering the infant's movements, love by stroking and fondling. Each emotion was characterized by a specific set of responses. These neonatal emotions matched Watson's model of behavior: specific stimuli elicited specific responses in a reliable and predictable manner.

Watson also found that many stimuli that had often been said to elicit "innate" fear reactions were ineffective. His infants showed no fear of the dark or fire and no fear of animals such as snakes, rats, and dogs. In fact, these stimuli often elicited curiosity and friendly investigation. Why, then, do so many older children fear the dark, fire, snakes, rats, and dogs? Because, Watson answered, they have learned to do so. In a 1917 paper Watson first suggested that the three basic emotional reactions can be transferred through conditioning to a range of stimuli (Watson & Morgan, 1917). Fears can be learned. Watson himself had a lifelong fear of the dark, a fear that at times was so strong that he could sleep only in a room with a light. He traced this fear to a nurse in Greenville who had told him that the devil goes around at night looking for naughty little boys. Watson was a dramatic confirmation of the truth of John Locke's prediction "Let but a foolish nurse..." (Chapter 2). In 1919 Watson made a direct test to see whether a fear could be conditioned in a human infant under controlled conditions. This was his experiment with "Albert B." or "Little Albert," one of the best-known experiments in the history of psychology.

Watson and Albert B.

Watson and his coworker Rosalie Rayner selected Albert B. because of his stolid temperament. He was the eleven-month-old son of one of the hospital's wet nurses, a healthy, happy boy who had lived all his life in the hospital and so was unafraid of the situation. Albert had few fears and reacted with friendly curiosity to the sight of a rat, a dog, a rabbit, a monkey, and even a fire. However, he did show an intense fear reaction when a metal bar was struck behind his head. Watson and Rayner set out to condition a fear of white rats in Albert. They showed him a white rat, and as soon as he reached out for it, they struck an iron bar. After only seven pairings of the rat and the loud noise made when the bar was struck, Albert cried and crawled away when he saw the rat, even without the noise. A strong fear had been conditioned.

Five days later Albert was shown the rat, a set of wooden blocks, a rabbit, a short-haired dog, a sealskin coat, a package of white cotton, the heads of Watson and his assistants, and a bearded Santa Claus mask. He showed a strong fear response to the rat, the rabbit, the dog, the cotton, and the sealskin coat. Albert's response to Watson's head was milder through still negative, but he played happily with the blocks. The conditioned fear had generalized to a variety of white, furry objects having some similarity to the rat. Five days later Albert was given an additional pairing of a rabbit and a dog with noise. Thirty-one days later he was tested for the last time and was found to show a fear of the Santa Claus mask, the sealskin coat, the rat, the rabbit, and the dog. At that time Albert's mother removed him from the hospital, and he was never tested again.

One of the most frequently cited experiments in psychology textbooks, the study of Albert B. has also been the subject of much distortion and misrepresentation. First, while the experiment is usually presented as an illustration of classical or Pavlovian conditioning of fear, from the way Watson described it, it is clear that it had a strong punishment component. Whenever Albert reached for the rat, a loud noise followed—a typical punishment procedure. Second, after Watson and Rayner's report, a number of attempts to replicate their results were published (English, 1929; Valentine, 1930; Bregman, 1934). These investigators found no evidence that fears could be conditioned in the way Watson and Rayner had described—results that are seldom mentioned in psychology texts. Third, Ben Harris (1979) pointed out that no detail of the original experiment has escaped misrepresentation and distortion: Albert's age and the object of his fear have been changed, and the range of generalization has been extended by imaginative writers to include a fur pelt, a man's beard, a cat, a puppy, the fur neckpiece supposedly worn by Albert's mother, and even a teddy bear. At times the story has been given a happy ending in which Albert's fear is removed or deconditioned. In addition, the significant information that Watson and Rayner knew that Albert's mother planned to remove him from the hospital a number of weeks before he left and yet did nothing to overcome his fear is not mentioned. Textbook accounts of this experiment have come to be based more on myth than on reality.

Watson and Rayner's experiment with Albert quickly became widely known. Watson regarded their results as a conclusive demonstration that fears can be conditioned and went on to argue that most fears are acquired in this manner. The graphic descriptions of Albert's behavior ensured wide publicity:

> The instant the rat was shown the baby began to cry. Almost instantly he turned sharply to the left, fell over on his left side, raised himself on all fours, and began to crawl away so rapidly that he was caught with difficulty before reaching the edge of the table. (Watson & Rayner, 1920, p. 3)

Later such conditioning procedures were to be described in sensational terms in Aldous Huxley's 1932 novel *Brave New World*, George Orwell's *Animal Farm* (1946) and *Nineteen Eighty Four* (1949), and Anthony Burgess's *A Clockwork Orange* (1963).

Watson's Separation from Psychology

By 1920 Watson was convinced that his career was going well. His experiment with Little Albert had confirmed his view that fears are acquired through conditioning. In 1919 he published a major book, *Psychology from the Standpoint of a Behaviorist*. Concerned that Watson might move to another university, the president of Johns Hopkins gave him a generous salary increase. Many younger psychologists found his behaviorism attractive. One of them, Mary Cover Jones, recalled:

> As graduate students at Columbia University, my husband Harold E. Jones and myself, and other members of our student group were among those to whom Watson "sold" behaviorism. I can still remember the excitement with which we greeted *Psychology from the Standpoint of a Behaviorist*. It shook the foundations of traditional European-bred psychology, and we welcomed it. That was in 1919; it pointed the way from an arm-chair psychology to action and reform and was therefore hailed as a panacea. (Jones, 1974, p. 582)

Despite this success 1920 also brought the end of Watson's academic career. The details of this sad and shattering episode read more like the script of a modern soap opera than the biography of a scientist (Cohen, 1979).

Throughout his marriage Watson had had affairs with many women, but then he fell hopelessly in love with his research assistant, Rosalie Rayner. He allowed his feelings to become known and wrote many passionate letters to Rayner. His wife, Mary Watson, obtained these letters by feigning illness while visiting Rayner's parents, asking for a few minutes to lie down, and using the time during which she was alone to search Rayner's bedroom. In this desperate ruse her motive was honorable, for she was trying to save her marriage and expected that once he knew she possessed the letters "she would be able to persuade Watson to come back" (Cohen, 1979, p. 149). Her mistake was to show the letters to her brother, John Ickes, a mercenary character whose reaction was to demand money from Watson and from

Rayner's rich and socially prominent family. When they refused, the letters mysteriously fell into the hands of President Goodnow of Johns Hopkins. With the support of the senior faculty, including Adolf Meyer, Goodnow concluded that Watson had disgraced himself, Johns Hopkins, and science and dismissed him from the university. In a letter to Meyer, Watson insisted that "both psychology and the university could do without me" and stated confidently that he would be able to find a position "that will not be as bad as raising chickens or cabbages" (Watson, 1920, in Buckley, 1982, p. 211).

Unfortunately, the sensational publicity surrounding the subsequent divorce case made it impossible for Watson to find another academic position. The newspapers had a field day reporting the court testimony in lurid detail and portraying Watson as the master behaviorist who had seduced his beautiful research assistant and betrayed his wife and children. The trial judge gave Watson a severe tongue-lashing, branding him among other things "an expert on misbehavior." Even today the circumstances surrounding Watson's dismissal and divorce continue to produce gossip and scandal (McConnell, 1980, pp. 326–327).

After Watson's divorce many of his friends and colleagues, with Yerkes and perhaps surprisingly Titchener as notable exceptions, abandoned him. He resolved to go into commercial work and to burn forever his bridges to psychology. *In Psychology from the Standpoint of a Behaviorist* Watson had claimed that the behaviorist's ability to predict and control behavior would allow important contributions to business and industry. Now, through the force of circumstance, he was about to test this claim. His friend William I. Thomas, a sociologist who had been dismissed from the University of Chicago amid charges of sexual impropriety, introduced him to Stanley Resor, the president of the J. Walter Thompson advertising agency of New York City. Resor's aim was to make his agency a "university of advertising," and so Watson was a good catch. Resor offered Watson the grand salary of $10,000 a year but insisted that he learn the advertising business from the ground up by working in the field.

Watson's first assignment was to survey the rubber boot market along the Mississippi River. He went from town to town and village to village, asking people which brand of rubber boots they wore and why. Next he surveyed grocers in large cities, trying to persuade them to stock and sell Yuban coffee. Watson referred to this thankless task as "Yubanning" and admitted that he had been "shown the door quite frequently" (Watson, 1936, p. 279). He was determined to succeed, but trudging around doing the surveys must have been depressing work. Resor also arranged for Watson to serve a stint as a counter clerk at Macy's so that he could observe consumer behavior firsthand. Later Watson was to be criticized by some academic psychologists for having sold out to commerce. One wonders how many of his critics finding themselves in his situation would have had the fortitude to do as well as he did.

Slowly Watson came to understand advertising. He discovered that

the consumer is to the manufacturer, the department stores and the advertising agencies, what the green frog is to the physiologist. (Watson, in Buckley, 1982, p. 212)

Behaviorism seemed ideally suited to predicting and controlling consumers' behavior. Watson became an innovative and creative advertising executive. He was the first person to use careful demographic surveys of target populations of consumers and to offer free samples in exchange for filling out questionnaires. In his advertising campaigns Watson stressed style over substance and insisted that the function of advertising was to make people reasonably dissatisfied with what they owned. He made large-scale use of testimonials and appeals to authority: Queen Marie of Rumania endorsed Pond's Cold and Vanishing Cream for him. Watson also tried to manipulate the consumer's motives and emotions. In a campaign for Johnson & Johnson Baby Powder aimed at first-time mothers, Watson stressed the purity and cleanliness of the product and the dangers of dirt and disease. A successful advertising campaign Watson directed changed the image of life insurance salesmen from "harbingers of death" to "bearers of life." In advertisements for the first underarm deodorants, Watson stressed personal hygiene. At times his manipulations of consumers' emotions were blatant. In an advertisement for the Scott Paper Company, Watson featured a photograph of a surgical team at work with the caption "And the trouble began with harsh toilet tissue." In one carefully controlled experiment Watson found that smokers were unable to discriminate one brand of cigarettes from another, so he used advertising slogans like "I'd walk a mile for a Camel" to stimulate brand loyalty in consumers. To increase the sales of Maxwell House coffee Watson devised the coffee break, which became a feature of American life. Watson was also one of the first advertisers to use radio effectively.

For many years Watson was the chief showpiece of the Thompson agency, the executive who had lived down the "stigma" of being an academician (Buckley, 1982). He was paid a very high salary—close to $70,000 in 1930—and enjoyed the executive perquisites, yet he missed psychology. In a poignant passage of his autobiography Watson wrote of those years:

> I began to learn that it can be just as thrilling to watch the growth of a sales
> curve of a new product as to watch the learning curve of animals and men.
> (Watson, 1936, p. 280)

Perhaps so, but at least until around 1930 it seems that had Watson been able to trade watching sales curves for Johnson & Johnson Baby Powder, Pond's Cold and Vanishing Cream, Maxwell House Coffee, and underarm deodorants for the opportunity to watch learning curves in the laboratory of a major university, he would willingly have done so. Unfortunately, no such opportunity was given to him.

During the 1920s and 1930s Watson published many books and articles on psychology for the general public. He became

> the first *pop* psychologist to the rapidly expanding middle class, assuming
> the role once held by the minister in a more rurally based society. (Buckley,
> 1982, p. 217)

Watson also wanted to carry on the research with children he had begun at Johns Hopkins. In 1923 he obtained a grant from the Laura Spellman Foundation for this research. With the assistance of Mary Cover Jones and Harold Jones, seventy children ranging in age from three months to seven years were studied. One of the most important investigations concerned the ways in which fears could be overcome, research initiated by Mary Cover Jones (Mussen & Eichorn, 1988, p. 818).

Overcoming Fears: The Case of Peter

A number of possible ways of overcoming fears were studied. Long periods during which a child did not encounter the feared object were usually ineffective. One little girl went more than two months without seeing a feared rabbit but burst into tears as soon as she saw the animal again. Thus time and disuse did not cure fears. In a method of verbal organization, children were encouraged to talk about their fears, but this method also proved ineffective. In a method of social imitation, a child met another child who had no fear of a feared object. Seeing this child play with the feared object did not overcome the fear. The most effective method for overcoming fear was direct conditioning.

This method was used in the case of Peter. Watson, using Mary Cover Jones's case notes (Jones, 1924a, 1924b), described Peter as follows:

> Peter was an active, eager child of approximately 3 years of age. The child was well adjusted to ordinary life situations except for his fear organization. He was afraid of white rats, rabbits, fur coats, feathers, cotton wool, frogs, fish and mechanical toys. From the description of his fears you might well think that Peter was merely Albert B.... grown up. Only you must remember that Peter's fears were "home grown," not experimentally produced as were Albert's. Peter's fears though were much more pronounced. (Watson, 1928a, p. 62)

When a rat was brought into the room, Peter screamed and fell on his back. In their method of direct conditioning Watson and Jones sat Peter in a high chair; just as he was about to begin his lunch, a caged rabbit was brought into the room and put down about twelve feet away from him. Care was taken not to disturb Peter's eating. The next day the rabbit was brought a little closer, and on succeeding days the same routine was followed, with care taken never to arouse Peter's fear. Finally, the uncaged rabbit could be placed on his table and Peter would eat with one hand while patting the rabbit with the other. His fears of cotton wool, a fur coat, and feathers were also found to have been eliminated, and his reactions to a rat and other animals greatly improved. Peter went home to a difficult environment, but Watson and Jones kept in touch with him and reported that he continued to be fond of rabbits and would often approach and play with them.

The case of Peter has often been cited as a classic in the development of behavioral techniques to treat fears or phobias (Eysenck, 1960). The similarity of Watson and Jones's technique to that suggested by John Locke (Chapter 2) for overcoming a "vain terror of frogs" is worthy of note. Such deconditioning or desensitization procedures are widely used today in behavioral treatments of fears and phobias (Wolpe, 1958, 1973).

Watson's Views on Nature versus Nurture

The fundamentals of Watson's behaviorist position changed little over the years, but he did modify some of his views. His changing conception of the relative roles of nature and nurture in determining behavior is a good example. Watson is often considered to have been an archenvironmentalist, an ardent advocate of nurture and the environmental control of behavior. That was certainly true of the later Watson, especially of his popular writings in the 1920s and 1930s, but it was not true of his earlier position. In his 1914 book *Behavior: An Introduction to Comparative Psychology*, Watson described instincts as important influences on an animal's behavior. He outlined the long and often confused history of uses of the term *instinct* in psychology but concluded that "in spite of its past the term is short, useful and convenient" (Watson, 1914, p. 106). Watson believed at the time that much animal behavior is best described as instinctive: "congenital responses unfolding serially under appropriate stimulation" (Watson, 1914, p. 106). Watson had often seen such instinctive behaviors in his studies of the terns of the Tortugas Islands.

In *Psychology from the Standpoint of a Behaviorist* (1919) his position had shifted. The book deals almost exclusively with human behavior, and though Watson described a long list of human behaviors as affected by instincts—hunting, fighting, maternal care, gregariousness, imitation, manipulation, and play—most of these behaviors are "really consolidations of instincts and habit" (Watson, 1919, p. 282). In *Behaviorism* (1924) the ascendancy of habit is complete. Watson included two chapters with the provocative title "Are There Any Instincts?" (chaps. 5 and 6). His answer was that instincts do not exist and habits are dominant. We are aggressive because we have learned to behave that way; to diminish aggressive behavior, parents must learn to care for their offspring, and children even have to learn how to play. How such habits are formed became central to Watson's behaviorism. Psychologists following his lead performed thousands of experiments on habit formation. Often these experiments were done with rats, leading some to conclude that magicians and psychologists have much in common:

> Magicians pull rabbits out of hats.
> Psychologists pull habits out of rats!

From 1924 on the term *instinct* had no place in Watson's psychology. Instincts had been abandoned. In addition, conceptions of inherited capacities, talents, abilities, penchants, and vocations were rejected. The environment was everything, and so Watson was led to offer his frequently quoted challenge:

> Give me a dozen healthy infants, well-formed and my own specified world to
> bring them up in and I'll guarantee to take any one at random and train him
> to become any type of specialist I might select—doctor, lawyer, artist,
> merchant, chief and, yes even beggarman and thief, regardless of the talents,
> penchants, tendencies, abilities, vocations, and race of his ancestors.
> (Watson, 1924, p. 82)

Thus behaviorism promised a remade world, free from the past, in which people could be conditioned to behave in acceptable ways. The question of who is to decide which behaviors are and are not acceptable and which people are to be the doctors, lawyers, artists, and even beggars never troubled Watson. He had faith in his vision of a new behaviorist utopia. But what of the challenge itself? Given a dozen healthy infants and total control over their nurture, would Watson have been able to make good his boast? Watson admitted that he had gone beyond the facts, and though he envisioned infant laboratories in preschools, he was never able to prove his theories. In his autobiography he rather wistfully recalled:

> I sometimes think I regret that I could not have a group of infant farms where I could have brought up thirty pure-blooded Negroes on one, thirty pure-blooded Anglo-Saxons on another, and thirty Chinese on a third—all under similar conditions. Some day it will be done but by a younger man. (Watson, 1936, p. 281)

The closest Watson came to such schemes was in his numerous experiments with his own children, leading Rosalie Rayner to write a whimsical article entitled "I Am the Mother of the Behaviorist's Sons" (Rayner, 1930). As adults, their two sons both found life difficult. Shortly after Watson's death, his son Jimmy went into psychoanalysis, and Billy committed suicide a few years later (Cohen, 1979).

There were many reasons for Watson's switch to an environmentalist position. First, his move from animal to human research influenced this change. Instinctive behaviors were much less apparent in humans than in animals, and when Watson investigated certain fears and tendencies such as handedness that previously had been ascribed to instincts or innate predilections, he found that learning and habit were involved. Second, an ever-increasing catalogue of human activities had been explained as instinctive. Often such explanations were circular: Why are there so many wars? Because humans are instinctively aggressive and territorial. How do we know that humans have such instincts? Because there have been so many wars. Such explanations explained nothing, and so Watson concluded that the best position for psychology was to deny that there are instincts at all. Third, animal researchers had questioned whether some behaviors described as instinctive were in fact instincts. Zing-Yang Kuo published a series of critiques of the concept of instinct in psychology (Kuo, 1921, 1924, 1930). Kuo studied under Edward Tolman (Chapter 13) at the University of California and then returned to China, where he made important contributions to psychology and embryology (Gottlieb, 1972). Kuo's conclusions were that many behaviors previously described as instincts are actually acquired habits and that it is possible to have a "psychology without heredity." In his best-known experiments Kuo raised kittens and young rats and kittens and birds together. As adults these animals not only tolerated each other but even showed each other some affection. The cats never killed the rats, and birds raised with kittens would ride around the laboratory on the cats' backs. The so-called rat- and bird-killing instincts of cats had not appeared. Such results proved conclusively to Watson that all behavior, including many actions formerly thought to be instinctive, is in fact learned. Fourth, the process of habit formation could be studied, whereas instincts were part of an animal's genetic makeup and could not be directly studied. For all these reasons Watson became more and more an environmentalist.

Behaviorism and Child Care

In 1928 Watson, with the assistance of Rosalie Rayner, published a book on child care, *Psychological Care of Infant and Child*. Within a few months of publication it had sold more than 100,000 copies and was a controversial best-seller. In many ways it reads like their revenge. The book's dedication "To the first mother who brings up a happy child" seems calculated to enrage many readers. The book presents a harsh, dogmatic behaviorist manual for raising children. Parental love and affection are minimized. The following passage is characteristic of the tone:

> There is a sensible way of treating children. Treat them as though they were
> young adults. Dress them, bathe them with care and circumspection. Let
> your behavior always be objective and kindly firm. Never hug or kiss them,
> never let them sit on your lap. If you must, kiss them on the forehead when
> they say good-night. Shake hands with them in the morning. Give them a
> pat on the head if they make an extraordinary good job of a difficult task.
> (Watson, 1928a, pp. 81–82)

For many readers this book was behaviorism gone mad, and even Watson and Rayner did not follow such harsh procedures with their own children. Later Mary Cover Jones was to say of *Psychological Care:*

> This is the book for which generations of mothers, including my own, have
> flayed Watson. He himself quoted one parent, a "dear old lady," who said,
> "Thank God, my children are grown up and that I had a chance to enjoy
> them before I met you." (Jones, 1974, p. 582)

Watson became quite defensive about the book and later admitted:

> *Psychological Care of Infant and Child* was another book I feel sorry
> about—not because of its sketchy form, but because I did not know enough
> to write the book I wanted to write. I feel that I had a right to publish this,
> sketchy as it is, since I planned never to go back into academic work.
> (Watson, 1936, p. 280)

Watson's Later Life

After 1930 Watson had little involvement with psychology. He did not read or contribute to psychology journals, seldom met academic psychologists, and was the forgotten man of psychology. He lived with his family on a large suburban estate in Connecticut and became, as his son Billy said, "suburbanized." He kept animals, built a magnificent barn, and made a great deal of money from his advertising career. Rayner died in 1936. Watson spent the 1940s doing essentially nothing professionally—looking after his animals and puttering in his garden.

In the 1950s Watson received two important recognitions. First, in 1956 Gustav Bergmann published a positive evaluation of Watson's contributions to psychology.

He described Watson as second only to Freud in the history of psychology and concluded:

> Yet I have not the slightest doubt that with all the light and all the shadow,
> he is very much a major figure. Psychology owes him much. His place in the
> history of our civilization is not inconsiderable and it is secure. Such men
> are exceedingly rare. We ought to accept them and appreciate them for what
> they are. (Bergmann, 1956, p. 276)

Bergmann also characterized Watson's understanding of science as "silly," his social philosophy as "deplorable," and much of his general philosophy as "patent nonsense." Forty years earlier such comments would have elicited a vigorous Watsonian response. In 1957 they met only suburban silence.

The other important recognition of Watson came from the APA. In 1957 he was awarded the association's gold medal for his contributions to psychology. Watson traveled to New York City to attend the APA convention and accept the award but at the last minute found himself so overwhelmed by anxiety that he sent his son Billy to the convention in his place. However, he was deeply moved by the award and the accompanying citation:

> To John B. Watson, whose work has been one of the vital determinants of
> the form and substance of modern psychology. He initiated a revolution in
> psychological thought and his writings have been the point of departure for
> continuing lines of fruitful research. (Karier, 1986, p. 148)

When a new reprint of *Behaviorism* was published in 1958, Watson dedicated it "in gratitude" to the members of the APA.

How different would the history of psychology have been if Watson had had a full academic career? One can only speculate, but surely with his brilliance, creativity, and aggressive personality, his contributions would have been important. Perhaps his behaviorism would have matured to be more like the psychologies discussed in Chapter 13.

As we have seen, a major influence on Watson's behaviorism was the work of Pavlov. However, Pavlov was an important figure in the history of psychology in his own right. Now we turn to a consideration of the career and contributions of Academician Pavlov.

IVAN PETROVICH PAVLOV (1849–1936)

Pavlov's Early Life

Pavlov was born on September 14, 1849, in the small town of Ryazan in central Russia, the son of a clerical family (Babkin, 1949; Asratyan, 1953). His mother was the daughter of a Russian Orthodox priest. Pavlov's paternal grandfather had been the village sexton, and his father was a parish priest in one of the poorer districts of Ryazan. In nineteenth-century Russia clerics formed a separate class of "pure Russians." Pavlov was proud of his family heritage and was intensely patriotic all his life. He was the oldest child of a family of eleven children, six of whom died when young. As a boy he attended the local school and then an ecclesiastical seminary. There he read two books that caused him to abandon his plans to enter the priesthood: Charles Darwin's *Origin of Species* (1859) and Ivan Mikhailovich Sechenov's *Reflexes of the Brain*. (More on the influence of Sechenov's book later.) Pavlov always acknowledged Darwin's influence and had an ecstatic, almost mystical regard for him. When Pavlov, in the last years of his life, organized a research station at Koltushi outside Leningrad, he established it on a large country estate he called the "Soviet Down," a reference to Darwin's country home.

Pavlov left the seminary in 1870 without qualifying as a priest. He enrolled in the faculty of natural science at the University of St. Petersburg. Nineteenth-century Russia was a largely agrarian society and most of the population were illiterate peasants. A large percentage of Russia's educated and cultured people lived in St. Petersburg, and the city was a center of intellectual, social, and artistic life. Czar Nicholas II held court there, and the city's Hermitage art museum was world-famous. Aleksandr Borodin, the composer of the opera *Prince Igor*, was a resident of the city; in addition to being a distinguished composer he was also a professor of biochemistry at the university. Dimitry Mendeleyev, who established the periodic table of the elements, was St. Petersburg's professor of chemistry. Pavlov's brother Dimitri worked in Mendeleyev's laboratory.

Sechenov was the professor of physiology. He had studied with the leading nineteenth-century French physiologist Claude Bernard (Chapter 3). In Bernard's Paris laboratory Sechenov had demonstrated that a salt crystal or electric current applied to the cut end of a frog's spinal cord inhibits spinal reflexes. "Sechenov's experiment" is a classic demonstration of inhibition by a higher center of the activity of a lower one. Such a hierarchical model of nervous activity was to be central to Pavlov's later theoretical ideas. In his book *Reflexes of the Brain*, published in 1866—publication was delayed because the ecclesiastical authorities feared that the book was so clearly written that it would be widely read and might undermine the faith of many people—Sechenov argued that all physical acts are reflexes resulting from a combination of excitation and inhibition. The key to an understanding of the human psyche would be an understanding of the reflexes of the brain:

> The new psychology will have as its basis, in place of the philosophizings whispered by the deceitful voice of consciousness, positive facts or points of departure that can be verified at any time by experiment. And it is only physiology that will be able to do this, for it alone holds the key to the truly scientific analysis of psychical phenomena. (Sechenov, 1866, in Frolov, 1938, p. 6)

Pavlov adopted such views as his own.

Pavlov's Early Research

Pavlov graduated in 1875 with the degree of candidate of natural science. He had a brilliant record as a research student and won a gold medal for his research on the nerves of the pancreas. He was appointed to the St. Petersburg Military Academy and the Veterinary Institute. In 1878 another St. Petersburg luminary, S. P. Botkin, a professor of internal medicine, invited Pavlov to take charge of a newly opened laboratory of experimental medicine. Botkin was best known for his theory of nervism, which held that most bodily functions are regulated by the nervous system. Botkin considered most diseases to be the result of failures of the central nervous system to adapt the organism to the demands of life; these failures are usually due to an excessive reaction or overreaction to stress and threat. Botkin also believed that all life shares common elements, for example, basic proteins, and that what distinguishes different life-forms is the way in which these elements are organized. Botkin taught a scientific approach to medicine and biology that started at the simplest levels of organization and worked toward more complex ones. It was the approach Pavlov would follow in his research.

The laboratory Botkin provided was nothing more than a shed in the garden of the medical clinic. The laboratory was small and poorly equipped, but in it Pavlov did important research on the cardiac nerves. Pavlov was the first investigator to train dogs to support venous and arterial cannulations without anesthesia (Giurgea, 1985, p. 8). He was able to demonstrate that the cardiac nerves are capable not only of increasing and decreasing heart rate but also of augmenting or diminishing the force of each heartbeat; they have a dual function. Pavlov was awarded an M.D. degree in 1883, and his cardiac research was recognized with a second gold medal. He then spent three years working in Germany. The four years following his return to Russia were a time of hardship. His applications for a number of academic positions were unsuccessful, and Pavlov was forced into a hand-to-mouth existence. Often he and his family had little food and sometimes no heat in their apartment during the Russian winter. Still he struggled to continue his research, often keeping experimental animals in his apartment. Once, while Pavlov was studying the transformation of chrysalides into butterflies, the insects died from the cold. When his wife complained about their poverty, Pavlov replied:

> Oh, leave me alone please. A real misfortune has occurred. All my
> butterflies have died, and you are worrying about some silly trifle. (Babkin,
> 1949, p. 26)

These difficult years ended when Pavlov was appointed to a chair of pharmacology at the St. Petersburg Military Academy. In 1891 he organized the Institute of Experimental Medicine in St. Petersburg, where he conducted his research for the next forty years. On seeing Pavlov's laboratory in 1901, B. P. Babkin (1949) recalled that it seemed an unimposing place. But that appearance was deceptive, for the research on digestive processes carried out in the laboratory was to win Pavlov the 1904 Nobel Prize. In 1895 Pavlov was appointed professor of physiology at the University of Saint Petersburg; in 1901 he was elected a corresponding member of the Russian Academy of Sciences, and in 1907 a full member, or Academician. Pavlov had reached the pinnacle of Russian academic and scientific life, but not without a struggle.

Pavlov's Conditioning Experiments

In his research Pavlov constantly sought "windows" onto functioning physiological systems—cardiac, digestive, and cortical. Acute vivisectional methods had their place, but all too often they seemed to shatter the body's inherent mechanisms. Pavlov's aim was to observe living systems. He developed stringent surgical procedures modeled on those used in humans; his dogs went through four surgery preparation rooms before an operation. Not one instance of sepsis occurred in his laboratory, and that in an era without antibiotics. Pavlov was a skilled surgeon who never lost an animal in surgery. His first major success came in 1888, when he isolated a functioning mammalian heart. For the first time the heart's action could be observed directly.

In his search for a window onto the digestive system, Pavlov developed an operation in which a miniature stomach was isolated in a pouch so that glandular activity in the dog's stomach could be studied without contamination from food being digested. Many experimenters before Pavlov had tried to develop such a pouch—in fact, one of the reasons Pavlov went to Germany was to study the procedures of R. Heidenhain in Breslau—but their attempts had been unsuccessful. Pavlov too initially encountered many difficulties. His first nineteen operations failed, but in the twentieth animal a miniature stomach was isolated in a pouch. Eventually Pavlov became so skilled at making this "Pavlov pouch" that the surgery was often over before people who had come to observe the operation realized it had begun. With a small part of the stomach externalized, Pavlov had a window onto the digestive system. He studied the composition of gastric juices when dogs ate different

Ivan Pavlov with his students and research assistants in his laboratory. The dog stands in a "Pavlov harness" for the conditioning experiments. (The Bettmann Archive)

foods and when the esophagus was severed so that food did not reach the dogs' stomachs. Under these sham feeding conditions the dog ate what Pavlov labeled a "fictitious meal," yet gastric juices began to flow some time after it began to eat. This gastric reflex occurred without food being present in the stomach; it was elicited by a higher center in the nervous system. Pavlov termed it a "psychical reflex."

Pavlov collected gastric juices from corked fistulas (tubes) implanted in the wall of the pouch. As much as twenty liters of pure gastric juices was produced by his dogs each day. Not for nothing did Pavlov refer to his laboratory as a "gastric juice factory." The ingenious Pavlov sold this juice to people with digestive problems as an aid to digestion, and these sales earned half the laboratory's annual research budget (Babkin, 1949, p. 69). Since the juice tasted vile and was of doubtful therapeutic value, Pavlov must have been a good salesman.

Pavlov reported his results in *Lectures on the Work of the Digestive Glands*, published in 1897. The work was a great success for which he gained an international reputation and the Nobel Prize for medicine in 1904. No doubt the audience for his address as a Nobel laureate expected Pavlov to describe his experiments on digestion. Instead he described what he had observed through his latest window: "psychical reflexes."

Starting in 1891 Pavlov and his students began to pay attention to the gastric juices and saliva secreted by dogs at times other than when they were fed. At first these responses were nothing more than "nuisances" that interfered with their studies of digestion (Anokhin, 1971, p. 48), but then Pavlov began to study them more systematically. In 1891 Georgi S. Ovsianitskii in his doctoral dissertation investigated the response of the salivary glands to a variety of stimuli (Windholz, 1986, p. 141). Ovsianitskii's method involved pumping serum into the salivary glands and observing the outflow from the salivary duct. To simplify the experiments, fistulas were implanted in the dogs' salivary glands, allowing saliva to be collected. Often dogs salivated when they saw but did not eat food, when they saw a bowl that often contained food, and even when they heard the footsteps of the laboratory personnel. Since these were not the physiologically appropriate stimuli for salivation, Pavlov (1897) referred to them as "psychical stimuli."

Pavlov believed that study of these stimuli and the responses they elicited would allow the secrets of the cerebral hemispheres to be brought to light. Others were not convinced, and some of his fellow physiologists regarded his experiments as at best quasi-scientific. The great English physiologist Charles Sherrington once advised Pavlov to return to real physiology, though he later acknowledged the importance of Pavlov's research (Sherrington, 1941, p. 286).

In his experiments Pavlov (1927) used a variety of stimuli to be conditioned, or conditioned stimuli (CSs): metronomes, buzzers, and tactile and thermal stimuli. He went to great lengths to isolate his animals from all stimuli other than the ones being studied. Pavlov designed a special laboratory, his "Tower of Silence," with walls insulated with two feet of turf, and tested his dogs in double chambers isolated from the experimenters. A CS was presented just before the dog was fed. After a number of these pairings Pavlov observed that the stimulus alone would elicit salivation. This response he termed the *conditioned reflex* (CR). Pavlov had established a procedure in which a variety of stimuli acquire the power to elicit reflex responses. Buzzers, metronomes, and tactile and thermal stimuli do not normally elicit salivation; it is only after conditioning that they have the power to do so.

Pavlov observed that once a CR had been established to one CS, other similar stimuli that had not themselves been paired with the food would elicit the response. A dog conditioned to respond to a metronome of 90 beats per minute (b.p.m.) would also give CRs to the sound of metronomes of 100 and 80 b.p.m. A dog conditioned to respond to a tactile stimulus on the middle of the leg would also respond to stimuli at other points on the leg. The CR had generalized from the original CS to other similar stimuli.

Pavlov also found that secondary conditioned reflexes could be established. Once a CR had been formed, a novel stimulus paired with the original CS a number of times could elicit the same CR. This was especially interesting, since the secondary CS had itself never been paired with the physiologically appropriate stimulus, the food.

Pavlov also found that if a CS was presented repeatedly without food, for example, it would weaken, a process he called *extinction*. He also discovered that this procedure could be used in conjunction with reinforcement to train a dog to discriminate between stimuli. If food always followed a metronome of 100 b.p.m. (CS+) and never followed a metronome of 60 b.p.m. (CS−), a dog would secrete little if any saliva to CS− and copious amounts of CS+. Pavlov believed that the two stimuli produced either excitation or inhibition in the cortex. At times the effects of this inhibition were obvious. When CS− was presented many times, some dogs became drowsy and eventually fell into a "deep, snoring sleep." When CS+ was again presented, it was necessary to "stir up the dog" before it would respond. Sleep was also seen when long intervals separated the CS and the food during conditioning.

Howard Liddell, an American student working in Pavlov's laboratory, did a fascinating variation of this discrimination procedure (Liddell, cited by Lorenz, 1969, in Pribram, 1969; additional details in Gantt, 1975). Liddell conditioned a dog to discriminate between accelerating (CS+) and decelerating (CS−) metronomes. Once the dog had learned this discrimination, Liddell freed it from the conditioning harness. When the CS+ was presented, the dog ran over to the metronome, barked, whined, and begged from it; when the decelerating CS− was presented, the dog placed its paw on the pendulum and appeared to be trying to speed up its back-and-forth motion.

Pavlov also tested the limits of his dogs' ability to discriminate between stimuli. He found that they could not discriminate between colors and so concluded that dogs are color-blind. A dog trained to discriminate between metronomes of different rates salivated to one of 82 b.p.m. but not to one of 78 b.p.m.—an exquisite discrimination. Similar fine discriminations were conditioned between different thermal and tactile stimuli and between wheels that rotated either clockwise or counterclockwise. Some discriminations, though, were too difficult for the dogs to make. The dramatic change in their behavior at such times led Pavlov to an interest in "experimental neuroses."

Pavlov's Research on Neuroses

In 1921 one of Pavlov's students, N. R. Shenger-Krestovnikova, trained a dog to discriminate between a circle and an ellipse. At first the figures were very different, and the dog easily learned the discrimination. Then the ellipse was made progressively more circular. The dog was finally able to discriminate between a circle and an ellipse with axes in a ratio of 8 to 7. This was a remarkably acute discrimination, but when Shenger-Krestovnikova changed the ratio to 9:8, she saw a dramatic change in the dog's behavior:

> The whole behavior of the animal underwent an abrupt change. The hitherto quiet dog began to squeal on its stand, kept wriggling about, tore off with its teeth the apparatus for mechanical stimulation of the skin, and bit through the tubes connecting the animal's room with the observer, a behavior which had never happened before. On being taken into the experimental room the dog now barked violently, which was also contrary to its usual custom; in short it presented all the symptoms of acute neurosis. (Pavlov, 1927, p. 291)

A second incident confirmed Pavlov's interest in neurotic behaviors. In September 1924, a big flood struck Leningrad (St. Petersburg's new Soviet name). Rising water trapped Pavlov's dogs in their kennels, and many of them had to swim to keep their heads above water. After their rescue the dogs huddled together in small groups without any of the usual biting, growling, or play. These behaviors apparently had been inhibited by the trauma of their near drowning. When returned to the conditioning apparatus, some of the dogs showed profound behavioral changes. Their CRs were erratic and easily disrupted, and they were acutely sensitive to certain stimuli, especially the sight and sound of water. When a mere trickle of water ran into the experimental chamber, a dog became disturbed and fought to escape from the conditioning harness. Water was an overwhelmingly powerful excitatory stimulus (Gantt, 1973).

Pavlov was so impressed by these stress-induced neurotic behaviors that at the age of seventy-five he decided to study human clinical disorders. He spent much of the last decade of his life trying to apply the lessons he had learned from his conditioning experiments with dogs to understanding the causes of human psychological disorders. One of Pavlov's last major presentations, an address to the International Neurological Congress in London in July 1935, was on neuroses and psychoses.

Pavlov's Views on Individual Differences

Early in his conditioning experiments Pavlov found large individual differences between animals in regard to the speed and strength of conditioning. Some dogs conditioned quickly, some slowly; some dogs extinguished quickly, in some extinction was slow; some dogs generalized freely, others very little; some dogs learned discriminations with ease, others with great difficulty; some dogs were resistant to experimental neurosis, others were not. Pavlov concluded that dogs differ in the strength, balance, and lability of the excitatory and inhibitory processes in their nervous systems. In describing the results of his research Pavlov paid close attention to individual differences. He never averaged the results over several dogs but always reported the results from single animals (Eysenck, 1983, p. 117).

Pavlov described four basic "types" of dog, using the ancient typology of Hippocrates (Chapter 1) (Pavlov, 1928):

1. *Sanguine dogs* were strong, lively, and active. They conditioned quickly, learned discriminations with ease, and generalized extensively. They had a "calm, business-like approach" to the conditioning experiments and were excellent experimental animals. Pavlov believed excitation and inhibition to be in balance in their nervous systems.
2. *Melancholic dogs* were slow and depressed. They conditioned slowly and showed poor generalization and discrimination. Inhibition seemed dominant in these dogs.
3. *Choleric dogs* were unstable and impetuous. They conditioned quickly and generalized widely but had difficulty with discriminations and showed little resistance to experimental neurosis. Pavlov believed that excitation was excessive in their nervous systems.
4. *Phlegmatic dogs* were inert and slothful. They conditioned slowly and showed poor generalization and discrimination but were resistant to experimental neurosis. In these dogs inhibition was believed to be dominant.

While Pavlov found sanguine and melancholic types to be the most common, all dogs were different. He believed that these differences were largely genetically determined, but he did not ignore environmental influences or what he termed the "education" dogs received early in life. Pavlov raised littermate puppies in two different conditions: (1) almost total freedom, with many and varied contacts with other dogs and humans and (2) isolation in individual cages with as little contact as possible. At the age of three months the "prisoners," as Pavlov called the isolated dogs, were afraid of everything and had a very strong orienting reflex that was difficult to extinguish compared with the dogs raised in the first condition. However, the "prisoners" habituated more easily to the isolation of a sound-deadened experimental room (Giurgea, 1985, p. 9). This research was a clear precursor of the investigations of Donald Hebb, Robert Melzak, and Mark Rosenzweig on the effects of deprived and enriched environments on behavior and brain chemistry.

Pavlov's Later Life

Pavlov lived before, during, and after the Bolshevik Revolution. Before 1917 he was a moderate liberal but had little interest in politics. Initially Pavlov was hostile to the Bolsheviks and once said of their revolution:

> It is the greatest misfortune sustained by Russia....If that which the Bolsheviks are doing with Russia is an experiment, for such an experiment I should regret giving even a frog. (Pavlov, quoted by Babkin, 1949, p. 161)

Pavlov had a personal reason for animus toward the new regime. He had deposited his Nobel Prize award of 73,000 gold rubles in a St. Petersburg bank. After the revolution the Bolsheviks liquidated the bank's assets, and Pavlov lost his money. Despite his hostility, the Bolsheviks flattered and supported Pavlov. They saw his research as proof that people could be conditioned to serve the worldwide proletarian revolution. In 1921 a decree over Lenin's signature stated:

> Taking into consideration the very exceptional services of Academician I. P. Pavlov, which have enormous significance for the workers of the whole world, the Soviet of People's Commissars has decided:
>
> 1)...to direct a committee to create as soon as possible the most favorable conditions for safeguarding the scientific work of Academician Pavlov and his collaborators.
>
> 2) To direct the Government Publishing House to print in the best printing house of the Republic an *édition de luxe* of the scientific work produced by Academician Pavlov and his collaborators.
>
> 3) To direct the Committee of Provisions for Workers to supply to Academician Pavlov and his wife special rations equal in caloric content to two academic rations.
>
> 4) To direct the Petrosoviet to assure to Professor Pavlov and his wife the perpetual use of the apartment occupied by them and to furnish it and Pavlov's laboratory with the maximum conveniences. (decree of the Soviet of the People's Commissars, January 24, 1921, in Babkin, 1949, p. 165)

Shortly after this decree was issued the Soviet Union was struck by famine. Pavlov refused to accept extra rations unless his coworkers and the laboratory animals were adequately fed. When the authorities refused, Pavlov rejected the extra food and cultivated a garden next to his laboratory.

By 1923 Pavlov was so unhappy with the new regime that he requested permission to leave Russia permanently. He had friends in both England and the United States and hoped to transfer his laboratory to either country. Permission was denied, but he was allowed to visit the United States in 1925. His visit was marred by his loss of $2,000 in New York City. An account in *Time* described the circumstances of his loss:

> Pavlov came to America. Confused by rush and roar he sat for a moment on a seat in Grand Central Station, Manhattan. A small handbag containing much of his money lay on the seat beside him. And with characteristic absorption in the seething human laboratory around him he forgot his worldly goods completely. When he rose to go the handbag was gone. It had been taken from under his very nose. "Ah well," sighed Pavlov gently, "we must not put temptation in the way of the needy." (*Time*, March 19, 1928, in Gerow, 1988, p. 12)

Fortunately, his hosts at the Rockefeller Institute compensated him for the loss. His second visit to the United States was made so that he could attend the 1929 International Congress of Psychology at Yale University. Pavlov was in his eightieth year, frail and gray, but he presented a lively paper entitled "Brief Sketch of the Highest Nervous Activity" outlining his experiments and results. He spoke in Russian with a translator, and his lecture was warmly received. A psychologist, Edna Heidbreder, who was in the audience remembered:

> Pavlov seemed to be speaking with great enthusiasm, and the empathizing audience broke into enthusiastic applause without waiting for the translation. When the translation came the applauded passage proved to be a description of some apparatus used in Pavlov's laboratory. (Heidbreder, in Duncan, 1980, p. 3)

During the conference Robert Yerkes showed Pavlov around the Yale Primate Center. Unfortunately, one of the chimpanzees greeted the distinguished visitor with a shower of "material" from the cage floor. The ever-logical Pavlov, noticing that he was the only bearded person in the group, asked, "How did you condition the chimpanzee only to throw at people with beards?" (Fletcher, 1980).

In 1927 sons of priests were expelled by the regime from Soviet medical schools. Pavlov condemned this action and said that if such students were expelled, he too, as the son of a priest, would have to leave. Despite such opposition the regime supported his research, and Pavlov became more tolerant. At the Fifteenth International Congress of Physiologists held in Moscow in 1935, Pavlov was hailed by the regime as the "world's greatest physiologist and a shining example of the triumph of Soviet science" (Asratyan, 1953). In his welcoming address to the delegates, Pavlov said:

> We, the directors of scientific institutions, are really uneasy and alarmed when we ask ourselves whether we shall be in a position to justify all the resources which the government places at our disposal. As you know, I am an experimenter from head to foot. My whole life has been given to experiment. Our government is also an experimenter, only in an incomparably higher category. I passionately desire to live, in order to see the completion of this historical social experiment. (Babkin, 1949, p. 162)

Why did Pavlov change his political views to accommodate the new regime? Two of his Soviet biographers, Aleksel Frolov (1938) and Ezras Asratyan (1953), explained Pavlov's change on ideological grounds. More convincing is the explanation of Boris Babkin (1949), who ascribed the change to Pavlov's intense patriotism and fear of Germany. All his life Pavlov was intensely anti-German; in 1927 he even refused to allow a German surgeon to remove his gallstones. When Hitler came to power in Germany in 1933, Pavlov, along with most Soviet intellectuals and scientists, saw Germany as a terrible threat to their country, and so they supported the only government they had, the Bolsheviks.

Pavlov's Diverse Research

Pavlov's conditioning experiments are known to all students of psychology and are at least vaguely familiar to members of the general public. However, they were not the experiments for which he received the Nobel Prize, and all his life he had varied research interests. A documentary film, *Scenes from Pavlov's Laboratory* (Stagner, 1972), shows Pavlov and his students engaged in a wide range of research in addition to conditioning experiments with dogs: comparative studies of the behavior of fish, birds, and tortoises; field studies of animal and human behavior; and ingenious studies of problem solving by chimpanzees. Pavlov's chimpanzee research, though not well known, is fascinating (Windholz, 1984). In 1933 Pavlov received a gift of two chimpanzees from Paris. For the next three years the animals were housed at the Koltushi research station, where they were given considerable freedom to roam the fields, parks, and forest. Experimental work with them was performed by P. K. Denisov but directed by Pavlov. The two chimpanzees were given tasks in which they had to overcome various difficulties to reach food: opening a locked box, putting out a fire barring their way, building a pyramid of boxes to reach food suspended from the roof, and tasks which required a combination of these acts (Windholz, 1984, p. 26). Pavlov knew of Wolfgang Köhler's chimpanzee problem-solving experiments (Chapter 7) and had visited Köhler's Berlin laboratory. In some ways his experiments were similar, but he rejected Köhler's account of insight learning. Pavlov was more sympathetic to Edward Thorndike's description of trial-and-error learning (Chapter 10). Pavlov saw his animals as accumulating "practical experience," which they used in solving problems. In addition to this animal research Pavlov, as we have seen, devoted the last decade of his life to clinical research.

Academician Pavlov

Pavlov had a self-described "passion for science." Carved in stone above the entrance to his new laboratory at Koltushi was the admonition "Observation—Observation." On the lawn Pavlov personally erected busts of his three scientific heroes: Mendel, Darwin, and Sechenov. He was punctual to a fault, totally devoted to science, and rather helpless outside the laboratory—he was never able to master train schedules and could never travel alone. As an example of Pavlov's dedication and priorities, Horsley Gantt (1975) recalled this incident during the Bolshevik Revolution:

> Pavlov had planned some experiments to be done with an assistant. They were planned for 9 A.M. and as was his custom Pavlov walked three miles from his home to his laboratory, arriving promptly at nine. To his extreme annoyance his assistant arrived ten minutes late. Pavlov angrily criticized the young man who explained: "But Professor there's a revolution going on with shooting in the streets!" Pavlov replied, "What the hell difference does a revolution make when you've work to do in the laboratory. Next time there's a revolution, get up earlier!" (Gantt, 1975)

Obviously Pavlov was a severe taskmaster. "Happiness is nothing," he often said, "the dogs mean all" (Gerow, 1988, p. 3). But Pavlov also had that most redeeming of human qualities, a sense of humor. On one occasion the demonstrations presented by his assistant L. A. Orbeli failed dismally during one of Pavlov's lectures. Pavlov was so angry that he castigated Orbeli in public. Orbeli resigned. That evening Pavlov, already a Nobel laureate, went to Orbeli's home and told him:

> I can't accept your resignation. You are my best assistant. Let us make a deal: you let me shout, don't pay attention, and do your work. (Giurgea, 1985, p. 8)

Orbeli worked as Pavlov's assistant for the rest of his life.

When Pavlov visited Cambridge University to receive a doctor of science degree, the irreverent undergraduates presented him with a toy dog festooned with glass fistulas. Pavlov was delighted and kept the dog on his desk when he returned to the Soviet Union (Frolov, 1938). He enjoyed hard work and athletics all his life—they gave him, he said, "muscular gladness" (Gantt, 1973, p. 135). At the age of eighty-six Pavlov stated that he needed just fifteen more years to complete his research. He worked until four days before his death of pneumonia on February 27, 1936, and is said to have made notes on his own reactions in the hours before he died. Pavlov was given an elaborate funeral with full honors as a hero of the Soviet state. In 1949 the Soviet government marked the centennial of his birth with two commemorative stamps.

CONDITIONING BEFORE PAVLOV

Early Descriptions of Conditioning

Pavlov's place in the history of psychology is secure, but it is also true that descriptions of conditioning antedate his work. Weston Bousfield (1955) called attention to one such explicit description of conditioning by the seventeenth-century Spanish playwright Lope de Vega. In his play *The Chaplain of the Virgin*, Lope de Vega described a young monk's ingenious solution to a taxing behavioral problem:

> Saint Ildefonso used to scold me and punish me lots of times. He would sit me on the bare floor and make me eat with the cats of the monastery. These cats were such rascals that they took advantage of my penitence. They drove me mad, stealing my choicest morsels. It did no good to chase them away. But I found a way of coping with the beasts in order to enjoy my meals when I was being punished. I put them all in a sack, and on a pitch black night took them under an arch. First I would cough and then immediately whale the daylights out of the cats. They whined and shrieked like an infernal pipe organ. I would pause for a while and repeat the operation— first a cough, and then a thrashing. I finally noticed that even without beating them, the beasts moaned and yelped like the very devil whenever I coughed. I then let them loose. Thereafter whenever I had to eat off the floor, I would cast a look around. If an animal approached my food, all I had to do was cough, and how that cat did scat. (Bousfield, 1955, p. 828)

Mark Rosenzweig (1959) gave other examples of descriptions of conditioning before Pavlov. In a textbook on physiology published in the mid-eighteenth century, Albrecht von Haller noted that hunger alone can provoke the flow of saliva. In 1763

Robert Whytt (Chapter 3) wrote in his *Essays on Voluntary and Involuntary Motions of Animals:*

> Thus the sight, or even the recalled *idea* of grateful food causes an uncommon flow of spittle into the mouth of a hungry person; and the seeing of a lemon cut produces the same effect in many people. (Whytt, 1763, p. 280)

In 1803 C. Dumas pointed out that copious saliva is often secreted at times when we are accustomed to eat. He termed such secretions *habits*. In 1852 F. Bidder and C. Schmidt reported that the sight or even the thought of food may provoke salivation. James Ward in an 1878 *Encyclopaedia Britannica* article explained that while the dog's mouth waters at the sight of food, the human gourmand's mouth waters at the thought of food. Claude Bernard in 1872 did an experiment in which a horse's parotid duct was exposed so that saliva could be collected. Bernard found that if he repeatedly waved his hand in front of the horse's face just before it was fed, eventually his hand movement alone elicited a copious flow of saliva (Rosenzweig, 1959).

Edwin B. Twitmyer's Conditioning Experiments

In addition to these accounts, an explicit description of conditioning in humans was given in 1902 by the psychologist Edwin B. Twitmyer. In his doctoral research directed by Lightner Witmer (Chapter 4) at the University of Pennsylvania, Twitmyer planned to study the effects of muscle tension on the magnitude of the knee-jerk (patellar) reflex in humans. He used a bell as a preparatory signal to warn his subjects that patellar hammers were about to fall on their patellar tendons. One day, while adjusting his apparatus, Twitmyer accidentally rang the bell without dropping the patellar hammers. To his very great surprise the subject jerked his knees. Twitmyer described the event as follows:

> During the adjustment of the apparatus for an earlier group of experiments with one subject (Subject A) a decided kick of both legs was observed to follow a tap of the signal bell occurring without the usual blow of the hammers on the tendons. (Twitmyer, 1902, in Twitmyer, 1974, p. 1059)

When questioned, the subject reported that he had been conscious of the knee jerks but that they had been involuntary and subjectively identical to the responses elicited by the hammers. Reflex knee jerks had resulted from a stimulus other than the usual one. Twitmyer realized the significance of this observation and made extensive tests with six additional subjects. After many presentations of the bell followed 150 milliseconds later by stimulation of the patellar tendon—the number varied between 150 and 238 pairings in different subjects—the bell alone elicited the knee jerk. The form of the responses to the bell was identical to that of the responses made when the patellar tendon was stimulated. When the subjects tried to inhibit their responses to the bell, they were unable to do so. Twitmyer wrote:

> The results of these experiments warrant the opinion that the occurrence of the kick without the blow on the tendons cannot be explained as a mere accidental movement on the part of the subjects. On the contrary the

phenomenon occurs with sufficient frequency and regularity to demand an inquiry into its nature. (Twitmyer, 1902, in Twitmyer, 1974, p. 1061)

Twitmyer promised to make such an inquiry but never did. Why not, and why has his work been so neglected?

Occasionally Twitmyer has been described as an example of a person who made an important discovery but did not appreciate its significance. Such descriptions are totally unfair to Twitmyer. His account of the conditioning phenomenon was explicit, and there is no doubt that he understood the significance of his finding. His dissertation was privately published and so was not widely read. Twitmyer presented a paper on his research at the 1904 meeting of the APA. His title, "Knee-Jerks Without Stimulation of the Patellar Tendon," should have alerted the delegates, but unfortunately it did not. He read his paper at the end of a long morning session that had produced much discussion of earlier papers. When Twitmyer's turn came, it was well past the scheduled lunch break. At the end of his presentation William James (Chapter 9), the session's chairman, described Twitmyer's result as "another interesting example of learning" (Dallenbach, 1959, p. 636). He asked for comments or questions and, as there were none, adjourned the session. Many years later Karl Dallenbach wrote in an eloquent appreciation of Twitmyer:

> His report, though presented before the elite of American psychology, fell dead. Not one of his hearers commented upon it after his presentation. The most important paper, as we now know, of that and many succeeding meetings of the Association was followed by—to Twitmyer—an embarrassing silence!...A good chairman, after throwing the paper open for discussion would, particularly in the case of a young man giving his first report, have asked the first question to thaw the audience's reticence and to start the discussion rolling. Had James done that, the audience's reaction might have been different. Had Twitmyer received a spark of encouragement, he would have continued his investigation. Had he done that, "conditioning" might have had its effective beginning in America instead of Russia. "Of all sad words...the saddest...it might have been!" (Dallenbach, 1959, p. 636)

Dallenbach's words were compassionate, but his attribution of priority to Twitmyer was incorrect. As we have seen, Pavlov and his students had begun their research in 1891, more than a decade before Twitmyer (Windholz, 1986). Twitmyer himself never claimed priority but always looked back on this experience with feelings of disappointment and dismay (Irwin, 1943, p. 452). Discouraged, he turned to other interests, especially the diagnosis and treatment of speech problems. He joined the staff of the psychological clinic at the University of Pennsylvania and in 1914 was made the director of the university's speech clinic.

As we have seen, the reaction to Pavlov's description of conditioning was very different. Pavlov spoke with the authority of a Nobel laureate; Twitmyer was an unknown young man. Pavlov coined an intriguing term, *the conditioned response;* Twitmyer's *knee jerk* was not compelling. Pavlov spent over forty years studying conditioning; Twitmyer never did another conditioning experiment. The contrast could hardly be more striking. However, Twitmyer's research was of high quality, and he was very much a victim of circumstance. In 1974 Twitmyer received well-deserved recognition when the *Journal of Experimental Psychology* reprinted his 1902 dissertation.

CONCLUSION

John Watson hoped to cause a revolution in psychology, and he succeeded. He aimed to replace earlier concerns about the structure and functions of consciousness with the study of behavior. His behaviorism was to have as its subject matter objective studies of behavior rather than introspective studies of consciousness. The goals of Watson's behaviorism were the observation, prediction, and control of behavior in humans and other animals. Watson saw behavior as a series of responses to stimuli (S-R) and believed that it could be understood without reference to what he termed the "mystery box" of the nervous system.

Watson's studies of animal learning, and later of human infants, were notable for their objectivity and precision. He regarded their results as compelling evidence that behavior is indeed a series of responses to stimuli. In answering the question of how stimuli acquire the power to elicit responses, Watson used the principles of classical conditioning established by Pavlov. His own demonstrations of classical conditioning and deconditioning of emotional responses in infants led Watson to conclude that classical conditioning is the basis of much human behavior.

Watson's career as an academic psychologist lasted only twenty years, yet his impact was enormous and his influence is still felt. To some psychologists, though, Watson was an archenvironmentalist whose mechanical conceptions ignored the complexities of human behavior. To others he seemed a radical who made rash and exaggerated claims for his behaviorism. Yet Watson's behaviorism clearly changed psychology.

Ivan Pavlov's classical conditioning research forms one of the foundations of contemporary psychology. His experiments were exemplary in their precision and objectivity. Pavlov also had a wide range of psychological interests: experimentally induced and clinical neuroses, field studies of human and animal behavior, and research on complex problem solving. Though his classical conditioning experiments were preceded by earlier observations, none of the earlier studies has had the lasting impact of Pavlov's research. Classical conditioning is still seen as one of the major ways in which behavior changes as a result of the experiences an animal or human undergoes (Roscorla, 1988).

Edward Tolman. (Archives of the History of American Psychology, University of Akron)

chapter

13

Four Neobehaviorist
Psychologists

With its founder John Watson exiled from psychology, behaviorism might have been expected to decline in importance and influence during the 1920s, 1930s, and 1940s. In fact, this was the era when the behaviorist position dominated American psychology. Watson's rejection of consciousness, his definition of psychology as the "science of behavior," and his insistence on objective, observational data—his methodological behaviorism—were accepted by most psychologists. However, behaviorism was never a tight little school of psychology, and different approaches to the study of behavior soon emerged, with a common theme being a concern for the level of behavioral analysis to be employed. Should the approach be *molar,* that is, concerned with purposive acts and cognition, or *molecular,* a search for a unit of behavioral analysis similar to the reflex arc of the physiologists. The four psychologists to be considered in this chapter—Edward Chace Tolman, Edwin Ray Guthrie, Clark Leonard Hull, and B. F. Skinner—formulated "neobehaviorist" approaches to psychology that addressed this issue and in doing so had some similarities but many differences. These differences gave vitality and impetus to the behaviorist movement in American psychology.

EDWARD CHACE TOLMAN (1886–1959)

Tolman's Early Life

Edward Chace Tolman was born in Newton, Massachusetts, in 1886, the third child and second son of an upper-class New England family. His father was president of a manufacturing company and a staunch believer in the Puritan ethic of

405

hard work and constant effort. One of his favorite mottoes was "tend to business." Tolman's mother had a Quaker background. She was a warm and caring person who loved her children deeply and tried to instill in them her Quaker values of plain living and high thinking. Tolman attended the excellent public schools in Newton and followed his older brother, Richard Tolman, to the Massachusetts Institute of Technology (MIT). In his autobiography Tolman explained his decision to enter MIT as having been due to family pressure. His father had been a member of MIT's first graduating class and was a university trustee.

Tolman majored in electrochemistry and graduated with a B.S. degree in 1911. During his senior year he read a book that changed his and many other people's lives, William James's *Principles of Psychology* (Chapter 9). Tolman had always been interested in "what makes people tick." He found James's psychology captivating and decided to abandon physics, chemistry, and mathematics for psychology and philosophy. As he admitted in his autobiography, an additional reason for the switch was his reluctance to compete with his older brother, who had graduated from MIT and quickly begun a promising career as a theoretical physicist and chemist. Richard Tolman's career culminated in his work as an associate of Robert Oppenheimer on the atomic bomb project at Los Alamos (Rhodes, 1986).

The summer after his graduation, Edward Tolman enrolled at Harvard and took a course in philosophy and one in psychology with Robert Yerkes (Chapter 11). He liked both courses but decided that he "did not have brains enough to become a philosopher" (Tolman, 1952, p. 323) and so enrolled as a graduate student in Harvard's Department of Psychology. For the rest of his life Tolman's devotion to psychology never wavered. At Harvard he worked in the laboratory of Hugo Münsterberg. As we saw in Chapter 5, by 1911 Münsterberg's interests were concentrated on applied topics, and he left the direction of the laboratory to his assistant, Herbert S. Langfeld. However, Münsterberg made a point of attending the laboratory's meetings, at which students presented and discussed their research.

Invariably Münsterberg opened these meetings with a brief lecture describing introspection as *the* method of psychology; then the students and research assistants would describe experiments in which introspection was seldom used. To Tolman's practical mind something was clearly wrong. If, as Münsterberg claimed, introspection was indeed *the* psychological method, why was it used so seldom in his laboratory? Tolman was also troubled by the thought that if Münsterberg were correct, he and the other graduate students at Harvard would be well advised to transfer to Cornell University, where they could be instructed in introspection by the master himself, Edward Titchener (Chapter 5). Since his fellow graduate students showed no inclination to leave for Cornell, Tolman concluded that something was amiss. It is easy to see Tolman's dilemma. Fortunately, he enrolled in a second course with Yerkes that helped resolve his conflict. Yerkes used as his text Watson's recently published *Behavior: An Introduction to Comparative Psychology* (Chapter 12) and defended Watson's definition of psychology as a science of behavior that has no need for introspection. When Tolman considered the work he and others in Münsterberg's laboratory were actually doing, he concluded that Watson's definition was appropriate.

At the end of his first year of graduate studies, Tolman went to Germany to prepare for his doctoral language examination in German. He spent a month with Kurt Koffka at the University of Giessen, where he was introduced to Gestalt psychology. As we saw in Chapter 7, in 1912 Gestalt psychology was full of vigor and excitement. Tolman was impressed, though he later recalled sensing only vaguely what Gestalt psychology was about. However, the Gestalt psychologists made a definite impression, and ten years later, in 1923, Tolman returned to Giessen to learn more about their approach to psychology. Kurt Lewin's views were especially important in influencing his decision, and Tolman always acknowledged his indebtedness to Lewin and the Gestalt psychologists.

Tolman's dissertation research at Harvard concerned memory for nonsense syllables learned in the presence of pleasant or unpleasant odors. He received a Ph.D. degree in 1915 and then taught as an instructor at Northwestern University for three years. During this period he published his first research papers on conventional problems of imageless thought, retroactive inhibition, and association times for pleasant and unpleasant words. He recalled later that "at the time the behavioristic point of view had not yet really got into my blood" (Tolman, 1952, p. 329). In 1918, Northwestern went through a wartime retrenchment in which the number of teaching positions was reduced. Tolman lost his position because, it was said, he had been an ineffective teacher, but Tolman always believed that the real reason had been his pacifist and antiwar activities. In any event, Tolman was dismissed by Northwestern and was fortunate to find a position at the University of California at Berkeley. He found California and the freedom of the West immediately appealing. Tolman believed that Berkeley provided an ideal academic environment and remained loyal to the University of California for the remaining four decades of his life.

Tolman's Cognitive Behaviorism

Thoughtful Maze-Learning Rats One product of Tolman's new sense of freedom was a resolve to break with conventional psychology and consider behaviorism. At Berkeley he developed a new course on comparative psychology that he taught with Watson's book as a text. Tolman also acquired some rats, built a number of mazes, and began to study maze learning by those animals. He quickly became convinced that accounts of maze learning that emphasized mechanical stamping in or out of connections between stimuli and responses did not adequately describe the behavior he was observing. There seemed to be more to the behavior of his rats than being prodded back and forth by stimuli, rewards, and punishments. Far from behaving in a mechanical, unthinking fashion, the rats appeared to Tolman to behave with intelligence and purpose. He treated maze learning as a cognitive molar phenomenon and believed that his rats learned the general pattern or layout of the maze. They learned what Tolman was to term a *cognitive map* of the maze (Tolman, 1948). Purpose and cognition were to be the central concerns of Tolman's molar behaviorism. They had been excluded by Watson, an exclusion Tolman considered a grave error. He aimed to develop a new, "sensible" behaviorism based on objective observations of behavior but including purpose and cognition. Tolman outlined his views in a series of papers published in the 1920s (Tolman, 1922, 1923, 1926) and then in his celebrated book *Purposive Behavior in Animals and Men,* published in 1932. Despite its title, he devoted most of the book to descriptions and analysis of the behavior of rats in mazes and with a nice sense of humor dedicated it to "MNA"— *Mus norvegicus albinus,* the white rat.

Tolman began *Purposive Behavior* with a vigorous attack on mentalistic psychologies and a strong endorsement of the behaviorist approach. Psychology, he argued, should be an objective science of behavior and have as its subject matter such molar behaviors as

> a rat running a maze; a cat getting out of a puzzle box; a man driving home to dinner; a child hiding from a stranger; a woman doing her washing or gossiping over the telephone; a pupil marking a mental-test sheet; a psychologist reciting a list of nonsense syllables; my friend and I telling one another our thoughts and feelings—*these are behaviors (qua molar).* (Tolman, 1932, p. 8)

Such molar acts, according to Tolman, are purposive, goal-directed, and cognitive. A rat in a maze learns not only that a reward will be in the goal box but that a specific reward will be there. Different rewards have different values and affect behavior differentially. In an experimental demonstration of such effects, one of Tolman's students, R. Simmons, ran groups of rats at the same level of hunger through a maze for different rewards. Rats running for bread and milk ran fastest, those given sunflower seeds ran the next fastest, and rats that simply were removed from the goal box when they reached the end of the maze ran the slowest. Certain rewards were more "demanded" than others, and they acted as "immanent determinants" of maze running (Simmons, 1924).

Tolman and his students were also able to show that the rats learned to expect a particular reward and were disappointed when a less demanded reward was found in its place. Attributions of "disappointment" to maze-running rats sound like behaviorist heresy, but in an elegant series of experiments Tolman claimed to have observed such reactions. When rats that had been trained with a highly demanded reward encountered a less demanded one on later trials, they ran more slowly and made more errors. Rats trained first with a less demanded reward improved their performance when the more demanded reward was substituted (Elliott, 1928). To Tolman such changed behavior after the substitutions constituted clear, objective evidence that his rats had acquired specific expectations and had been disappointed or elated when their expectations were not met.

Experiments by Otto Tinklepaugh showed such specific expectations in monkeys. From 1925 to 1927 Tinklepaugh had worked with Wolfgang Köhler (Chapter 7) before joining Tolman at Berkeley. With a research budget of $50 he ran memory experiments in which a piece of banana was placed under one of two cups in full view of a restrained monkey. Thus far the experiment was very much like the ones conducted by Köhler on Tenerife (Chapter 7); the difference was that in Tinklepaugh's experiment the experimenter, while hidden from the monkey's view, substituted a piece of lettuce for the banana. When released, the monkey jumps down from the chair, and rushes to the proper container and picks it up. She extends her hand to seize the food. But her hand drops to the floor without touching it. She looks at the lettuce, but (unless very hungry) does not touch it. She looks around the cup and behind the board. She stands up and looks under and around her. She picks the cup up and examines it thoroughly inside and out. She has on occasion turned towards observers present in the room and shrieked at them in apparent anger. (Tinklepaugh, 1928, p. 224)

Tolman believed that even an avowed behaviorist seeing the monkey's behavior would be forced to agree that she had "expected" to find the banana and was "disappointed" to find lettuce.

Latent Learning But what if animals first found no rewards and then encountered them? Would they be "surprised" and change their behavior? The first of an important series of experiments using this paradigm were reported in 1929 by Hugh Blodgett (1929). Three groups of rats were trained to run a maze. Group 1, the control group, was fed upon reaching the goal box. Group 2, the first experimental group, did not find food for the first six days of training but on the seventh day found food in the goal box and continued to find it there for the rest of the experiment. Group 3, the second experimental group, ran without food for two days, found food in the goal box on the third day, and continued to find it there for the rest of the experiment. Both experimental groups showed a marked reduction in the number of errors made in running the maze the day after the transition from nonreward to reward conditions, and this improved performance continued for the rest of the experiment. Clearly the rats had learned during the initial nonreward trials, and they were able to use this "cognitive map" of the maze when rewards were introduced.

Tolman termed the initial learning during the nonreward trials *latent learning* and argued that such learning is pervasive in the everyday experience of humans (Tolman, 1932, p. 343). We drive or walk along the same route each day and in so doing learn the locations of stores, parks, banks, bus stops, and the like, but this learning is latent. It is only when we need to find a park, store, or bus stop and are able to do so that such learning becomes manifest. This report of latent learning in rats stimulated a great volume of research. While there was some controversy, numerous investigators reported evidence that rats do in fact learn in the absence of rewards (Thistlethwaite, 1951). The phenomenon is both reliable and robust. Latent learning challenges assumptions that learning can occur only with reinforcement. Some law-of-effect learning theorists responded to this challenge by claiming that reinforcement must have been present during the initial "nonreward" trials. Since they believed that reinforcement is necessary for learning and since rats in latent learning experiments clearly do learn, such a claim was required of them. But what was the reinforcement? It was said that reduction of a rat's curiosity about the maze or a reinforcing feeling of freedom following removal from the goal box might have been "minimally reinforcing" and thus have supported learning during the initial trials. The details of such claims will not be considered here, but it should be noted that in postulating a "higher" curiosity drive and feelings of freedom, law-of-effect theorists had clearly been forced to broaden their positions, just as Tolman hoped they would.

Tolman's Insight-Learning Experiments In *Purposive Behavior*, Tolman also reported the results of a brilliant experiment on insight learning by rats. Tolman was familiar with Köhler's experiments on insight learning by apes (Chapter 7) and commented favorably on them. His aim was to show similar behaviors in maze-learning rats. Together with C. H. Honzik, Tolman conducted an experiment using an elevated maze that had paths without side walls so that a rat could see the whole maze from any point. There were three routes of different lengths from the starting point to the goal box, but they all had a final common path. First Tolman and Honzik allowed the rats to explore the maze. Then the rats were made hungry and most quickly learned to take the shortest and most direct path to food. They behaved in accordance with what Tolman termed the "law of least effort"; that is, given a choice between a number of paths to a reward, animals generally choose the one that requires the least effort. Next, a barrier was introduced so that the shortest path was blocked but the remaining two paths were open. When rats reached the barrier, they retreated and took the next shortest unblocked path. Finally, a second barrier was erected, blocking both of these paths. After encountering this barrier the rats immediately switched to the only remaining unblocked path. Tolman felt that his rats had shown insight. He believed they had learned a cognitive map of the maze that was not a narrow "strip map" of a particular path to the goal but a broad map of the maze as a whole. Finding one path to the goal blocked, the rats were able to use this map in selecting the next shortest unblocked path. This experiment was indeed an ingenious demonstration of insight learning by rats.

Place versus Response Learning Tolman was elected president of the APA in 1937. In his presidential address, "The Determiners of Behavior at a Choice Point," he described additional experiments designed to illustrate cognitive, purposive behavior in rats. In one of these experiments Tolman used this simple apparatus:

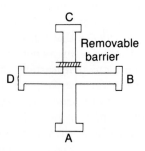

A is the start box, and **B** is the goal box. A hungry rat quickly learned to run without hesitation to **B**, but what was actually learned? One answer is that the rat had learned to make a specific response—turning right—because that response led to food. Tolman favored a different answer. He believed that the rat had developed a cognitive map of the maze in which the place of reward was marked. With only the results from initial learning, there is nothing to choose between these two answers. The "Tolmanians," or as they sometimes called themselves "Tolmaniacs," provided an ingenious test. Once a rat had learned to run from **A** to **B**, it was started from **C**. The two answers predict different behaviors at the choice point. The S-R answer predicts that the rat should make the learned response, that is, turn right and so reach **D**; the cognitive map view predicts that the rat should refer to its cognitive map, locate the marked reward location, and go to it, thus reaching **B**. On the test trial the majority of rats reached **B**, leading Tolman to conclude that in learning the maze they had acquired a spatial representation of the apparatus as a whole, a cognitive map, rather than specific responses to stimuli within the apparatus.

A second method of assessing response versus place learning was to determine which was more readily learned. Tolman, Ritchie, and Kalish (1946) built the elevated maze shown in the following diagram:

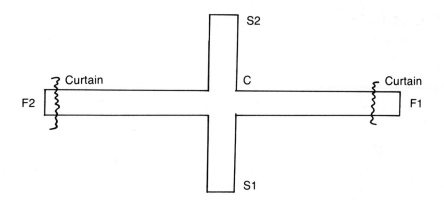

Response-learning rats started randomly from S1 and S2 but always found food by turning right; place-learning rats also started randomly from S1 or S2 but always found food in the same place. All eight rats in the place-learning group learned to run to the correct place within eight trials. None of the response-learning rats learned that quickly, and five of them did not learn after seventy-two trials. In this elevated maze, place learning was more rapid.

At choice points Tolman's rats often hesitated and vacillated, looking back and forth at the alternative paths before making a choice. Tolman described their behavior as "vicarious trial and error." According to Tolman, "VTE-ing," as it came to be called, reflects a rat's "search for the stimulus" and the experimenter's "instructions." It is part of the animal's attempt to learn "what leads to what" in a particular situation (Tolman, 1932, chap. XIII).

Tolman's Theoretical Model

While these were important investigations, they are only a small sample of the research program Tolman directed. He published over 100 papers and two books describing his research and theory of behavior. In "The Determiners of Behavior at a Choice Point" (Tolman, 1938), he described three classes of variables that influence behavior: *independent, intervening,* and *dependent variables.* Independent variables refer to conditions of the experiment, such as the animal's maintenance schedule, the type of goal object, the types and modes of stimuli provided, the responses required, and the number and distribution of trials. Each of these independent variables was seen to influence an intervening variable: demand, appetite, differentiation, motor skill, and hypotheses and biases, respectively. Tolman reported experimental investigations of the relationships between these independent and intervening variables.

A second class of independent variables referred to the individual: heredity, age, previous training, and special endocrine or drug conditions. In most experiments psychologists attempt to hold these variables as constant as possible by, for example, using large groups of standard animals, between the ages of 90 to 120 days, with no previous training and no special endocrine or drug conditions.

Finally, psychologists use various dependent variables: maze-running speed, number of errors, number of VTEs at choice points. These dependent variables allow the strength of intervening variables to be measured. Tolman's model of independent, intervening, and dependent variables has been widely used in psychological research.

Tolman's General Concerns

Tolman hoped to develop a comprehensive behavior theory that would have a broad range of applications. As he said, "Rats in mazes are very nice. But, after all, they do not constitute the whole universe of behavior" (Tolman, 1932, p. 182). He admired the Gestalt psychologists, especially Kurt Lewin, whose ideas he had "borrowed time and again and absorbed into my very blood" (Tolman, 1952, p. 339). Tolman's goal was a psychological system, like Lewin's, that would include the complexities of human thought and motivation together with such social problems as aggression and war. He hoped for something more than a "rat-runners' psychology." Chapters in the second half of *Purposive Behavior* discuss inventive ideation, speech, sensation, perception and image, feeling and emotion, and personality and include some conclusions for philosophers and psychologists. In a paper entitled "Psychological Man" written in 1941, in the midst of World War II, Tolman discussed human drives to aggression and the motives that lead to wars. This paper begins with a moving passage:

> There has come a frenzy in the tides of men. Social forces whose power we
> have not understood or, if we have understood, we have been helpless to
> control, have sucked us into a dark whirlpool. (Tolman, 1941, p. 205)

Tolman considered the question of what psychologists could say and do at such a terrible time. A year later, in 1942, he published *Drives Toward War*. In this book he combined his own concepts with certain Freudian ideas and used them to try to understand human drives that lead to the devastation of war. Tolman also considered such clinical phenomena as regression, fixation, and displaced aggression onto outgroups and tried to explain them using the concepts he had developed in his animal research.

A number of times during his long career Tolman supported causes he believed to be important. Perhaps the most dramatic was his support of colleagues, especially younger faculty members, during what came to known as the "year of the oath" (Stewart, 1950) at the University of California. In 1949 the California Regents decided that in addition to the traditional oath of loyalty to the state of California, university employees would be required to swear a codicil that read "I swear that I am not a member of the Communist Party or under any oath, or a party to any agreement, or under any commitment that is in conflict with my obligation under this oath." Faculty members were instructed to "sign or get out." Tolman refused. He pointed out that it would have been relatively easy for him to "get out" but much more difficult for younger people at the beginning of their careers. Tolman chose to stay and head the opposition that led to the eventual withdrawal of the oath by the Regents in 1950. A recognition of Tolman's integrity in this struggle is shown by the University of California Regents' decision in 1959 to confer upon him an honorary LL.D. degree.

Tolman wrote with wit and grace. In the sometimes ponderous literature of psychology his stylish writings stand out. While devoted to psychology and the scientific analysis of behavior, Tolman never took either himself or his experiments too seriously. He had a talent for neologisms, and many of the expressions he formulated are now part of the terminology of psychology: *sign-gestalt expectation, sign-significate relations, cognitive map, means-end readiness, discriminanda and manipulanda*, and perhaps most colorful of all, *schematic sowbug*, a term Tolman used in predicting VTE in discrimination learning (Tolman, 1939).

Tolman received many honors and awards. He was president of the APA in 1937 and chairman of Lewin's Society for the Psychological Study of Social Issues in 1940. He was a member of the Society of Experimental Psychologists and the National Academy of Sciences. In 1957 the APA gave Tolman an award for distinguished scientific contributions. The remarks he made upon receiving this award are characteristic:

> This is really all I have to say. It is not too brilliant an account; but I do
> want to point out that such experiments were fun to do, although they took
> a long time and although the results when we got them persisted in being
> slight, confused and somewhat sleazy. They did give us, anyway, a beautiful
> chance to speculate about vector models, and this, too, was fun. But,
> whether such experiments or such models will in the end have any world
> shattering importance seems doubtful. . . . But as it is, I am stuck with these
> sorts of data and these sorts of models, and I intend to go on playing with

them....In short, we will have a delightful time and absolutely no dull moments. (Tolman, 1957, quoted by Crutchfield, 1961, p. 141)

EDWIN RAY GUTHRIE (1886–1959)

Guthrie's Early Life

William McDougall (1933), the expatriate British psychologist, classified behaviorists as "strict, near, and purposive" types. Watson was the quintessential strict behaviorist, Tolman and McDougall himself were of the purposive variety, while Guthrie was a near or perhaps commonsense behaviorist. Edwin Ray Guthrie was born in Lincoln, Nebraska, in 1886, the oldest of five children. His father operated a piano store, and his mother had been a grade school teacher. Guthrie was a precocious child. He showed his academic talent early, and in the eighth grade he read Darwin's books. In high school his senior thesis was so well reasoned and written that his high school principal, H. K. Wolfe, interviewed him to make sure it had not been plagiarized. It had not, and Guthrie graduated from high school with a brilliant record.

In 1903 he entered the University of Nebraska, where he majored in mathematics. He also took several courses in philosophy and the only course in general psychology that was taught. Guthrie graduated in 1907 with Phi Beta Kappa honors and continued his studies as a graduate student at Nebraska. He earned a master's degree in philosophy while taking a number of graduate courses in mathematics and psychology. In a research course with Thaddeus Bolton he devoted a winter to

Edwin R. Guthrie. (Archives of the History of American Psychology, University of Akron)

measuring thresholds for the perception of "twoness," a psychophysical experience that quenched forever Guthrie's interest in that area of psychology. Fortunately, he also took a number of psychology courses with his former high school principal, H. K. Wolfe, that were more interesting. Wolfe obtained his Ph.D. from Wilhelm Wundt in 1886, returned to the United States in 1889, and took a position as chairman of the Department of Philosophy at the University of Nebraska. In addition to philosophy, Wolfe taught general, pedagogical, and experimental psychology. He also established a psychological laboratory that he constantly sought to equip and improve (Benjamin & Bertelson, 1975). In 1897 Wolfe was accused of being uncooperative and of "intermeddling" in the affairs of other departments. His appointment at Nebraska was terminated. Despite student petitions and a mass protest meeting in his behalf, he was forced to leave the university. Wolfe spent the next eight years as the principal of a number of high schools, including Guthrie's. In 1906 a new chancellor of the university invited Wolfe to return to the faculty. He was an inspirational teacher, and the Department of Psychology he established at Nebraska has had the distinction of seeing more of its undergraduate students go on to become president of the APA than any other college or university (Benjamin & Bertelson, 1975). Guthrie was one of the APA presidents from Nebraska. More than fifty years later Guthrie acknowledged his "good fortune to be his [Wolfe's] only student" (Guthrie, 1959, p. 160). During his three years as a postgraduate student at Nebraska, Guthrie also taught mathematics in a Lincoln high school.

In 1910 Guthrie entered the University of Pennsylvania as a postgraduate fellow in the Department of Philosophy. During his Christmas vacation he attended the annual meeting of the American Philosophical Association and heard a philosopher, Edgar Arthur Singer, deliver an address entitled "Mind as an Observable Object." Twenty-five years later Guthrie recalled Singer's address as "the most stirring event of my academic life" (Guthrie, 1935, p. vii). What captured his interest was Singer's contention that the mind can be studied objectively within the framework of science. Singer was on the faculty of the Department of Philosophy at the University of Pennsylvania, and so Guthrie was able to take a Ph.D. with him. Guthrie's thesis was in the area of symbolic logic and dealt with Bertrand Russell's paradoxes, that is, with propositions whose truth implies their falsity and whose falsity implies their truth, for example, "All generalizations are invalid." Guthrie received a Ph.D. in 1912 but found his interest in philosophy weakening. Such philosophical exercises as those of Bertrand Russell and Alfred North Whitehead in their *Principia Mathematica* required

> some 400 pages to establish the conclusion that one plus one equals two, and
> that every intervening step could be challenged and would require more
> proof, and that the steps of these added proofs would require still
> more....(Guthrie, 1959, p. 161)

Such exercises made Guthrie doubt that deduction alone could ever lead to an understanding of the human mind.

After receiving his Ph.D. Guthrie taught mathematics in a Philadelphia high school for three years before accepting a position as an instructor in philosophy at the University of Washington. He remained there from 1914 until his retirement in 1956, transferring to the Department of Psychology in 1919 and being appointed a professor in 1928, dean of the graduate school in 1943, and the university's executive officer in 1947. These administrative positions undoubtedly restricted his contributions to psychology. Nevertheless, his was an important neobehaviorist voice.

Learning through Contiguity

Guthrie's most important contribution to psychology was his theory of learning, or what he called with characteristic modesty his "point of view" or "rudiments" of a system of learning. He presented his position in two major theoretical papers in 1930 and 1934; in his best-known book, *The Psychology of Learning*, published in 1935; and in a third theoretical paper in 1940. Guthrie's view of learning was concise and simple: all learning is based on contiguity between stimuli and responses. "Stimuli which accompany a response tend, on their recurrence, to evoke that response" (Guthrie, 1930, p. 412). In *The Psychology of Learning* Guthrie stated this principle of contiguity in similar words: "A combination of stimuli which has accompanied a movement will on its recurrence tend to be followed by that movement" (Guthrie, 1935, p. 26). The last movements in a situation will be repeated when that situation recurs. The principle of contiguity is elegant and simple, especially in contrast to the complex accounts of learning given by other neobehaviorists. Even Tolman's view of learning became increasingly complex. In one of his last major statements (1959) he devoted many pages to complex diagrams showing multiple interactions and relationships between independent, intervening, and dependent variables. As we will see later in this chapter, Clark Leonard Hull's learning theory became very elaborate, and B. F. Skinner coauthored a 750-page book describing the effects of schedules of reinforcement, just one aspect of his operant approach. The principle of association through contiguity can be traced to Aristotle (Chapter 1). It received a full exposition by the British empiricists James Mill, Alexander Bain, and David Hartley (Chapter 2). Guthrie believed that a general account of learning could be based on this ancient principle.

At first sight Guthrie's principle of association through contiguity seems inadequate as an explanation of learning. What of the effects of reward and punishment and of practice? What of forgetting and the temporal conditioning experiments of Pavlov? In Pavlov's experiments minutes separated the conditioned and unconditioned stimuli, yet his dogs gave conditioned responses to the CS. Since there was no temporal contiguity between the CS and unconditioned stimulus (US), how could that be? At first glance these questions presented a serious challenge to Guthrie, but in fact he was able to answer all of them. Consider first his analysis of the effects of reward and punishment. Guthrie had no quarrel with the "popular and well-established view" that reward and punishment affect learning. What he did dispute was Thorndike's belief that they act to somehow stamp in or stamp out habits. According to Guthrie a cat in a puzzle box learns to escape because that response removes the animal from the stimulus situation of the puzzle box and so preserves an association between the stimulus and the escape response. Food does not stamp in or strengthen a stimulus-response connection; rather, it protects an association that has already been formed. Food does not cause learning; it protects against unlearning. Guthrie said:

> What encountering the food does is not to intensify a previous item of behavior but to protect that item from being unlearned. The whole situation and action of the animal is so changed by the food that the pre-food situation is shielded from new associations. (Guthrie, 1940, p. 144)

For Guthrie the ultimate function of reward is to remove an animal from a particular stimulus situation and thus prevent it from unlearning an association that has been formed. The role of rewards is to keep the response "faithful" to the stimulus.

But what of punishment? Surely annoyers and punishers produce learning. Responses leading to such negative consequences are usually suppressed. Guthrie agrees that indeed they are:

> Sitting on tacks does not discourage learning. It encourages one in learning to do something else than sit. It is not the feeling caused by punishment, but the specific action caused by punishment, that determines what will be learned. (Guthrie, 1935, p. 158)

Punishers elicit actions, and it is those actions which are learned:

> The animal on a charged grid, a barefoot boy on a hot pavement, a man sitting on a tack have as their goals mere escape from the intense stimulation that causes general tension and restlessness as well as specific movements. (Guthrie, 1935, p. 165)

When these "maintaining stimuli" are removed, there is contiguity between them and the response. When they recur, the response occurs again. Learning occurs through contiguity, but in this case with aversive stimuli.

Another well-established fact concerns the effects of practice. Guthrie acknowledged that both psychological research and everyday experience show that practice does indeed produce improved performance. How can that be since there should be contiguity on the first occasion when a response occurs and thus immediate learning independent of practice? In responding to this challenge Guthrie distinguished between movements and acts (Guthrie, 1940). He pointed out that our everyday language usually refers to acts—we sail a boat, eat dinner, ride a horse, play a piano, shoot a basketball—and to their results rather than to the movements that constitute them. Certainly all these acts improve with practice. There is an obvious difference between a maestro and a novice, a professional basketball player and a weekend player, and so on. But this difference, according to Guthrie, is a consequence of improvement in the numerous movements that underlie these complex acts. It is those movements which are refined with practice and whose association with the stimulus situation is established. The novice responds in a clumsy, uncertain, inefficient manner; the expert, in a smooth, sure, and efficient way. Their acts may be similar—they both play the piano or shoot the basketball—but their movements are very different. Practice works on these movements.

What of forgetting? Guthrie accounted for forgetting as being due to the formation through contiguity of new associations. If there were no new associations, there would be no forgetting. He stated that "learning does not disappear as the result of a mere lapse of time, but only when that lapse of time includes new learning which erases the old" (Guthrie, 1935, p. 117). Guthrie cited Pavlov's results showing that a conditioned response would often remain for many weeks without noticeable weakening. He argued that such conditioned responses are stable because the conditioned stimulus is not encountered by the experimental animal in its everyday life, and so the association is protected. Guthrie predicted that if Pavlov's dogs had encountered the CSs in their everyday life, forgetting (extinction) would have been much more rapid.

Guthrie also used the results of an experiment by John Jenkins and Karl Dallenbach (1924) on the effects of sleep on memory. These authors found that material learned just before a subject went to sleep was better retained than was material learned prior to waking activities. Sleep, said Guthrie, prevented learning of new associations, and so the old ones were protected.

Finally, Guthrie cited the everyday experience of putting on ice skates at the beginning of the winter. Usually one finds that skating is easy even though many months have passed since the last skating session. According to Guthrie, the movements involved in ice-skating are unique and thus are not reconditioned by our summertime activities.

The final challenge to Guthrie's contiguity view of learning we will consider seems the most serious at first sight. How could he account for trace conditioning? Pavlov found that conditioned responses can be established and maintained when the CS precedes the US by a long time interval, sometimes even minutes. How, then, can there be contiguity between the stimulus and response? Guthrie argued that when a CS such as a bell or buzzer is presented, the dog responds by listening to it, and the listening response continues when the bell is no longer ringing; that is, the response persists through the trace interval. Guthrie wrote:

> When the bell rings the dog responds by "listening" which is a series of
> movements, postural changes, turning of the head, pricking up the ears, and
> the like. When the salivary glands begin to secrete, the accompanying
> stimuli are not furnished by the bell but by these responses to the bell.
> (Guthrie, 1930, p. 418)

Guthrie's analysis of his results caused Pavlov to write "The Reply of a Physiologist to Psychologists" (Pavlov, 1932), the only paper he published in an American journal of psychology. Pavlov devoted almost half the paper to a highly critical rebuttal of Guthrie. First, Pavlov contrasted Guthrie's approach, in which the conditioned reflex is used to illustrate a principle of learning, with his own approach, in which the conditioned reflex is a phenomenon that must be analyzed and reduced to its physiological basis. Second, with reference to Guthrie's analysis of temporal conditioning, Pavlov reported that the "listening response" Guthrie had described is part of the "orienting reaction," a reaction that quickly disappears. Thus Guthrie had postulated a nonexistent reaction as the basis of temporal conditioning. Rather than a series of active, substitute responses, Pavlov reported that during long trace and delay intervals between the CS and the US a dog was often

completely indifferent and quiet in the first period of action of the
conditioned stimulus; or even (as is not seldom the case) immediately upon
the beginning of that stimulus, he drops into a drowsy and sometimes
abruptly into a sleeping state, with relaxation of the musculature. (Pavlov,
1932, p. 95)

Where, then, Pavlov asked, were the movement-produced substitute stimuli to which,
as Guthrie claimed, conditioning had occurred? According to Pavlov, trace conditioning and delay conditioning are based on active, central inhibition of the conditioned reflex. Guthrie, he said, had made "incorrect use" of the facts of conditioning. It is clear from the tone of Pavlov's reply that Guthrie had made him angry.
This is perhaps not a surprising reaction, for at one point Guthrie had characterized
Pavlov's explanations of delay conditioning as assuming "mysterious latencies in
the nervous system" (Guthrie, 1930, p. 418).

Guthrie, like Tolman, had a talent for coining descriptive phrases: Thorndike's
explanation of the effects of delayed rewards was said to assume a "cerebral hang-
over"; Tolman's rats VTE-ing at a choice point were described as being "lost in
thought." Guthrie also used many anecdotes and accounts of everyday events to
illustrate his concepts:

In a Pacific coast city recently a number of dogs succumbed to strychnine
poisoning. Poisoned chunks of beef were found in the neighborhood. Several
owners of good dogs undertook to train their animals not to indulge in stray
tidbits by scattering many pieces of beef to which were fastened small
mousetraps of the familiar spring variety. (Guthrie, 1935, p. 21)

The dogs quickly developed a "very supercilious attitude toward stray meat" as a
result, Guthrie concluded, of the almost perfect contiguity between eating and the
action of the mousetrap (Guthrie, 1935, p. 21).

A young mother once asked Guthrie how she could teach her daughter not to
throw her coat on the floor when she arrived home. Guthrie advised her to insist
that the girl put her coat back on, go out the door, return, remove her coat, and
hang it up. In this way contiguity between entering the house and hanging up the
coat would be preserved and the habit would be established. The mother reported
success with this procedure.

Guthrie also reported the example of

two small countryboys who lived before the day of the rural use of motor
cars and had their Friday afternoons made dreary by the regular visit of
their pastor whose horse they were supposed to unharness, groom, feed and
water and then harness again on the departure. (Guthrie, 1935, p. 48)

To preserve their afternoons, the two boys retrained the horse. One of them stood
behind the animal and shouted "Whoa," whereupon the other boy gave the horse
a sharp jab with a hayfork. Guthrie reported that the boys were "quite satisfied with
the results." When the pastor said "Whoa" the horse would lunge forward and the
boys were able to enjoy their Friday afternoons (Guthrie, 1935, p. 48). He also
described how nervous bird dogs can be trained by discharging a pistol at a great
distance, slowly moving closer, and then using a louder pistol. He also listed different methods of "breaking horses." One method favored by the military is to train

the horse first with a light blanket, then with a sack, then with a sack with a little sand, and then with more sand until the horse carries a saddle and finally a rider. In all these cases movements are associated with stimuli through contiguity. Guthrie considered the habit of smoking to be made up of many movements. Many stimuli have become signals to smoke: the sight and smell of tobacco, finishing a meal, and sitting down to work, among others. For a person to stop smoking, these stimuli must be associated with new movements. The habits must be sidetracked by, for example, eating an apple after dinner or chewing gum while working (Guthrie, 1935, chap. XI).

Descriptive phrases, stories, and anecdotes have an undeniable charm but are no substitute for experimental results. Guthrie was well aware of this deficiency and on one occasion set out to remedy it. From the autumn of 1936 to the spring of 1939, Guthrie and his colleague George P. Horton conducted an intensive study of contiguity learning by cats. At the time Guthrie was fifty years of age and had numerous administrative responsibilities, but he spent his late afternoons in the department of psychology's vivarium taking notes while Horton tested their cats. They first presented their results in a film distributed through the Psychological Cinema Register in 1938 and then in their monograph *Cats in a Puzzle Box*, published in 1946. As the title implies, they used a puzzle box and recorded approximately 800 escape responses. A conspicuous feature of their apparatus was a slender vertical rod or pole about one foot away from the front of the box. When the cat jostled or rubbed against the pole, the front door opened and the cat escaped. The moment the rod moved, a camera photographed the cat, thus making a permanent record of the cat's behavior at the moment of escape. Having this apparatus, they were able to ask:

> Does the behavior of the cat in the puzzle box go at any point contrary to,
> or in violation of, the principle of association through contiguity? (Guthrie &
> Horton, 1946, p. 1)

Since the box opened as soon as the pole moved, the principle of contiguity predicted that a specific movement, captured by the camera, would be learned. The same cat should show considerable stereotypy in its behavior from trial to trial. Individual cats' responses at the moment of release were indeed highly stereotyped, as illustrated by cat K:

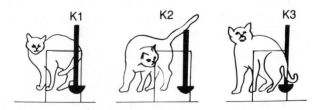

On its first trial it struck the pole while turning in the box after some 4 seconds. This was repeated after 13 and 17 secs. in the next two trials. In the fourth trial the movement was repeated but the mechanism failed to operate and the cat walked around the pole, striking it with its left shoulder. On trial 5 the first turning movement failed to operate the mechanism and the cat kept on turning, striking the pole with its rear foot. In trials 6, 7, 9, 10, 11, and 12 the same turning response brought release. (Guthrie & Horton, 1946, p. 27)

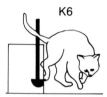

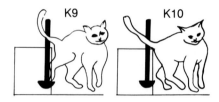
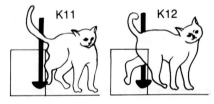

Later responses shown by this cat and other cats included rubbing against the pole and leaning into it while walking past. Responses contiguous with escape from the box had been learned.

In 1979 Bruce Moore and Susan Stuttard suggested that the stereotyped responses Guthrie and Horton had observed might in fact have been part of the cats' species-typical greeting for the human observers, a rubbing or brushing response that was redirected to the post in the box. In a replication of the earlier experiment they found that cats approached and rubbed the post when they could see human observers but did not do so when the observers were hidden. Guthrie's explanation might have been incorrect, but his experiment remains a classic study of animal learning.

Guthrie's Clinical Interests

In 1938 Guthrie published *The Psychology of Human Conflict*, a reflection of his long-standing interest in clinical psychology. He had read and studied the works of Sigmund Freud as a graduate student and had taught a course on the psychology of adjustment for many years. With his wife he translated Pierre Janet's *Principles* of Psychotherapy (1903) in 1924. He found Janet's views, especially his conception of the unconscious, much more appealing than Freud's "appeal to darkness" (Guthrie, 1948, p. 65). He also preferred Janet's notion of a *force mentale* to what he considered Freud's pseudo-physiological explanations. Janet believed that this force differs in strength in different people and also waxes and wanes at different times. When it is exhausted through a series of life crises, neurotic symptoms are likely. If the *force mentale* can be restored, neurotic symptoms will be alleviated. Janet's conception of humans as delicately balanced energy systems appealed to Guthrie. In 1903 Janet had published the first detailed descriptions of bulimia (Pope, Hudson, & Mialet, 1985). After Janet's death Guthrie stated that his contribution to psychology had been greater than that of Wundt and criticized psychologists for ignoring his work (Guthrie, 1948).

During World War II, Guthrie served as a civilian consultant in military intelligence and in the Office of War Information. In 1945 he was elected president of the APA. After the war he returned to the University of Washington and devoted most of his time to administrative duties. However, he did find time to coauthor *Educational Psychology* (1950) and to write *The State University: Its Function and Future* (1959). In 1958 the American Psychological Foundation awarded him a gold medal for his contributions to psychology. He died of a heart attack in 1959 at the age of seventy-three and was remembered as

> a witty and warm-hearted sage, who was not only wise but always ready with an apt way of phrasing his wisdom. (Sheffield, 1959, p. 642)

CLARK LEONARD HULL (1884–1952)

Hull's Early Life

Clark Leonard Hull was born on a farm near Akron, New York, in May 1884. He attended a one-room rural school, took all the courses it offered, taught there for a year, and then entered Alma Academy. Even as a young boy Hull had a strong drive to succeed, to do well and be something more than "an obscure chore boy," his reference to the odd jobs he took to earn his way through high school. Hull's diaries of those years contain frequent references to long periods of work and study and to his intense desire to succeed. This entry from May 2, 1903, is typical:

> Worked all day.... Got poor marks in Latin for three months. I have made up my mind that I will get 92 or more next month. I am going to work on that til I bust if I don't. Am going to commence tonight. This will be a test as to whether I have got the power to meet formidable obstacles. 92 or *bust*. I've done it once and I can do it again. (Hull, 1962, p. 811)

His dedication and high level of aspiration had their price. Hull was intensely self-critical and after taking the Latin test felt great disappointment because his score was "only 91.5." Financial pressures forced him to interrupt his high school education and work for a year as an apprentice mining engineer in Hibbing, Minnesota. He returned to Alma Academy, was graduated, but then suffered a severe bout of

Clark L. Hull. (Archives of the History of American Psychology, University of Akron)

typhoid fever which left him physically weak and delayed his entrance to college for a year.

At Alma College Hull studied mining engineering, but a severe attack of poliomyelitis at the end of his second year left one leg paralyzed and ruled out a career as a mining engineer. Hull decided to study either religion or psychology, finally choosing psychology because he felt it would allow both theoretical and practical work with apparatus. To save money for his education Hull taught for two years after his illness in a high school before entering the University of Michigan to complete his undergraduate studies. At twenty-seven years old, recently married and having overcome serious difficulties, Hull was more mature and dedicated but also more shy and reserved than the average student. He ascribed these characteristics to his strong desire to overcome the effects of polio and to show the world that though he was a man "who walked with a cane," he was as good as anyone.

At Michigan, Hull's interests turned more and more toward psychology. He graduated with a B.A. degree in 1913 and again taught for a year, this time at a normal school in Kentucky, to save money for graduate school. He was admitted to the University of Wisconsin as a graduate student and was assigned as a research assistant to Joseph Jastrow. Jastrow had taken his Ph.D with G. Stanley Hall (Chapter 9) and was an active experimental psychologist. However, in selecting his graduate students it is said that he chose talented ironworkers and engineers and with their assistance added an exotic Moorish room to his house (Meyer, 1978). Thus Hull's background might have had something to do with his appointment. In any event Hull was delighted to have this position, for his journey to graduate school had been long and arduous. Persistence, perseverance, and stick-to-itiveness characterized Hull all his life (Spence, 1952).

At Wisconsin, Hull's commitment to psychology, especially to experimental psychology, became firm. In 1916 he wrote in his diary:

> It seems almost certain now that I shall be a pure psychologist, and that my career will be spent in the free atmosphere of a great university. That this is settled is a very great advantage, for now I shall not need to waste energy preparing for work I shall never do. (Hull, 1962, p. 814)

In his dissertation research Hull used complex Chinese characters to which subjects learned specific responses. His dissertation, *Quantitative Aspects of the Evolution of Concepts*, demonstrating the development and use of concepts, came to be quoted extensively in the psychological literature. Hull was recognized as a creative and imaginative experimenter. He received a Ph.D. degree in 1918 when he was thirty-four years old and then accepted a position as an instructor at Wisconsin.

Hull's Research on Aptitude Testing

Almost immediately Hull began the first of what were to be three distinct phases of his research career, his work on aptitude testing. At Wisconsin he was assigned to teach a course on psychological testing. Knowing almost nothing about the topic, he read the literature on testing and was struck by what he considered the poverty of the field and especially by the weakness of attempts to validate different aptitude tests. In his characteristically thorough manner, Hull set out to develop a scientific body of knowledge on aptitude testing and even to develop a "universal aptitude test." Later he realized that the latter goal was unrealistic, but his work in this area did lead to his first book, *Aptitude Testing*, published in 1928.

In his attempt to validate various tests, Hull made extensive use of correlations between test scores and performance. The tedium of computing correlation coefficients with tables and by hand led Hull to build a correlation machine that would compute such correlations automatically. He was an accomplished tinkerer, gadgeteer, and mechanic who liked to design and build machines. A punched paper input provided data to the machine, which could be programmed to do correlations and other operations. While many people doubted that such a machine could be designed or would ever work, Hull's machine did calculate correlations. Today, with hand-held electronic calculators and desktop computers, Hull's achievement may not seem great. However, at the time it was a considerable achievement, and Hull's machine is now housed in the Smithsonian Museum in Washington, D.C. His book on aptitude testing was well received, but Hull concluded that what was needed was a large-scale study with thousands of workers. While such a study might be possible in a large city, it was not feasible in Madison, Wisconsin, and so Hull decided to end his work on aptitude testing. He turned to his second major research interest, hypnosis and suggestibility. Hull studied hypnosis first at Wisconsin and then at Yale after his move there in 1929.

Hull's Research on Hypnosis and Suggestibility

Once again this interest developed from a course Hull taught. In lectures to pre-medical students Hull discussed hypnosis and found that his students were fascinated with the material. He became interested in hypnosis and especially in the role suggestibility plays in medical cures. Jastrow too was interested in hypnosis, for he had often investigated psychical phenomena. An avowed skeptic, Jastrow delighted in exposing as charlatans and frauds the seers, soothsayers, psychics, clairvoyants, and fortune-tellers who visited Madison. Hull attended a séance and was impressed by the ardor and enthusiasm of the participants and the intensity of their belief that they had communicated with the "other side." However, true to his mentor Jastrow, Hull concluded that the whole thing was based on trickery and suggestion.

After reviewing the literature on hypnosis (Chapter 8), Hull concluded that this field too was in a "dilapidated state" (Hull, 1933, p. ix) and in dire need of objective experimental investigations. He began his research hoping to conduct "one hundred or at least ninety-nine systematic, empirical studies" and did publish 32 papers and one book on hypnosis (Hull, 1933, preface). Hull was well aware of the dangers and pitfalls of studying hypnosis and of the many earlier cases of error, deception, and even fraud (Chapter 11). He was determined to avoid the "wretched experiments" (Hull, 1933, p. 16) of the past and was successful in doing so. Hull described his results and theoretical views on hypnosis in his second book, *Hypnosis and Suggestibility*, published in 1933. He described hypnotic phenomena and experiments in which instruments were used to record physiological responses during the hypnotic trance and outlined techniques such as fixation and direct suggestion for the induction of a hypnotic trance. Hull believed that rather than being characteristic of certain people, susceptibility to hypnosis is a trait that has a normal distribution in the population as a whole. His research showed that women and girls were only slightly more susceptible to hypnosis than were men and boys. Children were somewhat more susceptible than were adults. In general normal people of average intelligence made the best subjects for experiments on hypnosis. Hull found little evidence of a relationship between high and low intelligence, various character traits, neuroses or psychoses and susceptibility to hypnosis. He concluded that hypnotic susceptibility was less special and restricted than had been thought.

Hull also found that hypnosis did not facilitate the recall of recent memories. Subjects were no more likely to recall the details of a recent event under hypnosis than they were in a normal, waking state. However, he did find that hypnosis allowed some childhood and other old memories to be recalled. Posthypnotic suggestions, a favorite demonstration of stage hypnotists, were found to be relatively ineffective. Hull concluded that hypnosis is best described as a state of hypersuggestibility.

The most important characteristic of all these conclusions was that they were based on objective, experimental evidence. When *Hypnosis and Suggestibility* was published, reviewers praised Hull's scientific approach and the manner in which he had opened hypnosis and suggestibility to experimental investigation. Nearly thirty years later, Ernest Hilgard, a leading contemporary investigator of hypnosis, said of Hull's book:

> It still stands as a model of clarity and objectivity in the approach to what remain even today puzzling and unresolved problems. (Hilgard, 1961, p. xv)

Today *Hypnosis and Suggestibility* is still used as a text in university courses on hypnosis. Despite its excellence, Hull's research did have one unfortunate consequence. A woman who had been hypnotized sued Hull and Yale University, where the experiment had been done, claiming that the experience had caused her to have a mental breakdown. The suit was settled out of court, but the university authorities instructed Hull to end his research on hypnosis.

Hull's Behavior System

While Hull's work on aptitude testing and hypnosis was of undeniable importance, his most significant contribution to psychology was his attempt to develop a comprehensive behavior system. This third phase of his research career began at Wisconsin and continued after his move to Yale in 1929. Hull was recruited by James Angell (Chapter 10), the president of Yale, to strengthen Yale's Institute of Psychology, which soon became the Institute of Human Relations. At the time of his move from Wisconsin Hull confided in his diary that he had "torn myself from the associations of fifteen years, to make a new start in my scientific life" (Hull, 1962, p. 826).

At Yale, Hull began to think seriously about writing a behavioristic account of psychology. In the summer of 1930 Hull was invited to lecture on aptitude testing at Harvard, where he acquired copies of Isaac Newton's *Principia* and Bertrand Russell and Alfred North Whitehead's *Principia Mathematica*. Unlike Guthrie, Hull found these works to be a model for the type of psychological system he hoped to develop. Returning to Yale, he began a serious study of the works of the classical epistemologists and philosophers; Democritus (Chapter 1), Thomas Hobbes, John Locke, David Hume, Immanuel Kant, and Gottfried Wilhelm von Leibnitz (Chapter 2). At the time Hull was in his forties, a professor at Yale and a man with a secure reputation in psychology; yet rather than resting on his laurels he began this study, a long and demanding series of experimental investigations, and work on the behavior system that filled the rest of his life. Hull was often troubled by forebodings of early death and feelings that there was not sufficient time to accomplish what he wanted to do. He was convinced that after the age of fifty he would no longer be able to make the contributions to psychology he expected of himself. His conviction that time was running out motivated his compulsive drive to work and produce.

Hull was sympathetic to John Watson's behaviorism and agreed that psychology should be the science of behavior. He had also been impressed with Ivan Pavlov's *Conditioned Reflexes* (1927) (Chapter 12) and found Pavlov's experiments admirable for the care with which they were conducted and the precision of their results. A third influence came from Robert Woodworth's (1918) imposition of the organism (O) between the stimulus (S) and the response (R), forming S-O-R (Chapter 10). One of Hull's most influential students, Kenneth Spence, described Hull's system as a "Herculean elaboration of this S-O-R formula" (Spence, 1952, p. 646).

Hull's first major theoretical paper on learning was published in 1929. In "A Functional Interpretation of the Conditioned Reflex," Hull described the conditioned reflex as

an automatic trial and error mechanism which mediates blindly and
beautifully, the adjustment of the organism to a complex environment.
(Hull, 1929, p. 498)

With his engineering background and fascination with machines and gadgets, Hull
was intrigued by the notion of the human organism as a machine. In *Principles of
Behavior* (1943), he recommended as "a prophylaxis against anthropomorphic sub-
jectivism" the device of regarding "from time to time, the behaving organism as a
completely self-maintaining robot, constructed of materials as unlike ourselves as
may be" (Hull, 1943, p. 27). Hull hoped that one day he would be able to design
and build a behaving machine that would match the success of his correlation machine. He was never able to do so, but this mechanistic view of behavior permeated
his behavior system. Hull saw the conditioned reflex as a mechanism that allows an
organism to react to environmental demands. He tried to extend the principles of
classical conditioning to instrumental and trial-and-error learning situations, that
is, to construct a single-factor theory of learning. He found this extension difficult
and after rereading Thorndike concluded that it was impossible. Instead he accepted the principle of reinforcement based on drive reduction, which had developed from studies of instrumental conditioning, as a second major factor in learning. From then on Hull became more and more of a law-of-effect or reinforcement
theorist, though he still employed Pavlovian concepts.

In 1936 Hull was elected president of the APA. For his presidential address
he planned originally to present a "Prospectus for Psychology Based Upon Habit."
Instead, he entitled the address "Mind, Mechanism and Adaptive Behavior" and
presented for the first time to a general audience of psychologists his organized,
deductive behavior system (Hull, 1937). Hull believed that a sound general theory
of behavior was vital to psychology. He was convinced that the most effective way
for psychology to progress as an experimental science was to have a well-developed
theory that would serve as a framework for research. Such a theory would not only
integrate and organize experimental results but indicate directions for future research. It would serve as the *Principia* of psychology. Hull used as his model theoretical systems employing a set of explicitly defined postulates from which certain
theorems could be deduced and tested through experimentation. Such systems had
worked well in physics. Hull described himself as being "docile to the data" and
saw the need for constant revision of the behavior system as its predictions were
tested and either confirmed or refuted. He considered his behavior system only a
first step, but it was the most ambitious attempt to construct a formal behavior
system we have encountered.

Hull's Learning Theory

As part of his presidential address Hull prepared and distributed a set of mimeo-
graphed sheets containing his first set of postulates, definitions, and derived theorems. Each derivation ended with the "QED" of mathematical proofs, an indication of the rigor with which Hull hoped to proceed. This system was further
extended and developed in his most important book, *Principles of Behavior,* pub-

lished in 1943. *Principles* represents Hull at his most readable and for more than two decades was one of the most frequently cited and quoted works in psychology. The book sold consistently from its publication to the mid-1960s, with its peak sales coming in 1949. From 1946 until his death in 1952, Hull's health deteriorated and he suffered increasingly frequent and severe angina pectoris attacks. Still, during those six years he was able to write *Essentials of Behavior* (1951) and *A Behavior System,* published posthumously (1952a).

Hull's final system consisted of seventeen postulates and seventeen corollaries. The central postulate related the strength of a habit [habit strength (S^HR)] to the number of times the habit was reinforced (N). This postulate read as follows:

> Habit strength, the tendency of a stimulus trace to evoke an associated
> response, increases as a positive growth function of the number of trials,
> provided that trials are evenly spaced, reinforcement occurs on every trial,
> and everything else remains constant. (paraphrased from Hull, 1943, p. 114,
> in Hilgard, 1956, p. 131)

Successive reinforcements were seen as contributing increments of "habs" to habit strength. However, habit strength is an intervening variable in Hull's system and cannot be measured directly. It combines with other intervening variables relating to drive level (D), stimulus intensity (V), and the incentive value of the reward (K) in a multiplicative function to yield a value for the reaction potential (S^ER):

$$S^ER = S^HR \times D \times V \times K$$

S^ER then combines with other intervening variables S^OR and L to determine the value of the output, dependent variables—reaction latency, reaction amplitude, and number of nonreinforced responses before extinction.

Other Hullian postulates relate habit strength to the nature and amount of the reinforcing agent, the time between response and reinforcement, and the temporal relationship between CS and CR. Hull showed that theorems could be derived from each of these postulates and then could be tested experimentally. The business of psychology was to analyze interactions between the system's variables in situations that were as simple as possible. Hull intended his system to be as general as possible, that is, one that would be successful in predicting both the amplitude of the galvanic skin response in humans and lever pressing by rats. He led an extensive program of experimental research on classical and instrumental conditioning with both human and animal subjects. Hull was open to critical tests of his system, though he did like to wager malted milks on their outcome. One of his former students, Carl Hovland, remembered that Hull had

> an unusual knack for getting his students so involved with their research
> problems that they continued related investigations when they took jobs at
> other institutions, and soon had students of their own carrying on similar
> research. There was a large number of enthusiastic fourth and fifth
> generation students throughout the country. (Hovland, 1952, p. 349)

These students used a psychological language of their own, and even today it is not unusual to hear references to "subscript S, superscript H, subscript R" and the multiplicative effects of "big D" in their discussions. Hull also attracted students from a number of foreign countries, especially Japan. The Japanese students took degrees with Hull at Yale, returned to Japan, and established a Hullian school of Japanese psychology. One result was that in the 1950s and early 1960s Japanese journals of psychology contained numerous "Hullian" articles reporting experimental investigations of the interactions between "Hullian" variables. When all else failed, Hull ruefully admitted that he would often make a specially definite prediction that would immediately send a dozen people rushing to their laboratories to prove him wrong.

Hull's System: An Evaluation

Hull's was clearly an ambitious and sophisticated attempt to develop a general system of behavior, but was it a success? Certainly in terms of its heuristic value in stimulating research it was. In his obituary for Hull, Kenneth Spence pointed out that approximately 40 percent of *all* experimental reports in the *Journal of Experimental Psychology* and the *Journal of Comparative and Physiological Psychology,* two prestigious APA journals, during the decade from 1941 to 1950 made reference to Hull (Spence, 1952, p. 641). In the areas of learning and motivation Spence found the citation figure to be 70 percent, more than twice that of any other behavior theorist. Harry Ruja (1956) tallied citation frequencies for psychologists in three major journals of experimental psychology from 1949 to 1952. Hull was by far the most frequently cited psychologist, followed by Spence, Hovland, Hilgard, and Neal Miller, all Hull's former students or close collaborators. Hull's behavior system and theory of learning clearly had a great impact.

However, Hull was not without his critics. On the one hand, there were those who questioned the limited range of experimental situations Hull used and claimed that they could not possibly form the basis of a general system or theory of behavior. In Hull's defense, in developing his system he used the best available materials, whatever their source. Thus, postulate II refers to eyelid conditioning, postulate X to the conditioned galvanic skin response, postulate IV to rats' bar pressing and the amplitude of the galvanic skin response, postulate VII to rats' running responses, and so on.

A second criticism concerns the artificial and limited situations Hull used to test his system. How could a psychologist who did not study people in situations outside the laboratory hope to develop a general system of behavior? Such critics, Hull maintained, misunderstood the process of science. Just as physicists use the unworldly and artificial conditions of the vacuum tube and biologists use the controlled environment of a test tube, psychologists who study behavior must begin with artificial, controlled situations. Hull hoped to go on to more complex learning situations and eventually to a broad range of human problems. He was never able to do so, though his students John Dollard and Neal Miller made one such attempt. In 1950 they published *Personality and Psychotherapy,* in which they tried to integrate Freud's psychoanalysis with Hull's learning theory. The Freudian concept of transference was seen as a case of stimulus generalization, repressed conflicts were seen as those which the patient is unable to label, and maladjustments were attributed to conflicts between incompatible habits and drives.

Other critics contended that while Hull's system had scored impressive successes in predicting the behavior of groups of rats, it was far from successful in predicting the behavior of individual animals. Consider postulate IV. Hull's derived theoretical curve for the growth of habit strength with successive reinforcements corresponded well to reports by Stanley Williams (1938) and C. Theodore Perin (1942). Their results showed that groups of rats given increasing numbers of reinforcements for lever pressing make increasing numbers of extinction responses. However, when one considers the behavior of individual animals in these experiments, we see that in Williams's results the two animals making the largest number of extinction responses were actually in the group given the smallest number of reinforcements (Williams, 1938, p. 512); four rats given the largest number of reinforcements actually made the smallest number of extinction responses. Similarly, in Perin's results, the two rats making the largest number of extinction responses were in the group receiving only thirty reinforcements, while three animals in the group receiving seventy reinforcements did not make a single extinction response (Perin, 1942, p. 99). While Hull's theory was successful in predicting the behavior of groups of animals, it was less useful in predicting the behavior of individuals.

Finally, there were psychologists, with B. F. Skinner in the forefront, who questioned the possibility and even the utility of a general system of behavior. Skinner's position will be considered in more detail later in this chapter.

What, then, can we conclude about Hull's behavior system? Perhaps that it was a magnificent failure—magnificent in its ambition and the rigorous program of experimental research it stimulated but a failure in that the goal of a comprehensive behavior system was not achieved and may in fact be impossible. The days of ambitious theories such as Hull's have passed. Perhaps a magnificent failure is too harsh and a fairer evaluation might be that of Ernest Hilgard, who wrote of Hull:

> It must be acknowledged that Hull's system, for its time was the best there was—not necessarily the one nearest to psychological reality, not necessarily the one whose generalizations were the most likely to endure—but the one worked out in the greatest detail, with the most conscientious effort to be quantitative throughout and at all points closely in touch with empirical tests. (Hilgard, 1956, p. 182)

Hull's contributions were recognized by his contemporaries. In addition to the presidency of the APA, he was elected to the National Academy of Sciences in 1936 and in 1945 received the Warren Medal from the Society of Experimental Psychologists in recognition of his "careful development of a systematic theory of behavior."

Hull died of a heart attack in May 1952, just weeks before he was to retire from Yale University. He had been hard at work on his behavior system until shortly before his final illness.

BURRHUS FREDERICK SKINNER (1904–)

B. F. Skinner is the best-known psychologist in the world today. In 1970 a random sample of 1,000 APA members ranked Skinner as the most important influence on contemporary psycholgy (Wright, 1970). That same year another poll included Skinner among the "100 most important people in the world today." A 1971 Johns Hopkins University survey of psychology faculties and graduate students found Skinner to be the social scientist whose work was most respected. Rae Goodell (1975) surveyed college students' recognition of the names of scientists: Skinner was identified correctly by 82 percent of the students, the highest visibility of any scientist, outranking such luminaries as Margaret Mead (81 percent), Jonas Salk (78 percent), Linus Pauling (50 percent), and James D. Watson (15 percent). Eugene Garfield (1978) found Skinner to be one of the most frequently cited authors in the social sciences. In addition to Skinner's extensive writings—twelve major books, numerous papers, and a multivolume autobiography—there are extensive writings about him, some favorable (Evans, 1968), some unfavorable (Machan, 1974), and some falling between these extremes (Carpenter, 1974). Finally, there are now two journals mainly devoted to a "Skinnerian" approach to psychology, the *Journal of the Experimental Analysis of Behavior*, first published in 1958, and the *Journal of Applied Behavior Analysis*, first published in 1968 (Laties, 1987).

As the modern spokesperson for radical behaviorism, Skinner has become well known through his popular books and writings, appearances on television talk shows and programs such as *Nova*, public lectures, debates, and discussions. He is an articulate, effective, and at times humorous defender of his position. Skinner is also opinionated and controversial: "I now present the devil," said a Harvard

B. F. Skinner. (James R. Holland Stock, Boston)

professor introducing Skinner to his class as a guest lecturer in the late 1940s (Gerow, 1988, p. 73). On his first television appearance he was posed Montaigne's hypothetical dilemma: "Would you, if you had to choose, burn your children or your books?" His answer was that he would burn his children because he believed "his contribution to the future would be greater through his work than through his genes." This reply provoked the predictably outraged response, much controversy, and many invitations for future appearances. It also prompted this wry comment from one of his two daughters, Julie S. Vargas, herself a psychologist: "Skinner fathered behavior analysis and me. I'm not sure which he considers the greater contribution" (Vargas, 1984). After publication of his 1971 book *Beyond Freedom and Dignity* Skinner was described by the then vice president of the United States, Spiro T. Agnew, as an "extreme radical attacking the very precepts upon which American society is based and an advocate of radical surgery on the national psyche" (Hall, 1972, p. 68); the theologian Richard L. Rubenstein described the same book as "less likely to be a blueprint for the Golden Age than for the theory and practice of hell" (Rubenstein, 1971, p. 53). Skinner estimated that 80 percent of the reviews of *Beyond Freedom* were unfavorable. In September 1971, Skinner reached the pinnacle as a media figure when he appeared on the cover of *Time* magazine. *Time*'s headline "B. F. Skinner Says We Can't Afford Freedom" was calculated to cause controversy, and it did (Skinner, 1971a). Fortunately, Skinner has survived the fame and notoriety, and as he said in a 1972 interview, "My hat still fits" (Hall, 1972, p. 68).

Skinner's Early Life

Skinner was born in Susquehanna, Pennsylvania, on March 20, 1904. In his autobiography Skinner gave a detailed, fascinating behaviorist account of his early years. He attended Hamilton College in upstate New York, hoping to become a writer and poet. Skinner took only one course in psychology. The course was taught by William Squires, who had taken his doctorate with Wundt at Leipzig, but the only thing Skinner remembered from the course was Squires's demonstration of the two-point discrimination threshold. Skinner graduated in 1926 with Phi Beta Kappa honors. As an undergraduate he wrote regularly for student publications, sometimes under the pen name of Sir Burrhus de Beerus. At a writer's conference he met Carl Sandburg and Robert Frost. Frost offered to read his work, and Skinner sent him three serious short stories. Frost replied with a warm, supportive letter commenting on Skinner's "niceties of observation" and ending "you are worth twice anyone else I have seen in prose this year" (Skinner, 1976, p. 249). Such praise strongly reinforced Skinner's ambition to be a writer, and he resolved to spend the year after his graduation testing his skills. He did all the correct things—built a "writer's study," subscribed to the literary magazines, read the great books, and even smoked a pipe—but all to no avail. At the end of this "dark year," Skinner concluded that he had nothing to say and changed his career plans.

Watson's *Behaviorism* had just been published and was being reviewed in the literary magazines Skinner received. In *Dial* Bertrand Russell described the book as "massively impressive" (Russell, 1927, in Skinner, 1979, p. 10), and in 1927 he said of Watson's approach in his *Outline of Philosophy*, "I think it contains more truth than most people suppose, and I regard it as desirable to develop the behaviorist method to the fullest possible extent" (Russell, 1927, in Russell, 1960, p. 73). Later Russell was to change his opinion of Watson's behaviorism (Russell, 1951), but at the time his praise was convincing to Skinner, for Russell had long been his favorite philosopher. The study of behavior appealed to Skinner, who had enjoyed observing the behavior of animals in the Susquehanna countryside and of people in the town itself. Perhaps the study of behavior would provide a career. Skinner purchased copies of Watson's book and Russell's works of philosophy. He read all of Watson and some of Russell, but not the last third, in which Russell undertook to refute behaviorism. Many years later Skinner thanked Russell for introducing him in his review and philosophy to behaviorism. "Good heavens," Russell replied, "I thought they had demolished behaviorism" (Skinner, 1976, p. 224).

H. G. Wells reviewed Ivan Pavlov's *Conditioned Reflexes* in *The New York Times*. He characterized the book as "difficult to read but momentous" and said that it provided a clear conception of the workings of the brain. Skinner read Pavlov's book and decided that his future lay in psychology, especially in conditioning. He applied for admission to Harvard University and was accepted. However, before enrolling as a graduate student, Skinner had one more brief fling at the life of an artist. He lived in Greenwich Village and Paris, but then it was on to Harvard and the beginning of his career as a psychologist.

Skinner's Training in Psychology

Skinner found most of his Harvard courses dull, uninteresting, and incompatible with his developing interest in behavior. Titchener's former student Edwin G. Boring was director of the Harvard laboratory. Skinner found structuralist psychology especially tedious in Boring's lectures and books. Paradoxically, however, it was Boring's book *The Physical Dimensions of Consciousness* (1933) that motivated Skinner to develop a different approach to psychology:

> Whenever I found myself losing interest in the work at hand or even simply feeling tired, a few pages of Boring's book had the effect of a dozen cups of coffee. (Skinner, 1979, p. 94)

A seminar with Walter S. Hunter, a Chicago Ph.D. who had worked with Watson, in which he discussed his delayed reaction experiments on animal memory, and courses in the department of biology with W. J. Crozier were more reinforcing. Crozier had been a student of Jacques Loeb (Chapter 12), whose book on tropisms Skinner had read. Two other aspects of Skinner's student days at Harvard proved to be of great importance. First, he met Fred S. Keller, and they became friends and lifelong colleagues. Second, in 1929, the International Congress of Physiology was held at the Harvard Medical School. Skinner heard Pavlov's address, which he found impressive. He also obtained an autographed portrait of Pavlov, which he hung above his desk.

During his eight years at Harvard, first as a graduate student, then as a postdoctoral fellow, and finally as a junior fellow in Harvard's prestigious Society of Fellows, Skinner established and developed his approach to the study of behavior and became more and more an avowed behaviorist. For his dissertation Skinner undertook to identify a unit of behavioral analysis. Influenced by both Ivan Pavlov and Charles Sherrington, he identified the reflex as that unit. He described the task of psychology as dividing behavior into reflexes and devising measures of their strength and of the variables that affect them. His commitment to a behavioristic approach was such that when Gordon Allport asked him during his dissertation examination to outline some objections to behaviorism, Skinner could not think of even one (Skinner, 1979, p. 75).

Skinner's Operant Conditioning

At Harvard Skinner developed the apparatus that most psychologists, following the lead of Hull and his students, refer to as the "Skinner box" but which Skinner himself always calls an "operant conditioning apparatus." In Skinner's early experiments, a hungry animal placed in the apparatus, a rat and later a pigeon, makes an arbitrary response—in the rat's case pressing a lever, in the pigeon's pecking an illuminated disk or key—and is reinforced for doing so. The rat or pigeon makes the response, food is delivered, and the probability of the response increases. The animal operates on its environment to produce a food reward; hence the term *operant conditioning*.

Skinner's apparatus had some similarities to Thorndike's instrumental conditioning (Chapter 10), and Skinner has often acknowledged that his contribution was to take Thorndike and the law of effect seriously. Still, there are differences, the most important of which is that in Thorndike's experiments the response rate was controlled by both the subject and the experimenter, whereas in Skinner's apparatus it was controlled solely by the subject. In Thorndike's instrumental conditioning, the cat's response latency and the intertrial interval selected by the experimenter determine how many responses can be made every hour; in Skinner's operant conditioning, the response rate is totally under the animal's control. Response rate quickly became the basic datum of Skinner's operant conditioning experiments.

Skinner's development of the operant conditioning apparatus and his use of the response rate were important steps toward his goal of an experimental analysis of behavior. How did Skinner come to take these steps? Fortunately, in his article "A Case History in Scientific Method" (1956), Skinner described these steps. Originally he set out to study habituation to a novel stimulus by using a running response in young rats. In accordance with what he termed his "four principles of scientific practice"—when you run into something interesting, drop everything else and study it; some ways of doing research are easier than others; some people are lucky; and apparatuses, especially complicated ones, break down—Skinner developed his apparatus through perseverance, good luck, and some accidents. In the apparatus an animal learned right before his eyes, and the response rate reflected that learning.

Skinner then studied extinction. When he disconnected the food dispenser so that lever pressing no longer produced food, the response rate decreased in an orderly manner. Spontaneous recovery and reconditioning could also be studied, as could the effects of deprivation and satiation. In all cases changes in the response rate were orderly and predictable. Specified operations led to predictable outcomes. Behavior could be predicted and controlled with precision.

In 1936 Skinner joined the faculty of the University of Minnesota and from there published his classic *The Behavior of Organisms* in 1938. The publisher, Appleton-Century-Crofts, having a contract with Hull for his *Principles,* was initially doubtful about "another rat book" (Skinner, 1979, p. 214). Another difficulty was that Skinner wanted to include more figures than the budget allowed. A favorable prepublication review by Tolman, who predicted that the book "will always have a very important place in the history of psychology" (Skinner, 1979, p. 211), and a grant of $500 from Harvard made publication possible. Skinner described his operant system of behavior, in which response consequences are crucial. Responses followed by positive outcomes—for example, presentation of food to a hungry animal or escape from or avoidance of electric shock—are reinforced, and their response rate increases; responses followed by such negative outcomes as removal of food and presentation of shock are punished, and their response rate decreases. Skinner also described experiments on extinction, spontaneous recovery, reconditioning, discrimination learning, and the effects of drives. In a retrospective review Travis Thompson described *The Behavior of Organisms* as "one of a handful of books that changed the face of modern psychology" (T. Thompson, 1988, p. 397). The research Skinner outlined is an example of what Thomas Kuhn (1970) termed a paradigm shift. For the first time the behavior of individual animals was subjected to intensive, dynamic analysis and control.

Forty years later *The Behavior of Organisms* is still a frequently cited work, but in the years following its publication it was not widely read. Most psychologists interested in animal learning were anticipating publication of Hull's "big book," his *Principles of Behavior,* and only 800 copies of *The Behavior of Organisms* were printed. By 1946, 252 copies had still not been sold. Some reviews of the book were negative (Wolf, 1939; Finan, 1940). Four main criticisms predominated. First, the title itself, *The Behavior of Organisms,* was held to be pretentious for a book that dealt exclusively with lever pressing by rats. Second, Skinner was accused of having neglected the works of others on learning and motivation, a criticism that was to a large degree warranted. Third, the book was said to deal with a restricted, limited, and artificial range of behavior. Fourth, the book was said to lack the "fortification of statistics" and to describe the behavior of a small number of subjects. Despite such criticisms Skinner's contribution was important. He had succeeded in specifying and measuring a functional unit of behavior, the operant, which was for Skinner a class of behavior having an orderly relationship to environmental effects.

Schedules of Reinforcement

In the 1940s Skinner began his research on the effects of different schedules of reinforcement. These experiments have proved to be of great importance. They began serendipitously when Skinner found myself on a Friday afternoon with only a few pellets on hand and did not want to spend part of the weekend making more. If I reinforced only an occasional response, my supply would last for many days. (Skinner, 1979, p. 97)

Skinner began to reinforce only some of the responses. He found that intermittent reinforcement maintained the frequency of responding; in fact, the animals responded more often than they did when every response produced reinforcement. Skinner and his students went on to conduct a massive program of research on the effects of schedules of reinforcement. This work was described by Ferster and Skinner in their monumental *Schedules of Reinforcement* (1957), a work showing records of hundreds of thousands of responses. Such schedules have predictable and reliable effects on responding and have proved to be a basic tool in the experimental analysis of behavior. The number of lever presses by rats and pecks by pigeons Skinner has inspired is awe-inspiring. Research on schedules has proved to be a major contribution, and it is the research of which Skinner himself is most proud. When asked in 1967 which of his contributions to psychology he would select as most important, Skinner replied that

> it would be the whole question of the contingencies of reinforcement arranged by schedules of reinforcement. . . . I think it is my basic scientific contribution. (Skinner, in Hall, 1967, p. 107)

Behavioral Control

In a paper entitled "How To Teach Animals," published in 1951, Skinner described what he termed *shaping*. When one trains a pigeon to peck a key for food, the bird is reinforced first for looking at the front wall of the chamber, then for moving toward it, then for lifting its head, and finally for pecking. Gradually the pigeon is shaped through reinforcement to make the response. Not only key pecking but also such behaviors as choosing one playing card from a deck or pecking at the keys on a piano can be shaped. Much as a sculptor molds clay, shaping allows the psychologist to mold behavior.

Shaping is a powerful procedure for establishing and changing behavior, and it surely is no coincidence that Skinner chose to entitle the second volume of his autobiography *The Shaping of a Behaviorist* (1979). Skinner became well known for his ingenious demonstrations of shaping. At Minnesota he shaped a rat to drop a marble through a hole. The student newspaper ran a story on the rat, which they named Pliny the Elder, and local newspapers and *Life* magazine did features on Skinner's "basketball-playing rat." In another demonstration, Skinner shaped two pigeons to "play table-tennis." The birds stood at either end of a table and vigorously pecked a ball back and forth. The general audience was intrigued by the spectacle of two birds "playing table-tennis." In his most ambitious demonstration of the power of shaping, Project Orcon, Skinner trained pigeons in simulators to act as missile guidance or organic control systems, hence the acronym (*organic control*) (Skinner, 1960). While the pigeons performed flawlessly in simulators, Skinner was never able to convince the military authorities that their behavior was reliable. Two of his coworkers on Project Orcon, Keller and Marian Breland, were so impressed by the outcome that they founded a company, Animal Behavior Enterprises, to train animals using operant principles for advertising displays. They have had both successes (Breland & Breland, 1950) and failures (Breland & Breland, 1961), but techniques of immediate reinforcement, shaping, and schedule control are now pervasive in training animals in commercial settings and for entertainment (Pryor, 1977).

Skinner's Utopia

Skinner spent the summer of 1945 writing a utopian novel, *Walden Two*. In it he described an imaginary community in which operant principles of behavioral control are used to produce a harmonious and happy society. The community of Walden Two is set in a beautiful and bountiful land, an idealized version of the Susquehanna River valley of Skinner's youth. The community has happy and productive workers and well-behaved children whose ethical and moral training is completed by the age of six. The standard of living is of such quality that community members spend their leisure time performing Bach's Masses, playing chess, and having scholarly discussions. It is a community where the Ten Commandments have been translated into explicit programs of behavioral control, indeed, a Skinnerian utopia.

Descriptions of utopias abound in Western literature, starting with that by Plato (Chapter 1). In his *Republic* Plato described a small city-state in which the culture and individualism of Athens were combined with the discipline of Sparta. The state was to be ruled by a small group of philosophers, the finest products of the educational system. Other people would be selected for different roles in accordance with their faculties and talents. Under the rule of a philosopher-king, *sub homine*, men and women would find happiness and satisfaction.

In *City of God* (A.D. 426), Saint Augustine described a supreme utopia, the Christian heaven. There happiness is found in the sight of God, *sub deo*, but only after death and only by a select group.

In his book *Utopia* (1517) Sir Thomas More, the lord chancellor of England, described the evils and horrors of life in the England of his time: crime, poverty, cruel punishments, invidious class distinctions, and a licentious court. His remedy was a just and fair system of codified law, a society that functioned *sub lege*.

Jean-Jacques Rousseau, in *The Social Contract* (1762), described a very different utopia. Inspired by descriptions of the seemingly idyllic societies of the South Pacific given by the first European explorers of that enchanted region, Rousseau described a society in which happiness is found by returning to nature, living *sub natura*. Only by living in harmony with nature and natural law could we ever find happiness.

Aldous Huxley's *Brave New World* (1932) is a satire in which the threat posed by psychology, especially by conditioning, is described. Huxley saw conditioning techniques as a threat to human freedom and wrote his book to point out the dangers of a society *sub psychologia*.

Skinner's aim in writing *Walden Two* was to describe a society *sub operando*. The community's leader is the character Frazier, and with him as an alter ego Skinner was able to say things about the possibilities and techniques of behavioral control that he was not prepared to say by himself at that time:

> I have only one important characteristic, Burris, I'm stubborn. I've had only one idea in my life—a true *idée fixe*...to put it as bluntly as possible, the idea of having my own way. "Control" expresses it, I think. The control of human behavior, Burris. In my early experimental days it was a frenzied, selfish desire to dominate. I remember the rage I used to feel when a prediction went astray. I could have shouted at the subjects of my experiments, "Behave, damn you! Behave as you ought!" Eventually I realized that the subjects were always right. They always behaved as they should. It was I who was wrong. I had made a bad prediction. (Skinner, 1948, pp. 288–289)

Skinner described a community so successful that the initially dubious Burris resigns his university position and joins Frazier at Walden Two at the end of the book. Together they dream of additional Walden Two–style communities and even of taking over the whole country. In fact, only one such community has been established, and it has been only modestly successful (Kinkade, 1973).

Skinner wrote *Walden Two* in just seven weeks, and it was rejected by several publishers before being published in 1948. Many of the first reviews were hostile:

> The only thing I'm sure I really like in *Walden Two* is the radio.—*Herald Tribune*

> A depressingly serious prescription for communal regimentation, as though the author had read Aldous Huxley's *Brave New World* and missed the point.—*Time*

> A slur upon a name, a corruption of an impulse...such a triumph of *mortmain*, or the dead hand, has not been envisaged since the days of Sparta.—*Life*

Sales of the book were disappointing at first, but in the 1960s and 1970s, with the burgeoning interest in alternative lifestyles and the counterculture, *Walden Two* became a best-seller. Skinner kept a neatly drawn cumulative record of the book's sales in his office. For many years of poor sales the curve hugs the abscissa, but then it accelerates as total sales exceed 2 million copies.

Skinner's Applied Research

In 1945 Skinner accepted the chairmanship of the Department of Psychology at Indiana University. There he continued his animal research and, after the birth of his daughter Deborah, began to think about the child-rearing environment provided by a suburban home. He concluded that it was far from ideal. The child fusses and receives attention, and so fussing increases in rate; the child explores a bright, attractive object that happens to be an expensive vase and is punished for doing so; the child makes constant demands on the parents, who are not able to respond as they would like to. Skinner set out to design a better environment for his daughter. He began by analyzing her needs. The first was warmth. Rather than wrapping her in bulky clothing and covering her crib with blankets, Skinner built a small, well-heated compartment in which Debbie lived. A child must also be protected from illness. Skinner believed that most childhood illnesses are caused by air-borne viruses, and so the air entering Debbie's compartment passed through a series of filters. Freedom from bulky clothing and the presence of attractive toys encouraged Debbie to exercise and play. Her need for social contacts and interaction was satisfied by ensuring that there were times each day when she was out of the compartment and had her parents' undivided attention.

In 1945 *The Ladies Home Journal* published an article describing this device and the experience of Skinner and his wife raising their daughter in it for two and a half years. Here was one behaviorist who had followed Watson's challenge, "Give me a dozen healthy infants..." (Chapter 12), and exercised great control over the environment of his own daughter. The article reported that Debbie was a healthy and happy child who had not cried for six months except when given inoculations. Photographs showed an obviously happy Debbie frolicking naked in her compartment. Newspapers, radio, and Pathé News ran stories on this device, and Skinner received letters from hundreds of harassed parents asking where they could purchase one. Some reactions, though, were predictably outraged. The article's title, "Baby in a Box," conjured up images of social isolation and a cagelike environment. Skinner was accused of having deprived Debbie of any social life and of the love and affection of her parents, of having treated her like one of his rats or pigeons. One critic went so far as to say that the only time human beings should be placed in a box is when they are dead. A mother who had used the box with her twins had a more pragmatic conclusion. "The box," she said, "is a boon to mothers because it cuts down on laundry and bathing" (Gerow, 1988, p. 45). In addition to its notoriety the baby device proved to be a financial embarrassment. Skinner invested $500 in a company to build these "Heir Conditioners" only to have his fellow investor, the man who was supposed to manufacture the devices, disappear with his money and the deposits of potential buyers. However, some air-cribs, as the devices came to be called, were built, and 130 babies were raised in them without ill effects (Skinner, 1979, pp. 293–317). For many years rumors circulated that Skinner's daughter had been permanently affected by her experience and even that she had become psychotic. Happily, such was not the case. Deborah Skinner graduated with Phi Beta Kappa honors from Radcliffe College and is now a successful artist. Looking back on her experience as the "baby in the box," she commented:

> It wasn't really a psychological experience but what you might call a
> happiness-through-health experiment. I think I was a very happy baby. Most
> of the criticisms of the box are by people who don't understand what it was.
> (D. Skinner, quoted in *Time*, 1971, p. 51)

Skinner's other daughter, Julie Vargas, who was not herself raised in the air-crib, decided to raise her two daughters in the device.

The next of Skinner's innovations was stimulated by his observations of the behavior of the teacher and children in his daughter's fourth-grade classroom. He was distressed by what he saw as "minds being destroyed." Very little learning appeared to take place, and what little there was seemed to Skinner to occur in spite of, rather than because of, classroom reinforcements. With so many children in the class, the teacher was unable to attend to each of them at once, and so many behaviors that should have been reinforced were not. The children worked primarily to avoid threatened aversive events: the teacher's displeasure, ridicule by classmates, poor test scores or grades, or a trip to the principal's office. Positive reinforcers were rare and, when administered at all, were usually delayed. Skinner's animal research had shown that delayed reinforcers are ineffective reinforcers, and so even these well-meaning attempts to provide positive reinforcers were probably ineffective. A further problem was that the teacher had to present information to be learned at the same pace for all the students. For some the pace was too fast, for others it was clearly too slow, yet they all had to proceed together. To Skinner the classroom, with its primarily aversive control procedures, few positive reinforcers (those which were there were usually delayed), lack of individual attention, and lockstep progression, seemed an environment guaranteed to produce learning difficulties. Skinner wrote:

> The condition in the average school is a matter of widespread concern.
> Modern children simply do not learn arithmetic quickly or well. Nor is the
> result simply incompetence. The very subjects in which modern techniques
> are weakest are those in which failure is most conspicuous and in the wake
> of an ever-growing incompetence come the anxieties, uncertainties, and
> aggressions, which in their turn present other problems in the school.
> (Skinner, 1954, in Skinner, 1961, p. 151)

What could be done to remedy this situation? Skinner's solution was the development of teaching machines.

While early, innovative teaching machines had been developed in the 1920s by Sidney L. Pressey, his work had been ahead of his time and his machines were not widely used (Benjamin, 1988). Skinner devised a teaching system based on the operant principles of behavioral control established in his animal research. First, reinforcement would be immediate. The child would be told right away whether his or her response was correct or incorrect. Second, each child would progress at his or her own rate, moving on only when material had been mastered. Third, the material to be learned would be presented in small steps, with additional information presented when an error was made. Learning would be shaped through a carefully constructed program of instruction.

Programmed learning with teaching machines and programmed texts has been used extensively in schools, colleges, and universities not only in the United States but also in more than seventy-two countries around the world (UNESCO, 1973). There are at least a dozen journals devoted to programmed instruction and many books on the topic. Crucial to the success of such instruction is the quality of the programs. While some excellent programs have been written, it seems that more attention has been paid to the machines and gadgetry than to the quality of the programs they use. Skinner (1961) predicted that programmed instruction could be used to teach such complex behaviors as calculus, musical composition, understanding the Bible, solving personal problems, and even thinking. His hopes have not been fulfilled. Programmed instruction has been used successfully to teach spelling and basic arithmetic in schools and even the principles of Skinner's experimental analysis of behavior in colleges (Holland & Skinner, 1961), but programs to teach many other subjects have been less successful. Still, Skinner's teaching machines and techniques of programmed instruction were an important innovation. Today his behavior system is widely taught to teachers. Teaching is seen as "reinforcement contingency management," teachers and students are encouraged to set "behavioral goals," classroom behavior is "shaped," and "token economy" systems, based on conditioned reinforcers, and "time-outs," in which the child is removed from all stimuli and reinforcers for a brief period, are used. Skinner's impact on education has been great.

Skinner's Behavior Modification

Skinner also stimulated innovative approaches to the behavior of people suffering from mental illness. His interest in the behavior of people diagnosed as neurotic or psychotic dates to 1932, when he explored the possibility of shaping psychotic patients at the Worcester State Hospital in Massachusetts to press levers for various reinforcers. This project was never instituted, but in 1948 Paul Fuller, a graduate student at Indiana University, trained a "vegetative idiot" to make an operant response. This eighteen-year-old man had been institutionalized for many years and was diagnosed as severely feebleminded. He lay on his back without moving, never made a sound, and did not eat or drink. Fuller shaped him to raise his right hand, using as a reinforcer milk injected into his mouth. After four conditioning sessions the young man raised his arm consistently three or four times a minute. Despite his physicians' conclusion that he was incapable of learning anything, the young man had clearly learned to make this operant response. Fuller (1949) claimed that had time permitted, it would have been possible to shape other responses, indeed to establish a small behavioral repertoire in this man.

Encouraged by Fuller's success, Skinner turned his attention to the diagnosis and treatment of mental illness. Freud's views were influential at the time (Chapter 8), but Skinner found Freud's concepts and treatment unacceptable. They were based, he claimed, on such "explanatory fictions" as id, ego, and supergo; repression; and catharsis. Skinner also questioned the effectiveness of psychoanalysis as a therapeutic procedure. He recommended an approach in which a patient's behavior would be observed and attempts would be made to change it through appropriate contingencies of reinforcement. He believed that many seemingly bizarre behaviors may in fact be orderly responses maintained by powerful reinforcers. Breaking these maladaptive reinforcement contingencies and substituting reinforcement of adaptive responses were the twin goals of the treatment procedures Skinner developed.

After Skinner's return to Harvard in 1948, two of his graduate students, Ogden S. Lindsley and Nathan H. Azrin, pioneered what has come to be known as *be-*

havior modification. With Skinner, Lindsley established lever-pressing stations at the Boston Metropolitan State Hospital, where psychotic patients responded for such reinforcers as candy and cigarettes. Their behavior was orderly and predictable. After graduating from Harvard, Azrin established a behavior modification program at Anna State Hospital in southern Illinois. There Teodoro Ayllon (1963) modified the behavior of a psychotic woman with a nine-year history of towel hoarding. Whenever she stole or hoarded a towel, the nursing staff members were instructed to give her many towels. After four weeks she was found to have 650 towels in her room. She then began to remove them and to resist being given more. The reinforcing value of towels had clearly been changed by this satiation procedure. Ayllon and Azrin went on to establish programs of behavioral management for entire wards of patients and in 1968 published *The Token Economy,* describing their procedures and outcomes.

Behavior modifiers have had reported success in controlling a wide variety of behaviors, including smoking, obesity, shyness, tics, speech problems, and autism (Ulrich, Stachnik, & Mabry, 1966; Bellack, Hersen, & Kazdin, 1982). In 1982, 852,000 mentally retarded children participated in special education programs in the United States (Schernberger, 1983), the vast majority of which were based on principles of behavioral control and management explicated by Skinner (Gaylord-Ross & Holvoet, 1985). Most residential programs for the mentally retarded employ operant principles as a standard part of their treatment.

There are now well over two dozen English-language journals devoted to behavior modification and many others in foreign languages, a division of the APA (Division 25) for "Skinnerian" psychologists, and several international behavior modification associations. Thompson (1988) stated:

> Interventions for human problems based on operant principles can be found from Auckland, New Zealand, to Reykjavik, Iceland, to Rome, Italy, as well as in every state in the United States. (T. Thompson, 1988, p. 399)

Despite these impressive achievements, numerous critics see behavior modification as a callous and even cruel attempt to manipulate and control people. Patients, it has been argued, have been deprived of basic rights to good food, exercise, and a clean bed so that these things could be used as reinforcers. Often such critics challenge a wide range of techniques including electroconvulsive shock, aversion therapy, isolation, and punishment procedures, labeling them all behavior modification. Skinner's repeated protests that the term *behavior modification* refers only to techniques using systematic application of positive reinforcers have been to no avail. In the face of this chorus of critics, behavior modification can now be used only under the most carefully controlled and supervised conditions.

Industrial Applications of Behavior Modification

Skinner has often commented on the similarity between certain schedules of reinforcement and the pay regimes used in business and industry. Piecework schedules appear to be similar to ratio schedules of reinforcement, and weekly pay schedules appear to be similar to interval schedules. At times the similarities are striking. Just as an animal after reinforcement on a fixed interval schedule often pauses before slowly increasing its response rate, workers paid on Fridays often show "Monday morning blues" and some reluctance to work on Mondays. A number of attempts have been made to apply Skinnerian principles of operant control in a variety of industrial and business settings, often with striking success (Feeney, 1973). Other impressive applications include the use of reinforcement principles in preventing industrial accidents (Fox, Hopkins, & Anger, 1987) and the development of airline "frequent flier" programs—a form of token economy—which originally were developed to increase loyalty to a specific airline but have had the effect of increasing air travel from 20 to 35 percent (T. Thompson, 1988, p. 399).

Skinner's Later Life

Skinner retired as Harvard's Edgar Pierce Professor of Psychology in 1974 and since that time has concentrated on writing his autobiography (Skinner, 1976, 1979, 1983) and editing a retrospective collection of his papers (Skinner, 1987). However, he regularly contributes papers to the psychological literature that are innovative and controversial (Skinner, 1989). In 1980 Robert Epstein, Robert Lanza, and Skinner responded to reports of symbolic communication between chimpanzees with an experimental demonstration of symbolic communication between operantly conditioned pigeons whimsically dubbed Jack and Jill. At the 1982 convention of the APA Skinner presented an elegant behaviorist account of his own behavior while growing old, a report later expanded into a book, *Enjoying Old Age*, published in 1983. Skinner has little to say about loss, fear of dying, or the meaning of life. Rather, it is a collection of behavioral prescriptions for the elderly:

> Hang an umbrella on a handy doorknob if rain is predicted; that way it will not be forgotten.

> Read pornography to extend and pep up the sex life.

> Prepare new tricks to amuse grandchildren when they visit.

> Construct the environment so that you are not bothered by the inevitable decline in vision, hearing, physical strength, and endurance.

> Risk the contempt of younger contemporaries by freely admitting that you read detective stories and watch soap operas.

Skinner's career has been a long and distinguished one, filled with awards, honors, and accomplishments: election to the Society of Experimental Psychologists in the early 1940s and receipt of the society's prestigious Warren Medal in 1942, the presidency of the Midwestern Psychological Association in 1949 and of the Pavlovian Society in 1966, the Humanist of the Year Award from the American Humanist Association in 1972. However, Skinner was never elected president of the APA.

Skinner has arranged his environment to be maximally reinforcing of those of his behaviors he considers important. His home office, with its carefully charted cumulative records of the time he spends at his desk and his scholarly productivity, is designed to place Skinner in a box. Yet with all this attention and care and the many reinforcers, has it been enough? Perhaps a clue to the answer can be found in this passage from Skinner's personal journal:

> Sun streams into our living room. My hi-fi is midway through the first act of "Tristan and Isolde." A very pleasant environment. A man would be a fool not to enjoy himself in it. In a moment I will work on a manuscript which may help mankind. So my life is not only pleasant, it is earned or deserved. Yet, yet, I am unhappy. (Skinner, quoted in *Time*, 1971, p. 53)

NEOBEHAVIORISM IN RETROSPECT

What can we conclude about these four neobehaviorist psychologists? They shared a definition of psychology as the science of behavior, but nevertheless, many differences have emerged. Of the four, Guthrie's importance and influence have remained the most stable. He has long been considered an interesting and stimulating learning theorist whose principle of contiguity provides a powerful explanation of behavior. Tolman's purposive behaviorism enjoyed a period of popularity, but with the rise of Hull and Skinner, with their avowedly mechanistic approaches to behaviorism, it went into something of a decline. In the 1970s, however, Tolman's position became increasingly attractive to psychologists interested in thinking and problem solving. To such cognitive psychologists, Tolman's experiments and concepts are of great value and interest. Figures cited earlier in this chapter showed clearly how Hull's theory of learning and behavior system have dominated the literature on learning. In addition, in 1940, 4 percent of the papers in the *Journal of Experimental Psychology* referred to the work of "Hullians." By 1950, the figure was a remarkable 37 percent, by 1960, it had fallen to 24 percent; and by 1970, it was back to 4 percent (Guttman, 1977, p. 323). In more recent years citations of Hull have been infrequent. As we have seen, Skinner has also had a great impact on psychology. However, citation counts of his works in the *Journal of Experimental Psychology*, and for that matter many other conventional psychology journals, would show percentages much lower than those of Hull. Skinner's impact has been outside such conventional psychology publications, often in journals such as the *Journal of the Experimental Analysis of Behavior* and the *Journal of Applied Behavior Analysis*, which were founded explicitly to publish "Skinnerian" research. In recent years Skinner has concentrated on philosophical and societal concerns and has become in the words of one of his former students, Norman Guttmann,

> as it were, the leading figure in a myth, a myth already made in the popular imagination and awaiting a new occupant. He has succeeded to the role of scientist-hero, the Promethean fire-bringer, the master technologist, and instructor of technologists. Also, his is the role of chief iconoclast, the image-breaker who liberates our thoughts from ancient restrictions. (Guttmann, 1977, p. 322)

Earlier Watson had filled that role, and Skinner is clearly his successor within psychology.

Epilogue

This book has reviewed the development of psychology from its roots in antiquity; through philosophy and the great advances in physiology and other life sciences in the seventeenth, eighteenth, and nineteenth centuries; and finally to Wilhelm Wundt's founding of psychology as an independent science late in the nineteenth century. Since then many psychologists have been part of the "short history" of psychology. In considering some of them we have emphasized not only their theoretical, empirical, and practical contributions to psychology but also their lives and careers, successes and failures, triumphs and frustrations. As a result this has been a personalistic history of psychology.

But what of the current status of psychology? In 1892 William James ended his *Psychology* with a consideration of psychology in his day and came to the pessimistic conclusion that it was

> a string of raw facts; a little gossip and wrangle about opinions; a little classification and generalization on the mere descriptive level; a strong prejudice that we *have* states of mind, and that our brain conditions them: but not a single law in the sense in which physics shows us laws, not a single proposition from which any consequence can causally be deduced. We don't even know the terms between which the elementary laws would obtain if we had them. This is no science, it is only the hope for a science. (James, 1892, p. 468)

Has psychology met James's criticisms? Has the hope for a true science of psychology been fulfilled, or do we still have little more than a collection of gossip and opinion? Toward the end of his career James became even more pessimistic about the status and prospects of psychology, and the field still has numerous critics who question not only the reality but even the prospect of a true science of psy-

445

chology. However, there is much in contemporary psychology that is interesting, important, and hopeful. Progress has been made, some psychological phenomena are now understood, and some laws of behavior have been established.

Knowledge of the structure and functions of the nervous system and of the biological bases of psychological phenomena has advanced rapidly. The pioneering research of Pierre Flourens, Pierre-Paul Broca, Gustav Fritsch, Eduard Hitzig, and even Roberts Bartholow has demonstrated that the brain can be studied scientifically and that some of its functions can be understood. Karl Lashley's *Brain Mechanisms and Intelligence,* published in 1929, directed the thinking and research of a generation of physiological psychologists. Donald Hebb's *The Organization of Behavior* (1949) provided a bridge between psychology and the rapidly developing neurosciences and a model for the effects of experience on the brain. Working in Hebb's laboratory, James Olds and Peter Milner in 1954 discovered "pleasure centers" in the brain, a dramatic and totally unexpected finding. David Hubel and Thorsten Wiesel in 1969 described precise relationships between cortical cell activity and perceptual phenomena, while Roger Sperry's research with "split-brain" subjects demonstrated the different psychological functions of the two hemispheres of the brain (Sperry, 1961). For their research Hubel, Wiesel, and Sperry shared the 1981 Nobel Prize for medicine. Finally, the discovery in the mid-1970s of endogenous morphinelike substances in the brain (the endorphins) promises to advance our understanding of pain and perhaps even pleasure (Snyder, 1977).

Recently developed statistical procedures allow the analysis and interpretation of psychological data in a way that was impossible as little as twenty years ago. For example, techniques of factor analysis have been used to analyze masses of data bearing on human personality and intellect and to develop empirically based descriptions of personality traits and models of intelligence. Raymond B. Cattell, one of the contemporary advocates of such an approach, predicts that factorial descriptions of personality will allow accurate predictions of behavior. Cattell's precise statistical approach to personality may be traced back to Sir Francis Galton in the nineteenth century, though the techniques Cattell used are incomparably more powerful than anything available to Galton (Cattell, 1965, 1977). Would this approach to the complexities of personality impress James? One can only speculate, but perhaps he would have seen in it a way of testing his own hunches about "tender- and tough-minded" personality types.

Today's electronic instruments make possible precise presentations of stimuli, accurate records of behavioral responses, detailed recordings of activity in the nervous system, and impressive modes of data acquisition, storage, and analysis. James professed a horror of the "brass instrument" psychology of his time, but surely even he would be impressed by the apparatus and equipment of a modern psychological laboratory and by what such equipment allows psychologists to do. Computers allow us to implement complex statistical analyses and develop causal models of psychological processes that were impossible before their development.

Computers have also changed psychologists' very conceptions of psychological phenomena. The switchboard models of stimulus-response connections proposed by the early behaviorists have been supplanted by computer models and an information-processing viewpoint concerned with the acquisition, storage, and retrieval of information. Herbert Simon's *The Sciences of the Artificial* (1969) described classical psychological problems by using computer analogies. Later Simon and his coworkers studied artificial intelligence. Their programs allowed computers to solve problems, to remember, and even to reason (Newell & Simon, 1972). In 1979 Simon won a Nobel Prize for this research.

Cognition has been restored to a central position in psychology, a development James would certainly have welcomed. In his time cognitive psychology was under active development by the psychologists of the Würzburg school. Disruptions caused by World War I and the behaviorist revolution of John B. Watson diminished the impact of such early cognitive psychologists as Franz Brentano and Carl Stumpf. For two to three decades behaviorism dominated psychology, and indeed, Watson's successor, B. F. Skinner, continues to have a strong influence on contemporary psychology. However, in recent decades interest in cognitive psychology has revived, leading to what has been termed psychology's cognitive revolution (Lachman, Lachman, & Butterfeld, 1979). The British psychologist Donald Broadbent developed a model of human attention which led to a productive research program (Broadbent, 1958). In the United States George Miller, Eugene Galanter, and Karl Pribram advocated a new cognitive psychology that would study plans, images, and other mental processes (Miller, Galanter, & Pribram, 1960). The decade of the 1960s also saw Noam Chomsky's influential conclusion that the structure of language is innate (Chomsky, 1965) and detailed studies of mental imagery (Paivio, 1969), short-term memory (Sternberg, 1966), and organizational processes in memory (Mandler, 1967; Bower, 1970). Finally, developments in linguistics, computer science, and artificial intelligence have been strong influences on psychology. Today cognitive psychology is one of the most dynamic and interesting areas of psychology. Franz Brentano, Carl Stumpf, and Edward Tolman would certainly have approved of that development.

Today's developmental psychology is very different from the field founded by G. Stanley Hall, though Hall's influence is still important. Hall's catalogues of child development proved to be of lasting value, as they were elaborated and extended by his student Arnold Gesell (1954), whose work led to developmental measures of intelligence. This normative approach to development was revolutionized by the work of Jean Piaget (1954), who used careful observations coupled with innovative tests of thinking to stimulate three decades of research on the development of cognition as well as moral development. Another area pioneered by Hall, the study of aging, has recently returned to prominence and with the aging of the population is a most important area of contemporary psychology. Today's life-span approach to developmental psychology is a direct legacy from Hall.

Social and industrial psychology have also developed apace since James's time. Kurt Lewin's ingenious experiments on social behavior find a contemporary reflection in Stanley Milgram's (1963, 1974) studies of compliance with authority, Bibb Latané and John Darley's (1970) investigations of the "unresponsive bystander," and the dramatic simulation of the prison experience by Zimbardo, Haney, and Banks (1973). The results of these investigations have challenged our expectations of human behavior and presented demanding questions. Hugo Münsterberg's pioneering research in industry and business founded industrial and organizational psychology. Today they are important and accepted applications of psychology.

Similar progress could be cited in other areas of psychology. In clinical psychology, for example, few would doubt that the 1980s are better times for the mentally ill than the 1880s or even the 1930s were. Yet much remains to be done in all areas of psychology, and some critics question whether psychologists will ever make the required progress. They consider psychology a "soft" science or even a "pseudoscience." Psychological research has at times been ignored or ridiculed as a waste of time and money. In the majority of these cases careful consideration of the research itself, especially in its historical context, has shown it to be serious and important (Atkinson, 1977). Even psychology's Nobel laureates would fail to impress such critics. The prizes, they might claim, were awarded to physiologists (Hubel and Wiesel), a neurosurgeon (Sperry), and an information-processing scientist (Simon) rather than to four psychologists. While it must be admitted that psychology has not attained the rigor of older sciences and that the number of psychological laws is still small, our review of the history of psychology shows that progress has been made.

One aspect of contemporary psychology that surely would amaze James is its size. After decades of slow growth, the number of psychologists has increased greatly, and there are now some 65,000 members of the APA and smaller but still significant numbers of psychologists overseas. James knew all the important psychologists of his time personally. Today no psychologist could make such a claim, and it is the fortunate few who know even the majority of psychologists in their own areas of specialization. There are now forty-seven divisions of the APA, more divisions than the number of psychologists who attended the APA's first meeting in 1892. These divisions were formed to meet the specialized needs of the association's members; in the meetings they organize and the journals they publish, they clearly do so. Yet with this increased specialization there is also the danger that psychology may be Balkanized into many competing and quarrelsome factions. One unifying force is a history that all psychologists *share*.

James would also surely be stunned by the size of today's national and regional conventions of psychologists. The APA's annual convention is held in a large city, often in more than one hotel or convention center, and has a program of more than 500 pages. Hundreds of papers, symposia, and lectures are presented on a great variety of topics. Were James to page through such a convention program or wander the convention halls overhearing snippets of the presentations, what would he think of today's psychology? How can such diverse people all be psychologists? Yet they do have something in common. One would hope, for example, that all these modern psychologists would recognize James. He and the other psychologists discussed in this book are our historical heritage. They should never be neglected, and if this book has in any way prevented such neglect or interested a reader in the history of psychology, its writing will have been worthwhile.

References

Ach, W. (1905). Über die Willenstätikeit und das Denken. *Archiv für die Gesamte Psychologie, 4,* 1–294.

Allen, G. W. (1967). *William James: A biography.* New York: Viking.

Altman, I. (1987). Centripetal and centrifugal trends in psychology. *American Psychologist, 42,* 1058–1069.

Altman, L. K. (1987). *Who goes first?* New York: Random House.

American Psychological Association. (1981). Ethical principles of psychologists. *American Psychologist, 36,* 633–638.

Angell, J. R. (1907). The province of functional psychology. *Psychological Review, 14,* 61–91.

Angell, J. R. (1909). The influence of Darwin. *Psychological Review, 16,* 152–169.

Angell, J. R. (1911). Preface to *Clever Hans* by O. Pfungst. New York: Henry Holt.

Angell, J. R. (1936). James Rowland Angell. In C. Murchison (Ed.), *A history of psychology in autobiography* (Vol. 3, pp. 1–38). Worcester, MA: Clark University Press.

Annin, E. L., Boring, E. G., & Watson, R. I. (1968). Important psychologists, 1600–1967. *Journal of the History of the Behavioral Sciences, 4,* 303–315.

Anokhin, P. K. (1971, March). Three giants of Soviet psychology. *Psychology Today,* pp. 43–78.

Aristotle. (1910). *De partibus animalium* (W. Ogle, Trans.). Oxford: Clarendon.

Aristotle. (1912). *Historia animalium* (D. W. Thompson, Trans.). Oxford: Clarendon.

Arnheim, R. (1988). Visual dynamics. *American Scientist, 76,* 585–591.

Arvidson, R. M. (1971). More about Wundt's doctorate students. *American Psychologist, 26,* 516.

Asratyan, E. A. (1953). *I. P. Pavlov: His life and work.* Moscow: Foreign Languages Publishing House.

Atkinson, R. C. (1977, March). Reflections on psychology's past and concerns about its future. *American Psychologist,* pp. 205–210.

Ayllon, T. (1963). Intensive treatment of psychotic behavior by stimulus satiation and food reinforcement. *Behavior Research and Therapy, 1*, 53–61.

Ayllon, T., & Azrin, N. (1968). *The token economy: A motivational system for therapy.* New York: Appleton-Century-Crofts.

Babkin, B. P. (1949). *Pavlov: A biography.* Chicago: University of Chicago Press.

Baer, A. (1905). Über gleichzeitige elektrische Reizung zweier Grosshirnstellen am ungehemmten Hunde. *Pflugers Archiv der Physiologie, 106*, 523–567.

Bailey, B. (1981, September). Freud's forerunner: Franz Anton Mesmer. *Historical Review,* pp. 71–75.

Bain, A. (1855). *The senses and the intellect.* London: Parker.

Bain, A. (1875). *The emotions and the will* (3rd ed.). New York: Appleton. (Original work published 1859)

Bakan, D. (1967). Is phrenology foolish? In *Readings in Psychology Today* (pp. 328–335). Del Mar, CA: CRM.

Baldwin, J. M. (1895). Types of reaction. *Psychological Review, 2*, 259–273.

Barash, D. P. (1977). *Sociobiology and behavior.* New York: Elsevier.

Barker, R., Dembo, T., & Lewin, K. (1941). Frustration and regression: An experiment with young children. *University of Iowa Studies in Child Welfare, 18*, 1–314.

Barlow, N. (Ed.). (1958). *The autobiography of Charles Darwin, 1809–1882.* London: Collins.

Barron, F. (1969). *Creative person and creative process.* New York: Holt, Rinehart & Winston.

Bartholow, R. (1874). Experimental investigations into the functions of the human brain. *American Journal of the Medical Sciences, 67*, 305–313.

Beers, C. W. (1908). *A mind that found itself.* New York: Longmans Green.

Bell, C. (1965). Idea of a new anatomy of the brain: Submitted for the observation of his friends. In R. J. Herrnstein & E. G. Boring (Eds.), *A source book in the history of psychology* (pp. 23–26). Cambridge, MA: Harvard University Press. (Original work published 1811)

Bellack, A. S., Hersen, M., & Kazdin, A. E. (Eds.). (1982). *International handbook of behavior modification and therapy.* New York: Plenum.

Bencivenga, J. (1987, November 30). Britain's conservative secretary has radical plans. *Christian Science Monitor,* p. 19.

Benjamin, L. T. (1987). A teacher is for ever: The legacy of Harry Kirke Wolfe (1858–1918). *Teaching of Psychology, 14*, 68–74.

Benjamin, L. T., Jr. (1988). A history of teaching machines. *American Psychologist, 43*, 703–712.

Benjamin, L. T., Jr., & Bertelson, A. D. (1975). The early Nebraska psychological laboratory, 1889–1930: Nursery for presidents of the American Psychological Association. *Journal of the History of the Behavioral Sciences, 11*, 142–148.

Bennett, A. H., & Godlee, R. J. (1885). Case of cerebral tumor. *Medico-Chirurgical Transactions (London), 68*, 243–275.

Bennett, W. R. (1977). How artificial is intelligence? *American Scientist, 65*, 674–702.

Bentley, M. (1925). The psychologies called "structural": Historical derivation. In C. Murchison (Ed.), *Psychologies of 1925* (pp. 383–393). Worcester, MA: Clark University Press.

Ben-Yehuda, N. (1980). The European witch craze. *American Journal of Sociology, 86*, 1–31.

Bergmann, G. (1956). The contribution of John B. Watson. *Psychological Review, 63*, 265–276.

Berkeley, G. (1820). *The works of George Berkeley.* 3 vols. London: Richard Priestley.

Berkeley, G. (1949–1957). *The works of George Berkeley.* 10 vols. (A. A. Luce & T. E. Jessop, Eds.). London: Thomas Nelson.

Berker, E. A., Berker, A. H., & Smith, A. (1986). Translation of Broca's 1865 report. *Archives of Neurology, 43,* 1065–1072.

Berliner, A. (1971). Letter to Professor F. Wesley of Portland State University. In Arvidson, R. M. (1971), More about Wundt's doctorate students. *American Psychologist, 26,* 516.

Bernard, C. (1957). *Introduction of the study of experimental medicine.* New York: Dover. (Original work published 1865)

Bernfeld, S. (1953). Freud's studies on cocaine, 1884–1887. *Journal of the American Psychoanalytic Association, 1,* 581–613.

Bernheim, H. (1964). *Hypnosis and suggestion in psychotherapy.* New Hyde Park, NY: University Books. (Original work published 1865)

Bertin, C. (1982). *Marie Bonaparte: A life.* San Diego: Harcourt Brace Jovanovich.

Bettelheim, B. (1965). *Love is not enough: The treatment of emotionally disturbed children.* New York: Free Press.

Bieliauskas, V. J. (1977). Mental health care in the USSR. *American Psychologist, 32,* 376–379.

Binet, A. (1892). *Les altérations de la personnalité.* Paris: Alcan.

Binet, A. (1903). *L'Étude expérimentale de l'intelligence.* Paris: Schleicher Frères.

Binet, A. (1904). Commission des anormaux. *Bulletin de la Société Libre pour l'Étude Psycholgique de l'Enfant, 15,* 406–408.

Binet, A. (1911). Nouvelles recherches sur la mesure du niveau intellectuel chez les enfants d'école. *L'Année Psychologique, 17,* 145–201.

Binet, A., & Simon, T. (1905). Méthodes nouvelles pour le diagnostic du niveau intellectuel des anormaux. *L'Année Psychologique, 11,* 191–244.

Bingham, W. V. (1941). Psychological services in the United States Army. *Journal of Consulting Psychology, 5,* 221–224.

Binz, C. (1885). *Doktor Johann.* Bonn: Weyer.

Blakemore, C. (1977). *Mechanics of the mind.* Cambridge: Cambridge University Press.

Blodgett, H. C. (1929). The effect of the introduction of reward upon the maze performance of rats. *University of California Publications in Psychology, 4,* 113–134.

Blum, T. (1978). *Pseudoscience and mental ability.* New York: Monthly Review Press.

Blumenthal, A. L. (1970). *Language and psychology: Historical aspects of psycholinguistics.* New York: Wiley.

Blumenthal, A. L. (1975). A re-appraisal of Wilhelm Wundt. *American Psychologist, 30,* 1081–1088.

Blumenthal, A. L. (1979). The founding father we never knew. *Contemporary Psychology, 24,* 547–550.

Blumenthal, A. L. (1985). Wilhelm Wundt: Psychology as the propaedutic science. In C. E. Buxton (Ed.), *Points of view in the modern history of psychology* (pp. 19–50). New York: Academic Press.

Boakes, R. (1984). *From Darwin to behaviorism: Psychology and the minds of animals.* Cambridge: Cambridge University Press.

Boffey, P. M. (1971, April 30). American Association for the Advancement of Science: Facing the question of what it should be and do. *Science,* pp. 453–458.

Bogen, J. E., De Zure, R., Tenhouton, W. D., & March, J. F. (1972). The other side of the brain: The A/P ratio. *Bulletin of the Los Angeles Neurological Society, 37,* 49–61.

Boring, E. G. (1923, April 25). Facts and fancies of immigration. *New Republic,* pp. 245–246.

Boring, E. G. (1927). Edward Bradford Titchener, 1867–1927. *American Journal of Psychology, 38,* 489–506.

Boring, E. G. (1952). Edward Garrigues Boring. In C. Murchison (Ed.), *A history of psychology in autobiography* (Vol. 4, pp. 27–52). New York: Russell & Russell.

Boring, E. G. (1953). John Dewey, 1859–1952. *American Journal of Psychology, 66,* 145–147.

Boring, E. G. (1929/1957). *A history of experimental psychology* (1st ed., 1929; 2nd ed., 1957). New York: Appleton-Century-Crofts.

Boring, M. D., & Boring, E. G. (1948). Masters and pupils among the American psychologists. *American Journal of Psychology, 61,* 527–534.

Bouchard, T. J., Jr. (1981, May). Unpublished colloquium. Ohio State University.

Bouchard, T. J., Jr. (1984). Twins reared together and apart: What they tell us about human heredity. In S. W. Fox (Ed.), *The chemical and biological bases of individuality* (pp. 147–178). New York: Plenum.

Bousfield, W. A. (1955). Lope de Vega on early conditioning. *American Psychologist, 10,* 828.

Bower, G. H. (1970). Organizational factors in memory. *Cognitive Psychology, 1,* 18–46.

Braid, J. (1843). *Neuropynology: Or the rationale of nervous sleep considered in relation to animal magnetism.* London: Churchill.

Brecher, E. M. (1972). *Licit and illicit drugs.* New York: Consumers Union.

Bregman, E. D. (1934). An attempt to modify the emotional attitudes of infants by the conditioned response technique. *Journal of Genetic Psychology, 45,* 169–198.

Breland, K., & Breland, M. (1950). A field of applied animal psychology. *American Psychologist, 5,* 115–124.

Breland, K., & Breland, M. (1961). The misbehavior of organisms. *American Psychologist, 16,* 681–684.

Brentano, F. (1973). *Psychology from an empirical standpoint* (L. L. McAlister, Ed.). New York: Humanities Press. (Original work published 1874)

Breuer, J., & Freud, S. (1957). *Studien über Hysterie.* New York: Basic Books. (Original work published 1895)

Brigham, C. C. (1923). *A study of American intelligence.* Princeton, NJ: Princeton University Press.

Brigham, C. C. (1930). Intelligence tests of immigrant groups. *Psychological Review, 37,* 158–165.

Brill, A. A. (1938). *The basic writings of Sigmund Freud.* New York: Random House.

Bringmann, W. G. (1979, September/October). Wundt's lab...humble but functioning. *American Psychological Association Monitor,* p. 13.

Bringmann, W. G., Balance, W. D. G., & Evans, R. B. (1975). Wilhelm Wundt (1832–1920): A brief biographical sketch. *Journal of the History of the Behavioral Sciences, 11,* 287–297.

Broadbent, D. E. (1958). *Perception and communication.* New York: Pergamon.

Bronowski, J. (1973). *The ascent of man.* Boston: Little, Brown. (Original work published 1879)

Brown, J. F. (1929). The methods of Kurt Lewin in the psychology of action and affection. *Psychological Review, 36,* 200–221.

Buckley, K. W. (1982). The selling of a psychologist: John Broadus Watson and the application of behavioral techniques to advertising. *Journal of the History of the Behavioral Sciences, 18,* 207–221.

Bühler, K. (1907). Tatsachen und Probleme zu einer Psychologie der Denkvorgänge: I. Über Gedanken. *Archiv der Psychologie, 9,* 297–305.

Bullock, A. (1952/1962). *Hitler: A study in tyranny* (1st ed., 1952; rev. ed., 1962). London: Pelican.

Burks, B. S., Jensen, D. W., & Terman, L. M. (1930). *Genetic studies of genius: Vol. 3. The promise of youth: Follow-up studies of a thousand gifted children.* Stanford, CA: Stanford University Press.

Burnham, J. C. (1972). Thorndike's puzzle boxes. *Journal of the History of the Behavioral Sciences, 78,* 159–167.

Burtt, H. E. (1980, May). *Seventy five years of psychology at the Ohio State University* [Videotaped lecture].

Burtt, H. E., & Pressey, S. L. (1957). Henry Herbert Goddard, 1866–1957. *American Journal of Psychology, 70,* 656–657.

Bynum, W. F., Porter, R., & Shepherd, M. (Eds.). (1985). *The anatomy of madness: Essays in the history of psychiatry* (Vol. 2). New York: Tavistock.

Candolle, A. de. (1873). *Histoire des sciences et des savants depuis deux siècles.* Geneva: Georg.

Cannon, W. B. (1927). The James-Lange theory of emotions: A critical examination and an alteration. *American Journal of Psychology, 39,* 106–124.

Caporael, L. (1976). Ergotism: The Satan loosed in Salem? *Science, 192,* 21–26.

Capshew, J. H., & Hearst, E. (1980). Psychology at Indiana University from Bryan to Skinner. *Psychological Record, 30,* 319–342.

Carpenter, F. (1974). *The Skinner primer: Behind freedom and dignity.* New York: The Free Press.

Carr, H. A. (1925). *Psychology: A study of mental activity.* New York: Longmans Green.

Carr, H. A. (1935). *An introduction to visual space perception.* New York: Longmans Green.

Carr, H. A. (1936). Harvey A. Carr. In C. Murchison (Ed.), *A history of psychology in autobiography* (Vol. 3, pp. 69–82). Worcester, MA: Clark University Press.

Carr, H., & Watson, J. B. (1908). Orientation in the white rat. *Journal of Comparative Neurology and Psychology, 18,* 27–44.

Carroll, L. (1871/1940). *Through the looking-glass* (1st ed., 1871; Miniature ed., 1940). London: Macmillan.

Cary, M., & Haarhoff, T. J. (1959). *Life and thought in the Greek and Roman world.* London: Methuen.

Cattell, J. M. (1885). Über die Zeit der Erkennung und Benennung von Schriftzeichen, Bildern und Farben. *Philosophische Studien, 2,* 635–650.

Cattell, J. M. (1886). The time it takes to see and name objects. *Mind, 11,* 63–65.

Cattell, J. M. (1890). Mental tests and measurements. *Mind, 15,* 373–381.

Cattell, J. M. (1895). Measurements of the accuracy of recollection. *Science, 2,* 761–766.

Cattell, J. M. (1903). Statistics of American psychologists. *American Journal of Psychology, 14,* 310–328.

Cattell, J. M. (1906). *American men of science.* New York: Science Press.

Cattell, J. M. (1909). The school and the family. *Popular Science Monthly, 74,* 84–95.

Cattell, J. M. (1921). In memory of Wilhelm Wundt. *Psychological Review, 28,* 155–159.

Cattell, J. M. (1929). Psychology in America (Address of the president of the Ninth International Congress of Psychology). *Science, 70,* 335–347.

Cattell, J. M. (1943). The founding of the Association. *Psychological Review, 50,* 61–64.

Cattell, R. B. (1965). *The scientific analysis of personality.* Chicago: Aldine.

Cattell, R. B., & Kline, P. (1977). *The scientific analysis of personality and motivation.* New York: Academic Press.

Chance, P. (1975, November). Ads without answers make the brain itch. *Psychology Today,* p. 78.

Chomsky, N. (1965). *Analysis of the theory of syntax.* Cambridge, MA: MIT Press.

Clark, R. W. (1980). *Freud: The man and the cause—a biography*. New York: Random House.

Clark, R. W. (1986). *The survival of Charles Darwin*. New York: Avon.

Clarke, E., & O'Malley, C. D. (1968). *The human brain and spinal cord*. Berkeley, CA: University of California Press.

Cohen, D. (1979). *J. B. Watson: The founder of behaviorism*. London: Routledge & Kegan Paul.

Cohen, P. J., & Dripps, R. D. (1970). History and theories of general anesthesia. In L. S. Goodman & A. Gilman (Eds.), *The pharmacology and bases of therapeutics* (4th ed., pp. 42–48). New York: Macmillan.

Cole, J. O., & Davis, J. M. (1975). Antidepressant drugs. In A. M. Freedman, H. I. Kaplan, & B. J. Saddock (Eds.), *Comprehensive textbook of psychiatry* (Vol.2, pp. 1941–1956). Baltimore: Williams & Wilkins.

Collins, N. (1932, January 25). Alice with the 15,000 pound look. *News Chronicle*.

Colp, R., Jr. (1977). *To be an invalid: The illness of Charles Darwin*. Chicago: University of Chicago Press.

Colp, R., Jr. (1979). Charles Darwin's vision of organic nature. *New York State Journal of Medicine, 79*, 1622–1629.

Comte, A. (1896). *Cours de philosophie positive* (H. Martineau, Trans.). London: G. Bell.

Conklin, E. G., Thorndike, E. L., Livingston, B. E., Carlson, A. J., Woodworth, R. S., Achilles, P. S., Davis W., Howard, L. O., Parker, G. H., Russell, N. H., & Swann, W. F. G. (1944). James McKeen Cattell—In memoriam. *Science, 99*, 151–165.

Copernicus, N. (1976). *On the revolutions of the heavenly spheres* (A. M. Duncan, Trans.). New York: Barnes & Noble.

Cox, C. M. (1926). *Genetic studies of genius: Vol. 2. The early mental traits of three hundred geniuses*. Stanford, CA: Stanford University Press.

Cox, J. M. (1811). *Practical observations on insanity*. Philadelphia: Thomas Dobson. National Library of Medicine, Washington, DC. Microfilm No. 25459, Reel 60–41.

Cranefield, P. F. (1974). *The way in and the way out: François Magendie, Charles Bell and the roots of the spinal nerves*. Mount Kisco, NY: Futura.

Crannell, C. W. (1970). Wolfgang Köhler. *Journal of the History of the Behavioral Sciences, 6*, 267–268.

Crawford, C. (1979). George Washington, Abraham Lincoln, and Arthur Jensen: Are they compatible? *American Psychologist, 34*, 664–672.

Creelan, P. G. (1974). Watsonian behaviorism and the Calvinist conscience. *Journal of the History of the Behavioral Sciences, 10*, 95–118.

Crewdson, J. (1987). *By silence betrayed*. Boston: Little, Brown.

Cromer, W., & Anderson, P. A. (1970). Freud's visit to America: Newspaper coverage. *Journal of the History of the Behavioral Sciences, 6*, 349–353.

Cronbach, L. (1975). Five decades of public controversy over mental testing. *American Psychologist, 30*, 1–14.

Crutchfield, R. S. (1961). Edward Chace Tolman, 1886–1959. *American Journal of Psychology, 74*, 135–141.

Crutchfield, R. S., & Krech, D. (1962). Some guides to the understanding of the history of psychology. In L. Postman (Ed.), *Psychology in the making* (pp. 3–27). New York: Knopf.

Dain, N. (1971). *Disordered minds: The first century of Eastern State Hospital in Williamsburg, Virginia*. Williamsburg, VA: Colonial Williamsburg Foundation.

Dallenbach, K. M. (1928). Bibliography of the writings of Edward Bradford Titchener, 1917–1927. *American Journal of Psychology, 40*, 121–125.

Dallenbach, K. M. (1959). Twitmyer and the conditioned response. *American Journal of Psychology, 72,* 633–638.

Danziger, K. (1979). The positivist repudiation of Wundt. *Journal of the History of the Behavioral Sciences, 15,* 205–230.

Danziger, K. (1985). The origins of the psychological experiment as a social institution. *American Psychologist, 40,* 133–140.

Darwin, C. (1899). *Origin of species* (6th ed.). New York: Hurst. (Original work published 1859)

Darwin, C. (1962). *The voyage of the Beagle* (L. Engel, Ed.). New York: Anchor. (Original work published 1860)

Darwin, C. (1871). *The descent of man.* London: John Murray.

Darwin, C. (1872). *The expression of the emotions in man and animals.* London: John Murray.

Darwin, C. (1877, July). A biographical sketch of an infant. *Mind,* pp. 258–294.

Darwin, C. (1958). *Autobiography* (N. Barlow, Ed.). London: Collins.

Davis, A. (1949). Poor people have brains too. *Phi Delta Kappa, 30,* 294–295.

De Beer, G., Rowlands, M. J., & Skramovsky, B. M. (Eds.). (1967). *Darwin's notebooks.* London: British Museum Natural Historical Series.

Delboeuf, J. L. R. (1889). *Le magnétisme animal à-propos d'une visite a l'école de Nancy.* Paris: Alcan.

Dennis, W., & Boring, E. G. (1952). The founding of the American Psychological Association. *American Psychologist, 7,* 95–97.

Descartes, R. (1908). *Discours de la méthode* (J. Veitch, Trans.). In B. Rand, *Modern classical philosophers* (pp. 101–116). Boston: Houghton Mifflin. (Original work published 1637)

Descartes, R. (1912). *The passions of the soul* (H. A. P. Torrey, Trans.). In B. Rand (Ed.), *The classical psychologists* (pp. 168–190). Houghton Mifflin. (Original work published 1649)

Descartes, R. (1972). *Treatise on man* (T. S. Hall, Trans.). Cambridge, MA: Harvard University Press. (Original work published 1637)

Deutsch, A. (1949). *The mentally ill in America.* New York: Columbia University Press.

Dewey, J. (1886). *Psychology.* New York: Harper & Brothers.

Dewey, J. (1894). The psychology of infant language. *Psychological Review, 1,* 63–66.

Dewey, J. (1896). The reflex arc concept in psychology. *Psychological Review, 3,* 359–370.

Dewsbury, D. A. (1984). *Comparative psychology in the twentieth century.* Stroudsburg, PA: Hutchinson Ross.

Dinnage, R. (1987, November 29). Against the master and his men. *The New York Times Book Review,* pp. 10–11.

Dollard, J., & Miller, N. E. (1950). *Personality and psychotherapy.* New York: McGraw-Hill.

Doorley, L. (1982, December). When Freud came to Worcester. *Yankee,* pp. 75–77, 139–145.

Dorfman, D. D. (1978, September 29). The Cyril Burt question: New findings. *Science,* p. 1117.

Doty, R. W. (1969). Electrical stimulation of the brain in behavioral context. *Annual Review of Psychology, 20,* 289–320.

Drake, S. (1975). The role of music in Galileo's experiments. *Scientific American, 232,* 98–104.

Dunbar, R. (1984, August). Mendel's peas and fuzzy logic. *New Scientist,* p. 38.

Duncan, C. P. (1980). A note on the 1929 International Congress of Psychology. *Journal of the History of the Behavioral Sciences, 16,* 1–5.

Dunlap, K. (1912). The case against introspection. *Psychological Review, 19,* 404–413.

Dunlap, K. (1919–1920). Are there any instincts? *Journal of Abnormal Psychology, 14,* 35–50.

Ebbinghaus, H. (1913). *Memory: A contribution to experimental psychology* (H. A. Ruger & C. E. Bussenius, Trans.). New York: Teachers College, Columbia University. (Original work published 1885)

Ebbinghaus, H. (1902). *Grundzüge der Psychologie.* Leipzig: Veit.

Ebbinghaus, H. (1910). *Abriss der Psychologie.* Leipzig: Veit.

Edman, I. (1970). John Dewey: America's philosopher attains an alert 90. In B. B. Seligman (Ed.), *Molders of modern thought* (pp. 99–106). Chicago: Quadrangle.

Ehrenfels, C. (1890). Über Gestaltqualitäten. *Vierteljahrschrift für Wissenschaftliche Philosophie, 14,* 1–256.

Eisenberg, L. (1977). The social imperatives of medical research. *Science, 198,* 1105–1110.

Eissler, K. R. (1978). Biographical sketch of Sigmund Freud. In E. Freud, L. Freud, & I. Grubrich-Smiltis (Eds.), *Sigmund Freud: His life in pictures and words.* New York: Harcourt Brace Jovanovich.

Elkind, D. (1974). *Children and adolescents: Interpretive essays on Jean Piaget.* London: Oxford University Press.

Elliott, M. H. (1928). The effect of change of reward on the maze performance of rats. *University of California Publications in Psychology, 4,* 19–30.

Engel, L. (Ed.). (1962). *The voyage of the Beagle by Charles Darwin.* Garden City, NY: Anchor.

English, H. B. (1929). Three cases of the "conditioned fear response." *Journal of Abnormal and Social Psychology, 34,* 221–225.

Epstein, R., Lanza, R. P., & Skinner, B. F. (1980). Symbolic communication between two pigeons. *Science, 207,* 543–545.

Erlenmeyer, A. (1886) Über die Wirkung des Cocain bei der Morphiumentziehung. *Centralblatt für Nervenheilkunde, Psychiatric und gerichtliche Psychopathologie, 8,* 289–299.

Esdaile, J. (1976). *Mesmerism in India and its practical application in surgery and medicine.* New York: Arno. (Original work published 1846)

Evans, R. B. (1968). *B. F. Skinner: The man and his ideas.* New York: Dutton.

Evans, R. B. (1972). E. B. Titchener and his lost system. *Journal of the History of the Behavioral Sciences, 8,* 168–180.

Evans, R. B. (1979, May). Manual labors: Titchener's contribution. *American Psychological Association Monitor,* p. 3.

Evans, R. B., & Koelsch, W. A. (1985). Psychoanalysis arrives in America. *American Psychologist, 40,* 942–948.

Eysenck, H. J. (1960). *Behavior therapy and the neuroses.* London: Pergamon.

Eysenck, H. J. (1977). Foreword to *The subnormal mind* by Cyril Burt. London: Oxford University Press.

Eysenck, H. J. (1979). *The structure and measurement of intelligence.* New York: Springer.

Eysenck, H. J. (1983). The social application of Pavlovian theories. *Pavlovian Journal of Biological Science, 18,* 117–125.

Fahie, J. J. (1903). *Galileo: His life and work.* London: John Murray.

Fancher, R. E. (1977). Brentano's psychology from an empirical standpoint and Freud's early meta-psychology. *Journal of the History of the Behavioral Sciences, 13,* 207–227.

Fancher, R. E. (1983). Alphonse De Candolle, Francis Galton, and the early history of the nature-nurture controversy. *Journal of the History of the Behavioral Sciences, 19,* 341–352.

Fancher, R. E. (1985). *The intelligence men: Makers of the IQ controversy.* New York: Norton.

Fancher, R. E. (1987). Henry Goddard and the Kallikak family photographs. *American Psychologist, 42,* 585–590.

Farras, V. (1988). *Heidegger et le Nazisme.* Paris: Editions Verdier.

Fearing, F. (1930). *Reflex action: A study in the history of physiological psychology.* Baltimore: Williams & Wilkins.

Fechner, G. F. (1912). *Elements of psychophysics.* In B. Rand (Ed.), *The classical psychologists* (pp. 562–572). Boston: Houghton Mifflin. (Original work published 1860)

Fechner, G. F. (1877). *In Sachen der Psychophysik.* Leipzig: Breitkopf und Härtel.

Feeney, E. L. (1933). At Emery Air Freight: Positive reinforcement boosts performance. *Organizational Dynamics, 1,* 41–50.

Feldman, S. (1932). Wundt's psychology. *American Journal of Psychology, 44,* 615–629.

Fernberger, S. W. (1932). The APA: A historical summary, 1892–1930. *Psychological Bulletin, 29,* 1–89.

Fernberger, S. W. (1933). Wundt's doctorate students. *Psychological Bulletin, 30,* 80–83.

Fernberger, S. W. (1943). The American Psychological Association, 1892–1942. *Psychological Review, 50,* 33–60.

Ferrier, D. (1886). *The functions of the brain* (2nd ed.). London: Smith, Elder.

Ferster, C. B., & Skinner, B. F. (1957). *Schedules of reinforcement.* New York: Appleton-Century-Crofts.

Finan, S. L. (1940). [Review of *The Behavior of Organisms*]. *Journal of General Psychology, 22,* 441–447.

Fine, R. (1985). Anna Freud (1895–1982). *American Psychologist, 40,* 230–232.

Flanagan, J. C. (1963). The definition and measurement of ingenuity. In C. W. Taylor & F. Barron (Eds.), *Scientific creativity: Its recognition and development* (pp. 89–98). New York: Wiley.

Fletcher, F. (1980, April). Reminiscences of Yerkes. Unpublished talk at the Ohio State University.

Flourens, P. (1965). Recherches expérimentales sur les propriétés et les fonctions du système nerveux dans les animaux vertébrés. In R. J. Herrnstein & E. G. Boring (Eds.), *A source book in the history of psychology* (pp. 220–223). Cambridge, MA: Harvard University Press. (Original work published 1823)

Flourens, P. (1843). *Examen de la phrénologie.* Paris: Paulin.

Flourens, P. (1864). *Psychologie comparée* (2nd ed.). Paris: Garnier Frères.

Fowler, O. S., & Fowler, L. N. (1859). *New illustrated self-instructor in phrenology and physiology.* New York: Fowler & Wells.

Fowler, R. D. (1987). Report of the Treasurer, 1986. *American Psychologist, 42,* 632–635.

Fox, D. K., Hopkins, B. L., & Anger, L. W. (1987). The long-term effects of a token economy on safety performance in open-pit mining. *Journal of Applied Behavior Analysis, 20,* 215–224.

Freeman, F.N. (1922). The mental age of adults. *Journal of Educational Research, 6,* 441–444.

Freeman, F. N. (1923). A referendum of psychologists. *Century Illustrated Magazine, 107,* 237–245.

Freeman, F. S. (1977). The beginnings of Gestalt psychology in the United States. *Journal of the History of the Behavioral Sciences, 13,* 352–353.

Freud, E., Freud, L., & Grubrich-Similtis, I. (Eds.). (1978). *Sigmund Freud: His life in pictures and words.* New York: Harcourt Brace Jovanovich.

Freud, S. (1884). Über Coca. *Centralblatt für gesamte Therapie, 2,* 289–314.

Freud, S. (1901). The psychopathology of everyday life. In A. A Brill (Ed.), *The basic writings of Sigmund Freud* (pp. 35–178). New York: Macmillan.

Freud, S. (1935). *An autobiographical study* (J. Strachey, Trans.). London: Hogarth.

Freud, S. (1959). *Collected papers of Sigmund Freud* (E. Jones, J. Riviere, J. Strachey, & A. Strachey, Eds.). 5 vols. New York: Basic Books.

Freud, S. (1961). *The interpretation of dreams* (J. Strachey, Ed.). New York: Science Editions. (Original work published 1900)

Freud, S. (1966). *The complete introductory lectures on psychoanalysis* (J. Strachey, Trans. and Ed.). New York: Norton.

Frolov, Y. P. (1938). *Pavlov and his school.* London: Kegan, Paul, Trench, Trubner.

Fromm, E. (1941). *Escape from freedom.* New York: Farrar & Rinehart.

Fromm, E. (1956). *The art of loving.* New York: Harper.

Fuller, P. R. (1949). Operant conditioning of a vegetative human organism. *American Journal of Psychology, 62,* 587–590.

Furumoto, L. (1979). Mary Whiton Calkins (1863–1930): Fourteenth president of the American Psychological Association. *Journal of the History of the Behavioral Sciences, 15,* 346–356.

Galen. (1968). *On the usefulness of the parts of the body* (M. T. May, Trans.). Ithaca, NY: Cornell University Press.

Galilei, Galileo. (1610). *Sidereus nuncius.* Venice: T. Baglionum.

Galilei, Galileo. (1927). Dialogue concerning the two great systems of the world. In W. S. Knickerbocker (Ed.), *Classics of modern science* (pp. 36–45). New York: Appleton-Century-Crofts. (Original work published 1632)

Gall, F. J. (1965). On phrenology, the localization of the functions of the brain. In R. J. Herrnstein & E. G. Boring (Eds.), *A source book in the history of psychology* (pp. 211–220). Cambridge, MA: Harvard University Press. (Original work published 1825)

Galli, G. (1964). *Sulle qualitata formali dell'area fisionomica.* Bologna: Istituto di Psicologia dell'Università.

Gallistel, C. R. (1981). Bell, Magendie, and the proposals to restrict the use of animals in neurobehavioral research. *American Psychologist, 36,* 357–360.

Galton, F. (1874). *English men of science: Their nature and nurture.* London: Macmillan.

Galton, F. (1879/1970). Psychometric experiments. *Brain, 2,* 148–162. Reprinted in H. F Crovitz (Ed.), *Galton's walk* (pp. 24–35). New York: Harper & Row.

Galton, F. (1880). *Hereditary genius* (2nd American ed.). New York: D. Appleton. (Original work published 1869)

Galton, F. (1907). *Inquiries into human faculty and its development* (2nd ed.). New York: Dutton. (Original work published 1883)

Galton, F. (1901, October 31). The possible improvement of the human breed under the existing conditions of law and sentiment. *Nature,* pp. 659–665.

Galvani, L. (1953). *De viribus electricitatis in motu muscularis commentarius* (R. Montraville, Trans.). Cambridge, MA: E. Licht. (Original work published 1850)

Gantt, W. H. (1973). Reminiscences of Pavlov. *Journal of the Experimental Analysis of Behavior, 20,* 131–136.

Gantt, W. H. (1975, April 25). Unpublished lecture on Pavlov given at the Ohio State University.

Garfield, E. (1978). The 300 most-cited authors. *Current Contents, 28,* 5–17.

Garrett, H. E. (1951). *Great experiments in psychology* (3rd ed.). New York: Appleton-Century-Crofts.

Garrett, H. E. (1955). *General psychology*. New York: American Book Co.

Garvey, C. R. (1929). List of American psychological laboratories. *Psychological Bulletin, 26*, 652–660.

Gay, P. (1988). *Freud: A life for our time*. New York: Norton.

Gaylord-Ross, R. J., & Holvoet, S. H. (1985). *Strategies for educating students with severe handicaps*. Boston: Little, Brown.

Gazzaniga, M. S. (1970). *The bisected brain*. New York: Appleton-Century-Crofts.

Geldard, F. A., & Sherrick, C. E. (1972). The cutaneous "rabbit": A perceptual illusion. *Science, 178*, 178–179.

Gerow, J. R. (Ed.). (1988). *Time: Psychology 1923–1988*. New York: Time.

Gesell, A. (1954). *The first five years of life*. London: Methuen.

Gesell, A., & Ilg, F. L. (1943). *Infant and child in the culture of today*. London: Hamish Hamilton.

Gibson, E. J. (1977). How perception really develops: A view from outside the network. In D. L. La Berge & S. J. S. Samuels (Eds.), *Basic processes in reading: Perception and comprehension* (pp. 155–173). Hillsdale, NJ: Lawrence Erlbaum.

Gillie, O. (1976, October 24). Pioneer of IQ faked his research findings. *Sunday Times of London*, pp. 1–2.

Gilman, S. L. (1979). Darwin sees the insane. *Journal of the History of the Behavioral Sciences, 15*, 253–262.

Giurgea, C. E. (1985). On facts and ideologies in the Pavlovian saga. *Pavlovian Journal of Biological Science, 20*, 7–10.

Gleitman, H. (1981). *Psychology*. New York: Norton.

Goddard, H. H. (1911a). *The Binet-Simon measuring scale for intelligence* (rev. ed.). Vineland, NJ: Training School.

Goddard, H. H. (1911b). Two thousand normal children measured by the Binet measuring scale of intelligence. *Pedagogical Seminary, 18*, 232–259.

Goddard, H. H. (1912). *The Kallikak family: A study in the heredity of feeble-mindedness*. New York: Macmillan.

Goddard, H. H. (1913). The Binet tests in relation to immigration. *Journal of Psychoasthenics, 18*, 105–107.

Goddard, H. H. (1917). Mental tests and the immigrant. *Journal of Delinquency, 2*, 243–277.

Goddard, H. H. (1920). *Human efficiency and levels of intelligence*. Princeton, NJ: Princeton University Press.

Goddard, H. H. (1928). *School training for gifted children*. Yonkers-on-Hudson, NY: World Book.

Goddard, H. H. (1942). In defense of the Kallikak study. *Science, 95*, 574–576.

Goodall, J. (1971). *In the shadow of man*. Boston: Houghton Mifflin.

Goodell, R. (1975). *The visible scientists*. Unpublished Doctoral dissertation, Stanford University. Reported in *American Psychological Association Monitor*, August 1975, p. 1.

Goodman, E. (1979, December). Margaret Floy Washburn: "A complete psychologist." *American Psychological Association Monitor*, p. 3.

Goodstein, L. D. (1988, September). Some final thoughts. *American Psychological Association Monitor*, p. 3.

Gottlieb, G. (1972). Zing-Yang Kuo: Radical scientific philosopher and innovative experimentalist (1898–1970). *Journal of Comparative and Physiological Psychology, 80*, 1–10.

Gould, J. L. (1982). *Ethology: The mechanisms and evolution of behavior*. New York: Norton.

Gould, S. J. (1978, October). Women's brains. *Natural History*, pp. 44–50.

Gould, S. J. (1981). *The mismeasure of man*. New York: Norton.

Grant, M. (1916). *The passing of the great race, or the racial basis of European history*. New York: Scribner's.

Gregory, R. L. (1974). *Concepts and mechanisms of perception*. London: Duckworth.

Guazzo, F. M. (1970). Compendium maleficarum (M. Sumners, Ed.; E. A. Ashwin, Trans.). New York: Barnes & Noble.

Guilford, J. P. (1954). *A factor analytical study across the domains of reasoning, creativity and evaluation: I. Hypothesis and description of tests: Reports from the psychological laboratory*. Los Angeles: University of Southern California Press.

Gur, R. C., & Reivich, M. (1980). Cognitive task effects on hemispheric blood flow in humans: Evidence for individual differences in hemispheric activation. *Brain and Language, 9*, 78–92.

Guthrie, E. R. (1930). Conditioning as a principle of learning. *Psychological Review, 37*, 412–428.

Guthrie, E. R. (1934). Pavlov's theory of conditioning. *Psychological Review, 41*, 199–206.

Guthrie, E. R. (1935). *The psychology of learning*. New York: Harper & Brothers.

Guthrie, E. R. (1938). *The psychology of human conflict*. New York: Harper.

Guthrie, E. R. (1940). Association and the law of effect. *Psychological Review, 47*, 127–148.

Guthrie, E. R. (1948). Pierre Janet, 1859–1947. *Psychological Review, 55*, 65–66.

Guthrie, E. R. (1959). Association by contiguity. In S. Koch (Ed.), *Psychology: A study of a science* (Vol. 2, pp. 158–195). New York: McGraw-Hill.

Guthrie, E. R., & Horton, G. P. (1946). *Cats in a puzzle box*. New York: Rinehart & Co.

Guthrie, R. V. (1976). *Even the rat was white: A historical view of psychology*. New York: Harper & Row.

Guttman, N. (1977). On Skinner and Hull: A reminiscence and projection. *American Psychologist, 32*, 321–328.

Hajal, F. (1983). Galen's ethical psychotherapy: Its influence on a medieval near-Eastern physician. *Journal of the History of Medicine and Allied Sciences, 38*, 320–333.

Hale, M., Jr. (1980). *Human science and order: Hugo Münsterberg and the origins of applied psychology*. Philadelphia: Temple University Press.

Hall, E. (1972, November). Will success spoil B. F. Skinner? *Psychology Today*, pp. 65–72, 130.

Hall, G. S. (1878). The muscular perception of space. *Mind, 3*, 433–450.

Hall, G. S. (1893). *The contents of children's minds on entering school*. New York: Kellogg.

Hall, G. S. (1894). Research, the vital spirit of teaching. *Forum, 17*, 558–570.

Hall, G. S. (1903). The relations between higher and lower races. *Proceedings of the Massachusetts Historical Society, 17*, 4–13.

Hall, G. S. (1904). *Adolescence: Its psychology and its relation to physiology, anthropology, sociology, sex, crime, religion and education*. New York: Appleton.

Hall, G. S. (1905a). The Negro question. *Proceedings of the Massachusetts Historical Society, 19*, 95–107.

Hall, G. S. (1905b). The Negro in Africa and America. *Pedagogical Seminary, 12*, 350–368.

Hall, G. S. (1906a). *Youth*. New York: Appleton.

Hall, G. S. (1906b). Undeveloped races in contact with civilization. *Washington University Association Bulletin, 4*, 145–150.

Hall, G. S. (1911a). Eugenics: Its ideals and what it is going to do. *Religious Education, 6*, 152–159.

Hall, G. S. (1911b). The teaching of sex in schools and colleges. *American Society for Sanitary and Moral Prophylaxis, 2*, 1–19.

Hall, G. S. (1911c). The problem of dependent races. *29th Annual Mohonk Conference Report.*

Hall, G. S. (1911d). *Educational problems.* 2 vols. New York: Appleton.

Hall, G. S. (1919). Some possible effects of the war on American psychology. *Psychological Bulletin, 16,* 48–49.

Hall, G. S. (1922). *Senescence: The last half of life.* New York: Appleton.

Hall, G. S. (1924). *Life and confessions of a psychologist.* New York: Appleton.

Hall, M. H. (1967, September). An interview with "Mr. Behaviorist" B. F. Skinner. *Psychology Today,* p. 20.

Haller, A. von. (1747). *Primae lineae physiologiae.* Göttingen: Vandenhoeck.

Hammond, A. (1984). The choosing of the 20. *Science 84, 5,* 9.

Harlow, H. F. (1949). The formation of learning sets. *Psychological Review, 56,* 51–65.

Harlow, J. M. (1869). *Recovery from the passage of an iron bar through the head.* Boston: Clapp.

Harrington, A. (1987). *Medicine, mind, and the double brain.* Princeton, NJ: Princeton University Press.

Harris, B. (1979). Whatever happened to Little Albert? *American Psychologist, 34,* 151–160.

Harris, M. (1975). *Cows, pigs, wars and witches—the riddle of culture.* New York: Vintage.

Harris, R. (1984). *The making of Neil Kinnock.* London: Faber.

Hartley, D. (1912). Observations on man. In B. Rand (Ed.), *The classical psychologists* (pp. 313–330). Boston: Houghton Mifflin. (Original work published 1749)

Hartmann, G. W. (1935). *Gestalt psychology.* New York: Ronald Press.

Hayek, F. A. (1951). *J. S. Mill and Harriet Taylor: Their friendship and subsequent marriage.* London: Routledge & Kegan Paul.

Hays, R. (1962). Psychology of the scientist: III. Introduction to "Passages from the idea books of Clark L. Hull." *Perceptual and Motor Skills, 15,* 803–806.

Hearnshaw, L. S. (1979). *Cyril Burt: Psychologist.* Ithaca, NY: Cornell University Press.

Hebb, D. O. (1949). *The organization of behavior: A neuropsychological theory.* New York: Wiley.

Hebb, D. O. (1959). Karl Spencer Lashley, 1890–1958. *American Journal of Psychology, 72,* 142–150.

Hefferline, R. F., Keenan, B., & Harford, R. A. (1959). Escape and avoidance conditioning in human subjects without their observations of the response. *Science, 130,* 1338–1339.

Heidbreder, E. (1961). *Seven psychologies.* New York: Appleton-Century-Crofts. (Original work published 1933)

Heider, F. (1970). Gestalt theory: Early history and reminiscences. *Journal of the History of the Behavioral Sciences, 6,* 131–139.

Heilbroner, R. L. (1985). Carnegie and Rockefeller. In *A sense of history: The best writings from the pages of American Heritage* (pp. 430–460). New York: Houghton-Mifflin.

Henle, M. (1978a). One man against the Nazis—Wolfgang Köhler. *American Psychologist, 33,* 939–944.

Henle, M. (1978b). Gestalt psychology and gestalt therapy. *Journal of the History of the Behavioral Sciences, 14,* 23–32.

Henle, M. (1986). *1879 and all that.* New York: Columbia University Press.

Herrmann, D. J., & Chaffin, R. (Eds.). (1988). *Memory in historical perspective: The literature before Ebbinghaus.* New York: Springer-Verlag.

Herrnstein, R. J. (1971). I.Q. *Atlantic Monthly, 228,* 43–64.

Herrnstein, R. J., & Boring, E. G. (Eds.). (1965). *A source book in the history of psychology.* Cambridge, MA: Harvard University Press.

Heyduk, R. G., & Fenigstein, A. (1984). Influential works and authors in psychology: A survey of eminent psychologists. *American Psychologist, 39*, 556–559.

Hilgard, E. R. (1956). *Theories of learning* (2nd ed.). New York: Appleton-Century-Crofts.

Hilgard, E. R. (1961). Introduction to a new edition of C. L. Hull, *Hypnosis and suggestibility*. New York: Appleton-Century-Crofts.

Hilgard, E. R. (1987). *Psychology in America: A historical survey*. New York: Harcourt Brace Jovanovich.

Hillix, W. A., & Broyles, J. W. (1980). The family trees of American psychologists. In W. G. Bringmann & R. D. Tweney, *Wundt studies* (pp. 422–434). Toronto: C. J. Hogrefe.

Hillix, W. A., & Marx, M. H. (1974). *Systems and theories in psychology: A reader*. New York: West.

Hinde, R. A., & Stevenson-Hinde, J. (1933). *Constraints on learning*. New York: Academic Press.

Hippocrates. (1952). Concerning the sacred disease. In R. M. Hutchins (Ed.), *Great books of the Western world: Vol. 10. The writings of Hippocrates*. Chicago: Encyclopaedia Britannica.

Hippocrates. (1955). The nature of man. In J. Chadwick & W. N. Mann (Eds.), *The medical works of Hippocrates* (pp. 202–213). Oxford: Blackwell.

Hobbes, T. (1651). *Leviathan, or the matter, forme and power of commonwealth, eccklesiasticall and civill*. London: A. Crooke.

Hobbes, T. (1951). Human nature. In R. S. Peters (Ed.), *Body and citizen* (pp. 182–244). New York: Collier. (Original work published 1650)

Hochberg, J. (1979). Sensation and perception. In E. Hearst (Ed.), *The first century of experimental psychology* (pp. 89–142). Hillside, NJ: Lawrence Erlbaum.

Hoffeld, D. R. (1980). Mesmer's failure: Sex, politics, personality and the Zeitgeist. *Journal of the History of the Behavioral Sciences, 16*, 377–386.

Hofmann, P. (1988, March 27). Freud's Vienna begins at Berggasse 19. *The New York Times*, p. 21.

Hofstadter, D. R. (1979). *Gödel, Escher, Bach: An eternal golden braid*. New York: Basic Books.

Holden, C. (1980). Identical twins reared apart. *Science, 207*, 1323–1326.

Holland, J. G., & Skinner, B. F. (1961). *The analysis of behavior*. New York: McGraw-Hill.

Hollender, M. H. (1980). The case of Anna O.: A reformulation. *American Journal of Psychiatry, 137*, 787–800.

Holt, E. B. (1911). *Founders of modern psychology*. New York: Appleton.

Horney, K. (1937). *The neurotic personality of our time*. New York: Norton.

Hovland, C. I. (1952). Clark Leonard Hull, 1884–1952. *Psychological Review, 59*, 347–350.

Hubel, D. H., & Wiesel, T. N. (1969). Receptive fields and functional architecture in two nonstriate visual areas (18 and 19) of the cat. *Journal of Neurophysiology, 28*, 229–289.

Hull, C. L. (1928). *Aptitude testing*. Yonkers-on-Hudson, NY: World Book.

Hull, C. L. (1929). A functional interpretation of the conditioned reflex. *Psychological Review, 36*, 498–511.

Hull, C. L. (1933). *Hypnosis and suggestibility*. New York: Appleton-Century.

Hull, C. L. (1937). Mind, mechanism and adaptive behavior. *Psychological Review, 44*, 1–32.

Hull, C. L. (1943). *Principles of behavior*. New York: Appleton-Century-Crofts.

Hull, C. L. (1951). *Essentials of behavior*. New Haven, CT: Yale University Press.

Hull, C. L. (1952). *A behavior system*. New Haven, CT: Yale University Press.

Hull, C. L. (1962). Psychology of the scientist: IV. Passages from the "idea books" of Clark L. Hull. *Perceptual and Motor Skills, 15,* 807–882.

Hull, C. L. (1968). Clark Leonard Hull. In E. G. Boring (Ed.), *A history of psychology in autobiography* (Vol. 4, pp. 143–162). New York: Russell & Russell. (Original work published 1952)

Hulse, S. H., & Green, B. F. (Eds.) (1986). *One hundred years of psychological research in America: G. Stanley Hall and the Johns Hopkins tradition.* Baltimore, MD: Johns Hopkins University Press.

Hume, D. (1911). *A treatise of human nature.* 2 vols. London: Dent. (Original work published 1739–1740)

Hume, D. (1748) *An enquiry concerning the human understanding.* London: Dent.

Iltis, H. (1932). *Life of Mendel.* (E. Paul & C. Paul, Trans.). New York: Norton.

Irwin, F. W. (1943). Edwin Burket Twitmyer, 1873–1943. *American Journal of Psychology, 56,* 451–453.

Itard, J. M. G. (1962). *The wild boy of Aveyron.* New York: Appleton-Century-Crofts. (Original work published 1894)

James, W. (1884, January). On some omissions of introspective psychology. *Mind, 9,* 1–2b.

James, W. (1935). Letter to Carl Stumpf. In R. B. Perry, *The thought and character of William James* (Vol. 2, pp. 68–71). Boston: Little, Brown. (Original work published 1887)

James, W. (1890). *The principles of psychology.* 2 vols. New York: Henry Holt.

James, W. (1892). *Psychology: A briefer course.* New York: Henry Holt.

James, W. (1899). *Talks to teachers on psychology and to students on some of life's ideals.* New York: Henry Holt.

James, W. (1902). *Varieties of religious experience.* New York: Longmans, Green.

James, W. (1907). *Pragmatism.* New York: Longmans, Green.

James, W. (1909). *The meaning of truth: A sequel to pragmatism.* New York: Longmans, Green.

James, W. (1910). The moral equivalent of war. New York: Association for International Conciliation.

Janet, P. (1903). *Les obsessions et la psychasthénie.* Paris: Alcan.

Jastrow, J. (1943). American psychology in the '80's and '90's. *Psychological Review, 50,* 65–67.

Jaynes, J. (1976). *The origin of consciousness and the breakdown of the bicameral mind.* Boston: Houghton Mifflin.

Jenkins, J. G., & Dallenbach, K. M. (1924). Oblivescence during sleep and waking. *American Journal of Psychology, 35,* 605–612.

Jensen, A. R. (1969). How much can we boost IQ and educational achievement? *Harvard Educational Review, 39,* 1–23.

Jessen, P. C. (1751). *De Siti* (University dissertation, Jena).

Johnson, R. C., McClearn, G. E., Yuen, S., Nagoshi, C. T., Ahern, F., & Cole, R. E. (1985). Galton's data a century later. *American Psychologist, 40,* 875–892.

Joncich, G. (1968). *The sane positivist: A biography of Edward Lee Thorndike.* Middletown, CT: Wesleyan University Press.

Jones, E. (1953/1955/1957). *The life and work of Sigmund Freud.* 3 vols. New York: Basic Books.

Jones, M. C. (1924a). The elimination of children's fears. *Journal of Experimental Psychology, 7,* 383–390.

Jones, M. C. (1924b). A laboratory study of fear: The case of Peter. *Pedagogical Seminary, 31,* 308–315.

Jones, M. C. (1974). Albert, Peter, and John B. Watson. *American Psychologist, 29,* 581–583.

Kamin, L. J. (1974). *The science and politics of IQ.* Potomac, MD: Lawrence Erlbaum.

Kamm, J. (1977). *John Stuart Mill in love.* London: Gordon & Cremonesi.

Kanner, L. (1964). *A history of the care and study of the mentally retarded.* Springfield, IL: Charles C. Thomas.

Kant, I. (1908a). *Critique of practical reason* (T. K. Abbott, Trans.). In B. Rand, *Modern classical philosophers* (pp. 457–485). Boston: Houghton Mifflin. (Original work published 1788)

Kant, I. (1908b). *Critique of pure reason* (J. Watson, Trans.). In B. Rand, *Modern classical philosophers* (pp. 376–456). Boston: Houghton Mifflin. (Original work published 1781)

Kant, I. (1965). *On the a priori nature of space* (J. Watson, Trans.). In R. Herrnstein & E. G. Boring (Eds.), *A source book in the history of psychology* (pp. 132–135). Cambridge, MA: Harvard University Press. (Original work published 1781)

Karier, C. J. (1976). *Testing for order and control in the corporate liberal state.* New York: Pantheon.

Karier, C. J. (1986). *Scientists of the mind.* Urbana: University of Illinois Press.

Keller, F. S. (1937). *The definition of psychology.* New York: Appleton-Century-Crofts.

Kellogg, R. (1972). Interview in *Development* [Film, CRM].

Kenyon, J. (1981). Brain stimulation and affective behavior: A note on an early demonstration of a "reward center." *Journal of the History of the Behavioral Sciences, 17,* 174–175.

Kessen, W., & Cathan, E. D. (1986). A century of psychology: From subject to object to agent. *American Scientist, 74,* 640–649.

Kesten, H. (1945). *Copernicus and his world.* New York: Roy.

Kevles, D. J. (1987). *In the name of eugenics: Genetics and the uses of human heredity.* New York: Knopf.

Kiley, S. (1987, November 30). An unheard cry for freedom. *The Times of London,* p. 15.

Kingsbury, F. A. (1946). A history of the department of psychology at the University of Chicago. *Psychological Bulletin, 43,* 259–271.

Kinkade, K. (1973). *A Walden Two experiment: The first five years of Twin Oaks Community.* New York: Morrow.

Kittredge, G. L. (1929). *Witchcraft in old and New England.* Cambridge, MA: Harvard University Press.

Knapp, T. J. (1985). Contributions to the history of psychology: T. V. Moore and his "Cognitive Psychology" of 1939. *Psychological Reports, 357,* 1311–1316.

Knapp, T. J. (1986a). The emergence of cognitive psychology in the latter half of the twentieth century. In T. J. Knapp & L. C. Robertson (Eds.), *Approaches in cognition: Contrasts and controversies* (pp. 13–15). Hillsdale, NJ: Lawrence Erlbaum.

Knapp, T. J. (1986b). Ralph Franklin Hefferline: The Gestalt therapist among the Skinnerians or the Skinnerian among the Gestalt therapists? *Journal of the History of the Behavioral Sciences, 22,* 49–60.

Koch, H. L. (1955). Harvey A. Carr, 1873–1954. *Psychological Review, 62,* 81–82.

Koenigsberger, L. (1906). *Hermann von Helmholtz* (F. A. Welby, Trans.). Oxford: Oxford University Press.

Koffka, K. (1922). Perception: An introduction to the Gestalt theories. *Psychological Bulletin, 19,* 531–585.

Koffka, K. (1935). *Principles of Gestalt psychology.* New York: Harcourt, Brace.

Köhler, W. (1925). An aspect of gestalt psychology. In C. Murchison (Ed.), *Psychologies of 1925* (pp. 163–195). Worcester, MA: Clark University Press.

Köhler, W. (1925). *The mentality of apes* (E. Winter, Trans.). New York: Harcourt, Brace.

Köhler, W. (1944). Max Wertheimer, 1880–1943. *Psychological Review, 51,* 143–146.

Köhler, W. (1947). *Gestalt psychology.* New York: Liveright.

Kohlstedt, S. D. (1980). Science: The struggle for survival, 1880–1894. *Science, 209,* 33–42.

Kraepelin, E. (1919). *Dementia praecox and paraphrenia* (R. M. Barclay, Trans.). Chicago: Chicago Medical Book.

Krantz, D. L. (1969). The Baldwin-Titchener controversy. In D. L. Krantz (Ed.), *Schools of psychology* (pp. 1–19). New York: Appleton-Century-Crofts.

Kraus, O. (1924). *Franz Brentano.* Munich: Beck.

Krech, D. (1961). Introduction to a new edition of Tolman's *Purposive behavior in animals and men.* New York: Appleton-Century-Crofts.

Krech, D. (1962). Cortical localization of function. In L. Postman (Ed.), *Psychology in the making* (pp. 31–72). New York: Knopf.

Kroc, R. (1987). *Grinding it out: The making of McDonald's.* New York: St. Martin's Press.

Krüger, J. G. (1756). *Versuch einer experimentellen Seelenlehre.* Halle and Helmstedt: Hemmerde.

Kuhn, T. S. (1970). *The structure of scientific revolutions* (2nd ed.). Chicago: University of Chicago Press.

Külpe, O. (1895). *Outlines of psychology* (E. B. Titchener, Trans.). New York: Macmillan. (Original work published 1893)

Kuo, Z. Y. (1921). Giving up instincts in psychology. *Journal of Philosophy, 18,* 645–664.

Kuo, Z. Y. (1924). A psychology without heredity. *Psychological Review, 31,* 427–448.

Kuo, Z. Y. (1930). The genesis of the cat's responses to the rat. *Journal of Comparative Psychology, 11,* 1–35.

Lachman, R., Lachman, J. L., & Butterfield, E. C. (1979). *Cognitive psychology and information processing.* Hillsdale, NJ: Lawrence Erlbaum.

Ladd, G. T., & Woodworth, R. S. (1911). *Elements of physiological psychology.* New York: Scribner's.

Lamb, W. R. M. (1967). *The works of Plato* (Vol. 2). Cambridge, MA: Harvard University Press.

La Mettrie, J. O. de. (1927). *L'Homme machine.* Chicago: Open Court. (Original work published 1748)

Landa, L. (1981). Phenomena, comment and notes. *Smithsonian, 12,* 22.

Lane, H. (1976). *The wild boy of Aveyron.* Cambridge, MA: Harvard University Press.

Langer, W. C., & Gifford, S. (1978). An American analyst in Vienna during the Anschluss, 1936–1938. *Journal of the History of the Behavioral Sciences, 14,* 37–54.

Langfeld, H. S. (1937). Carl Stumpf, 1848–1936. *American Journal of Psychology, 49,* 316–320.

Lapointe, F. H. (1970). Origin and evolution of the term "psychology." *American Psychologist, 25,* 640–646.

Larson, C. A., & Sullivan, J. J. (1965). Watson's relation to Titchener. *Journal of the History of the Behavioral Sciences, 1,* 338–354.

Lashley, K. S. (1929). *Brain mechanisms and intelligence.* Chicago: University of Chicago Press.

Lashley, K. S. (1950). In search of the engram. In *Society of Experimental Biology Symposium No. 4: Physiological mechanisms in animal behavior* (pp. 454–482). New York: Cambridge University Press.

Latané, B., & Darley, J. M. (1970). *The unresponsive bystander: Why doesn't he help?* New York: Appleton-Century-Crofts.

Laties, V. G. (1987). Society for the experimental analysis of behavior: The first thirty years (1957–1987). *Journal of the Experimental Analysis of Behavior, 48,* 495–512.

Leibniz, G. W. von. (1912). Philosophical works. In B. Rand (Ed.), *The classical psychologists* (pp. 208–228). Boston: Houghton Mifflin.

Lesch, J. F. (1984). *Science and medicine in France: The emergence of experimental physiology, 1790–1855.* Cambridge, MA: Harvard University Press.

Lesky, E. (Ed.). (1979). *Writings of Franz Joseph Gall.* Bern: Hans Huber.

Lewin, K. (1917). Krieglandschaft. *Zeitschrift für angewandte Psychologie, 12,* 440–447.

Lewin, K. (1931). Environmental forces in child behavior and development (D. K. Adams, Trans.). In C. Murchison (Ed.), *A handbook of child psychology* (pp. 94–127). Worcester, MA: Clark University Press.

Lewin, K. (1935). *A dynamic theory of personality.* New York: McGraw-Hill.

Lewin, K. (1936). *Principles of topological psychology.* New York: McGraw-Hill.

Lewin, K. (1937). Carl Stumpf. *Psychological Review, 44,* 189–194.

Lewin, K., Lippitt, R., & White, R. K. (1939). Patterns of aggressive behavior in experimentally created "social climates." *Journal of Social Psychology, 10,* 271–299.

Liddell, H. (1969). Personal communication to Konrad Lorenz, 1951, cited by K. Lorenz. In K. H. Pribram (Ed.), *On the biology of learning* (pp. 13–93). New York: Harcourt, Brace and World.

Limber, J. (1982). What can chimps tell us about the origin of language? In S. Kuczaj (Ed.), *Language development: Vol. 2. Language, thought and culture* (pp. 429–469). Hillsdale, NJ: Lawrence Erlbaum.

Lippitt, R. (1939). An experimental study of authoritarian and democratic group atmospheres. *University of Iowa Studies in Child Welfare, 16*(3), 43–195.

Lippmann, W. (1922a). The mental age of Americans. *New Republic, 32,* 213–215.

Lippmann, W. (1922b). The reliability of intelligence tests. *New Republic, 32,* 275–277.

Lippmann, W. (1922c). The abuse of tests. *New Republic, 32,* 297–298.

Lippmann, W. (1922d). A future for tests. *New Republic, 33,* 9–10.

Lippmann, W. (1923). The great confusion. *New Republic, 34,* 145–146.

Locke, J. (1960). *Two treatises on government.* Cambridge: Cambridge University Press. (Original work published 1689)

Locke, J. (1964). *Some thoughts concerning education* (F. W. Garforth, Ed.). Woodbury, NY: Barron's Educational Series. (Original work published 1693)

Locke, J. (1975). *An essay concerning human understanding* (P. Nidditch, Ed.). Oxford: Clarendon Press. (Original work published 1690)

Loftus, E. (1980). *Memory.* Reading, MA: Addison-Wesley.

Lorenz, K. (1935). Der Kumpan in der Umwelt des Vogels. *Journal of Ornithology, 83,* 137–213, 289–413.

Lorenz, K. (1950). The comparative method in studying innate behavior patterns. *Symposium of the Society for Experimental Biology, 4,* 221–268.

Lorenz, K. Z. (1969). Innate bases of learning. In K. H. Pribram (Ed.), *On the biology of learning* (pp. 13–94). New York: Harcourt, Brace & World.

Lotze, R. H. (1965). On local signs in their relation to the perception of space. In R. J. Herrnstein & E. G. Boring (Eds.), *A source book in the history of psychology* (pp. 135–140). Cambridge, MA: Harvard University Press. (Original work published 1852)

Lovejoy, A. O. (1936). *The great chain of being.* Cambridge, MA: Harvard University Press.

Luchins, A. S., & Luchins, E. H. (1970). *Wertheimer's seminars revisited: Problem solving and thinking.* 3 vols. Albany, NY: Faculty-Student Associates, SUNY at Albany.

Luther, M. (1907). *Table talks* (P. Smith, Ed.). New York: Columbia University Press. (Original work published 1652)

Lykken, D. T. (1979). The detection of deception. *Psychological Bulletin, 86,* 47–53.

Mach, E. (1914). Analysis of sensations. La Salle, IL: Open Court. (Original work published 1886)

Machan, T. R. (1974). *The pseudo-science of B. F. Skinner.* New Rochelle, NY: Arlington House.

Macmillan, M. B. (1979). Delboeuf and Janet as influences on Freud's treatment of Emmy von N. *Journal of the History of the Behavioral Sciences, 15,* 299–309.

Macmillan, M. B. (1986). A wonderful journey through skull and brains: The travels of Mr. Gage's tamping iron. *Brain and Cognition, 5,* 67–107.

Maddocks, M. (1986). Harvard was once unimaginably small and humble. *Smithsonian, 16,* 140–160.

Magendie, F. (1822). Experiences sur les fonctions des racines des nerfs rachidiens. *Journal de Physiologie Expérimentale et Pathologique, 2,* 276–279.

Mahaffy, J. P. (1880). *Descartes.* London: W. Blackwood.

Mandler, G. (1967). Organization and memory. In K. W. Spence & J. T Spence (Eds.), *The psychology of learning and motivation* (Vol. 1, pp. 327–372). New York: Academic Press.

Marrow, A. J. (1969). *The practical theorist: The life and work of Kurt Lewin.* New York: Basic Books.

Marx, M. H., & Hillix, W. A. (1979). *Systems and theories of psychology* (3rd ed.). New York: McGraw-Hill.

Marx, O. (1966). Aphasia studies and language theory in the 19th century. *Bulletin of the History of Medicine, 40,* 328–349.

Masson, J. M. (1984). *The assault on truth.* New York: Farrar, Straus & Giroux.

Matossian, M. K. (1982). Ergot and the Salem witchcraft affair. *American Scientist, 70,* 355–357.

May, M. T. (1968). *Galen on the usefulness of the parts of the body.* Ithaca, NY: Cornell University Press.

Mazlish, B. (1975). *James and John Stuart Mill: Father and son in the nineteenth century.* New York: Basic Books.

McConnell, J. V. (1980). *Understanding human behavior* (3rd ed.). New York: Holt, Rinehart & Winston.

McDougall, W. (1905). *Physiological psychology.* New York: Macmillan.

McDougall, W. (1912). *Psychology: The study of behavior.* London: Williams & Norgate.

McDougall, W. (1933). *The energies of men.* New York: Scribner's.

McGee, V. J., Huber, R. J., & Carter, C. L. (1983). Similarities between Confucius and Adler. *Individual Psychology, 39,* 237–246.

McGuire, W. (Ed.). (1974). *The Freud/Jung letters.* Princeton, NJ: Princeton University Press. Excerpts in *Psychology Today,* February 1974, pp. 37–42, 86–94.

McKinney, F. (1978). Functionalism at Chicago: Memories of a graduate student, 1929–1931. *Journal of the History of the Behavioral Sciences, 14,* 142–148.

McReynolds, P. (1987). Lightner Witmer: Little-known founder of clinical psychology. *American Psychologist, 42,* 849–858.

Mendel, G. (1866). Versuche über Pflanzenhybriden. *Verhandlungen des Naturforschenden Vereins in Brünn, 4,* 3–47.

Menninger, R. W. (1976). Psychiatry 1976: Time for a holistic medicine. *Annals of Internal Medicine, 84,* 603–604.

Merlan, P. (1949). Brentano and Freud: A sequel. *Journal of the History of Ideas, 10,* 451.

Meyer, D. R. (1978). Unpublished lecture on the history of psychology, Ohio State University.

Meyer, D. R. (1983). How to read Hearst. Unpublished lecture notes, Ohio State University.

Middleton, D. (1971). *Sir Francis Galton's* Art of Travel. Harrisburg, PA: Stackpole.

Middleton, W. S. (1928). Benjamin Rush. *Annals of Medical History, 10,* 434.

Milgram, S. (1963). Behavioral study of obedience. *Journal of Abnormal and Social Psychology, 67,* 371–378.

Milgram, S. (1974). *Obedience to authority: An experimental view.* New York: Harper & Row.

Mill, J. (1912). *Analysis of the phenomena of the human mind.* In B. Rand (Ed.), *The classical psychologists* (pp. 463–482). Boston: Houghton Mifflin. (Original work published 1829)

Mill, J. S. (1869). *The subjection of women.* London: Longmans, Green, Reader & Dyer.

Mill, J. S. (1875). *A system of logic* (9th ed.). 2 vols. London: Longmans, Green, Reader & Dyer.

Mill, J. S. (1909). *Essays on liberty.* New York: P. F. Collier. (Original work published 1859)

Mill, J. S. (1961). *The utilitarians and utilitarianism.* Garden City, NY: Doubleday. (Original work published 1861)

Mill, J. S. (1961). *Auguste Comte and positivism.* Ann Arbor: University of Michigan Press. (Original work published 1865)

Mill, J. S. (1961). *The early draft of John Stuart Mill's Autobiography* (J. Stillinger, Ed.). Urbana, IL: University of Illinois Press. (Original work published 1873)

Miller, G. A. (1962). *Psychology: The science of mental life.* New York: Harper & Row.

Miller, G. A. (1984). The test. *Science 84, 5,* 55–57.

Miller, G. A., Galanter, E., & Pribram, K. (1960). *Plans and the structure of behavior.* New York: Holt.

Miller, J. (1982). *The body in question.* New York: Vintage.

Mills, W. (1899). The nature of animal intelligence and the methods of investigating it. *Psychological Review, 6,* 262–274.

Mintz, A. (1954). An eighteenth century attempt at an experimental psychology. *Journal of General Psychology, 50,* 63–77.

Misiak, H., & Sexton, V. S. (1966). *History of psychology.* New York: Grune & Stratton.

Misiak, H., & Staudt, V. M. (1934). *Catholics in psychology: A historical survey.* New York: McGraw-Hill.

Momigliano, L. N. (1987). A spell in Vienna—but was Freud a Freudian? *International Review of Psychoanalysis, 14,* 373–389.

Montagu, A. (1977, December 11). [Review of *Origins: What new discoveries reveal about the emergence of our species and its possible future*]. *Saturday Review,* pp. 23–25.

Moore, B. R., & Stuttard, S. (1979). Dr. Guthrie and felis domesticus: Or, tripping over the cat. *Science, 205,* 1031–1033.

Moore, T. de R. (1980). *Galápagos: Islands lost in time.* New York: Studio/Viking.

Moore, T. V. (1938). *Cognitive psychology.* Philadelphia: Lippincott.

Moorehead, A. (1969a). *Darwin and the Beagle.* New York: Harper & Row.

Moorehead, A. (1969b, September 6). Annals of discovery: The Beagle II. *The New Yorker,* pp. 41–95.

More, T. (1965). *Utopia* (P. K. Marshall, Trans.). New York: Washington Square Press. (Original work published 1517)

Morgan, M. J. (1977). *Molyneux's question.* New York: Cambridge University Press.

Morley, J. (1915). *Rousseau.* London: Macmillan.

Moskowitz, M. J. (1977). Hugo Münsterberg:A study in the history of applied psychology. *American Psychologist, 32,* 824–842.

Moulton, F. R. (1944). James McKeen Cattell. *Scientific Monthly, 58,* 249–251.

Mueller, C. G. (1979). Some origins of psychology as science. *Annual Review of Psychology, 30,* 9–29.

Mueller, J. (1840). *Handbuch der Physiologie der Menschen.* Coblenz: J. Holscher.

Mueller, J. (1912). Elements of physiology. In B. Rand (Ed.), *The classical psychologists* (pp. 330–344). Boston: Houghton Mifflin.

Müller, G. E., & Pilzecker, A. (1900). Experimentelle Beiträge zur Lehre von Gedächtniss. *Zeitschrift für Psychologie und Physiologie der Sinnesorgane, 1,* 1–288.

Münsterberg, H. (1908). *On the witness stand.* New York: Clark Boardman.

Münsterberg, H. (1909). *Psychotherapy.* New York: Moffat, Yard.

Münsterberg, H. (1910). *Subconscious phenomena.* Boston: R. G. Badger.

Münsterberg, H. (1913). *Psychology and industrial efficiency.* New York: Houghton Mifflin.

Münsterberg, H. (1914). *Psychology: General and applied.* New York: D. Appleton.

Münsterberg, M. (1922). *Hugo Münsterberg: His life and work.* New York: D. Appleton.

Murphy, G., & Kovach, J. K. (1972). *Historical introduction to psychology* (3rd ed.). New York: Harcourt Brace Jovanovich.

Mussen, P., & Eichorn, D. (1988). Mary Cover Jones (1896–1987). *American Psychologist, 43,* 818.

Myers, G. E. (1986). *William James: His life and thought.* New Haven, CT: Yale University Press.

Nelson, K. R. (1980, February 23). Wire service reports.

Newell, A., & Simon, H. A. (1972). *Human problem solving.* Englewood Cliffs, NJ: Prentice-Hall.

Newman, J. R. (1956a). Descartes and analytical geometry. In J. R. Newman (Ed.), *The world of mathematics* (Vol. 1, pp. 235–237). New York: Simon & Schuster.

Newman, J. R. (1956b). Commentary on Sir Francis Galton. In J. R. Newman (Ed.), *The world of mathematics* (Vol. 2, pp. 1167–1172). New York: Simon & Schuster.

Newton, I. (1687). *Philosophiae naturalis principia mathematica.* London: W. Dawson.

Newton, I. (1704). *Opticks.* London: Smith and Walford.

Oden, M. H. (1968). The fulfillment of promise: 40-year follow-up of the Terman gifted group. *Genetic Psychology Monographs, 77,* 3–93.

O'Donnell, J. M. (1979). The crisis of experimentalism in the 1920's: E. G. Boring and his uses of history. *American Psychologist, 34,* 289–295.

Ogden, R. M. (1911). Imageless thought: Résumé and critique. *Psychological Bulletin, 8,* 183–197.

Ogden, R. M. (1951). Oswald Külpe and the Würzburg school. *American Journal of Psychology, 64,* 4–19.

Olds, J. M., & Milner, P. M. (1954). Positive reinforcement produced by electrical stimulation of septal area and other regions of rat brain. *Journal of Comparative and Physiological Psychology, 47,* 419–427.

Olivier, A., Bertrand, G., & Picard, C. (1983). Discovery of the first human stereotactic instrument. *Applied Neurophysiology, 46,* 84–91.

Olmsted, J. M. D. (1943). The aftermath of Charles Bell's famous "idea." *Bulletin of the History of Medicine, 14,* 341–351.

Olmsted, J. M. D. (1944). *François Magendie*. New York: Schuman.

Orne, M. T. (1962). On the social psychology of the psychological experiment with particular reference to demand characteristics and their implications. *American Psychologist, 17,* 776–783.

Ornstein, R. (1972). *The psychology of consciousness*. New York: W. H. Freeman.

Osgood, C., Suci, G., & Tannenbaum, P. (1957). *The measurement of meaning*. Urbana, IL: University of Illinois Press.

Overton, S. (1986, September 7). Inside Dix: "Wolves and lambs" create a volatile mix at Dix. *Raleigh News and Observer*, pp. 1, 32A, 33A.

Paivio, A. (1969). Mental imagery in associative learning and memory. *Psychological Review, 76,* 241–263.

Paivio, A. (1971). *Imagery and verbal processes*. New York: Holt.

Passingham, R. E. (1979). Brain size and intelligence in man. *Brain, Behavior and Evolution, 16,* 253–270.

Pastore, N. (1978). The army intelligence tests and Walter Lippmann. *Journal of the History of the Behavioral Sciences, 14,* 316–372.

Pauly, P. J. (1979). Psychology at Hopkins: Its rise and fall and rise and fall and . . . *Johns Hopkins Magazine, 30,* 36–41.

Pavlov, I. P. (1902). *Lectures on the work of the digestive glands* (W. H. Thompson, Trans.). London: Charles Griffin. (Original work published 1897)

Pavlov, I. P. (1928). *Lectures on conditioned reflexes* (W. H. Gantt, Trans.). New York: International.

Pavlov, I. P. (1932). The reply of a physiologist to psychologists. *Psychological Review, 39,* 91–127.

Pavlov, I. P. (1960). *Conditioned reflexes* (rev. ed.) (G. V. Anrep, Trans. and Ed.). New York: Dover. (Original work published 1927)

Payne, J. (1883). *Lectures on the science and art of education*. Boston: Willard Small.

Pearson, K. (1914–1930). *The life, letters and labours of Francis Galton*. 3 vols. Cambridge: Cambridge University Press.

Penfield, W., & Rasmussen, A. T. (1950). *The cerebral cortex of man*. New York: Macmillan.

Perin, C. T. (1942). Behavior potentiality as a joint function of the amount of training and the degree of hunger at the time of extinction. *Journal of Experimental Psychology, 30,* 93–113.

Perlman, D. (1986). SPSSI's publication history: Some facts and reflections. *Journal of Social Issues, 42,* 89–113.

Perls, F. (1969). *In and out the garbage pail*. New York: Bantam.

Perls, F. (1973). *The Gestalt approach and eyewitness to therapy*. Ben Lomond, CA: Science and Behavior Books.

Perls, F., Hefferline, R. F., & Goodman, P. (1951). *Gestalt therapy*. New York: Dell.

Perry, R. B. (1935). *The thought and character of William James*. 2 vols. Boston: Little, Brown.

Perry, R. B. (1948). *The thought and character of William James: Briefer version*. Cambridge, MA: Havard University Press.

Pfungst, O. (1911). *Clever Hans*. New York: Henry Holt.

Piaget, J. (1954). *The origins of intelligence in children*. New York: International Universities Press.

Pillsbury, W. B. (1955). Harvey A. Carr, 1873–1954. *American Journal of Psychology, 68,* 149–151.

Pinel, P. (1962). *A treatise on insanity*. Academy of Medicine, The History of Medicine Series. New York: Hafner. (Original work published 1801)

Plato. (1902). *The Republic of Plato* (J. Adam, Ed.). Cambridge: Cambridge University Press.

Poffenberger, A. T. (1962). Robert Sessions Woodworth, 1869–1962. *American Journal of Psychology, 75,* 677–689.

Pope, H. G., Jr., Hudson, J. I., & Mialet, J. P. (1985). Bulimia in the late nineteenth century: The observations of Pierre Janet. *Psychological Medicine, 15,* 739–743.

Pope John Paul II. (1980). *Science 80, 3,* 11.

Popenoe, P. (1921). [Review of Goddard's *Human efficiency and levels of intelligence*]. *Journal of Heredity, 12,* 231–236.

Porter, T. M. (1986). *The rise of statistical thinking, 1820–1900.* Princeton, NJ: Princeton University Press.

Posner, M. I. (1978). *Chronometric explorations of the mind.* Hillsdale, NJ: Lawrence Erlbaum.

Pressey, S. L. (1933). *Psychology and the new education.* New York: Harper & Brothers.

Pressey, S. L. (1974). Reminiscences of Harvard. Unpublished lecture at the Ohio State University.

Pressey, S. L. (1976). An afternoon with Sidney Pressey. Unpublished transcript of a lecture at Ohio State University.

Pribram, K. H. (Ed.). (1969). *On the biology of learning.* New York: Harcourt, Brace & World.

Price, D. M. (1988, April 17). For 175 years: Treating the mentally ill with dignity at a Philadelphia hospital. *The New York Times,* p. 29.

Price, H. L., & Dripps, R. D. (1970). General anesthetics. In L. S. Goodman & A. Gilman (Eds.), *The pharmacological basis of therapeutics* (4th ed., pp. 79–92). New York: Macmillan.

Pryor, K. (1977, February). Orchestra conductors would make good porpoise trainers. *Psychology Today,* pp. 61–64.

Puglisi, M. (1924). Franz Brentano: A biographical sketch. *American Journal of Psychology, 35,* 414–419.

Quetelet, L. A. (1968). *A treatise on man and the development of his faculties* (R. Knox, Trans.). New York: Burt Franklin. (Original work published 1842)

Quinn, S. (1987). *A mind of her own: The life of Karen Horney.* New York: Summit.

Rand, B. (1908). *Modern classical philosophers.* New York: Houghton Mifflin.

Rand, B. (1912). *The classical psychologists.* New York: Houghton Mifflin.

Rayner, R. (1930). I am the mother of the behaviorist's sons. *McCall's.*

Redondi, P. (1987). *Galileo heretic.* Princeton, NJ: Princeton University Press.

Reiser, S. J. (1979). The medical influence of the stethoscope. *Scientific American, 240,* 148–156.

Reisman, J. M. (1966). *The development of clinical psychology.* New York: Appleton-Century-Crofts.

Restak, R. M. (1988). *The mind.* New York: Bantam.

Rhodes, R. (1986). *The making of the atomic bomb.* New York: Simon & Schuster.

Riley, S. (1987, November 30). An unheard cry for freedom. *The Times of London,* p. 15.

Roazen, P. (1975). *Freud and his followers.* New York: Knopf.

Roback, A. A. (1961a). *History of psychology and psychiatry.* New York: Philosophical Library.

Roback, A. A. (Ed.). (1961b). Ebbinghaus, H: Pioneer in memory. In *History of psychology and psychiatry* (pp. 82–83). New York: Philosophical Library.

Roback, A. A., & Kiernan, T. (1969). *Pictorial history of psychology and psychiatry.* New York: Philosophical Library.

Robinson, D. B. (1970). *The 100 most important people in the world today.* New York: Putnam.

Robinson, D. N. (1976/1981). *An intellectual history of psychology* (1st ed., 1976; 2nd ed., 1981). New York: Macmillan.

Robinson, P. (1984, March 12). Freud's last laugh. *New Republic*, pp. 29–33.

Roediger, H. L. (1985). Remembering Ebbinghaus. *Contemporary Psychology, 30*, 519–523.

Romanes, G. J. (1912). *Animal intelligence*. New York: Appleton.

Root-Bernstein, R. S. (1983). Mendel and methodology. *History of Science, 21*, 275–295.

Roscorla, R. A. (1988). Pavlovian conditioning: It's not what you think it is. *American Psychologist, 43*, 151–160.

Rosenthal, R. (1966). *Experimenter effects in behavioral research*. New York: Appleton-Century-Crofts.

Rosenzweig, M. R. (1959). Salivary conditioning before Pavlov. *American Journal of Psychology, 72*, 628–633.

Rosenzweig, S. (1984, March). Hail to Hall. *American Psychological Association Monitor*, pp. 5–6.

Ross, D. (1972). *G. Stanley Hall: The psychologist as prophet*. Chicago: University of Chicago Press.

Rossi, A. S. (1970). *Essays on sex equality by John Stuart Mill and Harriet Taylor*. Chicago: University of Chicago Press.

Rothman, D. J., & Rothman, S. M. (1984). *The Willowbrook wars: A decade of struggle for social change*. New York: Harper & Row.

Rubenstein, R. (1971, September 20). Quoted in *Time*, p. 53.

Rubin, E. (1927). *Visuell wahrgenommene Figuren*. Presented at the Bonn Congress for Experimental Psychology, April 1927. (Original work published 1921)

Rubin, E. (1949). *Experimental psychologica*. Copenhagen: Enjer Munksgaard.

Ruckmick, C. A. (1937). Carl Stumpf. *Psychological Bulletin, 34*, 187–190.

Ruja, H. (1956). Productive psychologists. *American Psychologist, 11*, 148–149.

Rush, B. (1812). *Medical inquiries and observations upon the diseases of the mind*. Philadelphia: Kimber & Richardson.

Rush, F. (1980). *The best kept secret*. Englewood Cliffs, NJ: Prentice-Hall.

Russell, B. (1945). *A history of western philosophy*. New York: Simon & Schuster.

Russell, B. (1951). *The autobiography of Bertrand Russell (1914–1944)*. Boston: Little, Brown.

Russell, B. (1960). *An outline of philosophy*. New York: World. (Original work published 1927)

Ryan, T. A. (1982). Psychology at Cornell after Titchener: Madison Bentley to Robert Macleod, 1928–1948. *Journal of the History of the Behavioral Sciences, 18*, 347–369.

Sagan, C. (1979). *Broca's brain*. New York: Random House.

Sahakian, W. S. (Ed.). (1968). *History of psychology*. Itaska, IL: Peacock.

Samelson, F. (1977). World War I intelligence testing and the development of psychology. *Journal of the History of the Behavioral Sciences, 13*, 274–282.

Sanger, G., & Gilbert, E. (1950). Consumer reactions to the integration of Negro sales personnel. *International Journal of Attitude and Opinion Research, 4*, 57–76.

Sargent, S. S., & Stafford, K. R. (1965). Basic teachings of the great psychologists (rev. ed.). Garden City, NY: Doubleday.

Savage-Rumbaugh, E. S., Rumbaugh, D. M., & Boysen, S. (1978). Symbolic communication between two chimpanzees. *Science, 201*, 641–644.

Scarr, S. (1987). Three cheers for behavior genetics: Winning the war and losing our identity. *Behavior Genetics, 17*, 219–228.

Schank, R. C. (1976). The role of memory in language processing. In C. N. Cofer (Ed.), *The structure of human memory* (pp. 162–189). San Fransisco: Freeman.

Schernberger, R. C. (1983). *Public residential services for the mentally retarded.* Madison, WI: National Association of Superintendents of Public Residential Facilities for the Mentally Retarded.

Schiller, P. H. (1951). Figural preferences in the drawings of a chimpanzee. *Journal of Comparative and Physiological Psychology, 44,* 101–111.

Schilpp, P. A. (Ed.). (1939). *The philosophy of John Dewey.* New York: Tudor.

Schlosberg, H. (1954). Three dimensions of emotion. *Psychological Review, 61,* 81–88.

Schmemann, S. (1987, November 22). Eighty-five minutes that scarred history. *The New York Times,* p. 23.

Schwartz, S. (1986). *Classic studies in psychology.* Palo Alto, CA: Mayfield.

Schwartz, S. (1988, January 24). Intellectuals and assassins—annals of Stalin's killerati. *The New York Times Book Review,* p. 3.

Sears, R. M. (1977). Sources of life satisfactions of the Terman gifted men. *American Psychologist, 32,* 119–128.

Sears, P. S., & Barbee, A. H. (1977). Career and life satisfactions among Terman's gifted women. In J. C. Stanley, W. C. George, & C. H. Solano (Eds.), *The gifted and the creative: A fifty-year perspective* (pp. 28–65). Baltimore, MD: Johns Hopkins University Press.

Selltiz, C., Citron, A. F., Harding, J., Rosahn, O., & Wormser, M. H. (1950). The acceptability of answers to anti-Semitic remarks. *International Journal of Opinion and Attitude Research, 4,* 353–390.

Senden, M. von. (1960). *Space and sight: The perception of space and shape in the congenitally blind before and after operation.* New York: Free Press.

Shakespeare, W. (1923). King Lear. In St. John Ervine (Ed.), *The complete works of William Shakespeare* (pp. 1026–1064). London: Literary Press.

Shakow, D. (1930). Hermann Ebbinghaus. *American Journal of Psychology, 42,* 505–518.

Shattuck, R. (1980). *The forbidden experiment.* New York: Farrar, Straus & Giroux.

Sheffield, F. D. (1959). Edwin Ray Guthrie, 1886–1959. *American Journal of Psychology, 72,* 642–650.

Sherrington, C. S. (1906). *The integrative action of the nervous system.* New Haven, CT: Yale University Press.

Sherrington, C. S. (1941). *Man and his nature.* New York: Macmillan.

Shettleworth, S. J. (1973). Food reinforcement and the organization of behavior in golden hamsters. In R. Hinde & J. Stevenson-Hinde (Eds.), *Constraints on learning* (pp. 243–263). New York: Academic Press.

Silverman, J. (1964). The problem of attention in research and theory in schizophrenia. *Psychological Review, 71,* 352–379.

Simmons, R. (1924). The relative effectiveness of certain incentives on animal learning. *Comparative Psychology Monographs, 2*(7).

Simon, H. A. (1969). *The sciences of the artificial.* Cambridge, MA: MIT Press.

Simonoff, L. N. (1866). Die Hemmungsmechanismen der Säugethiere experimentell bewiesen. *Archiven der Anatomie und Physiologie, 33,* 545–564.

Skinner, B. F. (1938). *The behavior of organisms.* New York: Appleton-Century-Crofts.

Skinner, B. F. (1948). *Walden Two.* New York: Macmillan.

Skinner, B. F. (1951). How to teach animals. *Scientific American, 185,* 26–29.

Skinner, B. F. (1959). Has Gertrude Stein a secret? In B. F. Skinner, *Cumulative record* (pp. 261–271). New York: Appleton-Century-Crofts. (Original work published 1934)

Skinner, B. F. (1959). A case history in scientific method. In S. Koch (Ed.), *Psychology: A study of a science* (Vol. 2, pp. 359–379). New York: McGraw-Hill. (Original work published 1959)

Skinner, B. F. (1960). Pigeons in a pelican. *American Psychologist, 15,* 28–37.

Skinner B. F. (1961). *Cumulative record* (enlarged ed.). New York: Appleton-Century-Crofts.

Skinner, B. F. (1971a, September 20). B. F. Skinner says: "We can't afford freedom." *Time,* pp. 47–53.

Skinner, B. F. (1971b). *Beyond freedom and dignity.* New York: Knopf.

Skinner, B. F. (1976). *Particulars of my life.* New York: Knopf.

Skinner, B. F. (1979). *The shaping of a behaviorist.* New York: Knopf.

Skinner, B. F. (1983). *Enjoying old age.* New York: Knopf.

Skinner, B. F. (1987). *Upon further reflection.* Englewood Cliffs, NJ: Prentice-Hall.

Skinner, B. F. (1989). The origins of cognitive thought. *American Psychologist, 44,* 13–18.

Skinner, D. (1971, September 20). Quoted in *Time,* p. 51.

Small, W. S. (1901–1902). Experimental study of the mental processes of the rat, II. *American Journal of Psychology, 12,* 206–239.

Smith, J. D. (1985). *Minds made feeble: The myth and legacy of the Kallikaks.* Rockville, MD: Aspen Systems.

Smith, P. (1976). *A new age now begins* (Vol. 2). New York: McGraw-Hill.

Smith, P. (1985). *America enters the new world* (Vol. 7). New York: McGraw-Hill.

Snyder, S. H. (1977). Opiate receptors and internal opiates. *Scientific American, 236,* 44–56.

Snyder, S. H. (1984). Medicated minds. *Science 84, 5,* 141–142.

Snyderman, M., & Herrnstein, R. J. (1983). Intelligence tests and the immigration act of 1924. *American Psychologist, 38,* 986–995.

Sokal, M. M. (1971). The unpublished autobiography of James McKeen Cattell. *American Psychologist, 26,* 626–635.

Sokal, M. M. (1980a). Science and James McKeen Cattell, 1894–1945. *Science, 209,* 43–52.

Sokal, M. M. (1980b). *An education in psychology: James McKeen Cattell's journal and letters from Germany and England, 1880–1888.* Cambridge, MA: MIT Press.

Spanos, N. P., & Gottlieb, J. (1976). Ergotism and the Salem village witch trials. *Science, 194,* 1390–1394.

Spearman, C. (1904). "General intelligence" objectively determined and measured. *American Journal of Psychology, 15,* 201–292.

Spearman, C. (1961). C. Spearman. In C. Murchison (Ed.), *A history of psychology in autobiography* (Vol. I, pp. 299–333). New York: Russell & Russell. (Original work published 1930)

Spence, J. T. (1987). Centrifugal versus centripetal tendencies in psychology. *American Psychologist, 42,* 1052–1054.

Spence, K. W. (1952). Clark Leonard Hull: 1884–1952. *American Journal of Psychology, 65,* 639–646.

Sperry, R. W. (1961). Cerebral organization and behavior. *Science, 133,* 1749–1757.

Spoto, D. (1983). *The dark side of genius: The life of Alfred Hitchcock.* New York: Ballantine.

Stagner, R. (1972). *Scenes from Pavlov's laboratory* [Film]. Shown at the forty-fourth annual meeting of the Midwestern Psychological Association, Cleveland, Ohio.

Starkey, M. L. (1950). *The devil in Massachusetts.* New York: Knopf.

Steel, R. (1980). *Walter Lippmann and the American century.* New York: Atlantic–Little, Brown.

Stein, J. (Ed.) (1967). *The Random House dictionary of the English language*. New York: Random House.

Sternberg, S. (1966). High-speed scanning in human memory. *Science, 153*, 652–654.

Sternberg, S. (1969). The discoveries of processing stages: Extensions of Donders' method. *Acta Psychologica, 30*, 276–315.

Sternberg, S. (1975). Memory scanning: New findings and current controversies. *Quarterly Journal of Experimental Psychology, 27*, 1–32.

Stevens, L. A. (1971). *Explorers of the brain*. New York: Knopf.

Stevens, S. S. (1966). A metric for the social consensus. *Science, 151*, 530–541.

Stevens, S. S. (1968). Edward Garrigues Boring: 1886–1968. *American Journal of Psychology, 81*, 589–606.

Stewart, G. R. (1950). *The year of the oath*. Garden City, NY: Country Life Press.

Stone, I. (1980). *The origin: A biographical novel of Charles Darwin* (J. Stone, Ed.). New York: Doubleday.

Stookey, B. (1954). A note on the early history of cerebral localization. *Bulletin of the New York Academy of Medicine, 30*, 559–578.

Stookey, B. (1963). Jean Baptiste Bouillaud and Ernest Auburtin: Early studies on cerebral localization and the speech center. *Journal of the American Medical Association, 184*, 1024–1029.

Storr, A. (1984, February 12). Did Freud have clay feet? *The New York Times Book Review*, p. 3.

Street, R. F. (1931). *A Gestalt completion test*. New York: Teachers College, Columbia University.

Strouse, J. (1980). *A biography of Alice James*. New York: Houghton Mifflin.

Stumpf, C. (1890). *Tonpsychologie*. Leipzig: S. Hirzel.

Stump, C. (1961). Autobiography. In C. Murchison (Ed.), *A history of psychology in autobiography* (Vol. 1, pp. 389–441). New York: Russell & Russell. (Original work published 1930)

Sulloway, J. (1979). *Freud, biologist of the mind: Beyond the psychoanalytic legend*. New York: Basic Books.

Tatar, M. M. (1978). *Spellbound: Studies on mesmerism and literature*. Princeton, NJ: Princeton University Press.

Tellegen, A., Lykken, D. T., Bouchard, T. J., Jr., Wilcox, K. L., Segal, N. L., & Rich, S. (1988). Personality similarity in twins reared apart and together. *Journal of Personality and Social Psychology, 54*, 1031–1039.

Terman, L. M. (1916). *The measurement of intelligence*. New York: Houghton Mifflin.

Terman, L. M. (1922). The great conspiracy. *New Republic, 33*, 116–120.

Terman, L. M. (1924). The mental test as a psychological method (1923 American Psychological Association presidential address). *Psychological Review, 31*, 93–117.

Terman, L. M. (1926). *Genetic studies of genius: Vol. 1. Mental and physical traits of a thousand gifted children*. Stanford, CA: Stanford University Press.

Terman, L. M. (1932). Trails to psychology. In C. Murchison (Ed.), *A history of psychology in autobiography* (Vol. 2, pp. 297–332). Worcester, MA: Clark University Press.

Terman, L. M., & Oden, M. H. (1947). *Genetic studies of genius: Vol. 4. The gifted child grows up*. Stanford, CA: Stanford University Press.

Terman, L. M., & Oden, M. H. (1959). *Genetic studies of genius: Vol. 5. The gifted group at mid-life*. Stanford, CA: Stanford University Press.

Terrace, H. S. (1979). *Nim*. New York: Knopf.

Thistlethwaite, D. (1951). A critical review of latent learning and related experiments. *Psychological Bulletin, 48*, 97–129.

Thompson, G. (1978). Memories of Kurt Lewin at the University of Iowa. Unpublished lecture, Ohio State University.

Thompson, K. S. (1975). H.M.S. Beagle, 1820–1870. *American Scientist, 63*, 664–672.

Thompson, K. S. (1988). Ontogeny and phylogeny recapitulated. *American Scientist, 76*, 273–275.

Thompson, N. L. (1987). Early women psychoanalysts. *International Review of Psychoanalysis, 14*, 391–407.

Thompson, T. (1988). Retrospective review: Benedictus behavior analysis: B. F. Skinner's magnum opus at fifty. *Contemporary Psychology, 33*, 397–402.

Thorndike, E. L. (1898a). *Animal intelligence* [Monograph supplement]. *Psychological Review, 2*(8).

Thorndike, E. L. (1898b). Some experiments in animal intelligence. *Science, 8*, 818–824.

Thorndike, E. L. (1899). A reply to "The nature of animal intelligence and the methods of investigating it." *Psychological Review, 6*, 412–420.

Thorndike, E. L. (1906). *The principles of teaching: Based on psychology.* New York: A. G. Seiler.

Thorndike, E. L. (1911). *Animal intelligence.* New York: Macmillan.

Thorndike, E. L. (1913). *Educational psychology.* 3 vols. New York: Teachers College, Columbia University.

Thorndike, E. L. (1921). *The teacher's word book.* New York: Columbia University Press.

Thorndike, E. L. (1931). *A teacher's word book of the twenty thousand words found most frequently and widely in general reading for children and young people.* New York: Teachers College Bureau of Publications.

Thorndike, E. L. (1932). *A teacher's word book of the twenty thousand words found most frequently and widely in general reading for children and young people.* New York: Columbia University Press.

Thorndike, E. L. (1936). Edward Lee Thorndike. In C. Murchison (Ed.), *A history of psychology in autobiography* (Vol. 3, pp. 263–270). Worcester, MA: Clark University Press.

Thorndike, E. L. (1939). *Your city.* New York: Harcourt, Brace.

Thorndike, E. L. (1940). *One hundred forty-four smaller cities.* New York: Harcourt, Brace.

Thorndike, E. L., & Woodworth, R. S. (1899/1900). *The influence of special training on general ability.* Paper presented at the eighth annual meeting of the American Psychological Association, Yale University, 1899. Summary in *Psychological Review, 7*, 140–141.

Thorndike, E. L., & Woodworth, R. S. (1901). The influence of improvement in one mental function upon the efficiency of other functions, I. *Psychological Review, 8*, 247–261.

Tinker, M. A. (1932). Wundt's doctorate students and their theses, 1875–1920. *American Journal of Psychology, 44*, 630–637.

Tinklepaugh, O. L. (1928). An experimental study of representative factors in monkeys. *Journal of Comparative Psychology, 8*, 197–236.

Titchener, E. B. (1891). Dr. Münsterberg and his experimental psychology. *Mind, 16*, 594–598.

Titchener, E. B. (1898). Postulates of a structural psychology. *Philosophical Review, 7*, 449–465.

Titchener, E. B. (1899). Structural and functional psychology. *Philosophical Review, 8*, 290–299.

Titchener, E. B. (1901–1905). *Experimental psychology*. New York: Macmillan.

Titchener, E. B. (1905). [Review of Thorndike's *Elements of psychology*]. *Mind, 56,* 552–554.

Titchener, E. B. (1910). The past decade in experimental psychology. *American Journal of Psychology, 21,* 404–421.

Titchener, E. B. (1914). On "Psychology as the behaviorist sees it." *Proceedings of the American Philosophical Society, 53,* 1–17.

Titchener, E. B. (1916). *A beginner's psychology*. New York: Macmillan.

Titchener, E. B. (1921a). Brentano and Wundt: Empirical experimental psychology. *American Journal of Psychology, 32,* 108–120.

Titchener, E. B. (1921b). Wilhelm Wundt. *American Journal of Psychology, 32,* 161–178.

Titchener, E. B. (1921c). Functional psychology and the psychology of act, I. *American Journal of Psychology, 32,* 519.

Titchener, E. B. (1922a). Functional psychology and the psychology of act, II. *American Journal of Psychology, 33,* 43–83.

Titchener, E. B. (1922b). [Book review]. *American Journal of Psychology, 33,* 150–152.

Titchener, E. B. (1928). *A text book of psychology*. New York: Macmillan.

Todd, J. T., & Morris, E. K. (1986). The early research of John B. Watson: Before the behavioral revolution. *Behavior Analyst, 9,* 71–78.

Tolman, E. C. (1922). A new formula for behaviorism. *Psychological Review, 29,* 44–53.

Tolman, E. C. (1923). The nature of instinct. *Psychological Bulletin, 20,* 200–216.

Tolman, E. C. (1926). A behaviorist theory of ideas. *Psychological Review, 33,* 352–369.

Tolman, E. C. (1932). *Purposive behavior in animals and men*. New York: Century.

Tolman, E. C. (1938). The determiners of behavior at a choice point. *Psychological Review, 45,* 1–41.

Tolman, E. C. (1939). Prediction of vicarious trial and error by means of the schematic sowbug. *Psychological Review, 46,* 318–336.

Tolman, E. C. (1941). Psychological man. *Journal of Social Psychology, 13,* 205–218.

Tolman, E. C. (1942). *Drives toward war*. New York: Appleton-Century.

Tolman, E. C. (1948). Cognitive maps in rats and men. *Psychological Review, 55,* 189–208.

Tolman, E. C. (1952). Edward Chase Tolman. In E. G. Boring, H. S. Langfeld, H. Werrer, & R. M. Yerkes (Eds.), *A history of psychology in autobiography* (Vol. 4, pp. 323–339). Worcester, MA: Clark University Press.

Tolman, E. C. (1958). *Behavior and psychological man*. Berkeley: University of California Press.

Tolman, E. C. (1959). Principles of purposive behavior. In S. Koch (Ed.), *Psychology: A study of a science* (Vol. 2, pp. 92–157). New York: McGraw-Hill.

Tolman, E. C., Ritchie, B. F., & Kalish, D. (1946). Studies in spatial learning: II. Place learning versus response learning. *Journal of Experimental Psychology, 36,* 221–229.

Tuchman, B. W. (1979). *A distant mirror: The calamitous 14th century*. New York: Ballantine.

Tucker, W. H. (1987). The Kallikaks revisited: A trip worth taking. *Contemporary Psychology, 32,* 288.

Tuddenham, R. D. (1974). Fame and oblivion. *Science,* 1071–1072.

Tuke, D. H. (1885). *The insane in the United States and Canada*. London: Paul, Trench.

Tuke, D. H. (1892). *A dictionary of psychological medicine*. Philadelphia: P. Blakiston.

Turkington, C. (1985). First mental hospital in colonies restored at Williamsburg. *American Psychological Association Monitor, 16,* 38.

Turnbull, H. W. (1956). The great mathematicians. In J. R. Newman (Ed.), *The world of mathematics* (Vol. 1, pp. 75–168). New York: Simon & Schuster.

Twitmyer, E. B. (1902/1974). *A study of the knee-jerk.* (Doctoral dissertation, University of Pennsylvania). Republished in *Journal of Experimental Psychology, 103,* 1047–1066.

Twitmyer, E. B. (1905). Knee-jerks without stimulation of the patellar tendon. *Psychological Bulletin, 2,* 43–44.

Ulrich, R., Stachnik, T., & Mabry, J. (Eds.). (1966). Control of human behavior. 2 vols. Glenview, IL: Scott, Foresman.

UNESCO. (1973). *International directory of programmed instruction.* Paris: UNESCO.

Vaeth, J. G. (1958). *Graf Zeppelin.* New York: Harper.

Valenstein, E. S. (1986). *Great and desperate cures: The rise and decline of psychosurgery and other radical treatments for mental illness.* New York: Basic Books.

Valentine, C. W. (1930). The innate bases of fear. *Journal of Genetic Psychology, 37,* 394–420.

Van de Kemp, H. (1983). A note on the term "psychology" in English titles: Predecessors of Rauch. *Journal of the History of the Behavioral Sciences, 19,* 185.

Van Wagenen, B. (1914). Surgical sterilization as a eugenic measure. *Journal of Psychoasthenics, 18,* 185–196.

Vargas, J. S. (1984, November 9). Behavior analysis and microcomputer instruction. Unpublished Vance W. Cotter memorial address, Ohio State University.

Varon, E. J. (1935). *The development of Alfred Binet's psychology.* Princeton: Psychological Review Company.

Venezky, R. L. (1977). Research on reading processes: A historical perspective. *American Psychologist, 32,* 339–345.

Vernon, P. E. (1957). *Secondary school selection.* London: Methuen.

Viney, W., Michaels, T., & Ganong, A. (1981). A note on the history of psychology in magazines. *Journal of the History of the Behavioral Sciences, 17,* 270–272.

Waldrop, M. M. (1981). Let us now praise famous Boojums. *Science, 212,* 1378.

Wallach, H. (1976). Empiricist was a dirty word. *Swarthmore College Bulletin, 83,* 1–5.

Washburn, M. F. (1903). *The animal mind.* Chicago: University of Chicago Press.

Washburn, M. F. (1932). Some recollections. In C. Murchison (Ed.), *A history of psychology in autobiography* (Vol. 2, pp. 333–358). Worcester, MA: Clark University Press.

Wasserstein, J., Zappulla, R., Rosen, J., & Gerstman, L. (1987). In search of closure: Subjective contour illusions, Gestalt completion tests and implications. *Brain and Cognition, 6,* 1–14.

Watson, J. B. (1903). *Animal education.* Chicago: University of Chicago Press.

Watson, J. B. (1907). *Kinaesthetic and organic sensations: Their role in the reactions of the white rat to the maze* [Monograph supplement]. *Psychological Review 8*(33).

Watson, J. B. (1908). The behavior of noddy and sooty terns. *Publications of the Carnegie Institution, 2,* 187–255.

Watson, J. B. (1910, March). The new science of animal behavior. *Harper's,* pp. 346–353.

Watson, J. B. (1913). Psychology as the behaviorist sees it. *Psychological Review, 20,* 158–177.

Watson, J. B. (1914). *Behavior: An introduction to comparative psychology.* New York: Henry Holt.

Watson, J. B. (1916). *The place of the conditioned reflex in psychology* (American Psychological Association presidential address, 1915). *Psychological Review, 23,* 89–116.

Watson, J. B. (1919). *Psychology from the standpoint of a behaviorist.* Philadelphia: Lippincott.

Watson, J. B. (1924). *Behaviorism.* New York: Norton.

Watson, J. B. (1928a). *Psychological care of infant and child.* New York: Norton.

Watson, J. B. (1928b). *The ways of behaviorism.* New York: Harper & Brothers.

Watson, J. B. (1936). John Broadus Watson. In C. Murchison (Ed.), *A history of psychology in autobiography* (Vol. 3, pp. 271–281). New York: Russell & Russell.

Watson, J. B., & Morgan, J. J. B. (1917). Emotional reactions and psychological experimentation. *American Journal of Psychology, 28,* 163–174.

Watson, J. B., & Rayner, R. (1920). Conditioned emotional reactions. *Journal of Experimental Psychology, 3,* 1–14.

Watson, R. I. (1968/1978). *The great psychologists from Aristotle to Freud* (1st ed., 1968; 4th ed., 1978). New York: Lippincott.

Watt, H. J. (1903). Experimentelle Beiträge zu einer Theorie des Denken. *Archiv für die Gesamte Psychologie, 4,* 289–436.

Weindling, P. (1985). Weimar eugenics: The Kaiser Wilhelm Institute for Anthropology, human heredity and eugenics in social context. *Annals of Science, 42,* 303–318.

Wertheimer, M. (1912/1968). Experimentelle Studien über das Sehen von Bewegung. *Zeitschrift der Psychologie, 61,* 161–265. Excerpted in W. S. Sahakian (Ed.), *History of psychology* (pp. 418–422). Itaska, IL: Peacock.

Wertheimer, M. (1959). *Productive thinking* (enlarged ed.). New York: Harper & Row. (Original work published 1945)

Whytt, R. (1751). *An essay on the vital and other involuntary motions of animals.* Edinburgh: Hamilton, Balfour & Neill.

Wickens, C. (1980). *The University of Chicago department of psychology from the point of view of an undergraduate.* Unpublished memoir.

Wiggam, A. (1922). The new decalogue of science. *Century Magazine, 103,* 643–650.

Williams, D. H., Bellis, E. C., & Wellington, S. W. (1980). Deinstitutionalization and social policy: Historical perspectives and present dilemmas. *American Journal of Orthopsychiatry, 50,* 54–64.

Williams, L. L. (1914). The medical examination of mentally defective aliens: Its scope and limitations. *American Journal of Insanity, 71,* 257–268.

Williams, R. L. (1970). Black pride, academic relevance, and individual achievement. *Counseling Psychologist, 2,* 18–22.

Williams, S. B. (1938). Resistance to extinction as a function of the number of reinforcements. *Journal of Experimental Psychology, 23,* 506–522.

Windholz, G. (1984). Pavlov vs. Köhler: Pavlov's little-known primate research. *Pavlovian Journal of Biological Science, 19,* 23–31.

Windholz, G. (1986). A comparative analysis of the conditioned reflex: Discoveries of Pavlov and Twitmyer, and the birth of a paradigm. *Pavlovian Journal of Biological Science, 21,* 141–147.

Windholz, G., & Lamal, P. A. (1986). Pavlov and the concept of association. *Pavlovian Journal of Biological Science, 21,* 12–15.

Wolf, E. (1939). [Review of *The behavior of organisms*]. *Journal of Genetic Psychology, 54,* 475–479.

Wolf, T. H. (1973). *Alfred Binet.* Chicago: University of Chicago Press.

Wollheim, R. (1988, April 24). The mighty father. *The New York Times Book Review,* p. 3.

Wolman, B. B. (1960). *Contemporary theories and systems in psychology.* New York: Harper & Row.

Wolpe, J. (1958). *Psychotherapy by reciprocal inhibition.* Johannesburg: Witwatersrand University Press.

Wolpe, J. (1973). *The practice of behavior therapy* (2nd ed.). New York: Pergamon.

Woodworth, R. S. (1909). Hermann Ebbinghaus. *Journal of Philosophy, 6,* 253–256.

Woodworth, R. S. (1910). Racial differences in mental traits. *Science, 31,* 171–186.

Woodworth, R. S. (1915). A revision of imageless thought. *Psychological Review, 22,* 1–27.

Woodworth, R. S. (1918). *Dynamic psychology.* New York: Columbia University Press.

Woodworth, R. S. (1927). Dynamic psychology. In C. Murchison (Ed.), *Psychologies of 1925* (pp. 110–126). Worcester, MA: Clark University Press.

Woodworth, R. S. (1938). *Experimental psychology.* New York: Holt.

Woodworth, R. S. (1943). The adolescence of American psychology. *Psychological Review, 50,* 10–32.

Woodworth, R. S. (1944a). Some personal characteristics. *Scientific Monthly, 58,* 14–15.

Woodworth, R. S. (1944b). James Mckeen Cattell, 1860–1944. *Psychological Review, 51,* 1–10.

Woodworth, R. S. (1931/1948). *Contemporary schools of psychology* (1st ed., 1931; rev. ed., 1948). New York: Ronald Press.

Woodworth, R. S. (1958). *Dynamics of behavior.* New York: Holt.

Woodworth, R. S. (1959). John Broadus Watson, 1878–1958. *American Journal of Psychology, 72,* 301–310.

Woodworth, R. S. (1961). Robert S. Woodworth. In C. Murchison (Ed.), *A history of psychology in autobiography* (Vol. 2, pp. 359–380). New York: Russell & Russell. (Original work published 1932)

Woodworth, R. S., & Schlosberg, H. (1954). *Experimental psychology* (rev. ed.). New York: Holt.

Wright, G. D. (1970). A further note on ranking the important psychologists. *American Psychologist, 25,* 650–651.

Wundt, M. (1944). *Die Wurzeln der deutschen Philosophie in Stamm und Rasse.* Berlin: Junker und Dunnhaupt.

Wundt, W. (1902). *Outline of psychology* (C. Judd, Trans.). Leipzig: Wilhelm Engelmann.

Wundt, W. (1904). *Principles of physiological psychology* (5th ed.) (E. Titchener, Ed.). New York: Macmillan. (Original work published 1874)

Wundt, W. (1908). Kritiche Nachlese zur Ausfrage Methode. *Archiv für die gesamte Psychologie, 11,* 445–459.

Wundt, W. (1912). *An introduction to psychology* (2nd ed.). New York: Macmillan.

Wundt, W. (1914/1915). *Concerning true war.* Address at the University of Leipzig, 1914. Reprinted in *Oxford Pamphlets on the War,* No. XII. Oxford: Oxford University Press.

Wyatt, F., & Teuber, H. L. (1944). German psychology under the Nazi system, 1933–1940. *Psychological Review, 51,* 229–247.

Yerkes, R. M. (1904). Literary notices [Review of *Animal education*]. *Journal of Comparative Neurology and Psychology, 14,* 70–71.

Yerkes, R. M. (1916). The mental life of monkeys and apes: A study of ideational behavior. *Behavior Monographs, 3,* 1–145.

Yerkes, R. M. (Ed.). (1921). Psychological examining in the United States Army. *Memoirs of the National Academy of Sciences, 15,* 1–890.

Yerkes, R. M. (1943). Early days of comparative psychology. *Psychological Review, 50,* 74–76.

Yerkes, R. M. (1961). Psychobiologist. In C. Murchison (Ed.), *A history of psychology in autobiography* (Vol. 2, pp. 381–407). New York: Russell & Russell. (Original work published 1932)

Yerkes, R. M., Bridges, J. W., & Hardwick, R. S. (1915). *A point scale for measuring mental ability.* Baltimore: Warwick & York.

Yerkes, R. M., & Morgulis, S. (1909). The method of Pavlov in animal psychology. *Psychological Review, 6*, 257–273.

Yerkes, R. M., & Yerkes, A. W. (1929). *The great apes: A study of anthropoid life*. New Haven, CT: Yale University Press.

Young, R. M. (1985). *Darwin's metaphor: Nature's place in Victorian culture*. New York: Cambridge University Press.

Zeigarnik, B. (1927). Über Behalten von erledigten und unerledigten Handlungen. *Psychologische Forschung, 9*, 1–85.

Zilboorg, G., & Henry, G. W. (1941). *A history of medical psychology*. New York: Norton.

Zimbardo, P. G., Haney, C., & Banks, W. C. (1973, April 8). A Pirandellian prison. *The New York Times Magazine*, pp. 38–60.

Zusne, L. (1975). *Names in the history of psychology: A biographical source book*. Washington, DC: Halstead/Wiley.

Zwelling, S. S. (1985). *Quest for a cure: The public hospital in Williamsburg, Virginia, 1773–1885*. Williamsburg, VA: The Colonial Williamsburg Foundation.

Name Index

Subject Index

Abendberg institution, near Interlaken, Switzerland, 226–227

Ablation experiments by Flourens, 78–81

About the Parts of Animals (Aristotle), 24

Abstraction experiments, 172

Act psychology, Brentano's, 160

Action research, Lewin's, 208–211

Activity of the Will (Münsterberg), 129

Adolescence (Hall), 295

Advertising:
    Münsterberg's study of, 139
    Watson's career in, 382–383
    Zeigarnik effect in, 186

Afterimages, 54

Air-cribs, 439

Albert B. study, 380–381

Alpha (chimpanzee), 186–187

American Association for the Advancement of Science (AAAS), 277

American Journal of Psychology, 125–126, 291–292

American Psychological Association (APA):
    clinical psychologists in, 215
    current status of, 5, 448
    disaffection with, 5–6, 126
    founding of, 293

introspection demonstration for, 121

membership growth of, 125, 294

presidential addresses to, 307, 309, 315, 357, 378, 410, 427

and test development, 314

Tolman's award from, 413

Twitmyer's paper presented to, 401

Watson's gold medal from, 388

and World War I, 356, 357

American Psychological Society (APS), 6

American Traits (Münsterberg), 131, 141

Americans, The (Münsterberg), 141

Analysis of Sensations (Mach), 179

Analysis of the Phenomena of the Human Mind (James Mill), 58–59

Ancients, 2, 11–25
    atomism, 18
    challenges to, 15, 18–19
    importance of, 25
    mathematics, 16–17
    medicine, 12–16
    philosophy, 19–25

Anesthetic agents, 235

Animal Education (Watson), 370–371

Animal spirits, Descartes' concept of, 38, 39

Animals:
    Aristotle's beliefs about, 24
    brains, studies of, 79–81, 85–87, 90
    and cognitive behaviorism, 407–411
    Galton's interest in, 271
    Gestalt principles and, 186–187, 193–198
    in Guthrie's learning theory, 419–421
    individual behavior of, 394–395, 430
    as intelligent, interest in, 166–168
    and language use, 40, 121
    mental continuity, concept of, 260
    operant conditioning of, 434–437
    Pavlov's study of, 391–395, 398, 418–419
    Thorndike's learning experiments with, 194, 318–323, 434
    Watson's study of, 370–373
    Wundt's ideas about studying, 108–109

Anna O. case, 237–238, 241

Apes:
    Gestalt experiments with, 186–187, 195–198

490